W9-CPC-939

HANDBUCH ZUR DEUTSCHEN GRAMMATIK

LARRY D. WELLS
BINGHAMTON UNIVERSITY

WIEDERHOLEN UND ANWENDEN

SECOND EDITION

Houghton Mifflin Company Boston New York

Senior Development Editor: Katherine Gilbert
Project Editor: Helen Bronk
Production/Design Coordinator: Jennifer Meyer
Director of Manufacturing: Michael O'Dea
Marketing Manager: Elaine Uzan Leary

Cover Design: Harold Burch, Harold Burch Design, New York City.

Acknowledgments
p. 76: Poem by Uwe Timm: "Erziehung" from *Bundesdeutsch, lyrik zur sache grammatik,* ed. Rudolf Otto Wiemer. Reprinted by permission of Peter Hammer Verlag
p. 89: Article on Helga Schutz excerpted from "Was'n Kleinkariertes Volk," by Dieter E. Zimmer, *Die Zeit* 18, April 26, 1991, by permission of the publisher and the author.

Printed in the U.S.A.

Library of Congress Card Catalog Number: 96-76971

ISBN: 0-669-39902-7

123456789-MV-00 99 98 97 96

Table of Contents

Introduction ix
To the Instructor xiii
To the Student xix
Acknowledgments xxi

1 Word Order 1

1.1 Word Order in Main Clauses 1
1.2 Positions of the Conjugated Verb in Questions 4
1.3 Positions of the Conjugated Verb in Dependent Clauses 5
Tips zum Schreiben *Beginning the Sentence* 7
Wortschatz 8
vocabulary for activity instructions: **ändern, ausdrücken, sich äußern (zu),** etc.
Zusammenfassung 9

2 Present Tense 11

2.1 Present-Tense Conjugations 11
2.2 Uses of the Present Tense 14
Tips zum Schreiben *Using Familiar Verbs and Structures* 19
Wortschatz 20
wissen, kennen; lernen, studieren
Zusammenfassung 22

3 Present Perfect Tense 24

3.1 Principal Parts of Verbs 24
3.2 Present Perfect Tense 27
Tips zum Schreiben *Using the Present Perfect Tense* 32
Wortschatz 33
strong / weak verb pairs: **fahren, führen; fallen, fällen,** etc.
Zusammenfassung 36

4 Cases and Declensions 38

4.1 Cases 38
4.2 Regular Noun Declensions 38
4.3 Nominative Case 39
4.4 Accusative Case 40
4.5 Dative Case 41
4.6 Genitive Case 44
Tips zum Schreiben *Checking for Correct Cases 49*
Wortschatz 50
direct object complements for **machen: einen Ausflug machen, eine Reise machen,** etc.
Zusammenfassung 51

5 Articles and Possessive Adjectives / Articles Used as Pronouns 53

5.1 Definite Articles 53
5.2 Indefinite Articles 55
5.3 **Der-**Words 56

5.4 Possessive Adjectives 58
5.5 **Der-** and **ein-**Words Used as Pronouns 59
Tips zum Schreiben *Editing Your Writing* 65
Wortschatz 65
der Raum, der Platz, der Ort, die Stelle
Zusammenfassung 67

6 Negation / Imperatives 69
6.1 Negation 69
6.2 Imperatives 70
Tips zum Schreiben *Writing First Drafts and Checking for Common Errors* 76
Wortschatz 77
expressions of negation: **kein-, kein- . . . mehr, nicht,** etc.
Zusammenfassung 79

7 Simple Past Tense / Past Perfect Tense 80
7.1 Simple Past Tense 80
7.2 Past Perfect Tense 83
Tips zum Schreiben *Choosing Precise Verbs* 87
Wortschatz 89
Verbs of going: **gehen, fahren, fallen, fliegen,** etc.
Zusammenfassung 91

8 Future Tense / Future Perfect Tense 93
8.1 Future Tense 93
8.2 Future Perfect Tense 94
Tips zum Schreiben *Qualifying Statements About the Future* 97
Wortschatz 98
fortfahren, fortsetzen, weiter[tun]
Zusammenfassung 99

9 Modal Verbs 101
9.1 Present and Past Tenses of Modal Verbs 101
9.2 Meanings of Modal Verbs 102
9.3 Perfect Tenses of Modal Verbs 106
9.4 Future Tense of Modal Verbs 107
Tips zum Schreiben *Providing Explanation* 111
Wortschatz 112
verbs of liking and inclination: **gern haben, mögen, gefallen,** etc.
Zusammenfassung 114

10 Prepositions 116
10.1 Accusative Prepositions 116
10.2 Dative Prepositions 118
10.3 Two-Way Prepositions 124
10.4 Genitive Prepositions 127
Tips zum Schreiben *Adding Information Through Prepositions* 134
Wortschatz 136
bekommen, erhalten, kriegen, holen
Zusammenfassung 137

11 Conjunctions 138
11.1 Coordinating Conjunctions 138
11.2 Two-Part (Correlative) Conjunctions 139
11.3 Subordinating Conjunctions 140
Tips zum Schreiben *Writing with Conjunctions* 149
Wortschatz 151
verbs of thinking: **denken (an / von), meinen, glauben, halten (von / für)**
Zusammenfassung 153

12 Noun Genders, Noun Plurals, Weak Nouns 155

12.1 Noun Genders 155

12.2 Noun Plurals 158

12.3 Weak Noun Declensions 160

Tips zum Schreiben *Checking for Correct Genders and Plurals* 163

Wortschatz 164

animals: **der Affe, die Ameise, der Bär, die Biene,** etc.

Zusammenfassung 167

13 Adjectives 170

13.1 Adjectives Without Endings 170

13.2 Adjectives with Endings 170

13.3 Limiting Adjectives 173

13.4 Adjectives Governing Cases 175

13.5 Adjectives with Prepositional Complements 176

13.6 Adjective Suffixes 177

Tips zum Schreiben *Writing with Adjectives* 184

Wortschatz 185

positive and negative reactions: **ausgezeichnet, erstklassig, abscheulich, armselig,** etc.

Zusammenfassung 186

14 Comparative and Superlative 188

14.1 Comparative and Superlative Forms 188

14.2 Uses of the Comparative and Superlative 190

14.3 Other Types of Comparisons 192

14.4 Other Superlative Constructions 193

Tips zum Schreiben *Comparing and Contrasting* 196

Wortschatz 197

nouns derived from adjectives: **breit / die Breite, flach / die Fläche, groß / die Größe,** etc.

Zusammenfassung 198

15 Questions and Interrogatives 200

15.1 Yes-No Questions 200

15.2 Interrogative Words 201

15.3 Indirect Questions 203

Tips zum Schreiben *Asking Rhetorical Questions* 207

Wortschatz 207

verbs of stopping: **halten, anhalten, aufhalten; aufhören, stehenbleiben, stoppen**

Zusammenfassung 209

16 Personal, Indefinite, and Demonstrative Pronouns 211

16.1 Personal Pronouns 211

16.2 Indefinite Pronouns 212

16.3 Demonstrative Pronouns 214

Tips zum Schreiben *Using Pronouns in German* 219

Wortschatz 220

nur, erst; ein ander-, noch ein-

Zusammenfassung 221

17 Reflexive Pronouns / *Selbst* and *selber* / *Einander* 223

17.1 Reflexive Pronouns 223

17.2 Reflexive Verbs 224

17.3 **Selbst** and **selber** 227

17.4 The Reciprocal Pronoun **einander** 228
Tips zum Schreiben *Using Process Writing in German* 231
Wortschatz 232
entscheiden, sich entscheiden (eine Entscheidung treffen), sich entschließen (einen Entschluß fassen), beschließen
Zusammenfassung 234

18 Infinitives 236
18.1 Infinitives with **zu** 236
18.2 Adverbial Phrases with **um . . . zu, ohne . . . zu, and (an)statt . . . zu** 237
18.3 Infinitives without **zu** 237
18.4 **Lassen** + Infinitive 238
18.5 Infinitives as Nouns 238
18.6 Double Infinitives 239
Tips zum Schreiben *Expressing Your Own Views* 243
Wortschatz 243
lassen, verlassen, weggehen
Zusammenfassung 245

19 *Da*-Compounds/Uses of *es* 247
19.1 Prepositional **da-** Compounds 247
19.2 Anticipatory **da-** Compounds 248
19.3 Uses of **es** 249
Tips zum Schreiben *Avoiding Some Common Pitfalls* 254
Wortschatz 255
es handelt sich um, es geht um, handeln von
Zusammenfassung 256

20 Conditional Subjunctive (Subjunctive II) 257
20.1 Conditional Subjunctive 257
20.2 Present-Time Conditional Subjunctive Forms 257
20.3 Uses of the Present-Time Conditional Subjunctive 261
20.4 The Past-Time Conditional Subjunctive 264
20.5 Indicative Versus Subjunctive with **können, müssen,** and **sollen** 266
Tips zum Schreiben *Using the Conditional Subjunctive* 270
Wortschatz 271
sich benehmen, sich aufführen, sich verhalten, tun, als ob, handeln
Zusammenfassung 273

21 Adjective Nouns/Participial Modifiers 275
21.1 Adjective Nouns 275
21.2 Participles as Adjectives 277
21.3 Extended Modifiers 277
Tips zum Schreiben *Using Extended Modifiers* 281
Wortschatz 282
lernen, erfahren, herausfinden, entdecken, feststellen
Zusammenfassung 284

22 Numerals and Measurements 286
22.1 Cardinal Numerals 286
22.2 Ordinal Numerals 288
22.3 Units of Measurement 290
Tips zum Schreiben *Conveying Statistical Information* 295

Wortschatz 295
addieren, subtrahieren, multiplizieren, dividieren, hoch

Zusammenfassung 296

23 Seasons, Dates, and Time Expressions 298

23.1 Expressions of Time 298

23.2 Telling Time 303

Tips zum Schreiben *Beginning Sentences with Time Expressions* 306

Wortschatz 307
-mal, das Mal, die Zeit + Expressions with **Zeit**

Zusammenfassung 309

24 Adverbs 310

24.1 Descriptive Adverbs 310

24.2 Adverbs of Time 311

24.3 Adverbs of Place 312

24.4 Position of Adverbs and Adverbial Phrases 313

24.5 Adverbial Conjunctions 313

Tips zum Schreiben *Establishing a Sequence of Events* 315

Wortschatz 316
am Ende, zum Schluß, zuletzt, schließlich, endlich

Zusammenfassung 317

25 Particles 319

25.1 Particles 319

25.2 Uses of Various Particles 319

Tips zum Schreiben *Deciding When to Use Flavoring Particles* 327

Wortschatz 328
expressions with flavoring particles: **das ist aber / ja wahr!, das ist aber / ja lächerlich!,** etc.

Zusammenfassung 329

26 Relative Pronouns 331

26.1 Relative Clauses 331

26.2 Relative Pronouns 331

26.3 **Was, wo**-Compounds, and **wo** as Relative Pronouns 334

26.4 The Indefinite Relative Pronouns **wer** and **was** 335

Tips zum Schreiben *Using and Avoiding Relative Clauses* 342

Wortschatz 343
categories of things: **der Apparat, die Einrichtung, das Gerät,** etc.

Zusammenfassung 344

27 Indirect Discourse Subjunctive 346

27.1 Indirect Discourse 346

27.2 Forms of Present-Time Indirect Discourse Subjunctive 347

27.3 Present-Time, Past-Time, and Future-Time Indirect Discourse 349

27.4 Uses of Indirect Discourse Subjunctive 351

Tips zum Schreiben *Paraphrasing* 355

Wortschatz 356
verbs of speaking: **andeuten, ankündigen, antworten auf,** etc.

Zusammenfassung 358

28 Passive Voice 360

28.1 Passive Voice 360

28.2 True Passive Versus Statal Passive 364

28.3 Substitutes for the Passive Voice 365

Tips zum Schreiben *Avoiding Overuse of the Passive* 369

Wortschatz 370
schaffen (weak or strong verb)
Zusammenfassung 371

29 Verb Prefixes 373
29.1 Separable Prefixes 373
29.2 Inseparable Prefixes 376
29.3 Two-Way Prefixes 379
Tips zum Schreiben *Writing with Inseparable Prefix Verbs* 385
Wortschatz 385
verbs with **be-**, **er-**, and **ver-** prefixes: **arbeiten (bearbeiten, erarbeiten, verarbeiten),** etc.
Zusammenfassung 388

30 Prepositions as Verbal Complements 390
30.1 Prepositional Complements to Verbs 390
30.2 Prepositions with Particular Verbs 391
Tips zum Schreiben *Categories of Writing* 399
Wortschatz 399
es stellt sich heraus, sich herausstellen als, es zeigt sich, sich erweisen als
Zusammenfassung 401

Appendices 403
1 Capitalization and Punctuation 403
2 Letter-Writing 407
3 Cognates 410
4 Strong and Irregular Verbs 413

German-English Vocabulary 419

Index 441

Introduction

Handbuch zur deutschen Grammatik, Second Edition, is a reference and review grammar for second- and third-year German students who are familiar with the basics of German vocabulary and grammar. It can be used either as a primary text or as a reference manual in conjunction with other materials, such as literature readers. Its goal is two-fold: (1) to present clear and complete explanations of all major grammar topics, and (2) to provide meaningful, communicative practice of those topics. There is abundant oral group and pair work, as well as generous attention to writing strategies in each chapter. Depending upon instructor preference and student abilities, the material can be used in course sequences lasting anywhere from one to four semesters (one to six quarters).

Features of the Second Edition

- **Resequencing of Grammar.** ***Handbuch's*** thirty chapters have been re-ordered with the needs of intermediate / advanced students in mind. Instructors choosing to approach ***Handbuch*** sequentially will find the order of presentation optimal: material generally covered in lower-level courses comes in the earlier chapters, while material traditionally presented for the first time in intermediate / advanced courses comes later. However, ***Handbuch*** continues to lend itself to a modular approach as well. Each chapter is self-contained and can be presented in any order, depending on the needs of the class or student.
- **Improved Grammar Explanations.** Explanations have been improved for enhanced clarity. Cross-referencing has been revamped and improved design makes finding explanations even easier than before.
- **Streamlined *Wortschatz* sections.** Now even more closely tied to the grammar portion of the chapter, these simplified sections still include an *Übung* section to ensure thorough mastery of this vocabulary.
- **New *Zusammenfassung* sections.** Each chapter of ***Handbuch*** now ends with a *Zusammenfassung* section. These new sections include:

1. *Rules to Remember:* A concise summary of the most important structural points covered in the chapter.

2. *Learning Tips:* In selected chapters, hints to students on how to go about learning and remembering the important points of the chapter.
3. *Activities:* Learner-centered, task-oriented, pair, group, and individual activities designed to provide students with maximum opportunity for free expression and synthesis of the material in the chapter.

Chapter Organization

Handbuch is divided into thirty chapters. Each chapter is divided into three principal parts: *Grammar, Wortschatz,* and *Zusammenfassung.* Exercises and activities fall at the end of each chapter part.

Grammar Sections

This is the main part of each chapter. Grammar explanations, which are in English, are comprehensive and succinct. Frequent charts and numerous examples with English translations illustrate each point. Since the explanations are in outline form and carefully cross-referenced to other points in the text, instructors and students can easily select specific items for study or review.

At the end of the grammar explanations for each chapter are three sections of exercises and activities: *Übungen, Anwendung,* and *Schriftliche Themen.*

Übungen. This section contains exercises that range from controlled to open-ended. As much as possible the exercises are contextualized; many involve genuine transfer of information and personal views. Most of these exercises can be done at several levels. All of them can be assigned as written homework and many can also be done orally in class with partners or in groups.

Anwendung. These application activities, based on "real-world" topics, go beyond the specific grammatical focus of the *Übungen* by letting students practice their communication skills in German. Students are encouraged in these activities to express themselves. Helpful lists of functional expressions and conversation openers *(Redemittel),* useful vocabulary *(Vokabelvorschläge),* and possible conversation topics *(Themenvorschläge)* are frequently included.

Ideally, students prepare the *Anwendung* activities outside of class, jotting down ideas and gathering necessary vocabulary so that they are prepared to engage in intelligent conversation in class. As a follow-up activity to class discussion, many of these *Anwendungen* can be assigned as composition topics.

Schriftliche Themen. This activity section concludes the grammar part of each chapter. It always begins with a boxed *Tips zum Schreiben* note. This unique feature offers general, process-oriented writing strategies as well as specific suggestions for the effective use of selected grammar structures in writing. The *Tips* are put into action in composition assignments that involve specific use of the major grammar structures studied in the chapter.

Wortschatz *Sections*

The second major chapter division is the *Wortschatz* section. This vocabulary expansion section focuses on thematic vocabulary, synonyms, idioms, linguistic points, and words that pose special problems for nonnative German speakers. The vocabulary studied is related as closely as possible to the chapter grammar topic. The section concludes with *Übungen* that reinforce the material just presented. Some of these vocabulary activities are open-ended and can be done in pairs or groups.

Zusammenfassung *Sections*

Each chapter concludes with a *Zusammenfassung* section. The section opens with a concise list of the most important grammatical principles presented in the chapter (Rules to Remember). In some chapters, a Learning Tips section follows that offers helpful hints on how best to master the material in the chapter. The section concludes with some task-oriented and learner-centered activities. These activities encourage students to apply what they have learned in the chapter in a meaningful and creative way. Most activities involve pair or group work.

Components

Handbuch zur deutschen Grammatik is accompanied by all the components necessary for a complete intermediate- or advanced-level course.

Arbeitsheft

Each chapter of the ***Arbeitsheft*** corresponds to a chapter in the student text. The ***Arbeitsheft*** is divided into three sections: writing activities, listening activities (the laboratory manual), and directed grammar activities.

The *writing activities* of each chapter consist of a wide range of writing tasks, with a focus on developing process-writing skills. Students use the targeted grammar structures in a variety of creative, personalized, open-ended situations.

The *listening activities* are designed to accompany the Audiocassette program. They represent a wide range of unique listening tasks based on the dialogues or scenarios recorded on the Audiocassettes, including listening for key words or structures, solving puzzles, identifying situations, or giving personal reactions in writing.

The final section of the ***Arbeitsheft,*** *Aufgaben zur Grammatik,* contains a series of controlled exercises to reinforce each major grammar point. For self-correction, answers to these exercises are provided at the back of the ***Arbeitsheft.***

Audiocassette Program

Eight 60-minute tapes offer students an authentic listening experience. The laboratory manual (listening activities) portion of the ***Arbeitsheft*** is coordinated to the Audiocassettes. Semi-scripted, spontaneous conversations in natural German capture students' attention and expose them to real-life authentic speech.

Tapescript/Answer Key

This component contains a complete transcript of all recorded material as well as an answer key for all discrete-answer comprehension activities.

To the Instructor

While ***Handbuch*** can be used by instructors embracing any methodology, it was written from the conviction that successful acquisition of language depends less on how it is *taught* than on its being *practiced* in a meaningful way. Thus, ***Handbuch*** includes not only controlled, contextualized exercises, but also a wealth of open-ended activities leading to genuine communication through learner-generated exchange of information, experiences, and opinions. The following suggestions of effective ways to teach with ***Handbuch*** are intended as a helpful guide, useful to instructors with a variety of philosophies and teaching styles.

Grammar Sections

One of the key issues that arose during the development of this text concerned the level and amount of grammar to be included. Research has shown that there exists considerable disparity in intermediate-level classes from one institution to another. Even within a single language department, the knowledge and skills level of intermediate students can vary widely. Therefore, the decision was made to cover the basics thoroughly enough that the book could be used by those with very limited previous exposure to German grammar, yet would provide enough detail on some of the finer points to benefit more advanced students as well. As a result, ***Handbuch*** can be used as either a review or a reference grammar. The grammar can be treated sequentially or in a modular fashion, since neither grammar nor vocabulary building is cumulative from one chapter to the next.

How the instructor chooses to test the material in each chapter is a matter of personal choice. We recommend, however, that as much as possible written testing of grammar should be learner-generated rather than instructor-imposed. For example, instead of doing fill-in activities, multiple-choice questions, etc., students should be asked to produce their own sentences, statements, or compositions using specific structures indicated by the instructor.

The following are suggestions for working with the various activity types that are included in ***Handbuch.*** These suggestions are not exhaustive.

Übungen

The *Übungen* range from structural manipulations (and an occasional translation exercise) to more open-ended activities. Many, while controlled, are nevertheless real world–based and can be used to facilitate a genuine exchange of students' ideas, experiences, views, and knowledge. All of them can be done as homework, and many can be redone in class several times as pair or group activities, each time with a different partner.

Example I *(from Chapter 2, page 17):*

F **Wie lange schon.** Erzählen Sie, wie lange / seit wann Sie Folgendes tun.

Beispiel: Tennis spielen
Ich spiele (schon) seit fünf Jahren Tennis.

1. Deutsch lernen
2. etwas als Hobby betreiben (*do*)
3. Auto fahren
4. etwas besonders Interessantes tun
5. [noch eine Aktivität]

Here are five possible ways to work with this short, straightforward activity. You might choose to use any or all of these approaches.

1. *Homework task.* Students write or mentally prepare the exercise.
2. *Pair work.* Students do the exercise in class with a partner. Students monitor each other's output for grammatical accuracy.
3. *Partner-based communicative task.* Students ask various partners questions based upon the exercise. For example:
   Seit wann lernst du Deutsch?
   Hast du ein Hobby? Wie lange spielst du . . . ?
   etc.
4. *Class or group activity.* Working in groups or as a class, students generate additional questions to ask other students and the instructor.
5. *Task-based assignment.* Students research specific information about certain topics. They concentrate on discovering how long certain things have been going on (in their school, in their community, etc.). Students then share their information with the class. Some possible topic sentences might be:
   Diese Schule gibt es seit . . . Jahren.
   Deutsch lernt man in dieser Schule seit [date].

Example II *(from Chapter 3, page 30):*

B **Große Menschen, große Leistungen** (*accomplishments*). Erzählen Sie, wie diese Menschen berühmt geworden sind. Verwenden Sie die angegebenen Verben.

Beispiel: Alfred Nobel (das Dynamit)
Er hat das Dynamit erfunden.

entdecken (*to discover*)	schreiben
erfinden (*to invent*)	singen
essen	tragen
gründen (*to found*)	übersetzen
komponieren	

1. Friedrich Schiller (das Drama *Wilhelm Tell*)
2. Siegmund Freud (die Tiefenpsychologie)
3. Rudolf Diesel (Dieselmotor)
4. Marlene Dietrich (Lieder)
5. Gustav Mahler (*Das Lied von der Erde*)
6. Atlas (die Welt)
7. Maria Theresa (Kaiserin von Österreich)
8. Heinrich Schliemann (Troja)
9. Martin Luther (die Bibel)
10. Adam und Eva (Apfel)

Many of the *Übungen* are based on authentic situations and can be used as a springboard for broadening students' knowledge and cultural awareness. Here are five suggested ways for handling the above activity.

1. Students write five additional present perfect statements about one of the persons listed in the exercise.
2. Students prepare five to seven quiz questions in the present perfect about famous people and their accomplishments. The questions can be culturally specific. Students then quiz one another. Some possible questions might be:
   *Wer hat **Die Blechtrommel** geschrieben?* (Günther Grass)
   Welcher deutsche Autor hat 1972 den Nobelpreis erhalten? (Heinrich Böll)
   Was hat James Watt getan / erfunden? (die Dampfmaschine)
3. Students write five present perfect statements about the accomplishments of the most famous person they have met personally.
4. Students write five present perfect statements about the person (living or dead) they most / least admire.
5. Students create their own exercise for generating present perfect statements without talking about themselves.

In addition to the discrete-answer, structural exercises and the culturally based exercises, many *Übungen* are personal *wahre Aussagen*. In doing these activities, instructors should insist that students' responses be real, that is, that they provide genuine information or commentary, not simply make up responses. These activities allow for the recycling of information and opinions as well as of grammatical structures. For example, one student might make statements to another student, who restates what was said to a third party. Such recycling also simulates authentic situations in that people frequently repeat information in normal conversations. Students should treat these activities as conversational opportunities and be prepared to ask follow-up questions about the statements their partners make, while at the same time consciously practicing the specific grammar points of the exercise.

Anwendung

When using these *Anwendung* activities, instructors should be flexible in allowing students to talk about what interests them. If an activity holds little interest for them, perhaps the students themselves can suggest a different topic to discuss using the same *Redemittel* and grammar structures. Instructors should view all the *Anwendungen* in the text as suggestions and as prompts for devising additional activities and tasks of their own. Following are some points to keep in mind when designing such activities:

1. Activities should be learner-based and learner-centered rather than instructor- or textbook-centered.
2. Activities should involve *active* speech production (output) based upon recall of meaningful *input*. Types of input include:
   - "real-world" input based upon the recall abilities, knowledge, experiences, and opinions of the students
   - listening / viewing input from cassette tapes, videotapes, radio, television, movies, etc.
   - reading input from a wide variety of texts: literary, journalistic, etc.
3. Grammar-based activities should be linked in a meaningful way to language skills (reading, listening, writing, speaking) and to cultural understanding.
4. Activities should involve genuine transfer and communication of information, knowledge, opinion, or reaction.
5. Activities should be interactive (involve more than one person, though the other person may be either a listener or a reader).
6. Activities should provide for primary monitoring of at least *one* structure for accuracy.
7. Activities should facilitate more than simple one-sentence utterances.

8. Activities should avoid structures and vocabulary beyond the abilities of the learners.
9. Activities should encourage thinking in German rather than in one's native tongue.
10. Activities should be of interest to the learners.

Schriftliche Themen

Writing skills are frequently neglected in foreign language instruction, yet few activities better integrate the various facets of language learning. Writers have to combine content with vocabulary and structure, and form with (self-)expression. They also have to monitor carefully for grammatical accuracy. The writing activities in the *Schriftliche Themen* sections are designed as *Schreibproben* rather than as extensive compositions. In most instances, eight to twelve sentences per *Thema* should suffice. When doing the activities, students should concentrate on applying the major grammar points of the chapter. *Tips zum Schreiben* offers suggestions on how to do this naturally and effectively. Instructors should modify the topics as they see fit. For example, in the case of the *Bildgeschichten,* students might tell the stories not only from their own perspective, but also from the point of view of various characters in the stories.

In using the *Schriftliche Themen,* instructors may find the following guidelines helpful:

1. Keep writing tasks short (in most cases eight to twelve sentences). It is better to assign more short writing tasks rather than fewer long compositions.
2. Have students exchange ideas (brainstorm) in groups or as a class about particularly challenging writing assignments before they do them at home.
3. Emphasize development of a good writing style by reminding students to follow the suggestions in the *Tips zum Schreiben* paragraph in each chapter's writing section.
4. Reward personal creativity, but insist upon grammatical accuracy (monitoring).
5. Ask for at least two drafts, a rough draft for peer editing (in pairs or small groups) and a corrected final copy to be handed in for a grade.
6. Occasionally have students write a composition in pairs or small groups. This approach allows for considerable student interaction and peer correction.
7. Have students indicate at the top of every composition what reader(s) they "pictured" or had in mind when they wrote; writing to a specific audience will help students focus their thoughts and style.
8. Do not correct straightforward grammar errors on writing tasks; circle the most egregious ones and have students self-correct. Encourage students to use the index in the text for quickly locating grammar explanations to be reviewed.

9. Always write at least one comment or follow-up response to the *content* of every writing task. Students will be more willing to write if they think someone is interested in what they have to say.
10. Occasionally have students retell or explain orally what they have written, but only after they have handed in their compositions.

Instructors might consider saving copies of the best writing assignments for later publication in an *Aufsatzsammlung* to be distributed in that class or in other German classes. This approach may encourage students to put more effort into their compositions and be more rigorous in their self-correction.

Wortschatz *Sections*

The use of synonyms and words that translate identically into English but actually have different meanings poses considerable difficulty for many German learners. Students should be encouraged to write the words in the *Wortschatz* sections on cards and to develop their own list of synonyms of tricky words. The best way for students to learn these words is of course to use them, both when writing and when reading. Indeed, instructors might consider requiring that specific words from a *Wortschatz* section be included in a particular writing assignment.

Zusammenfassung *Sections*

Instructors may wish to have students quickly preview the material in each chapter by first having them look at the *Rules to Remember* in the *Zusammenfassung* section to see which grammar points they already know. Come test time, they can use the Rules for quick review. The activities in this section can be done at any time during the chapter when the instructor wishes to do oral or written group work. These activities make a nice break from the regular classroom routine. They are particularly appropriate for use in courses emphasizing conversation.

To the Student

If you have had one to two years of basic German instruction, either at the college or high-school level, and wish to refresh your knowledge of grammar, then this book is for you. For those of you who do well on grammar quizzes but have difficulty speaking the language, this book will also prove helpful. In language learning, understanding the concept is not enough: it is also necessary to remember the structures and practice them in contexts that are meaningful for you. Only then will you be able to recall these structures quickly and use them correctly.

This text provides exactly that kind of practice. The grammar is explained in small, manageable units for quick and easy reference. The exercises *(Übungen)* following these explanations let you practice specific grammar structures in a somewhat controlled situation, while at the same time drawing on your own ideas, knowledge, and experiences. Next, the more general application activities *(Anwendung)* provide an opportunity to communicate on a range of issues, while utilizing the grammar structures you have just learned. Finally, the writing sections *(Schriftliche Themen)* stress developing your writing skills in German in both content and form. The composition topics provide a variety of practical and creative writing tasks such as composing reports, letters, and short narratives. The *Wortschatz* sections focus mainly on synonyms and matters of word usage. Finally, the *Zusammenfassung* sections contain a concise list of *Rules to Remember* that summarize the highlights of the chapter. The activities in this section offer a variety of creative communicative activities that will encourage you to put what you have learned into practice.

Learning Vocabulary

In doing the exercises and activities in this book, you will find that the level of sophistication and accuracy of your spoken and written German depends in part on the amount and type of vocabulary you already know or are willing to learn. Since many of the activities in this book are open-ended, it is not possible to predict what words you will wish to use. Suggested vocabulary *(Vokabelvorschläge),* themes *(Themenvorschläge),* and conversational openers *(Redemittel)* accompany some of the activities; but you should also strive to expand your vocabulary base by looking up in a dictionary additional words and expressions that you need in order to express your thoughts and ideas. You might want to put clusters of vocabulary words for certain topics on $3'' \times 5''$ cards for quick and easy reference. Such clusters would consist mainly of nouns, verbs, adjectives, or adverbs. Since there are only a certain number of prepositions, conjunctions, and pronouns, you should learn these as soon as possible so that you can form more complex sentences and avoid redundancy when writing or speaking. All other words, expressions, and idioms can be learned as you need them.

Learning Grammar

Grammar should not be learned in isolation or for its own sake. If you wish to work on particular grammar structures, you should consciously use them when discussing or writing about things you have read, heard, or experienced. You should also practice listening for particular structures when people speak or when you work with the Audiocassettes that accompany the ***Arbeitsheft.*** These habits will help you reach what should be your goal: meaningful, accurate communication in German.

—Larry D. Wells

Acknowledgments

It takes many dedicated people to produce a book. I would like to acknowledge the various editors, designers, artists, and assistants who contributed to both the first and the second editions of ***Handbuch***. In particular, I wish to thank Katherine Gilbert, Senior Development Editor, for guiding this revision to its completion, and Helen Bronk, Project Editor, for overseeing the manuscript's preparation for press. Their input has made ***Handbuch*** a better book.

I would like to thank the following people for reviewing the first edition of ***Handbuch zur deutschen Grammatik***. Their comments and suggestions were invaluable during the development of the second edition.

Dr. John M. Jeep   Miami University, FL
Richard Spuler   Rice University, TX
Esther Enns   University of Calgary, Canada
Joanna Bottenberg   Concordia University—Loyola Campus, Quebec, Canada

Word Order

1.1 Word Order in Main Clauses

A. *First Sentence Elements*

1. The most common first element in a German sentence is the grammatical subject.

Dieser Zug fährt über Augsburg nach Frankfurt.	*This train travels to Frankfurt via Augsburg.*

2. Words modifying the subject are considered part of the first element.

Der letzte Zug aus München fährt über Nürnberg nach Frankfurt.	*The last train out of Munich travels to Frankfurt via Nürnberg.*

3. German speakers often put adverbial expressions or prepositional verbal complements (see 30.1) in first position for the sake of style or to draw attention to this information as the actual "topic" of the statement. When this happens, the subject, which would normally be in first position, moves to a position after the conjugated verb. NOTE: Adverbial first elements are not set off by a comma, as they may be in English.

In wenigen Minuten wird der Zug Frankfurt erreichen. *(adverbial expression)*	*In a few minutes, the train will reach Frankfurt.*
Auf unseren Besuch in Frankfurt freuen wir uns sehr. *(prepositional verbal complement)*	*We are very much looking forward to our visit to Frankfurt.*

4. Direct and indirect objects, infinitives, and participles can also occur in first position, but this is much less common. In such instances, they occur mainly (but not only) in response to specific questions asking for the information contained in these elements.

Blumen hat er gekauft. *(direct object)*	*He bought flowers.*
Meinen Eltern schreibe ich. *(indirect object)*	*I am writing my parents.*
Essen wollen wir jetzt nicht. *(infinitive)*	*We do not want to eat now.*
Verstanden habe ich vom Vortrag überhaupt nichts. *(past participle)*	*I didn't understand anything at all of the lecture.*

5. **Ja, nein,** and nouns of address are not considered first elements. They are set off by a comma, and the actual sentence begins after the comma.

Ja, das ist die Liechtensteiner Polka, mein Schatz.	*Yes, that is the Liechtenstein polka, my dear.*
Mein lieber Mann, das würde ich Ihnen nicht empfehlen.	*My dear fellow, I would not recommend that to you.*

B. *Position of the Conjugated Verb*

1. The second sentence element in a main clause is always the conjugated verb, regardless of which element occupies first position.

   Die Arbeit geht **jetzt** gut.
   Jetzt **geht** die Arbeit gut.
   Gut **geht** die Arbeit jetzt.
   } *Work is going fine now.*

2. Even if the first sentence element is a subordinate clause, the conjugated verb of the following main clause is still in second position within the overall sentence.

   1 Weil wir mehr Zeit haben, *2* **geht** die Arbeit jetzt gut.
   Because we have more time, the work is going fine now.

3. For purposes of word order, when two main clauses are connected by a coordinating conjunction **(aber, denn, oder, sondern,** and **und)** (see 11.1), the conjunction is not considered a first element of the second clause; thus the position of the conjugated verb in the second clause does not change.

Sie studiert in Heidelberg, *aber* ihre Familie **wohnt** in Köln.	*She is studying in Heidelberg, but her family lives in Cologne.*

C. *Subjects and Direct/Indirect Objects*

1. Generally, subjects not in first position come as close after the conjugated verb as possible, followed by indirect and/or direct objects, and then adverbial expressions.

Gestern kaufte **Tina** ein Geschenk in der Stadt. — *Tina bought a present in town yesterday.*

2. Indirect (dative) objects (see 4.5) normally precede direct (accusative) objects (see 4.4).

Gestern kaufte Tina **ihrer Mutter ein Geschenk.** — *Yesterday Tina bought her mother a present.*

3. An accusative object *pronoun* precedes dative objects, even if the dative object is also a pronoun.

Gestern kaufte Tina **es** (das Geschenk) **ihrer Mutter.** — *Yesterday Tina bought it for her mother.*

Gestern kaufte Tina **es ihr.** — *Yesterday Tina bought it for her.*

4. A German speaker may regard a direct object noun (but never a pronoun) as important enough to be a direct complement to the verb and place it in final sentence position or in a position immediately preceding another verbal complement (see 1.1 F).

Tina kaufte ihrer Mutter zum Geburtstag **ein Geschenk.**
Tina hat ihrer Mutter zum Geburtstag **ein Geschenk** gekauft.
} *Tina bought her mother a present for her birthday.*

D. *Adverbial Expressions After the Verb*

Adverbial expressions not in first position follow the sequence **Time—Manner—Place** (TMP rule).

Peter hat mich heute früh (*T*) nach Hause (*P*) gebracht.

Peter hat mich in seinem Auto (*M*) nach Hause (*P*) gebracht.

Peter hat mich heute früh (*T*) in seinem Auto (*M*) nach Hause (*P*) gebracht.
Peter brought me home early this morning in his car.

E. *The Position(s) of* nicht *(see 6.1)*

F. *Verbal Complements*

1. In German, the most important information complementing or completing the idea of the conjugated verb tends to be in final position within a sentence. Such elements are called *verbal complements.*

2. The most common verbal complements are separable prefixes (see 29.1), past participles (see 3.1), and infinitives (see 8.1, 9.1, and 18.1).

Sie schreibt seinen Namen **auf.** *(separable prefix)*	*She writes down his name.*
Wir haben keine Blumen im Garten **gefunden.** *(past participle)*	*We found no flowers in the garden.*
Wir werden viele Gäste zur Party **einladen.** *(infinitive)*	*We will invite many guests to the party.*
Die Katze hat alles **aufgefressen.** *(separable prefix + past participle)*	*The cat ate up everything.*

3. Verbal complements such as predicate nominatives (see 4.3) and adverbs modifying the verb (see 24.1) also belong in final position, but in front of any separable prefixes, past participles, or infinitives in final position.

Er wurde nach vielen Jahren **Chef der Firma.** *(predicate nominative)* Er ist nach vielen Jahren **Chef der Firma** geworden.	*He became head of the firm after many years.*
Sie haben die neuen Wörter **auswendig** gelernt. *(adverb)*	*They (have) learned the new words by heart.*

G. *Double Infinitives* *(see 18.6)*

1.2 Positions of the Conjugated Verb in Questions

1. The conjugated verb takes first position in yes-no questions, followed immediately by the subject.

Geht die Arbeit jetzt gut? *(yes-no question)*	*Is the work going well now?*

2. The conjugated verb follows an interrogative word or expression (see 15.2).

Was **macht** die Arbeit so schwer?	*What makes the work so difficult?*
Bei was für einer Firma **arbeitest** du?	*For what sort of a company do you work?*

3. In indirect questions, the question itself is a subordinate clause (see 1.3) and the verb stands in final position within this clause.

Sie fragt, bei was für einer Firma du **arbeitest.**	*She asks what sort of a company you work for.*

1.3 Positions of the Conjugated Verb in Dependent Clauses

A. Subordinate Clauses

1. The conjugated verb occupies final position in subordinate clauses (see 11.3), even if the subordinate clause comes first in the sentence.

   COMPARE:

   Main clause: Wir kennen niemanden dort.
   We don't know anyone there.

   Subordinate clause: Wir gehen nicht zur Party, weil wir niemanden dort **kennen.**
   We are not going to the party, because we don't know anyone there.

   Weil wir niemanden dort **kennen,** gehen wir nicht zur Party.
   Because we don't know anyone there, we are not going to the party.

2. The conjugated auxiliary verb in a subordinate clause follows final position elements such as infinitives and past participles.

   Sie gingen heim, nachdem sie Lebensmittel eingekauft **hatten.** — *They went home after they had shopped for groceries.*

3. The conjugated auxiliary verb in a subordinate clause precedes a double infinitive in final position (see 18.6).

   Wir wissen, daß er sie **hat besuchen wollen.** — *We know that he wanted to visit her.*

4. As in English, the subordinating conjunction **daß** *(that)* may be omitted. When this happens, the second clause is considered a main clause and the verb stays in second position.

   COMPARE:

   Ich weiß, daß er lieber zu Hause **ißt.**
   Ich weiß, er **ißt** lieber zu Hause.
   } *I know (that) he prefers to eat at home.*

B. Relative Clauses

A relative clause (see 26.2) is a subordinate clause; the conjugated verb occupies final position within this clause.

Menschen, die Sport **treiben,** bleiben fit. — *People who engage in sports stay fit.*

* Übungen

A **Die schwere Prüfung.** Schreiben Sie die Sätze um. Setzen Sie das kursivgedruckte *(in italics)* Element an erste Stelle.

Beispiel: Wir haben *gestern* eine schwere Prüfung geschrieben.
Gestern haben wir eine schwere Prüfung geschrieben.

1. Schwere Fragen waren *auf der Prüfung.*
2. Die Studenten konnten *die meisten dieser Fragen* nicht beantworten.
3. Die Professorin war *darüber* schwer enttäuscht.
4. Ihre Studenten hatten allerdings *(to be sure)* viel *gelernt.*
5. Sie hatten *aber* einige wichtige Punkte nicht verstanden.
6. Jetzt wußte die Professorin, *daß sie die Lektion würde wiederholen müssen.*

B **Antworten auf Fragen.** Beantworten Sie die folgenden Fragen. Stellen Sie die erwünschte Information an den Anfang Ihrer Antwort.

Beispiel: Wie alt sind Sie jetzt?
Achtzehn Jahre alt bin ich jetzt.

1. Seit wann lernen Sie Deutsch?
2. Wo wohnen Sie jetzt?
3. An welchen Tagen haben Sie einen Deutschkurs?
4. Was trinken Sie besonders gern oder ungern?
5. Was werden Sie heute abend nach dem Essen tun? (z.B. lesen, fernsehen, ein wenig schlafen usw.)

C **Ein schöner Nachmittag.** Stellen Sie das Akkusativobjekt an eine andere Stelle, aber nicht an den Anfang des Satzes.

Beispiel: Am Vormittag macht Melanie einige Einkäufe in der Kaufhalle.
Am Vormittag macht Melanie in der Kaufhalle einige Einkäufe.

1. Am Nachmittag trifft Melanie eine Freundin in der Stadt.
2. Sie entschließen sich *(decide),* einen Spaziergang in dem Park zu machen.
3. Im Park suchen sie sich in einem Gartenpavillon einen hübschen Platz zum Sitzen aus.
4. Dort bestellen sie nach einiger Zeit Kaffee und Kuchen.
5. Sie verlassen den Park gegen Abend und gehen nach Hause.

D **Fehlende Information.** Ergänzen Sie die Sätze durch die Information in Klammern.

Beispiel: Wir fahren morgen nach Bern. (mit dem Zug)
Wir fahren morgen mit dem Zug nach Bern.

1. Ich habe viel Zeit. (heute)
2. Sie gingen mit der Familie. (gestern; einkaufen)

3. Sie spricht mit anderen Passagieren. (während der Fahrt)
4. Die Jungen nahmen ihre Fahrräder auf die Exkursion. (mit)
5. Wir haben heute morgen gelesen. (mit großem Interesse; die Zeitung)
6. Sie muß heute eine Postkarte schicken. (ihren Eltern)
7. Er wollte gestern mit der Aufgabe nicht helfen. (uns)
8. Hat er seiner Freundin den Brief geschrieben?—Ja, er hat geschrieben. (ihr; ihn)

✱ Anwendung

A **Partnergespräch.** Erzählen Sie jemandem im Kurs Folgendes. Beginnen Sie Ihre Sätze mit der fettgedruckten *(boldface)* Information.

was Sie **manchmal** denken
was Sie **in diesem Kurs** lernen möchten
was Sie **besonders gern** tun
was Sie gern tun, **wenn Sie Zeit haben**
was Sie **gestern** . . .
was Sie **morgen** . . .
usw.

B Berichten *(report)* Sie im Kurs, was Sie in Anwendung A über Ihren Partner / Ihre Partnerin erfahren.

Beispiel: Meine Partnerin heißt Oksana. Manchmal denkt sie, daß Deutsch schwer ist. In diesem Kurs möchte sie mehr sprechen. Besonders gern geht sie abends ins Kino. usw.

✱ Schriftliches Thema

Tips zum Schreiben ***Beginning the Sentence***
In German, using a variety of first-sentence elements is essential for effective writing. In addition to the sentence subject, adverbs, prepositional phrases, and subordinate clauses work particularly well. As a rule, try not to begin more than two or three sentences in a row with the sentence subject.

Berlin: Geschichte einer Stadt. Ändern Sie den folgenden Text stilistisch, damit *(so that)* nicht jeder Satz mit dem Satzsubjekt beginnt.

Berlin war von 1871 bis 1945 die Hauptstadt des Deutschen Reichs. Die Stadt gehörte *(belonged)* vor dem Zweiten Weltkrieg mit mehr als 4,5 Millionen Einwohnern zu den wichtigsten Metropolen Europas. Diese Stadt lag aber am Ende des Krieges in Trümmern *(rubble)*. Die alliierten Mächte *(powers)* teilten die

Stadt nach ihrem Sieg *(victory)* in vier Besatzungszonen *(occupation zones)*. Der östliche Teil der Stadt wurde während der Berliner Blockade von 1948–1949 Teil der Deutschen Demokratischen Republik (DDR). Man baute 13 Jahre später die Berliner Mauer, um die Flucht *(flight)* von Bürgern aus der Ostzone zu verhindern. Berlin blieb bis zum Sturz *(fall)* der Mauer im November 1989 eine geteilte Stadt. Die DDR und Berlin wurden wenige Monate später Teil eines neuen vereinigten Deutschlands.

Wortschatz 1

ändern
ausdrücken
sich äußern
austauschen
beenden
berichten
beschreiben

\+ *other vocabulary for activity instructions*

The following words occur more than once in the direction lines for the exercises and activities in this text.

VERBEN

ändern	to change, modify	**erklären**	to explain
ausdrücken / **zum Ausdruck bringen**	to express, say	**ersetzen**	to replace, substitute
sich äußern (zu)	to express one's views, comment on	**erzählen**	to tell, narrate
austauschen	to exchange	**gebrauchen** / **verwenden**	to use, make use of
beenden	to end, complete	**mitteilen**	to communicate *or* impart, tell
berichten (über) + *accusative*	to report (on), tell about	**übersetzen**	to translate
beschreiben	to describe	**umformen**	to transform, recast
besprechen	to discuss	**unterstreichen**	to underline
betonen	to emphasize, stress	**verbinden**	to connect, combine
bilden	to form *(sentences)*	**wiederholen**	to repeat
einsetzen	to insert, supply *(missing words)*	**zusammenfassen**	to summarize
ergänzen (durch)	to complete (with)		

SUBSTANTIVE *(Nouns)*

der Ausdruck, ¨-e	expression	**der Inhalt, -e**	content(s)
die Aussage, -n	statement	**das Thema, -en**	topic
der Gebrauch	use	**der Vorschlag, ¨-e**	suggestion

ADJEKTIVE

fehlend	missing	**passend**	suitable, proper
fettgedruckt	printed in boldface	**unterstrichen**	underlined
kursivgedruckt	printed in italics	**verschieden**	various

ÜBUNG

Anweisungen *(instructions)* **zu Übungen.** Was soll man tun? Erklären Sie die folgenden Anweisungen auf englisch.

1. Ersetzen Sie die unterstrichenen Wörter durch andere Ausdrücke.
2. Ergänzen Sie die Sätze durch passende Verben.
3. Drücken Sie die Sätze anders aus. Wiederholen Sie keine Verben.
4. Äußern Sie sich zu den folgenden Themen.
5. Bilden Sie Sätze.
6. Machen Sie bitte fünf Aussagen zu dem folgenden Thema.
7. Fassen Sie den Inhalt eines Textes in wenigen Sätzen zusammen.
8. Stellen Sie fünf Fragen mit verschiedenen Fragewörtern an jemanden im Kurs. Berichten Sie darüber.
9. Beenden Sie die folgenden Sätze.

Zusammenfassung 1

Rules to Remember

1. The conjugated verb comes first in yes-no questions.
2. The conjugated verb comes second in main clauses.
3. The conjugated verb occupies final position in dependent clauses.
4. Verbal complements in main clauses are in final position.
5. Adverbial expressions follow the sequence time–manner–place (TMP).
6. Dative objects generally precede accusative objects unless the accusative object is a pronoun.

Activities

1 **Asking and responding to questions.** Write down five questions asking for specific information that you can ask of fellow students. Other students answer the

questions, putting the requested information in first position. (Remember, if the sentence begins with something other than the subject, the subject comes after the verb.)

2 **Changing word order.** Choose one paragraph from a German story. Read each sentence aloud, one at a time. Then reread each sentence while shifting one element to a different position within the sentence.

3 **Moving the verb in subordinate clauses.** Underline ten sentences in a story. Restate the contents of your sentences to the class using one or more of the following models.

Es steht im Text, daß . . .
Wir lesen im Text, daß . . .
In diesem Text erfahren wir, . . .

4 **Expanding sentences.** Write on the board a very short German statement, the shorter the better. Your fellow students now take turns, each adding *one* element to the sentence and making any necessary changes in sentence word order.

Beispiel:
STUDENT A: Ich arbeite.
STUDENT B: Ich arbeite abends.
STUDENT C: Manchmal arbeite ich abends.
STUDENT D: Manchmal arbeite ich abends zu Hause.
STUDENT E: Wenn ich manchmal abends zu Hause arbeite, schlafe ich ein.
usw.

5 **Sentence chains.** Taking turns at the board (or on a piece of paper), write a "shaggy dog," or run-on story. The first student writes the first sentence, the second student the second sentence, etc. Starting with the second sentence, the first element of each sentence must be the final element of the preceding one. If the final element of the preceding sentence is a noun, its case may be changed in the next sentence.

Beispiel:
STUDENT A: Es lebte *eine alte Hexe.*
STUDENT B: *Die alte Hexe* lebte *in einem dunklen Wald.*
STUDENT C: *Im dunklen Wald* gefiel es ihr *sehr gut.*
STUDENT D: *Sehr gut* fand sie die vielen Himbeeren *um ihr Haus.*
STUDENT E: *Ihr Haus* war *aus Zucker.*
STUDENT F: *Zucker* war die Lieblingsspeise *eines kleinen Jungen im Dorf.*
usw.

VARIATION: Invent your own run-on story of at least twenty sentences.

6 **Working with a text.** From memory, make ten statements about either a story or a non-literary text you have read recently for class. Begin all of your statements with something other than the grammatical subject.

Present Tense

2.1 Present-Tense Conjugations

A. *Regular Verbs*

1. Most German verbs form the present tense **(das Präsens)** by dropping the **-en** from the infinitive and adding personal endings to the remaining stem.

Singular		**kochen** *(to cook)*		**diskutieren** *(to discuss)*
1st pers.	ich	koch **e**	ich	diskutier **e**
2nd pers. (informal)	du	koch **st**	du	diskutier **st**
3rd pers.	er / sie / es	koch **t**	er / sie / es	diskutier **t**
Plural				
1st pers.	wir	koch **en**	wir	diskutier **en**
2nd pers. (informal)	ihr	koch **t**	ihr	diskutier **t**
3rd pers. / 2nd pers. sing. & pl. (formal)	sie / Sie	koch **en**	sie / Sie	diskutier **en**

2. If the verb stem ends in **-d** or **-t,** or if it ends in an **-m** or **-n** that is preceded by a consonant other than **l** or **r,** then an **e** is inserted before the **-st** and **-t** endings (second and third persons singular and second person plural). This change facilitates pronunciation.

	arbeiten *(to work)*				**öffnen** *(to open)*		
ich	arbeit **e**	wir	arbeit **en**	ich	öffn **e**	wir	öffn **en**
du	arbeit **est**	ihr	arbeit **et**	du	öffn **est**	ihr	öffn **et**
er / sie / es	arbeit **et**	sie / Sie	arbeit **en**	er / sie / es	öffn **et**	sie / Sie	öffn **en**

3. If the verb stem ends in a sibilant **(-s, -ss, -ß, -tz, -z),** the **s** of the second person singular **-st** ending is absorbed into the preceding sibilant.

reisen *(to travel)*	**grüßen** *(to greet)*	**sitzen** *(to sit)*
du rei**st**	du grü**ßt**	du sit**zt**

4. If the infinitive ends in **-ern** or **-eln,** the initial **e** in the first person singular stem is optional.

ärgern *(to annoy)*	**sammeln** *(to collect)*
ich ärg**(e)re**	ich samm**(e)le**

5. If the infinitive ends in **-n** (instead of **-en**), **-ern,** or **-eln,** then the first and third person plural endings are identical to the infinitive.

tun *(to do)*	**ärgern** *(to annoy)*	**sammeln** *(to collect)*
wir tu**n**	wir ärg**ern**	wir samm**eln**
sie / Sie tu**n**	sie / Sie ärg**ern**	sie / Sie samm**eln**

B. *Verbs with Stem-Vowel Shifts*

1. Some strong verbs (see 3.1) change a stem vowel **e** to **i** in the second and third persons singular. (see Appendix 4 for a complete listing)

brechen *(to break)*	
ich breche	wir brechen
du brichst	ihr brecht
er / sie / es bricht	sie / Sie brechen

Other common **e** > **i** *verbs*

essen *(to eat)* → du **i**ßt; er **i**ßt[1]
geben *(to give)* → du g**i**bst; sie g**i**bt
helfen *(to help)* → du h**i**lfst; er h**i**lft
nehmen *(to take)* → du n**i**mmst; sie n**i**mmt[2]
sprechen *(to speak)* → du spr**i**chst; er spr**i**cht
sterben *(to die)* → du st**i**rbst; sie st**i**rbt
treffen *(to meet)* → du tr**i**ffst; er tr**i**fft
treten *(to step; to kick)* → du tr**i**ttst; sie tr**i**tt
vergessen *(to forget)* → du verg**i**ßt; er verg**i**ßt
werfen *(to throw)* → du w**i**rfst; sie w**i**rft

1. The spelling **-ss-** occurs only between short vowels; in all other instances German uses **-ß.**
2. This verb also has a slight consonant change.

2. Some strong verbs change a stem vowel **e** to **ie** in the second and third persons singular.

	sehen *(to see)*		
ich	sehe	wir	sehen
du	s**ie**hst	ihr	seht
er / sie / es	s**ie**ht	sie / Sie	sehen

Other common **e** > **ie** *verbs*

befehlen *(to command)* → du bef**ie**hlst; sie bef**ie**hlt
empfehlen *(to recommend)* → du empf**ie**hlst; er empf**ie**hlt
geschehen *(to happen)* → es gesch**ie**ht
lesen *(to read)* → du l**ie**st; sie l**ie**st
stehlen *(to steal)* → du st**ie**hlst; er st**ie**hlt

3. Some strong verbs change a stem vowel **a** to **ä** in the second and third persons singular.

	fangen *(to catch)*		
ich	fange	wir	fangen
du	f**ä**ngst	ihr	fangt
er / sie / es	f**ä**ngt	sie / Sie	fangen

Other common **a** > **ä** *verbs*

anfangen *(to begin)* → du f**ä**ngst an; er f**ä**ngt an
einladen *(to invite)* → du l**ä**dst ein; sie l**ä**dt ein
fahren *(to go; to drive)* → du f**ä**hrst; er f**ä**hrt
fallen *(to fall)* → du f**ä**llst; sie f**ä**llt
gefallen *(to please)* → du gef**ä**llst; er gef**ä**llt
halten *(to hold)* → du h**ä**ltst; sie h**ä**lt
lassen *(to let; to leave)* → du l**ä**ßt; er l**ä**ßt
schlafen *(to sleep)* → du schl**ä**fst; sie schl**ä**ft
schlagen *(to hit, beat)* → du schl**ä**gst; er schl**ä**gt
tragen *(to carry; to wear)* → du tr**ä**gst; sie tr**ä**gt
wachsen *(to grow)* → du w**ä**chst; er w**ä**chst
waschen *(to wash)* → du w**ä**schst; sie w**ä**scht

4. Several strong verbs change their stem vowels as follows:

laufen *(to run)* → du l**äu**fst; sie l**äu**ft
saufen *(to drink, guzzle)* → du s**äu**fst; er s**äu**ft
gebären *(to give birth)* → du geb**ie**rst; sie geb**ie**rt
stoßen *(to push, bump)* → du st**ö**ßt; er st**ö**ßt

C. *Auxiliary Verbs and* wissen

The following very common verbs conjugate irregularly in the present tense:

	sein *(to be)*	**haben** *(to have)*	**werden** *(to become)*	**wissen** *(to know)*
ich	**bin**	habe	werde	**weiß**
du	**bist**	**hast**	**wirst**	**weißt**
er / sie / es	**ist**	**hat**	**wird**	**weiß**
wir	**sind**	haben	werden	wissen
ihr	**seid**	habt	werdet	wißt
sie / Sie	**sind**	haben	werden	wissen

D. *Modal Verbs* *(See 9.1)*

E. *Prefix Verbs*

1. Verbs with the inseparable prefixes **be-, emp-, ent-, er-, ge-, miß-, ver-,** and **zer-** (see 29.2) conjugate in the present tense just like their root verbs.

Sie **beschreibt** das Bild.	*She describes the picture.*
Franz **erzählt** eine Geschichte.	*Franz tells a story.*

2. Verbs with separable prefixes (**an-, aus-, fort-, mit-, weg-,** etc.) conjugate just like their root verbs, but in the present (and simple past) tenses the prefix separates from the verb and moves to the end of a main clause (see 29.1).

Wir **gehen** heute abend mit Freunden **aus.** *(prepositional prefix)*	*We are going out with friends this evening.*
Sie **wirft** die alten Zeitungen **weg.** *(adverbial prefix)*	*She throws away the old newspapers.*

3. A separable prefix does not separate from its verb in a subordinate clause.

Ich weiß, daß er heute abend mit Freunden **ausgeht.**	*I know that he is going out with friends this evening.*

2.2 Uses of the Present Tense

A. *Present Time*

English has three different ways to express present time; German has only one.

ich schreibe { *I write* (present tense) / *I am writing* (progressive present tense) / *I do write* (emphatic present tense)

B. *Continuing Past Actions*

English expresses the idea of a past action continuing into the present with *have been* + the *-ing* form of the verbs or *have* + the past participle + *for* or *since.* German expresses the same idea with the present tense followed by the adverb **schon** + a time expression in the accusative, the preposition **seit** + dative, (see 10.2I) or **schon seit** + dative.

Sie **warten schon** eine Stunde.	*They have already been waiting (for) an hour.*
Gerhard **arbeitet seit** einem Jahr bei Siemens.	*Gerhard has been working (has worked) at Siemens for a year.*
Wir **wohnen schon seit** dem Sommer hier.	*We have been living (have lived) here since the summer.*

C. *Narration*

The present tense is used frequently when recounting jokes, episodes, and plots of films or books, even though the context is clearly past time.

Am Anfang der Erzählung **sitzt** der Hauptcharakter in seinem Zimmer und **liest.** Kurz nach Mitternacht **klopft** plötzlich jemand . . .	*In the beginning of the story the main character is sitting in his room and reading. Shortly after midnight someone suddenly knocks . . .*

D. *Future Time*

The present tense can be used to indicate what someone *is doing* or *is going to do* in the future, provided that context or an adverb of time makes the future meaning clear (see 8.1B).

Wir **gehen** *morgen* einkaufen.	*We're going / going to go shopping tomorrow.*

* Übungen

A **In der Familie.** Wer tut was?

Beispiel: kochen (Vater)
Vater ***kocht.***

1. Musik hören (die Mutter)
2. in einem Büro arbeiten (der Vater)
3. Sport treiben (die Schwester)
4. basteln *(to do handicrafts)* (ich; die Eltern)

5. Feste feiern (alle in der Familie)
6. viel über Politik reden *(talk)* (der Onkel)
7. telefonieren (der Bruder)
8. Bierdeckel *(beer coasters)* sammeln (ich; die Tante)
9. verrückte *(crazy)* Dinge tun (die Großeltern)

B **Immer zuviel oder zuwenig.** Thomas kritisiert alle Leute, die er kennt. Was sagt er zu diesen Personen?

Beispiele: zu seinem Vater: Taschengeld geben
„Vati, du gibst mir zuwenig Taschengeld."

zu seinen Eltern: arbeiten
„Liebe Eltern, ihr arbeitet zuviel."

1. zu seiner Mutti: das Haus putzen
2. zu seinen Eltern: reisen
3. zum Haushund: fressen
4. zu seiner Freundin: herumsitzen und nichts tun
5. zu seinen Mitspielern in der Fußballmannschaft: laufen und Tore schießen *(shoot goals)*

C **Was andere Leute (gern)[3] tun.** Sie möchten einiges über andere Studenten erfahren. Stellen Sie Fragen mit den folgenden Verben. Berichten Sie nachher über die Antworten.

Beispiele: schlafen
*Wie lange **schläfst** du gewöhnlich?*

essen
*Was **ißt** du gern zum Frühstück?*

werden
***Wirst** du oft krank?*

1. schlafen
2. essen
3. waschen
4. tragen
5. sprechen
6. lesen
7. werden
8. laufen

D **Einiges über Sie.** Bilden Sie mit den folgenden Präfixverben Aussagen über sich selbst und andere Mitglieder *(members)* Ihrer Familie.

---

3. For the use of **gern,** see **Wortschatz 9.**

Beispiele: ausgehen
*Ich **gehe** am Wochenende oft mit Freunden **aus.***
verstehen
*Meine Eltern **verstehen** mich oft nicht.*

1. ausgeben *(to spend)*
2. besuchen
3. fernsehen
4. anrufen
5. einladen
6. verbringen *(to spend time)*

E **Wie lange schon?** Erzählen Sie, wie lange / seit wann Sie Folgendes tun.

Beispiel: Tennis spielen
Ich spiele (schon) seit fünf Jahren Tennis.

1. Deutsch lernen
2. etwas als Hobby betreiben *(do)*
3. Auto fahren
4. etwas besonders Interessantes tun
5. [noch eine Aktivität]

* Anwendung

A **Sich vorstellen und andere kennenlernen.** Erzählen Sie jemandem im Kurs von Ihren Hobbys, Interessen und Freizeitbeschäftigungen *(leisure time activities)*. Was tun Sie gern? Was tun Sie nicht so gern? Was tun Sie mit anderen Menschen zusammen? Merken Sie sich *(take note)*, was Ihr(e) Partner(in) erzählt (siehe **schriftliches Thema A**).

THEMEN- UND VOKABELVORSCHLÄGE

viel Sport treiben (z.B. Tennis / Golf / Fußball spielen)
radfahren
angeln *(to fish)*
reiten
segeln *(to sail)*
sammeln (z.B. Briefmarken, Münzen, Sammelbilder von Sportlern)
fotografieren
Fremdsprachen lernen
lesen (z.B. Bücher, Zeitungen, Zeitschriften)
mit Freunden zusammen etwas machen (z.B. spazierengehen, ins Kino / ins Museum / tanzen gehen, Videospielfilme / MTV sehen, Karten / Schach *(chess)* / Scrabble spielen)

REDEMITTEL

Weißt du, was mir besonders viel Spaß macht?
Ich [lese] besonders gern . . .
Am liebsten [gehe] ich . . . *(Most of all I like to [go] . . .)*
In meiner [Briefmarken]sammlung habe ich . . .
Abends gehe ich manchmal . . .
Wenn ich viel Zeit habe, dann [fahre] ich . . .

B **Pläne für das Wochenende.** Sprechen Sie mit jemandem im Kurs über Ihre Pläne für das kommende Wochenende. Verwenden Sie das Präsens.

REDEMITTEL

Das weiß ich noch nicht so genau.
Wahrscheinlich stehe ich am Samstag . . . auf.
Zu Mittag esse ich . . .
Am Nachmittag muß ich . . .
Ich gehe dann am Abend . . .
Und was hast *du* fürs Wochenende vor *(have in mind)*?

C **Wo ich mich gern aufhalte** *(spend time)*. Erzählen Sie anderen Studenten von einem Ort *(place)*, der Ihnen besonders gefällt. Erklären Sie, warum Sie diesen Ort so gern besuchen. Was gibt es dort? Was tut man dort?

THEMENVORSCHLÄGE

ein Strand *(beach)*
ein Park
ein Feriendorf
ein Geschäft
das Haus von einem Freund

REDEMITTEL

Ich finde . . . ganz fabelhaft.
Weißt du, was mir so daran gefällt?
Viele Leute kommen . . .
Dort sieht man auch, wie . . .
Manchmal gibt es . . .
Da findet man . . .
Besonders gut gefällt / gefallen mir . . . (+ *nominative*)

* Schriftliche Themen

Tips zum Schreiben ***Using Familiar Verbs and Structures***
Always plan your composition around verbs and structures you already know. Do not attempt to translate English ideas and structures into German. Jot down your ideas in German using familiar vocabulary, then look up any other necessary words in a dictionary. To avoid misuse, check the meaning of these words in German as well as in English. You should also avoid using **haben** and **sein,** if a specific verb will describe an activity more precisely. Try not to repeat verbs, unless you wish to emphasize a particular activity through repetition. A good variety of verbs will make your writing more interesting.

A **Darf ich vorstellen?** Stellen Sie jemanden im Kurs schriftlich vor. Geben Sie Alter und Wohnort an. Erzählen Sie unter anderem *(among other things)* von seinen / ihren Hobbys, Interessen und Freizeitbeschäftigungen.

Beispiel: Johann ist 20 Jahre alt und kommt aus . . . Im Sommer arbeitet er als Jugendberater *(youth counselor)* in einem Sportklub. Wenn er Zeit hat, segelt er gern mit seinen Freunden . . . Abends gehen er und seine Freunde oft . . . Er sammelt Schallplatten und möchte später . . . usw.

B **Ein Arbeitstag.** Wie stellen Sie sich *(imagine)* einen Tag im Leben Ihres Deutschprofessors / Ihrer Deutschprofessorin vor? Erzählen Sie davon.

Beispiel: Meine Deutschprofessorin arbeitet sehr schwer. Jeden Morgen fährt sie schon kurz nach acht Uhr zur Universität, wo sie drei Stunden unterrichtet. Danach macht sie eine Mittagspause und ißt oft in der Cafeteria. Am Nachmittag hält sie Sprechstunden, und manchmal nimmt sie an einer Arbeitssitzung mit Kollegen teil. Wenn sie abends nach Hause kommt, . . . usw.

C **Alltägliche Menschen, alltägliches Leben.** Schildern Sie *(portray)* kurz die Arbeit oder den Tag eines Menschen, der mit seiner / ihrer Arbeit zu unserem alltäglichen Leben gehört (z.B. die Busfahrerin, der Briefträger, der Verkäufer / die Verkäuferin im Geschäft, wo Sie manchmal etwas Kleines zum Essen holen, usw.).

Beispiel: der Schülerlotse *(school crossing guard)*
Jeden Morgen sieht man ihn an der Ecke stehen. Wenn die Schüler kommen, hält er die Autos an, und die Schüler gehen über die Straße. An kalten Wintertagen hofft er, daß die letzten Schüler bald kommen. Er denkt oft (daran), daß er auch einmal klein war und . . . Manchmal träumt er von . . . usw.

Wortschatz 2

wissen	lernen
kennen	studieren

WISSEN VERSUS **KENNEN**

1. The verb **wissen** means to *know* something *as a fact.* It can never be used in the sense of knowing persons.

Sie **weiß** die Antworten.	*She knows the answers.*
Wir **wissen** viel über Briefmarken.	*We know a lot about postage stamps.*

2. **Wissen** is always used with the objects **alles, etwas, nichts, viel,** and **wenig.**

Er denkt, daß er **alles** besser **weiß.**	*He thinks that he knows everything better.*

3. **Wissen** often prefaces clauses, particularly in questions.

Weißt du, wann die Gäste kommen?	*Do you know when the guests are coming?*

4. The verb **kennen** *(to know)* expresses familiarity with someone or something. It cannot have a clause as a direct object.

Wir **kennen** diesen Politiker nicht.	*We do not know this politician.*
Kennst du die Alpen?	*Are you familiar with the Alps?*

Note the difference between the following two sentences:

Sie **weiß** viele europäische Hauptstädte.	*She knows (the names of) many European capital cities.*
Sie **kennt** viele europäische Hauptstädte.	*She knows / is familiar with many European capital cities. (She has been there.)*

5. Neither **wissen** nor **kennen** can express the idea of *knowing* a language or knowing *how* to do something; the modal verb **können** must be used in these cases (see 9.2).

Ich **kann** Deutsch.	*I know German.*
Können Sie tanzen?	*Do you know how to dance?*

LERNEN VERSUS STUDIEREN

1. The verb **lernen** means *to learn* or *to acquire* specific subjects, skills, or information.

Was hast du in diesem Kurs **gelernt?**	*What did you learn in this course?*
Udo **lernt** seit zwei Jahren Spanisch.	*Udo has been studying Spanish for two years. (It is not his major.)*

2. The verb **studieren** means to study at a university-level institution; it cannot refer to learning taking place in elementary or high schools. **Studieren** also means to study or major in a particular field or discipline.

Barbara möchte in Heidelberg **studieren.**	*Barbara would like to study in Heidelberg.*
Ihr Bruder **studiert** Jura in Göttingen.	*Her brother is studying law in Göttingen. (It is his major.)*

ÜBUNGEN

A **Welches Verb paßt?** Sagen Sie, ob Sie Folgendes **wissen, kennen** oder **können.**

Beispiele: die Stadt Hamburg
Nein, die Stadt Hamburg ***kenne*** *ich nicht.*

wann Goethe gelebt hat
Ja, ich ***weiß,*** *wann Goethe gelebt hat.*

1. jemanden, der in Holland wohnt
2. das Geburtsjahr Goethes
3. wann der Zweite Weltkrieg geendet hat
4. alle europäischen Länder, in denen man Deutsch spricht
5. etwas Interessantes über die Schweiz
6. den Namen des deutschen Bundeskanzlers
7. die Frau des deutschen Bundeskanzlers
8. eine andere Fremdsprache außer Deutsch

B **Die Stadt, in der ich jetzt wohne.** Was *wissen* Sie von der Stadt, in der Sie jetzt wohnen? Was *kennen* Sie in dieser Stadt besonders gut? Machen Sie ein paar Aussagen mit jedem Verb.

Zusammenfassung 2

Rules to Remember

1. Conjugated verbs agree with their grammatical subjects in person and in number.
2. German has only one set of present-tense forms; English has three.

Learning Tip

Studies show that we retain words better in context than as isolated vocabulary elements. Associate with each new verb you encounter or wish to learn two or three logical objects or verbal complements. For example, **ankommen** *(to arrive):* am Bahnhof/mit Freunden/zu spät OR
schreiben *(to write):* einen Brief/einen Zettel/an Freunde

Activities

1 **Getting to know someone.** Make a list of present-tense questions to ask a partner in class. Ask your questions and create new ones every day. How much can you learn about your partner in one week? Find at least seven things you have in common with this person.

2 **Game: Recalling vocabulary.** Write a random German word of at least six letters on the board. Now write down as many verbs as you can think of in two minutes that begin with the letters in that word on the board. The person with the most verbs is the winner.

Variation: Use the same word on the board. For each letter in the word, write a present-tense sentence containing a verb beginning with this letter. The first student to finish is the winner.

3 **Generating statements.** Write on a card as many verbs as you can think of in one minute. Give your card to a partner who must make a statement about herself / himself or about other students with each verb.

Variation: Working with a partner, *rapidly* generate as many present-tense statements about yourself or other students as you can think of in one or two minutes.

4 **Generalizing observations.** Working with a small group of students, make generalizing statements or observations. Do not repeat any verb until you have run out of ideas. Share your statements with other groups.

Beispiele: *Vögel haben Federn.*
Im Sommer ist es in Griechenland sehr heiß.
Politiker versprechen immer (zu) viel.

Variation: Group your generalizing observations around contrasting themes such as day / night, summer / winter, in the country / in the city, etc.

5 **Practicing the present.** Take a text you have read recently for class that is not in the present tense. Read the text aloud, changing all verbs to the present tense.

6 **Working with a text.** Write on the board ten verbs from a short text you have read recently for class. Working with other students, generate present-tense statements about the content of the text using these verbs.

Variation: Generate present-tense statements about what is *not* told in this text.

Beispiel: *Wir wissen nicht, ob / wo / wer / usw.*
Es steht nicht im Text, ob / wo / wer / usw.

3 Present Perfect Tense

3.1 Principal Parts of Verbs

Every German verb has three principal parts:

1. an *infinitive,* from which the present tense is formed.
2. a *past tense* form.
3. a *past participle,* from which the present perfect tense is formed.

Verbs are classified as *weak, irregular weak,* or *strong,* depending on how they form their second and third principal parts.

A. Weak Verbs

1. A weak verb forms its past participle by adding an unstressed **ge-** prefix and the ending **-t** to the infinitive stem.

Infinitive	*Past Tense*[1]	*Past Participle*
lernen	lernte	**ge**lern**t**
tanzen	tanzte	**ge**tanz**t**

2. When the verb stem ends in **-d** or **-t,** or in **-m** or **-n** preceded by another consonant other than **l** or **r,** an **e** is inserted before the final **-t** in both the past tense and the past participle for the sake of pronunciation.

Infinitive	*Past Tense*	*Past Participle*
arbeiten	arbeit**e**te	gearbeit**e**t
öffnen	öffn**e**te	geöffn**e**t

1. Although this chapter focuses on past participles, the past tense forms are provided as well, since the principal parts of a verb are best learned together. Formation of the simple past tense is presented in Chapter 7.

3. Verbs with infinitives ending in **-ieren,** all of which are weak, do not have a **ge-** prefix in the past participle.

Infinitive	*Past Tense*	*Past Participle*
diskutieren	diskutierte	**diskutiert**

B. Irregular Weak Verbs

1. **Haben** is a weak verb with a slightly irregular past tense.

Infinitive	*Past Tense*	*Past Participle*
haben	**hatte**	gehabt

2. A few other verbs are also irregular. They are sometimes called *mixed verbs,* since the past participle ends in **-t,** but the infinitive stem undergoes a vowel change, which is also characteristic of strong verbs. An **ist** before the past participle indicates that the present perfect is formed with the auxiliary verb **sein** instead of **haben** (see 3.2).

Infinitive	*Past Tense*	*Past Participle*
brennen *(to burn)*	br**a**nnte	gebr**a**nnt
kennen *(to know)*	k**a**nnte	gek**a**nnt
nennen *(to name)*	n**a**nnte	gen**a**nnt
rennen *(to run)*	r**a**nnte	ist ger**a**nnt
bringen *(to bring)*	br**ach**te	gebr**ach**t
denken *(to think)*	d**ach**te	ged**ach**t
wissen *(to know)*	w**u**ßte	gew**u**ßt

3. Two verbs have interchangeable regular and irregular weak forms.[2]

Infinitive	*Past Tense*	*Past Participle*
senden *(to send)*	sendete / s**a**ndte	gesendet / ges**a**ndt
wenden *(to turn)*	wendete / w**a**ndte	gewendet / gew**a**ndt

4. Modal verbs are also weak and irregular. They are discussed in Chapter 9.

---

2. Regular weak forms of **senden** must be used to mean *to broadcast on radio or TV.* The regular weak forms of **wenden** are used to mean *to turn over, inside out,* or *in the opposite direction.*

Am Abend hat Radio Bremen Musik **gesendet.**	*In the evening Radio Bremen broadcast music.*
Die Schneiderin hat den Mantel **gewendet.**	*The seamstress reversed the material in the coat (the material on the inside was put on the outside).*

C. *Strong Verbs*

1. Strong-verb participles are formed with a **ge-** prefix, but the participle ends in **-en** instead of **-t.** The stem vowel is also often different from that of the infinitive. (The stem vowel in the simple past tense of these verbs will always differ from that of the infinitive; see 7.1). Since a good number of strong verbs in German describe daily activities, they occur quite frequently and should be memorized. Many strong verbs have strong-verb equivalents in English. (See Appendix 4 for a more comprehensive list of strong verbs.)

Infinitive	*Past Tense*	*Past Participle*
beißen *(to bite)*	biß *(bit)*	gebissen *(bitten)*
fliegen *(to fly)*	flog *(flew)*	ist geflogen *(flown)*
geben *(to give)*	gab *(gave)*	gegeben *(given)*
singen *(to sing)*	sang *(sang)*	gesungen *(sung)*

2. The auxiliaries **sein** and **werden** are strong verbs.

Infinitive	*Past Tense*	*Past Participle*
sein *(to be)*	war *(was)*	ist gewesen *(been)*
werden *(to become)*	wurde *(became)*	ist geworden *(become)*

3. A few strong verbs also have minor consonant changes.

Infinitive	*Past Tense*	*Past Participle*
gehen *(to go)*	ging *(went)*	ist gega**ng**en *(gone)*
nehmen *(to take)*	nahm *(took)*	geno**mm**en *(taken)*
stehen *(to stand)*	stand *(stood)*	gesta**nd**en *(stood)*
tun *(to do)*	tat *(did)*	getan *(done)*

4. Strong verbs are often called irregular because of the vowel changes in the second and third principal parts. However, many of these vowel shifts do follow set patterns. Note, for example, the patterns in the following verb groups.

Infinitive	*Past Tense*	*Past Participle*
finden *(to find)*	fand *(found)*	gefunden *(found)*
springen *(to jump)*	sprang *(jumped)*	ist gesprungen *(jumped)*
trinken *(to drink)*	trank *(drank)*	getrunken *(drunk)*
zwingen *(to force)*	zwang *(forced)*	gezwungen *(forced)*
essen *(to eat)*	aß *(ate)*	ge**g**essen *(eaten)*
lesen *(to read)*	las *(read)*	gelesen *(read)*
messen *(to measure)*	maß *(measured)*	gemessen *(measured)*
sehen *(to see)*	sah *(saw)*	gesehen *(seen)*

D. *Prefix Verbs*

1. Verbs with separable prefixes (see 29.1) insert **-ge-** between the separable prefix and its participle. Separable prefixes can occur with weak, irregular weak, or strong verbs.

Infinitive	*Past Tense*	*Past Participle*
ausatmen *(to exhale)*	atmete aus	aus**ge**atmet *(weak)*
abbrennen *(to burn down)*	brannte ab	ab**ge**brannt *(irregular weak)*
mitnehmen *(to take along)*	nahm mit	mit**ge**nommen *(strong)*

2. Verbs with the *inseparable* prefixes **be-, emp-, ent-, er-, ge-, miß-, ver-,** and **zer-** (see 29.2) do not add **ge-** to the past participle since the participle already begins with an unstressed prefix. Inseparable prefixes can also occur with weak, irregular weak, or strong verbs.

Infinitive	*Past Tense*	*Past Participle*
besuchen *(to visit)*	besuchte	**besucht** *(weak)*
erkennen *(to recognize)*	erkannte	**erkannt** *(irregular weak)*
versprechen *(to promise)*	versprach	**versprochen** *(strong)*

3.2 Present Perfect Tense

A. *Formation*

1. The German present perfect tense **(das Perfekt)** is formed with the conjugated auxiliary **haben** or **sein** + the past participle of the main verb.

	haben	**+ *Past Participle***		**sein**	**+ *Past Participle***
ich	**habe**		ich	**bin**	
du	**hast**		du	**bist**	
er / sie / es	**hat**	**+ gesehen**	er / sie / es	**ist**	**+ gekommen**
wir	**haben**		wir	**sind**	
ihr	**habt**		ihr	**seid**	
sie / Sie	**haben**		sie / Sie	**sind**	

2. Past participles are placed at the end of main clauses. In dependent clauses, however, the conjugated auxiliary moves to final position.

Sie **hat** eine interessante Nachricht **bekommen.** *(main clause)*	*She has received some interesting news.*
Wißt ihr, wer ihr diese Nachricht **geschickt hat?** *(dependent clause)*	*Do you know who sent her this news?*

B. Haben *Versus* sein

1. The conjugated auxiliary **haben** is used to form the present perfect in most instances, including whenever the main verb has a direct object or is used reflexively.

Sie **haben** gut geschlafen.	*They slept well.*
Sie **hat** die Zeitung gelesen.	*She read the newspaper.*
Wir **haben** uns verspätet.	*We were late.*

2. The auxiliary verb **sein** is used only when *both* of the following conditions are met:

a. the main verb expresses motion, change of location, or change of condition; *and*
b. the main verb is intransitive (does not have an accusative object).

Sie **ist** nach Hause **gegangen.** *(motion)*	*She went home.*
Er **ist** von einem Baum **gefallen.** *(change of location)*	*He fell from a tree.*
Sie **sind** reich **geworden.** *(change of condition)*	*They became rich.*
Er **ist gestorben.** *(change of condition)*	*He died.*

3. **Sein, bleiben,** and a few other intransitive verbs require the auxiliary **sein,** even though they do not appear to express motion or change of location or condition.

sein *(to be)*	gelingen *(to succeed)*
bleiben *(to stay)*	geschehen *(to happen)*
begegnen *(to meet, come across)*	passieren *(to happen)*

Er **ist** Professor **gewesen.**	*He was a professor.*
Sie **sind** zu Hause **geblieben.**	*They stayed at home.*
Mir **ist** etwas Schreckliches **passiert.**	*Something terrible happened to me.*

4. Some verbs, such as **fahren, fliegen, schwimmen,** etc., can take either **haben** or **sein** as the auxiliary, depending on whether the emphasis is on the activity itself or on motion or change.

COMPARE:

Lorenz and Heilke **haben** im Tanzsaal **getanzt.** *(no change of location)*	*Lorenz and Heilke danced in the dance hall.*
Paul und Paula **sind** aus dem Saal **getanzt.** *(change of location)*	*Paul and Paula danced out of the dance hall.*

Sein is never used, however, when such verbs have an accusative object.

COMPARE:

Ich **bin** im Mercedes auf der Autobahn **gefahren.** *(motion with* **no** *accusative object)*	*I drove on the highway in a Mercedes.*
Ich **habe** den VW in die Garage **gefahren.** *(motion* ***with*** *an accusative object)*	*I drove the VW into the garage.*

C. Use

1. The present perfect is primarily a *conversational tense* used when referring to actions in the past. It corresponds in meaning to several English forms:

ich habe . . . gehört { *I heard* / *I was hearing* / *I did hear* / *I have heard* / *I would hear* }

2. In most cases, the present perfect tense **(ich habe . . . gehört)** has the same meanings as the simple past tense **(ich hörte).** The present perfect, however, is used much more frequently in spoken German and in written conversational situations such as letters and diaries.[3]

3. As main verbs, **haben** and **sein** occur more often in the simple past. & MODALS

Wo **warst** du gestern nachmittag?	*Where were you yesterday afternoon?*
—Ich **hatte** einen Termin beim Zahnarzt.	*I had an appointment with the dentist.*

* Übungen

A **Fragen im Perfekt.** Theo war heute morgen nicht in der Deutschstunde. Jetzt fragt er jemanden, was man gemacht hat. Welche Fragen stellt er?

Beispiel: Professorin / ein Quiz geben
Hat die Professorin ein Quiz gegeben?

Schwache (weak) *Verben*

1. ihr / viel arbeiten
2. man / das Gedicht von Goethe interpretieren
3. alle Studenten / Hausarbeiten einreichen *(hand in)*
4. ich / etwas Wichtiges versäumen *(miss)*

3. The present perfect tense is particularly prevalent in Southern Germany, Austria, and Switzerland, even in narration, whereas in Northern Germany the past tense is preferred for narration and sometimes even for conversation (see 7.1B).

Gemischte (mixed) *Verben*

5. die Professorin / denken, daß ich krank bin
6. du / wissen, wo ich war
7. Gabi / ihren Freund zur Stunde mitbringen

Starke (strong) *Verben*

8. du / die Aufgabe für morgen aufschreiben
9. jemand / einen mündlichen Bericht geben
10. ihr / ein neues Kapitel anfangen
11. die Professorin / über die Prüfung sprechen

B **Große Menschen, große Leistungen** *(accomplishments).* Erzählen Sie, wie diese Menschen berühmt geworden sind. Verwenden Sie die angegebenen Verben.

Beispiel: Alfred Nobel (das Dynamit)
Er hat das Dynamit erfunden.

entdecken *(to discover)*	gründen *(to found)*	singen
erfinden *(to invent)*	komponieren	tragen
essen	schreiben	übersetzen

1. Friedrich Schiller (das Drama *Wilhelm Tell*)
2. Sigmund Freud (die Tiefenpsychologie)
3. Rudolf Diesel (Dieselmotor)
4. Marlene Dietrich (Lieder)
5. Gustav Mahler *(Das Lied von der Erde)*
6. Atlas (die Welt)
7. Maria Theresa (Kaiserin von Österreich)
8. Heinrich Schliemann (Troja)
9. Martin Luther (die Bibel)
10. Adam und Eva (Apfel)

C **Schlagzeilen** *(headlines)* **aus Boulevardzeitungen** *(tabloids):* ***haben*** **oder** ***sein?*** Erklären Sie, was passiert ist.

Beispiel: Tauber Professor spricht mit Marsmenschen!
Ein tauber Professor ***hat*** *mit Marsmenschen* ***gesprochen.***

1. Sechsjähriges Mädchen wird Mutter von Zwillingen!
2. Blinde Holländer besteigen Deutschlands höchsten Berg!
3. Junge mit zwei Nasen bekommt neues Gesicht!
4. Zwei Jumbos kollidieren vor dem Start; alle Passagiere überleben!
5. Hund läuft Marathonlauf; läuft sich zu Tode!
6. Junges Ehepaar tanzt von Regensburg nach Erfurt!

D **Oktoberfestbesuch.** Auf dem Oktoberfest ist Michaela Folgendes passiert. Erzählen Sie im Perfekt davon.

Michaela kommt in München an. Nachdem sie in einer Pension ein preiswertes Zimmer findet, trifft sie Freunde, und sie gehen zusammen zum Oktoberfest.

Dort bleiben sie einige Stunden, und alle benehmen sich *(behave)* sehr lustig. Sogar auf den Tischen tanzt man. Später passiert aber etwas Schreckliches *(terrible)*. Die Kellnerin bringt die Rechnung, aber Michaela findet ihre Handtasche nicht. O je, auch die Brieftasche ist weg. Die Freunde zahlen für sie, und den Verlust meldet sie *(reports)* bei der Polizei. Auf dem Heimweg verläuft sie sich *(gets lost)* dann auch noch. Als sie endlich in der Pension ankommt, siehe da! was erblickt *(sees)* sie auf dem Bett? Ihre Handtasche! Die Brieftasche ist auch dabei. Da freut sie sich, daß sie die Handtasche noch hat, und legt sich schlafen.

Beispiel: *Michaela ist in München angekommen . . .*

E **Übung zu zweit: starke Verben.** Schreiben Sie zehn starke Verbinfinitive auf (siehe Appendix 4), und tauschen Sie *(exchange)* Ihre Liste mit jemandem aus. Bilden Sie mit den Verben dieser Person wahre Aussagen oder Fragen im Perfekt. Beginnen Sie einige Aussagen mit den Redemitteln **Ich glaube, daß . . ., Ich hoffe, daß . . .** und **Weißt du, ob** *(whether)* . . .

Beispiele: finden
Weißt du, ob jemand meine Brille gefunden hat?
essen
Ich habe heute morgen kein Frühstück gegessen.

* Anwendung

A **Vom Aufstehen bis zum Schlafengehen.** Erzählen Sie jemandem von Ihrem gestrigen Tag. Machen Sie eine Aussage für jede Stunde, die Sie gestern wach waren. Wiederholen Sie keine Partizipien.

B **Aus meinem Leben.** Berichten Sie in einer Gruppe kurz über ein paar wichtige Daten, Ereignisse *(events)* oder bisherige Leistungen aus Ihrem Leben. Haben Sie vielleicht einmal etwas Ungewöhnliches getan? Erzählen Sie!

REDEMITTEL

Weißt du, was ich einmal getan habe?
Ich glaube, ich habe dir nie erzählt, daß . . .
Vor einigen Jahren ist mir etwas Unglaubliches passiert.
Zu den wichtigsten Ereignissen meines Lebens gehört . . .
Es hat sich nämlich so ereignet *(happened)*:

C **Ein berühmter Mensch.** Informieren Sie sich über einen berühmten Menschen. Schreiben Sie dann kurze Notizen, aber keine ganzen Sätze. (Wenn man Notizen macht, soll das Verb immer am Ende stehen.) Berichten Sie mündlich und mit Hilfe Ihrer Notizen in ganzen Sätzen. Sagen Sie noch nicht, wer es war. Man soll zuerst raten *(guess)*.

Beispiel: **Notizen**

1856 in Mähren geboren
war Jude (Jude gewesen)
in Wien gelebt und dort Medizin studiert
1885–1886 in Paris studiert und gearbeitet
Psychiater geworden
die Psychoanalyse mitbegründet *(co-founded)*
viele Werke zur Psychoanalyse verfaßt *(composed)*
1938 nach England geflohen
1939 in England gestorben

Wer war es?[4]

Mündlicher Bericht

„Er ist in Mähren geboren und war Jude. Er hat in Wien gelebt und hat dort Medizin studiert. 1885–1886 hat er in Paris studiert und dort gearbeitet. Er ist Psychiater geworden. Später hat er das Studium der Psychoanalyse mitbegründet und viele Werke zur Psychoanalyse verfaßt. 1938 ist er nach England geflohen und 1939 dort gestorben. Wer war es?"

* Schriftliche Themen

Tips zum Schreiben ***Using the Present Perfect Tense***

The present perfect tense is primarily for conversational or informal writing. You can intersperse it with the simple past tense (see 7.1) in order to avoid repeated use of the auxiliary verbs **haben** and **sein** or when the context is clearly one of narration. When explaining *why* or *in which sequence* something happened, link your ideas logically with conjunctions (**als, denn, da, weil,** etc.; see 11.3) or adverbial conjunctions (see 24.5).

A **Ein Brief.** Schreiben Sie jemandem (der Deutsch versteht) einen kurzen Brief, in dem Sie erzählen, was Sie in den letzten Tagen getan oder erlebt haben. (Zum Schreiben deutscher Briefe siehe Appendix 2, *Letter Writing.*)

4. Sigmund Freud

Beispiel: Liebe Eltern!

Vielen Dank für Euren[5] lieben Brief und das kleine Paket. In den letzten zwei Wochen war ich sehr beschäftigt *(busy)*, denn ich hatte Prüfungen in drei Kursen. Ich habe sie aber alle mit *sehr gut* bestanden. Am letzten Wochenende haben mich ein paar Freunde von zu Hause besucht, und mit ihnen bin ich abends essengegangen. Als wir im Restaurant saßen, . . . usw.

B **Danke.** Sie waren am Wochenende bei Bekannten *(acquaintances)* eingeladen. Jetzt schicken Sie eine Karte, in der Sie sich bei Ihren Gastgebern bedanken und ganz kurz erzählen, wie der Abend Ihnen gefallen hat.

Beispiel: Liebe Freunde!

Ich möchte mich für den schönen Abend bei Euch bedanken. Alle Gäste waren ganz nett, und ich habe mich fast eine Stunde mit Eurem Papagei *(parrot)* über Politik unterhalten. Besonders gut hat mir die schöne Atmosphäre bei Euch gefallen. Daß ich ein volles Glas Rotwein auf Euer neues Sofa umgekippt *(tipped over)* habe, tut mir natürlich leid. Hoffentlich gehen die Flecken *(spots)* weg. Die Brandlöcher im Orientteppich sind aber nicht von mir. Das war jemand anders. Ich hoffe, daß wir bald wieder Gelegenheit *(opportunity)* haben, eine paar nette Stunden zusammen zu verbringen. Nochmals vielen Dank!

Herzliche Grüße,

Peter

Wortschatz 3

fahren / führen
fallen / fällen
hängen / hängen / henken
liegen / legen
sinken / senken
sitzen / setzen
springen / sprengen

+ *other strong verb / weak verb pairs*

---

5. All forms of the personal pronouns **du** and **ihr** are capitalized in letters and notes (see Appendix 2).

German has a number of transitive weak verbs that evolved originally from strong verbs.[6] In each instance, the strong verb describes the basic activity and is usually intransitive (has no direct object). The weak verb expresses the idea of making this activity happen, takes the auxiliary **haben,** and can have a direct object.

1. **fahren, fuhr, ist / hat gefahren** to go, travel; to drive
   führen, führte, hat geführt (= fahren machen) to lead, conduct

Sie **sind** gestern nach Gera **gefahren.** Gabi **hat** (den Wagen) **gefahren.**	*They traveled to Gera yesterday. Gabi drove.*
Diese Straße **führt** nach Garmisch.	*This road leads (goes) to Garmisch.*
Sie **führt** ein sonderbares Leben.	*She leads a strange life.*

2. **fallen, fiel, ist gefallen** to fall
   fällen, fällte, hat gefällt (= fallen machen) to fell

Heute **ist** viel Schnee **gefallen.**	*Lots of snow has fallen today.*
Paul **hat** viele Bäume **gefällt.**	*Paul has felled many trees.*

3. **hängen, hing, hat gehangen**[7] to hang, be hanging
   hängen, hängte, hat gehängt (= hängen machen) to hang (up)
   henken, henkte, hat gehenkt to hang a person on the gallows

Das Bild **hing** an *der* Wand.	*The picture was hanging on the wall.*
Der Maler **hängte** Bilder an *die* Wand.	*The painter hung pictures on the wall.*
Man **henkte** die Mörder um sieben Uhr morgens.	*They hanged the murderers at 7:00 in the morning.*

4. **liegen, lag, hat gelegen** to lie, be situated
   legen, legte, hat gelegt (= liegen machen) to lay, put in a lying position

Sie **lag** in *der* Sonne.	*She lay in the sun.*
Sie **legte** die Decke in *die* Sonne.	*She laid the blanket in the sun.*

---

6. Most of these weak-verb infinitives developed from an umlauted form of the second principal part of the strong verb:
   liegen, lag ⟶ legen (lägen)
   fahren, fuhr ⟶ führen

7. The strong verbs **hängen, liegen,** and **sitzen** describe stationary actions **(Wo?)** and require the dative case after two-way prepositions, whereas their weak-verb counterparts **hängen, legen,** and **setzen** describe directional actions **(Wohin?)** and require the accusative case after two-way prepositions (see 10.3).

5. **sinken, sank, ist gesunken** to sink
senken, senkte, hat gesenkt (= sinken machen) to lower

Die Sonne **sinkt** hinter den Horizont.	*The sun is sinking behind the horizon.*
Der Fischer **senkte** seinen Angelhaken ins Wasser.	*The fisherman lowered his fishhook into the water.*

6. **sitzen, saß, hat gesessen** to sit, be sitting
setzten, setzte, hat gesetzt (= sitzen machen) to set, put in a sitting position

Er **hat** in *diesem* Sessel **gesessen.**	*He sat in this easy chair.*
Sie **hat** das Kind in *diesen* Sessel **gesetzt.**	*She set the child in this easy chair.*

7. **springen, sprang, ist gesprungen** to jump, leap
sprengen, sprengte, hat gesprengt (= springen machen) to blow up; to break open

Der Hund **sprang** über die Mauer.	*The dog jumped over the wall.*
Die Truppen **sprengten** die Mauer.	*The troops blew up the wall.*

Other such pairs include:

erlöschen, erlosch, ist erloschen	to be extinguished, die out
löschen, löschte, hat gelöscht	to extinguish, put out; to quench (one's thirst)
erschrecken, erschrak, ist erschrocken	to be frightened
erschrecken, erschreckte, hat erschreckt	to frighten
ertrinken, ertrank, ist ertrunken	to drown, die by drowning
ertränken, ertränkte, hat ertränkt	to drown, kill by drowning
verschwinden, verschwand, ist verschwunden	to disappear
verschwenden, verschwendete, hat verschwendet	to squander
winden, wand, gewunden	to wind
wenden, wendete, gewendet	to turn

ÜBUNGEN

A **Welches Verb paßt?** Ergänzen Sie die Sätze durch die richtigen Verben.

Beispiel: Wir müssen nach Hause. (fahren / führen)
*Wir müssen nach Hause **fahren**.*

1. Sie können das Buch auf den Tisch ____ . (liegen / legen)
2. Die Bücher ____ auf dem Boden. (liegen / legen)

3. Jetzt ____ die Preise wieder. (sinken / senken)
4. Das Kaufhaus ____ seine Preise jetzt. (sinken / senken)
5. König Ludwig II von Bayern ist im Starnberger See südlich von München ____ . (ertrinken / ertränken)
6. Manche Leute glauben, daß jemand den König ____ hat. (ertrinken / ertränken)
7. Das Gericht *(court)* hat ein Todesurteil *(death sentence)* über den Mörder ____ .(fallen / fällen)
8. Die Entscheidung *(decision)* ist kurz vor Mitternacht ____ . (fallen / fällen)
9. Mozart hat viel gefeiert und sein Geld gern ____ . (verschwinden / verschwenden)
10. Kein Wunder, daß sein Geld dann schnell ____ ist. (verschwinden / verschwenden)

B **Was ist geschehen?** Erklären Sie, was geschehen ist. Verwenden Sie starke oder schwache Verben aus **Wortschatz 3.**

Beispiel: Humpty Dumpty ist gestorben. Wie?
*Er **ist** von einer Mauer **gefallen.***

1. Das Kind schreit jetzt vor Angst. Warum?
2. Zwei Stunden in Las Vegas, und Onkel Freds Geld ist weg. Wieso?
3. Auf der ersten Fahrt der *Titanic* sind viele Menschen gestorben. Wie?
4. Zwei Drachenflieger *(hang gliders)* sind mit ihren Drachen auf die Jungfrau (Berg in der Schweiz) gestiegen. Und dann?
5. Mariko hat einen furchtbaren Sonnenbrand bekommen. Wieso?

Zusammenfassung 3

Rules to Remember

1. There are three types of past participles: weak, irregular weak, and strong.
2. Weak and irregular weak verb past participles end in **-t (gehört);** strong verb past participles end in **-en (gesehen).**
3. The present perfect tense is formed with the conjugated auxiliary verbs **haben** or **sein** + a past participle.
4. The auxiliary **haben** is used with most verbs **(hat gefunden).**
5. The auxiliary **sein** is used with intransitive verbs expressing a) motion resulting in change of location **(ist gefallen; ist gekommen)** or b) change of location or condition **(ist gestorben; ist geworden).**
6. The conjugated auxiliary verb is in second position in main clauses. The past participle is in final position.

7. The present perfect tense may be used to talk or write about the completed past, be it five seconds or five years ago.

Activities

1 **Practicing forms.** Find short narrative texts (stories, fairy tales, or anecdotes) written in either the present or the simple past tense. Read the texts aloud, changing them into the present perfect tense as you read.

2 **Getting to know more about someone.** Prepare ten questions to ask students about their past. Interview another student and report his / her responses.

Variation: Ask someone when they did ten specific things for the first time in their life.

Beispiel: *Wann hast du zum erstenmal in deinem Leben ein Auto gefahren?*
—Ich habe zum erstenmal ein Auto gefahren, als ich sechzehn war.

3 **A memorable event in your life.** Prepare and present to the class a report of no more than ten sentences about a memorable event in your life. For example: a wonderful trip, a terrible situation, a frustrating experience, etc.

4 **Introducing someone.** Prepare to introduce an outside person of your acquaintance to your class. Begin by deciding what you would like to learn about this person that would make an interesting introduction. Ask this person for the information. Write out your introduction. Read the introduction to the class.

5 **Challenge: Don't say "yes" or "no."** A volunteer gets up in front of the class and students fire questions (in the present perfect tense) at him / her, with the intent of getting the volunteer to answer "yes" or "no." The volunteer has to try to answer the questions truthfully, but if he / she uses the words "yes" or "no," he / she loses and must sit down. There is a two-minute time limit per volunteer.

6 **Working with a text.** Discuss in groups or with the class as a whole some of the things characters did or did not do in a story you read recently for class. Explain why they did or did not do these things.

4 Cases and Declensions

4.1 Cases

Every German noun has number (singular or plural), gender (masculine, feminine, or neuter; see 12.1), and case. The case of a noun indicates its function within a sentence. There are four cases in German:

Nominative: sentence subject
Accusative: sentence direct object
Dative: sentence indirect object
Genitive: possessive, relationship between nouns

Case is usually indicated by an article (see Chapter 5) accompanying the noun.

4.2 Regular Noun Declensions

1. A noun listed in all four cases with either its definite or indefinite article is called a declension. Most nouns[1] decline as follows:

	Masc.	***Fem.***	***Neut.***	***Pl.***
Nom.	der Tisch	die Vase	das Buch	die Tische
Acc.	den Tisch	die Vase	das Buch	die Tische
Dat.	dem Tisch(e)	der Vase	dem Buch(e)	den Tischen
Gen.	des Tisch(e)s	der Vase	des Buch(e)s	der Tische

1. For the declension of weak nouns, see 12.3.

2. In the dative singular, monosyllabic masculine and neuter nouns have an optional **-e** ending that is usually omitted, except in a few set expressions such as **nach Hause; auf dem Lande.**
3. If a noun plural does not already end in **-n,** an **-n** must be added in the dative plural **(auf den Tischen).**

   EXCEPTION: Noun plurals ending in **-s (mit den Autos).**

4. Masculine and neuter nouns add either **-s** or **-es** in the genitive. The **-es** is usually added when a noun is monosyllabic **(das Geld, des Geld(e)s);** it is required when the noun ends in **-s, -sch, -ß, -x,** or **-z (das Schulhaus, des Schulhauses).** Nouns ending in **-nis** double the **s** before the **-es (das Mißverständnis, des Mißverständnisses).**

   The ending **-s** is usually used when the noun has more than one syllable **(des Lehrbuchs** BUT **des Buches),** or ends in a vowel or a silent **h (der See, des Sees; der Schuh, des Schuhs).**

4.3 Nominative Case

A. *Subjects*

1. A noun or pronoun used as the *sentence subject*—that is, as the word that generates the action of the verb—is in the nominative case. A singular subject requires a singular verb; a plural subject, a plural verb.

   Singular

Der Hund *beißt* nicht.	*The dog does not bite.*
Die Temperatur *steigt* schnell.	*The temperature is climbing rapidly.*

   Plural

Die Leute verstehen uns nicht.	*The people do not understand us.*

2. In German, the subject does not always precede the conjugated verb, as it usually does in English.

Heute beginnt **die Vorlesung** um zehn nach neun.	*Today the class begins at ten after nine.*

B. *Predicate Nominatives*

A noun used to complete the activity expressed by the linking verbs **sein, bleiben,** or **werden** is in the nominative case and is called the *predicate nominative.* A predicate nominative renames or describes the sentence subject.

Dieses Haus *ist* **sein Wohnsitz.**	*This house is his official residence.*
Wir *bleiben* **Freunde.**	*We remain friends.*
Er *wurde* **ein alter Mann.**	*He became an old man.*

4.4 Accusative Case

A. Direct Objects

1. A noun or pronoun used to complete the activity of verbs other than linking verbs is called an object. A great many verbs take a *direct object,* also known as an *accusative object.*

Wir lesen **die Zeitschrift.**	*We read the magazine.*
Er hat **keinen Ausweis.**	*He has no identification.*

2. Two accusative objects may be used after the verbs **fragen, kosten,** and **lehren.**[2]

Sie fragt **den Lehrer etwas Interessantes.**	*She asks the teacher something interesting.*
Das Auto hat **mich ein Vermögen** gekostet.	*The car cost me a fortune.*
Die Frau lehrt **das Kind ein Lied.**	*The woman teaches the child a song.*

B. Other Uses of the Accusative

1. The accusative is used with verbs of motion to express a distance covered.

Wir sind **eine Meile** gelaufen.	*We ran a mile.*
Sie kam **die Treppe** hinunter.	*She came down the stairs.*

---

2. In colloquial German there is a strong tendency to put nouns of person after **kosten** and **lehren** in the dative case when another object is in the accusative. This practice is usually considered substandard.

Sie lehrt **ihn.**	*She teaches him.*
BUT:	
Sie lehrt **ihn** (OR **ihm**) Deutsch.	*She teaches him German.*

2. The accusative is used when expressing a measurement or amount.

Dieser Teppich ist nur **ein(en) Meter**[3] lang.	*This rug is only one meter long.*
Das Kind ist erst **einen Monat** alt.	*The child is only one month old.*

3. The accusative is used in many conventional greetings and wishes.

Guten Morgen / Tag / Abend; **Gute** Nacht.
Herzlichen Glückwunsch. *(Congratulations.)*
Angenehme Reise. *(Have a nice trip.)*
Vielen Dank. *(Many thanks.)*
Gute Besserung. *(Get well soon.)*

4. The accusative is used after the expression **es gibt** (see 19.3B); after numerous prepositions (see 10.1 and 10.3); in some time expressions denoting a period of time or a point in time (see 23.1C).

4.5 Dative Case

for test → HA

A. *Indirect Objects*

1. The noun or pronoun used to indicate the person (less often, the thing) *to* or *for whom* an activity is done is called the *indirect object*. An indirect object is in the dative case; it may occur alone or together with an accusative object.

DAT. OBJ. ACC. OBJ. Er hat **den Kindern einen Hund** gekauft.	*He bought the children a dog.*

2. Dative objects generally precede accusative nouns.

Sie schreibt **den Kindern.**	*She writes (to) the children.*
Sie schreibt **den Kindern** einen Brief.	*She writes the children a letter.*
Sie schreibt **ihnen** einen Brief.	*She writes them a letter.*

3. Dative objects always follow accusative pronouns.

Sie schreibt **ihn den Kindern.**	*She writes it to the children.*
Sie schreibt **ihn ihnen.**	*She writes it to them.*

3. **Meter** can be either masculine or neuter, although masculine seems to be more common.

4. Dative and accusative objects often occur together with the following types of verbs:

Verbs of giving: **bringen, geben, leihen** *(to lend),* **reichen** *(to hand, pass),* **schenken, spendieren** *(to buy, pay for, treat)*

Verbs of showing: **beibringen** *(to teach),* **beweisen** *(to prove),* **erklären, zeigen**

Verbs of telling: **beschreiben** *(to describe),* **erzählen, mitteilen** *(to inform),* **sagen**

Verbs of recommending: **empfehlen, vorschlagen** *(to suggest)*

Der Chef hat **seinen Kollegen eine Runde** spendiert.	*The boss paid for a round (of drinks) for his colleagues.*
Kann jemand **den Studenten diesen Satz** erklären?	*Can someone explain this sentence to the students?*

5. The idea of doing something *to* or *for* someone cannot be expressed by **zu** + an object. German uses **zu** to convey the idea of *motion* or *direction* toward a person or a specific place.

COMPARE:

Sie gibt ihrem Vater ein Hemd. *(giving)*	*She is giving a shirt to her father.*
Ich bringe das Buch **zur** Bibliothek. *(motion or direction)*	*I am bringing the book to the library.*

B. *Verbs with Dative Objects*

1. A fairly large yet limited number of verbs in German take a dative object instead of an accusative object to complete the action of the verb. Common verbs of this type include:

ähneln	*to resemble*	gratulieren	*to congratulate*
antworten	*to answer*	helfen	*to help*
begegnen (*aux.* sein)	*to encounter, meet*	imponieren	*to impress*
danken	*to thank*	nutzen / nützen	*to be of use to*
einfallen (*aux.* sein)	*to occur to, come to mind*	passen	*to suit, fit*
folgen (*aux.* sein)	*to follow*	passieren (*aux.* sein)	*to happen*
folgen	*to obey*	raten	*to advise*
gehorchen	*to obey*	schaden	*to harm*
gehören	*to belong to*	schmecken	*to taste, taste good*
genügen	*to suffice*	schmeicheln	*to flatter*
geschehen (*aux.* sein)	*to happen*	trauen	*to trust*
		weh tun	*to hurt, pain*
		widersprechen	*to contradict*

Sie ähnelt **ihrer Mutter.**	*She resembles her mother.*
Ihr Mut hat **allen** imponiert.	*Her courage impressed everyone.*
Was ist **dir** passiert?	*What happened to you?*

2. The verb **glauben** takes a dative object with persons but an accusative object with things.

Wir glauben **dem Sprecher** nicht.	*We do not believe the speaker.*
Ich glaube **seine Antwort** nicht.	*I do not believe his answer.*

3. With several common verbs, the dative object in German is expressed in English as the subject (see also impersonal expressions, 19.3A).

fehlen	Das Geld fehlt **uns.** *We lack the money.*
gefallen	Der Film hat **den Kritikern** nicht gefallen. *The critics did not like the film.*
gelingen	Die Aufgabe gelingt **den Kindern.** *The children succeed in doing the task.*
leid tun	Sie tun **uns** leid. *We feel sorry for them.*
reichen	Das reicht **mir** aber! *I've had enough!*

4. Verbs of motion with the prefixes **ent-** (inseparable) and **nach-** (separable) take dative objects. The most common combinations occur with **gehen, kommen,** and **laufen.**

entgehen	*to escape, elude, avoid*
entkommen	*to escape*
entlaufen	*to run away from*
nachgehen	*to walk behind; to pursue, investigate*
nachkommen	*to come or follow after*
nachlaufen	*to run after*

Der Dieb konnte **der Polizei** *entkommen.*	*The thief was able to escape from the police.*
Wir werden **der Sache** *nachgehen.*	*We will investigate the matter.*

5. Some common verbs with the separable prefixes **bei-** and **zu-** also take dative objects.

beistehen	*to help, aid*	beitreten	*to join (a party, club, etc.)*
beistimmen	*to agree, concur*	beiwohnen	*to attend (a meeting, lecture)*
zuhören	*to listen to*	zusagen	*to be to one's liking; to accept (an invitation)*
zulächeln	*to smile at*		
zureden	*to (try to) persuade, urge*	zusehen	*to watch, witness*
		zustimmen	*to agree with, concur with*

Hans *trat* **einem Schachverein** *bei.*	*Hans joined a chess club.*
Man *redet* **ihr** *zu,* länger zu bleiben.	*They are urging her to stay longer.*

C. *Other Uses of the Dative*

1. The dative may indicate *to whom* something belongs, i.e., *whose* it is. This is particularly the case with parts of the body and articles of clothing (see also 5.1B). This *dative of possession* normally precedes the thing possessed.

Er klopfte **dem Touristen** auf die Schulter.	*He tapped the tourist on the shoulder (that is, on the tourist's shoulder).*
Ziehe **dem Kind** die Schuhe an!	*Put the child's shoes on! (That is, put the child's shoes on the child!)*

2. The dative occurs after several prepositions (see 10.2 and 10.3), in time expressions with certain prepositions (see 23.1B), and with some adjectives (see 13.4A).

4.6 Genitive Case

A. *General Use*

1. The genitive case in German establishes a relationship between two nouns, one being part of or belonging to the other. The noun in the genitive normally follows the other noun and provides more information about it. In English, such a relationship is usually expressed with an *of*-phrase or with the possessive *'s*. German does not use an apostrophe + **s** to indicate possession.

der Name **des Mannes**	*the name of the man; the man's name*
die Lage **dieses Geschäfts**	*the location of this store; this store's location*
die Zensuren **der Schüler**	*the grades of the pupils; the pupils' grades*

2. With proper names and family-member terms used as names, German adds an **-s** without an apostrophe.

Wilhelms Wagen	**Bärbels Brief**
Vaters Vase	**Mutters Mantel**

3. If the name ends in an **s** sound **(-s, -ß, -z, -tz),** no **-s** is added. In writing, the omission of this **-s** is indicated by an apostrophe. When speaking, a construction with **von** + dative is often used instead of the genitive (see Section B).

Agnes' Garten *or* **der Garten von Agnes**

Die neue Sicht der Dinge:
Kommunikation.
Deutsche Bank

4. The genitive is *not used* after units of measurement, as it is in English.

Ich möchte eine Tasse **Kaffee.** (**Tasse** *and* **Kaffee** *are both accusative.*)	*I would like a cup* ***of*** *coffee.*
Sie hat eine Packung **Rosinen** gekauft.	*She bought a package of raisins.*

B. Von *as a Substitute for the Genitive Case*

1. The word **von** + dative is often used as a genitive substitute.

das Haus unsres Onkels das Haus **von** unsrem Onkel	*the house of our uncle / our uncle's house*
die Bürger **von** *Frankfurt*	*the citizens of Frankfurt*

2. **Von** is always used if there is no article or adjective before the noun to indicate case.

die Arbeit **von** Ausländern	*the work of foreigners*

C. Other Uses of the Genitive

1. At one time, quite a number of German verbs took genitive objects. In most of these instances, the genitive objects have been replaced by prepositional phrases, or German speakers simply use a different verb instead. A few common verbs with genitive objects do remain.

einer Sache bedürfen	*to need sth.*
sich einer Sache bedienen	*to use sth.*
der Toten gedenken	*to remember the dead*
sich einer Sache bemächtigen	*to seize, take control of sth.*
sich einer Sache entsinnen (*preferred:* sich an eine Sache entsinnen)	*to remember sth.*
sich einer Sache erwehren	*to refrain from (doing) sth.*
sich des Lebens (*preferred:* über das Leben) freuen	*to rejoice in life*
sich einer Sache erfreuen	*to enjoy, be the beneficiary of sth.*

2. The genitive case is used with certain adjectives and adverbs (see 13.4B), after some prepositions (see 10.4), and in some time expressions (see 23.1D).

* Übungen

A **Kluge Sprüche.** In welchen Fällen *(cases)* sind die Substantive in den folgenden Sprüchen? Erklären Sie Ihre Antworten.

1. Sprachkürze gibt Denkweite. (Jean Paul, 1763–1825)
2. Fleiß *(diligence)* ist aller Tugenden *(virtues)* Anfang. (Friedrich der Große, 1712–1786)
3. Aus faulen Eiern werden keine Küken *(baby chickens)*. (Wilhelm Busch, 1832–1908)
4. Dem Glücklichen gehört die Welt. (Sprichwort)
5. Keine Erfindung ist wohl dem Menschen leichter geworden als die eines Himmels. (Georg Lichtenberg, 1742–1799)
6. Jedem Tierchen sein Pläsierchen. (Sprichwort)
7. Es ist noch kein Meister vom Himmel gefallen. (Sprichwort)
8. Der Irrtum ist viel leichter zu erkennen, als die Wahrheit zu finden. (Johann Wolfgang Goethe, 1749–1832)

B **Nominativ oder Akkusativ?** Ergänzen Sie die Artikel.

1. Er hat d-____ Saft beim Sparmarkt gekauft.
2. Wo findet man hier e-____ Buchladen *(m.)?*
3. D-____ Student kennt e-____ Arzt hier im Ort.
4. Wie gefällt dir d-____ Wein?
5. D-____ Buch wurde e-____ Erfolg *(success) (m.)*.
6. In den Augen der Kinder war d-____ Lehrer auch e-____ Freund.

C **Das habe ich getan.** Machen Sie mit jedem Verb und einem Akkusativobjekt eine Aussage darüber, was Sie heute oder gestern getan (oder nicht getan) haben.

Beispiele: *Ich habe heute **eine Prüfung** in Deutsch geschrieben.*
*Ich habe gestern **den Deutschprofessor** in der Stadt getroffen.*

bekommen	lesen	sehen
kaufen	schreiben	treffen

D **Nachmittags in der Stadt.** Wer tut was? Verwenden Sie Akkusativ *und* Dativ mit Artikeln oder Possessivpronomen (siehe 5.4). Wiederholen Sie kein Substantiv.

Beispiel: Der Kellner bringt ____ (die Gäste / eine Getränkekarte)
*Der Kellner bringt **den Gästen eine Getränkekarte**.*

1. Die Kellnerin empfiehlt ____. (der Gast / ein Rotwein)
2. Großvater kauft ____. (seine Enkeltochter / eine Pizza)
3. Ein Touristenführer zeigt ____. (die Besucher / das Stadtzentrum)
4. Katrin schreibt ____. (ihre Kusine / ein Brief)
5. Einige Studenten schreiben ____. (ihre Eltern / Postkarten)
6. Eine Verkäuferin verkauft ____. (ein Kind / ein Eis)

E **Durch Pronomen ersetzen.** Ersetzen Sie in den Sätzen von Übung D zuerst alle Dativobjekte durch Pronomen, dann alle Akkusativobjekte durch Pronomen, und zum Schluß beide Objekte durch Pronomen.

Beispiel: Der Kellner bringt den Gästen eine Getränkekarte.
Der Kellner bringt ***ihnen*** *eine Getränkekarte.*
Der Kellner bringt ***sie*** *den Gästen.*
Der Kellner bringt ***sie ihnen.***

F **Der hilfreiche Hans.** Hans ist immer hilfsbereit. Erzählen Sie, was er heute alles getan hat. Drücken Sie die Sätze durch einen Dativ anders aus.

Beispiel: Hans macht ein Frühstück für seine Frau.
Hans macht ***seiner Frau*** *ein Frühstück.*

1. Er hat einen Brief an seine Eltern geschrieben.
2. Er hat Blumen für seine Frau mitgebracht.
3. Er hat den Computer für seinen Chef repariert.
4. Er hat ein Märchen für seine Kinder erzählt.
5. Er hat den Wagen für seinen Freund Otto gewaschen.

Und was haben Sie heute oder gestern gemacht? Haben Sie auch etwas jemandem getan?

G **Anders ausdrücken.** Verwenden Sie die folgenden Verben mit Dativobjekten.

Beispiel: Das ist mein Buch.
Das Buch gehört ***mir.***

ähneln *(resemble)*	danken	gehören
gehorchen *(obey)*	schmeicheln *(flatter)*	widersprechen *(contradict)*

1. Hans sieht wie sein Vater aus.
2. Kinder sollen tun, was die Eltern sagen.
3. Das ist der Wagen von meinem Lehrer.
4. Wenn der Professor *ja* sagt, soll man nicht *nein* sagen.
5. Otto sagt allen Leuten immer das, was sie gern über sich hören.
6. Ich möchte ihm meinen Dank für seine Hilfe aussprechen.

H **Worterklärungen.** Erklären Sie die Wörter. Verwenden Sie den Genitiv.

Beispiele: der Familienvater
Das ist ***der Vater der Familie.***

die Hosentaschen
Das sind ***die Taschen einer Hose.***

1. die Bleistiftspitze
2. der Berggipfel
3. der Hausbesitzer
4. die Bauernhöfe *(pl.)*
5. der Arbeiterstreik
6. die Autofahrer
7. die Lehrbuchpreise

I **Interessante Tatsachen.** Was wissen Sie? Machen Sie fünf Aussagen mit dem Genitiv oder mit **von** und dem Dativ.

Beispiele: *Das Leben* ***einer Fliege*** (fly) *ist sehr kurz.*
Die meisten Knochen ***eines Menschen*** *sind in den Händen und den Füßen.*
Die Zähne ***von einem Nilpferd*** (hippopotamus) *sind nicht sehr scharf.*

J **Filmtitel.** Wie könnten diese Filme auf deutsch heißen?

1. In the Name of the Father
2. Life of Brian (Monty Python film)
3. The Diary **(das Tagebuch)** of Anne Frank
4. The Hunchback (**der Glöckner** = *bell-ringer*) of Notre Dame
5. Star Wars (**der Stern, -e** = *star*)
6. Son of the Pink **(rosarot)** Panther
7. Robin Hood: Prince of Thieves

Anwendung

A **Fragen zum Überlegen.** Diskutieren Sie mit jemandem in Ihrem Kurs über die folgenden Fragen. Berichten Sie Ihre Ideen in einer größeren Gruppe.

1. Welche Gegenstände sind im Leben von Studenten am wichtigsten?
2. Welche größeren Käufe würden Sie machen, wenn Sie das Geld dafür hätten?
3. Welche vier Dinge möchten Sie unbedingt *(absolutely)* haben, wenn Sie allein auf einer kleinen Südseeinsel wären?
4. Welche fünf Erfindungen haben der Menschheit am meisten geholfen?

B **Ich kenne jenen Ort.** Jemand im Kurs hat vor *(plans),* einen Ort (z.B. eine Stadt, einen Park) zu besuchen, den Sie gut kennen. Erzählen Sie ihm / ihr, was es dort alles zu tun und zu sehen gibt.

REDEMITTEL

Du mußt unbedingt . . . sehen.
Vielleicht kannst du auch . . . besichtigen.
Dort gibt es . . .
Dort findet man auch . . .
Der . . . ist dort besonders gut / bekannt . . .
Empfehlen kann ich dir auch . . .

C **Familienverhältnisse** *(family relationships)*. Bringen Sie Familienphotos zur Deutschstunde mit. Zeigen Sie Ihre Bilder und erklären Sie die Familienverhältnisse.

VOKABELVORSCHLÄGE: FAMILIENMITGLIEDER

der Schwager	*brother-in-law*	die Schwägerin	*sister-in-law*
der Stiefvater	*stepfather*	die Stiefmutter	*stepmother*
der Stiefbruder	*stepbrother*	die Stiefschwester	*stepsister*
der Halbbruder	*half-brother*	die Halbschwester	*half-sister*
die Großeltern	*grandparents*	das Enkelkind	*grandchild*

REDEMITTEL

Wir sind [acht] in unserer Familie
Das sind . . .
Auf diesem Bild siehst du . . .
[X] ist der / die . . . von . . .

* Schriftliche Themen

Tips zum Schreiben ***Checking for Correct Cases***

After writing a first draft of your composition, be sure to check whether all the nouns (and pronouns) are in the correct cases. A common error is to put nouns following the linking verbs **sein** or **werden** in the accusative case when they are really predicate nominatives. Although prepositional phrases and adverbs setting a time or place make good sentence openers, dative and accusative objects normally do not, since they complete the idea of the verb and should thus logically follow it.

A **Eltern und Kinder.** Wie sehen Sie das ideale Verhältnis zwischen Eltern und ihren Kindern? Wie können / sollen Eltern und Kinder einander helfen?

Beispiel: Wenn Kinder jung sind, müssen ihre Eltern selbstverständlich für sie sorgen. Sie sollen ihren Kindern vieles erklären und ihnen auch manches beibringen. Dafür *(in return)* sollen die Kinder ihrerseits *(for their part)* ihren Eltern gehorchen und bereit sein . . .

B **Freies Thema.**

Wortschatz 4

machen

einen Ausflug machen
eine Reise machen
einen Spaziergang machen
eine Ausnahme machen

+ *other direct object complements for* **machen**

1. **Machen** can mean *to do.* In such instances it is synonymous with **tun.**

   Was **machen / tun** Sie jetzt? — *What are you doing now?*
   —Ich **mache / tue** nichts. — *I am doing nothing.*

2. **Machen** can mean *to make* or *build.*

   Die Wanderer **machten** ein Feuer. — *The hikers made a fire.*

3. **Machen** can mean *to make* or *cause to be.*

   Das **macht** ihn traurig, aber nicht böse. — *That makes him sad, but not angry.*

4. **Machen** occurs with a considerable number of direct object complements. Common examples include:

einen Ausflug machen	to go on an outing	**Musik machen**	to make music
eine Reise machen	to take a trip	**eine Pause machen**	to take a break
einen Spaziergang machen	to take a walk	**jemandem** *(dative)* **Platz machen**	to make room for someone
eine Wanderung machen	to go hiking	**ein Foto machen**	to take a photograph
eine Ausnahme machen	to make an exception	**einen Schritt machen**	to take a step
eine Aussage machen	to make a statement	**Schulden machen**	to incur debts
einen Fehler machen	to make a mistake	**jemandem** *(dative)* **Sorgen machen**	to cause someone worry
Fortschritte machen	to make progress	**Unsinn machen**	to do something stupid
jemandem *(dative)* **(große) Freude machen**	to make someone (very) happy	**einen Unterschied machen**	to make a difference
(einen) Lärm machen	to make noise	**ein Vermögen machen**	to make a fortune
		einen Versuch machen	to make an attempt

All of these expressions are negated with **kein-.**

Wir können **keine** Ausnahme machen.	*We cannot make an exception.*
Machen Sie **keinen** Unsinn!	*Don't do something foolish!*

ÜBUNGEN

A **Anders ausdrücken.** Drücken Sie die Sätze mit dem Verb **machen** anders aus.

1. Wir kommen mit der Arbeit schnell vorwärts.
2. Euer Besuch hat uns sehr gefreut.
3. Darf ich dich fotografieren?
4. Ohne Eintrittskarte darf man nicht ins Museum hinein, aber Herr Frei läßt eine Frau ohne Karte herein.
5. Auf ihrem Examen hat sie alles richtig gehabt.
6. Er borgt Geld und kauft allerlei Dinge.
7. Die Kinder waren sehr laut.
8. Sie hat vor Gericht *(court)* gegen den Angeklagten *(defendant)* gesprochen.
9. Im Laufe der Jahre wurde sie sehr reich.
10. Sie tut, was sie kann, um nach Europa zu kommen.

B **Was machen Sie?** Verwenden Sie Ausdrücke mit **machen** in Ihren Antworten.

Beispiel: Was machen Sie gern?
Ich mache gern Wanderungen.

1. Was machen Sie besonders gern?
2. Was machen Sie nicht besonders gern?
3. Was machen Sie oft?
4. Was machen Sie selten?

Zusammenfassung 4

Rules to Remember

1. There are four cases in German.
2. The cases of nouns are often indicated by preceding articles.
3. The cases of pronouns are indicated by the pronouns themselves.
4. The nominative case indicates the doer of an activity.
5. The accusative case indicates the object of an activity.
6. The dative case indicates *to* or *for* whom something is done.
7. A dative object comes before an accusative object unless the accusative object is a pronoun.
8. The genitive case indicates *whose.*

Activities

1 **Analyzing cases.** Select a paragraph from each of five different texts at your disposal. Underline and determine the case for each noun and pronoun in these paragraphs. For the time being, you may wish to exclude nouns that are objects of prepositions.

2 **Things you don't have.** Make a list of five or six things you don't have. Tell your partner whether or not you would like to have these things. Your partner then reports to other members of the class.

Beispiel: YOU: Ich habe keinen Computer, aber ich möchte (k)einen haben.
YOUR PARTNER: [Name] hat keinen Computer, aber er / sie möchte (k)einen haben.

3 **Today and tomorrow.** Tell yourself or another student some of the things you did yesterday or must do tomorrow that were *object directed;* that is, your statements should contain nouns in the accusative. You may include adjectives to make the sentences more natural. Practice beginning some sentences with time expressions rather than subjects. This is a good activity to do mentally while lying in bed before falling asleep.

Beispiele: *Ich habe heute einen (interessanten) Film gesehen.*
Zu Mittag habe ich ein schönes Essen gehabt.
Am Abend habe ich meine Aufgaben getan.
Morgen muß ich eine Prüfung in Deutsch schreiben.

4 **Things to see and do.** A new student has arrived in town and asks you about some of the things to see and do on campus and in town. What can you tell him / her?

5 **Be nice, be happy.** Think of four or five ways you can / could help or be nice to other people by doing something for them. Focus consciously on using objects in the dative and accusative cases. Remember, dative before accusative! Tell your ideas to other students.

Beispiele: *Ich könnte meiner Mutter einen Brief schreiben.*
Ich könnte meinem Freund / meiner Freundin Blumen schenken.

6 **Working with a text.** From a story read for class, select what you consider to be the ten most important nouns for retelling or summarizing this narrative. Give your list to another student to write or make statements about the story using your words. Monitor carefully for case accuracy.

Articles and Possessive Adjectives/ Articles Used as Pronouns

5.1 Definite Articles

A. Declension

The definite article **(der bestimmte Artikel)**—English *the*—has masculine, feminine, neuter, and plural forms. It declines with the noun it modifies (see 4.2).

	Masc.	*Fem.*	*Neut.*	*Pl.*
Nom.	**der** Tisch	**die** Vase	**das** Buch	**die** Tische
Acc.	**den** Tisch	**die** Vase	**das** Buch	**die** Tische
Dat.	**dem** Tisch(e)	**der** Vase	**dem** Buch(e)	**den** Tischen
Gen.	**des** Tisch(e)s	**der** Vase	**des** Buch(e)s	**der** Tische

B. Use

1. German includes the definite article in reference to a specific noun. This usage parallels English.

   Kennst du **den** Mann von nebenan? — *Do you know the man from next door?*

2. Definite articles are used instead of possessive adjectives with parts of the body and with articles of clothing when it is clear to whom they belong.

   Sie hat **den** Mantel ausgezogen und (sich) **die** Hände gewaschen. — *She took off* ***her*** *coat and washed* ***her*** *hands.*

   BUT:

   Sie hat **seinen** Mantel getragen. — *She wore* ***his*** *coat.*

3. The definite article is also used in the following instances where it is usually omitted in English:

a. With names of days, months, seasons, and meals.

Sie kommen **am** (= **an dem**) Mittwoch **zum** (= **zu dem**) Abendessen.	*They are coming for dinner on Wednesday.*
Der Frühling beginnt **im** (= **in dem**) März.	*Spring begins in March.*

b. With means of transportation.

Er fährt mit **dem** Zug, nicht mit **dem** Auto.	*He is traveling by train, not by car.*

c. With proper names of streets, intersections, squares, churches, schools, universities, etc., even when they are in English. Also with names of lakes, canyons, mountains, and rivers.

Der Stephansdom in Wien steht **am** (= **an dem**) Stephansplatz am Ende **der** Kärntnerstraße.	*St. Stephan's Cathedral in Vienna stands in Stephan's Square at the end of Kärntner Street.*
Freunde von uns wohnen **am** Eriesee.	*Friends of ours live on Lake Erie.*

Speakers of German are apt to use English words for places in English-speaking countries, but with the same genders as their German equivalents: **in der Third Avenue (= in der Straße); am Washington Square (= am [an dem] Platz).**

d. With names of certain masculine, feminine, or plural countries: **der Jemen, der Kongo, der Sudan,** (sometimes **der Iran** and **der Irak**); **die Schweiz, die Slowakei, die Tschechische Republik, die Türkei, die Vereinigten Staaten.**

Zürich ist die größte Stadt in **der** Schweiz.	*Zurich is the largest city in Switzerland.*

e. With geographical and proper names modified by preceding adjectives.

das alte Deutschland	*old Germany*
die junge Frau Scherling	*young Mrs. Scherling*

f. With nouns that denote concepts, abstractions, and beliefs.

Lenin war ein wichtiger Kämpfer für **den** Kommunismus.	*Lenin was an important fighter for communism.*
Das Christentum ist fast 2.000 Jahre alt.	*Christianity is nearly 2,000 years old.*

g. With a number of words such as **Arbeit, Kirche, Schule,** and **Stadt,** particularly after prepositions.

Nach **der** Arbeit muß ich in **die** Stadt.	*After work I have to go into town.*
Vor **der** Schule gehen sie **zur** Kirche.	*Before school they go to church.*

C. *Omission of the Definite Article*

1. German generally omits the definite article (a) with pairs of nouns and (b) before a musical instrument when expressing playing that instrument.

Es geht um **Leben und Tod.** *(pair of nouns)*	*It is a matter of life and death.*
Er spielt **Violine,** und sie spielt **Klavier.** *(playing an instrument)*	*He plays the violin and she plays the piano.*

2. German normally omits the definite article with personal names, even in those instances in the plural where English includes an article.

Höflechners haben uns zum Abendessen eingeladen.	*The Höflechners have invited us to dinner.*

3. However, in very colloquial German the article is often included with first and last names. This usage personalizes the reference.

Kennst du **die** Jutta oder **den** Klaus?	*Do you know Jutta or Klaus?*
Ich war gestern bei **der** Frau Gsoels.	*I was at Mrs. Gsoels' yesterday.*

5.2 Indefinite Articles

A. *Declension*

The endings of the indefinite article **(der unbestimmte Artikel)**—English *a(n)*—are very similar to those of the definite article. They differ only in the masculine nominative singular and the neuter nominative and accusative singulars, which have no endings.

	Masc.		*Fem.*		*Neut.*		*Pl.*	
Nom.	ein □	Vater	ein **e**	Mutter	ein □	Kind	kein **e**[1]	Väter
Acc.	ein **en**	Vater	ein **e**	Mutter	ein □	Kind	kein **e**	Väter
Dat.	ein **em**	Vater	ein **er**	Mutter	ein **em**	Kind (e)	kein **en**	Vätern
Gen.	ein **es**	Vaters	ein **er**	Mutter	ein **es**	Kindes	kein **er**	Väter

1. There is no plural for the article **ein;** for this reason **kein** is used here as the plural article.

B. *Use*

Indefinite articles generally refer to nonspecific nouns, that is, *a* book as opposed to *the* book, just as in English. A nonspecific noun normally has no article in the plural.

Wir suchen **eine Blume.**	*We are looking for a flower.*
Gibt es **Blumen** in deinem Garten?	*Are there flowers in your garden?*

C. *Omission of the Indefinite Article*

German does *not* use the indefinite article before nouns of *occupation, nationality,* or *general class of person* (religious denomination, military rank, marital status, etc.) when they are used as predicate nominatives or after **als** *(as).*

Erwin Rommel war **Deutscher** und **General.**	*Erwin Rommel was* ***a*** *German and* ***a*** *general.*
Bärbl arbeitet als **Steuerberaterin.**	*Bärbl works as* ***a*** *tax advisor.*

5.3 Der-Words

A. *Forms*

1. The following article modifiers **(Artikelwörter)** take the same endings as the definite article. For this reason they are called **der**-words.

all-	*all* (sing. and pl.)	**manch-**	*many a,* (pl.) *some*
dies-	*this;* (pl.) *these*	**solch-**	*such (a),* (pl.) *such*
jed-	*each, every*	**welch-**	*which*
jen-	*that;* (pl.) *those*		

2. **Der**-words decline as follows:

	Masc.	***Fem.***	***Neut.***	***Pl.***
Nom.	dies**er** (der)	dies**e** (die)	dies**es** (das)	dies**e** (die)
Acc.	dies**en** (den)	dies**e** (die)	dies**es** (das)	dies**e** (die)
Dat.	dies**em** (dem)	dies**er** (der)	dies**em** (dem)	dies**en** (den)
Gen.	dies**es** (des)	dies**er** (der)	dies**es** (des)	dies**er** (der)

B. *Use of* der-*Words*

1. **All-** by itself occurs mainly before plural nouns (see also 13.3C); its use in the singular is somewhat less common.[2]

---

2. For uses of **all-** *(sing.)* in phrases such as **alles Gute,** see 21.1B.

Alle Geschäfte sind jetzt geschlossen. — *All stores are now closed.*

BUT:

Wir haben **alle Hoffnung** aufgegeben. — *We have given up all hope.*

2. To express the idea of *all* or *all the* in the singular, German often uses a definite article plus the adjective **ganz.**

Er hat **die ganze** Arbeit selbst gemacht. — *He did all the work himself.*

3. When followed by a **der-** or **ein-**word, **all-** has no ending in the singular and an optional ending in the plural.

Was hat die Firma mit **all** *dem Geld* gemacht? — *What did the firm do with all the money?*

Sie hat **all(e)** *ihre Verwandten* in Luxemburg besucht. — *She visited all her relatives in Luxemburg.*

4. **Jed-** occurs only in the singular.

Jedes Kind kann das verstehen. — *Every child can understand that.*

5. **Jen-** is fairly uncommon as a noun modifier and used mainly in contrast to **dies-.**

Willst du **dieses** Getränk oder **jenes** (Getränk)? — *Do you want this drink or that one?*

6. **Manch-** is common in the plural, but much less frequent in the singular. When the singular does occur, it is often used in conjunction with **ein-.** In such instances, **manch-** is not declined and **ein-** takes indefinite article endings.

Manche Leute lernen nie von ihren Fehlern. — *Some people never learn from their mistakes.*

Ich habe **manch eine** Person / **manche** Person getroffen, die einfach nicht gern reist. — *I have met many a person who simply does not like to travel.*

7. **Solch-** is common in the plural, but less so in the singular, where speakers of German prefer **so ein- / solch ein-** (*such a* or *a [. . .] like that*).

Solche Leute wie Jim brauchen wir. Kennst du **so einen** Menschen / **solch einen** Menschen? — *We need such people as Jim. Do you know such a person / a person like him?*

Jedes Kind möchte **so ein** Fahrrad / **solch ein** Fahrrad haben. — *Every child would like to have such a bicycle / a bicycle like that.*

8. **Welch-** is most commonly used as an interrogative article (see 15.2), but the forms **welch ein-** or **was für ein-** occur often in exclamations.

   Welch ein / was für ein herrliches Wetter! — *What glorious weather!*

5.4 Possessive Adjectives

A. Forms

1. Every pronoun (see 16.1) and noun has a corresponding possessive adjective **(das Possessivpronomen).**[3]

Pronoun	*Noun*	*Possessive Pronoun*	
ich		**mein**	*(my)*
du		**dein**	*(your)*
er	**der**-*noun*	**sein**	*(his; its)*
sie	**die**-*noun*	**ihr**	*(her; its)*
es	**das**-*noun*	**sein**	*(his; its)*
man		**sein**	*(his; their)*
wir		**unser**	*(our)*
ihr		**euer**	*(your)*
sie	*plural noun*	**ihr**	*(their)*
Sie		**Ihr**	*(your)*

2. Possessive adjectives have the same endings as the indefinite article (see 5.2). For this reason they are called **ein**-words.

	Masc.	*Fem.*	*Neut.*	*Pl.*
Nom.	mein	mein **e**	mein	mein **e**
Acc.	mein **en**	mein **e**	mein	mein **e**
Dat.	mein **em**	mein **er**	mein **em**	mein **en**
Gen.	mein **es**	mein **er**	mein **es**	mein **er**
Nom.	unser	uns(e)r **e**	uns(e)r	uns(e)r **e**
Acc.	uns(e)r **en**	uns(e)r **e**	uns(e)r	uns(e)r **e**
Dat.	uns(e)r **em**	uns(e)r **er**	uns(e)r **em**	uns(e)r **en**
Gen.	uns(e)r **es**	uns(e)r **er**	uns(e)r **es**	uns(e)r **er**

3. German grammarians classify possessive adjectives as possessive pronouns, hence the term **Possessivpronomen.** A possessive adjective used as a pronoun (see 5.5B) is a **substantiviertes Possessivpronomen.**

3. Note that the **-er** of the plural forms **unser** and **euer** is part of the adjective, not an ending. When these words have endings, the interior unstressed **-e-** is often dropped.

B. Use

1. The choice of possessive adjective is determined by the noun or pronoun to which it refers; the *endings* by the case, number, and gender of the noun it modifies.

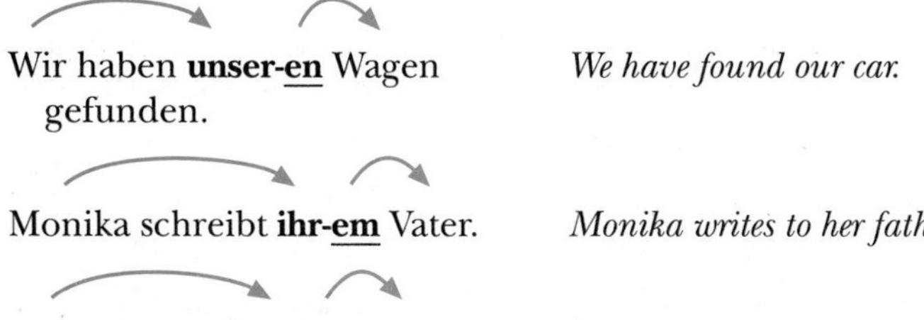

Wir haben **unser-en** Wagen gefunden.	*We have found our car.*
Monika schreibt **ihr-em** Vater.	*Monika writes to her father.*
Heinz besucht **sein-e** Mutter.	*Heinz visits his mother.*

2. Since **er, sie,** and **es** can refer to things as well as persons, the possessive forms **sein-** and **ihr-** can both mean *its* in English.

Der Ahorn verliert **seine** Blätter im Winter.	*The maple tree loses* ***its*** *leaves in the winter.*
Die Tanne verliert **ihre** Nadeln nicht.	*The fir does not lose* ***its*** *needles.*

3. Possessive adjectives are not normally used with articles of clothing and parts of the body (see 5.1B).

5.5 *Der-* and *ein-*Words Used as Pronouns

A. Der-*Word Pronouns*

1. When a noun is understood from context and thus not repeated, the accompanying definite article or **der**-word can function as a pronoun.

Ich nehme diese Lampe. **Welche** willst du?	*I'll take this lamp. Which one do you want?*
—Ich möchte **die** da.	*I'd like the one there.*
Manche mögen es heiß.	*Some (people) like it hot.*
Diese CD habe ich schon, und **jene** werde ich bald kaufen.	*This CD I already have, and that one I will buy soon.*

2. The pronouns **dies-** and **jen-** often express the idea of the *latter* and the *former,* respectively.

Der Kommunismus und der Sozialismus sind in Osteuropa verschwunden. Über **jenen** haben wir schon gesprochen, und mit **diesem** werden wir morgen anfangen.	*Communism and socialism have disappeared in Eastern Europe. We have already talked about the former, and we will begin with the latter tomorrow.*

3. The pronoun forms **dies** *(this, these)* and **das** *(that, those)* are commonly used as subject forms with the verb **sein** when pointing out objects. The verb will be either singular or plural, depending upon whether one or more items are being pointed out.

Dies ist mein Auto, **das** ist seins.	*That is my car, this is his.*
Dies / **Das** sind unsere Bücher.	*These / Those are our books.*

B. Ein-*Word Pronouns*

Ein-words, including **so ein-, manch ein-,** and **was für ein-,** can also function as pronouns as long as they retain their endings. In the three instances where the article **ein-** has no ending, a **der-**word ending must be added to indicate number, gender, and case, as highlighted in the following chart. The genitive forms occur rather infrequently.

Ein-Word Pronoun Declensions

	Masc.	***Fem.***	***Neut.***	***Pl.***
Nom.	mein **er**	mein **e**	mein **(e)s**	mein **e**
Acc.	mein **en**	mein **e**	mein **(e)s**	mein **e**
Dat.	mein **em**	mein **er**	mein **em**	mein **en**
Gen.	mein **es**	mein **er**	mein **es**	mein **er**

Hier ist mein Buch. Wo ist **dein(e)s?**	*Here is my book. Where is* ***yours?***
Ich brauche einen Bleistift. —Hier liegt **einer.**	*I need a pencil. Here is* ***one.***
Sie will Briefmarken kaufen, aber sie findet **keine.**	*She wants to buy stamps, but she can't find* ***any.***
Wir haben ein Zwei-Mann-Zelt. In was für **einem**[4] schlaft ihr?	*We have a two-person tent. What kind (of* ***one****) are you sleeping in?*

4. The use of **was für** does not influence the case, which in this instance depends upon the preposition **in** (see 15.2D).

✱ Übungen

A **Die Hansestadt[5] Hamburg.** Ergänzen Sie die Sätze durch passende Formen von **der** oder **ein.**

1. Im 9. Jahrhundert wurde „Hammaburg" an ____ Elbe *(f.)* gegründet.
2. Im Mittelalter entwickelte sich ____ Stadt Hamburg zu ____ wichtigen Handelsmetropole *(f.)*.
3. Mit ____ Aufkommen ____ Dampfschiffahrt *(steamboat travel)* wurde Hamburg ____ wichtiger Hafen für Seefahrer aus ____ ganzen Welt.
4. Trotz seines Alters ist Hamburg ____ moderne Stadt.
5. ____ Bombenangriffe *(bombing raids)* von 1943–45 zerstörten ____ Stadtzentrum sehr schwer. Fast 55.000 Menschen kamen ums Leben *(perished)*.
6. Heute umfaßt *(encompasses)* ____ Hafen ____ Gebiet *(n.)* von 16 km Länge.
7. In ____ Stadtteil Stellingen gibt es ____ sehenswerten Tierpark.
8. Im Westen ____ Stadt liegt ____ Hafenviertel St. Pauli mit ____ vielbesuchten *Reeperbahn (f.)*.[6]
9. Mit mehr als 1,8 Millionen Einwohnern gehört Hamburg zu ____ Weltstädten Europas.

B **Mit oder ohne Artikel?** Beantworten Sie die Fragen.

Beispiel: Wie heißt der größte See Österreichs?
Er heißt der Neusiedlersee.

1. In welchen Straßen oder Stadtteilen befinden sich
   a. das Weiße Haus?
   b. die besten New Yorker Modegeschäfte?
   c. die berühmten Jazzclubs von New Orleans?
2. Wie heißt der höchste Berg
   a. Deutschlands?
   b. der Schweiz?
   c. der USA?
3. Welcher Fluß fließt
   a. durch Paris?
   b. durch Hamburg?
   c. durch Kairo?
   d. durch St. Louis?

---

5. During the Middle Ages, Hamburg was a member of the Hanseatic League, a powerful alliance of key port cities along the North and Baltic Seas. It is still often referred to as **die Hansestadt Hamburg** (HH).
6. The *Reeperbahn* is a street known for its bars, nightclubs, arcades, and other forms of amusement.

4. Von welchem Land ist die Hauptstadt
   a. Prag?
   b. Teheran?
   c. Bern?
5. Womit kommt man am schnellsten
   a. von New York nach Philadelphia?
   b. von Athen nach Frankfurt?
   c. vom 2. Stock zum 99. Stock?
6. Wie heißt eine große Kirche in
   a. Köln?
   b. München?
   c. Wien?
7. Mit welchen -ismen (Religionen, politischen Bewegungen usw.) assoziieren Sie die Namen
   a. Karl Marx?
   b. Buddha?
   c. John Calvin?
   d. Martin Luther?

C **Gewohnheiten.** Was machen Sie in der Regel *vor, während* und / oder *nach* den folgenden Aktivitäten?

Beispiel: die Deutschstunde
Vor der Deutschstunde lerne ich gewöhnlich neue Vokabeln.

1. das Frühstück
2. die Schule
3. die Deutschstunde
4. die Arbeit
5. das Abendessen

Fragen Sie andere Studenten, was sie vor, während oder nach diesen Aktivitäten machen.

D **Beruf und Nationalität.** Ergänzen Sie die Sätze.

Beispiel: Mein Großvater war ____ und ____ .
Mein Großvater war ***Deutscher*** *und* ***Klavierbauer.***

1. Von Beruf ist mein Onkel / meine Tante ____ .
2. Meine Mutter ist ____ . Früher war sie ____ .
3. Ich bin jetzt ____ .
4. Mein Vater arbeitet als ____ .
5. Meine Vorfahren waren ____ .
6. Beruflich möchte ich ____ werden.

E **Welcher Artikel paßt?** Ergänzen Sie die Sätze durch passende Artikelwörter. Verwenden Sie jedes Artikelwort.

Beispiel: ___ Computer möchte ich kaufen.
***Diesen** Computer möchte ich kaufen.*

all-	manch-	solch-
dies-	so ein-	welch-
jed-		

1. Ich möchte ___ Buch kaufen.
2. ___ Leute sprechen immer zuviel. Ich mag ___ Leute nicht.
3. Amerika hat nicht ___ Kriege gewonnen.
4. Zu Weihnachten hat Sissi ___ Familienmitglied *(n.)* etwas geschenkt.
5. Mit ___ Zug wollen wir fahren?
6. Lilo trägt eine hübsche Bluse, und ihre Freundin möchte auch ___ Bluse haben.

F **Jeder für sich.** Bilden Sie mit jedem der folgenden Pronomen oder Substantive einen Satz, der auch ein Possessivpronomen enthält. Wiederholen Sie kein Verb.

Beispiele: sie
*Sie schreibt **ihrem** Freund.*
der Vogel
*Der Vogel baut **sein** Nest in einem Baum.*

1. ich
2. du
3. die Katze
4. der Mensch
5. das Mädchen
6. wir
7. ihr
8. die Arbeiter
9. Sie
10. man

G **Jedem das Seine.** *(To each his own.)* Wie kann es weitergehen? Setzen Sie die Reihe mit fünf bis sieben Ideen fort. Wer hat die besten Ideen?

dem Hund *(Dativ)* sein Knochen *(Nominativ)*
der Katze ihre Milch
dem Politiker seine Lügen
dem Basketballspieler seine Millionen
den Kindern ihre Spiele

H **Im Sportgeschäft.** Verwenden Sie jedes der folgenden Artikelwörter als Pronomen.

der- dies- welch- jen- so ein-

VERKÄUFERIN: Hier sind unsre Tennisschläger.
MARIA: ___ können Sie empfehlen?
VERKÄUFERIN: Besonders populär sind ___ .
MARIA: ___ hier gefällt mir vom Preis her, aber ich glaube, ich nehme lieber ___ .
VERKÄUFERIN: Mit ___ spiele ich auch.

I **Sind das deine Disketten?** Drücken Sie die Sätze auf deutsch aus.

1. This is my room, and that one belongs to my sister.
2. Are those your CDs?
3. These are mine, but those I borrowed from Robert.
4. Can we listen to **(hören)** this one?
5. Sure, but I like that one better.

J **Der Kassettenrecorder.** Setzen Sie passende Pronomen ein.

BERND: Mensch, du hast ja einen tollen Kassettenrecorder. ___ *(One like that / Such a one)* möchte ich auch haben.
UTA: Aber du hast doch ___ *(one),* nicht wahr?
BERND: Ja, aber ___ *(mine)* ist eigentlich zu groß zum Herumtragen, weißt du. ___ *(Yours)* kann man überallhin mitnehmen.
UTA: Ich würde dir gern ___ *(mine)* leihen, aber wir fahren morgen in Urlaub. Frage den Franz, vielleicht gibt er dir ___ *(his).*
BERND: Gute Idee. Was für ___ *(what kind of one)* hat er?

* Anwendung

Bei uns zu Hause. Erzählen Sie anderen Studenten im Kurs über das Leben bei Ihnen zu Hause. Berichten Sie, was Sie von diesen Leuten erfahren.

REDEMITTEL

Bei uns zu Hause muß jeder sein- / ihr- (eigenes) . . .
Vater hat sein- . . .
Mutter hat ihr- . . .
Von unserem . . . muß ich auch erzählen.
Und wie ist es bei euch?
Habt ihr auch eur- . . .?

* Schriftliche Themen

Tips zum Schreiben ***Editing Your Writing***
When preparing an introduction to or a description of a person or place, read aloud what you have written. Do the sentences provide essential information in a manner that is easy for your listeners to comprehend? Have you managed to avoid beginning every sentence with the name of the person or place or with the subject pronouns **er** and **sie?** When you use the possessive pronouns **sein** and **ihr,** do they match the nouns to which they refer in number and gender?

Wir stellen vor. Kennen Sie jemanden aus einem anderen Land, der jetzt in Ihrer Heimat studiert oder arbeitet? Stellen Sie diese Person in einem kurzen Bericht vor. Erwähnen *(mention)* Sie Nationalität, Beruf, Wohnort, Adresse (in welcher Straße, bei wem), Beruf der Eltern, besondere Interessen und Leistungen *(accomplishments)* usw.

Beispiel: Ich möchte meine Freundin Natsu Nemoto vorstellen. Sie ist Japanerin und Studentin. Abends arbeitet sie als Kassiererin in einem Studentencafé am University Square. Ihr Vater ist Ingenieur in Tokio, ihre Mutter Übersetzerin. Sie wohnt jetzt bei Familie Möller in der Grand Avenue. Nach ihrem Studium möchte sie Journalistin werden und . . . usw.

Wortschatz 5

der Raum	der Ort
der Platz	die Stelle

1. The noun **der Raum, ⸚e** means *space* or *room* as a general area or volume. It often occurs as a compound noun: **der Lebensraum** *(living space),* **der Weltraum** *(outer space),* **das Weltraumschiff, die Raumfahrt** *(space travel).* **Der Raum** can also mean *a room,* though **das Zimmer** is much more common.

Die Stadt braucht mehr **Raum** zum Bauen.	*The city needs more room for building.*
Wir müssen diesen kleinen **Raum** noch möblieren.	*We must still furnish this small room.*

2. The noun **der Platz, ¨-e** also means *space* or *room,* but in a more specific sense than **der Raum.** It often denotes a definite *space* or *place* that someone or something occupies or where an activity takes place. In this context it occurs frequently as a compound noun: **der Arbeitsplatz** *(place of work, work station),* **der Marktplatz** *(marketplace),* **der Parkplatz** *(parking lot),* **der Spielplatz** *(playing field),* **der Tennisplatz** *(tennis court).* **Der Platz** can also refer to a *seat* or a *square* in a town.

Ich brauche einen besseren **Platz** zum Arbeiten.	*I need a better place to work.*
Kannst du mich später am **Sportplatz** abholen?	*Can you pick me up later at the sports field?*
Nehmen Sie bitte **Platz.**	*Please take a seat.*

3. The noun **der Ort, -e** can mean a *place, spot,* or *site* but does not denote an exact point. It can also refer to a town, village, or hamlet.

Wir suchen einen **Ort,** wo wir allein sein können.	*We are looking for a spot where we can be alone.*
Hier ist nicht **der Ort,** über solche Dinge zu sprechen.	*Here is not the place to talk about such things.*
Sein **Geburtsort** ist Salzburg.	*His birthplace is Salzburg.*

4. The noun **die Stelle, -n** refers to a precise *spot, place,* or *location,* usually on or within a larger entity, such as the human body. It can occasionally occur interchangeably with **der Ort,** but always refers to a more defined *spot.* **Die Stelle** can also mean *stead* (that is, in someone's place). Finally, **die Stelle** can denote a *passage* in a book or a *job* or *position.*

An dieser **Stelle** im Wald wachsen besonders große Pilze.	*Particularly large mushrooms grow in this spot in the woods.*
An dieser **Stelle** (an meinem Arm) tut es weh.	*This spot (on my arm) hurts.*
An deiner **Stelle** würde ich anders handeln.	*In your position I would act differently.*
Lesen Sie diese **Stelle** im Buch noch einmal.	*Read this passage in the book once more.*
Sie sucht eine bessere **Stelle.**	*She is looking for a better position.*

5. The uses of **Ort, Stelle,** and **Platz** often overlap, but with subtle differences in meaning.

An dieser **Stelle** ist der Mann gestorben. *(the specific spot)*
An diesem **Ort** ist der Mann gestorben. *(the general location)*

ALSO:
In diesem **Ort** ist der Mann gestorben. *(village or town)*
Auf diesem **Platz** ist der Mann gestorben. *(the place / seat where he was sitting)*

ÜBUNGEN

A **Welches Wort paßt?** Ergänzen Sie durch passende Substantive. (Ab und zu paßt mehr als ein Wort hinein, aber dann hat der Satz auch eine etwas andere Bedeutung.)

1. Der Kommissar fuhr zu d- ____ ____ des Mordes.
2. Wer Golf spielen will, braucht ein- ____ ____ zum Spielen.
3. Sie erzählt gern von d- ____ ____ , wo sie aufgewachsen ist.
4. In vielen deutschen Städten gibt es kaum noch ____ zum Bauen.
5. An Ihr- ____ ____ hätte ich nicht so gehandelt.
6. An dies- ____ ____ ist der Unfall passiert.
7. Hier ist d- ____ richtige ____ für einen Garten.
8. Wir brauchen mehr ____ .

B **Von großer Bedeutung.** Nennen Sie jeweils zwei *Orte und zwei Plätze,* die für Sie große Bedeutung haben oder hatten.

Beispiel: *Seattle bedeutet mir viel, denn in diesem* ***Ort*** *bin ich geboren und aufgewachsen.*

Zusammenfassung 5

Rules to Remember

1. There are two types of articles, **der**-words and **ein**-words.
2. Articles mark the case, number, and gender of nouns.
3. The **der**-words are **all-, dies-, jed-, jen-, manch-, solch-,** and **welch-.**
4. The **ein**-words are the possessive adjectives **mein, dein, sein, ihr, unser, euer,** and **Ihr** plus **kein.**
5. **Der**-words and **ein**-words can be used as pronouns.

Activities[7]

1 **Analyzing.** Search through a non-literary text of at least two paragraphs for every occurrence of the possessive pronouns **sein-** and **ihr-.** Determine the *case* of each possessive pronoun and the *word* (not the modified noun!) to which it refers.

2 **His and hers.** Compare two people you know, one male, one female, who have different habits, personalities, or lifestyles. Focus on their families, friends, possessions, habits, activities, etc. Create at least five sentences using possessive adjectives.

7. Articles are so central to every German utterance that they cannot be easily isolated for focused practice. These activities will help you consciously distinguish the possessive adjectives **sein** and **ihr,** which cause problems for some learners.

Beispiele: ***Ihre** Eltern wohnen in New York, **seine** Eltern in Cleveland.*
***Ihre** Wohnung sieht immer hübsch aus. **Seine** Wohnung sieht katastrophal aus.*
***Sein** Auto ist neu. **Ihr** Auto ist sehr alt.*
usw.

3 **Group narrative.** Work in groups of eight to ten students. The first student says the first sentence of a story about a person or animal. Each following student continues the narrative in turn, but must use a possessive pronoun in his or her sentence. Go around the group and back to the first student, who then provides a concluding sentence. Now the next student begins a new narrative with a new character. Continue until each student has begun and completed a narrative cycle. Use either present or simple past tense.

Beispiel: STUDENT A: In Deggendorf an der Donau wohnt eine alte Großmutter in einem Schuh.
STUDENT B: In *ihrem* Schuh wohnen auch Kinder.
STUDENT C: *Ihre* Kinder haben nie genug zu essen. usw.

4 **Working with a text.** Make a list of the characters in a German story that you have already read. Make a factual or interpretative statement about each character and use the possessive pronouns **sein-** or **ihr-.**

Negation / Imperatives 6

6.1 Negation

A. Kein-

1. **Kein-** *(no, not a, not any)* is the negative form of the indefinite article **ein-** and takes the same endings (see 5.2). It is used only to negate nouns preceded either by **ein-** or by no article at all, although they may be preceded by adjectives.

Hat sie *einen* Computer?	*Does she have a computer?*
—Nein, sie hat **keinen** Computer.	*No, she does not have a computer.*
Gibt es gute Geschäfte hier in der Nähe?	*Are there any good stores around here?*
—Nein, hier gibt es **keine** guten Geschäfte.	*No, there are no / not any good stores here.*

2. **Kein-** cannot be used to negate a noun preceded by a definite article or a possessive pronoun. **Nicht** must be used instead.

COMPARE:

Sie findet **keinen** Computer.	*She finds **no** computer.*
Sie findet den / meinen Computer **nicht.**	*She does **not** find the / my computer.*

B. Nicht (nie, niemals)

1. **Nicht** *(not)* and **nie** / **niemals** *(never)* are used to negate all elements of a sentence other than nouns preceded by **ein-** or by no article at all.

2. **Nicht** *follows* conjugated verbs, dative and accusative objects, and specific time expressions.

Sie kauft das Kleid **nicht.** *(accusative object)*	*She isn't buying the dress.*
Er schreibt seinen Eltern **nicht.** *(dative object)*	*He isn't writing his parents.*
Wir sehen den Film heute **nicht.** *(specific time expression)*	*We're not going to see that film today.*

3. **Nicht** *precedes* adverbs and prepositional phrases that are not specific time expressions, and final-position verbal complements (see 1.1F).

Er kann **nicht** schnell rechnen. *(adverb)*	*He cannot calculate quickly.*
Wir gehen **nicht** mit ihnen tanzen. *(prepositional phrase)*	*We're not going dancing with them.*
Du kannst diesen Kurs **nicht** belegen. *(infinitive)*	*You cannot take this course.*
Sie haben die Gefahr **nicht** erkannt. *(past participle)*	*They didn't recognize the danger.*
Der Lärm hört **nicht** auf. *(separable prefix)*	*The noise does not stop.*
Sie ist **nicht** die richtige Frau für ihn. *(predicate nominative)*	*She is not the right woman for him.*
Das Wetter wird **nicht** besser. *(predicate adjective)*	*The weather is not getting any better.*

4. When **nicht** negates a specific element in contrast to something else, it *precedes* this element. The contrasting element is introduced by **sondern** (see 11.1).

Die Familie geht **nicht** *heute* wandern, **sondern** *morgen.*	*The family is going hiking not today, but rather tomorrow.*

6.2 Imperatives

A. Formation

1. The imperative **(der Imperativ),** has four forms in German.

du-form	*(familiar, singular)*
ihr-form	*(familiar, plural)*
Sie-form	*(formal, singular or plural)*
wir-form	*(first person plural: Let's . . .)*

2. Imperatives are generated from the present tense. The **du**-imperative consists of the present-tense stem + an optional **-e** that is usually omitted, particularly in colloquial German.

Schreib(e) bald!	*Write soon!*
Bring(e) deine Freunde **mit!**	*Bring your friends along!*

The final **-e** is *not* omitted if the infinitive stem ends in **-d, -t, -ig,** or in **-m** or **-n** preceded by a consonant other than **l** or **r.**

Antworte! Entschuldige! Atme!	*Answer! Pardon (me)! Breathe!*

3. Verbs with the present-tense vowel shifts **e** > **i** or **e** > **ie** also shift in the **du**-imperative, but they do not add an **-e.**

Du sprichst → **Sprich!**	*Speak!*
Du liest → **Lies** bitte schneller!	*Please read more quickly!*
EXCEPTION: **werden:** du wirst → Stirb und **werde!** (Goethe)[1]	*Die and become!*

However, verbs with the stem changes **a** > **ä, au** > **äu,** or **o** > **ö** do *not* have vowel shifts in the **du**-imperative and may take the optional **-e.**

Du trägst → **Trag(e)** es!	*Carry it!*
Du läufst → **Lauf(e)!**	*Run!*

4. The **ihr**-form imperative is the same as the **ihr**-form of the present tense, but the pronoun is omitted.

Gabi und Heidi, **kommt** bald **wieder!**	*Gabi and Heidi, come again soon!*
Sprecht deutlicher!	*Speak more clearly!*

5. German occasionally includes the pronouns **du** and **ihr** with the familiar imperative for emphasis or clarification.

Ich habe dreimal aufgeräumt. **Mach du** es mal! (**Macht ihr** es mal!)	*I have cleaned up three times. You do it for a change!*

6. The **Sie**-form imperative is the same as the **Sie**-form of the present tense, but the verb is always followed by the pronoun **Sie.**

Meine Damen und Herren, **treten Sie** bitte näher!	*Ladies and gentlemen, please step closer!*
Herr Ober, **bringen Sie** uns bitte eine Speisekarte.	*Waiter, please bring us a menu.*

---

1. From Goethe's poem "Selige Sehnsucht" in *Westöstlicher Divan.*

7. The **wir**-form imperative is the same as the **wir**-form of the present tense, but the verb is always followed by the pronoun **wir.**

Gehen wir heute einkaufen!	*Let's go shopping today!*
Nehmen wir nun **an,** daß niemand die Antwort weiß.	*Let's assume now that no one knows the answer.*

8. The imperatives for the verb **sein** are irregular.

Sei / **Seid** / **Seien Sie**	ruhig!	*Be quiet!*
Seien wir	vorsichtig!	*Let's be careful!*

B. *Use*

The imperative is used to express not only commands, but also requests, instructions, suggestions, or warnings. (See 20.3D for polite requests using the subjunctive and modal verbs.) Normally an imperative ends with an exclamation point, although a period is permissible if no emphasis is implied.

Passen Sie auf! *(command / warning)*	*Watch out! / Pay attention!*
Übersetzen Sie die Sätze. *(instruction)*	*Translate the sentences.*
Essen wir jetzt. *(suggestion)*	*Let's eat now.*

C. *Infinitives as Imperatives*

Directives for the general public, such as signs, announcements, and instructions, are often expressed with an infinitive and no pronoun. The infinitive is placed at the end of the command.

Bitte nicht **hinauslehnen!**	*Do not lean out!*
(Den) Rasen nicht **betreten!**	*Do not step on the grass!*

D. Bitte *and Flavoring Particles with the Imperative*

1. **Bitte** or any one of several flavoring particles (see 25.2) can accompany the imperative. **Bitte** makes a command more polite. When it begins a sentence, it is set off by a comma only when stressed. It also occurs in other positions, but it may not immediately precede pronouns.

Bitte tun Sie das!	*Please do that!*
Bitte, vergessen Sie die Nummer nicht!	*Please, don't forget the number!*
Zeigen Sie es ihnen **bitte** nicht!	*Please don't show it to them!*

2. **Doch** adds a sense of impatience to imperatives.

   Hilf mir **doch!** *Come on, help me!*

3. **Mal** adds a sense of mild impatience best expressed by the English word *just.*

   Hört **mal** zu! *Just listen!*
   Seien Sie **mal** ruhig! *Just be calm!*

4. **Nur** often adds a stipulative tone to imperatives, implying that consequences—either good or bad—will result.

   Versuchen Sie es **nur!** *Just try it (and see)!*

5. Several flavoring particles may accompany an imperative.

   Hören Sie **doch bitte mal** zu! *Come on, just listen, please!*

* Übungen

A **Alles falsch.** Berichtigen Sie die Aussagen. Verwenden Sie **kein-, nicht** oder **nie.**

1. Fische haben lange Beine.
2. Vancouver ist die Hauptstadt von Kanada.
3. Immanuel Kant hat an einer Universität in Japan studiert. Dort wurde er später Professor.
4. Es schneit oft in Miami.
5. Hasen fressen gern Mäuse.
6. Frankfurt hat 2 Millionen Einwohner.
7. Man soll den Tag vor dem Abend loben *(praise).*
8. Pferde geben den Menschen Milch.
9. *Alle* Studenten und Studentinnen in diesem Deutschkurs werden gute Noten bekommen.

B **Der ewige Neinsager.** Markus sieht alles negativ. Wie wird er wohl auf diese Fragen antworten?

Beispiele: Markus, macht dir das Leben Spaß?
*Nein, das Leben macht mir **keinen** Spaß.*

Markus, liest du gern?
*Nein, ich lese **nicht** gern.*

1. Bekommst du ein schönes Taschengeld?
2. Hast du deine verlorene Taschenuhr gefunden?
3. Verstehst du meine Fragen?
4. Möchtest du Sportler werden?
5. Kannst du deine Aufgabe morgen abgeben?
6. Bekommst du in Deutsch eine gute Note?

7. Gehst du morgen mit der Schulklasse schwimmen?
8. Ist dein Vater Chef dieser Bank?
9. Bist du glücklich?
10. Bist du mit deinem Leben zufrieden?
11. Telefonierst du gern mit deinen Freunden?

C **Das mache ich nicht.** Gibt es Dinge, die Sie nicht haben, nicht oder nie tun oder nicht gern tun? Machen Sie sieben Aussagen.

Beispiele: *Ich spiele kein Musikinstrument.*
Ich tanze nicht gern.

D **Nicht immer so höflich.** Frau Leis äußert ihre Bitten immer sehr höflich. Drücken Sie ihre Wünsche und Bitten durch den Imperativ der kursivgedruckten Verben stärker aus.

Beispiele: Du sollst lauter *sprechen.*
***Sprich** lauter!*

Würdet ihr uns bitte *helfen?*
***Helft** uns bitte!*

1. Herr Kollege, könnten Sie bitte den Projektor *holen?*
2. Leute, bitte etwas lauter *reden!*
3. Du kannst mich heute abend zu Hause *anrufen.*
4. Heinz, könntest du bitte die Tür *öffnen?*
5. Herr Moritz, darf ich Sie bitten, mir zu *helfen?*
6. Kinder, ihr sollt doch ruhiger *sein!*
7. Josef, ich hoffe, du *wirst* nicht böse.
8. Rainer, du sollst dich doch *beruhigen!*
9. Liebling, würdest du bitte nicht so schnell *fahren.*
10. Es wäre *(would be)* für uns gut, etwas fleißiger zu *sein.*

E **Situationen.** Was sagen Sie? Verwenden Sie auch passende Partikeln.

Beispiel: Ein Freund von Ihnen will Eintrittskarten für ein Rockkonzert kaufen und fragt Sie, ob er Ihnen auch welche kaufen soll.
Ja, kauf(e) mir bitte auch eine Karte!

1. Studenten plaudern *(chat)* neben Ihnen in der Bibliothek, während Sie zu lesen versuchen.
2. Sie haben die Frage Ihrer Deutschprofessorin entweder nicht gehört oder nicht verstanden.
3. Sie wollen mit jemandem irgendwo gemütlich zusammensitzen und plaudern.
4. Sie wollen, daß niemand Sie jetzt in Ihrem Zimmer stört, und hängen einen kleinen Zettel *(note)* an die Tür.
5. Sie haben eine schwierige Hausaufgabe und möchten, daß ein paar Freunde Ihnen dabei helfen.

6. Sie haben Ihre Mutter beim Sprechen unterbrochen und wollen sich entschuldigen.
7. Ihr deutscher Schäferhund bellt schon wieder, und das wollen Sie sich nicht mehr anhören.
8. Ihre kleine Schwester kommt mit ganz schmutzigen Händen zum Essen.

F **Bitten!** Was für Bitten haben Sie an die folgenden Personen?

Beispiel: an Ihren Vater
„Vati, schick mir bitte mehr Geld!"

1. an Ihre Eltern
2. an Ihre Geschwister (Bruder / Schwester)
3. an einen Freund / eine Freundin
4. an Ihren Deutschprofessor / Ihre Deutschprofessorin
5. an eine berühmte Person

* Anwendung

A **Faule Menschen.** Wer kann den faulsten Menschen beschreiben? Erzählen Sie von einem wirklichen oder erfundenen *(imaginary)* Menschen, der gar nichts hat und gar nichts tut.

REDEMITTEL

Mensch, kenne ich aber eine faule Person!
Er / sie ist so faul, daß er / sie . . .
Weil er / sie nie . . . [tut], hat er / sie auch kein- . . .
Natürlich [tut] er / sie auch kein- . . .
Meistens [tut] er / sie . . . und [tut] gar nicht(s).
Er / sie will nicht einmal *(not even)* . . .

B **Ratschläge** *(advice)* **fürs Leben.** Was für Ratschläge können Sie die anderen Studenten geben? Verwenden Sie bitte **du-** oder **ihr-**Imperative!

Beispiele: *Heirate / Heiratet nie!*
Sitz(e) / Sitzt nie ohne Helm (helmet) *unter Kokospalmen!*
Sei / Seid immer lustig!

Haben Sie Ratschläge für Ihren Deutschprofessor / Ihre Deutschprofessorin?

C **Wer nicht hören will, muß fühlen.** Das folgende Gedicht enthält Befehle *(commands),* die manche Kinder sicher schon öfter gehört haben. Welche Befehle (**du-**Imperative) mußten *Sie* sich als Kind anhören? Welche Befehle werden Ihre Kinder später wohl von Ihnen zu hören bekommen? Wie deuten Sie die Zeilen:

„Wer nicht hören will, muß fühlen"? Diskutieren Sie mit anderen Studenten darüber.

Erziehung

laß das
komm sofort her
bring das hin
kannst du nicht hören
hol das sofort her
kannst du nicht verstehen
sei ruhig
faß das nicht an
sitz ruhig
nimm das nicht in den Mund
schrei nicht
stell das sofort wieder weg
paß auf
nimm die Finger weg
sitz ruhig
mach dich nicht schmutzig
bring das sofort wieder zurück
schmier dich nicht voll
sei ruhig
laß das

wer nicht hören will
muß fühlen

—Uwe Timm

* Schriftliche Themen

Tips zum Schreiben ***Writing First Drafts and Checking for Common Errors***

Always jot down a few ideas in German before beginning a composition. Then write a first draft. Read through this draft to see whether you have used a variety of verbs. Now is also a good time to check for common errors such as misspellings, uncapitalized nouns, verbs not in second position, and the use of **nicht ein-** instead of **kein-** (see 6.1). Have you also kept your sentences concise and to the point, or do they tend to ramble on and on and on? When writing a second or final draft, be sure to vary your style by starting some sentences with elements other than the sentence subject.

A **Selbstanalyse.** Schreiben Sie eine Selbstanalyse mit dem folgenden Titel: „Was ich nicht bin, nicht habe, nicht tue und nicht will." (Siehe auch **Wortschatz 6.**)

Beispiel: Ich bin kein fauler Mensch, aber ich will nicht immer arbeiten. Ich will auch nicht . . . Natürlich habe ich auch keine Lust, . . . usw.

B **Reicher Mensch, armer Mensch.** Man kann sich leicht das Leben eines reichen Menschen vorstellen *(imagine)*. Wie ist es aber bei einem armen Menschen, der wenig oder nichts hat? Erzählen Sie davon.

C **Diese Stadt!** Gibt es manches, was Ihnen an der Stadt, in der Sie jetzt wohnen, nicht gefällt? Erzählen Sie aus einer etwas negativen Sicht davon. Verwenden Sie einige der Ausdrücke aus **Wortschatz 6.**

Beispiel: Diese Stadt gefällt mir nicht so sehr. Es gibt keine netten Studentenlokale, und nirgendwo kann man sich abends im Stadtzentrum gemütlich treffen. Aber ich gehe abends sowieso lieber nicht in die Stadt, denn es fahren nach zehn Uhr keine Busse zur Universität zurück. Außerdem gibt es nicht einmal . . . usw.

Wortschatz 6

kein-	nie / niemals
kein- . . . mehr	nicht einmal
nicht	noch nicht

\+ *other expressions of negation*

The most common expressions of negation include the following words and phrases.

kein-	no, not any	**nicht einmal**	not even
kein- . . . mehr	no more . . .	**nicht nur (sondern auch)**	not only (but also) (see 11.2)
nicht	not	**noch nicht**	not yet
nicht mehr	no more, no longer	**noch kein-**	not any . . . yet
nichts	nothing, not anything	**noch nie**	not ever (yet)
nie / niemals	never	**ich nicht**	not me / not I
niemand	no one, not anyone	**ich auch nicht**	me neither, nor (do) I
nirgends / nirgendwo	nowhere, not anywhere	**gar nicht** / **überhaupt nicht**	not at all

gar nichts / **überhaupt nichts**	nothing at all	**weder . . . noch**	neither . . . nor (see 11.2)
gar kein- / **überhaupt kein-**	not any . . . at all	**durchaus nicht** / **keinesfalls**	by no means, not at all
lieber nicht	(preferably) not, (would) rather not	**auf keinen Fall**	by no means

ÜBUNGEN

A **Keine Karten fürs Konzert.** Drücken Sie die Sätze auf deutsch aus.

1. Ariane wants to go to the concert, but she can't.
2. She doesn't have a ticket.
3. Her friends don't have any either.
4. Nor do I.
5. We don't even know where to purchase them.
6. However, Ariane hasn't given up all hope **(die Hoffnung)** yet.
7. Can't anyone give us some tickets?

B **Alles nur nein.** Antworten Sie mit kurzen Ausdrücken der Negation auf die Fragen. Verwenden Sie jeden Ausdruck nur einmal.

Beispiel: Hast du jemanden in meinem Garten gesehen?—Nein, . . .
Nein, niemanden.

1. Warst du je *(ever)* in Afrika?—Nein, . . .
2. Hast du dein Studium schon beendet?—Nein, . . .
3. Ich habe es nicht getan. Sie hat es nicht getan. Und du?—Nein, . . .
4. Hast du immer noch Probleme mit deinem Auto?—Nein, . . .
5. Tja, wer hat soviel Geld? Du?—Nein, . . .
6. Möchtest du an seiner Stelle *(in his place)* sein?—Nein, . . .

C **Aussagen.** Machen Sie Aussagen über sich *(yourself)* mit den folgenden Ausdrücken.

Beispiele: *Ich habe meinen Aufsatz in Deutsch* ***noch nicht*** *abgegeben.*
Ich war ***noch nie*** *in Europa.*

1. noch nie
2. noch nicht
3. gar kein- / überhaupt kein-
4. nie
5. durchaus nicht / keinesfalls

Zusammenfassung 6

Rules to Remember

1. **Kein-** negates nouns preceded by **ein-** or no article at all.
2. **Nicht** negates everything else.
3. **Nicht** *follows* verbs in second position, direct or indirect objects, and specific time expressions.
4. **Nicht** *precedes* other adverbial expressions that come after the verb.
5. No pronoun is used after **du-** and **ihr**-imperatives **(Komm; Kommt).**
6. Pronouns are always used after **wir-** and **Sie**-imperatives **(Gehen wir; Gehen Sie).**

Activities

1 **The way things used to be.** Discuss with other students how life was different ten, twenty, fifty, or one hundred years ago. What did people *not* have, *not* do? What did *not* exist?

Variation: Write out this assignment as a composition at home. Be prepared to share it with the class.

2 **You and your partner.** Find out what possessions your partner has that you do not. What activities does your partner do that you do not do? Report to the class the things your partner does not have or do, or that you do not have or do.

3 **A terrible day.** Tell a small group or the class about a really terrible day when nothing went right. Use either the present perfect or simple past tense. Use as many negatives as possible, including some of those in **Wortschatz 6.**

4 **Things to avoid.** By now you have gotten to know the town in which you are studying pretty well. Discuss with other students places to avoid, things not to do, etc. Give reasons. Give your comments a negative slant.

5 **Selling.** Page through a German magazine such as *Der Spiegel* or *Stern.* How many imperatives can you spot in the ads? Make a list. Bring some of the ads in to show to the class. Decide why some of these ads use the formal imperative and others the informal forms.

6 **Working with a text.** Make ten negative statements about a story or non-literary text you have read recently for class. For example, tell what characters did not do that they perhaps could or should have done.

Simple Past Tense / Past Perfect Tense

7.1 Simple Past Tense

A. *Formation*

1. The simple past tense **(das Präteritum)** is the second principal part of the verb (see 3.1). The simple past tense of *weak verbs* is formed by adding a **-t** plus a set of personal endings to the infinitive stem.

   If the infinitive stem ends in **-d, -t,** or in a single **-m** or **-n** preceded by a consonant other than **l** or **r,** then an **e** is added before the **-t** to facilitate pronunciation.

	lernen	**arbeiten**	**atmen** *(to breathe)*
ich	lernt **e**	arbeitet **e**	atmet **e**
du	lernt **est**	arbeitet **est**	atmet **est**
er / sie / es	lernt **e**	arbeitet **e**	atmet **e**
wir	lernt **en**	arbeitet **en**	atmet **en**
ihr	lernt **et**	arbeitet **et**	atmet **et**
sie / Sie	lernt **en**	arbeitet **en**	atmet **en**

2. *Irregular weak verbs* (see also 3.1B) form the simple past tense like the weak verbs, but they also change the stem vowel. The verbs **bringen** and **denken** have consonant changes as well. (The modal verbs are irregular; their tense formation is discussed in Chapter 9.)

	wissen		
ich	wußt **e**	wir	wußt **en**
du	wußt **est**	ihr	wußt **et**
er / sie / es	wußt **e**	sie / Sie	wußt **en**

also:			
brennen	bran**nte**	nennen	nan**nte**
bringen	bra**chte**	rennen	ran**nte**
denken	da**chte**	senden	san**dte** / sen**dete**[1]
kennen	kan**nte**	wenden	wan**dte** / wen**dete**[1]

3. *Strong verbs* (see also 3.1C) form the past-tense stem by changing the vowel and sometimes also the consonant of the infinitive stem; they *do not* add a **-t** to this stem, as do the weak verbs. There are no endings in the first and third persons singular of strong verbs.

	liegen	**gehen**	**sitzen**
ich	lag	ging	saß
du	lag **st**	ging **st**	saß **est**[2]
er / sie / es	lag	ging	saß
wir	lag **en**	ging **en**	saß **en**
ihr	lag **t**	ging **t**	saß **t**
sie / Sie	lag **en**	ging **en**	saß **en**

For a listing of strong verbs, see Appendix 3.

4. The auxiliaries **sein** and **werden** are strong verbs; **haben** is a weak verb, but slightly irregular.

	haben	**sein**	**werden**
ich	**hatte**	**war**	**wurde**
du	**hattest**	**warst**	**wurdest**
er / sie / es	**hatte**	**war**	**wurde**
wir	**hatten**	**waren**	**wurden**
ihr	**hattet**	**wart**	**wurdet**
sie / Sie	**hatten**	**waren**	**wurden**

5. In the past tense, all verbs with separable prefixes function as they do in the present tense (see 2.1E); the prefix goes to the end of a main clause, but reconnects to the verb in subordinate clauses.

1. For the use of these verb forms, see 3.1B, footnote 2.
2. Past-tense stems ending in **-s, -ss,** and **-ß** require an **e** before the **-st** in the second person singular. This **e** often occurs with many other strong verbs as well, particularly in poetry: **du fand(e)st; du hielt(e)st; du schnitt(e)st;** BUT **du kamst; du lagst; du warst.**

Gregor **schlief** oft während der Vorlesung **ein.**	*Gregor often fell asleep during the lecture.*
Alle wußten, daß er oft während der Vorlesung **einschlief.**	*Everyone knew that he often fell asleep during the lecture.*

B. Use

1. The German simple past tense is sometimes called the *narrative past;* it has several English equivalents.

   ich fragte { *I asked* / *I was asking* / *I did ask* / *I used to ask* / *I would ask (used to ask)*

2. The German simple past tense and present perfect tense (see 3.2C) usually have the same meaning. The present perfect tense, however, is normally used in conversation, whereas the simple past tense has a narrative flavor. The simple past is the preferred tense in stories, anecdotes, biographies, and historical accounts. It is also used in both written and spoken German to recount a series of connected past events—a practice that avoids the repeated use of the auxiliaries **haben** and **sein.**

Ich **kam, sah** und **siegte.**	*I came, saw, and conquered.*
Wir **fuhren** in die Stadt, **kauften** fürs Wochenende **ein, aßen** im Gasthof und **gingen** danach ins Kino.	*We drove to town, shopped for the weekend, ate in an inn, and went to the movies afterward.*

3. The simple past tense of **haben, sein,** and the modal verbs (see 9.1) is preferred over the present perfect tense, even in conversation (see 3.2C).

Er **war** gestern hier, aber ich **konnte** ihm nicht helfen, denn ich **hatte** keine Zeit.	*He was here yesterday, but I could not help him, for I didn't have any time.*

4. In actual practice, spoken German is usually a mixture of the two tenses—past and present perfect—dictated by a sense of rhythm and style.

   Am Sonntag **sind** wir aufs Land **gefahren.** In Pöllauberg **fanden** wir ein nettes Restaurant, von wo aus man fast die ganze Oststeiermark **sehen konnte,** da gutes Wetter **herrschte** *(prevailed).* Nachher **besichtigten** wir die Kapelle im Ort, und dann **sind** wir ein paar Stunden **gewandert.** Früh am Abend **waren** wir schon wieder in Wien. Die paar Stunden in der frischen Luft **haben** mir gut **getan.**

5. With the exception of **haben, sein,** and the modal verbs, the second person singular and plural forms **(du, ihr)** seldom occur in the simple past.

7.2 Past Perfect Tense

A. *Formation*

The *past perfect* tense **(das Plusquamperfekt** or **das Pluperfekt)** is a compound tense; it is formed with the *past tense* of either **haben** or **sein** + the past participle. The choice of **haben** or **sein** follows the same rules as in the present perfect (see 3.2B). The participle is placed at the end of the clause.

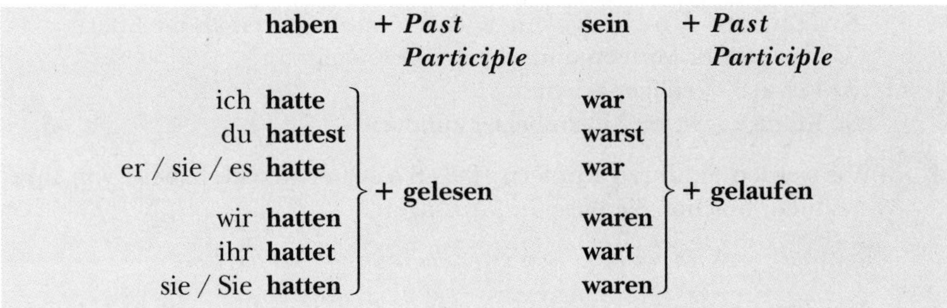

	haben	*+ Past Participle*	**sein**	*+ Past Participle*
ich	**hatte**		**war**	
du	**hattest**		**warst**	
er / sie / es	**hatte**	+ **gelesen**	**war**	+ **gelaufen**
wir	**hatten**		**waren**	
ihr	**hattet**		**wart**	
sie / Sie	**hatten**		**waren**	

B. *Use*

1. The German past perfect tense corresponds to the English past perfect; it expresses that an action had taken place *prior* to some other past-time event. The past perfect tense does not occur by itself; there is always some other past-time context, whether expressed or implied.

Als es zu regnen anfing, **hatte** Rolf gerade die Blumen **gegossen.**	*When it began to rain, Rolf **had** just **watered** the flowers.*
Silke **kam** ziemlich spät nach Hause. Sie **war** im Konzert **gewesen.**	*Silke came home rather late. She **had been** at a concert.*

2. The past perfect tense is *not* used when describing a sequence of events, even though some actions occurred prior to others.

Wir **fuhren** ins Stadtzentrum, **aßen** und **gingen** dann ins Kino.	*We drove to town, ate, and then went to the movies.*

3. The past perfect is very common, however, in dependent clauses introduced by **nachdem.**

Nachdem wir **gegessen hatten,** gingen wir ins Kino.	*After we had eaten, we went to the movies.*

* Übungen

A **Zu ihrer Zeit.** Mutter erzählt von ihrer Jugend. Damals machte man alles natürlich besser. Was sagt sie?

Beispiel: meine Mutter / uns jeden Morgen das Frühstück machen
*Meine Mutter **machte** uns jeden Morgen das Frühstück.*

1. junge Leute / nicht soviel rauchen
2. wir / mehr im Freien spielen
3. Studenten / nicht immer gegen alles demonstrieren
4. ich / mehr in der Schule aufpassen
5. Schüler / mehr Hausaufgaben machen
6. Teenager / nicht denken / daß / mehr wissen als die Eltern
7. wir / öfter Museen und Theater besuchen
8. Leute / fleißiger arbeiten
9. Kinder / ihren Eltern besser zuhören

B Was werden Sie Ihren Kindern (falls Sie später welche haben) von Ihrer Jugend erzählen? Machen Sie bitte fünf Aussagen.

Beispiel: *Als ich ein Kind war, war alles nicht so teuer wie heute.*

C **Amadeus.** Ergänzen Sie die Sätze durch die folgenden Verben im Präteritum.

arbeiten	hören	machen	spielen
bringen	kennenlernen	reisen	sterben
geben	kommen	schreiben	werden
heiraten	komponieren	sein	ziehen *(to move)*

1. Mozart ____ 1756 in der Stadt Salzburg zur Welt. 2. Schon mit drei Jahren ____ er Klavier. 3. Wenig später ____ Wolfgang sein erstes Musikstück. 4. Sein musikalisches Talent ____ ihn berühmt. 5. Als Wunderkind ____ er mit seiner Schwester durch Europa. 6. In vielen aristokratischen Häusern ____ man ihn spielen. 7. Im Jahre 1780 ____ er nach Wien. 8. Dort ____ er als Musiklehrer und ____ private Konzerte. 9. Er ____ Konstanze Weber im Jahre 1782. 10. Bald danach ____ er Haydn ____, und sie ____ gute Freunde. 11. Zwischen 1782 und 1791 ____ er Opern, Singspiele und Sinfonien. 12. Diese Werke ____ ihm Ruhm *(fame)*. 13. Als er 1791 ____, ____ er erst 35 Jahre alt.

D **Unser Jahrhundert.** Ergänzen Sie die Sätze mit jeweils zwei bis drei Aussagen.

Beispiel: In den 50er Jahren . . . *sahen die Autos ganz komisch aus.*
hörte man gern Rock und Roll.
wußte man noch nichts von Vietnam.

1. In den tollen 20er Jahren dieses Jahrhunderts . . .
2. Während des Zweiten Weltkriegs . . .

3. In den 50er Jahren . . .
4. In den 60er Jahren . . .
5. Während der 80er Jahre . . .

E **Kurzer Lebenslauf.** Schreiben Sie diesen Lebenslauf im Präteritum.

Günther Mohr spricht mit Kollegen:

Ich bin 1958 in Trier geboren. Dort bin ich aufgewachsen und in die Schule gegangen. In Göttingen und in München habe ich Philosophie und Volkswirtschaft *(economics)* studiert. Mein Studium habe ich 1986 mit einem Diplom in Volkswirtschaft beendet. Im Juni 1988 habe ich eine Amerikanerin geheiratet und bin mit ihr in die Vereinigten Staaten gegangen. Zuerst habe ich als Wirtschaftsplaner bei der Firma Texas Instruments gearbeitet. 1989 sind wir nach White Plains im Staate New York gezogen, wo ich eine Stelle bei der Firma IBM bekommen habe.

Beispiel: LEBENSLAUF FÜR GÜNTHER MOHR:
Günther Mohr wurde (ist) 1958 in Trier geboren.[3] *Dort . . .*

F **Ein Brand in der Brauerei.** Übersetzen Sie die Sätze ins Deutsche.

1. My uncle used to work in a brewery in Germany.
2. Every day he would go to work at seven o'clock and come home at three.
3. One day **(eines Tages)** a fire broke out.
4. Soon the entire brewery was burning.
5. By **(bis)** evening the brewery had burned down **(abbrennen).**
6. After that, my uncle didn't have a job in the brewery anymore.
7. He always used to say that he had been "fired" **(„gefeuert" worden war)** from his job.

G **Plusquamperfekt: Und wie war es vorher?** Setzen Sie die Sätze in die Vergangenheit.

Beispiel: Barbara spielt CDs, die sie in Europa gekauft hat.
Barbara ***spielte*** *CDs, die sie in Europa* ***gekauft hatte.***

1. Jemand hebt *(raises)* seine Hand, der noch nicht viel gesagt hat.
2. Herr Ulmer sitzt im Gasthaus. Er ist den ganzen Tag Ski gefahren.
3. Herr und Frau Meyer können ins Konzert gehen, weil sie Karten bekommen haben.
4. Nachdem du eingekauft hast, fährst du wohl mit der Bahn nach Hause.
5. Herr Schmied liegt tot in seinem blauen Mercedes. Jemand hat ihn erschossen.

---

3. Either **ist geboren** or **wurde geboren** can be used to tell when someone was born, if the person is still alive. The passive **wurde geboren** must be used if the person is dead.

H **Von Märchen, Sagen und Heldentaten.** Was war schon vorher geschehen? Ergänzen Sie die Sätze.

Beispiel: Dornröschen schlief ein, nachdem . . . (Finger stechen)
Dornröschen schlief ein, nachdem sie sich in den Finger gestochen hatte.

1. Als Rotkäppchen das Haus der Großmutter erreichte, . . . (der Wolf / Großmutter fressen)
2. Die Nibelungen machten Siegfried zu ihrem König, weil . . . (er / den Drachen Fafnir erschlagen)
3. Dornröschen wachte erst dann auf, nachdem . . . (hundert Jahre verfließen)
4. Die böse Hexe *(witch)* verbrannte, nachdem . . . (Gretel / sie in den Backofen stoßen)
5. Der Rattenfänger bekam die tausend Taler nicht, die *(which)* . . . (der Stadtrat *[city council]* von Hameln / ihm versprechen)

Anwendung

Tips zum mündlichen Erzählen ***Telling Stories***

Telling stories has nearly become a lost art. This is too bad, as it provides excellent language practice. Prepare for oral narratives by making only the most necessary chronological notes in telegram style, with verb infinitives last. Tell your story in many short, simple sentences. Avoid complex structures such as subordinating conjunctions or relative pronouns. The oral topics of activities A, B, and C can also be written as compositions.

A **Aus meinem Leben.** Erzählen Sie anderen Leuten von einem besonderen Ereignis aus Ihrem Leben oder aus dem Leben eines anderen Menschen, den Sie kennen.

THEMENVORSCHLÄGE

eine unvergeßliche Begegnung *(encounter)*
das Schlimmste, was mir je passierte
eine große Dummheit von mir
ein unglaubliches Erlebnis *(experience)*
der schönste Tag in meinem Leben
eine große Überraschung *(surprise)*

REDEMITTEL

Einmal / einst war(en) . . .
Früher [wohnte] ich . . .
Eines Tages / eines Morgens / eines Abends / eines Nachts . . .

Schon vorher waren wir . . . [gegangen].
Ich hatte auch vorher . . . [getan].
Und plötzlich . . .
Na ja, wie gesagt, ich . . .
Später . . .
Zu meinem Entsetzen *(fright)* / zu meiner Überraschung . . .
Kurz danach . . .
Zum Schluß . . .

B **Es war einmal.** Erzählen Sie im Kurs ein bekanntes Märchen oder eine von Ihnen erfundene Geschichte.

C **Münchhausen erzählt.** Der „Lügenbaron" von Münchhausen (1720–1797) war deutscher Offizier, kam viel in der Welt herum und erzählte gern und oft von seinen unglaublichen und erlogenen Abenteuern *(adventures)*. (Er erzählte sogar von seiner Reise zum Mond!) Erzählen Sie ein solches Abenteuer, in dem *Sie* die Hauptrolle eines Helden oder einer Heldin spielen. Je phantastischer, desto besser!

* Schriftliche Themen

Tips zum Schreiben ***Choosing Precise Verbs***
Verbs are the key! Avoid general verbs such as **haben, sein,** and **machen** in favor of verbs that precisely convey the actions or events you are describing. For example, **gehen** denotes activity but does not describe it. Consider how many different ways there are to *go* in English: walk, run, stumble, hobble, limp, race, etc. (See **Wortschatz 7**). Once you have a precise English verb, look up its German equivalent. Then cross-check this verb as a German entry, to see whether it really means what you think it does. Have in mind a person (not necessarily your instructor) for whom you are writing, and continually ask yourself how you can make your narrative more interesting to this reader.

A **Eine Bildgeschichte.** Erzählen Sie die Bildgeschichte auf Seite 88 im Präteritum. Benutzen Sie die Erzählskizze dabei.

Der Verdacht

bei Nacht • tragen • das Paket • die Brücke • ins Wasser werfen • Polizist sehen • glauben • stehlen • verhaften *(arrest)* • andere Polizisten • kommen • festhalten • telefonieren • das Baggerschiff • herausfischen • heraufholen • aufschneiden • eine Bowle • kitschig aussehen • erzählen • schenken • um Entschuldigung bitten • wieder ins Wasser werfen

Drawing by Gardner Rea; © 1932, 1960 The New Yorker Magazine, Inc.

B **Lebenslauf.** Schreiben Sie einen Lebenslauf von *sich* oder von einem bekannten *(well-known)* Menschen. Der Lebenslauf muß nicht lang sein, aber er soll die wichtigsten Informationen enthalten.

Beispiel: **Helga Schütz** wurde 1937 im schlesischen Falkenhain geboren und wuchs dann in Dresden auf. Nach einer Gärtnerlehre machte sie an der Potsdamer Arbeiter-und-Bauern-Fakultät ihr Abitur und studierte Dramaturgie an der Deutschen Hochschule für Filmkunst in Potsdam-Babelsberg. Für die Defa[4] schrieb sie Dokumentar- und Spielfilme–zum Beispiel „Die Leiden des jungen Werthers".

1970 erschien ihr erster Prosaband: „Vorgeschichten oder Schöne Gegend Probstein", eine Chronik von kleinen Leuten in der niederschlesischen Provinz. Im Westen erschienen im Luchterhand-Verlag ihre Erzählung „Festbeleuchtung" und die Romane „In Annas Namen" und „Julia oder Erziehung zum Chorgesang".

Helga Schütz wurde mit dem Heinrich-Greif-Preis, dem Heinrich-Mann-Preis und dem Theodor-Fontane-Preis ausgezeichnet. Dieses Jahr amtiert *(holds the position)* sie als „Stadtschreiberin" in Mainz. *(Die Zeit)*

Wortschatz 7

gehen	kommen
fahren	laufen
fallen	schwimmen
fliegen	steigen

\+ *synonyms for these verbs*

1. The following strong verbs express various basic types of *going;* they require the auxiliary **sein. Fahren** and **fliegen** take the auxiliary **haben** when used with direct objects (see 3.2B).

gehen	to go	**kommen**	to come
fahren	to go *(by vehicle);* to drive	**laufen**	to run
fallen	to fall	**schwimmen**	to swim
fliegen	to fly	**steigen**	to climb

4. **Defa: Deutsche Film-Aktiengesellschaft.** The official film company of the former German Democratic Republic.

2. A number of additional verbs prove very useful for telling precisely *how* a person or thing moves. Because they describe motion, these verbs also require the auxiliary **sein.** Strong verbs are marked with an asterisk, irregular verbs with a double asterisk.

eilen	to hurry, hasten	**schlendern**	to saunter, stroll
humpeln	to hobble, limp	**schreiten***	to stride
klettern	to climb *(a steep surface),* scramble	**springen***	to jump, leap, bound
		stolpern	to stumble
kriechen*	to creep, crawl	**stürzen**	to fall; to plunge, rush
rennen**	to run, race, dash	**treiben***	to drift, float
rutschen	to slip, slide	**treten***	to step, walk
sausen	to rush, whiz	**waten**	to wade
schleichen*	to creep, slink, sneak	**watscheln**	to waddle

Die Kinder **rutschten** auf dem Eis hin und her.	*The children slid back and forth on the ice.*
Eine große Ente *(duck)* **watschelte** durch den Hof.	*A large duck waddled through the yard.*
Der Herr **trat** vor den Spiegel.	*The gentleman stepped in front of the mirror.*

ÜBUNGEN

A **Genauer beschreiben.** Ersetzen Sie die fettgedruckten Teile der Sätze durch Verben, welche die Art des Gehens genauer oder stärker zum Ausdruck bringen.

Beispiel: *Autos fuhren schnell an uns vorbei.*
*Autos **sausten** an uns vorbei.*

1. Ein Boot **ging** ruderlos den Strom hinunter.
2. In der Dunkelheit **lief** das Kind **über einen Stein** und **fiel zu Boden.**
3. Einige Wanderer **gingen bis zu den Knien im Wasser** durch den Bach *(stream).*
4. Reinhold **stieg** gern steile Felsen *(steep cliffs)* hinauf.
5. Drei Menschen in schwarzen Mänteln **kamen** aus dem Fahrstuhl *(elevator).*
6. Als sie von dem Unfall erfuhr *(found out),* **ging** die Ärztin **schnell** ins Krankenhaus.
7. Feierlich *(ceremoniously)* **ging** die Königin durch die Halle.

B **Das passende Verb.** Bilden Sie Sätze mit den folgenden Subjekten und mit Verben, welche die Art des Gehens genau beschreiben.

Beispiel: ein Dieb
Ein Dieb schlich in das Haus.

1. Parkbesucher
2. einige Radfahrer in Eile
3. Autos auf dem Glatteis *(glare ice)*
4. die Preise *(prices)* während einer Depression
5. ein Hund mit verletztem *(injured)* Fuß
6. die Bewohner eines brennenden Hauses

Zusammenfassung 7

Rules to Remember

1. The simple past is primarily a narrative tense; it is used to tell stories, recite anecdotes, etc.
2. Weak and irregular weak verbs add **-t** + personal endings to the stem to form the simple past **(ich lernte; rannte;** *pl.* **wir lernten; rannten).**
3. Strong verbs form the simple past by changing the stem vowel and sometimes a consonant and adding endings **(ich ging; sah; wir gingen, sahen).** However, the first and third persons singular have no ending **(ich / er / sie / es ging).**
4. The second person simple past tense forms of most verbs **du lerntest (ranntest, gingst); ihr lerntet (ranntet, gingt)** are seldom used.
5. The past perfect tense is never used by itself, but rather only within the context of some other past time event, which it then precedes.

Activities

1 **Practicing forms.** Find a short narrative text in German (a story, fairy tale, or an anecdote), written in the present tense. Read the text aloud, but change all the present-tense verbs not in quotation marks to the simple past tense as you read.

2 **Words and stories.** Form groups of four–five students. Write ten words on a card and give the card to another group. This group writes a narrative using all ten words on your card. The results are read aloud to the class.

3 **Group chain story.** Write one noun, one verb, and one adjective on a slip of paper. Exchange your slip of paper with another student. Someone in class begins a story in past time, using the words on his / her card. Other students follow suit. You may say up to three sentences, as long as you use all three words on the card you have. The story ends when everyone has contributed.

4 **Historical report.** Working with a partner, prepare as homework a historical report on a person, place, event, or cultural phenomenon. Write out the report and hand it in for correction. Present an oral report in class without consulting the written narrative.

5 **A day in class.** Working in a group, write a narrative account of what happened in your German class yesterday.

6 **Working with a text.** Retell or summarize a story you have read, but take the point of view of one of the characters.

Future Tense/ Future Perfect Tense

8

8.1 Future Tense

A. Formation

1. The future tense **(das Futur)** is formed with the conjugated present tense of the auxiliary **werden** *(will)* + a main verb infinitive.

	werden	+ ***Main Verb Infinitive***		
ich	**werde**		*I*	
du	**wirst**		*you*	
er / sie / es	**wird**	+ **gehen**	*he / she / it*	*will go*
wir	**werden**		*we*	
ihr	**werdet**		*you*	
sie / Sie	**werden**		*they / you*	

2. In the future tense the main verb infinitive is at the end of the sentence or main clause.

Sie **wird** uns hoffentlich bald **einladen.**	*I hope she will invite us soon.*

3. In dependent clauses, however, the conjugated auxiliary **werden** moves to final position. However, if final position is occupied by a double infinitive (see 18.6), the auxiliary **werden** directly precedes the double infinitive.

Ich hoffe, daß sie uns bald einladen **wird.**	*I hope that she will invite us soon.*
BUT:	
Ich hoffe, daß sie uns bald **wird** einladen können.	*I hope that she will be able to invite us soon.*

B. *Use*

1. The future tense is used with or without time expressions to indicate that something *will* or *is going to* happen.

Wir **werden** eine bessere Wohnung **suchen.**	*We will look for a better apartment.*
Weißt du, ob Barbara auch nächstes Jahr hier **studieren wird?**	*Do you know whether Barbara is also going to study here next year?*

2. The present tense is often used in place of the future tense when an adverb of time (**bald, morgen, nächste Woche, im kommenden Jahr,** etc.) or the context indicates future time.

Das Semester **beginnt** *nächsten Montag.*	*The semester begins next Monday.*

3. The German future tense is also used with the particles **wohl** or **schon** to express *present probability.*

Das **wird** *schon* richtig **sein.**	*That's probably right.*
Die Polizei **wird** *wohl* etwas von dem Unfall **wissen.**	*The police probably know something about the accident.*

8.2 Future Perfect Tense

A. *Formation*

The future perfect tense (**das zweite Futur**) is formed by adding the conjugated auxiliary **werden** to a present perfect statement, thereby moving the present perfect auxiliary **haben** or **sein** to final position as an infinitive.

Present Perfect	*Future Perfect*
Sie **hat** die Arbeit **getan.** *She did the work.*	Sie **wird** die Arbeit **getan haben.** *She will have done the work.*
Sie **sind** nach Hause **gegangen.** *They have gone home.*	Sie **werden** nach Hause **gegangen sein.** *They will have gone home.*

B. *Use*

1. The future perfect is normally used with the particles **wohl** or **schon** to express *past probability,* the idea that something has probably already happened.

Inge **wird** ihr Auto wohl schon **verkauft haben.**	*Inge has probably already sold her car.*
Der Baum **wird** wohl während eines Sturms **umgestürzt sein.**	*The tree probably fell over during a storm.*

2. The future perfect may also express the idea that something *will have happened* by a certain time in the future. It is not used very often in this meaning.

Bis heute abend **wird** er unser Auto **repariert haben.**	*By this evening he will have repaired our car.*
Sie **werden** vor unserer Ankunft nach Bremen **abgeflogen sein.**	*They will have departed by plane for Bremen before our arrival.*

* Übungen

A **Lottogewinner!** In einem Fernsehinterview erzählen Herr und Frau Lindemann, was sie mit ihrem Lottogewinn machen werden. Sie sprechen im Präsens. Erzählen Sie *im Futur* von den Plänen der Familie Lindemann.

HERR UND FRAU LINDEMANN:
Mit unserem Lottogewinn von DM 500.000 machen wir erst mal eine Reise nach Amerika. Unsere Tochter reist mit. In Boston mieten wir uns einen Wagen und fahren durch Amerika nach San Francisco, und im Herbst eröffnen wir dann in Wuppertal eine Herrenboutique. Wir hoffen, daß viele Leute bei uns einkaufen.

B **Morgen.** Was werden Sie morgen tun? Was wird geschehen? Ergänzen Sie die Sätze.

Beispiele: Um acht Uhr . . .
Um acht Uhr werde ich aufstehen.

Um zehn Uhr . . .
Um zehn Uhr wird meine Deutschstunde beginnen.

1. Um acht Uhr . . .
2. Um halb zehn . . .
3. Zu Mittag . . .
4. Nach der Mittagspause . . .
5. Am späteren Nachmittag . . .
6. Am Abend . . .

Und jetzt drei weitere Aussagen im Futur. *Sie* sollen eine Zeit wählen.

7. Ich denke, daß . . .
8. Es ist möglich, daß . . .
9. Ich weiß noch nicht, ob . . .

C **Im Deutschkurs: Was wird wohl geschehen sein?** Erklären Sie, warum die Leute sich wohl so benehmen *(behave).*

Beispiel: Georg hat heute morgen einen schweren Kopf.
Er ***wird wohl*** *gestern abend zuviel* ***gelernt haben.***

1. Martina ist ganz böse auf den Lehrer.
2. Gabi ist heute untröstlich *(inconsolable).* Sie weint leise während des Unterrichts.
3. Stefan döst *(dozes)* in der letzten Reihe *(row),* während der Lehrer spricht.
4. Ulrich sitzt ganz still auf seinem Platz. Er hat ein blaues Auge.
5. Jörg kommt immer zur Deutschstunde. Heute ist er aber nicht da.

D **Zweites Futur: Bis dahin.** Was wird bis dahin schon geschehen sein?

Beispiel: Vor dem Ende dieses Jahres . . .
werde *ich ein Auto* ***gekauft haben.***
wird *Amerika einen neuen Präsidenten* ***gewählt haben.***
werden *Freunde von mir nach Europa* ***gereist sein.***

1. Bis *(by)* zum nächsten Freitag . . .
2. Vor dem Ende des Semesters . . .
3. Bevor ich 30 werde, . . .
4. Vor dem Jahre 2000 . . .
5. Bis man AIDS besiegt haben wird, . . .

Anwendung

A **Was andere machen werden.** Fragen Sie jemanden im Kurs nach seinen / ihren Plänen und berichten Sie darüber.

THEMENVORSCHLÄGE

nächsten Sommer
nach dem Studium
im späteren Leben
wenn alles nach Plan geht

REDEMITTEL

Weißt du schon, was du tun wirst, wenn . . . ?
Hast du dir überlegt *(thought about),* was . . . ?
Was hast du für . . . vor *(have in mind)*?
Wenn alles nach Plan geht, dann werde ich . . .
Vielleicht wird es mir gelingen *(succeed),* . . . zu [tun].
Ich werde wohl . . .

B **Prognosen für die Zukunft.** Diskutieren Sie mit anderen Studenten, wie die Welt Ihrer Meinung nach in 2, 5, 10, 20 oder 30 Jahren aussehen wird. Was wird wohl anders sein als heute? Was wird es (nicht mehr) geben?

THEMENVORSCHLÄGE

Umwelt (Stadt, Landschaft, Meer)
Medien (Zeitung, Radio, Fernsehen)
Technik und Informatik
Reiseverkehr
Film und Unterhaltung
Haus und Auto
Schule und Universität
Menschen, die heute sehr bekannt sind
Gesellschaft
Städte
AIDS

REDEMITTEL

In . . . Jahren wird . . .
Höchstwahrscheinlich werden wir (nicht) . . .
Ich denke, es wird wohl so sein: . . .
Es ist leicht möglich, daß . . .
Vielleicht werden die Menschen auch . . .
Es wird mich (nicht) überraschen, wenn . . .
Es kann sein, daß wir in (der) Zukunft . . .
Es wird wahrscheinlich (keine) . . . (mehr) geben.

* Schriftliche Themen

Tips zum Schreiben ***Qualifying Statements About the Future***
There is a saying in English: "Man proposes, God disposes." (German: **Der Mensch denkt, Gott lenkt.**) In other words, things may not always turn out as planned. Thus, when conjecturing about the future or when telling of your own plans, you may want to qualify some of your statements with adverbial expressions such as **eventuell** *(possibly, perhaps)*, **hoffentlich, unter Umständen** *(under certain circumstances)*, **unter keinen Umständen** *(under no circumstances)*, **vielleicht, wohl (schon)***(probably)*, and **(höchst)wahrscheinlich** *([most] likely)*. You can even stress the tentative nature of your future statements by beginning sentences with these qualifiers. Time expressions also work well in first position; they supply the reader with an immediate future context for what is to follow. Remember to use a mixture of present and future tense for the sake of stylistic variety, and be sure to vary your verbs.

A **Meine Zukunftspläne.** Erzählen Sie von Ihren Zukunftsplänen.

Beispiel: Ich bin jetzt im zweiten Studienjahr. In zwei Jahren werde ich mein Studium als *undergraduate* abschließen. Was danach kommt, weiß ich noch nicht ganz genau. Vielleicht werde ich weiterstudieren. Es kann aber sein, daß ich zuerst ein paar Jahre arbeite oder einen Beruf erlerne. Auf jeden Fall werde ich . . . usw.

B **Die Zukunft.** Wie sehen Sie die Zukunft Ihres Landes? Schreiben Sie entweder aus positiver oder negativer Sicht.

Wortschatz 8

fortfahren
fortsetzen
weiter[tun]

1. **Fortfahren** means *to continue doing.* It is intransitive and normally complemented by an infinitive phrase (see 18.1).

Fahren Sie bitte **fort** zu lesen.	*Please continue reading.*
Wir **fahren** heute **fort,** wo wir gestern aufgehört haben.	*We are continuing today where we stopped yesterday.*

2. **Fortsetzen** means *to continue something.* The verb is transitive and a direct object is required.

Sie **setzten** ihre Reise **fort.**	*They continued their trip.*
Setzen Sie die gute Arbeit **fort.**	*Continue the good work.*

3. The separable prefix **weiter** can be affixed to virtually any verb to express continuation of an activity.

Mach nur **weiter!**	*Just keep doing it.*
Wollen wir **weitergehen?**	*Do we want to continue on?*

ÜBUNG

Weitermachen. Beenden Sie die Sätze. Verwenden Sie die folgenden Verben.

fortfahren fortsetzen weiter[tun]

1. Es tut mir leid, daß ich Sie beim Lesen stören mußte. Sie können jetzt . . .
2. Diese Übersetzung ist gut. Du sollst . . .

3. Wir werden diese Diskussion morgen . . .
4. Wenn Sie zu der Brücke kommen, dann haben Sie den Campingplatz noch nicht erreicht. Sie müssen ein paar Kilometer . . .

Zusammenfassung 8

Rules to Remember

1. The future tense is formed with **werden** + an infinitive.
2. Infinitives are always in final position.
3. The future perfect tense is used primarily to speculate that someone probably did something or that something probably happened.

Activities

1 **Class activity.** Write five different future time expressions on a slip of paper. Exchange your slip with another student. Make future statements about yourself using the time expressions you have received.

2 **Plans.** Find someone in class who has interesting plans for the weekend. Then ask as many specific questions as you can think of about what he or she plans to do.

Beispiel: Monika is going home for the weekend.
Wie wirst du nach Hause fahren?
Wie lange wird die Fahrt dauern?
Was wirst du zu Hause tun?
usw.

Variation: Everyone in class poses one question to the person with the most interesting weekend plans.

3 **Interview.** Phone home and ask a family member (in English) about his / her future plans. Find out what the person will do *perhaps* **(vielleicht)** and what she / he will do *for sure* **(sicher).** Report the results to the class in German.

4 **Horoscope.** Make a list of five to seven names of well-known persons. Read your names in class. Other students make predictions about each person.

Beispiel: Liz Taylor
Im Jahre 2000 wird Liz Taylor sich von ihrem 15. Ehemann scheiden lassen.

5 **Predictions.** Write a date on one card and a topic on another. Cards are tossed in two separate hats. Draw a topic and a date and make a prediction for that topic and date.

Possible topics: **Familie, Politik, Gesellschaft** *(society),* **Wirtschaft** *(economy),* **Medien, Film, Sport** usw.

6 **Working with a text.** Write a paragraph in which you speculate as to what a character or characters in a novel or short story that you have read will be doing one year after the end of the story. Read your ideas to the class.

Modal Verbs

9.1 Present and Past Tenses of Modal Verbs

A. *Forms*

1. In the present tense, modal verbs conjugate like almost all other verbs in the plural, but the singular is irregular.

Present Tense of Modal Verbs

	dürfen	**können**	**mögen**	**müssen**	**sollen**	**wollen**
ich	**darf**	**kann**	**mag**	**muß**	**soll**	**will**
du	**darfst**	**kannst**	**magst**	**mußt**	**sollst**	**willst**
er / sie / es	**darf**	**kann**	**mag**	**muß**	**soll**	**will**
wir	dürfen	können	mögen	müssen	sollen	wollen
ihr	dürft	könnt	mögt	müßt	sollt	wollt
sie / Sie	dürfen	können	mögen	müssen	sollen	wollen

2. Modal verbs form their past tense like weak verbs (see 7.1), except that there are no umlauts carried over from infinitive stems and **mögen** undergoes a consonant change.

Past Tense of Modal Verbs

	dürfen	**können**	**mögen**	**müssen**	**sollen**	**wollen**
ich	durfte	konnte	mochte	mußte	sollte	wollte
du	durftest	konntest	mochtest	mußtest	solltest	wolltest
er / sie / es	durfte	konnte	mochte	mußte	sollte	wollte
wir	durften	konnten	mochten	mußten	sollten	wollten
ihr	durftet	konntet	mochtet	mußtet	solltet	wolltet
sie / Sie	durften	konnten	mochten	mußten	sollten	wollten

B. *Use*

1. Modal verbs are normally complemented by a main verb infinitive in final position.

Wir **müssen** morgen nach Ulm **fahren.**	*We have to drive to Ulm tomorrow.*

2. In dependent clauses, the conjugated modal of course moves to final position, like other verbs.

Er sagt, daß wir morgen nach Ulm **fahren müssen.**	*He says that we have to drive to Ulm tomorrow.*

3. When the main verb is obvious from previous context, it is often replaced by **das** or **es** or left out completely. This omission is also common in spoken English.

Wer kann hier gut rechnen? —Ich **kann** (es).	*Who here can calculate well?* *I can (do it).*
Wer sollte hier aufräumen? —Hans **sollte** (es).	*Who was supposed to clean up here?* *Hans was supposed to (do it).*

4. After modals, verbs of motion **(gehen, fahren, fliegen, laufen)** and the verbs **tun** and **machen** are usually inferred from context and thus are often omitted even though they cannot always be omitted in English.

Er **muß** aus geschäftlichen Gründen nach Zürich.	*He has to go to Zurich for business reasons.*
Unser Auto ist kaputt. Was **sollen** wir jetzt?	*Our car is shot. What are we (supposed) to do now?*

9.2 Meanings of Modal Verbs

A. Dürfen *(Permission)*

1. **Dürfen** means *may* in the sense of having permission or being allowed. It is commonly used in polite questions.

Sie **dürfen** nächste Woche zu Hause bleiben.	*They may / have permission to stay home next week.*
Darf ich Sie etwas fragen?	*May I ask you something?*

2. In the negative (with **nicht** or **kein-**), **dürfen** means *must not* or *may not.* (Compare with **müssen nicht** in Section C.)

In vielen Ländern **darf** man **nicht** ohne Führerschein Auto fahren. — *In many countries one must not / is not permitted to drive a car without a license.*

Du **darfst keinem** Menschen sagen, wie alt ich bin. — *You may not tell anybody how old I am.*

B. Können *(Ability; Possibility)*

1. **Können** means *can* or *to be able to* and expresses the idea of ability.

   Könnt ihr uns verstehen? — *Can / are you able to understand us?*

   Wir **konnten** das Rätsel nicht lösen. — *We were not able to solve the riddle.*

2. **Können** can also express possibility.

   So etwas **kann** passieren. — *Such a thing can happen.*

3. **Können** also has a special meaning of *to know* a language or *to know how to do* something.

   Sie **kann** Deutsch. — *She knows German. (She can speak German.)*[1]

   Er **kann** schwimmen. — *He knows how to swim.*

4. **Können** is sometimes used interchangeably with **dürfen,** just as *can* and *may* are often confused in English. Strict grammarians of German (and English) still regard this usage as substandard.

   Wo **kann** / **darf** ich hier parken? — *Where can / may I park here?*

C. Müssen *(Necessity; Probability)*

1. **Müssen** is the equivalent of English *must* or *have to* and expresses the idea of necessity.

   Die Schüler **müssen** jetzt schreiben. — *The pupils must / have to write now.*

   Gestern **mußten** die Geschäfte um halb sieben schließen. — *Yesterday the stores had to close at six-thirty.*

2. **Müssen** can also express probability, the idea that something must be or is probably true.

   Neuseeland **muß** sehr schön sein. — *New Zealand must be very beautiful.*

---

1. Like the verbs of motion (see 9.1B), the verb **sprechen** is understood and therefore usually omitted in this context.

3. When used negatively, **müssen nicht** means *not to have to.*

Mußt du die Aufgabe schreiben?	*Do you have to write the assignment?*
—Nein, ich **muß** sie **nicht** schreiben.	*No, I do not have to write it.*

Remember that *must not* is expressed by **nicht dürfen** (see Section A).

Ich **darf** es **nicht** tun.	*I must not do it.*

4. As an alternative to **müssen nicht,** German often uses **brauchen nicht** + a following infinitive which may or may not be preceded by **zu.**[2]

Sie **brauchen** uns nicht **zu schreiben.**	*You do not have to write to us.*
Du **brauchst** keine Angst **haben.**	*You don't have to be afraid.*

D. Sollen *(Obligation)*

1. **Sollen** means *supposed to* or *is to.* It implies a rather strong order or obligation.[3]

Du **sollst** aufstehen und auf die Kinder aufpassen.	*You are to get up and watch the children.*
Was **sollten** wir tun?	*What were we supposed to do?*

2. In questions or suggestions, **sollen** can express future time in the sense of English *shall.*

Wo **soll** ich dich heute abend treffen?	*Where shall I meet you this evening?*

3. **Sollen** can also mean *to be said to,* indicating that the statement is hearsay and thus may or may not be true.

Die Familie Krupp **soll** sehr reich sein.	*The Krupp family is said to be very rich.*
Lee Harvey Oswald **soll** als Sowjetagent gearbeitet haben.	*Lee Harvey Oswald is said to have worked as a Soviet agent.*

---

2. The use of **brauchen nicht** without **zu** was originally considered colloquial but is now acceptable.

3. The subjunctive II form **sollte(n)** *(should)* (see 20.5) is normally used instead of the indicative to express suggestion or recommendation (what one *ought to do*), as opposed to obligation (what one *is supposed to do*).

Du **sollst** hier bleiben. *(obligation)*	*You are to stay here.*
Du **solltest** hier bleiben. *(recommendation)*	*You ought to stay here.*

E. Wollen *(Desire; Wanting; Intention)*

1. **Wollen** means *to want to.* It can also mean *to intend to.*

Diese Firma **will** nach Braunschweig übersiedeln.	*This firm wants to / intends to move to Braunschweig.*
Niemand **wollte** das Risiko eingehen.	*No one wanted to take the risk.*

2. **Wollen** can also mean *to claim to.*

Hans **will** alles besser wissen.	*Hans claims he knows everything better (than we do).*
Hertha **will** die Vase nicht zerbrochen haben.	*Hertha claims not to have broken the vase.*

3. **Wollen** is often used as a main verb with a direct object.

Alle **wollen** den Frieden.	*Everyone wants peace.*

4. If the subject of a sentence wants someone else to do something, then a **daß**-clause is necessary.

COMPARE:

Sie will Golf spielen.	*She wants to play golf.*
Sie will, **daß er Golf spielt.**	*She wants him to play golf.*

F. Mögen *(Liking)*

1. The verb **mögen** is used mainly in its subjunctive II form **möchte(n)** *(would like)* (see 20.2D) to express a wish or request.

Er **möchte** im Sommer nach Italien fahren.	*He would like to travel to Italy in the summer.*
Herr Ober, ich **möchte** ein Glas Saft bitte.	*Waiter, I would like a glass of juice please.*

2. In positive statements in the indicative, **mögen** *(to like)* is used mainly with direct-object nouns and pronouns; it does not normally occur with a following infinitive.

Magst du solche Leute?	*Do you like such people?*
—Ja, ich **mag** sie.	*Yes, I like them.*

3. **Mögen** does occur frequently in negative statements, both with direct objects and with following infinitives. In a general statement, **nicht mögen** means *not to like (to);* in reference to a specific time, it means *not to want (to).*

Sie **mögen** Wein nicht. — *They do not like wine.*
Sie **mögen** *jetzt* keinen Wein. — *They do not want any wine now.*

Thomas **mag** nicht tanzen. — *Thomas does not like to dance.*
Thomas **mag** *jetzt* nicht tanzen. — *Thomas does not want to dance now.*

4. **Mögen** *(may)* is used occasionally in the indicative to express conjecture or possibility.

Das **mag** schon sein. — *That may very well be.*

5. As is the case with **wollen,** if the subject of a sentence would like someone else to do something, then a **daß**-clause must be used.

Ich möchte dir helfen. — *I would like to help you.*
Ich möchte, **daß du mir hilfst.** — *I would like you to help me.*

9.3 Perfect Tenses of Modal Verbs

A. *Formation*

1. The present perfect and past perfect of modal verbs are formed like those of other verbs.

haben +	***Past Participle (No Infinitive)***	
Er hat / hatte es	**gedurft.**	*He has / had been permitted to do it.*
	gekonnt.	*He has / had been able to do it.*
	gemocht.	*He has / had liked it.*
	gemußt.	*He has / had had to do it.*
	gesollt.	*He was / had been supposed to do it.*
	gewollt.	*He has / had wanted to do it.*

2. However, when a modal verb in the present or past perfect is accompanied by the infinitive of another verb, then the past participle of the modal is changed to an infinitive form. This results in a *double infinitive* construction in which the modal infinitive always comes last. The auxiliary verb is **haben.**[4]

haben +	***Double Infinitive***[5]	
Sie hat / hatte es	**tun dürfen.**	*She has / had been permitted to do it.*
	tun können.	*She has / had been able to do it.*
	tun müssen.	*She has / had had to do it.*
	tun sollen.	*She was / had been supposed to do it.*
	tun wollen.	*She has / had wanted to do it.*

4. Some speakers use an infinitive structure (**ich habe es dürfen / können,** etc.) *without* an accompanying main verb infinitive; such usage is considered regional.
5. **Mögen** is excluded here, since it is extremely rare in a double infinitive construction.

3. In dependent clauses, the conjugated auxiliary **haben** precedes the two infinitives.

Wer weiß, ob sie den Artikel **haben lesen können?**	*Who knows whether they have been able to read the article?*

B. Use

1. In the present perfect tense, modals usually occur without accompanying infinitives when the complementary verb is inferred from the context and thus unnecessary.

Hat sie gestern in die Stadt **gemußt?**	*Did she have to go into town yesterday?*
Kannst du Französisch?	*Do you know French?*
—Ja, aber ich habe es früher besser **gekonnt.**	*Yes, but I knew it better before.*

2. There is virtually no difference in meaning between the simple past tense and the present perfect tense of modals. The simple past tense is much more common.

Ich **habe** den Aufsatz noch nicht **schreiben können.**	*I* ***have*** *not yet* ***been able*** *to write the composition.*
MORE COMMON:	
Ich **konnte** den Aufsatz noch nicht **schreiben.**	*I* ***was*** *not yet* ***able*** *to write the composition.*

9.4 Future Tense of Modal Verbs

1. The future tense with modals is formed using the conjugated auxiliary **werden;** the modal becomes an infinitive and moves to final position, resulting in a double infinitive construction (see 18.6).

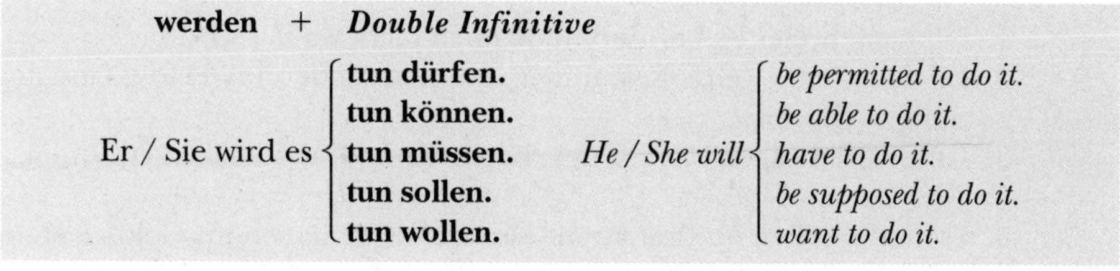

werden +	***Double Infinitive***		
Er / Sie wird es	**tun dürfen.**	*He / She will*	*be permitted to do it.*
	tun können.		*be able to do it.*
	tun müssen.		*have to do it.*
	tun sollen.		*be supposed to do it.*
	tun wollen.		*want to do it.*

COMPARE:

Er muß bald abfahren. *(modal statement)*	*He must depart soon.*
MUß →	
Er **wird** bald **abfahren müssen.** *(future modal statement)*	*He will have to depart soon.*

2. In dependent clauses, the conjugated future auxiliary is placed directly before the double infinitive.

Ute schreibt, daß sie uns im März nicht **wird besuchen können.**	*Ute writes that she will not be able to visit us in March.*

✱ Übungen

A **Auf englisch.** Drücken Sie die Sätze auf englisch aus.

1. Der Film ist zu Ende. Was sollen wir jetzt?
2. Was wollte der Fremde?
3. Morgen muß Hans nicht in die Schule.
4. Was soll das heißen?
5. Meine Eltern sind auf einer Europareise. Jetzt müssen sie in der Schweiz sein.
6. Wir können nach der Vorlesung nach Hause.
7. Darf man hier rauchen?
8. In Hamburg soll es oft regnen.
9. Das darf man hier nicht.

B **Ratschläge** *(advice)* **mit Modalverben.** Wie viele Ratschläge können Sie in den folgenden Situationen geben? Wer hat die besten Ratschläge?

Beispiele: Günther Dünnleib ist etwas zu dick geworden. (Er . . .)
*Er **soll** ein paar Kilo abnehmen.*
*Er **muß** viel laufen und Sport treiben.*

Ihre Freundin Monika sucht eine Arbeitsstelle. (Du . . .)
*Du **kannst** zum Arbeitsamt gehen.*
*Du **sollst** die Annoncen in der Zeitung lesen.*

1. Ich habe hohes Fieber und fühle mich nicht wohl. (Du . . .)
2. Ein Bekannter / eine Bekannte von Ihnen sucht ohne Erfolg eine neue Wohnung. (Er / Sie . . .)
3. Unser Briefträger, Herr Glück, hat im Lotto DM 500.000 gewonnen. (Sie *[you]* . . .)
4. Freunde wollen im Restaurant essen, aber sie haben ihr Geld zu Hause liegenlassen. (Ihr *[you]* . . .)
5. Wir (du und ich) haben morgen eine schwere Prüfung in Deutsch. (Wir . . .)
6. Ein Bekannter / eine Bekannte von uns hat einen schrecklichen Minderwertigkeitskomplex *(inferiority complex)*. Es wird jeden Tag mit ihm / ihr schlimmer. (Er / Sie . . .)
7. Die Eltern von einem / einer Bekannten fliegen nächste Woche zum ersten Mal nach Europa. (Sie *[they]* . . .)

C **Mit Modalverben geht's auch.** Drücken Sie den Inhalt dieser Sätze mit Modalverben aus.

Beispiel: Hier ist Parkverbot.
Hier darf man nicht parken.

1. Max spricht und versteht kein Serbokroatisch.
2. Die Studenten fanden die Leseaufgabe unmöglich.
3. Man sagt, daß zuviel Sonne ungesund ist.
4. Den Rasen bitte nicht betreten!
5. Tun Sie das lieber nicht!
6. Während des Flugs war das Rauchen verboten.
7. Fridolin behauptet immer, daß er alles besser weiß.
8. Erlauben Sie, daß ich eine Frage stelle?
9. Es ist nicht nötig, daß du mitkommst.

D **Schuhe kaufen.** Drücken Sie die Sätze auf deutsch aus.

1. I wanted to buy shoes yesterday, but I had to work and couldn't.
2. They are supposed to be quite inexpensive at the **(beim)** Kaufhof.
3. Gerda claims to have found a pair for less than **(weniger als)** 60 DM.
4. That I can hardly **(kaum)** believe.
5. Mother also wants me to buy some shoes for her.
6. I hope that you will be able to do that.

E **Forderungen!** *(Demands)* O weh! o weh! Was wollen oder möchten Leute von Ihnen? Machen Sie bitte vier Aussagen.

Beispiele: *Meine Mutter* ***will, daß*** *ich gute Noten bekomme.*
Mein Freund ***möchte, daß*** *ich ihn oft anrufe.*

Und was müssen Sie Gott sei Dank *nicht* tun? Machen Sie drei Aussagen.

Beispiele: *Ich* ***muß nicht*** *auf meine kleine Schwester aufpassen.*
Ich ***brauche nicht*** *beim Kochen* ***(zu)*** *helfen.*

F **Alles nur vom Hörensagen.** Ist es wahr, was andere vom Hörensagen berichten? Machen Sie vier Aussagen. Lesen Sie Ihre Aussagen im Unterricht vor.

Beispiele: *Elvis Presley soll noch am Leben sein.*
Friedrich der Große soll seinen Vater gehaßt haben.

REAKTIONEN

Das stimmt gewiß.
Das mag sein.
Sehr unwahrscheinlich!
Unsinn!

G **Damals.** Drücken Sie die Sätze im Perfekt aus.

Beispiel: Als Kind wollte ich oft meinen Eltern helfen.
Als Kind ***habe*** *ich oft meinen Eltern* ***helfen wollen.***

1. Früher mußte ich meinen Eltern oft helfen.
2. Manchmal durfte ich nicht ausgehen, wenn ich ihnen nicht geholfen hatte.
3. Es stimmte aber nicht, daß ich ihnen nicht helfen wollte.
4. Aber manchmal konnte ich es nicht, weil ich etwas anderes tun mußte.
5. Das konnten meine Eltern nicht immer verstehen.

H **Eine schöne Zukunft?** Erzählen Sie davon.

Beispiel: Heute muß ich noch (nicht) . . ., aber in zwei Jahren . . .
Heute ***muß*** *ich noch* ***studieren,*** *aber in zwei Jahren* ***werde*** *ich nicht mehr* ***studieren müssen.***

1. Heute muß ich (nicht) . . ., aber in vier Jahren . . .
2. Heute kann ich (nicht) . . ., aber ich weiß, daß ich in acht Jahren . . .
3. Heute will ich (nicht) . . ., aber in zwölf Jahren . . .
4. Heute darf ich (nicht) . . ., aber ich hoffe, daß ich in zwanzig Jahren . . .
5. Heute soll ich (nicht) . . ., aber in 30 Jahren . . .

Anwendung

A **Rollenspiel: Machen Sie mit?** Sie wollen etwas tun, aber Sie wollen es nicht allein tun. Versuchen Sie, jemanden dazu zu überreden *(persuade)*, mitzumachen. Diese andere Person will nicht und hat viele Ausreden *(excuses)*.

THEMENVORSCHLÄGE

Heute abend zum Essen oder zu einer Party ausgehen
Am Wochenende einen Ausflug *(excursion)* machen
Mit Ihnen zusammen die Hausaufgabe machen
An einer Protestaktion teilnehmen

REDEMITTEL

für

Du, ich habe eine tolle Idee! Willst du mitmachen?
Wir können / sollen . . .
Wir müssen nicht . . .

gegen

Ach, es tut mir furchtbar leid, aber ich muß / soll . . .
O, das klingt interessant, aber . . .
Leider kann ich nicht, denn . . .
Ach weißt du, ich möchte schon, aber . . .

B **Gebote** *(commands)* **und Verbote.** Als Kind gab es sicher manches, was Sie (nicht) tun *durften, konnten, mußten* oder *sollten,* aber doch (nicht) tun *wollten.* Erzählen Sie in einer Gruppe davon. Fragen Sie auch Ihren Professor / Ihre Professorin, wie es in seiner / ihrer Kindheit war. Machen Sie einige Aussagen im Präteritum **(ich mußte tun)** und einige Aussagen im Perfekt **(ich habe tun müssen).**

THEMENVORSCHLÄGE

beim Essen
in der Schule
im Haushalt
auf Reisen
mit Freunden

REDEMITTEL

Damals mußte ich . . .
Manchmal durfte ich nicht . . .
Es hat mich immer geärgert, daß ich . . . nicht habe [tun] dürfen.
Abends sollte ich . . ., aber . . .
Erst viel später durfte / konnte ich . . .

Variation: Was müssen oder sollen Sie *jetzt* tun, was Sie nicht gern tun? Was will man heute von Ihnen?

* Schriftliche Themen

Tips zum Schreiben ***Providing Explanation***
Modal verbs do not describe; they help provide reasons and motivations. Thus in explanations you can repeat them more frequently than you should other verbs. To link ideas by explaining *why* something happens, consider using adverbial conjunctions such as **daher, darum, deshalb,** and **deswegen** *(therefore, for that reason)* (see 24.5). These conjunctions are really adverbs and can either begin a clause or occur elsewhere in it.

Ich habe keine Zeit, (und) **daher** kann ich nicht kommen. Ich habe keine Zeit, und ich kann **daher** nicht kommen.	*I don't have any time, and thus I can't come.*

A **Bildgeschichte.** Erzählen Sie die folgende Bildgeschichte im Präteritum. Verwenden Sie mehrere Modalverben, und benutzen Sie die Erzählskizze dabei.

der Drachen • in den Baum fliegen • hängenbleiben • das Tor • der Pförtner *(gateman)* • nicht hineingehen • nach Hause • Vater bitten • holen • sich fein anziehen • denken, daß • auf den Baum klettern • der Junge wird in Zukunft . . . *(Modalverb im Futur)*

B **Motivationen.** Erklären Sie die Handlungsweise *(behavior)* eines Charakters in einem Buch, in einem Film oder aus der Geschichte. Warum wollte, konnte oder mußte dieser Mensch so handeln *(act)* oder sich so benehmen *(behave)*? (Siehe **handeln, Wortschatz 20.**)

Beispiel: Werther wollte die ganze Welt umarmen *(embrace)*, aber das konnte er nicht. Deshalb konnte er es auch nicht akzeptieren, daß Lotte ihn zwar liebte, ihn aber nicht heiraten wollte. Gegen Ende des Romans sollte er sie nicht mehr besuchen, aber . . . Zum Schluß nahm er sich dann deswegen das Leben. (Goethe, *Die Leiden des jungen Werthers*)

C **Sich entschuldigen.** Schreiben Sie einen Brief, in dem Sie sich bei jemandem dafür entschuldigen, daß Sie etwas *nicht tun können* oder *nicht getan haben* (z.B. nicht geschrieben; nicht angerufen; nicht zur Geburtstagsfeier gekommen). Nennen Sie die Gründe dafür. (Siehe Appendix 2, *Letter Writing*)

Beispiel: Es tut mir leid, daß ich gestern nicht auf Ihrer Geburtstagsfeier dabeisein konnte. Ich wollte kommen, aber ich war schon eingeladen worden und mußte deshalb . . . usw.

Wortschatz 9

Liking	*Inclination*
gern haben	möchten
mögen	hätte(n) gern
gefallen	würde(n) gern tun
gern tun	Lust haben auf / zu

1. The expressions **gern haben** and **mögen** mean *to like* in the sense of affection or approval. They express the emotions of someone toward the thing liked.

Sie **hat** dich **gern.** Sie **mag** dich.	} *She likes you.*

Ich **habe** es nicht **gern,** daß du hier bist. Ich **mag** es nicht, daß du hier bist.	*I don't like it that you are here.*

2. In English translation, **gefallen** is virtually synonymous with **gern haben** and **mögen.** However, **gefallen** describes the pleasing effect something has on someone, rather than the actual emotion of the person who likes. For this reason, the "liker" is in the dative case and receives the action; whether **gefallen** is singular or plural is determined by the subject, the thing(s) liked.

Dieser Film **gefällt mir.**	*I like this film. (It has a pleasing affect upon me.)*
Diese Filme **gefallen** mir.	*I like these films.*

3. The adverb **gern** used with a verb other than **haben** means *to like to do* the activity expressed by the verb.

Wir **wandern gern.**	*We like to hike.*
Sie **wohnt** nicht **gern** allein.	*She doesn't like to live alone.*

4. The subjunctive forms **möchte(n) (tun), hätte(n) gern,** and **würde(n) gern tun** (see 20.2) are polite ways of expressing inclination or asking what someone *would like (to do).*

Ich **möchte** einen Kaffee. Ich **hätte gern** einen Kaffee.	*I would like a coffee.*
Möchten Sie mitfahren? **Würden** Sie **gern** mitfahren?	*Would you like to come along?*

5. The expression **Lust auf / zu etwas haben** is commonly used to express what someone *feels like having or doing.* It is close in meaning to **möchte(n)** and can be made more polite by using the subjunctive form **hätte(n)** instead of **haben** (see 20.2). The preposition **auf** is used with objects and **zu** with activities.

Hast du **Lust auf** einen Apfelsaft? *(object)*	*Do you feel like (having) an apple juice?*
Hättest du **Lust auf** einen Apfelsaft?	*Would you like to have an apple juice?*
Wir **haben** keine **Lust zum** Tanzen. *(activity)* Wir **haben** keine **Lust zu** tanzen.	*We do not feel like dancing.*

ÜBUNGEN

A **Ja oder nein?** Wie reagieren Sie? Gefällt das Ihnen? Möchten Sie das tun? Verwenden Sie Ausdrücke aus diesem Wortschatz.[6]

Beispiele: tanzen
Ich tanze gern.

heute abend tanzen
Ich möchte heute abend nicht tanzen.
Ich habe / hätte keine Lust, heute abend zu tanzen.

1. die Universität, an der Sie jetzt studieren
2. Deutsch lernen
3. daß Sie für Ihre Kurse soviel lesen müssen
4. Rechtsanwälte *(lawyers)*
5. wenn jemand Ihnen Ratschläge *(pieces of advice)* gibt
6. eine schöne Wohnung für wenig Geld
7. zu einem Blues-Konzert gehen
8. ein Studiensemester im Ausland verbringen
9. der letzte Film, den Sie gesehen haben
10. die politische Stimmung *(mood)* in Ihrem Lande

B **So bin ich.** Erzählen Sie in jeweils *einem* Satz. Vergleichen Sie Ihre Sätze mit denen anderer Studenten.

1. was Sie überhaupt nicht gern haben
2. was Ihnen besonders gut gefällt
3. was Ihnen gar nicht gefällt
4. worauf Sie in diesem Augenblick Lust hätten
5. wozu Sie wirklich keine Lust haben
6. was Sie eines Tages unbedingt *(absolutely)* tun möchten
7. was Sie nicht mögen
8. was Sie am kommenden Wochenende gern tun würden

Zusammenfassung 9

Rules to Remember

1. Modal verbs conjugate irregularly in the present tense singular, but they conjugate like other verbs in the present tense plural.
2. *Must not* is **dürfen nicht; müssen nicht** means *not to have to.*

---

6. In most instances, several expressions are possible, but they may not always have exactly the same meanings. Discuss the various meanings in class with your instructor.

3. **Ich will / möchte gehen** means *I want / would like to go.* **Ich will / möchte, daß *sie* geht** means *I want / would like her to go.*
4. Modal verbs conjugate like weak verbs in the past tense, but without any infinitive stem umlauts **(wollen / wollte; müssen / mußte).**
5. German speakers normally use the simple past tense of modals rather than the present perfect.
6. The perfect tenses of modals require a double infinitive construction if there is also a main verb **(Sie hat gewollt,** but **Sie hat *gehen wollen*).**

Activities

1 **Do's and don'ts.** Discuss with 4–5 other students the do's and don'ts of doing something (being a good driver, learning a foreign language, hunting for wild turkeys, etc.).

2 **Ten commandments.** Make up ten commandments for a dictator, a politician, a good / poor student, a wise / unwise tourist, a person in the news, etc.

Beispiel: POLITIKER: Du sollst ehrlich sein.[7]
Du sollst nicht lügen.
Du sollst an deine Wähler denken.
usw.

3 **Requirements.** Working with 4–5 other students, tell what features you look for in a car, an apartment, a friend, etc. What must these things or persons have or not have?

4 **How to play.** Explain to a partner how to play your favorite game. Use modals.

5 **Semester blues.** Are you having a tough semester because you have to or ought to do so many things? Would you really like to be doing something else, but you can't right now? Tell the class about your semester.

6 **Advice.** Pick a character from a story you have read. Give this character five pieces of advice and use five different modals.

7. The Biblical Ten Commandments are in the **du** form, as God is perceived as speaking personally to each individual.

10 Prepositions

10.1 Accusative Prepositions

A. *Forms*

1. The accusative prepositions **(die Präposition, -en)** are as follows:

bis	*until, to, as far as, by*	ohne	*without*
durch	*through*	um	*around; at*
für	*for*	wider	*against*[1]
gegen	*against; toward*		

2. The following contractions are quite common:

durchs (durch das) **fürs** (für das) **ums** (um das)

B. *Use*

1. An accusative preposition is followed by an object noun or pronoun in the accusative case (see individual prepositions below).
2. A preposition with its object is called a *prepositional phrase.* Many prepositional phrases function as adverbs by telling *how* (with friends), *when* (after school), or *where* (in the park) something occurs. Other prepositional phrases provide *description* of persons and things (the man in the suit).
3. Prepositional phrases follow the time-manner-place word order rule (see 1.1D).

Wir gehen um acht Uhr ohne Freunde in die Stadt.	*We are going downtown without friends at eight o'clock.*

1. **Wider** is infrequent and used mainly in a few idiomatic phrases: **wider Erwarten** *(against all expectation).*

C. Bis

1. **Bis** means *until, as far as, up to,* or *by* a certain point or time.

Ich fahre nur **bis** Frankfurt.	*I am driving only as far as Frankfurt.*
Lesen Sie **bis** morgen **bis** Seite 50.	*Read up to page 50 by tomorrow.*
Ich bleibe **bis** nächsten Montag.	*I am staying until next Monday.*

2. **Bis** is frequently used in combination with other prepositions. In such constructions the case of the following objects is determined by the second preposition, not by **bis.**

Die jungen Leute tanzten **bis** spät **in die** Nacht (hinein).	*The young people danced until late into the night.*
Wir fanden alle Fehler **bis auf** einen.	*We found all the mistakes except for one.*
Die Spieler waren **bis vor** wenigen Tagen im Ausland.	*The players were abroad up until a few days ago.*
Die Arbeiter blieben **bis zur** letzten Stunde.	*The workers stayed until the last hour.*

D. Durch

Durch means *through.*

Diese Straße führt **durch** die Stadt.	*This road leads through the city.*
Einstein wurde **durch** seine Relativitätstheorie berühmt.	*Einstein became famous through his theory of relativity.*

E. Für

1. **Für** means *for.*

Ich kaufe einen Korb **für** meine Mutter.	*I buy a basket for my mother.*
Du kannst mein Fahrrad **für** DM 250 kaufen.	*You can buy my bicycle for 250 DM.*

2. **Für** is used to indicate for how long an activity *is* or *was intended.*

Wir gingen **für einen Tag** nach Wien.	*We went to Vienna for one day.*

3. To indicate for how long an activity *lasts* or *lasted,* German uses a time expression without any preposition.

Wir blieben aber **drei Tage** in Wien.	*However, we stayed in Vienna (for) three days.*

4. To indicate for how long an activity *has been going on,* German uses the preposition *seit* (see 10.2).

Wir sind **seit zwei Tagen** in Wien.	*We have been in Vienna for two days.*

F. Gegen

1. **Gegen** means *against* or *into.*

Sie warf den Ball **gegen** den Zaun.	*She threw the ball against the fence.*
Der LKW fuhr **gegen** einen Baum.	*The truck drove into a tree.*
Wir protestierten **gegen** den Bau des Atomkraftwerks.	*We protested against the construction of the nuclear plant.*

2. **Gegen** means *toward* in time expressions (see 23.2).

Gegen Abend hörte der Regen auf.	*Toward evening the rain stopped.*

Ich BIN GEGEN Alles

G. Ohne

Ohne means *without.*

Mach es **ohne** mich!	*Do it without me!*

H. Um

1. **Um** means *around* and is often used with an optional **herum.**

Sie gingen **um** die Ecke.	*They went around the corner.*
Diese Straßenbahn fährt **um** die Wiener Altstadt **(herum).**	*This streetcar travels around the old part of Vienna.*

2. For the use of **um** in time expressions, see 23.2.

10.2 } Dative Prepositions

A. Forms

1. The dative prepositions are as follows:

aus	*out of, of, from*	mit	*with, by*
außer	*except for; besides*	nach	*to, toward; after; according to*
bei	*by, near, at; with, in case of, during; upon, when, while doing*	seit	*since, for*
		von	*from, of; by; about*
		zu	*to; at*
gegenüber	*across from, opposite*		

2. The following contractions are quite common:

beim (bei dem) **vom** (von dem) **zum** (zu dem)
zur (zu der)

B. *Use*

Dative prepositions are followed by objects in the dative case.

C. Aus

Aus means *out of, (made) of,* or *from* the point of origin.

Herr Bühler fuhr den Ferrari **aus der** Garage.	*Mr. Bühler drove the Ferrari out of the garage.*
Wein wird **aus** Trauben gemacht.	*Wine is made from grapes.*
Diese Familie kommt **aus** der Stadt Essen.	*This family comes from the city of Essen. (that is, it is their hometown)*

D. Außer

1. **Außer** usually means *except for, besides,* or *in addition to.*

Alle sind verrückt **außer** dir und mir.	*Everyone is crazy except for you and me.*
Außer seiner Frau waren noch andere Leute im Zimmer.	*Besides (in addition to) his wife there were other people in the room.*

2. In a few idiomatic expressions **außer** means *out of.*

Ich bin jetzt **außer Atem.**	*I am now out of breath.*
Der Lift ist **außer Betrieb.**	*The elevator is out of order.*

E. Bei

1. **Bei** means *at, by,* or *near.*

Bei Hertie gibt es immer tolle Preise.	*There are always great prices at Hertie's (department store).*
In Böblingen **bei** Stuttgart arbeiten viele Leute **bei** (der Firma) IBM.	*In Böblingen near Stuttgart, many people work at IBM.*

2. **Bei** is used to indicate location at a person's place.

Wir essen heute abend **bei** Sigrid.	*We are eating at Sigrid's place this evening.*
BUT:	
Wir gehen **zu** Sigrid.	*We are going to Sigrid's.* *(see **zu**, p. 123)*

3. **Bei** can express the idea of *in case of, during,* or *with.*

Bei schlechtem Wetter geht man lieber nicht spazieren.	*In the case of / during bad weather it's better not to take a walk.*
Bei deiner Erkältung würde ich lieber zu Hause bleiben.	*With your cold I would rather stay home.*

4. **Bei** can also indicate *upon* or *while doing* an activity; in such instances, the activity itself is expressed by an infinitive used as a noun (see 18.5).

Herr Kohl schlief **beim** Lesen ein.	*Mr. Kohl fell asleep while reading.*
Beim Erwachen hörte sie Stimmen im Korridor.	*Upon awakening, she heard voices in the corridor.*

F. Gegenüber

1. **Gegenüber** means *across from* or *opposite.* It normally follows a pronoun but can either precede or follow a noun.

Sie saß ihm **gegenüber.**	*She sat opposite him.*
Er saß seiner Frau **gegenüber** / **gegenüber** seiner Frau.	*He sat across from his wife.*

2. When **gegenüber** precedes a noun or pronoun, the word **von** is often added.

Gegenüber vom Bahnhof ist ein Einkaufszentrum.	*Across from the train station is a shopping center.*

G. Mit

1. **Mit** means *with.*

Er spricht **mit** Freunden.	*He is talking with friends.*

2. **Mit** also indicates the instrument or means with which an activity is performed (see also 28.1C).

Sie wurde **mit** einem Messer getötet.	*She was killed with a knife.*

3. When describing means of transportation, **mit** means *by* and is normally used with a definite article.

In Deutschland reist man manchmal schneller **mit** der Bahn als **mit** dem Auto.	*In Germany one sometimes travels faster by rail than by car.*

H. Nach

1. **Nach** means *(going) to* and is used with proper names of geographical locations such as towns, cities, countries, and continents. It is also used with directions and points of the compass.

Dieser Flug geht **nach** Brasilien.	*This flight is going to Brazil.*
Die Straße führt zuerst **nach** rechts und dann **nach** Süden.	*The street goes to the right first and then to the south.*

2. **Nach** can also indicate motion *toward* a place or object, as opposed to motion *to* **(zu)** such locations.

COMPARE:

Die Kinder liefen **nach** dem Brunnen.	*The children ran* **toward** *the fountain. (in that general direction)*
Die Kinder liefen **zu** dem Brunnen.	*The children ran* **to** *the fountain. (to that goal and arrived there)*

3. **Nach** can mean *after* in either a temporal or a spatial sense.

Sie gingen **nach** dem Film in ein Restaurant.	*They went to a restaurant after the movie.*
Nach dem Feld kommt wieder Wald.	*After the field there are woods again.*

4. **Nach** sometimes means *according to* or *judging by,* in which case it usually follows its object.

Dem Wetterbericht **nach** soll es morgen in den Alpen schneien.	*According to the weather report it is supposed to snow in the Alps tomorrow.*
Ihrer Kleidung **nach** scheint sie Ausländerin zu sein.	*Judging by her clothing, she appears to be a foreigner.*

5. **Nach** occurs in a number of useful idiomatic expressions.

nach Bedarf *as needed*
nach Belieben *at one's discretion*
nach dem Gehör *by ear* (without notes)
nach Hause *(to go) home*
nach Wunsch *as you wish, as desired*
(nur) dem Namen nach kennen *to know by name (only)*
nach und nach *little by little, gradually*
nach wie vor *now as ever, the same as before*

I. Seit

1. **Seit** indicates *for how long* or *since when* an action that started in the past *has* or *had been going on.* German uses **seit** with the present tense, where English requires the present perfect (see 2.2), and **seit** with the simple past tense where English uses the past perfect. **Seit** often occurs with the adverb **schon.**

Es regnet **seit** gestern.	*It has been raining since yesterday.*
Wir wohnten **(schon) seit** einem Jahr in Braunschweig, als die Großmutter starb.	*We had (already) been living in Braunschweig for a year when Grandmother died.*

2. The preposition **seit** should not be confused with the conjunction **seit(dem)** (see 11.3). **Seit** is a preposition and precedes a noun. **Seit (dem)** precedes a dependent clause.

Seit / Seitdem er geheiratet hat, sehen wir ihn kaum.	*(Ever) since he got married, we scarcely see him.*

J. Von

1. **Von** means *from* a source, but not *out of* a point of origin (see **aus,** p. 119).

Deutsche Studenten bekommen ein Stipendium **vom** Staat.	*German students receive a scholarship from the state.*
Frau Salamun kommt **von** Wien nach Graz.	*Ms. Salamun comes from Vienna to Graz.*
BUT:	
Sie kommt **aus** Wien.	*Vienna is her hometown.*

2. **Von** means *of* when it expresses a relationship of belonging between two nouns. It is often a substitute for the genitive case (see 4.6).

Sie ist die Tante **von** meiner Freundin und eine Einwohnerin **von** Hameln.	*She is the aunt of my girlfriend and an inhabitant of Hameln.*

3. **Von** can also mean *by* (authorship) or *about* (topic of discussion).

Faust ist ein Drama **von** Goethe.	***Faust** is a drama by Goethe.*
Er spricht nicht gern **von** seinen Fehlern.	*He doesn't like to talk about his mistakes.*

4. **Von** in combination with **aus** indicates a vantage point or motion away from a particular location.

Vom Fenster **aus** sieht man den Parkplatz nicht.	*From the window one doesn't see the parking lot.*
Von Freiburg **aus** ist man in einer halben Stunde am Titisee.	*From Freiburg one is at the Titisee in half an hour.*

5. **Von** in combination with **an** indicates a point from which an activity starts and continues.

Von jetzt **an** keine Fehler mehr!	*From now on no more mistakes!*

K. Zu

1. **Zu** means *to* and is used to express motion toward persons, stores, objects, locales, and events.

Ein kranker Mensch sollte **zum** Arzt gehen.	*An ill person ought to go to the doctor.*
Wir gehen **zur** Sporthalle.	*We are going to the gym.*
Wir laufen **zum** Schillerplatz.	*We walk to Schiller Square.*

2. The contracted form **zum** commonly occurs with infinitives used as nouns.

Wir haben nichts **zum** Essen.	*We have nothing to eat.*
Ich brauche etwas **zum** Schreiben.	*I need something for writing.* (that is, *to write with*)

3. **Zu** occurs in a number of useful idiomatic expressions.

zu dritt / zu viert usw. *in threes, in fours, etc.*
zu Ende *over, at an end*
zu Fuß *on foot*
zu Hause *at home* (*compare with* nach Hause)
zu Ihnen / dir *(to go) to your place*
zu Eva *(to go) to Eva's place*
zu Mittag *at noon* (*but* am Abend)
zu Weihnachten, zu Ostern *for / at Easter, for / at Christmas*
zum Beispiel *for example*
zum Essen / Schreiben usw. *for eating / writing, etc.*
zum Frühstück / zum Mittagessen *for / at breakfast / the noonday meal*
zum Geburtstag *for one's birthday*
zum Kaffee (nehmen) *(to take) with one's coffee*
zum Schluß *in conclusion*
zum Wohl! *(Here's) to your health!*

4. **Zu** is sometimes used in the names of eating establishments.

(Gasthaus) zum Roten Bären *the Red Bear Inn*

5. **Zu** *cannot be used* with **geben** and other verbs of giving. Such verbs require an indirect object (see 4.5).

Sie gibt es **ihrem** Freund. *She gives it to her friend.*

10.3 Two-Way Prepositions

A. Forms

1. The following prepositions are called two-way prepositions *(Wechselpräpositionen)*.

an	*at, on, to*	über	*over, across; above; about*
auf	*on, upon, at*	unter	*under, beneath, below; among*
hinter	*behind*	vor	*before, in front of; ago*
in	*in, into, inside*	zwischen	*between*
neben	*beside, next to*		
entlang	*along*		

2. The following contractions are very common and often preferred to the separated forms:

ans (an das)	**am** (an dem)
aufs (auf das)	
ins (in das)	**im** (in dem)

Say, don't write

3. The following contractions are considered quite colloquial:

hinters (hinter das)	**hinterm** (hinter dem)
übers (über das)	**überm** (über dem)
vors (vor das)	**vorm** (vor dem)

B. Use

1. Two-way prepositions take the *dative case* when they indicate *location.*

Wo steht sie?	*Where is she standing?*
—**Im** Garten.	***In** the garden.*

2. Two-way prepositions take the *accusative case* when they indicate direction or motion toward an object or place.

Wohin geht er?	*Where is he going?*
—**In den** Garten.	***Into** the garden.*

3. Motion itself does not necessarily mean that the object must be in the accusative. The motion can be taking place within the area of the object, in which case the object is in the dative, since there is no change of position with respect to this location.

Wo laufen die Kinder?	*Where are the children running (around)?*
—**Im** Garten.	***In** the garden.*

C. An

1. **An** means *at* with the dative and *to* with the accusative.

Sie standen **an der** Tafel. *(location)*	*They stood at the board.*
Sie ging **an die** Tafel. *(direction)*	*She went to the board.*

D. Auf

1. **Auf** means *on (top of)* with the dative and *onto* with the accusative.

Sie sitzen **auf dem** Sofa. *(location)*	*They are sitting on the sofa.*
Sie setzten sich **auf das** Sofa. *(direction)*	*They sat down on the sofa.*

2. **Auf** is often used idiomatically to express being *at/in* or going *to* the countryside, public institutions, parties, weddings, and other festivities.

Sie arbeitet **auf dem** Land.	*She works in the country(side).*
Wir waren gestern **auf einer** Hochzeit.	*We were at a wedding yesterday.*
Ich gehe heute **auf die** Post.	*I am going to the post office today.*

3. With verbs of going, **zu** is frequently used instead of **an** and **auf.**

Wir gehen **ans** / **zum** Fenster.	*We go to the window.*
Sie fährt **auf die** / **zur** Bank.	*She drives to the bank.*

4. In actual usage, the distinction between **an** and **auf** is frequently blurred.

Sie sind **am** Bahnhof (*or* **auf dem** Bahnhof).	*They are at the train station.*
Er lag **am** Boden (*or* **auf dem** Boden).	*He was lying on the ground.*

E. Hinter

Hinter means *behind.*

Sie spielt **hinter dem** Haus. *(location)*	*She plays behind the house.*
Sie läuft **hinter das** Haus. *(direction)*	*She runs behind the house.*

F. In

1. **In** means *in* with the dative and *into* with the accusative. It is also used in certain contexts where English uses *at* or *to.*

Sie sind **in der** Schule. *(location)*	*They are at / in school.*
Die Familie reist morgen **in die** Berge. *(direction)*	*The family is traveling to / into the mountains tomorrow.*

2. In many instances **in** (accusative) and **zu** (dative) can be used interchangeably.

Er geht **in ein / zu einem** Konzert.	*He goes to a concert.*

3. In other instances, the meanings may differ slightly.

Sie geht **ins** Gebäude.	*She goes into the building.*
Sie geht **zum** Gebäude.	*She goes to (but not necessarily into) the building.*

4. **In** (accusative) is used instead of **nach** to indicate direction to countries used with articles.

Sie fliegt **in die** Türkei.	*She flies to Turkey.*
Viele Ausländer kommen jetzt **in die** USA.	*Many foreigners are now coming to the USA.*

G. Neben

Neben means *beside* or *next to.*

Der Spieler stand **neben dem** Tor. *(location)*	*The player stood next to the goal.*
Der Ball fiel **neben das** Tor. *(direction)*	*The ball fell beside the goal.*

H. Über

1. **Über** means *over, above, across,* or *about.*

Über der Stadt steht ein Schloβ. *(location)*	*A castle stands above the city.*
Eine Brücke führt **über den** Wassergraben. *(direction)*	*A bridge leads across the moat.*

2. When **über** means *about,* it requires the accusative case.

Sie sprachen **über seinen** Sieg.	*They were talking about his victory.*

I. Unter

Unter means *under, beneath, below,* or *among.*

Der Hund schläft **unter dem** Tisch. *(location)*	*The dog sleeps beneath the table.*

Der Hund kriecht **unter den** Tisch. *(direction)*	*The dog crawls under the table.*
Sie sind hier **unter** Freunden.	*You are among friends here.*

J. Vor

1. **Vor** means *in front of* or *ahead of.*

Wir treffen uns **vor dem** Museum. *(location)*	*We are meeting in front of the museum.*
Sie fährt **vor das** Museum. *(direction)*	*She drives in front of the museum.*

2. In a temporal sense, **vor** means *before* and takes the dative.

Du mußt **vor** acht Uhr aufstehen.	*You have to get up before eight o'clock.*
Sie aßen **vor** uns.	*They ate before us.*

3. With units of time (years, weeks, days, etc.) **vor** means *ago* and takes the dative (see 23.1E).

Sie rief **vor** einer Stunde an.	*She telephoned an hour ago.*

K. Zwischen

Zwischen means *between.*

Er sitzt **zwischen ihnen.** *(location)*	*He sits between them.*
Er setzt sich **zwischen sie.** *(direction)*	*He sits down between them.*

L. Entlang

Entlang means *along.* It normally precedes a noun in the dative case when indicating *position* along an object, but it follows a noun in the accusative case when indicating *direction* along an object.

Prächtige Bäume standen **entlang dem** Fluß. *(location)*	*Magnificent trees stood along the river.*
Die Straße führte **einen** Fluß **entlang.** *(direction)*	*The road led along a river.*

10.4 Genitive Prepositions

Frequent

(an)statt	*instead of*	während	*during*
trotz	*in spite of*	wegen	*because of, on account of*

Less Frequent

außerhalb	*outside of*	unterhalb	*beneath*
innerhalb	*inside of*	diesseits	*on this side of*
oberhalb	*above*	jenseits	*on the other side of*

There are also some fifty more genitive prepositions generally restricted to official or legal language: **angesichts** *(in light of)*, **mangels** *(in the absence of)*, etc.

A. (An)statt, trotz, während, wegen

1. **(An)statt, trotz, während,** and **wegen** are normally followed by objects in the genitive case, though in colloquial German the dative is also quite common.

Ich nehme das rote Hemd **(an)statt des** blauen / **dem** blauen.	*I'll take the red shirt instead of the blue one.*
Wir tun es **trotz des** Widerstands / **dem** Widerstand.	*We are doing it in spite of the resistance.*

2. When genitive prepositions are followed by masculine or neuter nouns without articles, the genitive **-s** is dropped.

Wir brauchen mehr Zeit **anstatt Geld.**	*We need more time instead of money.*

3. Genitive prepositions are used infrequently with pronouns. The one exception is **wegen,** which either takes dative pronouns or combines with special pronoun forms: **wegen mir / meinetwegen; wegen dir / deinetwegen; wegen uns / unseretwegen,** etc.

Ich tue es **seinetwegen.**	*I am doing it on his account / on account of him.*

4. The form **meinetwegen** is used idiomatically to mean *for all I care* or *it's okay by me.* It normally occurs either all by itself in response to a question.

Soll ich bleiben?	*Should I stay?*
—**Meinetwegen.**	*It's okay by me.*
Meinetwegen kannst du bleiben, wenn du willst.	*For all I care, you can stay if you want to.*

B. Außerhalb, innerhalb, oberhalb, unterhalb; diesseits, jenseits

1. **Diesseits, jenseits,** and the prepositions with **-halb** can be followed by either the genitive or **von** + the dative.

Jenseits der / von der Grenze wohnen auch Menschen.	*There are also human beings living on the other side of the border.*
Wir können die Brücke **innerhalb weniger / innerhalb von wenigen** Stunden erreichen.	*We can reach the bridge within a few hours.*

2. In the plural, however, **von** + the dative must be used if there is no article to indicate case.

Die Polizei war **innerhalb von** Minuten am Tatort.	*The police were at the scene of the crime within minutes.*

✱ Übungen

A **Anders ausdrücken.** Drücken Sie die Sätze anders aus. Verwenden Sie die folgenden Akkusativpräpositionen.

Beispiel: Er warf den Ball, und ein Fenster ging kaputt.
*Er warf den Ball **durch /gegen** das Fenster.*

bis	für	ohne
durch	gegen	um

1. Er ging in die Bank, aber er hatte keinen Ausweis dabei.
2. Karin deckte den Tisch, denn ihre Mutter hatte keine Zeit dazu.
3. Wir begannen um 9 Uhr zu arbeiten und waren um 11 Uhr fertig.
4. Der Politiker mochte das Projekt nicht, und er sagte es.
5. Auf allen Seiten des Parks steht eine Mauer.
6. Hemingway schrieb seine Romane *(novels)* und wurde berühmt.

B **Aussagen.** Machen Sie wahre Aussagen mit fünf der Präpositionen in Übung A.

Beispiel: *Ich habe **für** meine Kurse viel zu tun.*

C **Welche Präposition paßt?** Ergänzen Sie durch passende Dativpräpositionen und Endungen.

Beispiel: *Sie arbeitet **bei** Siemens.*

aus	gegenüber	seit
außer	mit	von
bei	nach	zu

1. Bist du ____ dein-____ Wohnung zufrieden?
2. Dieses Paket kommt ____ Deutschland.
3. Das Postamt befindet sich ____ d-____ Hauptbahnhof.
4. Wir essen heute abend ____ unser-____ Freund Karl.
5. ____ Wochen bekommen wir keine Briefe mehr.
6. Sie bauen ihr Haus ____ Holz.
7. Wir warten ____ ein-____ Monat auf eine Antwort.
8. Die Kinder kommen heute sehr früh ____ d-____ Schule ____ Hause.
9. Vater ist jetzt ____ d-____ Arbeit und nicht ____ Hause.
10. Sagt es niemandem ____ eur-____ Eltern!

D **Fragen zu Ihrer Person.** Beantworten Sie die Fragen mit den folgenden Präpositionen. Verwenden Sie jede Präposition mindestens einmal. Stellen Sie diese Fragen an andere Personen im Kurs. Berichten Sie die Antworten.

aus	nach	von
bei	seit	zu
mit		

1. Woher kommen Ihre Vorfahren (z.B. Ihre Großeltern) väterlicher- und mütterlicherseits?
2. Wie lange verdienen Sie schon Ihr eigenes Taschengeld?
3. Wohin würden Sie im Winter besonders gern in Urlaub fahren?
4. Wo arbeiten Ihre Eltern?
5. Wie fahren Sie am liebsten in den Urlaub? (Auto? Bahn? Bus? Flugzeug?)
6. Woher bekommen Sie das Geld für Ihr Studium oder für die Schule?
7. Wohin gehen Sie gern, wenn Sie abends ausgehen?
8. Wie kommen Sie jeden Tag zur Schule oder zur Uni?
9. Bei welchen Aktivitäten müssen Sie viel, wenig oder überhaupt nicht denken?

E ***Aus, von, nach,* oder *zu?*** Wie können die Sätze weitergehen?

1. Violinen baut man . . .
2. *Wilhelm Tell* ist ein historisches Drama . . .
3. Will man Tiger und Elefanten sehen, dann muß man . . .
4. Die Astronauten Aldrin und Armstrong reisten . . .
5. Die besten / teuersten Autos der Welt kommen . . .
6. Willst du eine wunderschöne Stadt sehen, dann geh . . .
7. Lungenkrebs kommt oft . . .
8. Zum Skilaufen reisen viele meiner Freunde . . .

F **Wechselpräpositionen.** Bilden Sie kurze Beispielsätze mit den folgenden präpositionalen Ausdrücken.

Beispiele: ins Stadtzentrum
Wir fahren ins Stadtzentrum.

neben dem Haus
Die Kinder spielen neben dem Haus.

1. hinter dem Supermarkt
2. in die Stadt
3. über dem Tisch
4. aufs Land
5. vor einem Computer
6. unter den Zeitungen
7. neben die Teller
8. den Rhein entlang
9. ans Meer
10. zwischen die Schiffe

G **Dativ oder Akkusativ?** Ergänzen Sie die Sätze mit passenden präpositionalen Ausdrücken. Ziehen Sie die Wechselpräpositionen und Artikel zusammen, wenn es geht.

1. Der Hund legt sich unter . . .
2. Ein Stein fiel in . . .
3. Abholen werden wir die Gäste an . . .
4. Stellen Sie die Bücher neben . . .
5. Unser Professor spricht morgen über . . .
6. Herumlaufen können wir zwischen . . .
7. Mechthild holt Briefmarken auf . . .
8. Oma spaziert jeden Tag eine halbe Stunde in . . .

H **Was macht Onkel Helmut?** Gehen Sie rechts um den Kreis herum. Bilden Sie einen Satz mit einer der Wechselpräpositionen. Wenn Sie zur nächsten Präposition kommen, bilden Sie einen weiteren Satz. Wenn Sie aber den ersten Satz mit einer Präposition *im Dativ* gebildet haben, dann sollen Sie mit der zweiten Präposition *den Akkusativ* verwenden, und umgekehrt *(vice versa)*. Und so geht es zwischen Dativ und Akkusativ weiter, bis Sie einmal um den ganzen Kreis gegangen sind. Bei dieser Übung sollen Sie auch kein Verb wiederholen!

Beispiele: *Onkel Helmut steht* ***am*** *Fenster.*
Er schaut ***auf den*** *Garten hinunter.*

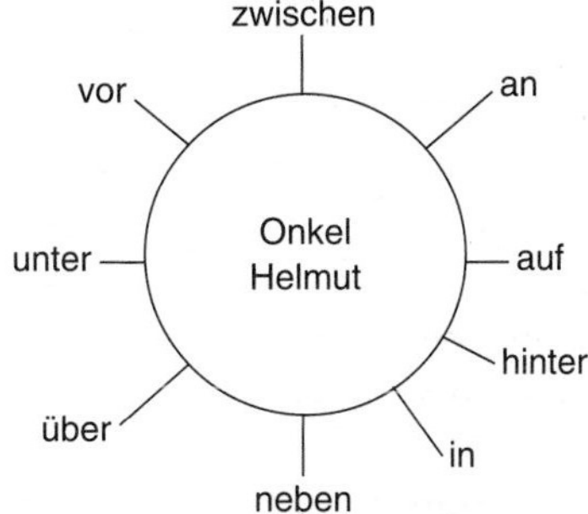

Gehen Sie noch einmal um den Kreis herum! Wo Sie vorhin den Dativ hatten, verwenden Sie jetzt den Akkusativ, und umgekehrt.

I **Bis wann oder wohin.** Ergänzen Sie die Sätze. Verwenden Sie die angegebenen Wörter. Übersetzen Sie die Sätze ins Englische.

Beispiel: Sie fuhr bis (der Bahnhof).
Sie fuhr ***bis zum Bahnhof.*** *(She drove as far as the train station.)*

1. Die Gäste waren bis (eine Stunde) hier.
2. Mein Freund Hans kann bis (zwei Minuten) den Atem anhalten.
3. Du mußt die Arbeit bis (der letzte Tag des Semesters) abgeben.
4. Ich fahre nur bis (die nächste Station).
5. Bis (ein alter Mann) starben alle an der Pest.

J **Anders ausdrücken.** Drücken Sie die Sätze mit den folgenden Genitivpräpositionen anders aus.

Beispiel: Die Arbeit war gefährlich, aber er machte sie.
Trotz der Gefahr *machte er die Arbeit.*

(an)statt	innerhalb	während
außerhalb	trotz	wegen / [-et]wegen

1. Barbara blieb, weil ihre Familie es wollte.
2. Ihr Mann blieb, damit sie nicht allein war.
3. Die Arbeit war in weniger als zehn Tagen fertig.
4. Wir können im Sommer reisen.
5. Das Wetter ist schlecht, aber wir gehen wandern.
6. Ich habe nichts dagegen, wenn du mitkommst.
7. Das liegt nicht in meiner Kompetenz.
8. Sie sollte Französisch lernen, aber sie lernte Deutsch.

K **Einiges über Sie.** Machen Sie Aussagen über sich mit vier der Präpositionen in Übung J.

Beispiele: *Ich werde **während** des Sommers arbeiten.*
Innerhalb *der nächsten Woche muß ich vier Aufsätze schreiben.*

L ***An, auf, in, nach* oder *zu?*** Wenn die Semesterferien endlich da sind, möchte jeder an einen schönen Urlaubsort fahren. Wohin möchten die Leute fahren?

Beispiele: Monika → Afrika
*Monika möchte **nach** Afrika.*

Ulrich → der Strand
*Ulrich möchte **an** den Strand.*

1. Jörg → Haus
2. Elisabeth → ihre Großeltern
3. Heidi → die Schweiz
4. Uwe → eine Südseeinsel
5. René → Skandinavien
6. Ed und Angelika → der Bodensee
7. Klaus → ein Ferienort in den Alpen
8. Bärbl → die Ostsee
9. 3 Studenten im Kurs → ?

M **Wohin?** Wohin gehen Sie, wenn Sie während des Semesters Folgendes tun wollen?

Beispiele: billig essen
Ich gehe zu Wendys.

schwimmen
Ich gehe zum Hallenbad auf der Universität.

1. fein essen
2. wandern
3. Sport treiben
4. tanzen
5. mit Freunden ausgehen
6. Hausaufgaben machen
7. Zeit vertreiben *(pass)*
8. Briefmarken kaufen
9. Geld holen
10. allein sein

N **Otto fuhr und fuhr und fuhr.** Mit wie vielen verschiedenen Präpositionen können Sie diesen Satz zu Ende schreiben? Mindestens zwölf bitte! Vergessen Sie auch den Genitiv nicht!

Beispiele: *Otto fuhr* ***in*** *den Park.*
Otto fuhr ***nach*** *Hamburg.*
Otto fuhr ***mit*** *seinen Freunden.*
usw.

* Anwendung

A **Wie kommt man dorthin?** Jemand im Kurs möchte Sie in den Ferien besuchen. Erklären Sie ihm / ihr, wie man zu Ihnen hinkommt.

REDEMITTEL

Wie komme ich (am besten) zu dir hin?
Wie fährt / kommt man von hier zum / zur / nach / in . . .?
Nimm die [dritte] Straße nach rechts / links.
Fahre . . .
- etwa eine halbe Stunde
- geradeaus
- nach links / nach rechts
- rechts / links in die [–]straße
- jene Straße entlang
- noch zwei Straßen weiter
- bis zur ersten Verkehrsampel *(traffic light)*
- bis zur Kreuzung
- an einem / einer . . . vorbei

Dort siehst du dann auf der linken / rechten Seite . . .

B **Rollenspiel: Auskunft geben.** Sie arbeiten bei der Touristeninformation im Zentrum *Ihres* Heimatorts. Jemand im Kurs ist Tourist(in) und stellt Ihnen viele Fragen. Verwenden Sie Präpositionen in Ihren Antworten.

FRAGENKATALOG

Wo kann ich hier [Blumen / Medikamente usw.] bekommen?
Wo finde ich hier [eine Kirche / eine Synagoge / eine Moschee]?
Können Sie hier in der Nähe [ein Restaurant / ein Kaufhaus usw.] empfehlen? Wie komme ich dorthin?
Wann schließen hier die Geschäfte?
Wo gibt es hier in der Nähe [eine Bank / eine Tankstelle usw.]?
Wir suchen [den Zoo / das Polizeiamt usw.].
Kann man hier irgendwo [baden / einkaufen usw.]?
Wie komme ich am besten von hier [zur Busstation / zum Flughafen / zur Autobahn usw.]. Ich bin ohne Auto unterwegs.
Wie lange arbeiten Sie heute schon hier?

C **Ausarbeitung eines Planes.** Sie haben morgen frei und wollen mit drei oder vier anderen Personen im Kurs etwas unternehmen (z.B. einen Ausflug machen, ein Projekt ausführen, Sport treiben). Diskutieren Sie, wohin Sie gehen wollen, was Sie dort machen können, und wann Sie es machen wollen. Teilen Sie anderen Gruppen im Kurs Ihren Plan mit. Verwenden Sie viele Präpositionen!

REDEMITTEL

Ich schlage vor, daß wir . . .
Wollen wir nicht . . . ?
Wir können auch . . .
Habt ihr nicht Lust, . . . ?
Was haltet ihr davon, wenn . . . ?

Variante: **Eine traumhafte Reise.** Machen Sie einen Plan für eine tolle fünftägige Reise. Wohin wollen Sie fahren? Wie wollen Sie dorthin kommen? Was können Sie dort unternehmen?

✱ Schriftliche Themen

Tips zum Schreiben ***Adding Information Through Prepositions***

Prepositions are important linking words within sentences, and prepositional phrases can add both color and detail to your writing. For example, **Die Frau lachte . . .** is not as descriptive and interesting as **Die Frau *in Rot* lachte *mit Vergnügen*** *(delight)*. When used at the beginning of a sentence, a prepositional phrase can provide a setting (a time and / or place) for the main action: **An einem kalten Schneetag in Berlin ging Herr Moritz mit seinem blauen Hut spazieren.** Just remember that in German, initial prepositional phrases are not followed by a comma, as they may be in English (see 1.1A).

A **Beim Friseur.** Erzählen Sie die Bildgeschichte mit vielen Präpositionen. Wenn Sie wollen, dürfen Sie auch erzählen, was zwischen den Bildern oder nach dem letzten Bild passiert. Verwenden Sie entweder das Präsens oder das Präteritum (siehe 7.1).

VOKABELVORSCHLÄGE

sitzen	riechen	Angst haben
der Friseur	gehen (wohin?)	rennen (wohin?)
die Flasche	die Biene, -n	nachfliegen
das Haarwasser	fliegen / kreisen	stecken
gießen	denken	das Waschbecken
sehr froh		

B **Besichtigung** *(sightseeing).* Erzählen Sie, wie man etwas Sehenswertes, was *Sie* schon kennen, wie z.B. eine Stadt, einen Stadtteil, ein Gebäude, einen Park usw., am besten besichtigt. Wo geht man hinein? An welchen sehenswürdigen Gebäuden kommt man vorbei? Durch welche Gebäude, Höfe *([court]yards)* oder dergleichen geht man? Was sieht man dort? Verwenden Sie verschiedene Präpositionen.

Beispiel: Wer nach München kommt, fährt am besten mit der Bahn zum Marienplatz und beginnt dort seine Stadtbesichtigung. An einer Seite des Platzes steht das Rathaus mit seinem berühmten Glockenspiel. Von hier aus geht man links am Rathaus vorbei und kommt nach etwa 100 Metern zur Frauenkirche, der bekanntesten Kirche der bayerischen Hauptstadt. Hinter der Frauenkirche kommt man in die Löwengasse . . . usw.

C **Verlaufen.** Haben Sie sich je verlaufen *(taken the wrong way),* so daß Sie Ihr Ziel nur mit großer Schwierigkeit oder gar nicht erreichten? Erzählen Sie davon. Beschreiben Sie auch Ihre Gefühle dabei. Verwenden Sie präpositionale Ausdrücke und auch Adjektive (siehe Kapitel 13), um alles noch genauer zu schildern *(depict).*

Wortschatz 10

bekommen kriegen
erhalten holen

1. **Bekommen** means *to get* or *receive.* It does not mean *to become.*

Sie **bekommt** ein neues Kleid zum Geburtstag.	*She gets a new dress for her birthday.*
Er hat einen Orden **bekommen.**	*He received a medal.*

2. **Erhalten** is close in meaning to **bekommen** but somewhat more formal.

Wir haben Ihren Brief **erhalten.**	*We have received your letter.*
Er **erhielt** drei Jahre Gefängnis.	*He received three years in prison.*

3. **Kriegen** is synonymous with **bekommen,** but very colloquial. It is avoided in formal writing.

Was hast du zum Geburtstag von deiner Tante **gekriegt?**	*What did you get from your aunt for your birthday?*

4. **Holen** means *to (go and) get* or *fetch* and is often used with the dative indicating *for whom.*

Hol (mir) bitte einen Stuhl.	*Please (go and) get (me) a chair.*
Er **holte** (sich) ein Hemd aus der Kommode.	*He (went and) got (himself) a shirt from the dresser.*

ÜBUNG

Welches Verb paßt? Ergänzen Sie den Text durch das richtige Verb.

bekommen erhalten holen kriegen

1. Euren netten Brief haben wir gestern ____ .
2. Wo kann ich Karten für den Vortrag *(lecture)* ____ ?
3. ____ dir etwas zum Essen und setz dich hin.
4. Linda ____ jetzt immer bessere Noten in Deutsch.
5. Ich ____ eine Wut *(rage),* wenn ich so was seh'.

Zusammenfassung 10

Rules to Remember

1. Prepositions govern cases.
2. The prepositions **bis, für, durch, gegen, ohne,** and **um** take an accusative object.
3. The prepositions **aus, außer, bei, mit, nach, seit, von, zu,** and **gegenüber** take a dative object.
4. The two-way prepositions **an, auf, hinter, in, neben, über, unter, vor, zwischen,** and **entlang** take the accusative when they indicate *change of position or state* and the dative when they indicate *location.*
5. The prepositions **(an)statt, trotz, während, wegen,** and a number of other less common prepositions take a genitive object.

NOTE: Prepositions are discussed in this chapter in their very literal meanings. Many prepositions, particularly the two-way prepositions, have idiomatic meanings dependent upon the verbs they complement. These meanings are discussed in Chapter 30.

Activities

1 **Analyzing.** Underline all of the prepositions in a text of one or two pages. Determine the meanings of these prepositions and the cases of their objects.

2 **The road home.** Describe step-by-step, road-by-road how you come to class or go home every evening. Mention means and route.

3 **From verbs to sentences.** Brainstorm with the class fifteen verbs to be written on the board. Using these verbs, write sentences that include prepositional phrases. Read your sentences aloud in class or give them to your instructor for correction. You should receive a point for each different preposition used correctly in a sentence. The person with the most points wins.

4 **Slice of life.** Divide into groups of four. Each person in turn shuts his / her eyes and pretends to be walking or driving alone to a favorite place. Each describes out loud changes of location, where she / he is going, what she / he is going by, etc.

5 **Working with a text.** Using fifteen different prepositions, make fifteen factual or interpretive statements about a text read recently for class. Try to do this from memory without consulting the text.

11 Conjunctions

11.1 Coordinating Conjunctions

A. Forms

The coordinating conjunctions are as follows:

aber[1]	*but, however*	sondern	*but rather*
denn[1]	*for, because*	und	*and*
oder	*or*		

B. Use

1. Coordinating conjunctions **(die koordinierende Konjunktion, -en)** link words, phrases, or independent clauses by adding information **(und)** or by showing a contrast **(aber, sondern),** a cause **(denn),** or an alternative **(oder).** For purposes of word order, a coordinating conjunction is not considered part of the clause that follows; therefore, any verb in the second clause is still in second position.

   Sie fuhren an den Strand, **und** wir gingen ins Gebirge.
   They drove to the shore, and we went to the mountains.

   Er blieb zu Hause, **denn** er wollte lesen.
   He stayed home, for he wanted to read.

---

1. **Aber** and **denn** can occur as flavoring particles (see 25.1). In addition, **aber** can be used as an adverb meaning *however.*

Viele beschwerten sich über das Wetter, er sagte **aber** nichts.	*Many were complaining about the weather; he said nothing, however.*

2. Generally, a comma separates all material linked by coordinating conjunctions. In the case of **und** and **oder,** if the two linked clauses share a common subject, no comma is used.

Sie fuhren aufs Land **und** machten eine lange Wanderung.	*They drove into the country and took a long hike.*
Willst du hier bleiben **oder** mit uns ins Kino gehen?	*Do you want to stay here or go to the movies with us?*

3. **Aber** *(but)* links clauses by providing *additional* information. The first clause can be either positive or negative.

Dieses Haus ist teuer, **aber** gut gelegen.	*This house is expensive but well-situated.*
Hans läuft nicht schnell, **aber** er denkt schnell.	*Hans does not run fast, but he thinks fast.*

4. **Sondern** *(but rather)* links clauses by providing information *contradictory* to information in the first clause. The first clause must contain a negating word such as **nicht, nie,** or **kein-** (see 6.1).

Dieses Haus ist nicht teuer, **sondern** billig.	*This house is not expensive, but (rather) inexpensive.*
Hanna arbeitet heute nicht, **sondern** sie bleibt zu Hause.	*Hanna is not working today, but (rather) she is staying home.*

11.2 Two-Part (Correlative) Conjunctions

1. The following two-part (correlative) conjunctions link words, phrases, or clauses in parallel fashion.

sowohl . . . als / wie (auch)	*both . . . and, as well as*
nicht nur . . . sondern auch	*not only . . . but also*
entweder . . . oder	*either . . . or*
weder . . . noch	*neither . . . nor*

Wir lernen **sowohl** Deutsch **als (auch)** Spanisch.	*We are learning German as well as Spanish.*
Nicht nur in Luxemburg spricht man Deutsch und Französisch, **sondern auch** in der Schweiz.	*Not only in Luxemburg do people speak German and French, but also in Switzerland.*
Sie spricht **weder** Spanisch **noch** Portugiesisch.	*She speaks neither Spanish nor Portuguese.*

2. When **entweder . . . oder** is used in two clauses, the position of **entweder** may vary.

Entweder *gehen wir* nach Dresden, **oder** wir bleiben hier.
Entweder *wir gehen* nach Dresden, **oder** wir bleiben hier.
Wir gehen **entweder** nach Dresden, **oder** wir bleiben hier.

Either we are going to Dresden, or we are staying here.

11.3 Subordinating Conjunctions

A. Forms

The following subordinating conjunctions are used frequently:

als	*when, as*	nachdem	*after*
als ob	*as if, as though*	ob	*whether, if*
bevor	*before*	obgleich	*although, even though*
ehe	*before*	obschon	*although, even though*
bis	*until, by*	obwohl	*although, even though*
da	*since, because*	seit(dem)	*since (temporal)*
damit	*so that (intent)*	sobald	*as soon as*
daß	*that*	solange	*as long as*
anstatt daß	*instead (of doing)* (*See also* anstatt zu; *18.2.*)	sooft	*as often as*
		während	*while*
		weil	*because*
ohne daß	*without (doing)* (*See also* ohne zu; *18.2.*)	wenn	*when, if, whenever*
		wenn . . . auch	*even if, even though*
so daß	*so that (result only)*	wenn . . . nicht	*unless*
falls	*in case, if*	wenn . . . kein-	*unless*
indem	*by (doing)*		

B. Use

1. A subordinating **(subordinierend)** conjunction connects a dependent or subordinate clause to a main clause. Subordinate clauses elaborate directly upon main clause statements, usually by telling when, how, why, or under what conditions the activity of the main clause occurs.

2. In a subordinate clause, the conjugated verb is always in final position. The two clauses are separated by a comma.

Main Clause	*Subordinate Clause*
Wir gehen heute im Park spazieren,	**wenn** *(if)* das Wetter schön *ist.*
	weil *(because)* wir Zeit dazu *haben.*
	obwohl *(although)* es heute stark *regnet.*

3. A subordinate clause can occur either before or after the main clause. If the subordinate clause comes first, the subsequent main clause must begin with a verb. In

other words, within the overall sentence the subordinate clause is the first element and the main clause verb is still in second position.

Subordinate Clause	*Main Clause*
Wenn das Wetter schön ist, Weil wir Zeit dazu haben, Obwohl es heute stark regnet,	**gehen** wir heute im Park spazieren.

4. Interrogative words (see 15.2) can also function as subordinate conjunctions. The conjugated verb is still in final position.

Niemand wußte, **warum** er sich das Leben genommen hatte.	*No one knew why he had taken his life.*

C. Als, wenn, wann

1. **Als** *(when, as)* refers only to *one-time* events or situations in the past. The one-time event can occur over a long period of time.

Als wir in Berlin ankamen, regnete es.	*When we got to Berlin, it was raining.*
Als ich ein Kind war, lebte meine Familie in Europa.	*When I was a child, my family lived in Europe.*

2. In narrative contexts, German speakers sometimes use **wie** instead of **als.**

Wie sie dann in das Zimmer kam, sah sie jemanden aus dem Fenster springen.	*As she came into the room, she saw someone leap out the window.*

3. **Wenn** *(when, whenever)* refers to recurring events in the past.

Es war immer viel los, **wenn** wir Berlin besuchten.	*There was always a lot going on when(ever) we visited Berlin.*

4. **Wenn** can also mean either *when* or *whenever (inevitable)* or *if (possible).*

Wenn dieser Mensch kommt, . . . *(inevitable)*	*When(ever) this person comes . . .*
Wenn dieser Mensch bald kommt, . . . *(possible)*	*If this person comes soon, . . .*

5. The interrogative **wann** (see 15.2) always refers to specific time and often occurs in indirect questions.

Weißt du, **wann** sie das Haus verlassen hat?	*Do you know when she left the house?*

D. Als ob / als wenn

1. **Als ob** *(less common:* **als wenn***)* means *as if* and is used to express conjecture or a contrary-to-fact condition. Clauses beginning with **als ob / als wenn** are normally in the subjunctive mood (see 20.3), and they frequently follow phrases such as **Es ist / war, Er tut / tat, Es scheint / schien.**

Es war ihm, **als ob** sie einander schon einmal getroffen hätten.	*It seemed to him as if they had already met each other once before.*

2. The word **ob** (or **wenn**) can be omitted and the meaning *as if* retained, providing **als** is followed immediately by the verb. This structure occurs frequently in poetry.

Es war, **als** hätt der Himmel die Erde still geküßt. (J. von Eichendorff)	*It was as if Heaven had quietly kissed the Earth.*

E. Bevor / ehe

Bevor and **ehe,** both of which mean *before,* can be used interchangeably. The conjunction **bevor** is not to be confused with the *preposition* **vor** (see 10.3), nor with the *adverb* **vorher** (see 24.2).

COMPARE:

Bevor / ehe Kai ins Bett ging, trank er ein Glas Milch. *(conjunction)*	*Before Kai went to bed, he drank a glass of milk.*
Vor dem Schlafengehen trank Maria eine Tasse Tee. *(preposition)*	*Before going to bed, Maria drank a cup of tea.*
Ulrich ging schlafen, aber **vorher** trank er ein Glas Saft. *(adverb)*	*Ulrich went to bed, but beforehand he drank a glass of juice.*

F. Bis

1. The conjunction **bis** *(until)* expresses the duration of an action *until* a certain time or place is reached. It also occurs as a preposition (see 10.1).

Wir arbeiten (solange), **bis** wir fertig sind. *(conjunction)*	*We are working until we are finished.*
Sie fahren **bis** Genf mit. *(preposition)*	*They are traveling (with us) as far as Geneva.*

2. **Bis** is often used to indicate the time *by when* an action is completed.

Bis der Winter kam, hatte ich den Pullover fertig gestrickt.	*By the time winter came, I had finished knitting the sweater.*

G. Da / weil

1. **Da** *(since, as)* and **weil** *(because)* are often used interchangeably to explain *why* an action occurs. However, **da** normally explains the situation leading to an action, whereas the more emphatic **weil** often indicates the reason for doing something.

Da er nichts Besseres zu tun hatte, ging Herr Ziegler in den Zoo.	*Since Mr. Ziegler had nothing better to do, he went to the zoo.*
Weil er die Schimpansen sehen wollte, ging Herr Ziegler in den Zoo.	*Because he wanted to see the chimpanzees, Mr. Ziegler went to the zoo.*

2. The conjunction **da** should not be confused with the adverb **da** (*then, there:* see 24.2).

H. Damit, so daß

1. **Damit** *(so that)* signifies a *purpose* for doing something.

Eltern sparen Geld, **damit** ihre Kinder studieren können.	*Parents save money so that their children can go to college.*

2. If both clauses have the same subject, German frequently uses a construction with **um + zu** + infinitive instead of **damit** (see 18.2).

Wir sparen Geld, **um** studieren **zu** können.	*We are saving money in order to be able to go to college.*

3. **So daß** indicates the *result* of an action.

Es regnete tagelang, **so daß** die Felder unter Wasser standen.	*It rained for days, so that the fields were under water.*
Es regnete **so** schwer, **daß** auch die Straßen überschwemmt waren.	*It rained so hard that even the streets were flooded.*

I. Daß

Daß *(that)* is often omitted, as in English, but then the clause is not subordinated and the verb remains in regular second position.

COMPARE:

Sie hofften, **daß** jemand sie besuchen *würde.* Sie hofften, jemand *würde* sie besuchen.	} *They hoped (that) someone would visit them.*

J. Falls

Falls *(in case, if, providing)* is sometimes used instead of **wenn** to express possibility.

Du kannst mitkommen, **falls** du Lust hast.	*You can come along if you feel like it.*

K. Indem

Indem *(by [-]ing)* expresses how someone achieves a result. Unlike English, German includes the subject again in the subordinate clause.

Du kannst viel Geld sparen, **indem** du das Auto selber reparierst.	*You can save a lot of money by repairing the car yourself.*
Indem er viel trainierte, wurde er ein schneller und erfolgreicher Läufer.	*By training a lot, he became a fast and successful runner.*

L. Nachdem

The conjunction **nachdem** *(after)* should not be confused with the *preposition* **nach** (see 10.2) or the *adverb* **nachher** (see 24.2).

COMPARE:

Sie geht ins Kino, **nachdem** sie gegessen hat. *(conjunction)*	*She is going to the movies after she has eaten.*
Sie geht **nach** dem Essen ins Kino. *(preposition)*	*She is going to the movies after the meal.*
Sie ißt jetzt, und **nachher** geht sie ins Kino. *(adverb)*	*She is eating now, and afterwards she is going to the movies.*

M. Ob

Ob *(if (=whether))* should not be confused with **wenn.**

COMPARE:

Weißt du, **ob** der Zug schon angekommen ist?	*Do you know whether/if the train has already arrived?*
Wenn der Zug hier ist, sollten wir sofort einsteigen.	*If the train is here, we should board immediately.*

N. Obgleich / obschon / obwohl

Obgleich, obschon, and **obwohl** all mean *although,* but **obwohl** is most common.

Der Redner sprach weiter, **obwohl** alle Zuhörer eingeschlafen waren.	*The speaker kept talking, although all members of the audience had fallen asleep.*

O. Seit(dem)

1. **Seitdem** (often abbreviated to **seit**) means *since* in a temporal sense. German uses the present tense with **seit(dem)** (see 2.2) to express an action that began in the past and continues into present time; English requires the present perfect.

2. If the action in the **seit(dem)** clause is not ongoing, then German uses the present perfect tense in that clause.

COMPARE:

Seit(dem) wir dieses Handbuch *benutzen, verstehen* wir die deutsche Grammatik besser. *(ongoing action)*	*Ever since we have been using this handbook, we understand German grammar better.*
Seit(dem) wir dieses Handbuch *gekauft haben,* verstehen wir die deutsche Grammatik besser. *(completed action)*	*Ever since we bought this handbook, we understand German grammar better.*

3. In addition to the conjunction **seit(dem),** there are the dative *preposition* **seit** *(since, for)* (see 10.2 and the *adverbs* **seitdem** and **seither**) (see 24.2).

Wir benutzen dieses Handbuch **seit** einigen Wochen, und **seitdem** / **seither** verstehen wir die deutsche Grammatik besser.	*We have been using this handbook for several weeks, and since then we understand German grammar better.*

P. Sobald, solange, sooft

The conjunctions **sobald** *(as soon as),* **solange** *(as long as),* and **sooft** *(as often as)* are often used to indicate the condition for doing an action.

Sobald sie kommt, könnt ihr gehen.	*As soon as she comes, you can go.*
Du mußt hier bleiben, **solange** es regnet.	*You must stay here as long as it is raining.*
Sie sprechen Deutsch, **sooft** sie können.	*They speak German as often as they can.*

Q. Während

1. The conjunction **während** *(while)* indicates the simultaneous occurrence of two actions. This conjunction should not be confused with the *preposition* **während** *(during)* (see 10.4).

COMPARE:

Während einige Kinder Fußball spielten, saßen andere im Sandkasten. *(conjunction)*	*While some children played soccer, others sat in the sandbox.*
Während der Ferien bleiben manche Leute zu Hause. *(preposition)*	*During school vacation some people stay home.*

2. The conjunction **während** can also be used to contrast two actions.

Im Rheinland trinkt man viel Wein, **während** man in Bayern oft Bier vorzieht.	*In the Rhineland people drink a lot of wine, while in Bavaria people often prefer beer.*

R. Weil *(see* da / weil, *p. 143)*

S. Wenn . . . auch / auch wenn

Wenn . . . auch and **auch wenn** mean *even if* or *even though.* **Wenn** and **auch** are normally separated by one or more words or phrases when **wenn** precedes **auch.** They normally occur together when **auch** comes first.

Ich lese Kafkas Geschichten gern, **wenn** ich sie **auch** nicht verstehe (*or:* **auch wenn** ich sie nicht verstehe).	*I like to read Kafka's stories, even though / even if I do not understand them.*

T. Wenn . . . nicht / wenn . . . kein-

There is no one-word German equivalent for *unless.* The most common way to express the same idea is by using **wenn** and the negating words **nicht** or **kein-.**

Wir werden nicht arbeiten, **wenn** Sie uns **nicht** bezahlen.	*We won't work unless you* (that is, *if you do not*) *pay us.*
Er kommt nicht, **wenn** er **keine** Zeit hat.	*He is not coming unless he has time.*

* Übungen

A ***Aber* und *sondern.*** Ergänzen Sie die Sätze durch **aber** und **sondern.**

Beispiel: Ich kann Deutsch nicht schreiben . . .
Ich kann Deutsch nicht schreiben, ***sondern*** *(ich kann) es nur sprechen.*
Ich kann Deutsch nicht schreiben, ***aber*** *ich verstehe es.*

1. Meine Nachbarin ist keine Ärztin, . . .
2. Wir wollen keinen Krieg, . . .
3. Frankfurt liegt nicht am Rhein, . . .
4. Man soll nicht alles glauben, was in der Zeitung steht, . . .
5. In diesem Teil der Stadt gibt es nicht viele Geschäfte, . . .

B **Ideen verbinden.** Drücken Sie die Sätze durch gepaarte Konjunktionen anders aus.

Beispiel: Ich habe ein rotes Fahrrad und ein blaues Fahrrad.
Ich habe ***sowohl*** *ein rotes Fahrrad* ***als auch*** *ein blaues.*
OR: *Ich habe* ***nicht nur*** *ein rotes Fahrrad,* ***sondern auch*** *ein blaues.*

nicht nur . . . sondern auch — entweder . . . oder
sowohl . . . als auch — weder . . . noch

1. In dieser Stadt wohnen viele reiche Menschen, aber auch viele arme.
2. Ich möchte keinen Tee. Ich möchte keinen Kaffee.
3. Wir wollen Deutschland besuchen. Wir wollen die Schweiz besuchen.
4. Du mußt Deutsch lernen, oder du mußt Französisch lernen, aber nicht beides.
5. Es gibt viele Fische im Meer, kleine und große.

Machen Sie wahre Aussagen mit jeder der gepaarten Konjunktionen.

C **Anders ausdrücken.** Drücken Sie die Sätze anders aus, indem Sie die präpositionalen Ausdrücke durch subordinierte Nebensätze ersetzen.

Beispiel: Ich komme nach dem Essen. (nachdem)
Ich komme, ***nachdem*** *ich gegessen habe.*

1. Beim Lesen schlafe ich manchmal ein. (wenn)
2. Man kann durch viel Arbeit zum Erfolg *(success)* kommen. (indem / wenn)
3. Sonia geht wegen der Krankheit ihrer Mutter nach Hause. (weil)
4. Trotz des Regens machen wir heute ein Picknick. (obwohl)
5. Die Menschen zahlen Steuern *(taxes)* bis zu ihrem Tod. (bis)
6. Man soll den Tag nicht vor dem Abend loben *(praise)*. (bevor)
7. Seit Beginn des Semesters sehe ich meine Eltern nicht mehr. (seit[dem])
8. Während ihres Studienjahres in Graz hat Pauline eine Reise nach Griechenland gemacht. (als)

D **Wie geht es weiter?** Beenden Sie die Aussagen mit den folgenden Konjunktionen. Beginnen Sie jeden zweiten Satz (2, 4, 6, 8) mit einem subordinierten Nebensatz.

Beispiel: Ich weiß, . . .
Ich weiß, daß manche Menschen sehr intolerant sind.
OR: *Daß manche Menschen sehr intolerant sind, weiß ich.*

als ob	damit	nachdem
bevor / ehe	daß	ob
bis	indem	wenn

1. Es gefällt mir überhaupt nicht, . . .
2. Ich lerne Deutsch, . . .
3. Man kann gute Noten bekommen, . . .

4. Meine Eltern fragen mich immer wieder, . . .
5. Am besten putzt man sich die Zähne, . . .
6. Es wird sicher noch eine Weile dauern, . . .
7. Manche Menschen können sich nicht konzentrieren, . . .
8. Man muß lange studieren, . . .
9. Manche Menschen tun so, . . .

E **Logisch weiterdenken.** Mit wie vielen verschiedenen Nebensätzen (koordinierend oder subordinierend) können Sie die folgenden Sätze beenden?

Beispiel: Karla bleibt zu Hause, . . .
weil *sie krank ist.*
denn *sie hat keine Lust, zur Uni zu fahren.*
obwohl *sie heute eine Prüfung hat.*
usw.

1. Man soll eine Fremdsprache lernen, . . .
2. Mein Freund Owen lernte Deutsch, . . .
3. Man lernt am besten segeln, . . .
4. Es steht in der Zeitung, . . .
5. Ich hole Geld von der Bank, . . .

F **Sie haben das Wort.** Machen Sie Aussagen auf deutsch.

Beispiel: Whenever I . . .
Wenn *ich ins Konzert gehe, tun mir die Ohren am Ende des Konzerts weh.*

1. When I was . . .
2. Ever since I . . .
3. By [-]ing, I . . .
4. Because I . . .
5. Before I . . .
6. As long as I . . .
7. Unless I . . .
8. Even though I . . .

G ***Als, wenn*** **und** ***wann.*** Machen Sie mit den Konjunktionen **als, wenn** und **wann** jeweils zwei Aussagen über sich oder über Ihr bisheriges Leben.

Beispiele: ***Als*** *ich ein Kind war, habe ich mich immer gefreut,* ***wenn*** *wir Schnee hatten.*
Ich bin nicht sicher, ***wann*** *ich mit meinem Studium fertig werde.*

H **Warum?** Beantworten Sie die Fragen mit Hilfe der Konjunktionen **da, weil, denn** und **damit.**

Beispiel: Warum sind wir hier?
Weil *wir nicht „dort" sind.*

1. Warum sind Frauen / Männer so kompliziert?
2. Warum gibt es nie genug Zeit?
3. Warum bekomme ich immer das kleinste Stück vom Kuchen?

4. Warum müssen wir sterben?
5. Warum stellen wir immer solche Fragen?

Stellen Sie fünf weitere solche Fragen an andere Studenten. Wer hat die besten Antworten?

* Anwendung

Taten und ihre Folgen. Haben Sie (oder jemand, den Sie kennen) einmal etwas besonders Großartiges / Wichtiges / Dummes getan? Erklären Sie jemandem, *wann* das war, *warum* es dazu kam und *was* die Folgen *(consequences)* davon waren.

REDEMITTEL

wann

Ja, das war damals, als . . .
Ehe ich . . .

warum

Vielleicht dachte ich, daß . . .
Ich habe es getan, damit / da / weil / denn . . .
Es war mir damals, als ob . . .

Folgen

Aber obwohl / sobald / indem ich . . .
Jedoch hatte ich nicht damit gerechnet *(figured)*, daß . . .
So kam es, daß . . .
Aber jetzt weiß ich . . .

* Schriftliche Themen

Tips zum Schreiben ***Writing with Conjunctions***

You can make your sentences more interesting by using coordinating and subordinating conjunctions. Coordinating conjunctions enable you to add information **(und)** or show a contrast **(aber)**, a cause **(denn)**, or an alternative **(oder)**. Subordinate conjunctions prove particularly useful when expressing intention **(damit)**, cause **(da)**, reason **(weil)**, or contrast **(obwohl, während)**.

Vary your writing style by mixing longer sentences with shorter ones. Complex sentences with more than one clause work well in explanations, but you might make key points and conclusions in shorter, simple sentences.

If a subordinate clause contains information you wish to stress, consider beginning the sentence with this clause. Remember that all clauses in German must be set off by commas, and that in subordinate clauses the inflected verb is placed in final position.

A **Rotkäppchen neu erzählt.** Verbessern Sie die folgende kleine Rotkäppchen-Geschichte durch den Gebrauch von Konjunktionen. Sie dürfen auch den Inhalt der Geschichte ändern oder sogar eine ganz neue Version schreiben.

Rotkäppchen sollte ihrer Großmutter einen Korb mit Wein und Kuchen bringen.
Die Großmutter fühlte sich nicht wohl. Sie lag im Bett.
Das Rotkäppchen fuhr in seinem Sportwagen durch den Wald.
Das Rotkäppchen sah seinen Nachbarn Herrn Wolf am Rande der Straße stehen.
Es bremste und fragte Herrn Wolf. „Wohin willst du?"
Er antwortete. Er wollte an den Strand fahren.
Er fragte. Wohin fuhr Rotkäppchen.
Es erzählte. Es sollte zur Oma fahren.
Jetzt hatte sie keine Lust mehr, ihre Oma zu besuchen.
Es wollte lieber an den Strand fahren.
Es lud Herrn Wolf ein, mitzufahren. Sie fuhren an den Strand.
Sie verbrachten einen wunderschönen Nachmittag.
Die arme Oma wartete vergebens *(in vain)* auf den Korb mit Wein und Kuchen.

B **Eine Bildgeschichte.** Erzählen Sie nicht nur, was geschieht, sondern auch, was das Mädchen Susi und der Hund Bello denken. Warum denken sie so? Verwenden Sie mindestens fünf verschiedene Konjunktionen.

VOKABELVORSCHLÄGE

die Wanne *(tub)*
füllen *(fill)*
der Schlauch *(hose)*
um die Ecke *(around the corner)*
zuschauen *(watch)*
ausziehen *(take off)*
glauben *(believe)*
neugierig *(curious)*
näher kommen *(to come closer)*
stecken *(to stick)*
packen *(to grab, seize)*
die Bürste *(brush)*
sehr böse *(very angry)*
in Zukunft *(in the future)*
nie wieder *(never again)*

C **Einen Standpunkt vertreten.** Schreiben Sie über ein Thema, wofür Sie sich besonders interessieren. Erklären Sie nicht nur, *wie* Sie dazu stehen, sondern auch *warum.*

THEMENVORSCHLÄGE

Sollten Kinder und Erwachsene weniger fernsehen?
Brauchen wir eine Energiesparpolitik?
Sollten alle Kinder eine Fremdsprache lernen?
Atomkraftwerke: ja oder nein?
Sollten Ausländer unbegrenzt in die USA / nach Deutschland einwandern dürfen?
Sollte man Euthanasie erlauben?

Beispiel: *Obwohl* ich Fremdsprachen für sehr wichtig halte, bin ich nicht der Meinung, *daß* alle Schulkinder unbedingt eine Fremdsprache lernen sollten. Manche Kinder wollen es tun, *denn* sie interessieren sich für andere Länder und Kulturen. Aber es gibt andererseits Kinder, die . . . *Indem* man sie dazu zwingt, Fremdsprachen zu lernen, . . . usw.

Wortschatz 11

denken	glauben
denken an	halten von
denken von	halten für
meinen	

1. **Denken** means *to think, believe* or *think something possible.*

Sie **denkt** viel.	*She thinks a lot.*
Er **denkt,** daß es morgen regnen wird.	*He believes that it will rain tomorrow.*
Wer hätte das **gedacht?**	*Who would have thought that possible?*

2. **Denken an** means *to think of, remember,* or *call to mind.*

Wir **denken an** die Folgen des Krieges.	*We are thinking of the results of the war.*
Du mußt doch **an** deine Gesundheit **denken.**	*After all, you have to think of your health.*

3. **Denken von** means *to think of* or *have an opinion.*

Was **denkst** du **von** seinem Plan?	*What do you think of his plan?*
Sie **denkt** nicht viel **von** ihm.	*She does not think much of him.*

4. **Meinen** means *to think, be of the opinion, mean,* or *say.*

Was hat er damit **gemeint?**	*What did he mean by that?*
Sie **meinte,** daß wir jemanden um Rat bitten sollten.	*She said / thought that we should ask someone for advice.*

5. **Glauben (an)** means *to think* or *believe (in)* and expresses belief as opposed to reasoned opinion.

Glaubst du an Gott?	*Do you believe in God?*
Ich **glaube,** daß es einen Gott gibt.	*I believe there is a God.*

6. **Halten von** means *to think of, have an opinion.* (It is synonymous with **denken von** and is often used to ask for an opinion.)

Was **halten** Sie **von** solchen Leuten?	*What do you think of such people?*

As a statement, **halten von** can only be used with **viel, wenig, etwas,** or **nichts.**

Ich **halte wenig von** solchen Leuten.	*I think little of such people.*

7. **Halten für** means *to think someone or something is, regard as, consider (to be).* In statements, this expression is completed either with a noun in the accusative case (after **für**) or with an adjective.

Wofür hältst du mich?	*What do you think I am?*
Ich **halte** dich **für** einen Narren / **für** närrisch.	*I think you are a fool / foolish.*

Compare the following uses of **halten von** and **halten für:**

Was **hältst** du **von** dem Plan des Bürgermeisters?	*What do you think of the mayor's plan?*
Ich **halte** nicht viel **von** seinem Plan.	*I do not think very highly of his plan.*
Ich **halte** seinen Plan **für** ganz geschickt.	*I consider his plan (to be) quite clever.*

ÜBUNGEN

A ***Denken, glauben, meinen* oder *halten?*** Welche Verben würden Sie verwenden?

Beispiel: an den Teufel ____
an den Teufel (nicht) ***glauben***

1. nichts von der Politik ____
2. oft an seine Kindheit ____
3. an die Güte im Menschen ____
4. für gefährlich ____
5. ____ , daß es einen Gott gibt
6. es mit jemandem gut ____
7. etwas Besonderes damit ____

B **Nach Meinungen fragen.** Fragen Sie jemanden im Kurs nach seiner / ihrer Meinung über bekannte Menschen und Ereignisse aus den Tagesnachrichten. Stellen Sie zwei oder drei Fragen mit Verben aus Wortschatz 11. Bei den Antworten sollen Sie auch Ausdrücke aus diesem Wortschatz verwenden.

Beispiel: *Was denkst / hältst du von der Politik der USA in Bosnien?*
Ich halte sie für nicht so gut.

Zusammenfassung 11

Rules to Remember

1. The conjunctions **aber, denn, oder, sondern,** and **und** are *coordinating;* they do not affect the position of the conjugated verb in the clauses that follow them.
2. Almost all other conjunctions are *subordinating;* the conjugated verb moves to final position within the subordinated clause.

Activities

1 **Providing plausible explanations.**[2] Find an article in the newspaper. Tell in German what a person or persons in this article did. Other students provide as many plausible explanations as possible for this behavior.

2. The idea for this activity comes from Mario Rinvolucri, *Grammar Games. Cognitive, affective, and drama activities for EFL students,* Cambridge University Press, 1984. Activity V.6.

Beispiel: *Eine Frau erschoß ihren Ehemann.*
Ich glaube, die Frau erschoß ihren Ehemann,
denn er hatte sie geschlagen.
weil er sie nicht mehr liebte.
damit sie einen anderen heiraten konnte.
obwohl . . .
um . . . zu . . .

2 **Talking about the past.** Divide into groups of four. Students then take turns telling about something they used to do when younger. Use **wenn** and **als** as appropriate. Go around the group as many times as possible.

3 **Writing about yourself.** Write a sketch or short description of yourself. Tell about your behavior and feelings and the reasons for them. Use at least eight different conjunctions.

4 **A sales pitch.** Make a sales pitch for a particular product. Use various conjunctions in building a persuasive argument. Bring in the product (or a picture) and make your sales pitch to the class.

5 **Working with a text.** Discuss with other students the behavior of the main characters in a story you all know. Speculate as to possible reasons for this behavior.

Noun Genders, Noun Plurals, Weak Nouns

12

12.1 Noun Genders

All German nouns, whether they represent persons, things, or ideas, have *grammatical* gender **(das Genus)** that is indicated by the definite article: **der** = masculine, **die** = feminine, **das** = neuter. While the nouns for male beings are usually masculine and the nouns for female beings feminine (examples of *natural* gender), all other nouns can be any of the three genders. For example, a tree is **der Baum,** a plant **die Pflanze,** and a leaf **das Blatt.** Although there is no apparent rationale for this classification, guidelines for predicting genders do exist. The most useful ones are listed in the following sections.

A. *Masculine Nouns*

The following types of nouns are usually masculine:

1. Words designating male beings, their professions, and their nationalities

der Mann, ¨-er	der Arzt, ¨-e	der Engländer,-
der Sohn, ¨-e	der Chemiker, -	der Franzose, -n

2. Agent nouns derived from verbs by adding the suffix **-er** to the infinitive stem

der Arbeit**er**, - (arbeiten)	der Mal**er** , - (malen)
der Fahr**er**, - (fahren)	der Schreib**er**, - (schreiben)

3. Days of the week, months of the year, seasons, and most weather elements

(der) Montag	der Frühling	der Regen
(der) Mai	der Herbst	der Schnee

4. Names of most *non-German* rivers

der Mississippi	der Nil
der Mekong	der Delaware

EXCEPTIONS: **die Wolga** **die Themse** **die Seine**

5. Nouns ending in the suffixes **-ig, -ling, -or,** or **-us**

der Käf**ig**, -e *(cage)*	der Lieb**ling** , -e
der Hon**ig**, -e	der Schwäch**ling**, -e *(weakling)*
der Mot**or**, -en	der Sozialism**us**
der Fakt**or**, -en	der Zirk**us**, -se

6. Most nouns ending in **-en**

der Gart**en**, ¨	der Krag**en**, - *(collar)*	der Ost**en**
der Haf**en**, ¨ *(harbor)*	der Mag**en**, - *(stomach)*	der Süd**en**

B. *Feminine Nouns*

The following types of nouns are usually feminine:

1. Words designating female beings, their professions, and their nationalities

die Frau, -en	die Ärztin, -nen	die Französin, -nen
die Tochter, ¨	die Chemikerin, -nen	die Engländerin, -nen

2. Agent nouns with the feminine suffix **-in** corresponding to masculine agent forms

die Arbeiter**in**, -nen	die Maler**in**, -nen
die Fahrer**in**, -nen	die Schreiber**in**, -nen

3. Most nouns ending in **-e** (plural **-n**)

die Krawatt**e**, -n	die Maschin**e**, -n	die Sprach**e**, -n

4. Nouns ending in the suffixes **-anz, -ei, -enz, -ie, -ik, -ion, -heit, -keit, -schaft, -tät, -ung,** or **-ur**

die Disson**anz**, -en	die Mus**ik**	die Land**schaft** , -en
die Konditor**ei** , -en	die Relig**ion**, -en	die Rivali**tät**, -en
die Frequ**enz**, -en	die Dumm**heit**, -en	die Bedeut**ung,** -en
die Demokrat**ie**, -en	die Schwierig**keit**, -en	die Prozed**ur**, -en

5. Names of many rivers in Germany

die Donau	die Elbe	die Havel	die Isar	die Mosel

EXCEPTIONS: **der Rhein** **der Inn** **der Lech** **der Main** **der Neckar**

C. *Neuter Nouns*

The following types of nouns are usually neuter:

1. Names of continents, cities, and most countries. However, they only require an article when modified by adjectives.

   Ich gehe nach Frankfurt / Europa / Deutschland. *(no article)*
   Es gibt heute **ein** vereinigt**es** Europa. *(article)*

2. Nouns for many metals

das Blei *(lead)*	das Eisen *(iron)*	das Gold
das Metall	das Silber	das Uran

   EXCEPTIONS: **der Stahl** **die Bronze**

3. Letters of the alphabet

   ein kleines G das große H

4. Infinitives and other parts of speech when used as nouns

(das) Lesen *(reading)*	das Ich *(ego)*
(das) Schreiben *(writing)*	das Für und Wider *(arguments for and against)*

5. Nouns ending in the suffix **-tum**

   das Christen**tum** das Juden**tum** das Eigen**tum,** ¨-er *(possession)*

   EXCEPTIONS: **der Reichtum, ¨-er** *(wealth)* **der Irrtum, ¨-er** *(error)*

6. Nouns with the diminutive suffixes **-chen, -lein** (and their dialect variations **-erl, -el, -le, -li**). Also nouns with the suffixes **-ment** and **-(i)um.**

das Mäd**chen**, -	das Experi**ment**, -e
das Büch**lein**, -	das Dat**um**, die Daten
das Buss**erl**, - *(kiss, smooch)*	das Muse**um**, die Museen
das Häus**le**, -	das Med**ium**, die Medien

7. Most collective nouns beginning with the prefix **Ge-**

Berge → das **Ge**birge	Wolken → das **Ge**wölk
Büsche → das **Ge**büsch	Schreie → das **Ge**schrei *(screaming)*

D. *Compound Nouns*

In compound words, both gender and plural are governed by the last word in the compound.

das Eisen *(iron)*
die Eisen**bahn** *(railroad)*
der Eisenbahn**schaffner** *(railroad conductor)*
die Eisenbahnschaffner**uniform** *(railroad conductor's uniform)*

E. *Nouns with Dual Gender*

1. Some words appear to have two separate genders, depending on meaning. Here are some common examples:

der Band, ¨e *(volume)*	**das Band, ¨er** *(ribbon, tape)*
der Flur, -e *(hallway)*	**die Band, -s** *(band, music group)*
der Gefallen, - *(favor)*	**die Flur, -en** *(meadow, pasture)*
der Gehalt, -e *(content[s])*	**das Gefallen** *(pleasure)*
der Kunde, -n *(customer, client)*	**das Gehalt, ¨er** *(salary, wages)*
der Messer, *(gauge)*	**die Kunde** *(news, notice, information)*
der Moment, -e *(moment)*	**das Messer, -** *(knife)*
der Schild, -e *(shield)*	**das Moment, -e** *(factor)*
der See, -n *(lake)*	**das Schild, -er** *(sign, signboard)*
der Tor, -en *(fool)*	**die See, -n** *(sea)*
	das Tor, -e *(gate)*

2. The word **Teil, -e** *(part, element, share)* is usually masculine. When it refers to a mechanical part, it is often used with the neuter article. Some compounds with **-teil** are masculine—**der Vorteil** *(advantage),* **der Nachteil** *(disadvantage);* others are neuter—**das Gegenteil** *(opposite),* **das Urteil** *(verdict).* Be sure to learn each compound with its article.
3. **Meter** and its compounds and **Liter** are now usually treated as masculine, although some dictionaries still list neuter as the officially preferred gender. (See 22.3B)

12.2 Noun Plurals

There are five basic plural endings for German nouns: **–, -e, -er, -en,** and **-s.** In some instances, the stem vowel of the noun also has an umlaut. In the plural, all nouns take the same article **(die).** The following guidelines should be considered rules of thumb only, for there are exceptions.

A. *No Plural Ending* (– or ¨)

Most masculine and neuter nouns ending in **-el, -en, -er** take no plural ending, though many that are masculine do take an umlaut.

der Sessel, **die Sessel**	der Mantel, **die Mäntel**
der Wagen, **die Wagen**	der Garten, **die Gärten**
der Fahrer, **die Fahrer**	der Vater, **die Väter**
das Kissen *(pillow),* **die Kissen**	
das Fenster, **die Fenster**	

EXCEPTION: **der Stachel, -n** *(thorn, prickle, stinger)*

B. Plural Ending **-e** *or* **¨-e**

1. A large number of monosyllabic masculine and neuter nouns take an **-e** ending in the plural. Some of these masculine nouns also take an umlaut.

   der Tisch, **die Tische** — der Bach, **die Bäche**
   das Jahr, **die Jahre** — der Stuhl, **die Stühle**

   EXCEPTIONS: der Mann, **die Männer;** der Wald, **die Wälder**

2. About thirty monosyllabic feminine nouns also take the plural ending **-e;** all also have an umlaut in the plural.

   die Angst, **die Ängste** — die Bank, **die Bänke**
   die Hand, **die Hände** — die Wand, **die Wände**

   ALSO: **die Brust, die Faust** *(fist),* **die Frucht, die Haut** *(skin; hide),* **die Kraft** *(strength),* **die Kuh, die Kunst, die Laus, die Luft, die Macht** *(power),* **die Maus, die Nacht, die Wand, die Wurst,** and a few others.

C. Plural Ending **-er** *or* **¨-er**

Many monosyllabic neuter words take an **-er** plural ending and also have an umlaut when possible.

das Buch, **die Bücher** — das Bild, **die Bilder**
das Dorf, **die Dörfer** — das Kleid, **die Kleider**

D. Plural Ending **-(e)n**

1. Almost all feminine nouns, including all those with feminine suffixes, take an **-(e)n** plural ending, but no umlaut.

   die Mauer, **die Mauern** — die Zeitung, **die Zeitungen**
   die Stunde, **die Stunden** — die Universität, **die Universitäten**

2. Nouns with the feminine suffix **-in** double the **-n** before the plural ending.

   die Autorin, **die Autorinnen** — die Polizistin, **die Polizistinnen**

E. Plural Ending **-s**

Many foreign words, particularly those ending in the vowels **-a** or **-o,** take an **-s** plural ending.

das Büro, **die Büros** — die Kamera, **die Kameras**

F. Nouns Without Plurals

1. Some categories of German nouns, for example nouns designating materials (sugar, wool, steel) or abstract concepts (love, hate, intelligence) have no plural.

2. Many collective nouns beginning with **Ge-** exist also only in the singular. Their English forms are often plural.

das Gebirge *(mountains)*	**das Geschirr** *(dishes)*
das Gebüsch *(bushes)*	**das Gewölk** *(clouds)*

3. In addition, a few other nouns usually occur only in the singular, though their English equivalents are often expressed in the plural.

die Brille *(eyeglasses)*	**die Schere** *(scissors)*
die Hose *(pants, trousers)*	**das Vieh** *(one or more head of cattle)*

12.3 Weak Noun Declensions

1. A particular group of masculine nouns adds **-(e)n** to all cases singular and plural except the nominative singular.

	Sing.	***Pl.***
Nom.	der Mensch	die Mensch**en**
Acc.	den Mensch**en**	die Mensch**en**
Dat.	dem Mensch**en**	den Mensch**en**
Gen.	des Mensch**en**	der Mensch**en**

Nouns of this type include:

a. Some nouns denoting male beings in general

der Bauer	der Herr[1]	der Kunde *(customer)*
der Bote *(messenger)*	der Junge	der Nachbar[2]
der Experte	der Knabe *(boy)*	der Riese *(giant)*

b. A number of nouns indicating nationality or religious affiliation

der Chinese	der Russe	der Buddhist	der Katholik
der Grieche	der Türke	der Jude	der Protestant

c. All nouns designating male beings and ending in the foreign suffixes **-ant, -arch, -ast, -ege, -ent, -ist, -oge, -om, -oph, -ot**

der Komödi**ant**	der Stud**ent**	der Astron**om**
der Mon**arch**	der Poliz**ist**	der Philos**oph**
der Enthusi**ast**	der Psychol**oge**	der Pil**ot**
der Koll**ege**		

---

1. **Herr** takes **-n** in the singular (**des Herrn, dem Herrn,** *etc.*), but **-en** in the plural (**der Herren, den Herren,** *etc.*).
2. **Nachbar** can also be declined regularly in the singular: **des Nachbars, dem Nachbarn,** etc.

2. Most weak nouns designating male beings have feminine equivalents with the suffix **-in.**

die Expertin	die Herrin *(mistress)*	die Russin
die Jüdin	die Bäuerin	die Pilotin

3. A few weak nouns have a genitive singular ending in **-ens.**

	Sing.	*Pl.*
Nom.	der Name	die Namen
Acc.	den Namen	die Namen
Dat.	dem Namen	den Namen
Gen.	des Nam**ens**	der Namen

Other common nouns of this type include:

der Friede(n) *(peace)*	**der Glaube** *(belief)*
der Gedanke *(thought)*	**der Wille** *(will)*

4. The weak neuter noun **das Herz** is irregular in the singular.

	Sing.	*Pl.*
Nom.	**das Herz**	die Herzen
Acc.	**das Herz**	die Herzen
Dat.	**dem Herzen**	den Herzen
Gen.	**des Herzens**	der Herzen

* Übungen

A ***Der, die* oder *das?*** Geben Sie Genus und Plural.

1. Diktatur
2. Spitze *(point)*
3. Winter
4. Pessimist
5. Männlein
6. Schreibkunst
7. Meldung *(announcement)*
8. Getränk
9. Käfig *(cage)*
10. Häftling *(prisoner)*
11. Name
12. Baustelle
13. Nation
14. Portugiese
15. Wissenschaft *(science)*
16. Bogen *(bow, arch)*
17. Trainerin
18. Partei
19. Kollege
20. Herz
21. Geldverdiener *(wage earner)*
22. Delaware *(river)*
23. Anachronismus
24. Fabrik *(factory)*
25. Schläfchen
26. Anwalt *(lawyer)*
27. Band
28. Mosel *(river)*

B **Männlich, weiblich oder sächlich (Neutrum)?** Welches Wort paßt auf Grund des Genus nicht in die Reihe? Warum nicht?

Beispiel: Christentum, Judentum, Heldentum, Irrtum
Irrtum ist ***der*** *(männlich), die anderen sind alle* ***das*** *(sächlich).*

1. Kirche, Jude, Riese, Junge
2. Brust, Macht, Kunst, Gehalt
3. Winter, Sommer, Herbst, Frühjahr
4. Klugheit, Vehemenz, Soziologe, Legalität
5. Gebäck, Gemüse, Geschmack, Getränk
6. Garten, Wagen, Ofen, Laufen
7. Neckar, Elbe, Oder, Mosel
8. Schreiber, Bäcker, Elektriker, Tochter
9. Präsident, Dissident, Experiment, Agent

C **Plural.** Welche Wörter in Übung B haben eine Pluralform? Nennen Sie diese Formen.

D **Adam und Eva.** Machen Sie aus männlichen Substantiven weibliche Substantive.

Beispiel: der Herr *(master)*
die Herrin (mistress)

1. der Jude	4. der Afrikaner	7. der König
2. der Polizist	5. der Biologe	8. der Methodist
3. der Tänzer	6. der Russe	9. der Nachbar

E **Substantive mit schwacher Deklination.** Ergänzen Sie die Sätze mit passenden Substantiven.

Beispiel: Hannibal ritt auf einem ____ über die Alpen.
Hannibal ritt auf einem ***Elefanten*** *über die Alpen.*

1. Im Weißen Haus findet man den ____ .
2. Bei einem Verbrechen *(crime)* ruft man einen ____ .
3. Fliegen ist der Beruf eines ____ .
4. Wenn wir Paßfotos brauchen, gehen wir zu einem ____ .
5. Eine Person, die an die Lehren von Karl Marx glaubt, nennt man einen ____ .
6. Der Papst im Vatikan ist das geistliche Oberhaupt *(head)* der ____ .
7. Im Geschäftsleben hat der ____ immer recht.

* Anwendung

Themenbereiche *(topic areas)*. Wählen Sie *(choose)* ein Thema, das Sie interessiert. (Sie müssen sich nicht unbedingt *[absolutely]* an die Themenvorschläge halten.) Schlagen *(Look up)* Sie acht bis zehn Substantive zu diesem Thema nach. Merken

Sie sich Genus und Plural von diesen Wörtern. Schreiben Sie Ihre Wörter *ohne* Genus und Plural auf eine Karte oder ein Blatt Papier. Nennen Sie auch den Themenbereich, zu dem Ihre Wörter gehören. Geben Sie die Karte an jemanden im Kurs weiter, der dieses Thema nicht gewählt hat. Er / sie soll versuchen, Bedeutung, Genus und Plural von diesen Wörtern zu erraten *(guess)*. Wenn er / sie ein Wort nicht erraten kann, erklären Sie es ihm / ihr auf deutsch.

THEMENVORSCHLÄGE

das Auto
Blumen und Pflanzen
der Computer
die Elektronik (Elektrowaren)
das Fliegen
(das) Haus und (die) Wohnung
Krankheiten
die Landschaft
der menschliche Körper
die Musik
die Politik
(die) Reise und (der) Urlaub
(der) Sport und Sportarten
die Tierwelt (siehe **Wortschatz 12**)

Beispiel: Thema: *der Garten*

Spaten	der Spaten, - *(spade)*
Harke	die Harke, -n *(rake)*
Pflanze	die Pflanze, -n *(plant)*
Samen	der Samen, - *(seed)*
Beet	das Beet, -e *(bed, patch)*
Schlauch	der Schlauch, ¨e *(hose)*
Erde	die Erde, -n *(soil)*
Dünger	der Dünger, - *(fertilizer, manure)*

* Schriftliche Themen

Tips zum Schreiben ***Checking for Correct Genders and Plurals***

After writing the first draft of a composition, go back and reread it for meaning. Make any revisions necessary so that your ideas are clear. Then check to make sure all nouns and articles are used in the proper gender and with the correct plural endings.

A **Beschreibung eines Ortes oder eines Gegenstands.** Beschreiben Sie ausführlich *(in detail)* einen Gegenstand oder einen Ort mit allem, was dazu gehört *(belongs)*.

THEMENVORSCHLÄGE

Ihr Auto
ein Garten (mit Gemüse und Blumen)
Ihr Heimcomputer
ein Spielplatz
etwas Besonderes, was Sie besitzen

Beispiel: Mein Computer ist ein Laptop-Gerät mit Festplatte *(hard disk)* und einem 3,5 Diskettenlaufwerk *(disk drive)*. Der Schirm ist farbig und recht klein. Im Computer befinden sich aber viele Software-Programme, darunter ein Textverarbeitungsprogramm *(word processing program)* und einige Videospiele. Zum System gehört auch ein Laserdrucker mit einer Druckgeschwindigkeit *(printing speed)* von acht Seiten pro Minute. Mir gefällt besonders die Tastatur *(keyboard)*, denn . . . usw.

B **Kurze Einleitung** *(introduction)*. Schreiben Sie eine kurze Einleitung zu einer Aktivität, die Sie besonders interessiert. Sie können z.B. erklären, welche Gegenstände man dazu braucht und wozu man sie braucht.

Beispiel: Zum Bergsteigen braucht man eine gute Ausrüstung. Dazu gehören vor allem stabile Schuhe und ein Rucksack. Man darf eine Wanderkarte, einen Kompaß, Wanderproviant *(hiking rations)* und eine warme Jacke auch nicht vergessen. Wer in felsige *(rocky)* Regionen hoch hinaufkommt, soll auch . . .

Wortschatz 12

der Affe	der Bär
die Ameise	die Biene

\+ *other animal names*

How many of these animal names do you already know or can you guess? Weak nouns (see 12.3) are indicated by *wk.* in parentheses. Where appropriate, sounds made by these animals are indicated. Write in plurals based upon the guidelines in this chapter. Answers are printed upside down on the last page of this chapter.

Animal	*Plural*	*Sound*
der Affe *(wk.)*		schreien
die Ameise *(ant)*		—
der Bär *(wk.)*		brüllen
die Biene		summen
der Bock		meckern
der Delphin		—
der Drache *(wk.)*		brüllen
das Eichhörnchen *(squirrel)*		—
die Ente *(duck)*		quaken, schnattern
der Esel		schreien
die Eule *(owl)*		schreien
der Falke *(wk.)*		schreien
der Fink *(wk.) (finch)*		zwitschern
die Fliege		summen
der Floh		—
der Frosch		quaken
der Fuchs		bellen
die Gans		schnattern
die Gemse *(chamois)*		
die Giraffe		
der Hai(fisch)		
der Hahn; das Huhn		krähen / gackern
der Hund		bellen
der Igel *(hedgehog)*		quieken
der Jaguar		brüllen
das Kamel		—
die Katze; der Kater		miauen
die Kröte *(toad)*		quaken
die Kuh		muhen
das Lamm		blöken
der Löwe *(wk.)*		brüllen
der Maulwurf *(mole)*		—
die Maus		quieken
die Motte		—
die Mücke (der Moskito)		surren
das Nilpferd		—
der Orang-Utan		brüllen

Animal	***Plural***	***Sound***
der Panther		brüllen
der Papagei		sprechen
der Pinguin		—
das Pferd		wiehern
die Ratte		—
das Schaf		blöken
die Schlange		zischen
der Schmetterling *(butterfly)*		—
das Schwein; die Sau		grunzen
der Seehund		bellen
die Spinne		—
der Stier		brüllen
das Stinktier		—
der Strauß *(ostrich)*		—
der Tausendfüßler		—
der Tiger		brüllen
der Uhu *(large owl)*		schreien
der Vogel		zwitschern; piepsen
der Wal(fisch)		—
der Waschbär *(wk.) (raccoon)*		—
der Wellensittich *(parakeet)*		piepsen
der Wolf		heulen
die Ziege *(goat)*		meckern

ÜBUNGEN

A **Welche Tiere kennen Sie?** Nennen Sie . . .

ein Tier, das Federn hat, aber nicht fliegen kann,
zwei Tiere, die sechs Beine haben,
drei Tiere, die den Menschen etwas geben,
vier Tiere, die gut schwimmen,
fünf Tiere, die fliegen,
sechs Tiere, die wir im Haus haben können,
sieben Tiere, die im Dschungel leben,
acht Tiere, die kleiner sind als eine Katze.

B **Ausdrücke mit Tiernamen.** Ergänzen Sie die Ausdrücke mit den angegebenen Tiernamen. Erklären Sie, was die Ausdrücke bedeuten.

Beispiel: Aus einer ___ einen ___ machen
Aus einer ***Mücke*** *einen* ***Elefanten*** *machen* (to make a mountain out of a mole hill)

Bock	Fliegen *(pl.)*	Katze
Elefant	Hühner *(pl.)*	Säue *(pl.)*
Eulen *(pl.)*	Hunde *(pl.)*	Stier

1. die ___ aus dem Sack lassen
2. vor die ___ gehen
3. Perlen vor die ___ werfen
4. den ___ zum Gärtner machen
5. sich wie ein ___ im Porzellanladen benehmen *(behave)*
6. mit den ___ schlafen gehen
7. zwei ___ mit einer Klappe *(swatter)* schlagen
8. ___ nach Athen tragen
9. den ___ bei / an den Hörnern packen *(grab)*

Zusammenfassung 12

Rules to Remember

1. There are three genders, usually indicated by the definite articles **der, die, das.**
2. Most male beings are **der;** most female beings are **die.** Other nouns can be any of the three genders.
3. There is no gender distinction in the plural; all nouns take the article **die.**
4. Weak nouns take **-(e)n** in all forms but the nominative singular: **der Experte, des Experten;** *pl.* **die Experten. Der Herr, des Herrn;** *pl.* **die Herren.**
5. Most nouns ending in **-e** are feminine and take **-n** in the plural: **die Tasche, -n.**
6. Nouns ending in the suffixes **-chen** and **-lein** are neuter and undergo no change in the plural: **das Mädchen -; das Männlein, -.**
7. The five German noun plural endings are **(¨), -e(¨e), -er (¨er), -en,** and **-s.**

Learning Tips
Learn nouns that you will probably use when speaking and writing. Familiarize yourself with common phrases containing articles or inflected adjectives: **ein herrlicher Tag; aus der Flasche; schönes Wetter.** It will also help if you learn nouns in thematic clusters (animals, foods, clothing, household furnishings, etc.).

Activities

1 **Thematic clusters.** Working alone or in a group, create several noun clusters (with gender and plural) around topics that interest you. Read your nouns to other students or groups. Let them guess the gender and plural of the nouns you choose.

Beispiel:

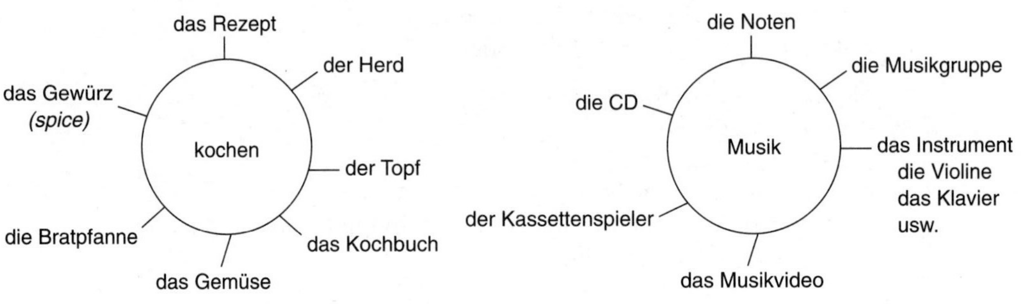

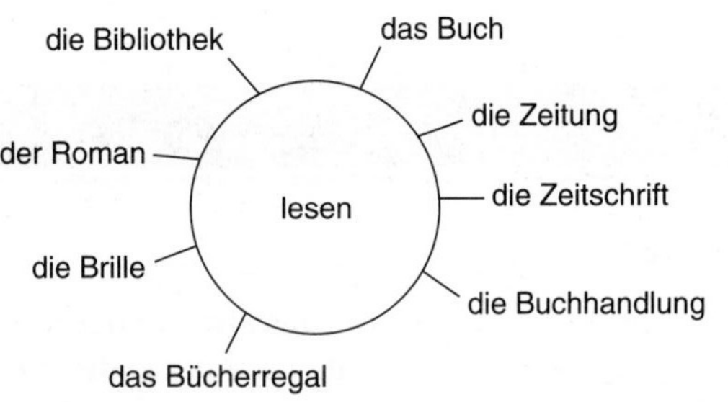

2 **Recall practice.** In ninety seconds, write down as many nouns as you can that begin with a particular letter. Now write gender and plural of these nouns. Repeat this activity with other letters.

3 **What do you see?** Give the gender and plural for every object you can see from the classroom window. Compare your list with those of other students.

4 **Brainstorming noun complements.** Write ten verbs. Brainstorm three nouns you associate with each verb. Do you know the gender and plural of these words? Exchange your verb list with a partner who then brainstorms words for your verbs.

5 **Arranging into thematic groupings.** Organize the nouns in a story you have read in thematic categories or groupings (i.e., persons, activities, mode of transport, etc.). Determine the gender and plural of these nouns.

6 **Working with a text.** Determine the gender and plural of what you consider the ten most important nouns in a story you have read. Use any information the text provides. Summarize the text using all ten nouns.

Animal Plurals (see p. 164): Affen, Ameisen, Bären, Bienen, Böcke, Delphine, Drachen, Eichhörnchen, Enten, Esel, Eulen, Falken, Finken, Fliegen, Flöhe, Frösche, Füchse, Gänse, Gemsen, Giraffen, Haie (Haifische), Hähne, Hühner, Hunde, Igel, Jaguare, Kamele, Katzen, Kater, Kröten, Kühe, Lämmer, Löwen, Maulwürfe, Mäuse, Motten, Mücken (Moskitos), Nilpferde, Orang-Utans, Panther, Papageien, Pinguine, Pferde, Ratten, Schafe, Schlangen, Schmetterlinge, Schweine, Säue (Sauen), Seehunde, Spinnen, Stiere, Stinktiere, Strauße, Tausendfüßler, Tiger, Uhus, Vögel, Wale (Walfische), Waschbären, Wellensittiche, Wölfe, Ziegen

13 Adjectives

13.1 Adjectives Without Endings

1. Adjectives (**das Adjektiv, -e**) provide additional information about nouns and pronouns. When they provide this information via the linking verbs **sein, werden,** and **bleiben,** that is, as *predicate adjectives,* they do not have endings.

Die Stadt Rosenheim *ist* **klein.**	*The city of Rosenheim is small.*
Dieses Problem *wird* jetzt **kompliziert.**	*This problem is now becoming complicated.*

2. In German, many adjectives can also be used without endings as adverbs.

Der Schnee fiel **leise.**	*The snow fell gently.*
Du mußt **fleißig** lernen.	*You must study diligently.*

13.2 Adjectives with Endings

When adjectives are followed by the nouns they modify, they are called *attributive adjectives* and require endings. To learn these endings, it is first necessary to know the endings of the articles (**der-** and **ein-**words).

A. *Articles* (der- *and* ein-*Words*)

1. The **der**-words are all the forms of the definite article and of **dieser, jeder, jener, mancher, solcher,** and **welcher** (see 5.3). The endings of **der**-words are called *primary* endings, since they signal specific information about the number, gender, and case of a following noun.

2. The **ein**-words are all forms of the indefinite article and of **mein, dein, sein, ihr, unser, euer, Ihr,** and **kein** (see 5.4). Except for three instances where **ein**-words have no ending (see next section), the endings of the **ein**-words are identical with those of the **der**-words and are thus also *primary.*

B. *Adjectives After* der- *and* ein-*Words*

1. If a **der**-word precedes an attributive adjective, the adjective no longer has to provide specific information about the number, gender, and case of the modified noun and thus takes a so-called *secondary* adjective ending. There are only two possible secondary endings: **-e** and **-en.**

Adjective Endings After **der-**Words

	Masc.	***Fem.***	***Neut.***
Nom.	der blau **e** Kuli	die klein **e** Lampe	das neu **e** Heft
Acc.	den blau **en** Kuli	die klein **e** Lampe	das neu **e** Heft
Dat.	dem blau **en** Kuli	der klein **en** Lampe	dem neu **en** Heft
Gen.	des blau **en** Kulis	der klein **en** Lampe	des neu **en** Heftes

	Pl.
Nom.	die alt **en** Bücher
Acc.	die alt **en** Bücher
Dat.	den alt **en** Büchern
Gen.	der alt **en** Bücher

2. If an **ein**-word has an ending and precedes an attributive adjective, the adjective takes a *secondary* ending (either **-e** or **-en**). If an **ein**-word has no ending, the following adjective takes a *primary* ending to signal information as to the number, gender, and case of the modified noun.

Adjective Endings After **ein-**Words

	Masc.	***Fem.***	***Neut.***
Nom.	ein jung **er** Lehrer	eine gut **e** Ärztin	ein lieb **es** Mädchen
Acc.	einen jung **en** Lehrer	eine gut **e** Ärztin	ein lieb **es** Mädchen
Dat.	einem jung **en** Lehrer	einer gut **en** Ärztin	einem lieb **en** Mädchen
Gen.	eines jung **en** Lehrers	einer gut **en** Ärztin	eines lieb **en** Mädchens

	Pl.
Nom.	seine klug **en** Freunde
Acc.	seine klug **en** Freunde
Dat.	seinen klug **en** Freunden
Gen.	seiner klug **en** Freunde

C. *Adjectives Without Preceding* der- *or* ein-*Words*

If no **der-** or **ein-**word precedes an adjective and a noun, then the adjective must have a *primary* ending to signal number, gender, and case of the noun. (The two exceptions, highlighted in the chart below, are the genitive singular endings in the masculine and neuter. In these instances, primary endings are not needed, since the **-(e)s** ending of the noun itself provides the necessary information.)

Primary Endings of Adjectives

	Masc.	***Fem.***	***Neut.***
Nom.	gut **er** Saft	warm **e** Milch	kalt **es** Wasser
Acc.	gut **en** Saft	warm **e** Milch	kalt **es** Wasser
Dat.	gut **em** Saft	warm **er** Milch	kalt **em** Wasser
Gen.	gut **en** Saftes	warm **er** Milch	kalt **en** Wassers

	Pl.
Nom.	frisch **e** Getränke
Acc.	frisch **e** Getränke
Dat.	frisch **en** Getränken
Gen.	frisch **er** Getränke

D. *Adjective Ending Summary*

At least one modifier before a noun, either an article or an adjective, must have a primary ending. Compare the following examples.

	Singular		
	der-*Word*	**ein-*Word***	***No article***
	der alte Wein	ein alt**er** Wein	alt**er** Wein
	die große Macht	unser**e** große Macht	groß**e** Macht
(durch)	**das** echte Glück	ein echt**es** Glück	echt**es** Glück
(mit)	**dem** starken Willen	ein**em** starken Willen	stark**em** Willen
(mit)	**der** leisen Stimme	dein**er** leisen Stimme	leis**er** Stimme
	Plural		
	die neuen Städte	kein**e** neuen Städte	neu**e** Städte
(wegen)	**der** guten Spieler	sein**er** guten Spieler	gut**er** Spieler

E. *Additional Rules*

1. All adjectives in a series take the same ending.

Du hast schön**e** blau**e** Augen.	*You have beautiful blue eyes.*
Ich mag deine schön**en** blau**en** Augen.	*I like your beautiful blue eyes.*

2. Adjective stems ending in **-er** and **-el** drop the stem **e** when they have adjective endings.

   teuer: ein teu**res** Auto   dunkel: eine dun**kle** Farbe

3. The adjective **hoch** drops the **c** when it has an adjective ending.

   hoch: ein **hoher** Berg

4. The adjectives **rosa** *(pink),* **lila** *(lilac),* and **prima** *(great)* are invariable; they do not take endings.

   ein **rosa** Kleid   das **lila** Hemd   eine **prima** Idee

5. The adjectives **halb** and **ganz** do not take endings before names of towns, countries, and continents, unless the name requires an article (see 5.1).

   halb Europa *(half of Europe)*
   ganz Frankreich *(all of France)*
   BUT:
   die **ganze** Türkei *(all of Turkey)*
   die **halbe** Schweiz *(half of Switzerland)*

6. Adjectives of nationality behave like all other descriptive adjectives (**die Schweiz** is an exception; see below). They are capitalized only when used in proper names.

   deutsche Kultur   **französische** Städte   **russischer** Wodka
   BUT:
   Die **Deutsche** Bank   Die **Französischen** Eisenbahnen

7. Adjectives based on the names of cities or towns are formed by adding the suffix **-er** to the noun. All capitalization is retained. The adjective of nationality based on **die Schweiz** also follows this rule.

   Dieser Zug fährt zum **Frankfurter** Flughafen.
   Er hat ein **Schweizer** Bankkonto.

13.3 Limiting Adjectives

A. Andere, einige, mehrere, viele, wenige

The *plural* limiting adjectives **andere** *(other),* **einige** *(some),* **mehrere** *(several),* **viele** *(many),* and **wenige** *(few)* function like other adjectives when used attributively. They take either primary or secondary endings, depending upon whether or not there is a preceding **der**-word or **ein**-word with a primary ending. Any following adjectives take the same endings as well.

Hier gibt es viel**e** interessant**e** Geschäfte.	*There are many interesting stores here.*
Hast du seine viel**en** interessant**en** Briefmarken gesehen?	*Have you seen his many interesting stamps?*

B. Viel, wenig, etwas

The *singular* limiting adjectives **viel** *(much)*, **wenig** *(little)*, and **etwas** *(some)* usually do not take endings; any subsequent adjectives require primary endings.[1]

Wir hörten **viel** laut**es** Gelächter.	*We heard much loud laughter.*
Er trank **wenig** kalt**e** Milch aber **etwas** frisch**en** Saft.	*He drank little cold milk, but some fresh juice.*

C. All-

1. **All-** functions as a **der**-word. It seldom occurs in the singular (see 5.3).
2. In the plural, **all-** takes primary endings; any adjectives following **all-** take the secondary ending **-en.**

Alle groß**en** Geschäfte haben jetzt Sommerschlußverkauf.	*All (the) large stores are now having summer sales.*

3. When **all-** (plural) precedes an article or possessive adjective, its ending is often omitted. The articles and possessive pronouns remain unaffected by **all(e),** but any following adjectives still require the secondary ending **-en.**

Hast du **all(e)** die komisch**en** Bilder gesehen?	*Did you see all the strange pictures?*
Er hat die Namen **all(er)** seiner neu**en** Schüler aufgeschrieben.	*He wrote down the names of all his new pupils.*

D. Ganz *Instead of* all-

Instead of **all-** (singular and plural), German often uses an article or possessive pronoun followed by **ganz** *(all, whole, complete)*. **Ganz** takes primary and secondary endings like most descriptive adjectives.

Er hat **den ganzen** Tag gearbeitet.	*He worked all day.*
Wir haben **unsere ganzen** nassen Sachen draußen gelassen.	*We left all our wet things outside.*

---

1. Occasionally **viel** and **wenig** do occur in the accusative and dative with optional endings: **mit viel(em) Ärger** *(with much aggravation)*; **nach wenig(em) Erfolg** *(after little success)*. The ending is not optional in the expression **vielen Dank.**

13.4 Adjectives Governing Cases

A. *Adjectives with the Dative or with* für + *Accusative*

1. The following adjectives normally require a noun or pronoun in the dative when used as predicate adjectives. The adjective follows the noun or pronoun.

(un)ähnlich	*(dis)similar, (un)like*	(un)klar	*(un)clear*
(un)bekannt	*(un)known*	nahe	*near, close*
(un)bequem	*(un)comfortable*	schuldig	*in debt (to owe)*
(un)bewußt	*(un)known (to)*	teuer	*expensive, valuable*
(un)dankbar	*(un)grateful*	überlegen	*superior*
fremd	*strange, alien*	wert	*worth, of value*
gehorsam	*obedient*		

Sie sieht *ihrer Mutter* sehr **ähnlich.**	*She looks very much like her mother.*
Sie war *ihrem Mann* in manchen Dingen **überlegen.**	*She was superior to her husband in many things.*
Deine Hilfe ist *mir* viel **wert.**	*Your help is worth a lot to me.*

2. Some common adjectives can be used either with the dative or with **für** + the accusative.

(un)angenehm	*(un)pleasant*	nützlich	*useful*
leicht	*easy*	peinlich	*embarrassing*
(un)möglich	*(im)possible*	(un)wichtig	*(un)important*

Dein Besuch war *ihm / für ihn* recht **angenehm.**	*Your visit was quite pleasant for him.*
Sein Benehmen ist *der Familie / für die Familie* sehr **peinlich.**	*His behavior is very embarrassing to/for the family.*
Es ist *mir / für mich* sehr **wichtig** zu wissen, ob sie kommt.	*It is very important to/for me to know whether she is coming.*

B. *Adjectives with the Genitive*

The following adjectives normally require a genitive noun or pronoun when used as predicate adjectives. The adjective follows the noun or pronoun. The three adjectives marked with an asterisk are also used with the dative, but with slightly different meanings (see A, above).

*sich *(dat.)* bewußt	*conscious of, aware of*	müde	*tired of*
gewiß	*certain of*	*(un)schuldig	*(not) guilty of*
		*wert	*worth, worthy of*

Ich war mir *der Folgen* einer solchen Tat **bewußt.**	*I was aware of the consequences of such an action.*
Die Mannschaft war *ihres Sieges* **gewiß.**	*The team was sure of its victory.*
Der Plan war *unserer Unterstützung* **wert.**[2]	*The plan was worth our support.*

13.5 Adjectives with Prepositional Complements

1. Some common adjectives occur in combination with a complementing prepositional phrase. The preposition is often different from what one might expect based upon English usage. The adjective comes either before or after the prepositional phrase.

arm / reich an *(dat.)*	*poor / rich in*
gewöhnt an *(acc.)*	*accustomed to*
interessiert an *(dat.)*	*interested in*
böse auf *(acc.)*	*angry at*
gespannt auf *(acc.)*	*in suspense about*
neidisch auf *(acc.)*	*envious of*
neugierig auf *(acc.)*	*curious about*
stolz auf *(acc.)*	*proud of*
verrückt auf *(acc.)*	*crazy about*
wütend auf *(acc.)*	*furious at*
durstig / hungrig nach	*thirsty / hungry for*
abhängig von	*dependent on*
begeistert von	*enthusiastic about*
überzeugt von	*convinced of*
blaß vor *(dat.)*	*pale from / with*
sicher vor *(dat.)*	*safe from*
bereit zu	*ready to do*
fähig zu	*capable of (doing)*

Manche Leute sind **verrückt auf** Sport.	*Many people are crazy about sports.*
Die Regierung war **von** ihrer Politik **überzeugt.**	*The government was convinced of its policy.*

2. In some instances, German speakers use the adjective **wert** with the accusative.

Berlin ist *eine* Reise **wert.** *Berlin is worth a trip.*

2. Many of these adjectives can also be used with an anticipatory **da**-construction (see 19.2), though the **da**-compound is often optional.

Bist du **(dazu)** bereit, uns zu helfen?	*Are you ready to help us?*
Ich bin **(darauf)** gespannt, was morgen geschehen wird.	*I am anxious to know what will happen tomorrow.*

13.6 Adjective Suffixes

Many descriptive adjectives are formed by adding suffixes to noun stems (and sometimes verb stems). Each suffix denotes some quality or aspect of the stem word. Knowing what the suffixes denote can aid in determining the meanings of adjectives.

A. *The Suffixes* -ig, -lich, -isch

These three suffixes denote *having the quality* expressed by the noun stem. Some nouns used with these suffixes require an umlaut.

1. **-ig** often corresponds to English *-y.*

das Blut:	**blutig**	*bloody*
die Lust:	**lustig**	*funny*
der Schatten:	**schattig**	*shadowy*
der Schlaf:	**schläfrig**	*sleepy*

2. **-lich** indicates that the adjective has the quality or appearance denoted by the noun stem.

der Ärger:	**ärgerlich**	*annoying*
der Frieden:	**friedlich**	*peaceful*
die Gefahr:	**gefährlich**	*dangerous*
die Natur:	**natürlich**	*natural*

COMPARE:
der Geist: **geistlich** *spiritual* **geistig** *intellectual*

3. **-isch** often corresponds to English *-ish, -cal,* or *-ic.* It is also common with nationalities and religions.

die Chemie:	**chemisch**	*chemical*
der Narr:	**närrisch**	*foolish*
der Franzose:	**französisch**	*French*
der Jude:	**jüdisch**	*Jewish*
der Katholik:	**katholisch**	*Catholic*

COMPARE:
das Kind: **kindisch** *childish* **kindlich** *childlike*

B. Other Common Suffixes

1. **-bar** corresponds to English *-ible, -able,* or *-ful.* It is often added to nouns or verb stems.

   der Dank: **dankbar** *thankful*
   die Sicht: **sichtbar** *visible*
   tragen: **tragbar** *portable*
   trinken: **trinkbar** *drinkable*

2. **-(e)n / ern** are used to create adjectives from nouns for materials, such as wood, metal, cloth. Some of these nouns require an umlaut in the adjective form.[3]

   das Glas: **gläsern** *of glass*
   das Holz: **hölzern** *wooden*
   das Silber: **silbern** *silver(y)*
   der Stahl: **stählern** *of steel*
   die Wolle: **wollen** *woolen*

3. **-haft** (*from* **haben**) denotes *having the quality or nature* of the stem noun.

   der Meister: **meisterhaft** *masterful / masterly*
   die Fabel: **fabelhaft** *fabulous*
   die Tugend: **tugendhaft** *virtuous*

4. **-los** indicates a *complete lack* of the quality expressed by the stem. It corresponds to English *-less.*

   die Hoffnung: **hoffnungslos** *hopeless*
   die Kraft: **kraftlos** *powerless*

5. **-reich / -voll** mean *full of* the quality expressed by the stem.

   die Hilfe: **hilfreich** *helpful* die Lehre: **lehrreich** *instructive*
   die Liebe: **liebevoll** *loving* der Wert: **wertvoll** *valuable*

6. **-sam** sometimes corresponds to English *-some.* It normally indicates a tendency to do the action expressed by a verb or noun stem.

   biegen: **biegsam** *flexible, pliable*
   die Mühe: **mühsam** *tiresome, laborious*
   sparen: **sparsam** *thrifty, frugal*

---

3. With some materials, German speakers often prefer a compound word to an adjective + noun.

   ein Glasauge (*instead of* **ein gläsernes Auge**)
   ein Holzbein (*instead of* **ein hölzernes Bein**)

* Übungen

A **Welche Endung fehlt?** Ergänzen Sie die Adjektive durch die fehlenden Endungen.

1. der jung___ Nachbar; unser alt___ Lehrer; jung___ Freund
2. aus einem voll___ Glas; aus der leer___ Flasche; aus warm___ Milch
3. durch ein groß___ Feld; durch das hoh___ Gras; durch tief___ Wasser
4. trotz des heiß___ Wetters; trotz eines klein___ Sturms; trotz groß___ Kälte *(f.)*
5. die reich___ Familien; ihre verwöhnt___ *(spoiled)* Kinder; arm___ Leute
6. während der lang___ Nächte; keine warm___ Nachmittage; kurz___ Wintertage
7. ein braun___ Tisch; sein rot___ Buch; blau___ Himmel

B **Anders ausdrücken.** Beenden Sie die Sätze. Verwenden Sie Adjektive ohne Artikelwörter.

Beispiel: Der Wein, den er trinkt, ist sehr herb. Er trinkt . . .
Er trinkt herben Wein.

1. Das Wetter ist heute recht heiß. Wir haben heute . . .
2. Die Blumen in meinem Garten sind sehr schön. In meinem Garten wachsen . . .
3. Die Leute, bei denen er wohnt, sind sehr freundlich. Er wohnt bei . . .
4. Der Schnee vor dem Haus ist sehr hoch. Vor dem Haus liegt . . .
5. Ihre Familie ist sehr gut. Sie kommt aus . . .
6. Wenn das Wetter schlecht ist, wandern wir nicht. Wir wandern nicht bei . . .

C **Kluge Sprüche.** Die folgenden Sprüche sind noch nicht ganz richtig. Berichtigen Sie die Sprüche, indem Sie passende Adjektive aus der Liste einsetzen.

Beispiel: Liebe rostet nicht.
***Alte** Liebe rostet nicht.*

alt	schlecht
geschenkt *(given as a gift)*	still
gut	voll
lang	

1. Ein Bauch *(m. belly)* studiert nicht gern.
2. Rat *(m. advice)* ist teuer.
3. Lügen haben Beine.
4. Einem Gaul *(m. horse)* schaut man nicht ins Maul.
5. Wasser sind tief.
6. Wer aus Liebe heiratet, hat Nächte aber Tage.

D **Nützliche Ausdrücke.** Ergänzen Sie die Ausdrücke durch passende Adjektive aus der Liste.

best-	gut	laut	offen
falsch	hoch	nett	schön
groß	lang	niedrig	zweit

Beispiel: Freunde haben
nette Freunde haben

1. ein Gesicht machen
2. Schulden *(debts)* machen
3. Menschen kennenlernen
4. einen Nachmittag verbringen
5. mit Stimme schreien
6. in den Jahren sein
7. wegen des Preises kaufen
8. mit Karten spielen
9. eine Note bekommen
10. die Geige spielen
11. aufs Pferd setzen
12. Lärm *(noise)* machen

E **Altersstufen.** Wie geht's weiter? Verwenden Sie Adjektive mit oder ohne Artikelwörter.

Beispiel: Mit fünf Jahren spielt man mit . . .
Mit fünf Jahren spielt man mit hübschen Spielsachen.

1. Mit zehn Jahren freut man sich auf *(acc.)* . . .
2. Zwanzig kommt, und man träumt von . . .
3. Dreißigjährige hoffen auf *(acc.)* . . .
4. Vierzig ist man und plant . . .
5. Erreicht hat man mit fünfzig . . .
6. Mit sechzig genießt man . . .
7. Was hat man mit siebzig schon alles gesehen! Zum Beispiel, . . .
8. Achtzig Jahre zählt man und denkt an *(acc.)* . . .
9. Wer neunzig wird, freut sich über . . .

F **Ein prima Leben.** Für Ines gibt es immer nur das Beste. Ergänzen Sie die Sätze mit Adjektiven aus der Liste.

ganz	Paris
hoch	prima
holländisch	teuer
lila	Schweizer

Beispiel: Ihre Kleidung kommt direkt aus Paris. Sie trägt ____ Kleidung.
*Sie trägt **Pariser** Kleidung.*

1. Ihr Geld hat sie in einem ____ Sparkonto in Zürich.
2. Sie trägt Schuhe von ____ Qualität.

3. Für Kleidung gibt sie sehr viel Geld aus. Selbstverständlich trägt sie einen ____ Ledermantel.
4. Der Käse, den sie einkauft, kommt aus Holland, denn sie ißt ____ Käse besonders gern.
5. Sie fährt einen ____ BMW.
6. Auf ihren Einkaufstouren reist sie jedes Jahr durch ____ Europa.
7. Ines führt ein ____ Leben!

G **Ob *viel* oder *wenig*, Graz hat's!** Ergänzen Sie die Endungen.

In der Grazer Altstadt gibt es viel____ sehr gut____ Restaurants. Dort kann man vor allem im Sommer einig____ nett____ Stunden im Freien sitzen und mit Leuten plaudern. Abends sucht man vielleicht am besten einig____ der nicht wenig____ gemütlich____ Studentenkneipen auf, wo eine gut____ Stimmung herrscht *(prevails)*. Die viel____ Touristen, die nach Graz kommen, können diese Hauptstadt der Steiermark mit wenig____ Geld aber viel____ Zeit schon richtig genießen.

H ***Alles* und *ganz*.** Machen Sie fünf Aussagen mit **all-** + Possessivpronomen (**mein-**, **dein-**, usw.). Dann drücken Sie Ihre Aussagen durch den Gebrauch von **ganz-** anders aus.

Beispiele: *Ich habe **all mein** Taschengeld für dieses Semester schon ausgegeben.*
*Ich habe **mein ganzes** Geld für dieses Semester schon ausgegeben.*

***Alle meine** Freunde lieben Brahms.*
***Meine ganzen** Freunde lieben Brahms.*

I **Dativ oder Genitiv?** Drücken Sie die Sätze durch den Gebrauch von Adjektiven aus der Liste anders aus. Einige Adjektive müssen Sie mehr als einmal benutzen.

(un)bekannt	müde
dankbar	nützlich
fremd	(un)schuldig
gewiß	wert

Beispiel: Dieser Vorschlag hilft den Leuten wenig.
Dieser Vorschlag ist den Leuten nicht sehr nützlich.

1. Von den finanziellen Schwierigkeiten unseres Nachbarn wußten wir nichts.
2. Der Angeklagte *(accused)* konnte beweisen, daß er den Mord nicht begangen *(committed)* hatte.
3. Er muß einem Sportgeschäft noch viel Geld zahlen.
4. Wir sind sehr froh, daß du uns geholfen hast.
5. Deine Ausreden *(excuses)* möchten wir uns nicht mehr anhören.
6. Ihr Verständnis für seine Probleme bedeutete ihm viel.
7. An eine solche Arbeitsweise war die Frau nicht gewöhnt.
8. Sie zweifelte nicht an ihrem Erfolg.
9. Sein neuer Roman verdient *(merits)* unsere Aufmerksamkeit.

J **Welche Präposition?** Schreiben Sie Modellsätze mit den folgenden Adjektiven + Präposition.

Beispiel: interessiert
Ich bin ***an*** *der europäischen Politik interessiert.*

1. arm; reich
2. böse; stolz
3. verrückt; wütend
4. begeistert; überzeugt
5. bereit; sicher

K **Exportdefizite.** Welche ausländischen Produkte kaufen oder benutzen Sie und Ihre Familie? Machen Sie fünf Aussagen.

Beispiele: *Wir haben einen japanischen Fernseher.*
Zu Hause essen wir gern holländischen Käse.

L **Was ist das?** Suchen Sie eine passende Aussage aus der zweiten Spalte *(column).*

Beispiel: ein schweigsamer Mensch
Man hört ihn selten.

1. sparsame Menschen	a. Vorsicht!
2. eine friedliche Epoche	b. Das Leben ist immer schön.
3. ein lehrreicher Satz	c. 25 Jahre!
4. ein bissiger Hund	d. Davon kann man etwas lernen.
5. traumhafter Schnee	e. Sie sind sicher nicht faul.
6. eine krankhafte Person	f. Endlich keine Kriege mehr!
7. ein schwächlicher Mensch	g. Wer den Pfennig nicht ehrt . . .
8. sorgenlose Kinder	h. Waren Sie schon beim Psychiater?
9. arbeitsame Menschen	i. Der heißt sicher nicht Arnold S.
10. silberne Hochzeit	j. Ja, Pulver bis zu den Knien!

M **Anders ausdrücken.** Drücken Sie den Inhalt der Sätze mit Adjektiven anders aus.

Beispiele: Manche Wörter kann man nicht übersetzen.
Manche Wörter sind nicht ***übersetzbar.***

Meine Eltern sparen viel.
Meine Eltern sind sehr ***sparsam.***

1. Man kann dieses Radio leicht tragen.
2. Es hat keinen Sinn, mehr Atomwaffen zu produzieren.
3. Die Zahl 12 kann man durch 2, 3, 4 und 6 teilen.
4. Während einer Rezession haben manche Menschen keine Arbeit.
5. Ein gutes Medikament wirkt sofort.
6. Willi hat ein Bein aus Holz.
7. Der Weltraum hat keine Luft.
8. Wir fuhren gestern auf einer Bergstraße mit vielen Kurven.
9. Ideen kann man nicht sehen, aber man kann sie denken.

* Anwendung

A **Alles verrückt!** Vielleicht kennen Sie die Geschichte auf englisch, die so beginnt: *There was a crooked man and he went a crooked mile.* Erzählen Sie eine solche Geschichte mündlich und mit dem Adjektiv **verrückt** oder mit einem anderen Adjektiv, das Ihnen besonders gefällt.

Beispiel: Es waren einmal ein verrückter Herr und eine verrückte Frau. Sie wohnten in einem verrückten Haus und hatten verrückte Kinder. Ihre verrückten Kinder gingen in eine verrückte Schule, wo sie mit anderen verrückten Kindern spielten. Sie trugen auch . . .

B **Sich etwas genau merken.** Arbeiten Sie mit einem Partner / einer Partnerin. Er / sie zeigt Ihnen etwa zehn Sekunden lang ein Bild. Was können Sie jetzt mit Adjektiven noch genau beschreiben, wenn Sie das Bild nicht mehr sehen?

Variante: Ihr Professor / Ihre Professorin zeigt allen im Kurs kurz ein Bild. Welche Partnergruppe kann sich die meisten Dinge merken und sie danach mit Adjektiven beschreiben?

C **Von der guten (oder schlechten) Seite sehen.** Diskutieren Sie mit anderen Leuten im Kurs die guten oder schlechten Seiten Ihrer Universität / Schule und der Stadt, in der Sie jetzt leben. Betonen Sie positive *und* negative Aspekte und verwenden Sie viele Adjektive.

REDEMITTEL

positiv

Ich finde, die Stadt hat . . .
Besonders [schön] finde ich . . .
Warst du schon in . . .?
Mir gefällt / gefallen hier vor allem . . .
Die vielen . . . finde ich . . .
Man darf auch . . . nicht vergessen.

negativ

Das meinst du, aber ich sehe das anders.
Aber and(e)rerseits gibt es nur wenig / wenige . . .
Besonders deprimierend *(depressing)* finde ich . . .
Vor allem stört / stören mich . . .
Die vielen . . . finde ich . . .
Man darf auch nicht übersehen, daß . . .

* Schriftliche Themen

Tips zum Schreiben ***Writing with Adjectives***

A text with just nouns and verbs is like a picture in black and white; only adjectives can turn it into color. With adjectives you can convey *how* you view or react to the persons, things, or events you write about. When beginning a composition, write the first draft without adjectives. Next, check to see that all articles and nouns are in the proper cases. Then add the adjectives that best describe your topics and situations.

A **Werbung.** Sie studieren ein Jahr an einer deutschsprachigen Universität und organisieren eine Ferienreise für interessierte Studenten. Sie müssen eine kurze Werbeschrift *(prospectus)* zusammenstellen. Beschreiben Sie das Ferienziel so positiv wie möglich.

Beispiel: Wir fliegen im April nach Minorca! Unser preiswertes Hotel–selbstverständlich mit Vollpension!–liegt an einem traumhaft schönen Strand in der Nähe des sonnigen Städtchens Ciudadela. Tag und Nacht bietet das Hotel ein reiches Angebot an Sport- und Unterhaltungsmöglichkeiten. Auch für seine vorzügliche Küche ist das Hotel weit und breit bekannt . . . usw.

GANZJAHRESZIEL DOMINIKANISCHE REPUBLIK

Vom Geheimtip zum Ferientip

Wir liegen an einem zauberhaft schönen Strand. Das warme, blaue Meer rollt in sanften Wellen heran. Hoch über uns wiegen sich als natürliche Sonnenschirme die Wipfel der Palmen in der leichten Brise. Eine barfüßige Schönheit bringt einen Rumdrink mit gestoßenem Eis. Das Glas is der Anblick mach der Dominika

B **Ein merkwürdiger** *(remarkable)* **Traum.** Beschreiben Sie einen merkwürdigen Traum, den Sie einmal hatten. Wenn Sie sich an keinen Ihrer Träume erinnern, können Sie vielleicht einen tollen Traum erfinden.

Beispiel: Einmal hatte ich einen ganz tollen Traum. Ich fuhr an einem warmen Sommerabend in einem kleinen Boot auf einem dunklen See. Um den See herum standen hohe Berge, und im Westen ging eine rote Sonne gerade hinter den Bergen unter. Wie ich nun dort saß, erschien *(appeared)* plötzlich über mir ein riesiger *(gigantic)* schwarzer Vogel mit . . . usw.

C **Bildhaft beschreiben.** Gehen Sie an einen Ort, der Ihnen gut gefällt. Nehmen Sie Papier und etwas zum Schreiben mit. Beschreiben Sie diesen Ort. Beginnen Sie Ihre Beschreibung mit *einem* Gegenstand an diesem Ort. Erweitern Sie dann

Ihr Blickfeld allmählich *(gradually)*, bis Sie in die Ferne blicken. Nennen Sie erst im letzten Satz Ihrer Beschreibung diesen Ort.

Beispiel: An diesem Ort steht ein kleiner Baum mit graugrünen Nadeln. Der Baum ist so groß wie ein erwachsener Mensch, und um den Baum liegt ein breiter Rasen. Hinter dem Rasen kommt ein steinernes Haus mit einem hübschen Blumengarten davor. Vom Haus aus hat man einen Ausblick auf . . . usw.

Wortschatz 13

ausgezeichnet	abscheulich
erstklassig	armselig
glänzend	böse
+ *other positive reactions*	+ *other negative reactions*

1. The following adjectives and adverbs describe very positive reactions and emotions.

ausgezeichnet excellent
erstklassig first-rate
fabelhaft fabulous, marvelous, incredible
glänzend splendid, magnificent, brilliant
großartig splendid, magnificent, marvelous
herrlich splendid, magnificent, lovely
klasse great
phantastisch fantastic
prächtig splendid, magnificent, sumptuous
prima great, first-rate
toll fantastic, incredible, terrific
vorzüglich superior, excellent choice, exquisite
wunderbar splendid, wonderful, marvelous

2. The following adjectives and adverbs describe very negative reactions and emotions.

abscheulich disgusting, revolting, repulsive
armselig poor, pitiful, wretched, miserable
böse bad, evil, wicked
gräßlich, **grauenhaft** dreadful, ghastly, hideous
grausig ghastly, gruesome, horrid
häßlich ugly, nasty, hideous

entsetzlich, **fürchterlich**, **furchtbar**, **schrecklich** — dreadful, frightful, horrible, awful, terrible

erbärmlich pitiful, miserable, wretched

gehässig spiteful, hateful, malicious

lächerlich ridiculous, ludicrous, absurd

scheußlich abominable, revolting, foul

widerlich disgusting, repugnant, repulsive, nauseating

ÜBUNGEN

A **Ein toller Mensch.** Drücken Sie die Sätze viel stärker aus.

Beispiel: Sie ist ein netter Mensch.
Sie ist ein großartiger Mensch.

1. Sie wohnt in einem schönen Haus mit einem hübschen Garten.
2. Sie fährt auch einen guten Wagen.
3. Sie schreibt interessante Bücher.
4. Sie hat einen angenehmen Ehemann.
5. Sie kann auch gut Klavier spielen.

Wie können Sie diese Frau in einigen weiteren Sätzen beschreiben?

B **Ach schrecklich!** Erfinden Sie eine böse Hexe für ein Märchen. Beschreiben Sie Aussehen, Stimme, Wohnung, Kinder usw. Verwenden Sie Adjektive aus **Wortschatz 13** und mindestens sechs verschiedene Verben.

Beispiel: Im Wald wohnte eine schreckliche alte Hexe in einer armseligen Hütte. Sie hatte . . . und trug . . . usw.

Zusammenfassung 13

Rules to Remember

1. Attributive adjectives have endings.
2. The endings of the definite articles (**der, die, das**) are so-called *primary* endings; they indicate case, number, and gender of the modified noun.
3. The article **ein** with no ending is not a primary ending, but all other **ein**-endings are primary endings.
4. If an article (**der**-word or **ein**-word) with a primary ending precedes an adjective, the adjective takes a so-called *secondary* ending (**-e** or **-en**).
5. If no article with a primary ending precedes an adjective, the adjective takes a primary ending.

Activities

1 **Class game.**[1] While music is playing or the instructor is clapping, walk around the room observing the other students' clothes, hair, rings, etc. When the music or clapping stops, pair up back-to-back with the person standing nearest to you and make statements about that person's clothing and general appearance from memory. Your partner will correct you as necessary. Use adjectives attributively.

Beispiel: STUDENT A: Du trägst eine grüne Bluse und goldene Ohrringe, nicht wahr?
STUDENT B: Meine Bluse ist grün, aber ich trage keine goldenen Ohrringe!

2 **Adding adjectives.** Read aloud a page from a story in German with which you are already familiar. As you read, insert adjectives before every noun that does not already have a modifying adjective. Vary your choice of adjectives, but try to remain true to the story. Through your choice of modifiers, give the story your own particular slant.

3 **Associations.** Write on a piece of paper the names of one country or location, one famous person, and one event (concert, athletic contest, etc.). Divide into groups of four. Read one item from your list and have everyone in the group give an immediate association with that word. Go around the group as many times as possible reading your cues.

Beispiel: STUDENT A: die Alpen
STUDENT B: hohe Berge, viel Schnee, schöner Urlaub

4 **Describing.** Describe to the class what you like / dislike about your hometown or the town you are now living in. Use adjectives attributively.

5 **Describing persons.** Describe out loud someone you admire. Use some attributive adjectives.

6 **Working with a text.** Discuss or describe the physical and personality traits of the main characters in a story you know. Use attributive adjectives whenever possible.

---

1. For this activity, I am indebted to Friederike Klippel, *Keep Talking. Communicative fluency activities for language teaching.* (translation), Cambridge University Press, 1984. Activity No. 11.

14 Comparative and Superlative

14.1 Comparative and Superlative Forms

A. *Regular Forms*

1. In German, almost all adjectives and adverbs, regardless of length, add **-er** to form the comparative and **-(e)st** to form the superlative.

2. German does *not* have forms equivalent to English *more* and *most* used with adjectives and adverbs of more than two syllables.

lächerlich	*ridiculous*
lächerlich**er**	*more ridiculous*
lächerlich**st-**	*most ridiculous*

3. German does occasionally use the comparative **weniger** + adjective, which corresponds to English *less.*

   Sie ist **weniger fleißig** als er. *She is less diligent than he.*

4. Adjectives and adverbs ending in **-e** add only an **r** in the comparative, while adjectives and adverbs ending in **-el** or **-er** drop the interior **e** in the comparative, but not in the superlative.

dunkel	*dark*	dunk**ler**	dunkelst-
leise	*faint*	leise**r**	leisest-
teuer	*costly*	teu**rer**	teuerst-

5. Adjectives and adverbs ending in **-d, -t, -s, -ß, -z,** or **-sch** generally add an **e** before the **-st** superlative suffix.

laut	*loud*	laut**est-**
stolz	*proud*	stolz**est-**

heiß	*hot*	heiß**est-**
hübsch	*pretty*	hübsch**est-**

6. Adjectives and adverbs ending in **-end** or **-isch** do not add an **e** before the **-st** suffix.

spannend	*exciting*	spannend**st-**
altmodisch	*old-fashioned*	altmodisch**st-**

B. Umlauted and Irregular Forms

1. A limited number of monosyllabic adjectives and adverbs take an umlaut in the comparative and superlative.

alt	*old*	**ä**lter	**ä**ltest-
jung	*young*	j**ü**nger	j**ü**ngst-
kalt	*cold*	k**ä**lter	k**ä**ltest-
warm	*warm*	w**ä**rmer	w**ä**rmst-
klug	*smart*	kl**ü**ger	kl**ü**gst-
dumm	*dumb*	d**ü**mmer	d**ü**mmst-
kurz	*short*	k**ü**rzer	k**ü**rzest
lang	*long*	l**ä**nger	l**ä**ngst-
schwach	*weak*	schw**ä**cher	schw**ä**chst-
stark	*strong*	st**ä**rker	st**ä**rkst-
hart	*hard*	h**ä**rter	h**ä**rtest-
krank	*sick*	kr**ä**nker	kr**ä**nkst-
oft	*often*	**ö**fter	**ö**ftest-
scharf	*sharp*	sch**ä**rfer	sch**ä**rfst-

2. Several adjectives form the comparative and superlative either with or without an umlaut.

gesund	*healthy*	ges**ü**nder / gesunder	ges**ü**ndest- / gesundest-
rot	*red*	r**ö**ter / roter	r**ö**test- / rotest-
schmal	*narrow*	schm**ä**ler / schmaler	schm**ä**lst- / schmalst-

3. Several adjectives have an irregular comparative or superlative or use different forms altogether.

groß	*large*	gr**ö**ßer	gr**ö**ßt-
gut	*good; well*	**besser**	**best-**
hoch	*high*	h**ö**her	h**ö**chst-
nahe	*near*	n**ä**her	n**ä**chst-
viel	*much*	**mehr**	**meist-**

4. The adverb **gern** (used with verbs to express the idea of liking to do something) has a comparative and a superlative derived from the adjective **lieb** *(dear)*.

   gern *gladly* **lieber** **am liebsten**

Steffi tanzt **gern,** aber ihre Schwester spielt **lieber** Skat.	*Steffi likes to dance, but her sister prefers to play skat.*
Boris spielt Schach **am liebsten.**	*Boris likes to play chess most of all.*

14.2 Uses of the Comparative and Superlative

A. *Comparative of Adjectives and Adverbs*

1. Comparatives of adjectives used as adverbs or as predicate adjectives do not take endings.

Sie spricht **lauter.** *(adverb)*	*She speaks louder.*
Er wird **größer.** *(predicate adjective)*	*He is becoming larger.*

2. Comparatives used attributively, that is, before nouns, take the same primary or secondary endings as any other adjective (see 13.2).

Sie hat ein **billigeres** Auto gekauft.	*She bought a less expensive car.*
Hans wohnt in einem **kleineren** Haus als seine Eltern.	*Hans lives in a smaller house than his parents.*

3. **Mehr** and **weniger** do not take adjective endings.

B. *Superlative of Adjectives*

1. Attributive adjectives in the superlative take the same primary or secondary endings as any other adjective (see 13.2).

Sie hat den **längsten** Aufsatz geschrieben.	*She wrote the longest composition.*
Jutta ist seine **älteste** Tochter.	*Jutta is his eldest daughter.*

2. If the noun after an adjective in the superlative is omitted but understood, the adjective still requires an ending.

Alle Studenten haben einen Aufsatz geschrieben, aber Franz hat den **interessantesten** eingereicht.	*All students wrote a composition, but Franz handed in the most interesting one.*

3. The prefix **aller-** *(of all)* is often added to superlatives for emphasis without any comparison necessarily implied, though one may be implied.

Er hat die **allerliebsten** Kinder.	*He has the most dear children.*

Spiegel, Spiegel an der Wand! Wer ist die **allerschönste** Frau im Land?	*Mirror, mirror on the wall! Who is the fairest woman of all?*

4. The superlative adjective **meist-** requires a definite article in situations where English *most* does not.

Es stimmt, daß **die meisten** Kinder in Amerika zuviel fernsehen.	*It is true that most children in America watch too much television.*

C. Superlative of Adverbs and Predicate Adjectives

1. Adverbs in the superlative require the prepositional construction **am (-)sten.**

Sie weiß es **am besten.**	*She knows it (the) best.*
Dieser Sessellift fährt **am schnellsten.**	*This chairlift goes (the) fastest.*

2. Predicate adjectives in the superlative may be expressed either attributively with endings or adverbially with the **am (-)sten** construction.

Von den Spielern in der Mannschaft ist Lothar **am stärksten** (*or:* **der stärkste**).	*(Of the players on the team, Lothar is the strongest.)*
Ich habe drei Söhne. Eric ist **am ältesten** (*or:* **der älteste**).	*I have three sons. Eric is the oldest (one).*

3. When two aspects of the same noun are compared in the superlative, only the **am (-)sten** construction is used.

Der Rhein ist in Deutschland **am längsten** und in Holland **am breitesten.**	*The Rhine is (at its) longest in Germany and (at its) widest in Holland.*

D. Absolute Comparatives and Superlatives

1. Comparatives can be used with no explicit comparison implied.

Sie war eine (etwas) **ältere** Frau.	*She was a (somewhat) older woman.*
Wir werden eine **längere** Reise machen.	*We will be taking a (somewhat) longer trip.*

2. Superlatives can be used to express a high degree of quality with no comparison implied.

Sie schreibt die **schönsten** Erzählungen.	*She writes the most beautiful stories.*
Ich habe gestern den **lustigsten** Witz gehört.	*I heard the funniest joke yesterday.*

E. Comparatives with als

1. German makes comparisons by combining the comparative with **als** *(than).*

Das Matterhorn ist **höher als** andere Berge in der Schweiz.	*The Matterhorn is higher than other mountains in Switzerland.*
Ein Tiger läuft **schneller als** ein Wildschwein.	*A tiger runs faster than a wild boar.*

2. In comparisons, the **als** phrase normally comes after verbal complements (see 1.1F).

Er kann höher springen **als** ich.	*He can jump higher than I.*
Sie hat den Satz genauer übersetzt **als** wir.	*She translated the sentence more precisely than we did.*

14.3 Other Types of Comparisons

1. German makes comparisons *without* the comparative by using **(nicht) so . . . wie** *([not] as / so . . . as).*

Die Schweiz ist **so groß wie** Ohio.	*Switzerland is as large as Ohio.*

2. This type of comparison can be modified by other adverbs such as **ebenso, genauso, fast, nicht ganz so, zweimal so,** etc.).

Düsseldorf wächst **nicht ganz so schnell wie** Köln.	*Dusseldorf is not growing quite as fast as Cologne.*

3. German expresses the equivalent of English phrases like *better and better, more and more, faster and faster* with **immer** plus an adjective or adverb in the comparative.

Es fällt **immer mehr** Schnee.	*More and more snow is falling.*
Unsere Professorin gibt uns **immer längere** Aufgaben.	*Our professor is giving us longer and longer assignments.*

4. German uses **je** + the comparative, followed by **desto** or **um so** and another comparative to express comparisons of the type *"The more the better"* or *"The bigger they are, the harder they fall."*

Je höher der Berg, **desto tiefer** / **um so tiefer** der Sturz.	*The higher the mountain, the farther the fall.*

5. The **je**-clause in a comparison is a dependent clause; any conjugated verb in this clause is in final position. The verb in the follow-up clause comes immediately after **desto** / **um so** + comparative.

Der Reichtum gleicht dem Seewasser; **je mehr** man davon *trinkt,* **desto durstiger** *wird* man. (A. Schopenhauer)

14.4 Other Superlative Constructions

1. The following superlative adverbs occur frequently in German.

frühestens *at the earliest*
höchstens *at (the) most*
meistens / meist *mostly*
mindestens *at least (with amounts)*
wenigstens / zumindest *at (the very) least*
möglichst *as . . . as possible*
spätestens *at the latest*

Hier kann man **frühestens** Ende November Ski laufen.	*Here one can ski at the earliest at the end of November.*
Hier wohnen **meistens / meist** Leute, die keine Kinder haben.	*There are mostly people living here who have no children.*

2. The adverb **mindestens** is used with amounts only; **wenigstens** (OR **zumindest**) is used in all other instances.

COMPARE:

Sie könnte uns **mindestens** *eine* Postkarte schicken.	*She could send us at least* ***one*** *postcard.*
Sie könnte uns **wenigstens** / **zumindest** eine Postkarte schicken.	*She could at (the very) least send us a postcard.*

3. The adverbs **äußerst** *(extremely, most)* and **höchst** *(highly)* add superlative emphasis to the base forms of adjectives.

Albert Schweitzers Leben war **äußerst / höchst** merkwürdig.	*Albert Schweitzer's life was extremely / most / highly remarkable.*

* Übungen

A **Formen üben.** Setzen Sie die Ausdrücke zuerst in den Komparativ, dann in den Superlativ.

Beispiele: ein alter Freund sein
ein ***älterer*** *Freund sein;* ***der älteste*** *Freund sein*

schnell laufen
schneller *laufen;* ***am schnellsten*** *laufen*

1. leise sprechen
2. mit großem Interesse zuhören
3. teuere Kleidung tragen

4. meiner jungen Tochter schreiben
5. gern bleiben
6. viel verdienen
7. ein warmes Herz haben
8. spannende Bücher lesen
9. gut arbeiten
10. in einem schönen Haus wohnen

B **Vergleiche.** Machen Sie jeweils zwei vergleichende Aussagen, eine mit **(nicht) so . . . wie** und eine mit **als** + Komparativ. Verwenden Sie die angegebenen Verben!

Beispiel: zwei Tiere
Ein Nilpferd ist ***nicht so*** *groß* ***wie*** *ein Elefant.*
Eine Spinne hat ***mehr*** *Beine* ***als*** *eine Biene.*

1. zwei Tiere
2. zwei Automarken *(makes of car)*
3. zwei Filmschauspieler(innen)
4. zwei Politiker(innen)
5. zwei Sportler(innen)
6. zwei Menschen, die Sie kennen

C **Mehr Vergleiche.** Bilden Sie fünf Aussagen mit attributiven Adjektiven im Komparativ. Wiederholen Sie kein Verb!

Beispiele: *Wir fahren ein* ***größeres*** *Auto als unsere Nachbarn.*
Mein Vater verdient ***mehr*** *Geld als meine Mutter.*

D **Unsere moderne Welt.** Die Welt ändert sich! Wird sie *immer besser* oder *immer schlechter?* Geben Sie bitte drei Argumente für jeden Standpunkt.

Beispiele: Besser: *Die Menschen leben jetzt immer länger.*
Schlechter: *Immer mehr Menschen sterben jetzt an AIDS.*

E **Sprüche machen.** Was meinen Sie?

Beispiel: Je älter . . .
Je älter man wird, desto mehr weiß man.

1. Je größer . . .
2. Je mehr man . . .
3. Je länger . . .
4. Je älter . . .
5. ein Spruch, der *Sie* besonders gut charakterisiert
6. ein Spruch, der einen Bekannten oder eine Bekannte von Ihnen treffend *(accurately)* charakterisiert
7. ein Spruch, der Ihre Professorin / Ihren Professor gut charakterisiert

F **Eine Welt der Superlative.** Machen Sie mindestens acht Aussagen. Verwenden Sie kein Adjektiv und kein Adverb mehr als einmal.

Beispiele: *Mt. Everest ist* ***der höchste*** *Berg.*
Der Jaguar läuft ***am schnellsten,*** *aber der Elefant hat* ***den längsten*** *Rüssel* (trunk).

THEMENVORSCHLÄGE

Edelsteine und Metalle (ein Diamant, das Gold, das Platin usw.)
Tiere (der Elefant, der Strauß *[ostrich]*, der Walfisch *[whale]* usw.)
Geographie (Berge, Seen, Länder, Flüsse, Meere, Wüsten *[deserts]* usw.)

G **Eine tolle Erbschaft** *(inheritance)*. Kurt hat DM 30.000.000 von einem reichen Onkel in der Schweiz geerbt. Wie lebt er jetzt? Machen Sie sechs Aussagen.

Beispiele: *Er fährt den* ***teuersten*** *Wagen.*
Er wohnt in dem ***schönsten*** *Haus.*
Er spielt Golf mit ***äußerst wichtigen*** *Politikern.*

Und was für ein Leben der Superlative würden *(would) Sie* mit einer solchen Erbschaft führen?

H **Aussagen.** Machen Sie fünf wahre Aussagen mit Adverbien im Superlativ (siehe 14.4).

Beispiele: *Ich stehe am Wochenende* ***meistens*** *erst sehr spät auf.*
Man sollte ***mindestens*** *eine Fremdsprache lernen.*

* Anwendung

A **Enthusiastischer Bericht.** Haben Sie neulich etwas besonders Schönes oder Interessantes erlebt? Erzählen Sie jemandem davon. Übertreiben *(exaggerate)* Sie ruhig ein bißchen, indem Sie Komparative und Superlative verwenden! Je enthusiastischer, desto besser! (Siehe auch **Wortschatz 13.**)

THEMENVORSCHLÄGE

eine Person	ein Film	eine Reise
ein Ort	eine Party	ein Kauf

Beispiel: Du, ich habe einen äußerst interessanten Tag erlebt. Wir waren in den tollsten Geschäften und haben die schönsten Sachen gesehen. Es war alles viel schöner, als ich mir vorher gedacht hatte. Das Beste habe ich aber noch gar nicht erwähnt . . . usw.

B **Eine bessere Alternative.** Versuchen Sie, jemanden im Kurs von einem Vorhaben *(plan of action)* abzubringen, indem Sie eine „bessere" Alternative vorschlagen.

THEMENVORSCHLÄGE

ein bestimmtes Auto kaufen
an einer bestimmten Universität studieren
eine bestimmte Fremdsprache lernen
in einer bestimmten Stadt wohnen
eine bestimmte Reise machen

REDEMITTEL

Ich finde . . . viel schöner / interessanter usw. als . . .
Ich glaube, das ist nicht so . . . wie . . .
Würdest du nicht lieber . . .?
Allerdings hat . . . schönere / nettere / interessantere usw. . . .
Eigentlich ist . . . besser / schöner usw.

KONZESSIONEN UND GEGENARGUMENTE

Das mag wohl richtig sein, was du sagst, aber . . .
Na gut, aber meinst du nicht, daß . . .?
Das schon *(that's true)*, aber du mußt auch . . .

* Schriftliche Themen

Tips zum Schreiben ***Comparing and Contrasting***

Comparisons and contrasts are often used to point out the similarities or differences between two subjects. You can contrast specific aspects of two subjects by alternating between them from sentence to sentence. Alternatively, you may choose to deal first with one subject at more length and then switch to the second subject, thereby dividing your paragraph or composition into two contrasting halves. In both methods, you can use the comparative of adjectives and adverbs to measure and contrast two subjects with respect to each other. When such comparisons express your opinion rather than absolute fact, then you should indicate this situation with phrases such as **ich finde,** or **meiner Meinung nach,** or **mir scheint es.**

A **Größer oder kleiner?** Möchten Sie lieber an einer großen oder einer kleinen Universität studieren? Führen Sie überzeugende *(convincing)* Argumente an. Verwenden Sie den Komparativ und den Superlativ.

Beispiel: Ich würde lieber an einer größeren Universität studieren, denn je größer die Universität, desto breiter das Angebot an interessanten Kursen und Programmen. Auf einem großen Campus findet man . . . Auf einem kleineren Campus dagegen *(on the other hand)* . . . usw.

B **Lieber Tierfreund!** Schreiben Sie einen Brief an die Zeitschrift *Der Tierfreund,* in dem Sie erzählen, warum Ihrer Meinung nach ein bestimmtes Tier (z.B. eine Katze) sich als Haustier besser eignet *(is suited)* als ein anderes (z.B. ein Hund).

Beispiel: Lieber Tierfreund,
meiner Meinung nach sind Fische die besten Haustiere, denn sie lernen viel schneller als Hunde, weil sie so oft in Schulen schwimmen. Sie miauen nicht so laut wie Katzen und fressen weniger als die meisten anderen Haustiere. Außerdem *(moreover)* sind Fische äußerst . . . Aus diesem Grunde empfehle ich . . . usw.

C **Heute und damals.** Ist Ihr Leben oder das Leben überhaupt im Laufe der letzten Jahre besser, schlechter, einfacher, komplizierter usw. geworden? Begründen Sie Ihre Antwort mit Vergleichen.

Beispiel: Ich glaube, daß es mir im Vergleich zu früher jetzt viel besser geht. Mir macht das Studium mehr Spaß als die Jahre in der Schule, und ich lerne interessantere Menschen kennen. Allerdings muß ich intensiver arbeiten, und ich habe weniger Freizeit. Im großen und ganzen aber finde ich . . . usw.

Wortschatz 14

breit / die Breite
flach / die Fläche
groß / die Größe

\+ *other adjective* ⟶ *noun derivations*

A number of common German feminine nouns ending in **-e** are derived from adjectives. Most of these nouns indicate dimension, size, strength, or personal quality.

breit	wide, broad	**die Breite**	width, breadth
flach	flat, level	**die Fläche**	surface
groß	large, great	**die Größe**	size, greatness
gut	good	**die Güte**	goodness
hart	hard	**die Härte**	hardness
hoch	high	**die Höhe**	height
kalt	cold	**die Kälte**	cold
kurz	short	**die Kürze**	shortness, brevity
lang	long	**die Länge**	length
nah	near	**die Nähe**	nearness, proximity
schwach	weak	**die Schwäche**	weakness
stark	strong	**die Stärke**	strength
tief	deep	**die Tiefe**	depth
warm	warm	**die Wärme**	warmth
weit	far; wide	**die Weite**	distance; width

ÜBUNGEN

A **Anders ausdrücken.** Drücken Sie die Sätze anders aus.

Beispiel: Dieser Brunnen *(well)* ist fünf Meter tief.
Dieser Brunnen hat eine Tiefe von fünf Metern.

1. Sie wohnt nah der Grenze.
2. Das Paket darf höchstens 60 cm breit sein.
3. Wir mögen es nicht, wenn es so kalt ist.
4. Ein Diamant ist unglaublich hart.
5. Wir haben kein Hemd *(shirt),* das für Sie groß genug ist.

B **Aussagen.** Machen Sie wahre Aussagen mit acht der Substantive in Wortschatz 14.

Beispiele: *Ich habe eine* ***Schwäche*** *für alte Uhren.*
Das Matterhorn hat eine ***Höhe*** *von mehr als 4.000 Metern.*
In der ***Kürze*** *liegt die Würze* (spice). (Brevity is the soul of wit).

Zusammenfassung 14

Rules to Remember

1. The comparative is formed by adding **-er** to the stem of an adjective or adverb **(klar, klarer).**
2. The superlative is formed by adding **(e)st-** to the stem of an adjective or adverb **(klar-, klarst-).**
3. Roughly twenty adjectives require a stem vowel umlaut in the comparative and superlative **(alt, älter, ältest-).**
4. The comparative and superlative forms of adjectives take adjective endings according to the normal adjective ending rules.
5. Adverbs must use the **am [-]sten** construction in the superlative **(am ältesten).** Predicate adjectives may use this construction as well.

Activities

1 **Comparisons.** One person calls out the name of a famous person to be compared with as many other famous people as possible. Other students make comparative statements, but they cannot repeat the verb **sein** or any adjective used by another student. The wittier the comparisons the better.

Beispiel: Madonna *macht bessere Interviews als . . .?*
Sie sieht exotischer aus als . . .?
Sie springt nicht so hoch wie . . .?
Sie singt schöner als . . .?

2 **Dead or alive.** Write a statement about a person, real or fictional, living or dead, who became famous by doing something better or worse than others. The class will try to guess who the famous person is.

Beispiele: *Er kämpfte klüger als Goliath.* (David)
Er tötete mehr Ehefrauen als andere Könige. (Heinrich der Achte von England)

3 **Comparing yourself with others.**[1] Find ten ways to compare yourself to a partner. Do not restrict yourself to physical characteristics. Ask as many questions as necessary. Your partner will also make a list of comparisons to you.

4 **Comparing things.** Pick two totally disparate objects (for example, **ein Elefant und ein Bleistift; ein Auto und ein Schuh**). Brainstorm with other students for possible ways of comparing these objects. The more outlandish the better.

Beispiele: der Elefant / der Bleistift
Ein Elefant ist dicker als ein Bleistift.
Mit einem Bleistift kann man besser schreiben als mit einem Elefanten.

der Schuh / das Auto
Ein Schuh ist nicht so groß wie ein Auto.
Es können mehr Leute in einem Auto sitzen als in einem Schuh.

5 **Superlatives in your life.** Make a list of superlatives in your life (your best friend, your favorite course, the worst book you ever read, etc.). Share these superlatives with other students.

6 **Working with a text or film.** Conduct a class discussion on the comparative merits of several stories or films you have read or seen this year.

---

1. For this and the following activity I am indebted to Penny Ur and Andrew Wright, *Five-Minute Activities. A resource book of short activities.* Cambridge University Press, 1992.

15 Questions and Interrogatives

15.1 Yes-No Questions

1. Questions requiring a *yes* or *no* answer begin with the conjugated verb, which is followed by the subject. Separable prefixes retain their normal position at the end of the sentence.

Hast du Franz gesehen?	*Have you seen Franz?*
Nehmen Sie unser Angebot **an?**	*Do you accept our offer?*

2. In conversation, yes-no questions are frequently posed as statements in an inquiring tone, often followed by **nicht wahr?** or **nicht?** *(isn't it? don't you? haven't they?* etc.)[1]

Liechtenstein liegt südlich von Deutschland, **nicht (wahr)?**	*Liechtenstein is south of Germany, isn't it?*

3. German uses the particle **doch** (see 25.2) to provide a *yes* answer to a question posed negatively.

Habt ihr keine Bananen?	*Don't you have any bananas?*
—Doch!	*Oh yes, we do!*

1. In Southern Germany and Austria, **gelt?** or **gel?** are often used colloquially instead of **nicht wahr?**

Du kommst morgen, **gel?**	*You're coming tomorrow, aren't you?*

15.2 Interrogative Words

Questions requiring an answer other than *yes* or *no* begin with an interrogative word and are followed immediately by the conjugated verb in second position.

Wann kommt der nächste Zug?	*When does the next train come?*
Wer hat den Tisch gedeckt?	*Who set the table?*

A. Wer *and* was

1. The interrogative pronoun **wer** *(who)* has masculine case forms only, but it refers to people of either gender. **Was** *(what)* has only one form, which is both nominative and accusative; it is also occasionally used after dative and genitive prepositions.

	Persons		***Objects or Ideas***	
Nom.	**wer?**	*who?*	**was?**	*what?*
Acc.	**wen?**	*who(m)?*	**was?**	*what?*
Dat.	**wem?**	*(to) who(m)?*	**(mit) was?**	*(with) what?*
Gen.	**wessen?**	*whose?*	**(wegen) was?**	*(on account of) what?*

Wer kann uns helfen? *(nominative / subject)*	*Who can help us?*
Wen habt ihr im Restaurant getroffen? *(accusative / object)*	*Whom did you meet in the restaurant?*
Wem hat er die Theaterkarten gegeben? *(dative / indirect object)*	*To whom did he give the theater tickets?*
Wessen Buch liegt auf dem Boden? *(genitive / possessive)*	*Whose book is lying on the floor?*
Was macht solchen Lärm? *(nominative / subject)*	*What is making such a noise?*
Was siehst du? *(accusative / direct object)*	*What do you see?*

2. **Wer** and **was** are used with either singular or plural forms of the verb **sein,** depending upon whether the subsequent subject is singular or plural.

Wer *war* Konrad Adenauer?	*Who was Konrad Adenauer?*
Wer / **Was** *sind* die Grünen?	*Who / What are the Greens (German environmental party)?*

3. Prepositions are placed directly before the forms of **wer.** They cannot occur at the end of the sentence in interrogatives, as frequently happens in colloquial English.

An wen denkst du?	***Whom*** *are you thinking* ***about?***
Von wem hast du heute einen Brief bekommen?	***Whom*** *did you get a letter* ***from*** *today?*

4. Prepositions do not normally appear before **was** (see Section B, below).

5. Prepositions appearing before **wessen** determine the case of the subsequent noun, as indicated in the following examples by the adjective ending.

Für wessen neues Album hat Udo diese Lieder geschrieben? *(accusative)*	*For whose new album did Udo write these songs?*
Mit wessen großer Hilfe machte er diese Entdeckung? *(dative)*	*With whose great help did he make this discovery?*

B. Wo-*Compounds*

1. Using a preposition with **was** is considered quite colloquial and somewhat substandard; German normally uses a prepositional **wo(r)**[2]-compound instead. **Wo**-compounds refer to things, not to people.

Woran denkst du? (*very colloquial:* **An was** denkst du?)	*What are you thinking about?*
Worüber sprecht ihr? (*very colloquial:* **Über was** sprecht ihr?)	*About what are you talking?*
BUT:	
Über wen sprecht ihr?	*About whom are you talking?*

2. **Außer, hinter, ohne, seit, zwischen,** and the genitive prepositions cannot be used in **wo**-compounds. On the rare occasion when one might wish to pose a question with one of these prepositions, **was** must be used instead.

Ohne was bist du in die Schule gegangen?	*You went to school without what?*

C. Welch-

The interrogative article **welch-** *(which, what)* declines like the definite article (see 5.3B) and agrees with the noun to which it refers in gender, number, and case.

Welche Zeitung möchtest du lesen?	*Which newspaper would you like to read?*
Mit welchen Leuten haben Sie gesprochen?	*With which people did you speak?*

---

2. When the preposition begins with a vowel, an **r** is inserted for pronunciation purposes.

D. Was für (ein)

The preposition **für** in **was für (ein)** *(what kind of [a])* does not affect the case of a following article and noun; their case is determined by their function within the sentence.

Was für ein Mann war er? *(subject)*	*What kind of (a) man was he?*
Was für einen Wagen willst du kaufen? *(direct object)*	*What kind of a car do you want to buy?*
In **was für einem** Haus wohnt ihr? *(object of preposition)*	*In what kind of a house are you living?*
Was für Leuten hat Therese geholfen? *(dative plural)*	*What kind(s) of people did Theresa help?*

E. Adverbs

The following interrogative adverbs are quite common.

wann	*when*
wo	*where*
wohin; woher	*to where; from where*
warum, weshalb	*why*
wie	*how*
wie lange	*how long*
wieso	*how is it that*
wieviel	*how much*
wie viele	*how many*

Wohin gehen Sie? *(colloquial:* **Wo** gehen Sie **hin?)**	*Where are you going (to)?*
Woher kommen diese Leute? *(colloquial:* **Wo** kommen diese Leute **her?)**	*Where do these people come from?*
Wieso versteht sie deine Frage nicht?	*How is it that she does not understand your question?*

15.3 Indirect Questions

1. Indirect questions are introduced by a clause or question opener. The interrogative word functions like a subordinating conjunction (see 11.3) and the conjugated verb is in final position.

COMPARE:

Wo hast du das gelernt? *(direct)*	*Where did you learn that?*
Ich möchte gern wissen, **wo** du das gelernt **hast.** *(indirect)*	*I would like to know where you learned that.*

2. Indirect yes-no questions require **ob** *(if, whether)* as a subordinating conjunction.

Habt ihr den Vortrag verstanden? *(direct)*	*Did you understand the lecture?*
Darf ich fragen, **ob** ihr den Vortrag verstanden **habt?** *(indirect)*	*May I ask whether you understood the lecture?*

* Übungen

A ***Ja, nein,* oder *doch?*** Beantworten Sie diese Fragen. Vorsicht, manchmal ist mehr als eine Antwort möglich. Es kommt darauf an, wie *Sie* die Fragen verstehen, und was *Sie* sagen wollen.

1. Lebt Ihr Großvater nicht mehr?
2. Wissen Sie nicht, wie die Hauptstadt von Togo heißt?
3. Trinken Sie gewöhnlich keinen Wein zum Abendessen?
4. Hat Goethe nicht das Drama *Wilhelm Tell* geschrieben?
5. Hat Mozart nicht *Die Zauberflöte* komponiert?
6. Arbeiten in der Schweiz keine Ausländer?
7. Finden Sie diese Aufgabe nicht lustig?

B **Fragen.** Ergänzen Sie die Fragen durch passende **wer**-Formen **(wer, wen, wem, wessen).**

Beispiel: ____ hat das beste Examen geschrieben?
Wer hat das beste Examen geschrieben?

1. ____ hat Ihnen mit der Aufgabe geholfen?
2. ____ sind die anderen Leute in Ihrer Gesprächsgruppe?
3. Von ____ haben Sie von diesem Kurs erfahren?
4. Für ____ machen Sie Notizen?
5. ____ Aufsatz hat die Professorin für den besten gehalten?
6. ____ würden Sie in diesem Kurs gern näher kennenlernen?
7. ____ würden Sie diesen Kurs empfehlen?

C ***Wer, wen* und *wem.*** Stellen Sie drei Fragen an jemanden im Kurs. Verwenden Sie die Fragewörter **wer, wen** und **wem.** Sie können auch Präpositionen gebrauchen.

D **Bernds Entschluß.** Sie können das, was Sie gerade über Bernd gehört haben, kaum glauben und fragen noch einmal nach dem Satzteil in Kursivschrift.

Beispiele: Bernd hört jetzt *mit seinem Studium* auf.
***Womit** hört Bernd jetzt auf?*

Er will *mit seiner Freundin* auf eine Kommune ziehen.
***Mit wem** will er auf eine Kommune ziehen?*

1. Bernd interessiert sich *für einen alternativen Lebensstil.*
2. *An eine große Karriere* denkt er nicht mehr.
3. Er träumt *von einem idyllischen Leben auf dem Land.*
4. *Von einem Bauern* hat er ein Stück Land gepachtet *(leased).*
5. Dort möchte er *ohne Streß und Verpflichtungen (obligations)* leben.
6. Natürlich will er noch Kontakt *zu seinen Freunden* haben.
7. *Über Besuche von Bekannten* wird er sich jederzeit freuen.
8. Aber *von seiner bisherigen (previous) Lebensweise* nimmt er jetzt Abschied.

E **Gabis Eltern möchten einiges wissen.** Gabi kommt während des Semesters auf kurzen Besuch nach Hause. Ihre Eltern möchten einiges wissen. Ergänzen Sie die Fragen ihrer Eltern durch **welch-.**

1. ____ Kurse hast du belegt?
2. ____ Kurs gefällt dir am besten?
3. An ____ Tagen hast du Deutsch?
4. ____ Kurs findest du am schwierigsten?
5. Mit ____ Studentin wohnst du zusammen?

F **Mehr erfahren.** Sie möchten mehr über jemanden im Kurs wissen. Stellen Sie Fragen.

Beispiel: In was für . . .
In was für einem Haus wohnst du?

1. Was für . . .
2. In was für . . .
3. Mit was für . . .
4. Für was für . . .
5. Zu was für . . .

G **Fragen zu einem Thema stellen.** Stellen Sie Fragen an jemanden im Kurs über eine interessante Reise oder schöne Ferien, die er / sie einmal gemacht hat. Verwenden Sie die folgenden Fragewörter.

1. wohin
2. wer
3. wen
4. *Präposition* + wem / wen
5. was
6. wo-
7. wo
8. wie lange
9. warum
10. was für (ein-)

H **Ja, das möchte ich mal wissen.** Beenden Sie die Sätze, so daß die Aussagen für Sie eine Bedeutung haben. Verwenden Sie einige der folgenden Fragewörter.

Beispiele: Ich möchte wissen, . . .
Ich möchte wissen, ob wir morgen eine Prüfung haben.

Weiß jemand, . . .
Weiß jemand, wie alt unser(e) Professor(in) ist?

ob	was	wie viele
wann	wie	wer / wen / wem / wessen
warum	wieviel	wo / woher / wohin

1. Ich möchte wissen, . . .
2. Manchmal frage ich mich, . . .
3. Frag mich bitte nicht, . . .
4. Wer weiß, . . .
5. Ich weiß nicht, . . .
6. Ich möchte gar nicht wissen, . . .

* Anwendung

A **Interview.** Sie sollen für die Studentenzeitung jemanden im Kurs interviewen. Versuchen Sie jetzt im Gespräch, einiges über diese Person und ihre Interessen zu erfahren (etwa acht bis zehn Fragen). Gebrauchen Sie möglichst viele verschiedene Fragewörter! Verwenden Sie Redemittel in einigen Fragen und Reaktionen.

REDEMITTEL

Fragen	*Reaktionen*
Sag mal: . . .?	Das ist aber interessant!
Darf ich fragen, . . .?	Erzähl doch mehr davon!
Ich möchte (gern) fragen / wissen, . . .	Wirklich?
Kannst du sagen, . . .?	Echt? *(slang: Really?)*
Ich hätte gern gewußt, . . .	Ach was! *(Come on, really!)*
Stimmt es *(Is it true)*, daß . . .?	Das wußte ich gar nicht!

B **Gruppenarbeit: Fragen an Prominente.** Sie wollen in einem Brief Fragen an eine prominente Person stellen. Wem wollen Sie schreiben? Einigen Sie sich mit drei oder vier anderen Personen in einer Gruppe über acht bis zehn Fragen (mit acht bis zehn verschiedenen Fragewörtern!), die Sie an diese Person stellen könnten. Erzählen Sie im Kurs, welche Person Sie ausgewählt *(selected)* haben, und welche Fragen Ihre Gruppe stellen möchte.

VORSCHLÄGE

Politiker	Geschäftsleute	Filmschauspieler
Wissenschaftler	Autoren	Sportler

✱ Schriftliche Themen

Tips zum Schreiben ***Asking Rhetorical Questions***

When writing expository prose, you will normally formulate statements rather than posing questions. Sometimes, however, questions can be effective rhetorical devices, as they address readers directly, thus eliciting their involvement or response. With rhetorical questions, you should strive for a stylistic balance between direct and indirect questions.

A **Das möchte ich gern wissen.** Im Leben gibt es viele Fragen aber wenige Antworten. Was für Fragen haben Sie? Erzählen Sie. Verwenden Sie direkte und indirekte Fragen dabei.

Beispiel: Ich möchte gern wissen, warum die Völker der Erde nicht glücklich zusammenleben können. Wieso müssen sie einander hassen und sooft Krieg gegeneinander führen? Ich verstehe auch nicht, wodurch man diese Situation vielleicht ändern könnte. Wie lange werden wir Menschen . . .? usw.

B **Standpunkt.** Äußern Sie sich zu einem Problem an Ihrer Universität / Schule, in Ihrer Stadt, in Ihrem Land oder in der Welt, das Sie für besonders dringend *(urgent)* halten *(consider)*. Bringen Sie Ihren Standpunkt durch den Gebrauch von rhetorischen Fragen und Fragen an die Leser ganz deutlich zum Ausdruck.

Beispiel: Ich halte die Armut in diesem Land für ein großes Problem. Warum können wir dieses Problem nicht lösen? Weil die Menschen . . . Manchmal muß ich mich fragen, . . . Stimmt es also doch *(after all)*, daß wir . . .? Zum Schluß *(in the end)* bleibt noch die große Frage: „Wann . . .“

Wortschatz 15

halten	aufhören
anhalten	stehenbleiben
aufhalten	stoppen

1. **Halten** *(intransitive)* means *to come to a stop* (with persons or vehicles).

Hier wollen wir nicht länger **halten.**	*We do not want to stop here any longer.*
Wissen Sie, ob der Bus hier **hält?**	*Do you know whether the bus stops here?*

2. **Anhalten** *(transitive or intransitive)* means *to come* or *to bring something to a brief or temporary stop* (with persons or vehicles). In the case of vehicles, such a stop is usually unscheduled.

Während der Fahrt haben wir mehrmals **angehalten.** *(intransitive)*	*During the drive we stopped several times.*
Weil Kühe auf der Straße standen, **hielt** der Fahrer den Wagen **an.** *(transitive)*	*Because cows were standing in the road, the driver stopped the car.*

3. **Aufhalten** *(transitive)* means *to stop* or *hold up someone or something temporarily.*

Ich will dich nicht länger **aufhalten.**	*I do not want to hold you up any longer.*
Die Katastrophe war nicht länger **aufzuhalten.**	*The catastrophe could not be stopped any longer.*

4. **Aufhören (mit etwas)** *(intransitive only)* means *to stop (doing something), cease.*

Wann **hat** der Lärm endlich **aufgehört?**	*When did the noise finally stop?*
Die Kapelle **hörte auf** zu spielen.	*The band stopped playing.*
Ich **habe mit** dem Rauchen **aufgehört.**	*I have stopped smoking.*

5. **Stehenbleiben** *(intransitive only)* means *to (come to a) stop.* When used with vehicles and machinery, **stehenbleiben** implies that the stopping occurs for mechanical reasons.

Das Mädchen lief in das Haus und **blieb** vor dem Spiegel **stehen.**	*The girl ran into the house and stopped before the mirror.*
Das Auto **ist** plötzlich einfach **stehengeblieben.**	*The car suddenly simply came to a stop.*

6. **Stoppen** *(intransitive)* means *to come to a stop* and is synonymous with **(an)halten. Stoppen** *(transitive)* means *to bring someone or something to a stop.*

Der Autofahrer **stoppte** kurz vor der Kreuzung.	*The driver stopped shortly before the intersection.*
Die Grenzpolizei **stoppte** mehrere Autos an der Grenze.	*The border police stopped several cars at the border.*
Der Arzt mußte zuerst den Blutverlust **stoppen.**	*The doctor first had to stop the loss of blood.*

ÜBUNGEN

A **Stopp, Stopp, Stopp.** Drücken Sie die Sätze auf deutsch aus.

1. Stop this train!
2. Does this train stop between Salzburg and Bischofshofen?
3. Where can we stop and eat?
4. They stopped a car and asked whether they could have a ride **(mitfahren dürfen).**
5. This quarreling **(das Streiten)** has to stop.
6. The car rolled across the street and came to a stop beside a tree.

B **Situationen.** Sagen Sie, was Sie in den folgenden Situationen machen.

Beispiel: Ein Freund fährt mit Ihnen in Ihrem Wagen. Er möchte an der nächsten Ecke aussteigen.
Ich halte den Wagen an der nächsten Ecke.

1. Sie arbeiten seit Stunden und sind jetzt sehr müde.
2. Sie fahren in Ihrem Auto. Jemand, den Sie kennen, steht am Straßenrand und winkt Ihnen zu.
3. Beim Fußballspiel sind Sie im Tor. Ein Gegenspieler schießt aufs Tor.
4. Sie gehen im Tiergarten spazieren. Plötzlich ruft ein Affe Ihnen zu: „Wie geht's, Herr / Frau Kollege *(colleague)*?"
5. Jemand hat sich tief in den Arm geschnitten und blutet stark.

Zusammenfassung 15

Rules to Remember

1. Yes-no questions begin with a conjugated verb.
2. Other questions begin with an interrogative word + conjugated verb.
3. The word **doch** is a *yes* answer to a question posed negatively: **Verstehst du kein Deutsch?—Doch! (Ich verstehe Deutsch.)**
4. Indirect questions are subordinate clauses; the conjugated verb comes last.

Activities

1 **Interviewing.** Working with a partner, ask questions, then more questions, then follow-up questions about some aspect of his / her life. Use a variety of interrogatives.

2 **How many questions?** Write down a statement of "fact": true or invented, wise or absurd, perhaps even taken from a story. How many different questions can you (or other students) generate about this one statement without repeating an interrogative expression?

Beispiele: Eine Frau sitzt unter einem Baum im Park.
Wie alt ist die Frau?
Hat sie Kinder?
Wann sitzt sie unter dem Baum?
Warum sitzt sie unter dem Baum?
Wo steht der Baum im Park?
Was für Kleider trägt sie?
usw.

3 **Interrupting with questions.** Prepare a small anecdote or text to read aloud in class. After every sentence, other students in class interrupt to ask as many questions as they can think of about that sentence.

4 **Mad science.** Make up questions about the world we live in to which you do not know the answers. Share your questions with the class.

Beispiele: *Warum ist der Himmel blau?*
Wie viele Bazillen gibt es in einem Kuß?

5 **Getting to know you.** Ask your partner two different personal questions every day for a week. At the end of the week, write a brief portrait of him / her based on what you've learned.

6 **Working with a text.** Make up seven or eight questions about things left unsaid or unanswered in a story you and your class have recently read. Pose your questions to the rest of the class. Discuss with the class as a whole the merits of the answers you receive as a basis for understanding the story better.

Personal, Indefinite, and Demonstrative Pronouns

16

16.1 Personal Pronouns

A. *Forms*

Personal pronouns **(das Personalpronomen, -)** have four cases.

	Nom.	*Acc.*	*Dat.*	*Gen.*[1]
1st Pers. Sing.	**ich**	**mich**	**mir**	(meiner)
2nd Pers. Sing.	**du**	**dich**	**dir**	(deiner)
3rd Pers. Sing.	**er**	**ihn**	**ihm**	(seiner)
	sie	**sie**	**ihr**	(ihrer)
	es	**es**	**ihm**	(seiner)
1st Pers. Pl.	**wir**	**uns**	**uns**	(unser)
2nd Pers. Pl.	**ihr**	**euch**	**euch**	(euer)
3rd Pers. Pl.	**sie**	**sie**	**ihnen**	(ihrer)
2nd Pers. Formal Sing. & Pl.	**Sie**	**Sie**	**Ihnen**	(Ihrer)

B. *Use*

1. The familiar **du** (*you,* singular) and **ihr** (*you,* plural) are used when addressing God, family members, children up to about the age of fourteen, animals, friends, fellow students, or other persons with whom you are on a first-name basis.

1. Genitive case pronoun forms have become archaic. They do, however, form the basis for the possessive adjectives (see 5.4).

2. The familiar plural **ihr** is often used instead of the formal **Sie** when referring to people as representatives of a group rather than individuals.

   Wie macht **ihr** Schweizer das? — *How do you (Swiss) do that?*

3. The formal **Sie** (*you,* singular and plural) is used when addressing one or more strangers or people with whom one is either not on a first-name basis or toward whom one wishes to maintain a certain distance or respect, as people in German-speaking countries tend to do. In classrooms, this distinction becomes blurred when instructors address students by their first name but still address them as **Sie.** Historically, **Sie** is a capitalized **sie** *(they);* thus as a subject it always takes a third-person plural form of the conjugated verb, even when referring to only one person.

4. The third-person pronouns **er, sie,** and **es** can refer to persons. However, they also substitute for all **der-, die-,** and **das**-nouns respectively, whether persons or things. Thus, depending upon the noun, **er, sie,** or **es** can all be equivalent to English *it.* (For other uses of **es** see 19.3.)

Woher hast du den Ring?	*Where did you get the ring?*
—Ich habe **ihn** in Ulm gekauft. **Er** war gar nicht so teuer.	*I bought **it** in Ulm. **It** was not all that expensive.*
Hast du deine Jacke hier?	*Do you have your jacket here?*
—Nein, ich habe **sie** nicht dabei.	*No, I do not have **it** with me.*

5. After prepositions, pronouns are subject to the same case rules as nouns. However, if a third-person pronoun refers to inanimate objects, German generally requires a **da**-construction instead of preposition + pronoun (see 19.1).

   COMPARE:

Er ist mein Freund. Ich arbeite **mit ihm.**	*He is my friend. I work with him.*
Das ist mein Bleistift. Ich arbeite **damit.**	*That is my pencil. I work with it.*

16.2 Indefinite Pronouns

A. *Forms*

The following indefinite personal pronouns **(das Indefinitpronomen, -)** are masculine in form, but they refer to persons of either sex. Their possessive is **sein,** their reflexive **sich.** For **jedermann, jemand,** and **niemand** the relative pronoun is the masculine **der** (see 26.2).

	man *(one)*	**jedermann** *(everyone)*	**jemand** *(someone)*	**niemand** *(no one)*
Nom.	man (einer)	jedermann (jeder)	jemand	niemand
Acc.	(einen)	jedermann (jeden)	jemand(en)	niemand(en)
Dat.	(einem)	jedermann (jedem)	jemand(em)	niemand(em)
Gen.	(——)	jedermanns (——)	jemands	niemands

B. Use

1. **Man** is normally used when talking about *one, you, they,* or *people* in general. It often occurs as a substitute for the passive voice (see 28.3). **Man** is a subject form only; in other cases the pronoun forms **einen** (accusative) or **einem** (dative) are often used.

Man weiß nie, was **einem** passieren kann.	*You (one) never know(s) what can happen to you (one).*

2. When **man** is used in a sentence, it cannot be subsequently replaced by **er.**

Wenn **man** nichts zu sagen hat, soll **man** (*not:* **er**) schweigen.	*If one has nothing to say, one (he) should remain silent.*

3. **Jedermann** *(everyone, everybody)* and **jeder** are interchangeable in general statements, although **jeder** is more common.

Jedermann / Jeder, der Zeit hat, sollte mitkommen.	*Everyone who has time should come along.*

4. When referring to women, German speakers sometimes avoid **jedermann** and use **jede** (feminine) with the possessive **ihr-** or the relative pronoun **die.**[2] This makes the reference specific rather than general.

Jede, *die* Zeit hat, soll *ihre* Komposition heute abend schreiben.	*Everyone (feminine) who has time is to write her composition this evening.*

5. **Jemand** *(somebody, someone, anybody, anyone)* and **niemand** *(nobody, no one)* can be used with or without endings in the accusative and dative. They take no endings when followed by forms of **anders.**

Sie sagte **niemand(em)** die Wahrheit.	*She told no one the truth.*
Wir haben dich gestern mit **jemand anders** gesehen.	*We saw you yesterday with someone else.*

---

2. It has become trendy for the moment in circles that consider **man** and **jedermann** blatantly sexist to replace them with **frau** and **jedefrau. Jemand** and **niemand** are also used occasionally with the feminine possessive **ihr-** and the feminine relative pronoun **die** (instead of the masculine **der**).

6. The word **irgend** *(any, some)* is often added to **jemand** to stress its indefiniteness.

Irgendjemand (OR **irgend jemand**) muß doch zu Hause sein.	*Well, somebody (or another) must be home.*
Kann mir nicht **irgendjemand** (OR **irgend jemand**) helfen?	*Can't anybody (at all) help me?*

7. **Irgend** is also used in the following combinations:

irgendwer *(somebody or other)*
irgendein-/irgendwelch- + *noun* *(any, some)*
irgend(et)was *(something or other)*

Irgendwer soll **irgend(et)was** tun.	*Somebody (or other) ought to do something (or other).*
Hast du in letzter Zeit **irgendwelche** interessanten Filme gesehen?	*Have you seen any interesting films lately?*

16.3 Demonstrative Pronouns

A. Forms

The demonstrative pronoun **(das Demonstrativpronomen, -)** is essentially a definite article used as a pronoun; only the forms of the genitive and the dative plural differ slightly from those of the definite article.

	Masc.	***Fem.***	***Neut.***	***Pl.***
Nom.	der	die	das	die
Acc.	den	die	das	die
Dat.	dem	der	dem	**denen**
Gen.	**dessen**	**deren**	**dessen**	**deren**

B. Use

1. Demonstrative pronouns are used instead of personal pronouns to indicate stress or emphasis. German speakers often use them when pointing out someone or something, frequently with vocal emphasis or in combination with a strengthening **da** or **hier.**

Ich suche einen Computer. Darf ich **den da** probieren?	*I am looking for a computer. May I try that one there?*
Du, nimm die große Wurst.	*Hey, take the large sausage.*
—Welche?	*Which one?*
—Die hier.	*This one here.*

2. Demonstratives are also used with or without emphasis to indicate familiarity with specific persons or things. In such instances, they often begin the sentence. This usage is quite colloquial.

Kennst du Eva Schmidt? —Ja, **die** (*instead of* **sie**) kenne ich.	*Do you know Eva Schmidt?* *Yes, I know her.*
Siehst du Udo und Gabi oft? —Ja, mit **denen** (*instead of* **ihnen**) bin ich viel zusammen.	*Do you often see Udo and Gabi?* *Yes, I am with them a lot.*

3. The genitive demonstratives **dessen** *(his)* and **deren** *(her)* are used mainly to eliminate the ambiguity of **sein** or **ihr** when they could refer to either of two preceding nouns of the same gender. **Dessen** and **deren** refer only to the last previously mentioned male noun or female noun.

Der Arbeiter hat den Chef mit **seiner** Frau gesehen. *(ambiguous)*	*The worker saw the boss with his wife.*
Der Arbeiter hat den Chef mit **dessen**[3] Frau gesehen.	*The worker saw the boss with his (the boss's) wife.*
Julia hörte Stefanie mit **ihrem** Vater sprechen. *(ambiguous)*	*Julie heard Stefanie speaking with her father.*
Julia hörte Stefanie mit **deren** Vater sprechen.	*Julia heard Stefanie speaking with her (Stefanie's) father.*

C. *The Demonstrative* derselbe

1. The demonstrative pronoun **derselbe** *(the same one[s])* consists of two parts: the first part **(der- / die- / das-)** declines as an article, the second part **(selb-)** and any subsequent adjectives take secondary adjective endings (see 13.2).

	Masc.	*Fem.*	*Neut.*	*Pl.*
Nom.	**der** selbe	**die** selbe	**das** selbe	**die** selben
Acc.	**den** selben	**die** selbe	**das** selbe	**die** selben
Dat.	**dem** selben	**der** selben	**dem** selben	**den** selben
Gen.	**des** selben	**der** selben	**des** selben	**der** selben

Ich habe diese Bilder gekauft. Sind das **dieselben,** die du gestern gesehen hast?	*I bought these pictures. Are they the same ones that you saw yesterday?*

3. Literally, **dessen Frau** means *the wife of that one,* that is, the latter-mentioned person.

2. **Derselbe** *(the same)* is used more often as an adjective than as a pronoun. It indicates *the very same.* **Der gleiche** indicates *one that is similar.* This distinction is often ignored in colloquial German, but should be observed in writing.

Klaus und Angela wohnen in **demselben** Haus.	*Klaus and Angela live in the (very) same house.*
Sie fahren auch **den gleichen** Wagen.	*They also drive the same (make of) car.*

✱ Übungen

A **Welches Pronomen paßt?** Ergänzen Sie durch Personalpronomen.

1. Heinz und Heidi suchen Hilfe und fragen: „Wer hilft ____ ?“
2. Siggi fühlt sich mißverstanden und lamentiert: „Ach, niemand versteht ____ .“
3. Bärbl spricht enthusiastisch von ihrem neuen Freund: „Er liebt ____ und spricht immer von ____ .“
4. Die Kinder fragen: „Wer will mit ____ spielen?“
5. Die Lehrerin fragt: „Kinder, wie geht es ____ ?“
6. Ich schreibe: „Werner, wir besuchen ____ bald.“
7. „Herr Braun, wann kommen ____ uns besuchen?“
8. Ich möchte mit Frau Seidlhofer sprechen: „Frau Seidlhofer, darf ich mit ____ sprechen?“

B **Situationen: *du, ihr* oder *Sie?*** Welche Anredeform gebrauchen Sie in den folgenden Situationen in einem deutschsprachigen Land?

1. Sie sprechen im Zugabteil mit einer Mutter und ihrer kleinen Tochter.
2. Sie sprechen mit einer Verkäuferin im Kaufhaus.
3. Sie sind in ein Studentenheim eingezogen und treffen einige Studentinnen zum ersten Mal.
4. Sie treffen zum ersten Mal die 24-jährige Schwester eines Studienfreundes.
5. Sie spielen Volleyball im Sportverein, aber Sie kennen die anderen Spieler nicht. Es sind Jugendliche und Erwachsene dabei.
6. Bei einem Tanzabend im Studentenheim bitten Sie eine Person in Ihrem Alter um einen Tanz. Sie kennen diese Person nicht.
7. Sie sprechen mit den Tieren im Tierpark.
8. Sie treffen (ganz unerwartet) Ihren Deutschprofessor aus Amerika.
9. Sie sitzen im Gasthaus, und ein Betrunkener, den Sie nicht kennen, redet Sie mit *du* an.

C **Fragen.** Beantworten Sie die folgenden Fragen. Ersetzen Sie in Ihren Antworten die kursivgedruckten Wörter durch Pronomen.

Beispiel: Kennen Sie *die Musikgruppe Phish?*
Ja, ich kenne sie.

1. Sehen Sie *Filme* gern?
2. Wie hieß *der erste James-Bond Film?*
3. Haben Sie *diesen Film* einmal gesehen?
4. Kennen Sie einen James-Bond Film mit *Roger Moore?*
5. Lesen Sie oft *Filmrezensionen (film reviews)?*
6. Wie heißt *Ihre Lieblingsband?*
7. Haben Sie *diese Band* im Konzert gesehen?
8. Haben Sie einmal *an diese Band* geschrieben?

D **Personalpronomen.** Machen Sie über jeden Gegenstand *eine* Aussage mit einem Pronomen im Nominativ und *eine* mit einem Pronomen im Akkusativ.

Beispiel: mein Computer
***Er** ist acht Jahre alt.*
*Ich finde **ihn** noch gut.*

1. deine Geldtasche
2. dein Lieblingshut *(m.)*
3. deine Familie
4. dein Wagen (oder dein Fahrrad)
5. dein Zimmerschlüssel *(m.)*

E **Was bedeuten diese Sprüche?** Können Sie die Sprichwörter erklären oder anders ausdrücken? Verwenden Sie Strukturen mit **man, jemand** oder **niemand.**

Beispiel: Morgenstunde hat Gold im Munde.
Wenn man früh aufsteht, kann man den Tag besser nützen.
OR: *Wenn jemand früh aufsteht, kann er / sie den Tag besser nützen.*

1. Wer im Glashaus sitzt, soll nicht mit Steinen werfen.
2. Wie man sich bettet, so schläft man.
3. Es ist noch kein Meister vom Himmel gefallen.
4. In der Kürze liegt die Würze.
5. Kleider machen Leute.

F **Fragen.** Beantworten Sie die Fragen. Verwenden Sie Demonstrativpronomen.

Beispiel: Wie gefallen dir deutsche Filme?
***Die** gefallen mir gut.*

1. Siehst du die Fernsehsendung *60 Minuten* oft?
2. Hast du einmal den Film *Das zauberhafte Land* (The Wizard of Oz) gesehen?
3. Wie gefallen dir die Romane von Stephen King?

4. John Grisham ist dir sicher bekannt. Hast du von ihm schon etwas gelesen?
5. Kennst du die deutsche Autorin Christa Wolf?

G **Wer ist gemeint?** Ändern Sie die Sätze so, daß klar wird, daß mit dem Possessivpronomen die zuletzt genannte Person gemeint ist.

Beispiel: Sie fuhren mit Freunden in ihrem Auto.
*Sie fuhren mit Freunden in **deren** Auto.*

1. Annette saß mit Monika in ihrem Zimmer.
2. Zwei Arbeiter sahen einige fremde Männer mit ihren Kindern spielen.
3. Herr Schroeder rief seinen Nachbarn an und sprach mit seiner Tochter.
4. Johanna sprach mit ihrer Mutter in ihrem Schlafzimmer.
5. Herr Schmidt sprach mit Herrn Weiß über seine Kinder.

H **Ich auch.** Hans Auch macht und erlebt immer dasselbe, was andere machen und erleben. Oder so sagt er. Was sagt er, wenn er Folgendes hört?

Beispiel: Uschi hat gute Noten bekommen.
*Ich habe **dieselben** guten Noten bekommen.*

1. Fred hat einen dummen Fehler gemacht.
2. Susi hat von einer interessanten Frau erzählt.
3. Micha hat die Frau eines berühmten Schauspielers gesehen.
4. Wir haben heute nette Leute aus Österreich kennengelernt.
5. Das sage ich ja immer.

* Anwendung

A **Das habe ich mitgebracht.** Bringen Sie etwas (oder ein Foto davon) mit, was Sie im Kurs gern zeigen würden. Erklären Sie anderen Studenten diesen Gegenstand, und stellen Sie Fragen über die Gegenstände anderer Studenten.

REDEMITTEL

Ich möchte dir / euch mein- . . . zeigen / vorstellen.
Er / sie / es ist / kann . . .
Sein- / ihr- . . . sind aus Holz / Metall usw.
Ich habe ihn / sie / es . . . bekommen / gekauft / gebaut usw.
Hast du auch . . .?
Wie sieht dein . . . aus? Hast du ihn / sie / es auch dabei?
Und nun möchte ich dir / euch etwas anderes zeigen.

B **So macht man das.** Suchen Sie jemanden im Kurs, der etwas nicht macht oder machen kann, was Sie können. Geben Sie Ihrem Partner / Ihrer Partnerin eine genaue Anleitung *(instruction)* für diese Tätigkeit *(activity)*.

THEMENVORSCHLÄGE

ein Karten- oder Brettspiel	ein Garten
ein Hobby	eine Reise
ein Sport	ein bestimmtes Projekt

REDEMITTEL

Wenn man / jemand . . . will, dann muß man . . .
Man macht das so: Jemand muß . . .
Jeder / jedermann versucht, . . . [zu tun].
Niemand darf . . .
Wenn jemand gewinnt / verliert, muß er . . .

* Schriftliche Themen

Tips zum Schreiben ***Using Pronouns in German***

German generally uses the indefinite pronoun **man** instead of the editorial *we* or *you* characteristic of English *(If you want to succeed, you have to . . .).* Remember, however, that if you begin a sentence with **man,** you must not shift to **er** or to **du / Sie** in the same sentence. This rule does not mean that you cannot have a variety of pronouns in one passage. In subsequent sentences you might use a range of words such as other indefinite pronouns **(jemand, niemand),** nouns designating persons or people **(Leute, Mensch[en], Person[en]),** or the relative pronoun **wer** (*whoever, he who;* see 26.4). Keep in mind, however, that frequent use of a masculine noun and the pronoun **er** in general statements might be regarded as sexist, since it seems to exclude women, as in the example **Wenn *ein Mensch* erfolgreich sein will, muß *er* fleißig arbeiten.** *(If a person wants to be successful, **he** must work hard).* You can avoid this dilemma by using plural nouns and pronouns: **Wenn *Menschen* erfolgreich sein wollen, müssen *sie* fleißig arbeiten.**

A **Kommentar.** Äußern Sie sich im allgemeinen *(in general)* zu einer Tätigkeit, einer Handlung oder einer Handlungsweise.

THEMENVORSCHLÄGE

Menschen, die immer . . .
die Politik einer Regierung
Fremdsprachen lernen
gesund / ungesund leben
wie man Glück im Leben findet

Beispiel: Wer dauernd vorm Fernseher hockt *(crouches)* und Kartoffelchips ißt, lebt ungesund. Aber leben Menschen, die *(who)* täglich joggen und so ihre Knie ruinieren, auch nicht genauso ungesund? Zwar behauptet man, daß Joggen gesund sei, aber dasselbe könnte man vielleicht auch vom ständigen *(constant)* Fernsehen sagen. Jedenfalls kenne ich niemanden, der sich beim Fernsehen die Knie verletzt hat oder von einem Hund gebissen wurde. Irgendjemand hat einmal geschrieben, daß . . . usw.

B **Das sollte man nicht tun.** Erklären Sie, warum man eine gewisse Tätigkeit **nicht** ausüben *(do)* soll. Was sind die Folgen von einer solchen Tätigkeit?

Beispiel: Ich glaube, man sollte nicht Fallschirm *(parachute)* springen. Wenn jemand aus einem Flugzeug abspringt und der Fallschirm sich nicht öffnet, hat er / sie großes Pech gehabt. Es kann aber auch passieren, daß man sich beim Landen verletzt *(injures)* und . . . usw.

Wortschatz 16

nur	ein ander-
erst	noch ein-

1. **Nur** means *only* in the sense of *that is all there is.*

Er ist **nur** fünf Jahre alt geworden.	*He lived only to the age of five.*
Wir haben **nur** ein Auto.	*We have only one car.*

2. **Erst** means *only* in the sense of *up until now* or *so far* and implies that more is to come.

Sie ist **erst** fünf Jahre alt geworden.	*She has only turned five (so far).*
Wir haben **erst** ein Auto.	*We have only one car (so far).*

Erst can also mean *only* in the sense of *not until.*

Sie ist **erst** gestern angekommen.	*She arrived only yesterday.* (That is, *she did not arrive until yesterday.*)

3. **Ein ander-** and **noch ein-** can both mean *another (an other),* but the former implies *another kind* and the latter an *additional one.*

Wir brauchen **ein anderes** Auto.	*We need another (different) car.*
Wir brauchen **noch ein** Auto.	*We need another (additional) car.*

ÜBUNGEN

A **Aussagen.** Machen Sie zwei Aussagen mit **nur** und vier mit **erst** über sich oder andere Menschen, die Sie kennen.

B ***Ein ander-* oder *noch ein-?*** Was sagen Sie in diesen Situationen?

Beispiel: In der Kleiderabteilung probieren Sie ein Hemd an, aber der Schnitt *(cut)* des Hemdes gefällt Ihnen nicht.
Ich möchte bitte ***ein anderes*** *Hemd anprobieren.*

1. Ein Stück Kuchen hat so gut geschmeckt, daß Sie Lust auf ein zweites Stück haben.
2. Sie haben für vier Eintrittskarten bezahlt aber nur drei Karten bekommen.
3. Sie wollen in den zoologischen Garten gehen, aber man hat Ihnen eine Karte für das Aquarium gegeben.
4. Ihr Zimmer ist zu klein geworden.

Zusammenfassung 16

Rules to Remember

1. **Du** (*you,* sing.) and **ihr** (*you,* pl.) are informal; **Sie** (*you,* sing. & pl.) is formal and always takes a plural verb form.
2. The pronouns **er, sie,** and **es** refer to **der-, die-,** and **das**-nouns respectively; **sie** refers to all plural nouns.
3. The pronoun **man** refers to persons in general without gender distinction. Thus it cannot be replaced with **er.**
4. The demonstrative pronouns **der, die, das,** and **die** are often used instead of the personal pronouns **er, sie, es,** and **sie** when referring to persons and things with which one is familiar.

Activities

1 **Talking to two or more persons.** Talk with a pair of students about a topic of your choice (films they have seen, weekend plans, etc.). Ask lots of questions using the informal plural **ihr.**

2 **What is it?** Make three statements about an object that is either a **der**-word or a **die**-word, but do not tell what "it" is. Other students try to guess what "it" is. If they cannot guess the item, provide one more obvious tip.

Beispiel: *Er ist klein. Er ist lang, aber dünn. Man trägt ihn oft in der Tasche. Man schreibt damit.*
—Es ist ein Kugelschreiber.

3 **Unusual objects.** Look up the German word and gender for ten unusual objects that you would like to know in German. See if other students can guess their meanings. Help them along with statements about your objects.

Beispiel: (der Dudelsack)
Er ist ein Musikinstrument. Er macht laute Musik.
Schotten spielen ihn gern. usw. (= a bagpipe)

4 **Generalizing statements.** Prepare the first half of five generalizing **"Wenn man . . ."** statements. Read your half statements in class and let other students provide possible conclusions.

Beispiel: *Wenn man Wachs in den Ohren hat, . . .*
dann hört man schlecht.
sollte man sich die Ohren waschen.
hat man vielleicht Bienen im Kopf.
usw.

5 **Observations.** Make five observations that characterize your outlook or views on life. Use pronouns such as **man** and **jemand.** Compare your observations with those of other students.

Beispiel: *Man soll immer fleißig sein und wenig fernsehen.*
Jemand, der Alkohol getrunken hat, soll nicht Auto fahren.

6 **Reactions and comments.** Make a list of five famous persons, living or dead. Call out the names in class. Other students should react to these names using demonstrative pronouns.

Beispiel: Ronald Reagan: ***Der*** *war . . . /* ***Den*** *halte ich für . . .*
Madonna: *Ja,* ***die*** *finde ich . . .*

Reflexive Pronouns / *Selbst* and *selber* / *Einander*

17

17.1 Reflexive Pronouns

A. Forms

In English, reflexive pronouns are indicated by adding *-self / -selves* to the object pronoun: *She hurt herself.* In German, the reflexives for the first person **(ich, wir)** and second person **(du, ihr)** pronouns are the same as regular accusative and dative forms; all third person forms plus the formal **Sie** take the reflexive **sich.**[1]

	Nom.	*Acc.*	*Dat.*	
1st pers. sing.	**ich**	**mich**	**mir**	*myself*
1st pers. pl.	**wir**	**uns**	**uns**	*ourselves*
2nd pers. fam. sing.	**du**	**dich**	**dir**	*yourself*
2nd pers. fam. pl.	**ihr**	**euch**	**euch**	*yourselves*
3rd pers. sing.	**er** (der Mann)	**sich**	**sich**	*himself*
	sie (die Frau)	**sich**	**sich**	*herself*
	es (das Kind)	**sich**	**sich**	*itself*
3rd pers. pl.	**sie** (die Leute)	**sich**	**sich**	*themselves*
2nd pers. formal sing. & pl.	**Sie**	**sich**	**sich**	*yourself / yourselves*

1. The interrogative pronouns **wer** and **was** (see 15.2) and the indefinite pronouns (**man, jemand, niemand, etwas, jedermann,** etc.) (see 16.2) are third person pronouns and also take the reflexive **sich.**

B. Positions of Reflexive Pronouns

1. A reflexive pronoun comes immediately after the conjugated verb and before any remaining elements of the sentence.

Er kauft **sich** ein Fahrrad.	*He is buying himself a bicycle.*

2. When a subject follows the verb, the reflexive pronoun can either precede or follow a subject *noun,* but it must always follow a subject *pronoun.*

Heute kauft **sich** *der Nachbar* ein Fahrrad. Heute kauft *der Nachbar* **sich** ein Fahrrad.	*Today the neighbor is buying himself a bicycle.*
Heute kauft *er* **sich** ein Fahrrad.	*Today he is buying himself a bicycle.*

17.2 Reflexive Verbs

A. Accusative Reflexives with Verbs

lies dich frei

. . . Bücher von Leykam

1. An accusative reflexive pronoun can be used with virtually any transitive verb if the subject directs an activity at himself / herself / itself. The accusative reflexive pronoun functions as a *direct* object (see 4.4) and refers to the sentence subject.

COMPARE:

Nonreflexive	*Reflexive*
Ich wasche **das Kind.** *I wash the child.*	Ich wasche **mich.** *I wash myself.*
Du rasierst **den Kunden.** *You shave the customer.*	Du rasierst **dich.** *You shave (yourself).*
Er sieht **ihn** im Spiegel. *He sees him (another person) in the mirror.*	Er sieht **sich** im Spiegel. *He sees himself in the mirror.*
Die Frau schnitt **die Blumen.** *The woman cut the flowers.*	Die Frau schnitt **sich.** *The woman cut herself.*

Wir waschen **die Kinder.** *We wash the children.*	Wir waschen **uns.** *We wash ourselves.*
Sie hörten **sie** auf dem Tonband. *They heard them (other people) on tape.*	Sie hörten **sich** auf dem Tonband. *They heard themselves on tape.*

2. Some transitive German verbs are used with an accusative reflexive when they indicate that an activity refers back to the subject, even though the English equivalent does not require a reflexive.

Nonreflexive	*Reflexive*
Sie **ändert** das Spiel. *She changes the game.*	Die Zeiten **ändern sich.** *Times change.*
Er **dreht** das Rad. *He turns the wheel.*	Das Rad **dreht sich.** *The wheel turns.*
Die Frau **öffnet** / **schließt** die Tür. *The woman opens / shuts the door.*	Die Tür **öffnet** / **schließt sich.** *The door opens / closes.*

3. With certain meanings, a significant number of German verbs are always used with an accusative reflexive, even though the English equivalent may not include a reflexive. They are generally referred to as reflexive verbs. Reflexive verbs take the auxiliary **haben** in the perfect tenses. Here are some common examples.

sich amüsieren	*to enjoy oneself*
sich ausruhen	*to take a rest*
sich beeilen	*to hurry*
sich benehmen	*to behave*
sich entschuldigen	*to apologize*
sich erholen	*to recover*
sich erkälten	*to catch a cold*
sich (wohl / schlecht) fühlen	*to feel well / ill*
sich langweilen	*to be bored*
sich (hin)legen	*to lie down*
sich setzen	*to sit down*
sich umsehen	*to take a look around*
sich verlaufen	*to get lost, go the wrong way*
sich verspäten	*to be late, come too late*

Habt ihr **euch** gut **amüsiert?**	*Did you enjoy yourselves?*
Die Schüler haben **sich** auf dem Weg zur Party **verlaufen.**	*The pupils got lost on the way to the party.*
Haben wir noch Zeit, **uns** ein bißchen **umzusehen?**	*Do we still have time to look around a bit?*

4. Many German verbs, including a number of accusative reflexive verbs, often complete their meaning with a prepositional phrase. Here are some common examples; you will find more in Chapter 30.

sich ärgern über *(acc.)* — *to be annoyed at*
sich beschäftigen mit — *to be occupied with*
sich erinnern an *(acc.)* — *to remember*
sich freuen auf *(acc.)* — *to look forward to*
sich freuen über *(acc.)* — *to be happy about*
sich fürchten vor *(dat.)* — *to be afraid of*
sich gewöhnen an *(acc.)* — *to get used to*
sich interessieren für — *to be interested in*
sich kümmern um — *to attend to, concern oneself with*
sich umsehen nach — *to look around for*
sich verlieben in *(acc.)* — *to fall in love with*
sich wundern über *(acc.)* — *to be amazed at*

Ich kann **mich** nicht mehr **an** ihn **erinnern.** — *I can no longer remember him.*

Wir **freuen uns auf** deinen Besuch. — *We are looking forward to your visit.*

5. The object of a prepositional phrase after a reflexive verb can also be a reflexive pronoun.

Ich ärgere mich **über mich.** — *I am annoyed at myself.*

Sie kümmert sich nur **um sich.** — *She is only concerned about herself.*

UNSERE MITARBEITER FREUEN SICH AUF IHRE BESTELLUNG
Minerva
Wissenschaftliche
Buchhandlung
A-1010 Wien, Schottengasse 7
Tel. 533 02 38, 533 02 39, 535 32 23, 535 34 76, Telex 114 506 spriw a, Telefax 535 34 10 28

B. *Dative Reflexives with Verbs*

1. Dative reflexives are used when the subject does something on his / her / its own behalf. In such instances, the sentence normally has a direct object as well. The dative reflexive pronoun functions as an *indirect* object (see 4.5) referring to the sentence subject.

COMPARE:

Ich ziehe **mich** an. *(accusative reflexive object)* — *I dress myself.* (that is, *I get dressed*)

Ich ziehe **mir** die Jacke an. *(dative reflexive object)* — *I put on the jacket.* (literally, *I pull the jacket on myself*)

Hast du **dir** einen neuen Mantel gekauft? — *Did you buy yourself a new coat?*

Mutter schrieb **sich** *(dative)* einen Zettel. — *Mother wrote herself a note.*

2. With some verbs, German often uses optional dative reflexives, even when the meaning is clear without them.

Kauft ihr **(euch)** neue Kleidung?	*Are you buying (yourselves) new clothing?*
Was hast du **(dir)** schon bestellt?	*What have you already ordered (for yourself)?*

3. Dative reflexive pronouns and definite articles are commonly used instead of possessive adjectives when referring to parts of the body (see 5.1).

Ich wasche **mir** die Hände.	*I wash my hands.*
Die Kinder haben **sich** die Finger verbrannt.	*The children burned their fingers.*

4. Some verbs always take dative reflexives with particular meanings.

sich etwas ansehen	*to take a look at something*
sich etwas einbilden	*to imagine or think something of oneself that is not true*
sich etwas leisten	*to afford something*
sich etwas merken	*to take note of something*
sich etwas überlegen	*to think something over*
sich etwas vorstellen	*to imagine, conceive of something*

Ich möchte **mir** einige Gemälde genauer **ansehen.**	*I would like to take a closer look at several paintings.*
Kannst du **dir** einen Flug nach Europa **leisten?**	*Can you afford a flight to Europe?*
Sie können **sich** *(dative)* gar nicht **vorstellen,** wie lange wir **uns** *(dative)* diese Entscheidung **überlegt** haben.	*You cannot imagine how long we thought this decision over.*

5. Sometimes the direct object accompanying the dative reflexive is actually a following *clause.*

Ich muß (es) **mir** überlegen, was wir tun können.	*I must think (it) over what we can do.*

17.3 *Selbst* and *selber*

1. **Selbst** and **selber** both mean *-self;* they are intensifying adverbs, not reflexive pronouns. They can occur either by themselves or in combination with reflexive pronouns.

Hast du dieses Haus **selber** / **selbst** gebaut?	*Did you build this house yourself?*
Sie hat *sich* **selbst** / **selber** angezogen.	*She got dressed (by) herself.*

2. **Selbst** and **selber** often occur together with reflexive pronouns after some verbs that take only dative objects (see 4.5B).

Du mußt *dir* **selbst** / **selber** helfen.	*You will have to help yourself.*
Er hat *sich* **selbst** / **selber** widersprochen.	*He contradicted himself.*

3. When **selbst** precedes the words it intensifies, it means *even*. **Selber** cannot be used in this context.

Selbst am Mittelmeer hatten wir mieses Wetter.	*Even on the Mediterranean we had lousy weather.*

17.4 The Reciprocal Pronoun *einander*

1. Plural reflexive pronouns can be used to express reciprocal actions, that is, actions done by persons ***to*** *each other* or *one another.* This structure, however, may result in ambiguity, which is best eliminated by using **einander** *(each other)*.

Wir kauften **uns** kleine Reiseandenken.	*We bought each other (OR: ourselves) little travel souvenirs.*
Sie kauften **einander** auch Reiseandenken.	*They also bought each other travel souvenirs.*

2. When used with prepositions, **einander** must be attached to the preposition to form one word.

Die Mannschaften spielen jetzt **gegeneinander.**	*The teams are now playing against each other.*
Fürchten sich Geister **voreinander?**	*Are ghosts afraid of one another?*

Übungen

A **Nicht reflexiv → reflexiv.** Machen Sie die Sätze reflexiv, indem Sie die kursivgedruckten Wörter ersetzen.

Beispiel: Narzissus sah *Bäume* im Wasserspiegel.
Narzissus sah ***sich*** *im Wasserspiegel.*

1. Man sollte *die Kleider* öfter waschen.
2. Ich habe *die Zeitung* auf das Sofa gelegt.

3. Sie zog *ihre Kinder* schick an.
4. Zieh *ihm* die Jacke aus.
5. Wir legten *die Decken* in die Sonne.
6. Kinder, was habt ihr *euren Eltern* zu Weihnachten gewünscht?
7. Was hat sie *ihm* versprochen?
8. Haben Sie *die Kinder* schon angezogen?
9. Niemand konnte *der Polizei* den Unfall erklären.
10. Der Arzt hat *ihm* die Wunden verbunden.

B **Mit und ohne Reflexivpronomen.** Bilden Sie jeweils zwei Sätze, einen mit und einen ohne Reflexivpronomen. Übersetzen Sie Ihre Sätze.

Beispiel: (sich) bewegen
Die Blätter bewegten sich im Wind.
(The leaves were moving in the wind.)
Der Wind bewegte die Blätter.
(The wind moved the leaves.)

1. (sich) ändern
2. (sich) fühlen
3. (sich) (hin)legen
4. (sich) öffnen
5. (sich) setzen

C **Situationen.** Beenden Sie die Sätze. Verwenden Sie die folgenden Verben.

Beispiel: Seit Stunden bellt der Hund von nebenan.
Vielleicht sollte Herr Franzen . . .
Vielleicht sollte Herr Franzen sich bei seinem Nachbarn oder bei der Polizei beschweren.

sich amüsieren	sich erkälten	sich bewerben um *(to apply for)*
sich ausruhen	sich umsehen	sich entschuldigen *(to apologize)*
sich beeilen		sich irren *(to be mistaken)*

1. Hans lief letzte Woche dauernd ohne Mantel im Regen herum.
   Kein Wunder, daß . . .
2. Der Bus fährt in zehn Minuten, und die Kinder sind noch nicht da.
   „Kinder, . . .!“
3. Lufthansa hat jetzt Stellen frei, und Monika sucht Arbeit.
   Vielleicht kann sie . . .
4. Morgen gibt es eine tolle Party bei Franz.
   Sicher werden wir . . .
5. Es tut mir leid, mein Herr, aber das stimmt nicht.
   Ich glaube, daß . . .
6. Verkäuferin: „Suchen Sie etwas Bestimmtes?“
   „Nein, ich will . . .“

7. Klaus hat seinen Kollegen beleidigt *(insulted).*
   Jetzt möchte er . . .
8. Ich bin sehr müde.
   „Dann solltest du . . .“

D **Aus meiner Vergangenheit.** Machen Sie fünf Aussagen über Ihr vergangenes Leben. Verwenden Sie reflexive Verben mit Präpositionen. Beginnen Sie zwei Ihrer Aussagen mit: **Ich glaube, daß . . .**

Beispiel: *Als Kind habe ich mich vor Schlangen gefürchtet.*
OR: *Ich glaube, daß ich mich als Kind vor Schlangen gefürchtet habe.*

E **Akkusativ → Dativ.** Verwenden Sie Reflexivpronomen im Dativ.

Beispiel: Du wäschst dich. (Hände)
Du wäschst dir die Hände.

1. Ziehe dich aus! (die Schuhe)
2. Habt ihr euch gewaschen? (die Füße)
3. Ich muß mich abtrocknen. (die Hände)
4. Sie kämmt sich. (die Haare)
5. Sie sollen sich anziehen. (andere Kleider)

F **Ein neues Auto.** Drücken Sie diese Sätze durch den Gebrauch von Reflexivpronomen im Dativ auf deutsch aus.

1. I want to buy (myself) a car.
2. Buy (yourself) a BMW!
3. I don't believe that I can afford such a car.
4. You are just imagining that. Take a look at one!
5. I'll think it over.
6. I can just imagine you in a beautiful sport convertible **(das Sportkabriolett).**

G **Selbst und selber.** Drücken Sie die Sätze auf englisch aus.

1. Hilf dir selbst, so hilft dir Gott.
2. Selbst Tiere haben das Recht auf eine saubere Umwelt.
3. Die Tiere haben selber mit vielen Schwierigkeiten zu kämpfen.
4. Manchmal ärgere ich mich über mich selber.
5. Diese Schaukel *(swing)* haben die Kinder selbst gebaut.
6. Selbst Politiker sagen manchmal etwas Kluges.

H **Einander.** Drücken Sie die Sätze anders aus.

Beispiel: Wann habt ihr euch kennengelernt?
*Wann habt ihr **einander** kennengelernt?*

1. Wir haben uns öfter gesehen.
2. Die Schüler helfen sich mit den Aufgaben.
3. Habt ihr nicht an euch geschrieben?

* Anwendung

A **Beim Aufstehen und vor dem Schlafengehen.** Erzählen Sie jemandem im Kurs, wie Sie sich morgens nach dem Aufstehen und abends zum Schlafengehen fertig machen. Was machen Sie zuerst? Was kommt danach? Was machen Sie zuletzt? Berichten Sie dann, was jemand Ihnen erzählt hat.

VOKABELVORSCHLÄGE

sich anziehen / ausziehen
(sich) duschen
sich die Haare kämmen
sich rasieren
sich strecken *(stretch)*
sich schminken
sich abtrocknen
sich waschen

B **Gefühle, Interessen und Reaktionen.** Erkundigen Sie sich bei jemandem nach der folgenden Information. Berichten Sie darüber.

Fragen Sie . . .

1. wann er / sie sich besonders ärgert.
2. wovor er / sie sich fürchtet.
3. wofür er / sie sich besonders interessiert.
4. woran / an wen er / sie sich (un)gern erinnert.
5. worauf er / sie sich ganz besonders freut.
6. worüber er / sie sich ganz besonders freut.

* Schriftliche Themen

Tips zum Schreiben ***Using Process Writing in German***

Conceptualize what you want to say in German, not English. Begin by making a list of German verbs that describe the actions you wish to discuss. Write short statements with these verbs, using a subject-verb-object or subject-verb-prepositional phrase format. Next, expand your basic statements by adding descriptive or qualifying adjectives (see Chapter 13), adverbs (see Chapter 24), or prepositional phrases (see Chapter 10). Finally, read what you have written to see in which sentences you can improve the style of your composition by putting elements other than subjects in first position.

A **Nacherzählen.** Erzählen Sie diese Bildgeschichte *in der Vergangenheit* nach. Gebrauchen Sie Verben mit Reflexivpronomen.

VOKABELVORSCHLÄGE

die Straßenbahn
die Werbung, -en *(advertisement)*
sich vorstellen
sich kaufen / holen
sich waschen
sich im Spiegel anschauen
sich das Gesicht einreiben
sich die Zähne putzen
sich freuen, (daß)
sich interessieren
sich fragen

B **Menschenbeschreibung.** Kennen Sie jemanden, der sehr begabt, exzentrisch oder eigenartig ist? Beschreiben Sie diesen Menschen. Womit beschäftigt er / sie sich? Wie benimmt er / sie sich? Wofür interessiert er / sie sich? Worüber ärgert er / sie sich?

Beispiel: Mein Freund Kuno ist sehr exzentrisch. Er langweilt sich nie, denn dauernd beschäftigt er sich mit Fragen, die ich mir nicht einmal vorstellen kann. Er hat z.B. einmal ausgerechnet, daß ein Mensch sich im Laufe seines Lebens mehr als hundertmal erkältet. Obwohl er sich einbildet, . . . usw.

Wortschatz 17

entscheiden }
sich entscheiden } (= eine Entscheidung treffen)
sich entschließen (= einen Entschluß fassen)
beschließen

1. **Entscheiden** means *to decide (for or against), settle a question* intellectually.

Ein Richter muß diesen Fall **entscheiden.**	*A judge must decide this case.*

2. **Sich entscheiden** means *to decide* or *choose* between various options. **Sich entscheiden (für)** means *to decide on one option,* to choose.

Hast du **dich entschieden,** ob du mitfahren willst oder nicht?	*Have you decided whether or not you want to go along?*
Ich habe **mich für** den grünen Mantel **entschieden.**	*I have decided on the green coat.*

3. **Eine Entscheidung treffen** means *to come to a decision.* It is roughly synonymous with **(sich) entscheiden,** though stylistically more emphatic.

Hast du schon **eine Entscheidung getroffen,** welchen Beruf du erlernen willst?	*Have you come to a decision as to which profession you want to learn?*

4. **Sich entschließen** means *to decide to take a course of action, to make up one's mind to do* something.

Er konnte **sich** nicht (dazu)[2] **entschließen,** ein neues Auto zu kaufen.	*He could not make up his mind to buy a new car.*

5. **Einen Entschluß fassen** means *to make a decision or resolution.* It is roughly synonymous with **sich entschließen,** but more emphatic.

Sie hat **den Entschluß gefaßt,** ein anderes Studium anzufangen.	*She made the decision to begin a different course of study.*

6. **Beschließen** means *to resolve to take a course of action* or *to pass a resolution* by virtue of some authority.

Wir haben **beschlossen,** eine neue Wohnung zu suchen.	*We have decided to look for a new apartment.*
Der Senat hat **beschlossen,** einen neuen Wohnblock bauen zu lassen.	*The senate has resolved to have a new apartment complex built.*

ÜBUNGEN

A **Eine schwierige Entscheidung.** Drücken Sie die Sätze auf deutsch aus.

1. The city council **(der Stadtrat)** decided to raise **(erhöhen)** our taxes.
2. For this reason my parents decided to move to the countryside **(aufs Land umziehen).**
3. But since they had made the decision to move, they had to decide where we were to **(sollten)** live.

---

2. The anticipatory **dazu** is optional with **sich entschließen.**

4. They could not decide where to go or whether they should buy or rent **(mieten)** a house.
5. They wanted me to make the decision.

B **Wer die Wahl** *(choice)* **hat, hat die Qual** *(torment)*. Beantworten Sie die folgenden Fragen.

Beispiel: Was war die schwerste Entscheidung in Ihrem Leben?
Ich mußte mich entscheiden, an welcher Universität ich studieren wollte.

1. Was war die beste / schlechteste Entscheidung, die Sie je getroffen haben?
2. Wann ist es für Sie schwer / leicht, sich zu entscheiden?
3. Haben Sie sich je zu etwas entschlossen, was Sie später bereut *(regretted)* haben?
4. Haben Sie einmal einen ganz klugen Entschluß gefaßt?
5. Wofür würden Sie sich nie entscheiden?

Zusammenfassung 17

Rules to Remember

1. A reflexive pronoun refers back to the sentence subject.
2. The dative and accusative reflexive of all third-person pronouns and **Sie** is **sich.** COMPARE: **Er sieht sie.** *(He sees her.)* **Er sieht sich.** *(He sees himself.)*
3. Some German verbs are always reflexive, even though the English equivalent may not be: **Ich erinnere mich.** *(I remember.)*
4. Many reflexive verbs complete their meaning with a prepositional phrase: **Ich erinnere mich an ihn.** *(I remember him.)*

Activities

1 **Analysis.** Underline ten verbs used reflexively in a German story or text. Determine whether or not the English equivalents for these verbs are also reflexive. Share your examples with the rest of the class.

2 **Statements about oneself.** Using reflexive verbs from this chapter or from Chapter 30, write five to seven statements about yourself. Read your statements to other students. See if you can find students with similar statements.

Beispiel: *Ich putze mir die Zähne immer nach dem Essen.*
Ich fürchte mich vor Schlangen.
usw.

3 **Personal improvement.** What are some of the things you could do more or less of to improve yourself? Focus on reflexive activities. Share your thoughts with other

students. Do you have any personal improvement suggestions for other students in class?

Beispiel: *Ich könnte / sollte mich beim Arbeiten besser konzentrieren.*

4 **Working with a text.** Discuss the behavior of a certain character in a story. Use reflexive statements as much as possible.

Beispiel: *Ich finde, X macht sich zu viele Sorgen um seine Ehe.*
Ich glaube, X kümmert sich zuwenig um ihren Mann.
usw.

18 Infinitives

18.1 Infinitives with *zu*

1. As verbal complements, infinitives normally occur in final position, preceded by **zu.** In the case of separable-prefix verbs, the **zu** comes between the prefix and the infinitive and links them together as one word.

Der Redner begann **zu lachen.**	*The speaker began to laugh.*
Sie versuchen **aufzustehen.**	*They try to get up.*

2. Two-word infinitive complements (**zu** + infinitive) may either precede or follow past participles and separable prefixes.

Das Kind fing **zu schreien** an. Das Kind fing an **zu schreien.**	*The child began to scream.*
Er hat versprochen **zu schreiben.** Er hat **zu schreiben** versprochen.	*He promised to write.*

3. Infinitive phrases of more than two words are usually perceived as separate clauses; they follow all other elements of a sentence and are set off by a comma.

Der Redner versuchte, **die schreckliche Lage in Bosnien zu schildern.**	*The speaker attempted to portray the terrible situation in Bosnia.*

4. If infinitive phrases of more than two words are perceived as directly complementing the main predicate, the comma is often omitted.

Der Redner **versuchte** seine Rede **zu beenden.**	*The speaker tried to conclude his talk.*

anstatt - a little more formal

18

18.2 Adverbial Phrases with *um . . . zu, ohne . . . zu,* and *(an)statt. . . zu*

Um *([in order] to),* **ohne** *(without),* and **(an)statt** *(instead of)* can introduce infinitive phrases with **zu.** These phrases are set off by a comma. When the phrase begins with **ohne** or **(an)statt,** its English equivalent uses a verb form ending in *-ing.*

Sie gingen nach München, **um** das Deutsche Museum **zu besuchen.**	*They went to Munich (in order) to visit the German Museum.*
Man sollte nichts kaufen, **ohne** es vorher **zu sehen.**	*One should not buy anything without seeing it first.*
Sie sehen Videofilme zu Hause, **(an)statt** ins Kino **zu gehen.**	*They watch videos at home, instead of going to the movies.*

18.3 Infinitives without *zu*

1. Infinitives accompanying modal verbs (see 9.1) and the future auxiliary **werden** (see 8.1) do not take a preceding **zu.**
2. Infinitives accompanying the verbs of perception **fühlen, hören, sehen, spüren** *(to perceive, feel),* as well as the verbs **heißen** *(to bid, command)* and **lassen** (see 18.4) do not take a preceding **zu.**

Wir **sehen** sie mit Freunden **sprechen.**	*We see them speaking with friends.*
Sie **fühlte / spürte** etwas auf ihrer Schulter **kriechen.**	*She felt something crawling on her shoulder.*
Der König **heißt** die Soldaten **eintreten.**	*The king bids the soldiers (to) enter.*

3. Infinitives accompanying **helfen, lehren,** and **lernen** can occur either with or without a preceding **zu.**

Sie **hilft** ihm den Text **(zu) übersetzen.**	*She helps him translate the text.*
Er **lehrte** die Kinder **(zu) schwimmen.**	*He taught the children (how) to swim.*

4. With **fühlen, hören, sehen, spüren,** and with **lernen** and **lehren,** a subordinate clause is often used instead of an accompanying infinitive phrase.

Sie spürte, **wie etwas auf ihrer Schulter kroch.**	*She felt how / that something was crawling on her shoulder.*
Er hörte, **wie jemand die Tür leise öffnete.**	*He heard someone quietly open the door.*

5. The verb **gehen** is also often used with a following infinitive without **zu.**

Wir **gehen** täglich **schwimmen.**	*We go swimming daily.*

18.4 *Lassen* + Infinitive

1. When **lassen** is complemented by an infinitive, it means *to let* or *to have someone do something.* Context determines which meaning is intended. The infinitive is not preceded by **zu.**

Sie **läßt** ihren Sohn ihr Auto zur Schule **fahren.**	*She lets her son drive her car to school.*
Sie **läßt** ihren Sohn ihr Auto **waschen.**	*She has her son wash her car.*

2. If **lassen** has no direct object agent (like **ihren Sohn** in the preceding examples), its English equivalent is *to let be done* or *to have done.*

Sie **läßt** ihr Auto zur Schule **fahren.**	*She lets her car be driven to school.*
Sie **läßt** ihr Auto **waschen.**	*She has her car washed (by someone else).*

3. A dative object (see 4.5) is sometimes used with **lassen** to indicate *to* or *for whom* the activity is done.

Frau Schwarz ließ **ihrer Tochter** ein Haus bauen.	*Mrs. Schwarz had a house built for her daughter.*
MORE COMMON: Frau Schwarz ließ ein Haus **für ihre Tochter** bauen.	

4. The dative *reflexive* pronoun (see 17.1) is commonly used with **lassen.**

Ich **muß** *mir* die Haare **schneiden lassen.**	*I have to have my hair cut.*
Sie **läßt** *sich* nicht **helfen.**	*She doesn't let anybody help her.* (literally, *she does not let herself be helped*)

18.5 Infinitives as Nouns

Virtually any infinitive can be capitalized and used as a neuter noun. Such nouns usually correspond to English gerunds (the *-ing* form).

Das Skifahren wird immer beliebter (und teurer).	*Skiing is becoming more and more popular (and expensive).*

Die Kinder haben jetzt keine Zeit **zum Spielen.**	*The children have no time now for playing.*

18.6 Double Infinitives

A. *Double Infinitives with the Perfect Tenses*

1. When used together with another verb, the verbs **fühlen, hören, sehen, spüren,** and **lassen** generally form the perfect tenses with a so-called double infinitive construction rather than with a past participle.

   COMPARE:

Sie **hat** die Mannschaft **gesehen.**	*She saw the team.*
Sie **hat** die Mannschaft **spielen sehen.**	*She saw the team play.*
Er hat den Brief auf dem Tisch **gelassen.**	*He left the letter on the table.*
Er hat den Brief **übersetzen lassen.**	*He had the letter translated.*

2. There is a tendency among some German speakers to use a past participle rather than the double infinitive construction with the four verbs of perception in the section above.

   COMPARE:

Wir haben ihn kommen **hören.** Wir haben ihn kommen **gehört.**	*We heard him come.*

   Some speakers would consider this usage of the past participle to be substandard, but at the present time either construction is acceptable.

3. The verb **helfen** can also form its perfect tense with a double infinitive. However, the tendency among German speakers is to use the past participle in combination with an infinitive phrase with **zu.**

   COMPARE:

Niemand hat dem Kind die Aufgabe **lösen helfen.** Niemand hat dem Kind **geholfen,** die Aufgabe **zu lösen.**	*Nobody helped the child solve the problem.*

4. German speakers often avoid a double infinitive construction by using a simple past tense instead.

Wir **hörten** ihn kommen.	*We heard him come.*
Niemand **half** dem Kind die Aufgabe lösen.	*Nobody helped the child solve the problem.*

5. In dependent clauses, the auxiliary verb comes before a double infinitive.

Ich weiß, daß er den Brief *hat* **übersetzen lassen.**	*I know that he had the letter translated.*

B. *Double Infinitives with the Future Tense*

The future tense of all verbs accompanied by infinitives without **zu** (including modal verbs) results in a double infinitive construction.

Wir werden die Kinder **schwimmen lehren.**	*We will teach the children to swim.*
Sie weiß, daß sie **wird gehen müssen.**	*She knows that she will have to go.*

* Übungen

A **Wie geht es weiter?** Beenden Sie die Sätze einmal mit **zu** plus Infinitiv und einmal mit mehr als zwei Wörtern.

Beispiel: Ich habe vor . . . (arbeiten)
Ich habe zu arbeiten vor. OR *Ich habe vor zu arbeiten.*
Ich habe vor, im Sommer zu arbeiten.

1. Die Touristen haben die Absicht *(intention)* . . . (weiterfahren)
2. Wann fängst du an . . .? (übersetzen)
3. Es scheint jetzt . . . (regnen)
4. Mein Nachbar versucht . . . (singen)
5. Du sollst auch nicht vergessen . . . (schreiben)

B **Mit oder ohne Komma? Ihre Meinung bitte.** Beenden Sie die Sätze mit Infinitivkonstruktionen.

Beispiel: Es macht mir Spaß, . . .
Es macht mir Spaß, Deutsch zu lernen.

1. Ich möchte jemanden bitten . . .
2. Alle Länder der Erde sollten versuchen . . .
3. Manche Leute wünschen nur . . .
4. Jeder Mensch sollte das Recht haben . . .
5. Unsere Regierung sollte aufhören . . .
6. In unserem Land sollten wir endlich einmal beginnen . . .

C **Anders ausdrücken.** Drücken Sie die Sätze anders aus. Verwenden Sie die Präpositionen **um, ohne** und **(an)statt** mit Infinitiven.

Beispiel: Ich lerne Deutsch, weil ich es mit meinen Verwandten sprechen will.
Ich lerne Deutsch, um es mit meinen Verwandten zu sprechen.

1. Manche Menschen denken nicht, wenn sie reden.
2. Wir gehen ins Ausland, wir bleiben nicht hier.
3. Die meisten Menschen arbeiten, damit sie essen können.
4. Wie kann man im Ausland studieren, wenn man die Sprache des Landes nicht versteht?
5. Viele Studenten schreiben ihre Arbeiten am Computer und benutzen keine Schreibmaschine.
6. Viele Touristen reisen ins Ausland, weil sie andere Länder und andere Menschen kennenlernen wollen.

D **Aussagen.** Machen Sie mit den Präpositionen **um, ohne** und **(an)statt** und einer Infinitivkonstruktion jeweils eine Aussage über sich selbst oder andere Menschen, die Sie kennen.

Beispiele: *Meine Schwester redet manchmal, ohne zu denken.*
Ich lerne Deutsch, um es mit meinen Verwandten (relatives) *zu sprechen.*

E **Sätze mit Infinitiven.** Machen Sie aus zwei Sätzen einen Satz.

Beispiel: Hans spielt. Ich sehe es.
Ich sehe Hans spielen.

1. Barbara kocht das Essen. Niemand hilft ihr.
2. Ihr Herz schlägt heftig *(heavily)*. Sie fühlt es.
3. Wir kaufen Lebensmittel ein. Wir gehen oft.
4. Der Baum fällt im Sturm um. Niemand sieht es.
5. Fritz lernt gern. Er lernt, wie man Schach spielt.
6. Sie macht einen Fehler. Niemand hört es.

Schreiben Sie Ihre Sätze jetzt im Perfekt.

Beispiel: *Ich habe Hans spielen sehen.*

F **Einiges über mich.** Ergänzen Sie die Aussagen. Verwenden Sie Infinitive.

Beispiel: Morgens höre ich . . .
Morgens höre ich meine Eltern frühstücken.

1. Ich sehe gern . . .
2. Wenn ich morgens aufwache, höre ich als erstes . . .
3. Als ich noch ganz klein war, lehrte mich jemand . . .
4. Gestern habe ich . . . (sehen / hören)
5. Ich würde gern . . . lernen.

G **Anders ausdrücken.** Drücken Sie Ihre Aussagen in Übung F durch den Gebrauch von Nebensätzen *(clauses)* anders aus.

Beispiel: *Morgens höre ich, wie meine Eltern frühstücken.*

H **Machen lassen.** Bilden Sie mit den Wörtern Sätze, in denen man etwas machen läßt. Verwenden Sie auch die angegebenen Zeitformen. Übersetzen Sie Ihre Sätze.

Beispiel: Professorin / Studenten / Text / übersetzen *(Präsens)*
Die Professorin läßt die Studenten den Text übersetzen.
(The professor has / lets the students translate the text.)

1. Die Eltern / Arzt / holen *(Präsens)*
2. Studentin / Freund / ihr Fahrrad / reparieren *(Präteritum)*
3. Stadt / eine Firma / mehrere alte Häuser / abreißen *(Perfekt)*
4. morgen / Lehrer / seine Schüler / eine Prüfung / schreiben *(Futur)*
5. Lehrerinnen / wollen / ihren Schülern / Film / zeigen *(Präsens)*
6. König / Besucher / eintreten *(Präteritum)*

I **Man kann doch nicht alles selber machen.** Beantworten Sie die Fragen. Verwenden Sie das Verb **lassen.**

1. Was machen Sie, wenn Ihre Haare zu lang sind?
2. Was muß man machen, wenn der Kühlschrank kaputt ist?
3. Was haben Sie in der letzten Woche machen lassen?
4. Was ließen Ihre Eltern Sie früher oft machen?
5. Was lassen Sie gern machen?
6. Was würden Sie gern machen lassen?
7. Was würden Sie nie machen lassen?

* Anwendung

Ungewöhnliche Erfahrungen und Erlebnisse. Tauschen *(exchange)* Sie ungewöhnliche Erfahrungen mit anderen Studenten im Kurs aus. Wer hat das Ungewöhnlichste gesehen oder gehört?

REDEMITTEL

Ja, weißt du, daß ich einmal . . . habe [tun] sehen?
Das ist interessant, aber einmal sah / hörte ich . . . [tun].
Das ist doch gar nichts. Ich habe sogar . . . [tun] sehen / hören.
[X] hat erzählt, daß er / sie einmal . . . hat [tun] sehen.

✱ Schriftliche Themen

Tips zum Schreiben ***Expressing Your Own Views***

When writing about your own views, get to the point quickly. To let readers know that you are expressing your opinions rather than indisputable facts, use phrases such as the following:

ich finde, (daß)
ich glaube, (daß)
meiner Meinung / Ansicht nach
ich halte es für . . . (*See* Wortschatz 11.)

A **Verpflichtungen** *(obligations).* Was wollen oder sagen andere Leute (z.B. Ihre Eltern oder Lehrer), daß Sie tun sollen? Macht es Ihnen Spaß, das zu tun? Tun Sie es ungern? Was lassen Ihre Eltern Sie nicht tun? Verwenden Sie in Ihrem Aufsatz grammatische Strukturen aus diesem Kapitel.

Beispiel: Meine Eltern sagen immer, daß ich ihnen mehr helfen soll. Sie lassen mich z.B. jeden Tag vor dem Essen den Tisch decken. Ich helfe meiner Mutter auch manchmal das Abendessen kochen. Nun, ich finde es schön, zum Haushalt etwas beizutragen *(contribute),* aber ich habe keine Lust, das jeden Tag zu tun. Schließlich will ich mein eigenes Leben führen, und niemand kann von mir erwarten, daß . . . usw.

B **Was man ungern tut.** Müssen Sie manchmal etwas tun, was Sie als besonders schwierig oder unangenehm empfinden? Erzählen Sie davon.

Beispiel: Ich finde es besonders unangenehm, in eine neue Wohnung umzuziehen. Natürlich versuche ich, Leute zu finden, die mir dabei helfen, aber wenn meine Freunde mich kommen sehen . . . usw.

Wortschatz 18

lassen
verlassen
weggehen

1. **Lassen** followed by a noun or pronoun object but no subsequent infinitive means *to leave* someone or something in a place or condition.

Die Kinder **lassen** ihre Bücher in der Schule.	*The children are leaving their books at school.*
Seine Worte **haben** mich kalt **gelassen.**	*His words left me cold.* (that is, *I was not moved by them*)

2. **Verlassen** means *to leave* or *depart* from a person, place, or activity. This verb is transitive and must always be used with a direct object.

Um wieviel Uhr hast du die Party **verlassen?**	*At what time did you leave the party?*
Ich **verließ** ihn in Hamburg.	*I left him in Hamburg.* (that is, *I went away*)

3. **Verlassen** can also imply permanent separation.

Ingeborg hat ihren Mann **verlassen.**	*Ingeborg left her husband.*

COMPARE:

Er **verließ** seine Frau in Rom.	*He left his wife in Rome.* (that is, *he went away, perhaps for good*)
Er **ließ** seine Frau bei Verwandten in Rom.	*He left his wife with relatives in Rome. (no permanent separation implied)*

4. **Weggehen** means *to leave, depart,* or *go away.* This verb is intransitive and cannot be used with a direct object.

COMPARE:

Er hat Berlin **verlassen.**	*He left Berlin.*
Er ist von Berlin **weggegangen.**	*He left / went away from Berlin.*

ÜBUNGEN

A ***Lassen, verlassen* oder *weggehen?*** Ergänzen Sie die Sätze durch passende Verben.

1. Die Frau hat Ehemann und Kinder ____ .
2. Der Mann hat seine Frau für ein paar Tage ____ .
3. Die Frau hat ihre Kinder für ein paar Tage in Bern ____ .
4. Der Mann hat seine Frau zu Hause ____ .
5. Ach, wo habe ich nur meine Schlüssel ____ ?
6. Wann möchtest du von hier ____ ?

B **Fragen.** Stellen Sie drei Fragen an andere Studenten. Verwenden Sie die drei Verben in diesem Wortschatz. Berichten Sie die Antworten.

Zusammenfassung 18

Rules to Remember

1. Infinitives and infinitive phrases are normally in final position within a clause or sentence.
2. Most infinitives require a preceding **zu.**
3. Infinitive phrases of more than two words are normally set off by a comma.
4. Infinitives used in combination with the verbs **fühlen, hören, sehen, spüren, heißen,** and **lassen,** generally take no preceding **zu.**
5. **Fühlen, hören, sehen, spüren,** and **lassen** in combination with other verbs normally form the present perfect tense with an infinitive rather than a participle: **Ich habe ihn kommen sehen** (*not* **gesehen**).

Activities

1 **Sayings.** Invent **Sprüche** for different persons according to the model **„Sein oder nicht sein, das ist die Frage.“**

Beispiel: DEUTSCHSTUDENT(IN): „Vokabeln lernen oder eine schlechte Note bekommen, das ist die Frage.“
FAULER MENSCH: „Essen oder schlafen, das ist die Frage.“

2 **I would rather.** Walk around the class and ask five other students what they would rather be doing than what they are doing now.

Beispiel: Was würdest du jetzt lieber tun, anstatt hier zu sitzen?
Anstatt im Klassenzimmer zu sitzen, würde ich lieber . . .

3 **What's important?** What is important for you in life? What do you not need to do? Make a list of seven or more statements, then share your feelings with a group of four–five other students.

Beispiele: *Für mich ist es wichtig, ein paar gute Freunde zu haben.*
Ich brauche nicht viele Freunde zu haben.

4 **Recipe for success.** Using infinitives, make a list of things you consider important for success in life. Remember to put the infinitive last.

Beispiele: *viele Freunde haben*
einen guten Job finden
fleißig sein
usw.

5 **Likes and dislikes.** What are some of the things you most or least like to see and hear? What do you like or not like to go do? Make a list, then discuss in a group of four or five students.

Beispiel: *Ich sehe gern Leute singen / tanzen / Eishockey spielen,* usw.
Ich höre ungern Hunde bellen, Türen schlagen, usw.
Ich gehe gern tanzen, aber ich gehe ungern wandern.

6 **Opinions for improvements.** Discuss with other students some of the things your school or university should let be or have done **(sollte tun lassen)** to improve the educational experience for students.

Da-Compounds / Uses of *es*

19

19.1 Prepositional *da*-Compounds

A. Forms

1. **Da**-compounds are formed like **wo**-compounds (see 15.2); the prefix **da(r)**- precedes the preposition. They occur with many, but not all prepositions.

da *+ preposition*	***dar-*** *+ preposition*	*colloquial*
dabei	dar**a**n	dran
dadurch	dar**a**uf	drauf
dafür	dar**a**us	draus
dagegen	dar**i**n	drin
damit[1]	dar**ü**ber	drüber
danach	dar**u**m	drum
davon	dar**u**nter	drunter
davor		
dazu		
dazwischen		

ALSO:
daher *(from there, from that)*
dahin *(to there)*

2. **Da**-compounds cannot be formed with **außer, gegenüber, ohne, seit,** or with genitive prepositions.

---

1. There is also the *conjunction* **damit,** which means *so that* (see 11.3).

B. *Use*

1. In prepositional phrases, personal pronouns are used when referring to *persons* or *animals.* However, if a prepositional phrase refers to *one or more inanimate things,* a **da**-compound is normally used.

   COMPARE:

Wartest du auf Ines / Edi?	*Are you waiting for Ines / Edi?*
—Ja, ich warte auf **sie** / **ihn.**	*Yes, I am waiting for her / him.*
Wartest du auf einen Brief von Margaret?	*Are you waiting for a letter from Margaret?*
—Ja, ich warte **darauf.**	*Yes, I am waiting for it.*

2. Occasionally a **da**-compound may be used to refer to living beings as belonging to a group, although the pronoun forms are usually preferable.

In dieser Klasse sind zwanzig Studenten, **darunter** / **unter ihnen** einige recht gute.	*In this class there are twenty students, among them some quite good ones.*

3. A **da**-compound can also refer to an entire previous clause.

Bald werden wir ausziehen müssen, aber **daran** möchte ich jetzt nicht denken.	*Soon we will have to move out, but I don't want to think about it / that now.*

4. In addition to referring to specific inanimate things, **da**-compounds also occur idiomatically in phrases and expressions. Here are some common examples.

Ich kann nichts **dafür.**	*I can't do anything about that.*
Es kommt **darauf** an.	*It all depends.*
Darauf kommt es an.	*That's what counts.*
Dabei bleibt es.	*That's how it's going to be.*
Was sagen Sie **dazu?**	*What do you have to say about that?*
Es ist **damit** aus.	*It's over.*
Heraus **damit!**	*Out with it!*
Was haben wir **davon?**	*What good does it do us?*

19.2 Anticipatory *da*-Compounds

1. Many verbs require prepositional phrases to complete their meanings (see 17.1 and 30.1).

Meine Eltern **freuen sich auf** meinen Besuch.	*My parents are looking forward to my visit.*

2. When the object of the preposition is not a noun, but rather a dependent clause (often introduced by **daß, ob,** or **wie**) or an infinitive clause, a **da**-compound is inserted before the clause. This somewhat redundant **da**-compound anticipates the following clause. In English such clauses are often rendered by a gerund construction, as in the first example below.

Meine Eltern freuen sich **darauf, daß** wir sie bald besuchen.	*My parents are looking forward to our visiting them soon.*
Sie sprechen **darüber, wie** man der Familie am besten helfen kann.	*They are talking about how people can best help the family.*
Es kommt jetzt **darauf** an, keinen Fehler zu machen.	*It is now a matter of not making a mistake.*

3. Sometimes an optional anticipatory **da**-compound is added even when the prepositional phrase is not essential for completing the meaning of the verb.

Sie erzählten **(davon),** wie sie ihre Ferien verbracht hatten.	*They told (about) how they had spent their vacation.*

4. The adverbs **dahin** and **daher** are used with **gehen** and **kommen** to anticipate subsequent clauses and cannot be omitted.

Die Schwierigkeiten kommen **daher,** daß es zu wenige Plätze im Studentenheim gibt.	*The difficulties stem from the fact that there are too few places in the student dormitory.*
Die Tendenz geht jetzt **dahin,** drei Studenten in einem Zimmer unterzubringen.	*The tendency is now to put three students in one room.*

5. **Da**-compounds can also be used with a number of adjectives that often take prepositional complements (see 13.5).

Wir sind **dazu** bereit, Ihnen eine Stelle anzubieten.	*We are prepared to offer you a position.*

19.3 Uses of *es*

A. *Impersonal* es

1. **Es**, like English *it,* can be used impersonally to indicate the occurrence of activities without any specific doers. It occurs frequently in weather and time expressions, as well as with numerous other impersonal verbs.

Es regnet (blitzt, donnert, friert, hagelt, schneit, stürmt).	*It is raining (lightning, thundering, freezing, hailing, snowing, storming).*
Es ist fünf Uhr.	*It is five o'clock.*
Es riecht (stinkt, duftet).	*It smells (stinks, gives off an aroma).*
Es klopft.	*There is a knocking.* (literally, *"it" is knocking*)
Es brennt.	*Something is burning.* (literally, *"it" is burning*)

2. **Es** also occurs in numerous so-called impersonal expressions in which *it* **(es)** is the subject of the German phrase or sentence but not of its English equivalent.

Wie geht **es?**	*How are you?*
Es geht mir gut.	*I am fine.*
Es ist mir heiß / kalt.	*I am hot / cold.*
Es gelingt mir.	*I succeed.*
Es wird mir schlecht.	*I feel sick.*
Es tut mir leid.	*I am sorry.* (literally, *it pains me*)
Es fehlt mir an *(dative)* . . .	*I am missing / lacking* . . .

B. Es gibt; es ist / sind

1. The expression **es gibt** means *there is* or *there are* and normally refers to the *existence* of something. The **es** is impersonal, but it originally referred to Nature, Providence, or Fate, which "gave" such things as weather and rich harvests. Thus **es** is always the subject, the verb form is always singular, and the object of the verb is always in the accusative.

Gibt es einen Gott?	*Is there a God?*
Vielleicht **wird es** Probleme **geben.**	*Perhaps there will be problems.*

2. The expression **es ist / sind** *(there is / are)* is often used interchangeably with **es gibt.** However, **es ist / sind** actually refers to the *presence* of something in a specific place, whereas **es gibt** refers more to general existence.

COMPARE:

Es gibt Kirchen in jeder deutschen Stadt.	*There are churches in every German town.*
Es sind / es gibt fünf Kirchen in unserer Stadt.	*There are five churches in our town.*
Es war / (less common) **es gab** niemand zu Hause.	*There was no one at home.*

3. In main clauses, the impersonal **es** may introduce a sentence in which the true subject follows the inflected verb. The verb agrees with this subject, not with **es.** This construction has a somewhat literary flavor. (See also **es** with the passive, 28.1).

Es wohnen drei Familien in diesem Haus. — *There are three families living in this house.*

Es kam ein Brief. *(literary narrative)* — *There came a letter.*

4. When the sentence begins with a different element, **es** is no longer introductory and cannot be used.

Es blieben nur noch wenige Bücher übrig. — *There were only a few books left over.*

Dann blieben nur noch wenige Bücher übrig. — *Then there were only a few books left over.*

C. *Anticipatory* es

Es may anticipate what is still to come in a subsequent clause. It can be either a subject or a direct object and is often optional after a verb. The same usage occurs in English.

Es freut / ärgert mich, daß . . . OR: Mich freut / ärgert **(es),** daß . . .	*It pleases / annoys me that . . .*
Es macht Spaß, wenn . . .	*It is fun when . . .*
Es ist möglich / schade / wichtig, daß	*It is possible / too bad / important that . . .*
Wir haben **(es)** gewußt, daß . . .	*We knew that . . .*
Ich kann **(es)** nicht glauben, daß . . .	*I can't believe (it) that . . .*

* Übungen

A **Gegenstände *(objects)* des Lebens.** Was kann man mit diesen Gegenständen alles tun? Verwenden Sie Konstruktionen mit **da-.**

Beispiele: ein Haus
*Man kann **darin** wohnen.*

ein Fernseher
*Man kann **davor** einschlafen.*

1. Zeitungen
2. Bleistift und Papier
3. Lebensmittel
4. ein Computer
5. alte Weinflaschen

Erzählen Sie von weiteren Gegenständen.

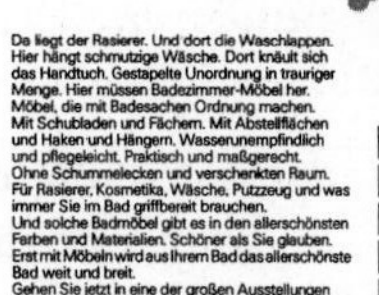

B **Fragen: Mit oder ohne *da*-Konstruktion?** Antworten Sie bitte mit ganzen Sätzen und ganz ehrlich auf die folgenden Fragen.

Beispiele: Sind Sie mit der jetzigen Politik in Ihrer Heimat einverstanden?
*Ja, ich bin **damit** einverstanden.*

Haben Sie Respekt vor Politikern?
*Nein, ich habe keinen Respekt vor **ihnen**.*

1. Freuen Sie sich über das Glück anderer Menschen?
2. Haben Sie etwas gegen Menschen, die anderer Meinung sind als Sie?
3. Haben Sie Vertrauen zu der Regierung Ihres Landes?
4. Haben Sie Angst vor Menschen mit AIDS?
5. Zählen Sie sich zu den Leuten, die fast jeden Tag etwas für die Umwelt tun?
6. Sind Sie bereit, ohne Styroporpackung und Spraydosen zu leben?
7. Sind Sie mit Ihrem bisherigen Leben zufrieden?

C **Knapper sagen.** Drücken Sie die Idee in den folgenden Sätzen viel knapper *(more succinctly)* und stärker aus. Verwenden Sie Ausdrücke mit **da**-Konstruktionen.

Beispiel: Wir haben es so gemacht, und wir können es jetzt nicht mehr ändern.
Dabei bleibt es.

1. Ob ich morgen komme? Tja, wenn ich Zeit habe, komme ich vielleicht, aber ich weiß es noch nicht so genau.
2. Du hast es ja gehört, und jetzt möchte ich deine Meinung wissen.
3. Ich bitte Sie jetzt noch einmal um den Brief.
4. Ich möchte Ihnen helfen, aber ich hatte mit der Entscheidung nichts zu tun.
5. Was für einen Vorteil *(advantage)* soll mir das bringen?
6. Sie haben sich auf unsere Kosten gut amüsiert, aber jetzt hört der Spaß auf.

D **Sätze ergänzen.** Ergänzen Sie die Sätze durch passende **da**-Konstruktionen.

Beispiel: Wir freuen uns . . . unsere Freunde uns besuchen. (über)
*Wir freuen uns **darüber, daß** unsere Freunde uns besuchen.*

1. Unsere Professorin ärgert sich . . . ein paar Studenten nicht zuhören. (über)
2. Ich erinnere mich . . . sie uns geholfen hat. (an)
3. Wir gewöhnen uns . . . früh aufzustehen. (an)
4. Er interessiert sich . . . ein Automotor funktioniert. (für)
5. Wir sprechen . . . wir unsere Sommerferien verbringen wollen. (über)
6. Denke . . . viel Spaß das Spiel machen wird. (an)

E **Anders formulieren.** Drücken Sie die Sätze durch den Gebrauch von **da**-Konstruktionen anders aus.

Beispiel: Du kannst dich auf unsere Hilfe verlassen. (helfen)
*Du kannst dich **darauf** verlassen, daß wir dir helfen werden.*

1. Wir möchten uns für Eure Hilfe bedanken. (helfen)
2. Unsere Professorin beklagt sich *(complains)* über unser häufiges Zuspätkommen. (zu spät kommen)
3. Auswanderer haben oft Angst vor dem Verlust *(loss)* ihrer Muttersprache. (verlieren)
4. Ein Automechaniker hat uns zum Kauf eines neuen Autos geraten. (kaufen)

F **Eigene Sätze bilden.** Bilden Sie wahre Aussagen über sich selbst oder über Menschen, die Sie kennen. Verwenden Sie die angegebenen Verben mit **da**-Konstruktionen.

Beispiel: sich freuen auf
Ich freue mich ***darauf,*** *im Sommer nach Europa zu fahren.*

1. Angst haben vor
2. sich ärgern über *(to be annoyed)*
3. überreden zu *(to persuade to do)*
4. sorgen für *(to see to it)*
5. zweifeln an *(to doubt)*

G **Was gibt's?** Drücken Sie die Sätze anders aus. Verwenden Sie die angegebenen Ausdrücke.

Beispiel: Man findet im Ruhrgebiet viele Großstädte.
Im Ruhrgebiet gibt es viele Großstädte.

es gibt es fehlt es ist / sind es + [Verb]

1. Ich habe im Moment leider kein Geld.
2. Ich höre draußen vor der Tür jemanden klopfen.
3. Am Marienplatz in München befinden sich elegante Geschäfte.
4. Feuer!
5. Daß der Schnee vor morgen kommt, ist höchst unwahrscheinlich.
6. Kein Grund ist vorhanden *(exists),* die Aussage dieses Polizisten zu bezweifeln.

* Anwendung

A **Etwas vorführen** *(demonstrate).* Bringen Sie einen Gegenstand (oder das Bild eines Gegenstandes) zum Unterricht mit. Erklären Sie, wie dieser Gegenstand funktioniert, was man damit machen kann usw. Verwenden Sie Kombinationen mit **da-**.

REDEMITTEL

Das hier ist . . .
Ich möchte euch ein bißchen darüber informieren, wie . . .

Damit kann man . . .
Ich möchte euch auch zeigen, wie . . .
Habt ihr jetzt Fragen darüber?

B **Räumlich beschreiben.** Erkundigen Sie sich bei jemandem im Kurs danach, wie ein bestimmter Raum (z.B. ein Schlafzimmer, ein Garten, die Küche) bei ihm oder ihr aussieht.

Beispiel: STUDENT 1: Wie sieht dein Zimmer im Studentenheim aus?
STUDENT 2: Mein Zimmer ist recht groß. In einer Ecke steht mein Arbeitstisch. Darauf steht mein Computer, und ich schreibe meine Aufgaben damit. Links davon . . . usw.

* Schriftliches Thema

Tips zum Schreiben ***Avoiding Some Common Pitfalls***

Use the first-person-singular **ich** sparingly when presenting your views and opinions on a subject in writing. You can occasionally include your reader or other persons in the solutions you propose by using **wir**. Readers can become confused, however, if you shift between the pronouns **ich** and **wir** for no apparent reason. Also, make sure you have not used the neuter or impersonal pronoun **es** to refer to nouns that are masculine (*pronoun:* **er**) or feminine (*pronoun:* **sie**).

After writing a first draft, reread it to see whether use of an occasional **da**-compound instead of a preposition plus a previously mentioned noun will tighten your text without sacrificing its clarity.

Einen Standpunkt vertreten *(represent).* Äußern Sie sich schriftlich zu einem Thema, zu dem es gewiß viele Meinungen gibt. Versuchen Sie, Ihre Argumente durch einige der folgenden Wendungen *(expressions / phrases)* einzuführen und zu betonen.

REDEMITTEL

Das Problem liegt meiner Meinung nach darin, daß . . .
Wir müssen uns vor allem darüber klar sein, wie / was / wer / inwiefern . . .
Ich möchte daran erinnern, daß . . .
Ich glaube, man kann sich nicht darauf verlassen *(rely upon)*, daß . . .
Ja, das kommt daher / davon, daß . . .
Sind wir uns jetzt darüber einig, daß . . .?
Ich halte es für wichtig / richtig, daß . . .
Daher gibt es keinen Grund, . . . zu [tun]

THEMENVORSCHLÄGE

Weltpolitik
Sozialprobleme
ideologische und politische Konfrontation an der Universität
Wirtschaftspolitik *(economic policy)*
Konflikte auf der Welt

Wortschatz 19

es handelt sich um
es geht um
handeln von

1. The expressions **es handelt sich um** and **es geht um** are synonymous. They indicate what something *is about* and have a number of English equivalents. The subject of these expressions is always **es,** and they are often used with an anticipatory **da**-compound.

	it is a question of	*we are dealing with*
es handelt sich um	*it is a matter of*	*we are talking about*
es geht um	*at issue is*	*it concerns*
	at stake are	

Es handelt sich um deine Zukunft.	*We are talking about your future.*
Um was für einen Betrag **geht es** denn?	*Well, what (kind of an) amount are we talking about?*
Es handelt sich darum, möglichst schnell zu arbeiten.	*It is a matter of working as quickly as possible.*

2. **Handeln von** is used to express the idea that a book, poem, play, movie, etc. *is about* something.

Dieser Film **handelt von** (der) Politik.	*This film is about politics.*
Wovon handelt dieses Fernsehspiel?	*What is this television play about?*

ÜBUNG

Auf deutsch. Drücken Sie die Sätze auf deutsch aus.

1. This story is about a woman with five children.
2. It is a matter of his pride **(der Stolz).**
3. "Have you read Peter Handke's *Wunschloses Unglück*?" "No, what is it about?"

Subjunctive I

indirect discourse or reported speech, objective

Subjunctive II

- cast a little doubt
- extremely polite
- dreams, wishes

ether we should support **(unterstützen)** the war or not.
n all about?

refer only to things, not to persons and animals.
ised to anticipate a following infinitive clause or subordi-

e is) is always in the accusative.
to the existence of an action, not to a specific thing: **Es**

Activities

Es and **da-** do not readily lend themselves to specific activities. However, you can practice the anticipatory **da-**construction in connection with reflexive verbs by doing **Anwendung B** in Chapter 17. Additional exercises with anticipatory **da-** can be found in Chapter 30.

Conditional Subjunctive (Subjunctive II)

20

20.1 Conditional Subjunctive

In both English and German, the *indicative* mood is used to express a real condition and its conclusion or result.

CONDITION *CONCLUSION / RESULT*
Wenn er Zeit **hat, geht** er zum Picknick.
If he has time, he is going / will go to the picnic.

The *conditional subjunctive,* known also as Subjunctive II **(der zweite Konjunktiv),** is used to express an unreal, hypothetical, or contrary-to-fact condition and its possible conclusion or result. There are no tenses in the conditional subjunctive, only times. A conditional clause (beginning with **wenn**) and its resultant clause are either in a hypothetical present / future time or in past time.

CONDITION *CONCLUSION / RESULT*
Wenn er Zeit **hätte, ginge** er zum Picknick.
If he ***had*** *time (either now or in the future), he* ***would go*** *to the picnic.*

Wenn er Zeit **gehabt hätte, wäre** er zum Picknick **gegangen.** *(past time)*
If he had had time (in the past), he would have gone to the picnic.

20.2 Present-Time Conditional Subjunctive Forms

The present-time conditional subjunctive is formed from the second principal part (the past-tense indicative stem) of a verb, hence the grammatical designation "Subjunctive II."

A. *Regular Weak Verbs*

The present-time conditional subjunctive of weak verbs is formed by adding the subjunctive endings **-e, -est, -e; -en, -et,** and **-en** to the past-tense stem. Since these endings are identical to the past-tense endings, the present-time conditional subjunctive is identical to the past tense of these verbs. For this reason, weak verb conditional subjunctive forms are very often replaced by an alternate subjunctive construction consisting of conjugated forms of **würde(n)** (the Subjunctive II of **werden**) + the weak verb infinitive, particularly in a resultant clause.

	Past Indic. /Subj. II	*Alternate Construction*
	lernen	
ich	lernt **e**	**würde . . . lernen**
du	lernt **est**	**würdest . . . lernen**
er / sie / es	lernt **e**	**würde . . . lernen**
wir	lernt **en**	**würden . . . lernen**
ihr	lernt **et**	**würdet . . . lernen**
sie / Sie	lernt **en**	**würden . . . lernen**

Wenn ich Deutsch lernte, **reiste** *(uncommon)* ich nach Österreich.
Wenn ich Deutsch lernte, **würde** ich nach Österreich **reisen.**
} *If I were learning German, I would travel to Austria.*

B. *Strong Verbs*

1. The present-time conditional subjunctive of strong verbs is formed by adding the subjunctive endings **-e, -est, -e; -en, -et,** and **-en** to the past-tense stem. In addition, the past-tense stems take an umlaut when the stem vowel is **a, o,** or **u.**

	Past Indicative			*Subjunctive II*	
	gehen	**kommen**			
ich	ging	kam	ich	ging **e**	käm **e**
du	gingst	kamst	du	ging **est**	käm **est**
er / sie / es	ging	kam	er / sie / es	ging **e**	käm **e**
wir	gingen	kamen	wir	ging **en**	käm **en**
ihr	gingt	kamt	ihr	ging **et**	käm **et**
sie / Sie	gingen	kamen	sie / Sie	ging **en**	käm **en**

Other examples:

Infinitive	*Past Indic.*	*Subj. II*
bleiben	blieb	er / sie **bliebe**
fliegen	flog	er / sie **flöge**
schneiden	schnitt	er / sie **schnitte**
werden	wurde	er / sie **würde**

Wenn unsere Freunde jetzt **kämen,** **blieben** wir zu Hause. — *If our friends came now, we would remain at home.*

2. With the exception of very common verbs such as **sein, werden, gehen, kommen,** and **tun,** the present-time conditional subjunctive of these verbs occurs mainly in written German. In spoken German, and to some extent in written German, there is a strong tendency to use the alternate construction with **würde(n),** particularly in the resultant clause, but even in the **wenn**-clause.

Wenn er schneller **führe, würde** er das Rennen **gewinnen.**
Wenn er schneller **fahren würde,** **würde** er das Rennen **gewinnen.**
} *If he drove / would drive faster, he would win the race.*

3. A number of strong verbs with the past-tense stem vowel **a** have alternative subjunctive forms with **ö** or **ü.** In some instances, **ö** or **ü** are the only forms. These forms sound obsolete and are normally replaced by **würde(n)** + the verb infinitive.

Infinitive	*Past Indic.*	*Subj. II*	
beginnen	begann	er / sie **begönne**	(*or* **begänne**)
empfehlen	empfahl	er / sie **empföhle**	(*or* **empfähle**)
gewinnen	gewann	er / sie **gewönne**	(*or* **gewänne**)
stehen	stand	er / sie **stünde**	(*or* **stände**)
helfen	half	er / sie **hülfe**	
sterben	starb	er / sie **stürbe**	
werfen	warf	er / sie **würfe**	

C. *Irregular Weak Verbs*

1. In the present-time conditional subjunctive of irregular verbs, the vowel of the past-tense stem either takes an umlaut or changes to **e,** depending on the verb.[1]

Infinitive	*Past Indic.*	*Subj. II*
brennen	brannte	er / sie **brennte**
bringen	brachte	er / sie **brächte**
denken	dachte	er / sie **dächte**
kennen	kannte	er / sie **kennte**
nennen	nannte	er / sie **nennte**
rennen	rannte	er / sie **rennte**
senden	sendete / sandte	er / sie **sendete**
wenden	wendete / wandte	er / sie **wendete**
wissen	wußte	er / sie **wüßte**

1. The **e** in the subjunctive of these verbs is really an umlauted **a (ä).** The sound is the same; only the orthography is different.

2. With the exception of **wissen,** these conditional subjunctive forms are usually replaced by **würde(n)** + the verb infinitive.

Wenn ich das täte, **würde** sie schlecht von mir **denken.**	*If I did that, she would think badly of me.*
Wenn ich mehr lesen würde, **wüßte** ich mehr.	*If I would read more, I would know more.*

D. Modal Verbs

Modal verbs with an umlaut in the infinitive take an umlaut in the present-time conditional subjunctive; **sollen** and **wollen** do not. The subjunctive forms of these verbs are *not* normally replaced by **würde(n)** + the verb infinitive. Note the meanings of the modals in the conditional subjunctive.

Infinitive	*Past Indic.*	*Subj. II*	
dürfen	durfte	er / sie **dürfte**	*would / might be permitted to*
können	konnte	er / sie **könnte**	*could / would be able to*
mögen	mochte	er / sie **möchte**	*would like to*
müssen	mußte	er / sie **müßte**	*would have to*
BUT:			
sollen	sollte	er / sie **sollte**	*should*
wollen	wollte	er / sie **wollte**	*would want to*

E. Haben, sein, werden

Haben, sein, and **werden** are the verbs most commonly used in the present-time conditional subjunctive. They all require an umlaut. Their alternative forms with **würde(n)** + infinitive are infrequent.

Infinitive	*Past Indic.*	*Subj. II*	*Alternate Construction*
haben	hatte	er / sie **hätte**	**würde . . . haben**
sein	war	er / sie **wäre**	**würde . . . sein**
werden	wurde	er / sie **würde**	**würde . . . werden**

F. Conditional Subjunctive Forms Versus würde(n) + *Infinitive*

1. In spoken German, only the present-time conditional subjunctive forms of **haben, sein, werden, gehen, tun, wissen,** and the modal verbs are still very common and preferred. With most other verbs, there is an increasing tendency to substitute

conjugated forms of **würde(n)** *(would)* + an infinitive, particularly in a resultant clause.

Wenn sie hier **wäre, würde** sie uns **helfen.**	*If she were here, she would help us.*
Wenn er uns nur **schreiben würde!**	*If he would only write us!*

2. Until a few years ago, **würde(n)** + infinitive in **wenn**-clauses was considered poor style, particularly in written German. In many instances this opinion no longer holds true.

Wenn Sie **mitkommen würden,** würden wir uns sehr freuen.	*If you would come along, we would be very happy.*

3. Present-time conditional subjunctive forms occur with greatest frequency in formal writing, where excessive repetition of **würde(n)** + an infinitive would be poor style. As a rule, stylists frown upon the use of **würde(n)** in both clauses of a conditional statement, unless the conditional subjunctive forms of both verbs sound stilted or obsolete. The less common a strong verb, the greater the probability that its conditional subjunctive forms will be avoided.

20.3 Uses of the Present-Time Conditional Subjunctive

A. *Hypothetical Conditions and Conclusions*

1. The present-time conditional subjunctive is most often used to express an unreal or contrary-to-fact condition and conclusion. Such "hypothetical" statements consist of two parts: a **wenn**-clause and a concluding clause. Since the **wenn**-clause is a subordinate clause, the verb is placed at the end of this clause (see 11.3). The following clause begins either with a conjugated verb or with an optional **dann** or **so** followed by the conjugated verb. The English equivalent is *If. . ., then . . .*

COMPARE:

Wenn wir besser **verdienen würden,** (dann / so) **könnten** wir ein Haus **kaufen.**	*If we earned more, (then) we could buy a house.*
Wenn sie mehr Zeit **hätte,** (dann / so) **würde** sie uns **besuchen.**	*If she had more time, (then) she would visit us.*

2. The order of the main clause and the **wenn**-clause can be reversed, just as in English, in which case **dann** is omitted.

Wir **könnten** ein Haus kaufen, wenn wir besser **verdienen würden.**	*We could buy a house if we earned more.*

3. Occasionally a **wenn**-clause begins with a verb and no **wenn.** In such instances, the **dann** or **so** in the concluding clause is optional but normally included. In English, this usage is restricted to the verbs *to have* and *to be,* but not in German.

Hätte sie mehr Zeit, (dann / so) würde sie uns besuchen.	*Had she more time, (then) she would visit us.*
Käme er jetzt, (dann / so) könnte er uns helfen.	*If he came now, (then) he could help us.*

B. *Conclusions Without Expressed Conditions*

It is possible to use the conditional subjunctive without any condition expressly stated, though one is often implied by the context. In such instances, German uses **würde(n)** + an infinitive with weak verbs, Subjunctive II with **haben** and modals, and either form with most strong verbs.

Das **würde** ich nicht **sagen!**	*I wouldn't say that!*
Das **könnte** sein.	*That could be.*
Wir **blieben** lieber zu Hause. BETTER: Wir **würden** lieber zu Hause **bleiben.**	*We would prefer to stay home.*

C. *Wishes*

1. Since wishes are inherently contrary to fact, they are also expressed by a present-time conditional subjunctive. The intensifying adverb **nur** is added, sometimes in combination with the flavoring particle **doch** (see 25.2E).

Wenn er (doch) nur **käme** / **kommen würde!** (fact: *he is not coming*)	*If only he were coming!*

2. As in conditional statements, **wenn** can be omitted; the verb in first position then expresses the idea of *if.*

Wäre es **(doch)** nur wärmer!	*If it were only warmer!*

3. German often prefaces contrary-to-fact wishes with the verbs **wollen** or **wünschen.** In such instances, **wollen** or **wünschen** are also put in the conditional subjunctive.

Ich **wollte / wünschte,** wir **hätten** mehr Zeit!	*I wish we had more time!*

D. Polite Requests

The present-time conditional subjunctive is used to make very polite requests.

Würden Sie bitte etwas leiser sprechen?	*Would you please speak more softly?*
Ich **hätte gern / möchte** einen Nachtisch.	*I would like some dessert.*
Könnten Sie mir bitte 20 Mark wechseln?	*Could you please change 20 marks for me?*
Dürfte ich Sie bitten, ihm zu helfen?	*Might I ask you to help him?*
Wäre es möglich, noch etwas zu bestellen?	*Would it be possible to order something else?*

E. After **als (ob) / als (wenn)**

1. A clause introduced by the conjunctions **als (ob)** or **als (wenn)** (see 11.3) often describes a situation that *appears* to be the case but in the speaker's view may not be true. If the **als ob** clause refers to the same time as the main clause, then the present-time conditional subjunctive is used, and sometimes even the alternate construction with **würde(n)** + infinitive, although the latter might be considered substandard by some grammarians.

Er tut (so), *als ob* er den Chef nicht **verstünde.**	*He acts as if he does not understand the boss (but he probably does).*
Er tat (so), *als ob* er nichts **hören würde.**	*He acted as if he didn't hear anything.*

2. Often the **ob** or **wenn** is omitted and the verb placed directly after **als.**

Das Haus sieht aus, *als* **wohnte** jetzt niemand dort.	*The house looks as if no one were living there now.*

3. In present time, the indicative is often used if in the speaker's view the impression is a correct one.

Er benimmt sich, als ob er krank ist.	*He is behaving as if he is sick* (that is, *he probably is sick*).

20.4 The Past-Time Conditional Subjunctive

A. *Forms*

1. The conditional subjunctive in past time is formed with the subjunctive auxiliary forms **hätte(n)** or **wäre(n)** + past participle.

Ich **hätte gearbeitet.**	*I would have worked.*
Sie **wären gegangen.**	*They would have gone.*

2. Alternative forms with **würde(n)** + **haben / sein** + past participle **(Ich würde gearbeitet haben; Sie würde gegangen sein)** are grammatically possible, but usually avoided.

B. *Use*

1. The past-time conditional subjunctive is used to express unreal past conditions and past conclusions that were contrary to fact.

COMPARE:

Wenn sie früher **käme, würde** sie den Zug nicht **verpassen.** *(present)*	*If she came earlier* (hypothetical condition), *she would not miss the train.*
Wenn sie früher **gekommen wäre, hätte** sie den Zug nicht **verpaßt.** *(past)*	*If she had come earlier, she would not have missed the train.*

2. Past-time subjunctive and present-time subjunctive can be used in the same sentence.

COMPARE:

PAST TIME	*PAST TIME*
Wenn Mozart länger **gelebt hätte,**	**hätte** er mehr Sinfonien **komponiert.**
If Mozart had lived longer,	*he would have composed more symphonies.*

PAST TIME	*PRESENT TIME*
Wäre er nicht so jung **gestorben,**	**gäbe** es jetzt mehr Kompositionen von ihm.
If he had not died so young,	*there would now be more compositions by him.*

3. As with the present-time conditional subjunctive, the order of the two clauses in the past-time conditional subjunctive can be reversed.

Vielleicht **wäre** Mozart nicht so jung **gestorben,** wenn er sich mehr **geschont hätte.**	*Perhaps Mozart would not have died so young if he had taken better care of himself.*

4. The past-time conditional subjunctive can also be used to describe conclusions without expressed conditions.

So etwas **hätten** unsere Studenten nie **getan.**	*Our students would never have done such a thing.*

5. Wishes about past time require past-time conditional subjunctive.

Wenn er nur länger auf Godot **gewartet hätte!**	*If only he had waited longer for Godot!*

C. Modals in the Past-Time Subjunctive

1. When no infinitive accompanies a modal verb, the past-time conditional subjunctive is formed with the subjunctive auxiliary **hätte(n)** + past participle.

Ihre Mutter **hätte** das nicht **gewollt.**	*Her mother would not have wanted that.*
Wir **hätten** es nicht **gekonnt.**	*We would not have been able to do it.*

2. If an infinitive accompanies the modal verb, the past-time conditional subjunctive is formed with the auxiliary **hätte(n)** + a double infinitive (see 9.3). The subjunctive double infinitive construction is quite common with the three modals **können, müssen,** and **sollen** but less so with the others.

Common

Sie **hätte gehen können.**	*She could have gone (but didn't).*
Sie **hätte gehen müssen.**	*She would have had to go (but didn't).*
Sie **hätte gehen sollen.**	*She should have gone (but didn't).*

Less Common

Sie **hätte gehen dürfen.**	*She would have been permitted to go.*
Sie **hätte** nicht **gehen mögen.**	*She would not have liked to go.*
Sie **hätte gehen wollen.**	*She would have wanted to go.*

3. The double infinitive always comes last, even in subordinate clauses; the auxiliary **hätte(n)** precedes it.

Wer weiß, ob sie die Prüfung **hätte bestehen können.**	*Who knows whether she could have passed the exam.*

D. After als (ob) / als (wenn)

The past-time conditional subjunctive is used after **als (ob) / als (wenn)** if the **als ob** clause refers to a time prior to that of the main clause.

Er tat so, *als ob* er den Chef nicht **verstanden hätte.**	*He acted as if he had not (previously) understood the boss.*

20.5 Indicative Versus Subjunctive with *können, müssen,* and *sollen*

Compare the following indicative and subjunctive forms.

	Indicative	*Subjunctive*
können	Sie **konnte** es **tun.** Sie **hat** es **tun können.**	Sie **könnte** es **tun.**
	She was able to do it.	*She could / would be able to do it.*
	Sie **kann / konnte** es **getan haben.**	Sie **hätte** es **tun können.**
	She could have done it. (that is, *it is possible that she did it*)	*She could have done it.* (that is, *she was capable of doing it, but didn't*)
müssen	Wir **mußten** es **tun.** Wir **haben** es **tun müßen.**	Wir **müßten** es **tun.**
	We had to do it.	*We would have to do it.* OR: *We (really) should do it.*
	Wir **müssen** es **getan haben.**	Wir **hätten** es **tun müssen.**
	We must have done it.	*We would have had to do it.* OR: *We (really) should have done it.*
sollen	Du **solltest** es **tun.** Du **hast** es **tun sollen.**	Du **solltest** es **tun.**
	You were supposed to do it.	*You should / ought to do it.*
	Du **sollst** es **getan haben.**	Du **hättest** es **tun sollen.**
	You are said to have done it.	*You should have done it (but you didn't).*

* Übungen

A **Formen üben.** Sagen Sie es anders.

Beispiele: er ginge
er würde gehen

sie würde uns schreiben
sie schriebe uns

1. du würdest denken
2. sie fielen
3. er würde sitzen
4. sie würde stehen
5. wir trügen es
6. sie würde fliegen
7. er schnitte sich
8. sie fänden uns
9. ich träfe ihn
10. ihr würdet froh sein
11. wir läsen es
12. ich würde dir helfen
13. er würde laufen
14. es würde kalt werden
15. sie verließe ihn

B **Formen in der Vergangenheit** *(past).* Setzen Sie die Formen in Übung A in die Vergangenheit.

Beispiele: er ginge
er wäre gegangen

sie würde uns schreiben
sie hätte uns geschrieben

C **Wie schön wäre das!** Stefan denkt, wie schön es wäre, wenn er morgen keine Schule hätte. Setzen Sie seinen Brief an Gabi in den Konjunktiv.

Liebe Gabi,

ach, wie schön wäre das, wenn wir morgen keine Schule hätten! Ich *stehe* erst gegen neun Uhr *auf.* Nach dem Frühstück *kommen* dann Freunde zu mir, und wir *gehen* in der Stadt bummeln. Vielleicht *essen* wir zu Mittag in einem Straßencafé. Danach *kaufen* wir im Musikgeschäft ein paar CDs, wenn wir noch genug Geld *haben.* Wenn nicht, dann *wissen* wir auch etwas anderes zu tun. Wir *können* uns zum Beispiel einen Film ansehen. Du *darfst* mitkommen, wenn du *willst,* aber du *mußt* schon um zehn Uhr bei mir sein. Es *ist* dann sicher sehr lustig.

Dein Stefan

D **Wie schön wäre das gewesen!** Setzen Sie Stefans Brief von Übung C in den Konjunktiv der Vergangenheit.

Beispiel: *Ach, wie schön wäre das gewesen, wenn wir* **gestern** *keine Schule gehabt hätten . . .*

E **Wie wäre es, wenn . . .?** Erzählen Sie in ein bis zwei Sätzen davon.

Beispiel: wenn das Semester schon zu Ende wäre
Wenn das Semester schon zu Ende wäre, würde ich nach Hause fahren und arbeiten. Ich würde auch fast jeden Abend mit Freunden ausgehen (ginge . . . aus).

1. wenn Sie mehr Zeit hätten
2. wenn Sie im Lotto viel Geld gewinnen würden
3. wenn Sie die Gelegenheit *(opportunity)* hätten . . . [zu tun]
4. wenn Sie Minister im Kabinett des US-Präsidenten wären
5. wenn Ihr Deutsch perfekt wäre

Machen Sie fünf weitere Aussagen dieser Art *(type)* über sich selbst oder über Menschen, die Sie kennen.

F **Ach, solche Studenten!** Frau Professor Schwerenote überlegt, wie ihr Kurs vom letzten Jahr gewesen wäre, wenn die Studenten nur mehr gearbeitet hätten. Was denkt sie?

Beispiel: Udo lernte nicht fleißig und bekam deswegen eine schlechte Note.
Wenn Udo fleißig gelernt hätte, hätte er sicher eine gute Note bekommen.

1. Sara schlief manchmal während der Stunde ein und störte den Unterricht dauernd durch lautes Schnarchen *(snoring)*.
2. Heinz hat seine Aufgaben nie rechtzeitig abgegeben *(handed in)* und verlor deswegen Punkte bei der Bewertung seiner Arbeit.
3. Josef schwänzte *(cut class)* manchmal und schrieb deswegen oft die falschen Hausaufgaben.
4. Angelika hat oft während der Stunde mit anderen Studenten gesprochen und deswegen oft den Unterricht gestört *(disturbed)*.
5. Vicki hörte oft nicht zu und wußte deshalb oft nicht, was andere gerade gesagt hatten.

Und was denken diese fünf Studenten wahrscheinlich über Frau Professor Schwerenote?

G **Ach, wenn es nur anders wäre!** Drücken Sie Wünsche zu den folgenden Themen aus. Verwenden Sie möglichst viele verschiedene Verben.

Beispiel: zu Ihrem Deutschkurs
Ach, wenn es im Deutschkurs nicht so viele Prüfungen gäbe!

1. zu Ihrem Leben
2. zum Leben Ihrer Eltern
3. zu einer Situation auf Ihrer Uni oder in Ihrer Schule
4. zum Leben in Ihrem Heimatland
5. zur Sozialpolitik in Ihrem Land
6. zur Weltpolitik
7. zu einem weiteren Thema

H **O je.** Haben Sie als Kind manches (nicht) getan, was Sie jetzt bereuen *(regret)*? Machen Sie fünf Aussagen.

Beispiele: *Ich wünschte, ich hätte meine Eltern nicht so viel geärgert.*
Ach, wenn ich nur meinen Eltern mehr geholfen hätte!

I **Wir bitten höflichst.** Was sagen Sie in diesen Situationen?

Beispiel: Im Zug raucht eine Frau neben Ihnen eine Zigarette. Das stört Sie.
Würden Sie bitte so nett sein und jetzt nicht rauchen?
OR: *Dürfte ich Sie bitten, jetzt nicht zu rauchen?*

1. Sie essen mit anderen Leuten zusammen und wollen die Butter haben.
2. Sie wollen $10 von jemandem borgen.
3. Bei einer Prüfung haben Sie die Anweisungen Ihres Professors / Ihrer Professorin nicht verstanden.
4. Sie bitten am Informationsschalter im Bahnhof um Auskunft.
5. Sie sind in einer Buchhandlung und suchen ein bestimmtes Buch.

J **Berühmte Menschen.** Erzählen Sie, was fünf berühmte Menschen (lebend oder tot) vielleicht anders hätten tun können oder sollen.

Beispiel: Abraham Lincoln
Er hätte an einem anderen Tag ins Theater gehen können (oder *sollen*).

K **Ich hätte helfen sollen.** Drücken Sie die Sätze auf deutsch aus.

1. I was supposed to help with the garden yesterday.
2. I could have helped, if I had had the time.
3. I probably should have helped.
4. But since I didn't have the time, I couldn't help.
5. My parents had to work without me.
6. If I had helped them, they would not have had to do everything alone.

L **Menschen, die so tun, als (ob).** Machen Sie fünf Aussagen über Menschen, die Sie kennen und die so tun, *als ob.* Machen Sie bitte ein paar Aussagen über die Gegenwart *(present)* und ein paar über die Vergangenheit.

Beispiele: *Mein Bruder tut / tat immer so,* ***als ob*** *er alles besser wüßte als ich.*
Meine Lehrer taten früher immer so, ***als*** *hätte ich etwas Dummes gesagt.*

✱ Anwendung

A **Was wäre, wenn?** Diskutieren Sie mit anderen Leuten, wie die Welt und das Leben anders wären, wenn gewisse Dinge anders wären.

THEMENVORSCHLÄGE

Wenn niemand ein Telefon / einen Fernseher hätte.
Wenn Sie unsichtbar wären.
Wenn es keinen Strom mehr gäbe.
Wenn es noch keine Computer gäbe.

REDEMITTEL

Wenn (das) so . . . wäre, ja dann . . .
Ja, erstens würde ich . . .
Ich glaube, ich würde . . .
Für mich wäre dann die Hauptsache / das Wichtigste . . .
Dann müßte / könnte man auch . . .
Und schließlich würde man / ich . . .

Wenn der Strom nicht wäre.

B **Änderungsvorschläge.** Diskutieren Sie mit anderen Studenten eine Situation im heutigen Leben, die anders werden sollte oder könnte. Geben Sie Ihre Meinung darüber, wie man diese Situation ändern sollte, könnte oder müßte, damit alles besser wäre oder sein könnte.

THEMENVORSCHLÄGE

Ihr eigenes Leben
die AIDS-Erkrankungen
die große Armut *(poverty)* auf der Welt
das Drogenproblem

die Zerstörung *(destruction)* der Umwelt
eine Situation auf Ihrer Universität oder an Ihrer Schule
die politische Lage irgendwo auf der Welt

REDEMITTEL

Meiner Meinung / Ansicht nach müßte / könnte / sollte man . . .
Ich glaube, wir müßten / könnten . . .
Ich bin der Meinung / Ansicht, daß . . .
Es wäre besser, wenn . . .
Ich wünschte, wir könnten . . .
So wie ich die Sache sehe, müßte man . . .
Man kann ja auch umgekehrt *(conversely)* argumentieren und sagen, daß . . .

C **Wenn das anders verlaufen wäre.** Besprechen Sie mit anderen Leuten ein politisches, kulturelles oder historisches Ereignis. Diskutieren Sie, was vielleicht geschehen wäre, wenn man anders gehandelt hätte. Was wären die Folgen *(results)* für heute?

THEMENVORSCHLÄGE

Wenn Amerika 1776 den Unabhängigkeitskrieg nicht gewonnen hätte.
Wenn Franzosen im Jahre 1789 die Bastille nicht gestürmt hätten.
Wenn der Norden im amerikanischen Bürgerkrieg nicht gesiegt hätte.
Wenn Lenin die Werke von Karl Marx nicht gelesen hätte.
Wenn Japan Pearl Harbor nicht angegriffen hätte.
Wenn es in der Sowjetunion weder Glaznost noch Perestroika gegeben hätte.

* Schriftliche Themen

Tips zum Schreiben ***Using the Conditional Subjunctive***

If you are presenting facts, you will use the indicative. If you are conjecturing, you *must* use the conditional subjunctive. In your writing, strive for a stylistic balance between conditional subjunctive forms and the alternate construction with **würde(n)** + an infinitive (see 20.3). As a rule, avoid the conditional subjunctive of weak verbs and less commonly used strong verbs (for example, **hülfe, schöbe, löge,** etc.). If at all possible, however, you should not include **würde(n)** + infinitive in both clauses of a conditional statement. Sometimes you can substitute the modals **könnte(n)** and **dürfte(n) / müßte(n)** for **würde(n)** without changing the meaning significantly (see below). Avoid too many **hätte**'s and **wäre**'s; they add little to a composition. Finally, once you have initiated conjecture with a **wenn**-clause, there is no need to keep repeating this condition; continued use of the subjunctive signals continuing conjecture: **Wenn ich eine Uhr *wäre*, dann *würde* ich gern an einer Wand im Bahnhof *hängen*. Ich *dürfte*** (*instead of* **würde**) **nie *schlafen*, denn ich *müßte*** (*instead of* **würde**) **die Zeit *messen* und den Menschen *zeigen*, wie spät es ist.**

A **Wenn ich [X] wäre.** (Ihr Professor / Ihre Professorin wird Ihnen sagen, was in Ihrem Fall das X sein soll.)

B **Mal was anderes.** Erzählen Sie, wie es wäre, wenn Sie einmal aus der Routine Ihres täglichen Alltags ausbrechen könnten. Was würden / könnten Sie anders tun? Wo? Mit wem? Warum?

C **Der Wunsch.** In was für einer Welt würden Sie gern leben?

Beispiel: Ich würde gern in einer Welt leben, in der alle Menschen in Frieden leben und arbeiten dürften. Alle würden glücklich sein, und niemand müßte sterben, weil er nicht genug zu essen bekäme. In einer solchen Welt gäbe es auch keine Rechtsanwälte *(lawyers)*, denn niemand würde gegen andere Menschen einen Prozeß führen, und ein weiser Richter *(judge)* würde alle Streitfälle *(disputes)* schlichten *(settle)* . . . usw.

D **Ein Bittbrief.** Schreiben Sie einen kurzen aber höflichen Brief, in dem Sie eine Person, eine Firma, ein Fremdenverkehrsamt *(tourist bureau)* usw. um etwas bitten.

Beispiel:

Steierischer Landesfremdenverkehrsverband
Herrengasse 16 (Landhaus)
A-8010 Graz
Österreich / Europa

Sehr geehrte Herren,

ich möchte meinen Winterurlaub in Österreich verbringen und bitte Sie deswegen um Auskunft über Winterferienorte in der Steiermark. Vor allem hätte ich gern Auskunft über Skiorte und über günstige Zugverbindungen. Ich wäre Ihnen auch sehr dankbar, wenn Sie mir diese Information umgehend *(promptly)* per Luftpost schicken könnten, damit ich Fahrt und Unterkunft bald buchen kann.

Mit herzlichen Grüßen

Ihr

Wortschatz 20

sich benehmen	tun, als ob
sich aufführen	handeln
sich verhalten	

1. **Sich benehmen** means *to act, behave (according to notions of socially good or bad behavior)*. It is usually used with adverbs such as **anständig** *(decently)*, **gut, schlecht, unmöglich,** etc.

Kinder, **benehmt euch** bitte!	*Children, please behave!*
Auf der Party haben **sich** ein paar Gäste sehr schlecht **benommen.**	*At the party a few guests behaved very badly.*

2. **Sich aufführen** means *to act, behave,* or *carry on.* It expresses *conspicuous* behavior. It requires an adverb.

Du hast **dich** aber komisch **aufgeführt.**	*You certainly behaved strangely.*

3. **Sich verhalten** means *to act, react, behave* in a given situation. It suggests controlled behavior.

Wie **verhalten sich** Menschen in solchen Streßsituationen?	*How do people behave in such stressful situations?*
Er wartete, was kommen sollte, und **verhielt sich** ganz ruhig.	*He waited to see what was to come and acted very calmly.*

4. **Tun, als ob** means *to act* or *behave as if.*

Der Hund **tut** (so), als ob er uns verstünde.	*The dog is acting as if he understands us.*

5. **Handeln** means *to act, take action.*

Manche Leute **handeln** nur im eigenen Interesse.	*Some people act only in their own interest.*

ÜBUNGEN

A **Welche Verben passen?** Ergänzen Sie die Sätze durch passende Verben aus **Wortschatz 20.**

1. Während der Operation ____ sich der Patient ganz ruhig.
2. Wenn niemand seine Bitte erhört, dann muß er selber ____ .
3. Während des Unterrichts hat sich das Kind unmöglich ____ .
4. Die anderen Partygäste waren schockiert, weil Fred sich so unmöglich ____ .
5. Gernot ____ immer sehr schnell, wenn er eine Entscheidung getroffen hat.
6. Hilda weiß nicht alles, sie ____ nur so.
7. Das Tier ____ sich ganz still, bis die Gefahr vorüber war.

B **Situationen.** Erklären Sie, was man in diesen Situationen tun muß oder soll. Es gibt manchmal mehr als nur eine Möglichkeit. Verwenden Sie Verben aus **Wortschatz 20.**

Beispiel: Man will guten Eindruck machen.
Man muß / soll sich höflich (politely) *benehmen.*

1. Andere Leute im Bus wollen schlafen.
2. Andere Leute brauchen dringend Hilfe.

3. Man will nicht verraten *(reveal),* daß man Angst hat.
4. Man hat sich um eine Stelle beworben *(applied)* und stellt sich jetzt beim Personalchef einer Firma vor.
5. Man will nicht für einen Narren *(fool)* gehalten werden.

Zusammenfassung 20

Rules to Remember

1. The conditional subjunctive (Subjunctive II) expresses an unreal, hypothetical or contrary-to-fact condition.
2. There are no tenses in the subjunctive. Instead, there are two time frames, present and past.
3. The present-time conditional subjunctive is formed from the past-tense indicative of a verb: **ging** → **ginge** *(would go);* **kam** → **käme** *(would come);* **lernte** → **lernte** *(would learn).*
4. The verbs **haben, sein, werden, gehen, kommen, tun** and the modal verbs regularly occur in the present-time conditional subjunctive: **hätte(n) / wäre(n) / würde(n) / ginge(n) / käme(n) / täte(n); dürfte(n) / könnte(n) / müßte(n) / möchte(n) / sollte(n) / wollte(n).**
5. Most other verbs (strong and weak) often or even regularly express the present-time conditional subjunctive with **würde(n)** + infinitive, particularly in spoken German.
6. The past-time conditional subjunctive is formed with the conditional subjunctive of the auxiliary verbs **haben** or **sein** + a past participle: **hätte(n) getan** *(would have done);* **wäre(n) gegangen** *(would have gone).*

Activities

1 **What if?** If you could, what are some things that you would do that you presently either are not able or not allowed to do? Use present-time subjunctive.

Beispiel: *Wenn ich könnte / dürfte, würde ich . . .*

2 **Why might you do?**[2] Suggest an unusual action and ask other students why they might perform this action. Compare student answers (the zanier the better!).

Beispiel: STUDENT A: Warum würdest du einen Affen zur Deutschstunde mitbringen?

STUDENT B: Ich würde einen Affen zur Deutschstunde mitbringen, wenn ich eine schwere Deutschprüfung hätte und der Affe Deutsch könnte.

2. From Ur and Wright, *Five-Minute Activities.*

3 **Do it over.** Tell three things you would do either differently or the same if you could relive the past year. Use present-time subjunctive.

Beispiel: *Wenn ich das vergangene Jahr wiederholen könnte, würde ich . . .*

4 **I wish I had known.**[3] Pick an age in your past and write five sentences expressing your regrets about that time. Compare your regrets with those of two other students.

Beispiel: *Ich wünschte, ich hätte damals die Ratschläge meiner Eltern besser befolgt.*

5 **If I had only.** Tell how things would be different now (use present-time subjunctive) if you had pursued other interests or a different course of action in previous years (use past-time subjunctive).

Beispiel: *Ach, wenn ich damals besser gelernt hätte, würde ich heute . . .*

6 **Working with a text.** Speculate about how events in a story you and your class recently read might have been different, had characters in the story acted differently.

---

3. From Rinvolucri, *Grammar Games.*

Adjective Nouns / Participial Modifiers

21

21.1 Adjective Nouns

A. *Masculine and Feminine Adjective Nouns*

1. Masculine and feminine nouns designating persons are sometimes formed from adjectives or from participles used as adjectives. Such nouns are capitalized, and they require the same primary or secondary endings that they would have as adjectives (see 13.2).

	Masc.	***Fem.***	***Pl.*** *(preceded / unpreceded)*
Nom.	der Fremd **e** (ein Fremd **er**)	die Fremd **e** (eine Fremd **e**)	die Fremd **en** / Fremd **e**
Acc.	den Fremd **en**	die Fremd **e**	die Fremd **en** / Fremd **e**
Dat.	dem Fremd **en**	der Fremd **en**	den Fremd **en** / Fremd **en**
Gen.	des Fremd **en**	der Fremd **en**	der Fremd **en** / Fremd **er**

Wir konnten **den Fremden** (*that is,* **den fremden Mann**) nicht finden.	*We could not find the stranger.*
Einige **Fremde** (*that is,* **fremde Menschen**) traten in den Hof.	*Some strangers walked into the courtyard.*

2. The following adjective nouns are quite common. Those marked with an asterisk are derived from either present or past participles (see 21.2).

der / die Angestellte*	*employee*	der / die Bekannte	*acquaintance*
der Beamte / die Beamtin	*official / female official*	der / die Deutsche	*German person*
		der / die Erwachsene*	*adult*

der / die Reisende*	*traveler*	der / die Verwandte*	*relative*
der / die Tote	*dead person*	der / die Vorgesetzte*	*supervisor, superior*
der / die Verlobte*	*fiancé(e)*		

B. Neuter Adjective Nouns

1. Neuter nouns derived from adjectives take either primary or secondary neuter adjective endings. Such nouns refer only to ideas, collective concepts, or abstractions.

		Neut.	
Nom.	das Gut **e**	ein Gut **es**	Gut **es**
Acc.	das Gut **e**	ein Gut **es**	Gut **es**
Dat.	dem Gut **en**	einem Gut **en**	Gut **em**
Gen.	des Gut **en**	eines Gut **en**	——

Er hat nur **Gutes** getan. — *He did only good (things).*

Der Pfarrer sprach vom **Guten** im Menschen. — *The pastor spoke of the good (things) in people.*

2. Sometimes neuter nouns are formed using comparative or superlative forms of adjectives (see 14.1).

Wir haben **Schlimmeres** erwartet. — *We expected worse (things).*

Sie hat ihr **Bestes** getan. — *She did her best.*

3. Adjectives following the pronouns **etwas, nichts, viel,** or **wenig** become neuter nouns with primary endings.

Tun Sie was Gutes.

Nom.	etwas Nett **es**
Acc.	etwas Nett **es**
Dat.	etwas Nett **em**
Gen.	——

Zum Geburtstag möchte ich sie mit **etwas Nettem** überraschen. — *For her birthday I would like to surprise her with something nice.*

Hast du **nichts Neues** erfahren? — *Didn't you find out anything new?*

4. **Ander-** is the only adjective noun not capitalized after **etwas, nichts, viel, wenig,** and **alles:**

Sprechen wir von etwas **anderem.** — *Let's talk about something else.*

5. After the declinable pronoun **alles** *(everything),* adjective nouns take secondary neuter endings.

Nom.	alles Wunderbar **e**
Acc.	alles Wunderbar **e**
Dat.	allem Wunderbar **en**
Gen.	alles Wunderbar **en**

Wir haben schon **alles Brauchbare** gefunden.	*We have already found everything usable.*

21.2 Participles as Adjectives

A. Present Participles as Adjectives

Present participles **(das Partizip Präsens)** are formed by adding **-d** to the infinitive; the **-(e)nd** ending corresponds to English *-ing*. Present participles describe an *action in progress* and are often used as attributive adjectives with endings.

eine **helfende** Hand	*a helping hand*
fließendes Wasser	*running water*
die **abfallenden** Blätter	*the falling leaves*

B. Past Participles as Adjectives

1. Past participles **(das Partizip Perfekt)** (see 3.1) describe a *completed action* and occur often as predicate adjectives.

Das Fenster war **geschlossen.**	*The window was closed.*
Sein Computer ist jetzt **repariert.**	*His computer is now repaired.*

2. Past participles can also be used attributively to modify nouns.

das **verwöhnte** Kind	*the spoiled child*
ein **gebrauchtes** Auto	*a used car*
aus **abgebrannten** Häusern	*out of burned-down houses*

21.3 Extended Modifiers

A. Extended Participial Modifiers

1. By including additional words in front of a participial adjective or any other adjective, it is possible to create a so-called *extended modifier* **(eine erweiterte Partizipialkonstruktion).**

eine **renovierte** Wohnung	*a renovated apartment*
eine **neulich renovierte** Wohnung	*a recently renovated apartment*

2. In German, the number of modifying words and phrases inserted before the adjective and noun can continue to expand and can include other parts of speech, such as prepositional phrases. In English, more than one or two modifiers are usually placed after the noun or in a relative clause.

   eine **neulich von der Stadt renovierte** Wohnung
   an apartment (that was) recently renovated by the city (literally, *a "recently-by-the-city-renovated" apartment*)

3. Within an extended modifier, adverbial phrases follow the Time-Manner-Place rule (see 1.1D).

   TIME (seit mehr als zehn Jahren) — *PLACE* (in Lübeck)

   die **seit mehr als zehn Jahren in Lübeck wohnende** Malerin
   the painter who has been living in Lübeck for more than ten years (literally, *the "for-more-than-ten-years-in-Lübeck-living" painter*)

4. Extended modifiers are also possible without participles.

   Die Stadt hat die **für den Bau eines neuen Spielplatzes nötigen finanziellen** Mittel.
   The city has the financial means for the construction of a new playground. (literally, *the city has the "for-the-construction-of-a-new-playground-necessary" means*)

5. The use of longer extended modifiers in German is a matter of stylistic preference. They usually sound quite official or formal.

   Die Beerdigung des **gestern im Alter von 95 Jahren in Prag gestorbenen italienischen** Komponisten Roberto Pinnza wird morgen in Mailand stattfinden.
   The burial of the Italian composer Roberto Pinnza, who died yesterday at the age of 95 in Prague, will take place tomorrow in Milan.

B. *Extended Modifiers with* zu + *Present Participle*

In very official or technical language, one occasionally encounters **zu** + a present participle used as part of an extended modifier to indicate that something *is to be, can be,* or *must be* done.

Der Professor schrieb die **zu lösenden** Aufgaben an die Tafel.	*The professor wrote the problems to be solved on the board.*
Die Arbeiter warten auf die **an sie auszuzahlenden** Löhne. MORE COMMON: Die Arbeiter warten auf die Löhne, die an sie auszuzahlen sind.	*The workers are waiting for the wages (that are) to be paid out to them.*

* Übungen

A **Adjektiv → Substantiv.** Ergänzen Sie durch passende Adjektivsubstantive.

Beispiel: In den Großstädten gibt es viele ____. (arm)
In den Großstädten gibt es viele ***Arme.***

angestellt	reich	verlobt
blind	tot	verwandt
einäugig		

1. Im Zweiten Weltkrieg gab es Millionen von ____ .
2. Viele meiner ____ kommen aus Deutschland.
3. Ein ____ kommt nicht leicht in das Himmelreich.
4. Diese Firma hat mehr als fünftausend ____ .
5. Ein ____ gibt seiner ____ einen Ring.
6. Im Reich der ____ ist der ____ König.

B **Anders ausdrücken.** Verwenden Sie Adjektive als Substantive im Neutrum. Übersetzen Sie Ihre Sätze.

Beispiel: Er hat etwas gesagt, was sehr gut war.
Er hat etwas sehr Gutes gesagt.
(He said something very good.)

1. Wir wünschen, daß euch nur gute Dinge passieren.
2. Auf unserer Reise durch die Schweiz haben wir viele interessante Dinge gesehen.
3. Alles, was wichtig ist, wird dir der Chef erklären.
4. Die Dame spricht von nichts, was neu ist.
5. Die Tagesschau brachte wenige neue Nachrichten.
6. Was machst du jetzt?—Nichts, was besonders wäre.
7. Sie hat eine morbide Faszination für das, was krank ist.

C **Was paßt am besten?** Ergänzen Sie die Substantive durch passende Partizipien des Präsens.

Beispiel: die Sonne
die ***aufgehende*** *Sonne*

1. die Temperatur
2. ein Wald
3. viele Kinder
4. alle Zuschauer
5. eine Hand
6. Kohlen *(coals)*

D **Länger und noch länger machen.** Erweitern Sie die Ausdrücke in Übung C zuerst durch einen adverbialen Ausdruck, dann durch mehrere Wörter.

Beispiel: *die aufgehende Sonne*
*die **am Morgen aufgehende** Sonne*
*die **ganz früh am Morgen im Osten aufgehende** Sonne*

E **Partizip Präsens → Partizip Perfekt.** Hier sind einige Phrasen mit Partizip Präsens. Bilden Sie Phrasen mit denselben Wörtern, aber mit *Partizip Perfekt.* Übersetzen Sie beide Phrasen ins Englische.

Beispiel: die **ab**fallenden Blätter
*die **ab**fallenden Blätter: the falling leaves*
*die **abgefallenen** Blätter: the fallen leaves*

1. ein abbrechender Ast *(branch)*
2. wachsende Städte
3. aussterbende Kulturen
4. einladende Familien
5. der jagende *(hunting)* Mensch
6. die besuchenden Kinder

F **Länger machen.** Erweitern Sie die Phrasen von Übung E durch ein weiteres Element.

Beispiele: die abfallenden Blätter
*die **schnell** abfallenden Blätter*
die *abgefallenen* Blätter
*die **während des Sturms** abgefallenen Blätter*

G **Partizipialkonstruktionen.** Drücken Sie die Relativkonstruktionen durch Partizipialkonstruktionen (entweder Partizip Präsens oder Partizip Perfekt) anders aus.

Beispiele: der Zug, der schnell abfährt
der schnell abfahrende Zug

ein Bus, der schon abgefahren ist
ein schon abgefahrener Bus

1. die Theorie, die von Einstein aufgestellt wurde
2. die Steuern *(taxes),* die dauernd steigen
3. der Preis, der rasch gesunken war
4. der Brief von einer Mutter, die in Rostock wohnt
5. in einem Auto, das neulich repariert wurde
6. eine Autorin, die von Millionen gelesen wird

H **Erweiterte Partizipialkonstruktionen.** Unterstreichen Sie erweiterte Partizipialkonstruktionen in den folgenden Sätzen. Übersetzen Sie die Sätze ins Englische.

Beispiel: Die nicht durch die Hermes-Exportkredit-Versicherung gedeckten Forderungen deutscher Exporteure belaufen sich auf etwa eine Milliarde Mark. (*Deutschland Nachrichten*)

The claims of German exporters (that are) not covered by Hermes Export Credit Insurance amount to roughly a billion marks.

1. Endlich rief das seit Jahren brutal unterdrückte *(suppressed)* Volk zur Revolution auf.
2. Der wegen mehrerer Berglawinen *(avalanches)* vorübergehend *(temporarily)* geschlossene Sankt-Gotthard-Paß soll heute abend gegen 18 Uhr für den Verkehr wieder freigegeben werden.
3. Von den 96 beim Absturz *(crash)* der „Mozart" der Lauda Air ums Leben gekommenen Österreichern konnten bisher 72 Opfer *(victims)* identifiziert werden.
4. Achtung, Achtung, eine Durchsage! Der aus Stuttgart kommende Intercity-Zug 511 wird wegen in der Nähe von Augsburg noch nicht abgeschlossener Gleisreparaturen *(track repairs)* mit zwanzigminutiger Verspätung auf Gleis 7 ankommen.
5. Am Ende seines Vortrags *(lecture)* faßte der Professor die wichtigsten, dennoch von mehreren Forschern *(researchers)* in Frage gestellten Ergebnisse *(results)* seiner Untersuchungen zusammen und wies auf einige noch durchzuführende *(carry out)* Experimente hin.

* Anwendung

Partizipialkonstruktionen im Gebrauch. Suchen Sie aus Zeitungen, Zeitschriften oder anderen Quellen *(sources)* drei bis fünf erweiterte Partizipialkonstruktionen. Stellen Sie diese Konstruktionen im Kurs vor.

* Schriftliche Themen

Tips zum Schreiben ***Using Extended Modifiers***

Lengthy extended modifiers are rarely a sign of good style. Shorter extended modifiers, however, can be used to good effect to avoid short relative clauses that might interrupt the flow of a sentence. From a German point of view, the phrase **der von Gleis fünf abfahrende Intercity-Zug** is simply more to the point than the relative clause construction **der Zug, der von Gleis fünf abfährt,** particularly when additional information is still to come. Perhaps this is why extended modifiers occur frequently in official announcements, both written and spoken.

A **Eine Mitteilung** *(notification).* Sie arbeiten für ein Studentenreisebüro und schreiben eine Mitteilung in Amtsdeutsch *(officialese)* über eine Reise an die Adria *(Adriatic Sea),* die nicht mehr stattfinden wird.

DIE INFORMATION

Eine Ferienreise an die Adria war geplant.
Diese Reise wird nicht mehr stattfinden.
Man konnte nicht alle Hotelzimmer buchen, die nötig waren.
Hinzu *(in addition)* kamen auch einige Schwierigkeiten bei der Buchung des Fluges.
Diese Schwierigkeiten waren unerwartet.
Außerdem dauern *(continue)* die politischen Spannungen *(tensions)* in den balkanischen *(Balkan)* Ländern noch an.
Deswegen hat Ihr Reisebüro die Reise abgesagt *(cancelled)*.
Für die Reise nach Kreta (Griechenland) sind noch einige Plätze frei.
Diese Reise findet auch zu Ostern statt.

B **Eine Meldung** *(announcement)*. Schreiben Sie in Amtsdeutsch eine Meldung für Ihren Deutschkurs oder für Ihre Schule / Universität. Hier wäre ein bißchen Humor am Platz *(in order)*.

Beispiel: Der von allen Studenten bewunderte und geliebte Deutschprofessor Joseph Bart wird in Zukunft seinen mit Arbeit überlasteten *(overburdened)* Studenten keine schweren Prüfungen mehr geben. Er hat außerdem mitgeteilt, daß . . . usw.

Wortschatz 21

lernen	entdecken
erfahren	feststellen
herausfinden	

1. **Lernen** (see also **Wortschatz 2**) means *to acquire knowledge or ability* through study or experience.

Sie hat einen Beruf **gelernt.**	*She learned a profession.*
Er **lernt** gerade, wie man einen Computer bedient *(uses)*.	*He is learning right now how to use a computer.*

2. **Erfahren** means *to learn* or *find out* without any study or searching necessarily implied.

Ich habe aus der Zeitung von ihrem Tod **erfahren.**	*I learned / found out about her death from the newspaper.*

Wir haben diese Nachricht von einem Freund **erfahren.**	*We learned / heard this news from a friend.*

3. **Herausfinden** means *to learn, find out,* or *discover* through effort or inquiry.

Kannst du **herausfinden,** wo sie wohnt?	*Can you find out where she lives?*
Die Polizei hat den Dieb noch nicht **herausgefunden.**	*The police have not yet found out who the thief is.*

4. **Entdecken** means *to discover.*

Immer wieder **entdeckt** man in dieser Stadt etwas Neues.	*Again and again one discovers something new in this city.*
Kolumbus hat Amerika **entdeckt.**	*Columbus discovered America.*

5. **Feststellen** means *to ascertain* or *determine* and implies that information is acquired through directed effort or inquiry. It is more formal than **herausfinden.**

Es wurde **festgestellt,** daß Franz Gelder unterschlagen hatte.	*It was ascertained that Franz had embezzled monies.*
Der Arzt muß die Ursache der Krankheit noch **feststellen.**	*The doctor still has to ascertain the cause of the sickness.*

ÜBUNGEN

A **Das passende Verb.** Welche Verben in **Wortschatz 21** könnte man mit den folgenden Wörtern oder Ausdrücken verwenden?

Beispiel: ein neues Computergeschäft
ein neues Computergeschäft entdecken

1. etwas Neues über Computer
2. einen Fehler im Softwareprogramm
3. woher der Fehler im Softwareprogramm kommt
4. wo man Computer am günstigsten reparieren läßt
5. daß es meistens zuviel kostet, einen älteren Computer reparieren zu lassen
6. wie man einen Computer selbst repariert

B **Eigene Erfahrungen.** Was haben Sie in diesem Semester erfahren, herausgefunden, entdeckt oder festgestellt? Machen Sie eine Aussage mit jedem Verb.

Beispiel: *Ich habe **erfahren,** daß Deutsch nicht immer leicht ist.*

Zusammenfassung 21

Rules to Remember

1. Many adjectives can be capitalized and made into adjective nouns.
2. Masculine adjective nouns always refer to male persons, female adjective nouns to female persons, and neuter adjective nouns to abstractions: **der Gute** *(the good man);* **die Gute** *(the good woman);* **das Gute** *(that which is good).*
3. Adjective nouns take the same primary or secondary endings they would as adjectives.
4. Present and past participles can function as adjectives: **eine helfende Hand, das verlorene Paradies.**
5. Most extended modifiers contain either a present participle or a past participle.
6. The modifiers within an extended modifier construction follow normal word order rules. Thus the participle is usually the last element before the noun: **Der von seinen Freunden geliebte Mann.**

Activities

1 **Recognizing participial modifiers.** Skim or read through a German-language newspaper such as the weekly *Deutschland Nachrichten*[1] or *Die Zeit.* Search for sentences containing ten present participles or past participles used as modifiers. Share your examples with the class.

2 **Associations.** Working with a partner or in a small group, write four or five phrases you associate with each of the four seasons, using present and/or past participles in short modifier constructions. Compare your phrases with those of other groups.

Beispiel: Herbst: *abfallende Blätter, zur Schule gehende Kinder* usw.

3 **Expanding sentences.** Working in groups of four to five, each student writes a short and simple sentence on a piece of paper that contains at least three nouns, including one in a prepositional phrase. Students pass their papers to the left, and the next student expands the sentence. Only additions of one word or phrases of two or three words may be added. Papers are then passed to the left again until sentences have been expanded as much as possible.

Beispiel: Der Mann sprach mit seiner Frau im Supermarkt.
Der ***alte*** *Mann sprach mit seiner Frau im Supermarkt.*
Der ***alte, hinkende*** *Mann sprach . . .*

---

1. The *Deutschland Nachrichten* is available on a free subscription basis from the German Information Center, 950 Third Avenue, New York, NY 10022.

*Der alte, **auf Krücken hinkende** Mann sprach . . .*
*Der alte, **auf Krücken hinkende** Mann sprach mit seiner **hübschen** Frau im Supermarkt.*
usw.

4 **Shrinking sentence.** Search through texts, preferably from German newspapers or scientific writing, for the longest extended modifier you can find. Take turns subtracting elements from this sentence, one element at a time, until only a core sentence remains. After each subtraction, the sentence must still be grammatically correct.

22 Numerals and Measurements

22.1 Cardinal Numbers

A. *Forms*

German words for cardinal numbers (**die Grundzahl, -en**) are always single words, no matter how complicated the number, with the exception of numbers over a million.

0	null				
1	eins	11	elf	21	**ein**undzwanzig
2	zwei	12	zwölf	22	zweiundzwanzig
3	drei	13	dreizehn	30	dreißig
4	vier	14	vierzehn	40	vierzig
5	fünf	15	fünfzehn	50	fünfzig
6	sechs	16	**sech**zehn	60	**sech**zig
7	sieben[1]	17	**sieb**zehn	70	**sieb**zig
8	acht	18	achtzehn	80	achtzig
9	neun	19	neunzehn	90	neunzig
10	zehn	20	zwanzig	99	neunundneunzig

1. In German-speaking countries the numeral 7 is usually handwritten with a slash through the middle (7̶) to distinguish it from the numeral *1*.

100	(ein)hundert
101	hunderteins
102	hundertzwei
200	zweihundert
999	neunhundertneunundneunzig
1.000	(ein)tausend
2.000	zweitausend
9.999	neuntausendneunhundertneunundneunzig
100.000 (OR 100 000)	hunderttausend
1.000.000 (OR 1 000 000)	eine Million
2.000.000	zwei Million**en**
1.000.000.000	eine Milliarde *(billion)*
2.000.000.000	zwei Milliard**en**
1.000.000.000.000	eine Billion *(trillion)*
2.000.000.000.000	zwei Billion**en**

B. Use

1. The word **eins** is used in counting and mathematics. Before a noun, **ein-** takes article endings. To distinguish **ein-** meaning *one* from **ein-** meaning *a*, German speakers stress the word when speaking. In written texts, this stress can be indicated by italics, underlining, or spacing.

Ich habe das alles in **e i n e m** Buch gefunden.	*I found all that in* ***one*** *book.*

2. **Ein** has no ending in the expression *one or two* and *one to two,* etc.

Wir fahren in **ein bis zwei Jahren** nach Deutschland.	*We are traveling to Germany in one to two years.*

3. **Ein** is optional before **hundert** and **tausend.** If used, the number is still one word.

125	(ein)hundertfünfundzwanzig
1.500	(ein)tausendfünfhundert

4. Either a period or a space is inserted to separate thousands.

37.655 or 37 655 = *English 37,655*

5. **Million, Milliarde,** and **Billion** take endings in the plural.

Deutschland hat fast 80 **Millionen** Einwohner.	*Germany has almost 80 million inhabitants.*

6. In percents or decimals, German uses commas where English uses periods.

4,5 (vier Komma fünf)	*four point five (= 4.5)*
8,9% (acht Komma neun Prozent)	*eight point nine percent (= 8.9%)*

7. Whole numbers plus one-half have no endings and are written as follows:

anderthalb / eineinhalb	*one and a half*
zweieinhalb, dreieinhalb usw.	*two and a half, three and a half, etc.*

Der Film hat **anderthalb** Stunden gedauert.	*The film lasted one and a half hours.*

C. *Approximations*

Numbers and amounts are approximated with words such as **etwa, rund,** or **ungefähr,** which all mean *roughly, around, about,* or *approximately.*

Es sind **etwa / rund / ungefähr** 800 Kilometer von München nach Hamburg.	*It is about / around / approximately 800 kilometers from Munich to Hamburg.*

D. *Adjective Suffixes with Numbers*

1. The suffix **-mal** means *times* and is often added to numbers to create adverbs. Its adjective form **-malig** takes endings.

einmal	*once*	**zigmal**	*umpteen times*
fünfmal	*five times*	ein **einmaliges** Angebot	*a one-time offer*
hundertmal	*a hundred times*	**mehrmaliges** Lesen	*repeated reading*

2. The suffix **-erlei** indicates *kinds of* and is often used with numbers. This suffix takes no adjective ending.

zweierlei Bücher	*two kinds of books*
zehnerlei Bäume	*ten kinds of trees*
allerlei Probleme	*all kinds of problems*

3. The suffix **-fach** corresponds to English *-fold.* It takes endings when used as an attributive adjective.

eine **zweifache** Summe	*a twofold sum*
ein **zehnfacher** Gewinn	*a tenfold profit*

22.2 Ordinal Numbers

A. *Forms*

From 1 to 19, the ordinal numbers **(die Ordnungszahl, -en)** (first, second, third) end in **-t** plus an adjective ending; from 20 on, they end in **-st** plus an adjective ending. Several are slightly irregular and are highlighted in the following chart.

1.	(der, die, das)	**erste**
2.	(der, die, das)	zweite
3.	(der, die, das)	**dritte**
4.	etc.	vierte
5.		fünfte
6.		sechste
7.		**siebte** (*less common:* **siebente**)
8.		**achte** (*no second* **t** *added*)
9.		neunte
10.		zehnte
11.		elfte
12.		zwölfte
19.		neunzehnte
20.		zwanzigste
21.		einundzwanzigste
30.		dreißigste
100.		hundertste
1.000.		tausendste

B. *Use*

1. Ordinal numbers always take either primary or secondary adjective endings (see 13.2).

das **erste** Mal	*the first time*
ihr **zweites** Buch	*her second book*

2. A period after a cardinal numeral indicates **-t** / **-st** plus adjective ending.

Heute ist der 1. Mai (der erste Mai).	*Today is May 1st.*
Wir feiern heute seinen 100. Todestag (seinen hundertsten Todestag).	*Today we are celebrating the 100th anniversary of his death.*

3. To enumerate points, German speakers use the adverbial forms **erstens** *(first of all),* **zweitens** *(in the second place / secondly),* **drittens** *(in the third place / thirdly),* etc.

Er kann uns nicht helfen. **Erstens** ist er nicht hier, **zweitens** hätte er keine Lust dazu, und **drittens** wüßte er nicht, was er tun sollte.	*He can't help us. First of all, he isn't here; secondly, he wouldn't want to; and thirdly, he wouldn't know what to do.*

C. *Fractional Amounts*

1. With the exception of **die Hälfte** *(one-half),* fractions are neuter nouns and therefore capitalized. They are formed by adding **-tel** (from **Teil,** *part*) to the stems of

ordinal numbers. Since this construction would yield two **t**'s (or even three in the case of **dritt-**), one **t** is dropped.

ein Dritt + tel → **Drittel**	*one-third*
fünf Zwanzigst + tel → **Zwanzigstel**	*five-twentieths*

2. *Half a(n)* is expressed in German by **ein- halb-**.

Sie bestellten **ein halbes** Huhn.	*They ordered half a chicken.*

3. *Half (of) the* is most often expressed by **die Hälfte** plus the genitive or by **die Hälfte von** with the dative, particularly in reference to more than one item.

Er verkaufte **die Hälfte** der Orangen / **von** den Orangen.	*He sold half (of) the oranges.*

4. German sometimes uses **d- halb-** *(half the)* instead of **die Hälfte** when referring to a single entity.

Ich habe schon **den halben** Roman (OR **die Hälfte** des Romans / **von** dem Roman) gelesen.	*I have already read half of the novel.*

22.3 Units of Measurement

A. *Currencies, Denominations, and Decades*

1. Most currencies, including **Mark, Pfennig** (Germany), **Schilling** (Austria), and **Dollar,** are singular when used with numbers.

DM 4,80	vier **Mark** achtzig
öS 6,10	sechs **Schilling** zehn
$7,25	sieben **Dollar** fünfundzwanzig

2. To indicate denominations of bills, coins, and stamps, German uses numbers with an **-er** suffix.

Bitte, drei **Sechziger** (Briefmarken) und **eine**[2] **Achtziger.**	*Three sixties and an eighty, please.*
Ich brauche hundert Mark: **einen**[3] **Fünfziger, zwei Zwanziger** und **einen Zehner.**	*I need one hundred marks: a fifty, two twenties, and a ten.*

---

2. **Achtziger** is feminine because **die Briefmarke** is understood.
3. **Fünfziger** is masculine because **der Schein** *(bill)* is understood.

3. Decades are also indicated with an **-er** suffix.

John F. Kennedy wurde in den **sechziger (60er)** Jahren Präsident der USA.	*John F. Kennedy became President of the U.S. in the sixties.*

B. Distances, Weights, Quantities, and Temperatures

1. The metric system is used in Europe and throughout the world as the International System of Units. It provides a logical and interconnected framework for all measurements in science, industry, and commerce.
The following metric units of measurement are very common.

Distance

der / das Kilometer[4] (km)	*(= 0.62 mile)*
der / das Meter (m)	*(= 39.37 inches)*
der / das Zentimeter (cm)	*(= 0.39 inch)*
der / das Millimeter (mm)	*(= 0.039 inch)*
der / das Quadratmeter (m^2)	*(= 10.76 square feet)*

Weight

das Gramm (g)	*(= 0.035 ounce)*
das Kilogramm (kg)	*(= 2.2 pounds)*
der Zentner	*(= 50 kilograms) (a hundredweight)*

Liquid Measure

der / das Liter *(= 1.057 quarts)*

2. The following English units of measurement are also common in German.

das Pfund	*(= 500 grams)*[5]
der Zoll	*(= 2.54 centimeters or 1 inch)*
die Meile, -n	*(= 1.6 kilometers)*
die Gallone, -n	*(= 3.79 liters)*

3. In German, masculine and neuter nouns of measurement used after numerals take no ending in the plural, while feminine nouns ending in **-e** do.

zwei Kilometer	*two kilometers*
zwei Gramm	*two grams*
zwei Meile**n**	*two miles*

4. With **Meter** and its compounds and with **Liter,** the masculine gender is normally used, although some dictionaries still list neuter as the preferred gender (see 12.1E).
5. An English troy pound is 450 grams; a German **Pfund** is 500 grams.

4. Unlike English, German does *not* use the word *of* in expressions of measurement.

	vier Flaschen Wein	*four bottles of wine*
	drei Glas Bier	*three glasses of beer (measure of quantity)*
BUT:	drei **Gläser**	*three glasses (not a measure of quantity)*

5. The Celsius / Centigrade system is used in Europe and throughout the world to measure temperatures. Thirty-two degrees Fahrenheit equals 0 degrees Celsius. To convert Fahrenheit to Centigrade, subtract 32 and multiply by 5/9. To convert Centigrade to Fahrenheit, multiply by 9/5 and add 32.

Degrees Celsius (Centigrade)	*Degrees Fahrenheit*
–40	–40
–35	–31
–30	–22
–25	–13
–20	–4
–15	5
–10	14
–5	23
0	32
5	41
10	50
15	59
20	68
25	77
30	86
35	95
40	104

* Übungen

A **Grundzahlen üben.** Schreiben Sie fünf sechsstellige Zahlen auf. Lesen Sie jemandem im Kurs Ihre Zahlen vor. Er / sie schreibt die Zahlen auf. Hat er / sie die richtigen Zahlen geschrieben?

B **Vom ersten bis zum?** Sagen Sie das mündlich! Vergessen Sie die Adjektivendungen nicht.

1. der 1. Mensch
2. der 2. Weltkrieg
3. beim 3. Mal
4. am 4. Juli
5. das 5. Rad am Wagen
6. mit meinem 6. Sinn *(sense)*
7. das 7. Siegel *(seal)*
8. ein 8. Weltwunder
9. Beethovens 9. Sinfonie
10. im 19. Bond-Film
11. die 20. Olympiade
12. am Ende seines 33. Lebensjahrs
13. jede 100. Person
14. das 254. Buch von Isaac Asimov

C **Fakten.** Schreiben Sie sieben historische oder kulturelle Tatsachen *(facts)* mit Ordnungszahlen. Lesen Sie Ihre Tatsachen im Kurs vor.

Beispiele: *Harry Truman war der 33. Präsident der U.S.A.*
Den internationalen Tag der Arbeit feiert man am 1. Mai.

D **Kombinationen.** Wie viele Kombinationen von Dollar- oder Markscheinen ergeben hundert Dollar / Mark?

Beispiele: *Zwei Fünfziger machen hundert Dollar.*
Hundert Einser machen hundert Dollar.

E **Schlagzeilen** *(headlines)*. In welchem Jahrzehnt war das? (Die Antworten finden Sie unten.)

Beispiel: ERSTE MENSCHEN AUF DEM MOND!
Das war in den sechziger Jahren.

1. LUFTANGRIFF AUF PEARL HARBOR!
2. PANIK AUF DER WALL STREET! MILLIARDEN VERLOREN!
3. HAWAII WIRD FÜNFZIGSTER BUNDESSTAAT!
4. DIE BERLINER MAUER GIBT'S NICHT MEHR!
5. JERRY GARCIA GESTORBEN!
6. VIERTE GOLDMEDAILLE FÜR JESSE OWENS!

Erfinden Sie weitere Schlagzeilen aus diesem Jahrhundert. Andere Studenten sollen erraten, in welchem Jahrzehnt diese Ereignisse *(events)* geschehen sind.

F **Auf deutsch bitte.** Wie sagt man das auf deutsch?

1. a two-time winner **(der Gewinner)**
2. a threefold increase **(die Steigerung)**
3. one-and-a-half hours
4. two kinds of people
5. half an hour
6. about fifty percent
7. half of the time
8. two-thirds of the voters **(der Wähler)**
9. two billion
10. umpteen times

Antworten: 1. 1941 2. 1929 3. 1959 4. 1989 5. 1995 6. 1936

G **Fragen.** Beantworten Sie die Fragen mit metrischen Maßeinheiten.

1. Wie groß *(tall)* sind Sie?
2. Wie weit ist es von Ihrer Universität zu Ihrer Heimatstadt?
3. Wieviel wiegen Sie?
4. Wie viele Quadratmeter hat Ihr Schlafzimmer? Ihre Wohnung? Ihr Haus?
5. Wie viele Kilometer hat Ihr Auto schon?
6. Wieviel Flüssigkeit trinken Sie durchschnittlich *(on the average)* pro Tag?
7. Wieviel Benzin faßt *(holds)* der Benzintank Ihres Autos?
8. Welche Größe hat ein normales Blatt Schreibmaschinenpapier?
9. Was war bisher *(up to now)* Ihr höchster Punkt auf der Erde?
10. Was ist die kälteste / heißeste Temperatur, die Sie je erlebt haben? Wo und wann war das?
11. Was ist die beste Zimmertemperatur zum Schlafen?
12. Was ist die normale Körpertemperatur eines Menschen?

H **Tatsachen aus der Welt.** Geben Sie zehn interessante Fakten in metrischen Maßeinheiten.

VORSCHLÄGE

die Höhe eines Berges
die Höhenlage einer Stadt
die Tiefe eines Sees
die Länge eines Flusses
das Gewicht *(weight)* eines Tieres usw.

* Anwendung

Zahlen und Statistiken. In einem Almanach oder in einem Atlas gibt es viele Zahlen und Fakten. Es gibt auch besondere Bücher mit vielen nützlichen (und nutzlosen) Statistiken. Wer kann die interessantesten Fakten und Statistiken finden? Berichten Sie im Kurs.

Beispiele: *In Luxemburg wohnen rund 365.000 Menschen.*
Ein Glas Rotwein enthält 156 Kalorien.
Bei einem einzigen Kuß werden rund 20.000.000 Bazillen übertragen (transferred).
Fast Zwei Drittel (66 Prozent) aller neuen Ehen in Amerika werden geschieden (end in divorce).

* Schriftliches Thema

Tips zum Schreiben ***Conveying Statistical Information***
Some repetition of the verbs **sein** and **haben** is unavoidable in texts containing statistical information. Before using **sein,** always consider whether the same idea can be expressed by describing the action rather than telling what "is." Numbers and statistics are easier to comprehend in shorter sentences; complex sentences with subordinate clauses and relative clauses should be kept to a minimum. Lists, charts, and graphs are also useful tools for illustrating or interpreting numbers or statistics.

Bericht mit Zahlen und Statistiken. Schreiben Sie einen Bericht mit Zahlen und Statistiken.

Beispiel: Mit einer Fläche von 83.855 km^2 (Quadratkilometern) ist Österreich nicht viel größer als die Schweiz. Österreich besteht aus 9 Bundesländern und hat eine Bevölkerung von rund 7,5 Millionen Einwohnern. Zwei Drittel des Landes liegen in den Alpen. Nur ein Viertel ist Hügelland *(hilly country)* und Flachland. Mit etwa 90 Einwohnern pro km^2 hat das Land eine relativ niedrige Bevölkerungsdichte *(population density).* Acht Nachbarstaaten grenzen an Österreich. Der höchste Berg ist der Großglockner mit 3.797 m, und mit seinen 13.972 m zählt der Arlberg-Straßentunnel zu den längsten Tunneln in den Alpen. Jährlich kommen mehr als 5 Millionen Besucher nach Österreich.

THEMENVORSCHLÄGE

Städte, Länder oder Staaten
Firmen und Geschäfte
Schulen oder Universitäten
Sport
Verkehrsmittel (Auto, Flugzeug, Schiff, Zug usw.)
Bauten (Kirchen, Hochhäuser, Pyramiden usw.)

Wortschatz 22

addieren	dividieren
subtrahieren	hoch
multiplizieren	

The basic mathematical operations are expressed as follows:

1. **addieren** to add

   vier **plus** acht ist / gleich zwölf
   $4 + 8 = 12$

2. **subtrahieren** to subtract

   sechzehn **minus** drei ist / gleich dreizehn
   $16 - 3 = 13$

3. **multiplizieren (mit)** to multiply (by)

   acht **mal** neun ist / gleich zweiundsiebzig
   $8 \times 9 = 72$

4. **dividieren (durch)** to divide (by)

   vierzig **durch** acht (geteilt) ist / gleich fünf
   $40 \div 8 = 5$

5. **hoch** raised to the [nth.] power

   vier **hoch** drei ist / gleich 64
   $4^3 = 64$

ÜBUNGEN

A **Mathematik.** Lösen Sie die Aufgaben mündlich und auf deutsch.

1. $11 \times 11 = ?$
2. $16^2 = ?$
3. $2^6 = ?$
4. $253 - 147{,}88 = ?$
5. $1 + 2 + 3 + 4$ [bis 15] $= ?$
6. $75 \div 15 = ?$
7. $213 \div 11 = ?$
8. $1{,}5 \times 1{,}5 = ?$

B Stellen Sie weitere Aufgaben dieser Art mündlich an andere Personen im Kurs.

Beispiel: STUDENT 1: Wieviel ist zwölf mal vierzig?
STUDENT 2: Zwölf mal vierzig ist vierhundertachtzig.

Zusammenfassung 22

Rules to Remember

1. In German, periods separate thousands, and commas are used in percents and decimals. **2.000.000; 4,5% (vier Komma fünf Prozent).**
2. Ordinal numbers from *second* to *nineteenth* are formed by adding a **-t** suffix + adjective ending to the cardinal number **(der fünfte Mann).**

3. The ordinal numbers from *twentieth* on are formed by adding an **-st** + adjective ending to the cardinal number **(der fünfundzwanzigste Mann).**
4. A period after a written ordinal number replaces the **-t** / **-st** + adjective ending **(der 25. Mann).**
5. Masculine and neuter nouns take no ending in measurements **(zwei Kilogramm),** but feminine nouns do **(zwei Meilen).**

Activities

1 **Questions.** Ask other students personal questions to which the answers will contain numbers of two or more digits. Can you come up with ten such questions?

2 **Personal profile.** Create a personal profile for yourself consisting mainly of numbers (height, weight, shoe size, SAT scores, important numbers in your life, cost of your education, etc.). Present your profile orally in class.

3 **Games.** Play a game of Monopoly or a card game such as pinochle with other students. Speak only German.

4 **Shopping.** Make a shopping list. Write down in addition the approximate cost of the items you need. Read your list out loud in German, then estimate how much money you'll need to withdraw from the bank before you go to the store.

5 **Numbers and statistics.** Compile a file of interesting statistics regarding sports, politics, history, geography, or science. Find other students who have chosen the same or similar fields and form a group. Share your statistics, then report to the class the three most interesting facts your group found.

6 **Working with a text.** Find an article or book chapter (preferably in German) containing statistics or numbers. Write down what you regard as the most interesting numbers or statistics and present them orally to the class.

23 Seasons, Dates, and Time Expressions

23.1 Expressions of Time

A. *Months and Seasons*

The names of seasons and months are masculine, and the definite article must be used with them. In expressions of time, they take the dative contraction **im (in dem).**

Seasons		*Months*	
im Frühling[1]	*in (the) spring*	im Januar	*in January*
im Sommer	*in (the) summer*	im Februar	*in February*
im Herbst	*in (the) fall*	im März	etc.
im Winter	*in (the) winter*	im April	
		im Mai	
		im Juni	
		im Juli	
		im August	
		im September	
		im Oktober	
		im November	
		im Dezember	

Der Herbst ist für mich die schönste Jahreszeit, denn **im November** habe ich Geburtstag. — *(The) fall is the best season of the year for me, for my birthday is in November.*

1. **Das Frühjahr** can also be used for spring.

Wir fahren **im Winter** oft in die Berge. — *We often travel to the mountains in (the) winter.*

B. Days of the Week and Parts of the Day

1. Names of the days of the week and parts of the day are masculine. They take the dative contraction **am (an dem)** in time expressions (exceptions: **in der Nacht, zu Mittag, um Mitternacht**). With days only, **am** may be omitted.

(am) Sonntag	*on Sunday*	am Morgen	*in the morning*
(am) Montag	*on Monday*	am Vormittag	*in the late morning*
(am) Dienstag	*on Tuesday*	zu Mittag	*at noon*
(am) Mittwoch	*on Wednesday*	am Nachmittag	*in the afternoon*
(am) Donnerstag	*on Thursday*	am Abend	*in the evening (until about 10:00 P.M.)*
(am) Freitag	*on Friday*		
(am) Samstag	*on Saturday*	in der Nacht	*at night (after 10:00 P.M.)*
		um Mitternacht	*at midnight*

Das Spiel findet **(am) Samstag** statt. — *The game is taking place (on) Saturday.*

Sie hat einen Termin **am Vormittag.** — *She has an appointment in the late morning.*

2. When combined with days of the week, parts of the day (other than **Nacht**) are not capitalized.

Wir wollen uns **(am) Donnerstag abend** in der Stadt treffen. — *We want to meet downtown on Thursday evening.*

BUT:

Der Unfall ereignete sich **in der Nacht von Freitag zum Samstag.** — *The accident occurred (on) Friday night. (after 10:00 P.M.)*

3. Adding an **-s** to the uncapitalized forms of days and parts of the day creates adverbs denoting repeated or habitual occurrences.

Diese Geschäfte sind **sonntags** zu. — *These stores are closed on Sunday(s).*

Sie arbeitet nur **nachmittags.** — *She only works afternoons.*

4. **Heute** *(today)*, **gestern** *(yesterday)*, **morgen** *(tomorrow)*, and occasionally **vorgestern** *(the day before yesterday)* and **übermorgen** *(the day after tomorrow)* can be combined with parts of the day.

heute		***gestern***	
heute morgen	*this morning*	gestern morgen	*yesterday morning*
heute vormittag	*this morning*	gestern vormittag	*yesterday morning*
heute mittag	*this noon*	gestern mittag	*yesterday at noon*
heute nachmittag	*this afternoon*	gestern nachmittag	*yesterday afternoon*
heute abend	*this evening*	gestern abend	*yesterday evening*
heute nacht	*tonight (after 10 P.M.)*	gestern nacht	*last night*

morgen[2]

morgen früh	*tomorrow morning*
morgen vormittag	*tomorrow morning*
morgen mittag	*tomorrow at noon*
morgen nachmittag	*tomorrow afternoon*
morgen abend	*tomorrow evening*
morgen nacht	*tomorrow night*
vorgestern abend	*the day before yesterday in the evening*
übermorgen früh	*the day after tomorrow in the morning*

C. Duration of Time and Specific Time (Accusative Case)

1. Duration of time is normally expressed in the accusative case with an article but without a preposition. The adjective **ganz** *(all, whole, entire)* is frequently included, but it must always be preceded by an article.

Sie blieben **den ganzen Monat** bei Verwandten.	*They stayed with relatives the entire month.*
Es hat **die ganze Nacht** geregnet.	*It rained all night.*

2. Specific time is also often expressed in the accusative case instead of with **an** or **in** plus the dative (see Sections A and B). Such expressions often include the adjectives **jed-** *(every),* **letzt-** *(last),* **nächst-** *(next),* and **vorig-** *(previous).*

Die Kinder haben **jeden Sonntag** Religionsunterricht. Die Kinder haben **an jedem Sonntag** Religionsunterricht.	*The children have religious instruction every Sunday.*
Es hat **letzte Woche** stark geschneit.	*It snowed heavily last week.*

D. Indefinite Time Expressions (Genitive Case)

The genitive case is used with the word **Tag (eines Tages)** and parts of the day **(eines Morgens, eines Nachmittags, eines Nachts)**[3] to express indefinite time. This structure is common in narratives.

Als Gregor Samsa **eines Morgens** aus unruhigen Träumen erwachte . . . (Franz Kafka, „Die Verwandlung“)	*As Gregor Samsa awoke* ***one morning*** *from restless dreams . . .*

---

2. The adverb **morgen** by itself or *before* another time expression means *tomorrow.* It means *morning* only if it follows other time expressions.
3. Although **Nacht** is feminine, **eines Nachts** is used by analogy to **eines Tages.** This construction occurs only in this phrase.

Ein Werwolf **eines Nachts** entwich . . . (Christian Morgenstern, „Der Werwolf")	*A werewolf sneaked off* ***one night*** *. . .*

E. Units of Time

1. The most common measurements of time are as follows:

die Sekunde, -n	*second*	die Woche, -n	*week*
die Minute, -n	*minute*	das Wochenende, -n	*weekend*
die Stunde, -n	*hour*	die Jahreszeit, -en	*season*
der Tag, -e	*day*	das Jahr, -e	*year*
		das Jahrzehnt, -e	*decade*
		das Jahrhundert, -e	*century*

2. To express *for days, for years,* etc., German adds the suffix **-lang** to the plural of units of time. As adverbs, such words are not capitalized.

Wir haben **stundenlang** / **tagelang** / **monatelang** gewartet.	*We waited for hours / for days / for months.*

3. To indicate *how long ago* something happened, German uses the preposition **vor** + the dative (see 10.3J).

Sie hat ihr Studium **vor einem Jahr** abgeschlossen.	*She completed her studies a year ago.*
Sie war **vor wenigen Stunden** hier.	*She was here (just) a few hours ago.*

4. The following expressions with units of time are quite common.

tagsüber	*during the day*
während / unter der Woche	*during the week*
an Wochentagen	*on weekdays*
am Wochenende	*on the weekend*
im Laufe des Jahres	*during the year*
alle drei Tage / Wochen / Jahre	*every three days / weeks / years*

F. Adjectives of Time

1. Appended to a noun, the suffix **-lich** creates an adjective indicating *how often* something occurs. The stem vowel of the noun has an umlaut in most instances.

ein **jährliches** Einkommen	*a yearly income*
ein **monatliches** Treffen	*a monthly meeting*
eine **wöchentliche** Zeitung	*a weekly newspaper*
ein **stündlicher** Glockenschlag	*an hourly chime, stroke of the hour*

2. With units of time, the suffix **-ig** creates adjectives expressing *how old* someone or something is or *how long* something occurs. The stem vowel of the noun has an umlaut in most cases.

ein **zweijähriges** Kind	*a two-year-old child*
eine **einstündige** Prüfung	*a one-hour exam*
eine **sechstägige** Reise	*a six-day trip*
ein **zehnminutiges / minütiges** Schläfchen	*a ten-minute nap*
BUT:	
ein **zweimonatiger** Kurs *(no umlaut)*	*a two-month course*

3. A number of adverbs of time form adjectives by adding the suffix **-ig.**

heute: die **heutige** Deutschstunde	*today's German class*
gestern: die **gestrige** Zeitung	*yesterday's newspaper*
damals: die **damalige** Zeit	*(the) time back then*
jetzt: die **jetzigen** Schwierigkeiten	*the present difficulties*
ehemals: die **ehemalige** DDR	*the former GDR*
vor: am **vorigen** Abend	*(on) the previous evening*

G. Dates and Years

1. One asks for and gives dates in either of two ways in German.

Der wievielte ist heute?
—Heute ist der 4. Juli.
Den wievielten haben wir heute?
—Heute haben wir den 4. Juli.

What is the date today?
Today is the 4th of July.

2. Dates after a day of the week preceded by **am** can be in either the dative or accusative case.

Das Konzert findet **am Montag, dem / den 10. September,** statt.	*The concert takes place on Monday, September 10th.*

3. Dates on forms and in letters are given in the order *day, month,* and *year.* If the article is used, it is in the accusative case.

Geboren: 3.6.1976 (den 3. Juni 1976)

4. Years are indicated by either **im Jahre** followed by the year or by the year alone.

Der Erste Weltkrieg brach **1914** / **im Jahre 1914** aus.	*The First World War broke out in 1914.*

23.2 Telling Time

A. *Colloquial Time*

1. In colloquial language, the following expressions are used to tell time. Everything *before* the hour is **vor,** everything *after* the hour **nach.** A period separates hours and minutes.

Written	***Spoken***
8.00 Uhr	acht Uhr
8.10 Uhr	zehn (Minuten) nach acht
8.15 Uhr	(ein) Viertel nach acht OR: (ein) Viertel neun (that is, *a quarter of the way to nine*)
8.20 Uhr	zwanzig (Minuten) nach acht OR: acht Uhr zwanzig
8.30 Uhr	halb neun (that is, *halfway to nine*)
8.35 Uhr	fünfunddreißig (Minuten) nach acht
8.40 Uhr	zwanzig (Minuten) vor neun
8.45 Uhr	(ein) Viertel vor neun OR: acht Uhr fünfundvierzig OR: drei Viertel neun (that is, *three quarters of the way to nine*)
8.50 Uhr	zehn (Minuten) vor neun
8.55 Uhr	fünf (Minuten) vor neun

2. The preposition **um** means *at* in time expressions.

Wir kommen heute abend **um** acht. — *We are coming this evening at eight.*

3. Approximate time is indicated by either **gegen** *(toward)* or **um . . . herum** *(around).*

Der Film endete **gegen** Mitternacht. — *The film ended toward midnight.*
Sie rief **um** neun **herum** an. — *She phoned around nine.*

4. Adverbs of time are used to indicate whether the hour is A.M. or P.M.

Er kommt **um acht Uhr morgens / abends.** — *He is coming at eight o'clock in the morning / evening.*

B. *Official Time*

Official time (transportation schedules, performances, TV and radio times, official announcements, hours of business, etc.) is given according to a 24-hour clock without **Viertel, halb, vor,** or **nach.**

9.15 Uhr	neun Uhr fünfzehn (Minuten)
11.24 Uhr	elf Uhr vierundzwanzig (Minuten)
18.30 Uhr	achtzehn Uhr dreißig (= 6:30 P.M.)
22.45 Uhr	zweiundzwanzig Uhr fünfundvierzig (Minuten) (= 10:45 P.M.)
0.15 Uhr	null Uhr fünfzehn (Minuten) (= 12:15 A.M.)

English A.M. = 0.00 Uhr bis 12.00 Uhr
English P.M. = 12.00 Uhr bis 24.00 Uhr

* Übungen

A **Verschiedene Zeiten.** Drücken Sie die Zeitausdrücke auf deutsch aus.

1. in the spring
2. afternoons
3. in the evening
4. tomorrow morning
5. in July
6. on Thursday
7. Friday evening
8. Tuesday night (after midnight)
9. on Sundays
10. Tuesday mornings
11. for hours
12. during the week
13. two weeks ago
14. on the weekend
15. all day

B **Einiges über Sie und andere Leute.** Machen Sie sechs wahre Aussagen mit Zeitausdrücken wie **vorig- / letzt-, nächst-, jed-,** und **d- ganz-.**

Beispiele: *Ich gehe fast* ***jeden Abend*** *in die Bibliothek.*
Letzte Woche *besuchte meine Freundin ihre Oma in Frankfurt.*

C **Wie ist es bei Ihnen?** Beantworten Sie die Fragen mit Zeitausdrücken. Stellen Sie dann diese Fragen auch an andere Leute im Kurs. Berichten Sie die Antworten.

1. Welche Jahreszeit haben Sie am liebsten?
2. In welchem Monat haben Sie Geburtstag?
3. Wann lernen Sie gewöhnlich am fleißigsten für Ihre Kurse?
4. Wann gehen Sie gewöhnlich mit anderen Leuten aus?
5. Was machen Sie in den einzelnen Jahreszeiten am liebsten?
6. Zu welcher Tageszeit sind Sie ganz frisch und munter *(wide awake)*? Wann sind Sie müde oder schläfrig?
7. Wann haben Sie zum letzten Mal etwas Warmes gegessen?

D **Anders ausdrücken: *-ig* oder *-lich*?** Drücken Sie Sätze anders aus, indem Sie die kursivgedruckten Wörter als Adjektive verwenden.

Beispiel: Herr Schmidt ist *jetzt* Besitzer des Hauses.
Herr Schmidt ist der ***jetzige*** *Besitzer des Hauses.*

1. Wo liegt die Zeitung *von gestern*?
2. Ich muß *jeden Tag* mein Brot verdienen.
3. Wann beginnt die Deutschstunde *morgen*?
4. Hast du die Nachrichten *heute* im Fernsehen gesehen?

5. Der Angestellte bekommt seinen Arbeitslohn *(wage) jede Woche.*
6. Ich hatte eine Vorlesung, *die zwei Stunden dauerte.*
7. Die Glocke läutet *jede Stunde.*

E **Geregeltes Dasein** *(existence).* Erzählen Sie in fünf bis sieben Sätzen, was Sie regelmäßig tun oder tun müssen. Wie regelmäßig tun Sie das?

Beispiele: *Ich muß* ***täglich*** *zur Deutschstunde.*
Ich zahle meine Miete ***monatlich.***

F **Wichtige Daten.** Was sind für Sie die drei wichtigsten Daten im Jahr? Was geschieht an diesen Tagen?

Beispiel: Der 4. Juli.
Am 4. Juli *fahre ich immer mit Freunden ans Meer.*

G **Wichtige Jahre.** Haben Sie in der Schule aufgepaßt? Wann war das? (Die Antworten finden Sie unten.)

Beispiel: Die ersten Menschen landeten auf dem Mond.
Das war im Jahre 1969.

1. Die Normannen eroberten England.
2. Kolumbus kam nach Amerika.
3. Die Vereinigten Staaten von Amerika erklärten ihre Unabhängigkeit *(independence).*
4. Die Französische Revolution brach aus.
5. Die Russen stürzten *(overthrew)* den Zaren Nikolaus II.

H **Wieviel Uhr ist es?** Im Winter ist es in Mitteleuropa sechs Stunden später als an der Ostküste der USA. Sagen Sie *informell und formell,* wieviel Uhr es jetzt in Luxemburg ist.

Beispiel: 12:15 P.M. (USA)
INFORMELL: *In Luxemburg ist es jetzt Viertel nach sechs / Viertel sieben abends.*
FORMELL: *In Luxemburg ist es jetzt achtzehn Uhr fünfzehn.*

A.M.	2:30	4:15	6:39	8:45	11:37	12:00
P.M.	1:45	3:25	5:18	8:45	10:01	11:57

I **Stundenplan.** Wie sieht Ihr Stundenplan für morgen aus? Welche Kurse haben Sie? Haben Sie auch andere Termine? Verwenden Sie verschiedene präpositionale Zeitausdrücke in Ihren Antworten.

Beispiel: *Ich habe* **um** *halb neun meine erste Vorlesung.* ***Von*** *zehn Uhr* **bis** *Viertel nach elf bin ich im Biologie-Labor.* ***Gegen*** *halb eins esse ich . . . usw.*

Antworten: 1. 1066 2. 1492 3. 1776 4. 1789 5. 1917

* Anwendung

A **Zeit zum Leben?** Wir leben heutzutage oft von einem Termin zum anderen und haben manchmal wenig Zeit für uns selber. Wie ist es bei Ihnen persönlich? Erzählen Sie davon.

REDEMITTEL

Bei mir ist es so:
Morgens muß ich immer . . .
Am Wochenende gibt's (gibt es) dann . . .
Abends habe ich selten Zeit für / zum . . .
Gestern abend zum Beispiel . . .
Eines Tages mußte ich sogar . . .
Alle paar Tage muß ich . . .

B **Vom Aufstehen bis zum Schlafengehen.** Erzählen Sie von Ihrem gestrigen Tag. Verwenden Sie möglichst viele verschiedene Zeitausdrücke.

REDEMITTEL

Zwischen acht und neun bin / habe ich . . .
Um neun bin / habe ich . . .
Am Vormittag mußte ich . . .
Zu Mittag war ich . . .
Gegen eins bin / habe ich wieder . . .
Am Nachmittag war ich eine Stunde . . .
Abends bin / habe ich . . .
In der Nacht habe ich dann . . .

* Schriftliche Themen

Tips zum Schreiben ***Beginning Sentences with Time Expressions***

For the sake of stylistic variety, time expressions are frequently the first element in a sentence. Remember, however, that in German a first element is not separated from the rest of the sentence by a comma unless this first element is a clause.

A **Keine Zeit zum Briefeschreiben.** Sie schreiben einem / einer Bekannten in Deutschland und erzählen in einem ersten Abschnitt *(paragraph),* warum Sie jeden Tag so beschäftigt sind, daß Sie erst jetzt (nach mehreren Wochen) auf seinen / ihren Brief antworten.

Beispiel:

Liebe Trudi,

sei herzlich gegrüßt! Schon vor Wochen wollte ich auf Deinen netten Brief vom Sommer antworten, aber ich hatte einfach keine Zeit dazu. Morgens muß ich schon um sieben aus dem Bett 'raus, denn meine erste Vorlesung beginnt schon um halb neun Uhr. Tagsüber bin ich . . . usw.

B **In die Zukunft schauen.** Unser Leben verläuft in Phasen. Nach den Kinderjahren kommt die Schule, und danach beginnt das Studium an einer Universität. Nach dem Studium beginnen für viele Leute die Jahre der eigenen Familie und der beruflichen Tätigkeit, und am Ende kommen die Pensionsjahre. Stellen Sie sich den Tages- und Jahresverlauf in einer der Phasen vor, die Sie noch nicht erlebt haben. Verwenden Sie das Futur (siehe 8.1) und verschiedene Zeitausdrücke.

Beispiel: Nach dem Studium beginnt für mich die Zeit der Arbeit und der Familiengründung. Morgens werde ich zur Arbeit ins Büro fahren. Zu Mittag werde ich . . . und am Abend . . . Manchmal werde ich am Wochenende . . . Wenn die Ferien kommen, dann . . . usw.

Wortschatz 23

-mal
das Mal
die Zeit
expressions with Zeit

1. The suffix **-mal** (see 22.1D) is used adverbially to express the *number of times* something happens. It occurs in the following common expressions:

einmal, zweimal, dreimal, usw.	once, twice, three times, etc.
diesmal	this time
ein paarmal	a few times
jedesmal	every time
manchmal	sometimes

2. The noun **das Mal** refers to a *number of times or occurrences.*

das erste / zweite / dritte / letzte Mal	*the first / second / third / last time*
zum ersten / zweiten / dritten / letzten Mal OR: zum erstenmal; zum zweitenmal	*for the first / second / third / last time*

3. The word **die Zeit** refers to *specific time* or *duration of time.* It occurs in a large number of time expressions including the following:

für einige Zeit	for a while	**zur Zeit**	at the present time, now
in unserer Zeit	in our time (now)		
in früheren Zeiten	in earlier times	**zu d e r** (*or:* **jener**) **Zeit**	at that time, back then
in kurzer Zeit	in a short time	**zu meiner / deiner / ihrer Zeit**	in my / your / her day
in letzter Zeit	lately, as of late		
in der nächsten Zeit	in the near future	**zu jeder Zeit (jederzeit)**	(at) anytime
nach einiger Zeit	after some time		
nach kurzer Zeit	after a brief time	**zu gewissen Zeiten**	at certain times
nach langer Zeit	after a long time		
von Zeit zu Zeit	from time to time	**zu bestimmten Zeiten**	at certain times
vor der Zeit	prematurely		
vor einiger Zeit	some time ago	**zu gleicher Zeit**	at the same time
vor kurzer Zeit	a short time ago	**zu rechter Zeit**	at the right moment
vor langer Zeit	a long time ago		

ÜBUNGEN

A **Alles mit *-mal.*** Machen Sie vier Aussagen über sich. Verwenden Sie die angegebenen Ausdrücke.

Beispiel: zum ersten Mal
Ich war vor zwei Jahren ***zum ersten Mal*** *in Europa.*

1. zum ersten Mal
2. das erste Mal
3. manchmal
4. zum letzten Mal
5. das letzte Mal

B **Damals und jetzt.** Machen Sie vier Aussagen über die Vergangenheit und drei Aussagen über das Präsens. Verwenden Sie verschiedene Ausdrücke mit dem Wort **Zeit.**

Beispiele: ***Vor kurzer Zeit*** *habe ich einen interessanten Film über Katzen gesehen.* (Vergangenheit)
Ich bin ***jederzeit*** *bereit, anderen Menschen zu helfen.* (Präsens)

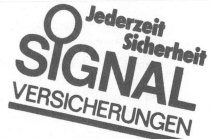

Zusammenfassung 23

Rules to Remember

1. Prepositional combinations with names of seasons and months are generally formed with **im: im Januar, im Frühling,** etc. Days of the week and parts of the day are preceded by **am: am Sonntag, am Morgen,** etc. (*but:* **in der Nacht**).
2. Duration of time and specific time are in the accusative case if there is no preposition **(diesen Monat, den ganzen Tag).**
3. Years stand alone or are preceded by **im Jahre,** never simply **in.**
4. Dates on forms and letters are always written in the order *day, month,* and *year:* If the article is used, it is in the accusative case. **3.11.1940** or **den 3. Nov. 1940.**

Activities

1 **Favorite times of year.** What is your favorite season **(Ihre liebste Jahreszeit)?** Tell some of the things you do during that season and on what days and at what times you do them. What is your favorite month? What do you do then?

2 **How many time expressions?** Write down as many time expressions as you can think of in thirty seconds or one minute. Exchange your paper with a partner. Check your partner's expressions for accuracy. Make statements about events and activities in your life using each of your partner's expressions.

3 **Significant dates.** Look up seven significant historical or cultural dates, including day, month, and year. See if other students can identify your dates.

Beispiel: *der 8. Dezember 1941 (der japanische Angriff auf Pearl Harbor)*
der 9. August 1995 (der Tod von Jerry Garcia)

4 **Weekly schedule.** Ask another student about his or her class schedule this term.

5 **Family.** Prepare a short oral report of three statements on each member of your immediate family. Each statement should contain a time expression. Suggestions: birthdays, anniversaries, trips, schools, new jobs, etc.

6 **Favorite programs.** Give days, times, and length of your favorite radio and TV programs.

24 Adverbs

An adverb tells *how, why, when,* or *where* an activity takes place. Virtually every prepositional phrase can and does function as an adverb (see 10.1). In addition to prepositional phrases, there are also other adverbial words.

24.1 Descriptive Adverbs

1. A descriptive adverb **(das Adverb, -ien)** is a descriptive adjective without an ending. When such an adverb modifies a verb, it often indicates *how, in which manner,* or *to what degree* an activity is done.

Sie arbeitet **fleißig.**	*She works diligently.*
Unsere Blumen wachsen **langsam.**	*Our flowers are growing slowly.*

2. Descriptive adverbs can also modify adjectives or other adverbs.

Sie wohnen in einem **schön** möblierten Haus. *(adjective modified)*	*They live in a beautifully furnished house.*
Er sprach **erstaunlich** gut. *(adverb modified)*	*He spoke remarkably well.*

3. Some adverbs of *manner* have no adjective equivalents.

Ich esse **gern** Eis.	*I like to eat ice cream.*
Die Musik war **kaum** zu hören.	*The music was scarcely to be heard.*

4. A few descriptive adverbs conveying attitude or reaction are formed by adding the suffix **-erweise** to descriptive adjectives.

bedauerlicherweise	*regrettably*
dummerweise	*stupidly*

erstaunlicherweise	*amazingly*
glücklicherweise	*fortunately*
möglicherweise	*possibly*

Erstaunlicherweise wurde niemand in dem Unfall verletzt. — *Amazingly, no one was injured in the accident.*

Descriptive adverbs can also occasionally be formed by adding the suffix **-weise** to nouns.

fallweise	*case by case*	stückweise	*piece by piece*
paarweise	*in pairs*	teilweise	*partially*

Wir sind mit der Arbeit schon **teilweise** fertig. — *We are already partially finished with the work.*

24.2 Adverbs of Time

1. Some adverbs of time tell *when* or *how often* an activity occurs. Some examples are:

ab und zu	*now and then*
bald	*soon*
immer	*always*
manchmal	*sometimes*
nie	*never*
oft	*often*
schon	*already*
wieder	*again*

2. Some adverbs of time indicate *when an activity begins* and are particularly useful for introducing narratives.

anfangs	*in the beginning*	einmal	*one time*
damals	*(back) then*	neulich, vor kurzem	*recently*
eines Morgens	*one morning (see 23.1D)*	zuerst, zunächst	*(at) first*
eines Tages	*one day*		
eines Abends	*one evening*		
einst	*once (past); some day (future)*		

3. Some adverbs of time help establish *sequences within activities* or narratives.

auf einmal, plötzlich	*suddenly*	immer noch	*still*
bis dahin	*up until then; by then*	inzwischen, mittlerweile, unterdessen	*meanwhile*
bald darauf	*soon (thereafter)*	vorher	*first, beforehand*
kurz darauf	*shortly thereafter*		

da / dann	*then*	nachher	*afterwards*
danach	*after that*	später	*later*

4. Some adverbs of time indicate the *conclusion of an activity* or narrative.

seitdem / seither	*(ever) since then, (ever) since that time*	schließlich	*finally; in the final analysis*
am Ende[1] / zum Schluß	*finally, in the end, in conclusion*	endlich	*finally, at long last*
		zuletzt	*at last, finally; last*

24.3 Adverbs of Place

1. Many adverbs of place tell *where*. Some common examples are:

anderswo	*somewhere else*
da	*there*
da drüben	*over there*
hier / dort	*hier / there*
innen / außen	*(on the) inside / (on the) outside*
links / rechts	*left / right*
nirgendwo	*nowhere*
oben / unten	*above / below*
überall	*everywhere*
vorn / hinten	*in front / behind*

2. Some adverbs of place combine with the prefixes **hin-** and **her-** (see 29.1C) to indicate direction to or from: **anderswohin** *(to someplace else)*, **überallher** *(from everywhere)*.
3. Some adverbs of place are used with the prepositions **nach** and **von** to indicate *to* or *from where:*

nach links / rechts	*to the left / right*
von links / rechts	*from the left / right*
nach oben	*upward, (to go) upstairs*
nach unten	*downward, (to go) downstairs*
von oben	*from above*
von unten	*from below / beneath*
nach / von vorn(e)	*to / from the front*

1. See **Wortschatz 24.**

24.4 Position of Adverbs and Adverbial Phrases

1. When adverbial expressions answer the questions *how, when,* or *where,* they follow a word order sequence of Time-Manner-Place (see also 1.1D). Even when one of these elements is missing, the sequence remains the same.

TIME *PLACE* Er war **gestern abend im Kino.**	*He was at the movies yesterday evening.*
MANNER *PLACE* Sie ist **zu Fuß in die Stadt** gegangen.	*She went into town on foot.*

2. General time precedes specific time.

GEN. TIME *SPEC. TIME*
Das Kind fährt **jeden Tag um acht Uhr** mit dem Rad zur Schule.
The child travels to school by bike every day at eight o'clock.

3. German adverbs and adverbial phrases often appear at the beginning of a sentence; they are not set off by a comma.

Glücklicherweise habe ich meinen Zug nicht verpaßt.	*Fortunately, I did not miss my train.*
Nach dem Film wollen wir essen gehen.	*After the movie we want to go eat.*

24.5 Adverbial Conjunctions

German has a number of adverbs that link a train of thought from one sentence or clause to the next by providing additional information, explanation, or contrast.

außerdem	*moreover, furthermore (additional information)*
daher darum deshalb deswegen aus diesem Grunde	*therefore, thus, for this / that reason (explanation)*
dennoch	*nevertheless, yet* } *(contrast)*
stattdessen	*instead* } *(contrast)*
trotzdem	*in spite of this / that*

Sie ist krank, (und) **daher / darum** kann sie nicht kommen.	*She is ill, and for this reason she cannot come.*
Sie ist krank und kann **deshalb / deswegen** (etc.) nicht kommen.	*She is ill and cannot come for this reason.*

Übungen

A **Zeitadverbien.** Erzählen Sie von sich mit den folgenden Adverbien.

Beispiel: neulich *(recently)*
Neulich habe ich einen guten Film gesehen.

1. ab und zu *(now and then)*
2. bisher *(up until now)*
3. stets *(continually, always)*
4. niemals *(never)*
5. einst *(once)*
6. kürzlich / vor kurzem *(recently)*

B **Wo und wohin?** Drücken Sie die Sätze auf deutsch aus.

1. Come over here!
2. She's at the front.
3. They ran to the rear.
4. They are going upstairs.
5. I can't find the book anywhere (use *nowhere*).
6. Did you look everywhere?
7. We'll have to go somewhere else.
8. "Which way do we go?" "Left."
9. They are over there.

C **Meinungen.** Bilden Sie Meinungsaussagen mit den folgenden Adverbien.

Beispiel: vergebens *(in vain)*
Ich finde, die meisten Menschen suchen ***vergebens*** *nach Glück.*

1. auswendig *(by heart)*
2. sicherlich *(certainly, for sure)*
3. hoffentlich *(hopefully)*
4. glücklicherweise *(fortunately)*
5. leider *(unfortunately)*
6. zufällig *(per chance)*

D **Wortstellung der Adverbien.** Schreiben Sie fünf Sätze, die adverbiale Ausdrücke der Zeit, des Ortes und der Beschreibung enthalten. Schreiben Sie die Sätze noch einmal, indem Sie *einen* adverbialen Ausdruck an andere Stelle setzen.

Beispiel: *Wir gehen oft mit Freunden im Park spazieren.*
Mit Freunden *gehen wir oft im Park spazieren.*

E **Adverbiale Konjunktionen.** Machen Sie fünf Aussagen über Taten, Situationen oder Gedanken und die Folgen davon. Verwenden Sie die angegebenen adverbialen Konjunktionen.

Beispiele: *Ich habe für meine Deutschprüfung intensiv gelernt, und* ***deswegen*** *werde ich eine gute Note bekommen.*
Ich habe in diesem Semester wenig gearbeitet. Ich habe aber ***trotzdem*** *gute Noten bekommen.*

deswegen / daher
aus diesem Grunde
dennoch
stattdessen
trotzdem

* Anwendung

A **Es kam aber anders.** Erzählen Sie von einem Unternehmen *(undertaking)* aus Ihrem Leben, das anders verlief als geplant. Verwenden Sie Zeitadverbien und Adverbien, die Ihre Reaktionen zum Ausdruck bringen.

REDEMITTEL

Einmal wollte ich . . .
Ich habe zuerst gedacht . . .
Leider war es so, daß . . .
Wir konnten aber trotzdem . . .
Da kam zufällig . . .
Glücklicherweise hat niemand gemerkt . . .
Wir mußten dann schließlich . . .

B **Wie ich etwas mache.** Erklären Sie, in welcher zeitlichen Folge Sie etwas tun oder sich auf etwas vorbereiten *(prepare)*.

THEMENVORSCHLÄGE

eine schwere Prüfung
eine schriftliche Arbeit für einen Kurs
ein Auto suchen und kaufen
eine Wohnung suchen
eine Ferienreise planen

Beispiel: eine schwere Prüfung
Zuerst frage ich die Professorin, was ich für die Prüfung lernen muß. Dann lese ich das alles noch einmal durch. Danach wiederhole ich die Kapitel, die ich für besonders wichtig halte, und zum Schluß überlege ich mir Fragen, die man in der Prüfung stellen könnte, und versuche, diese Fragen zu beantworten.

* Schriftliche Themen

Tips zum Schreiben ***Establishing a Sequence of Events***
To establish a chronology of events from one sentence or clause to another, you should use adverbs of time. Remember that time expressions normally precede expressions of manner and place and can also begin a sentence. You can also use adverbial conjunctions to establish logical links of explanation or contrast between sentences and clauses.

A **Der Verlauf eines schrecklichen, bedeutenden oder wichtigen Ereignisses** *(event)*. Berichten Sie über ein wichtiges historisches Ereignis (z.B. eine Katastrophe, einen Unfall, die Karriere eines berühmten Menschen). Verwenden

Sie dabei einige Adverbien, die den chronologischen Verlauf dieses Ereignisses verdeutlichen und die Folgen davon deutlich zum Ausdruck bringen.

Beispiel: Im Jahre 1906 ereignete sich in San Francisco ein schreckliches Erdbeben. Anfangs spürte man nur leichte Erschütterungen *(tremors),* aber kurz darauf kam die große Katastrophe, die vieles zerstörte und auch vielen Menschen das Leben kostete. Besonders schlimm war es nachher, als . . . Dennoch *(nevertheless)* konnten viele Leute . . .

B **Aus meinem Leben.** Erzählen Sie von einem merkwürdigen Erlebnis *(experience)* aus Ihrem Leben. Wie sind Sie zu diesem Erlebnis gekommen? Wie verlief es? Was waren die Folgen *(results)* davon?

Wortschatz 24

am Ende	schließlich
zum Schluß	endlich
zuletzt	

1. **Am Ende** and **zum Schluß** express the idea of conclusion in general terms and are synonymous in most instances.

Er hatte sein ganzes Leben gearbeitet, aber **am Ende** / **zum Schluß** hatte er nichts.	*He had worked his entire life, but in the end he had nothing.*

2. **Zuletzt** usually introduces the final event in a series.

Sie ging in die Bibliothek, dann in die Mensa und **zuletzt** nach Hause.	*She went to the library, then to the student cafeteria, and finally home.*

3. **Schließlich** and **endlich** can both express the idea that after a considerable period of time or series of events, something *finally* happens.

Nach langer Wanderung kamen wir **schließlich** / **endlich** ans Ziel.	*After a long hike we finally / at last reached our destination.*

4. **Schließlich** can also mean *in the final analysis* or *after all.*

Sie haben uns **schließlich** eine Menge Arbeit erspart.	*After all, they saved us a lot of work.*

5. **Endlich,** when stressed, is stronger than **schließlich** and conveys the idea that something has *finally* or *at (long) last* happened.

Endlich haben wir einen Brief bekommen.	*At long last, we received a letter.*

ÜBUNG

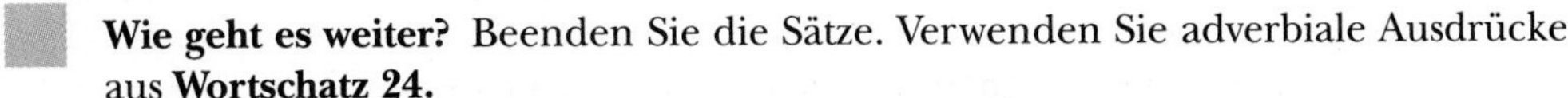

Wie geht es weiter? Beenden Sie die Sätze. Verwenden Sie adverbiale Ausdrücke aus **Wortschatz 24.**

Beispiel: Wir arbeiteten den ganzen Tag, und . . .
Wir arbeiteten den ganzen Tag, und ***am Ende*** *hatten wir nichts.*

1. Wir warten schon seit Stunden, aber ich möchte jetzt . . .
2. Die Party wird bis Mitternacht dauern, und . . .
3. Wir sollten uns nicht über ihn ärgern. Er hat uns . . .
4. Ich habe heute einiges vor. Zuerst muß ich arbeiten, dann muß ich einkaufen, danach muß ich zur Uni, und . . .
5. Viele Menschen schuften *(toil)* ihr ganzes Leben lang, und . . .

Zusammenfassung 24

Rules to Remember

1. A descriptive adverb is an adjective without an ending **(schnell, fleißig).**
2. In addition to descriptive adverbs, the most common adverbs are of time **(heute, oft)** or place **(hier, überall).**
3. A series of adverbs follows the word order rule of Time-Manner-Place.
4. A few adverbs (**deshalb, trotzdem,** etc.) function like conjunctions and link thoughts in two separate clauses or sentences.

Activities

1 **How many adverbs?** Write down as many adverbs of *place* as you can think of in one minute without consulting the chapter. Give your list to another student who then makes statements using your adverbs.

2 **Time-manner-place.** In three separate columns, write down five adverbs of *time,* five of description or *manner,* and five of *place.* Give your list to a partner who may use any combination of your adverbs to write five sentences, each of which contains adverbs of time, manner, and place. Your partner must use all of your adverbs, but in any combination.

3 **Sequencing.** Pick a time span of three hours within the past several days that you can remember clearly. Write or prepare a blow-by-blow description of the things you did during that time period. Use a variety of time adverbs.

4 **Shifting adverbs.** Pick a text of at least two paragraphs. Read through the text, underlining all adverbs of time, manner, and place. Restate the respective sentences by shifting one of these adverbs to a different position. For example, if an adverb comes after the conjugated verb, perhaps you can move it to the beginning of the sentence or vice versa.

5 **Working with a text.** Prepare an oral or written synopsis of a story you have read for class. At least one out of every three statements should begin with an adverbial expression.

Particles 25

25.1 Particles

German has a number of so-called "flavoring" particles **(die Abtönungspartikel, -n** or **die Modalpartikel, -n)** that convey various degrees of interest, surprise, impatience, irritation or indignation, reassurance, agreement, skepticism, resignation, casualness, and other feelings or reactions. Particles lend colloquial German much of its color, emotion, and idiomatic flavor, but they are not always readily translatable into English and frequently derive their nuances from the tone of voice in which they are spoken. The following explanations touch on some of the most common uses and functions of particles.

25.2 Uses of Various Particles

A. Aber

Aber has two uses. As a conjunction it means *but;* as a flavoring particle it makes the thought expressed more forceful.

Das ist **aber** nett von dir.	*That's really nice of you.*
Hast du etwas gegen unseren Besuch?	*Have you got anything against our visit?*
—**Aber** nein!	*Of course not!*

B. Also

Also does not mean *also;* it normally means *so* and suggests reassurance or reinforcement of the idea expressed.

Es ist **also** wahr, was du gesagt hast.	*So what you said is true.*

C. Auch

1. **Auch** has a wide range of uses, all related to the idea of *also, what's more,* or *too.*

Er wollte Deutsch lernen, und er hat es **auch** getan.	*He wanted to learn German and, what's more, he did.*
Wollt ihr uns **auch** helfen?	*And do you want to help us too?*

2. **Auch** is sometimes used in the sense of *even.* With this meaning it is interchangeable with **sogar.**

Auch / **Sogar** in den Alpen fiel letztes Jahr weniger Schnee.	*Even in the Alps less snow fell last year.*

D. Denn

Denn as a particle occurs only in questions; it adds a tone of either mild or strong impatience, surprise, or interest. It also makes questions sound less abrupt.

Kommst du **denn** nicht mit?	*Well, aren't you going to come along?*
Was habt ihr **denn** die ganze Zeit gemacht?	*Well, what did you do the whole time?*
Was ist **denn** hier los?	*What in the world is going on here?*

E. Doch

1. **Doch** is used in a variety of situations. Within its wide range of emphasis, it commonly conveys:

a. indignation.

Das ist **doch** Wahnsinn!	*That's really crazy!*

b. surprise or contradiction.

Sie haben aber **doch** alle Fragen richtig beantwortet.	*You answered all questions correctly after all. (surprise)* OR: *But you* **did** *answer all of the questions correctly. (contradiction)*

c. disbelief in negative statements.

Das kann **doch** nicht dein Ernst sein!	*You can't really be serious!*

2. **Doch** intensifies the sense of impatience or urgency in imperatives, usually in combination with **mal** (see 6.2).

Hör **doch** (mal) zu!	*Hey, come on, listen!*

3. **Doch** is also the proper response when countering the negative implication of a statement or question (see also 15.1).

Für uns hast du sicher keine Zeit. **—Doch.**	*You surely have no time for us.* *Oh yes (I do).*

F. Eben

1. As an adverb, **eben** means *just (now) / (then)*. It is synonymous with **gerade.**

Die Gäste gingen **eben** weg, als wir ankamen.	*The guests were just (then) leaving, as we arrived.*

2. As an intensifier, **eben** indicates resigned acceptance of a fact.

Wenn niemand mit ins Kino will, bleiben wir **eben** zu Hause.	*If no one wants to go to the movies, we'll just (have to) stay home.*
So sind die Dinge **eben.**	*That's just the way things are.*

3. **Eben** can also imply agreement, the idea that a statement is *precisely* or *exactly* the point.

Das war aber ein schwieriger Vortrag. **—Eben!**	*That was really a difficult lecture.* *Precisely!*

4. **Halt** is synonymous with **eben** in the sense of resigned acceptance. It is very colloquial.

Wir müssen **halt** warten, bis der Regen vorübergeht.	*We'll just have to wait until the rain passes.*

G. Eigentlich

1. **Eigentlich** means *actually, to tell the truth,* or *when you get right down to it.*

Eigentlich sollten wir froh sein, daß niemand uns gestört hat.	*When you get right down to it, we should be happy that no one disturbed us.*
Du hast **eigentlich** recht.	*You are right, actually.*

2. **Eigentlich** is not nearly as strong as the adverb **wirklich,** which implies that something *really* is the case.

   COMPARE:

Es ist **wirklich** sein Auto.	*It really is his car.*
Eigentlich ist es sein Auto.	*Actually, it is his car.*

H. Ja

1. **Ja** expresses the obviousness of a fact, sometimes with a slight tone of impatience; it is best rendered in English by *you know, don't you see?,* or *of course.*

Sie wissen **ja,** was ich meine.	*You know what I mean, of course.*
Das tue ich **ja** schon.	*I'm already doing that, don't you see?*

2. **Ja** adds a sense of urgency to imperatives. In this function it is often followed by **nur.**

Komm **ja (nur)** nicht zu spät nach Hause!	*Don't you dare come home too late!*

3. **Ja,** like **doch,** can also convey surprise.

Da ist sie **ja / doch.**	*Hey, there she is!*
Du hast **ja / doch** eine schöne Wohnung!	*You really have a nice apartment!*

4. **Ja** or **doch** can express that something is *of course* obvious.

Wir wollen **ja / doch** nicht vergessen, wie schwer das Leben manchmal sein kann.	*Of course, we don't want to forget how difficult life can sometimes be.*

I. Mal

Mal comes from **einmal** *(once / one time).* It adds a sense of casualness to statements and questions, similar to the idea of *hey* or *just.* It is very common in commands and suggestions.

Ich werde es **mal** versuchen.	*I'll just give it a try.*
Schauen wir **mal** nach, was in der Zeitung steht.	*Let's just see what the paper says.*
Hör **mal** zu!	*Hey, listen!*

J. Nun

Nun (often combined with **[ein]mal**) implies resigned acceptance of a situation. With this meaning it is virtually synonymous with **eben** and **halt.**

Was sollten wir **nun (ein)mal** tun?	*Well, what should we do?* (that is, *in a particular situation)*
Die Dinge stehen im Augenblick **nun (ein)mal** so.	*This just is the way things are at the moment.*

K. Nur

1. **Nur** conveys a variety of feelings including anxiety, indifference, encouragement, disappointment, and anger.

Das macht die Situation **nur** schlimmer.	*That only makes the situation worse.*
Wie kann man **nur** so unvorsichtig sein?	*How can one ever be so careless?*

2. In imperatives, **nur** adds a sense of urgency or warning.

Denke **nur** nicht, daß wir diese Beleidigung bald vergessen werden!	*Just don't think that we'll soon forget this insult!*
Tu(e) das **nur!**	*Just do it (and see what happens)!*

L. Schon

1. As an adverb, **schon** means *already.*

Wir haben es **schon** gemacht.	*We have already done it.*

2. In adverbial usage, **schon** is often used with **mal** to mean *ever before.*

Waren Sie **schon mal** Gast in diesem Hotel?	*Were you ever a guest in this hotel before?*

3. As a particle, **schon** expresses confidence or reassurance.

Hat sie es schon gemacht?	*Did she already do it?*
—Ich glaube **schon.**	*Oh, I think so.*
Ich werde es **schon** machen.	*Don't worry, I'll do it.*

4. The particle **schon** can also convey a somewhat reserved concession, the idea that although a statement is undoubtedly true, there is also another consideration.

Du hast ja eine gute Wohnung.	*You have a good apartment, you know.*
—Das **schon,** aber keine Möbel.	*Well, yes, but no furniture.*
Das ist **schon** richtig, was du sagst, aber . . .	*What you say is true, but . . .*

5. **Schon** gives a sense of impatient encouragement to requests.

Setz dich **schon** hin!	*Come on now, sit down!*

6. **Schon** can also be used to add a sense of confirmation or persuasive emphasis to questions.

Was kann man in so einem Fall **schon** sagen?	*What can you ever say in such a case?*
Wer möchte **schon** allein auf einer Südseeinsel leben?	*Who would ever want to live alone on a South Sea island?*

M. Überhaupt

1. In statements, **überhaupt** implies the idea of *in general* or *on the whole,* but these translations never truly capture the tone of this particle.

Es ist **überhaupt** schwierig, mit ihnen zu sprechen.	*On the whole, it is difficult to talk with them.*
Man sollte **überhaupt** mit seinen Behauptungen etwas vorsichtiger sein.	*One should in general be more careful with one's assertions.*

2. **Überhaupt** intensifies questions by conveying the idea of *ever* or *at all.*

Wie habt ihr das **überhaupt** gemacht?	*How did you ever do that?*
Versteht sie **überhaupt** Deutsch?	*Does she understand German at all?*

3. Used with negatives, **überhaupt (nicht)** means *not / nothing / anything at all.* It is synonymous with **gar nicht** (see **Wortschatz 6**).

Sie wissen **überhaupt** nichts.	*They do not know anything at all.*

N. Wohl

1. The particle **wohl** suggests probability (see also 8.1). Its English equivalents are *no doubt, quite likely,* or *probably.*

Diese Häuser gehören **wohl** der Gemeinde.	*These houses no doubt belong to the municipality.*
Das wird **wohl** wahr sein.	*That's probably true.*

2. In some expressions, **wohl** conveys a sense of certainty.

Das kann man **wohl** sagen!	*You can say that again!*
Du bist **wohl** nicht bei Sinnen!	*You must be out of your mind!*

O. Zwar

1. **Zwar** means *to be sure* or *of course* and is usually balanced by an **aber** *(however)* in the following clause.

Es gab **zwar** noch genug zu essen, aber niemand hatte Hunger. — *There was, to be sure, still enough to eat, but no one was hungry.*

2. **Zwar** cannot be used as an affirmative response to a question. Instead, German uses **allerdings** *(oh yes; by all means)* or **freilich** *(of course; by all means),* depending upon the type of response required.

COMPARE:

Haben Sie verstanden?	*Did you understand?*
—Allerdings.	*Oh, yes!* (that is, *I know what you are getting at*)
—Freilich.	*Of course!* (that is, *did you think I wouldn't?*)

* Übungen

A **Partikeln im Gebrauch.** Lesen Sie die folgenden Texte einmal ohne die kursivgedruckten Abtönungspartikeln und einmal mit diesen Partikeln. Erklären Sie dann auf englisch, wie die Partikeln den Text ändern und was sie zum Ausdruck bringen.

1. Deutsche Vereinigung: Vater Stratmann hat die Vereinigung mit gemischten Gefühlen erlebt. Wenn er ganz ehrlich sein soll, dann ist er *ja nun mal* Deutscher. Er weiß *zwar* nicht, ob er einen besonderen Nationalstolz hat, aber er ist *doch* ein bißchen geschichtsbewußt *(historically aware),* und als er im Fernsehen die Demonstrationen in Leipzig und die Leute auf der Mauer gesehen hat, das war *schon* ein erhebendes *(uplifting)* Gefühl, muß er ganz ehrlich sagen, da lief es ihm *doch* den Rücken runter *(chills ran down his spine). (Die Zeit)*
2. Eine kaputte Küchenuhr: Kaputt ist die Uhr, das weiß ich *wohl.* Aber sonst ist sie *doch* noch ganz wie immer: weiß und blau. Und was das Schönste ist, das habe ich Ihnen *ja* noch *überhaupt* nicht erzählt. Denken Sie *mal,* sie ist um halb drei stehengeblieben. (Wolfgang Borchert, „Die Küchenuhr“)

B **Viele haben es getan.** Lesen Sie die Sätze mit richtiger Betonung vor. Erklären Sie die Unterschiede zwischen den Sätzen. Drücken Sie die verschiedenen Nuancen auf englisch aus.

1. Sie hat es doch getan.
2. Er hat es nun einmal getan.
3. Du hast es also getan.
4. Du hast es also doch getan.
5. Habt ihr es überhaupt getan?
6. Sie haben es wohl getan.
7. Haben Sie es denn getan?
8. Sie hat es ja getan.
9. Wir haben es halt getan.
10. Haben Sie es schon einmal getan?
11. Er hat es eben getan.

C **Besonders betonen.** Bringen Sie die folgenden Aussagen durch den Gebrauch von Abtönungspartikeln stärker zum Ausdruck. Erklären Sie die Nuancen auf englisch. Bei einigen Sätzen gibt es mehrere Möglichkeiten.

aber	eben	nun
also	eigentlich	nur
auch	halt	schon
denn	ja	überhaupt
doch	mal	wohl

1. Das verstehe ich nicht! Wie hast du das gemacht?
2. Kommen Sie mit! Sie werden Interessantes erleben.
3. Aha, du bist es!
4. Das Leben im Ausland ist manchmal problematisch.
5. Hören Sie zu!
6. Du wolltest jetzt arbeiten gehen, nicht wahr?
7. Waren Sie einmal in Südtirol?
8. Diesen Zug haben wir verpaßt. Wir müssen auf den nächsten warten.
9. Mensch, du hast einen schönen Wagen!
10. Ihr wollt nicht mit uns mitgehen?
11. Sehen Sie, was die Leute hier alles zerstört haben.
12. Verstehen Sie, was er meint?
13. Er hat dich nicht verstanden.
14. Das hat sie gesagt.

Anwendung

Argumentation. Die Klasse einigt sich über eine These oder Behauptung, zu der es sicher viele Argumente pro und kontra gibt. Alle im Kurs sollen ihre Meinung sagen. Versuchen Sie, Ihre Argumente und Meinungen durch den Gebrauch von Adverbien *(siehe Kapitel 24)* und Abtönungspartikeln zu verstärken. Bei Meinungsäußerungen spielen auch Modalverben *(siehe Kapitel 9)* eine wichtige Rolle.

THESENVORSCHLÄGE

Man soll lieber nicht heiraten.
Die Politik eines Landes können einzelne Bürger nicht ändern.
In unserem Staat haben nicht alle Menschen die gleichen Chancen.
Geld regiert die Welt.
Gleiche Arbeit, gleicher Lohn *(wage)*.

REDEMITTEL

Es ist durchaus (nicht) so, daß . . .
Hoffentlich seht ihr doch ein, daß . . .
Wir sollten / müssen endlich mal . . .
Eigentlich ist das nicht ganz so falsch . . .
Das ist ja lauter Unsinn!
Ich sehe es leider, leider ganz anders.
Das ist doch überhaupt kein Argument!
Natürlich kann man das, aber . . .
Das sollte / kann man sowieso nicht sagen.
Es ist nun einmal eine Tatsache *(fact)*, daß . . .

Schriftliche Themen

Tips zum Schreiben ***Deciding When to Use Flavoring Particles***
The choices you make about which particles or adverbs to use when writing will vary with your intentions and with the types of readers you have in mind. Most particles are clearly for colloquial usage and would not be appropriate in a critical essay. In less formal writing, for example, in letters to friends or local newspapers or in speeches, particles can lend emotion to your opinions and strengthen the rhetorical persuasiveness of your arguments.

A **Stilebenen** *(Levels of style)*. Suchen Sie ein aktuelles Thema aus der Presse (Zeitung oder Zeitschrift). Schreiben Sie zuerst einen Aufsatz, in dem Sie sich in einem sachlichen *(objective, unbiased)* Stil zu diesem Thema äußern. Schreiben Sie dann einen Leserbrief, in dem Sie sich nicht mehr so sachlich äußern. In Ihrem Brief können Sie Gefühle und Meinungen durch Abtönungspartikeln, Adverbien und rhetorische Fragen stärker zum Ausdruck bringen.

Beispiel (Aufsatz):

Viele junge Leute benehmen sich heutzutage sehr schlecht. Man sagt, daß die Erziehung *(upbringing)* zu Hause anfangen soll, aber das ist nicht immer der Fall. Manche Eltern kümmern sich *(concern themselves)* zu wenig um ihre Kinder. Auch in der Schule fehlt oft die nötige Disziplin. Unter solchen Umständen *(circumstances)* ist es oft für junge Menschen schwierig . . .

Beispiel (Leserbrief):

An die Redaktion *(editorial staff)*

Ich finde es *doch* eine Schande *(disgrace)*, wie sich viele junge Leute heutzutage benehmen. *Zwar* sagt man, daß die Erziehung zu Hause anfangen soll, aber das ist leider *doch* nicht immer der Fall. Manche Eltern kümmern sich wenig oder *überhaupt* nicht um ihre Kinder. Auch in der Schule fehlt *ja* oft die nötige Disziplin. Wie sollen *denn* junge Menschen unter solchen Umständen . . . ? usw.

B **Bewertung** ***(evaluation)*** **des Unterrichts.** Schreiben Sie eine informelle Bewertung Ihres Deutschkurses. Weisen Sie auf *(point out)* gute und weniger gute Aspekte dieses Kurses hin. Haben Sie einige Vorschläge, wie man den Kurs vielleicht auch anders gestalten *(structure)* könnte?

Wortschatz 25

das ist aber / ja wahr!
das ist aber / ja lächerlich!
aber nein!

\+ *other expressions with flavoring particles*

Flavoring particles are particularly common in colloquial responses to things people say or do.

das ist aber / ja wahr!	that's sure true!	**das ist es eben!** / **das ist es ja!**	that's just it, that's just what I mean
das ist aber / ja lächerlich!	that's ridiculous!	**so ist es eben**	that's just how it is
aber nein!	oh no!	**ja, was ich sagen wollte,**	by the way, what I wanted to say
also gut / also schön	well, OK (I'll do it)	**mal sehen**	we'll just have to (wait and) see
na also!	what did I tell you!	**das wird schon stimmen**	I'm (pretty) sure that's right
also doch!	it's true what I said after all!	**es wird schon gehen / werden**	I'm (pretty) sure it'll work out okay
na (nun) ja	oh well, okay	**das habe ich mir (auch) schon gedacht**	that's just what I figured (too)
ich denke / glaube schon	I should think so		
was ist denn?	what's the matter?		
was ist denn hier los?	what's going on here?		
das darf doch nicht wahr sein!	that can't be (true)!		

ÜBUNGEN

A **Weniger formell.** Drücken Sie die Ideen in diesen Sätzen durch Ausdrücke mit Abtönungspartikeln informeller aus.

Beispiel: Das habe ich richtig gesagt!
Also doch!

1. Was ist los?
2. Ich bin ziemlich sicher, daß die Antwort richtig ist.
3. Genau das meine ich.
4. Sehen Sie? Es stimmt, was ich gesagt habe.
5. Ich bin sicher, daß es dir gelingen wird, das zu tun.

B **Reaktionen.** Was sagen Sie in diesen Situationen? Verwenden Sie Ausdrücke mit Abtönungspartikeln.

Beispiel: Ein Freund sagt etwas, was Sie sich auch schon gedacht haben.
Das ist es eben!
OR: *Das ist aber wahr.*

1. Jemand bringt in einer Diskussion ein Argument vor, das Sie für ziemlich überzeugend *(convincing)* halten.
2. Jemand macht eine Behauptung *(assertion)*, von der Sie meinen, daß man noch abwarten muß, ob sie stimmt oder nicht.
3. Jemand berichtet Ihnen etwas Unglaubliches. Sie sind sehr überrascht.
4. Jemand fragt Sie, ob es eine gute Idee wäre, noch eine Fremdsprache zu lernen.
5. Jemand bittet Sie, an einem Spiel teilzunehmen. Anfangs wollen Sie nicht, aber nachdem man Sie mehrmals bittet, können / wollen Sie nicht mehr nein sagen.
6. Jemand macht eine Behauptung *(assertion)*, die Sie für einen völligen Blödsinn *(nonsense, rubbish)* halten.

Zusammenfassung 25

Rules to Remember

1. Particles "flavor" colloquial German by conveying various feelings and reactions of the speaker.
2. Particles often derive their nuances from the tone of voice in which they are spoken.
3. Particles frequently do not have English equivalents.

Activities

Particles do not lend themselves to specific oral practice. The best way to learn them is by spotting or hearing them in colloquial German.

1. **Recognizing particles.** Look for particles in the dialogue sections of texts you read. First read these sections without the particles, then with particles. After a while, you should begin to hear the difference.

2. **Listening for particles.** Develop a feel for particles by listening for them in very colloquial conversations. The tape cassette series *Papa, Charly hat gesagt* (Langenscheidt Verlag, Bestellnummer 84515) contains a number of humorous father and son dialogues replete with particles. It is also available in book form. Vignettes by the German comedian Loriot (available commercially in Germany on audio cassette and videotape) are another excellent source of dialogue laden with particles.

3. **Building a repertoire.** Keep a list of useful expressions with particles that you either hear or encounter in your reading.

Relative Pronouns

26

26.1 Relative Clauses

The relative clause **(der Relativsatz, ⸚e)** supplies specific information about a previously mentioned person, thing, or idea. Since it is a clause, it must have a subject and a verb, and thus usually provides more information than an adjective.

COMPARE:

Dieses **kleine** Land hat einen hohen Lebensstandard. *(adjective modifier)*	*This small country has a high standard of living.*
Dieses Land, **das viel kleiner ist als seine Nachbarländer,** hat einen hohen Lebensstandard. *(relative clause modifier)*	*This country, which is much smaller than its neighbors, has a high standard of living.*

26.2 Relative Pronouns

A. *Forms*

1. In English, relative clauses are normally introduced by the relative pronouns *who, whom, whose, that* (for persons), and *which, that* (for things). The noun or pronoun to which they refer is called the *antecedent.*

Antecedent	*Relative clause*
The man	*who* came to dinner
The children	(to) *whom* we gave the presents
The book	*that* they read

In German, a relative clause is introduced by a relative pronoun **(das Relativpronomen, -)** that has *number, gender,* and *case.* With the exception of the dative plural and the four genitives, the forms of the relative pronoun are identical to those of the definite article.[1]

	Masc.	***Fem.***	***Neut.***	***Pl.***
Nom.	der	die	das	die
Acc.	den	die	das	die
Dat.	dem	der	dem	**denen**
Gen.	**dessen**	**deren**	**dessen**	**deren**

2. There is an alternative set of relative pronouns using the declined forms of **welch-** *(which)* (see 5.3). These forms are somewhat uncommon and used primarily to avoid repetition of identical words.

   Da kommt die, **welche** die Vasen gekauft hat. — *Here comes the one who bought the vases.*

   INSTEAD OF:
   Da kommt die, die die Vasen gekauft hat.

B. Use

1. A relative clause is a subordinate clause; the inflected verb therefore moves to final position within this clause.

   COMPARE:
   Ihr Freund wohnt in Marburg. **Er** *ist* ein bekannter Journalist.
   Ihr Freund, **der** ein bekannter Journalist *ist,* wohnt in Marburg.
   Her friend, who is a well-known journalist, lives in Marburg.

2. A relative pronoun has the same *gender* and *number* as the word to which it refers (its antecedent).

Ihr Freund, **der** in Marburg wohnt, . . .

Ihre Schwester, **die** in Bremen studiert, . . .

---

1. Historically, both relative pronouns and definite articles evolved from the demonstrative pronouns; the genitive articles **des** and **der** and the dative plural article **den** are simply shortened forms of the demonstratives **dessen, deren,** and **denen.**

3. The *case* of a relative pronoun is determined not by the case of its antecedent, but by its grammatical function within its own clause. Relative pronouns can occur as subjects of clauses (nominative), as accusative or dative objects, as objects of prepositions, or as genitive constructions.

Wir brauchen einen Politiker, . . .	*We need a politician . . .*
der unsere Interessen vertritt. *(subject)*	*who represents our interests.*
den jedermann respektiert. *(accusative object)*	*whom everyone respects.*
mit dem man auch reden kann. *(object of a preposition)*	*with whom one can also speak.*
dessen Politik nicht zu konservativ ist. *(genitive)*	*whose politics aren't too conservative.*
Sie sollten zu einer Ärztin gehen, . . .	*You should go to a doctor . . .*
die Sprechstunden auch am Abend hat. *(subject)*	*who also has office hours in the evening.*
die Sie besser kennen. *(accusative object)*	*whom you know better.*
zu der Sie Vertrauen haben. *(object of a preposition)*	*in whom you have trust.*
deren Klinik in der Nähe ist. *(genitive)*	*whose clinic is nearby.*
Er hat ein Problem, . . .	*He has a problem . . .*
das nicht weggehen will. *(subject)*	*that / which won't go away.*
das er lösen muß. *(accusative object)*	*that / which he has to solve.*
über das er nicht gern spricht. *(object of a preposition)*	*about which he does not like to talk.*
dessen Ursache wir nicht kennen. *(genitive)*	*the cause of which we do not know.*
Das Buch schildert Völker, . . .	*The book portrays peoples . . .*
die in Osteuropa wohnen. *(subject)*	*that / who live in Eastern Europe.*
die man im Westen nicht gut kennt. *(accusative object)*	*that / whom people in the West do not know well.*
denen wir helfen sollten. *(verb with dative object)*	*that / whom we should help.*
deren Sitten uns ganz fremd vorkommen. *(genitive)*	*whose customs seem quite foreign to us.*

4. Relative clauses in German must be set off by commas.

5. Prepositions used before **dessen** or **deren** do not affect their cases. The noun following the genitive relative pronoun is the object of the preposition and takes the appropriate case.

Kennst du *die Familie,* **in** *deren* **altem Haus** wir übernachten werden?	*Do you know the family in whose old house we will spend the night?*
Da kommt *der Mann,* **von** *dessen* **schrecklichem Unfall** du uns erzählt hast.	*Here comes the man whose terrible accident you told us about.*

26.3 *Was, wo*-Compounds, and *wo* as Relative Pronouns

A. Was

1. **Was** is used as a relative pronoun to refer to the antecedents **etwas, nichts, alles, viel(es), wenig(es), manches, einiges,** and the demonstratives **das** and **dasselbe.**

Es gibt fast nichts, **was** ihn überrascht.	*There is almost nothing that surprises him.*
Er tut dasselbe, **was** sie tut.	*He does the same thing (that) she does.*

2. **Was** is used to refer to neuter adjective nouns (see 21.1B), usually in the superlative, and to neuter ordinal numbers.

Das ist das Beste, **was** er je geschrieben hat.	*That is the best thing (that) he has ever written.*
Das erste, **was** wir tun müssen, ist Folgendes: . . .	*The first thing (that) we must do is the following: . . .*

3. **Was** is used to refer to an antecedent that is an entire clause or activity.

Ihre Gesundheit ist das Beste, was Sie haben.

COMPARE:

Im Tiergarten haben wir einen Eisbären gesehen, **der** sehr interessant war.	*At the zoo we saw a polar bear* **that** *was very interesting.* (that is, *the polar bear itself was interesting)*
Im Tiergarten haben wir einen Eisbären gesehen, **was** sehr interessant war.	*At the zoo we saw a polar bear,* **which** *was very interesting.(the experience of seeing a polar bear was interesting)*

B. Wo-*Compounds*

1. Prepositions are not normally used with the relative pronoun **was; wo-**combinations **(worauf, wodurch, womit,** etc.) are used instead.

Gib mir etwas, **womit** ich schreiben kann.	*Give me something with which I can write.*
Sie hat den ersten Preis gewonnen, **worauf** sie sehr stolz ist.	*She won first prize, of which she is very proud.* (that is, *she is proud of the fact that she won first place*)

2. A **wo**-compound may also be used to refer to a specific antecedent that is *not a person.* However, the preposition + relative pronoun **(der, die, das,** etc.) is generally preferred.

Acceptable	*Preferable*
Hier ist die Flasche, **woraus** er getrunken hat.	Hier ist die Flasche, **aus der** er getrunken hat.

3. Neither **da**-compounds (see 19.1) nor **wo**-compounds (see 15.2) can be used when the antecedent is a person.

C. Wo

The adverb **wo** *(where)* functions as a relative pronoun referring to an antecedent that is a place or location.

Wir haben die Fabrik besucht, **wo** (*or:* **in der**) sie arbeitet.	*We visited the factory where* (or: *in which*) *she works.*

26.4 The Indefinite Relative Pronouns *wer* and *was*

A. Wer *and* was *(Who/What)*

1. The indefinite relative pronoun **wer (wen, wem, wessen)** meaning *who (whom, whose)* is used when there is no antecedent referring to a specific person.

Er will nicht sagen, **wer** den Krug zerbrochen hat. *(nominative)*	*He does not want to say who broke the jug.*
Ich weiß nicht, **wen** sie heiratet. *(accusative)*	*I do not know whom she is going to marry.*
Sag uns, **mit wem** du gesprochen hast. *(dative)*	*Tell us with whom you spoke.*
Die Polizei konnte nicht feststellen, **wessen** Hund das Kind gebissen hatte. *(genitive)*	*The police were not able to ascertain whose dog had bitten the child.*

2. **Was** functions like **wer** but refers to things or concepts.

Er hat nie gesagt, **was** er wirklich gedacht hat.	*He never said what he really was thinking.*

B. Wer *and* was *(Whoever/Whatever)*

1. **Wer** and **was** can also be used to mean *whoever (he / she who)* and *whatever* respectively. In this usage, the first clause begins with **wer** or **was,** and the second clause generally begins with an optional demonstrative pronoun (see 16.3).

Wer ihm hilft, **(der)** bekommt ein freies Essen.	*Whoever helps him gets a free meal.*

2. The demonstrative pronoun must be used if it is not in the same case as **wer.**

Wer mich um Hilfe bittet, **dem** werde ich helfen.	*Whoever asks me for help, I will help.*

3. Both **wer** and **was** occur frequently in proverbs and sayings.

Wer aus der Haut fährt, **(der)** lebt außer sich.	*He who leaps out of his skin lives beside himself.*
Was ich nicht weiß, **(das)** macht mich nicht heiß.	*What I don't know won't hurt me.*

* Übungen

A **Am Rhein.** Verbinden Sie die beiden Sätze durch Relativpronomen.

Beispiel: Der Rhein ist ein Fluß. Er fließt durch mehrere Länder.
Der Rhein ist ein Fluß, der durch mehrere Länder fließt.

1. Am Rhein stehen viele alte Burgen *(castles)*. Sie stammen aus dem frühen Mittelalter.
2. Hoch oben auf einem Rheinfels *(cliff)* sitzt die Lorelei. Sie singt ein altes Lied.
3. Auf beiden Seiten des Rheins wächst der Wein. Den trinken die Rheinländer so gern.
4. Der Rhein fließt durch einige große Städte. In ihnen gibt es jetzt viel Industrie und auch viel Umweltverschmutzung *(air pollution)*.
5. Die Mosel mündet *(empties)* bei der Stadt Koblenz in den Rhein. Sie ist über zweitausend Jahre alt.
6. Touristen können mit Schiffen auf dem Rhein fahren. Sie wollen die Romantik dieses Flusses näher kennenlernen.

B **Eine gute Wanderausrüstung.** Sie und ein paar Freunde wollen eine Woche in den Bergen wandern. Sie sprechen mit dem Verkäufer im Sportgeschäft.

Beispiel: Wir brauchen Anoraks *(parkas)*, ____ wasserdicht sind.
Wir brauchen Anoraks, die wasserdicht sind.

1. Wir brauchen Bergschuhe, ____ aus Leder sind.
2. Wir suchen Rucksäcke, ____ leicht sind und in ____ man viel tragen kann.
3. Wir möchten eine Wanderkarte, auf ____ auch schwierige Touren eingezeichnet *(marked)* sind.
4. Es wäre auch gut, einen Kompaß zu haben, ____ man auch bei Nacht lesen kann.
5. Haben Sie auch ein Zelt *(tent)*, in ____ drei Personen schlafen können?
6. Zuletzt muß jeder von uns eine Brille tragen, ____ unsere Augen vor der Höhensonne schützt *(protects)*.

C **Personenbeschreibung.** Was wissen wir über Anita und Willi? Verwenden Sie Relativpronomen.

Beispiel: Sie kann mehrere Sprachen.
Sie ist eine Frau, die mehrere Sprachen kann.
OR: *Sie ist eine Person, die mehrere Sprachen kann.*

Anita

1. Alle Leute mögen sie.
2. Sie spricht gern über Politik.
3. Sie treibt viel Sport.
4. Zu ihr kann man kommen, wenn man Probleme hat.
5. Willi könnte ohne sie nicht glücklich sein.
6. Ihr Lachen ist ansteckend *(contagious)*.

Beispiel: Er arbeitet sehr fleißig.
Er ist ein Mann, der sehr fleißig arbeitet.
OR: *Er ist jemand, der sehr fleißig arbeitet.*

Willi

1. Alle Leute mögen ihn.
2. Mit ihm kann man sich gut unterhalten *(converse)*.
3. Er kocht sehr gern.
4. Man hört über ihn nur Positives.
5. Man kann ihm trauen.
6. Sein Englisch ist recht gut.

Beschreiben Sie jetzt jemanden, den Sie kennen. Schreiben Sie fünf bis sechs Sätze mit verschiedenen Relativpronomen.

D **Die Dinge nur loswerden.** In Ihrer Garage gibt es noch viel altes Gerümpel *(junk)*, das Sie gern loswerden möchten. Versuchen Sie, andere Leute zum Kauf dieser Dinge zu überreden *(persuade)*.

Beispiele: *Hier ist ein Fahrrad,* ***das*** *noch gut fährt.*
Hier sind ein paar alte Hobby-Zeitschriften, ***in denen*** *es interessante Artikel gibt.*

1. ein Kinderwagen mit nur drei Rädern
2. Plakate *(posters)*
3. ein leeres Aquarium
4. eine Öllampe
5. Autoreifen *(tires)*
6. ein kleines Modellflugzeug mit Motor
7. ein künstlicher Weihnachtsbaum
8. alte Kleidungsstücke

Und was für unwiderstehliche *(irresistible)* Dinge gibt es wohl auch noch in Ihrer Garage?

E **Tolle Dinge erfinden.** Welche fünf Dinge möchten Sie erfinden? Je toller (oder verrückter), desto besser!

Beispiele: *Ich möchte einen Hut erfinden,* ***der*** *sich automatisch vom Kopf hebt, wenn sein Besitzer „Guten Tag" sagt.*
Ich möchte eine Brille erfinden, ***die*** *Scheibenwischer hat.*

F **Situationen.** Wie drücken Sie die folgenden Ideen aus?

Beispiel: You are looking for a pencil with which to write.
Ich suche einen Bleistift, mit dem ich schreiben kann.

1. You can't find the coat you just bought.
2. You have a friend *(masculine or feminine)* for whom you would like to buy a present.
3. You want to buy a couple of pets **(Haustiere)** you can play with.
4. You want to learn a foreign language many people speak.
5. There is much **(viel)** you simply don't understand.

Machen Sie jetzt drei bis vier Aussagen über Dinge, die Sie wirklich brauchen oder haben möchten, die Sie aber jetzt nicht haben.

G **Tips für Europabesucher.** Machen Sie aus zwei Sätzen einen Satz mit Relativpronomen im Genitiv. Übersetzen Sie die neuen Sätze.

Beispiel: Auf dem Land gibt es viele Pensionen. Ihre Zimmer sind nicht so teuer.
Auf dem Land gibt es Pensionen, ***deren*** *Zimmer nicht so teuer sind.*
(In the countryside there are bed-and-breakfast establishments whose rooms are not so expensive.)

1. Im Herbst fahren viele Touristen in den Kaiserstuhl (Weingebiet in Südbaden). Seine Weine genießen einen besonders guten Ruf.
2. Man soll unbedingt auf den Dachstein (im Land Salzburg) hinauffahren. Von seinem Gipfel *(summit)* aus hat man einen herrlichen Panoramablick auf die umliegende Alpenwelt.
3. Im Sommer pilgern viele Touristen zum Kitzsteinhorn (Berg in Österreich). Auf seinen Gletschern *(glaciers)* kann man auch im Sommer Ski laufen.
4. Zu den großen Natursehenswürdigkeiten *(natural attractions)* Europas gehört die Adelsberger Grotte (in Slovenien). Ihre Tropfsteine *(stalactites)* bewundern Tausende von Besuchern jedes Jahr.
5. Besonders beliebt sind überall im Alpengebiet die Kurorte *(health resorts)*. Ihre Bergluft ist besonders gesund.

Gibt es denn auch in Ihrem Land oder in anderen Ländern, die Sie kennen, Sehenswürdigkeiten, die man unbedingt besuchen sollte? Schreiben Sie bitte drei Sätze mit **dessen** oder **deren.**

H ***Der, die, das, was* oder *wo?*** Beenden Sie die Sätze mit passenden Relativsätzen.

Beispiele: Ich habe einen Computer, . . .
Ich habe einen Computer, ***der*** *mir Spaß macht.*

Ich tue alles, . . .
Ich tue alles, ***was*** *mir Spaß macht.*

1. Ich möchte das tun, . . .
2. Ameisen *(ants)* sind Insekten, . . .
3. Manche Menschen sind intolerant, . . .
4. Deutsch ist eine Sprache, . . .
5. Liechtenstein ist ein Land, . . .
6. Es gibt viele Dinge, . . .
7. Ich weiß viel, . . .
8. Eine schwere Krankheit wäre *(would be)* das Schlimmste, . . .
9. Es gibt noch manches, . . .
10. Ich möchte an einen Ort reisen, . . .

I **Was ich alles möchte.** Ergänzen Sie die Sätze. Verwenden Sie entweder Präpositionen aus der Liste mit Relativpronomen oder **wo-** plus Präposition.

an	für	über
bei	in	von
durch	mit	zu

Beispiele: Ich möchte einen Freund haben, . . .
Ich möchte einen Freund haben, ***mit dem*** *ich über alles sprechen kann.*

Ich möchte nichts tun, . . .
Ich möchte nichts tun, ***worüber*** *ich mich später schämen müßte.*

1. Ich möchte Professoren haben, . . .
2. Ich möchte etwas studieren, . . .
3. Ich würde gern einen Beruf erlernen, . . .
4. Ich möchte später viel(es) sehen, . . .
5. Ich möchte später in einer Stadt wohnen, . . .

J **Was die Eltern nicht wissen.** Es gibt gewiß einiges, was Ihre Eltern über Sie nicht wissen. Erzählen Sie in etwa fünf Sätzen davon. Verwenden Sie **was** und Formen von **wer.**

Beispiel: Meine Eltern wissen nicht, . . .
Meine Eltern wissen nicht, ***wer*** *mein fester Freund ist.*
mit wem *ich jeden Tag zu Mittag esse.*
was *ich abends tue, wenn ich keine Hausaufgaben habe.*

K **Sprüche und Antisprüche.** Was bedeuten diese bekannten Sprüche? Erfinden Sie eigene Varianten (Antisprüche!) dazu. Je cleverer, desto besser!

Beispiel: Wer im Glashaus sitzt, soll nicht mit Steinen werfen.
Wer im Glashaus sitzt, ***(der)*** *soll keinen Krach* (noise, racket) *machen.*
(den) *sieht jeder.*
(der) *braucht gute Vorhänge* (curtains).

1. Wer *a* sagt, muß auch *b* sagen.
2. Wer den Pfennig nicht ehrt *(respects),* ist des Talers nicht wert.
3. Wer nichts wagt *(dares),* gewinnt nichts.
4. Wer zuletzt lacht, lacht am besten.
5. Was ich nicht weiß, macht mich nicht heiß.
6. Was man nicht im Kopf hat, muß man in den Beinen haben.

Erfinden Sie ein paar „weise" Sprüche dieser Art! Es gibt doch tausend Möglichkeiten!

* Anwendung

A **Fotos.** Bringen Sie ein paar Fotos oder Dias *(slides)* von einer Reise oder einer Episode aus Ihrem Leben zur Unterrichtsstunde mit. Erklären Sie die Orte und Menschen auf Ihren Bildern. Sie sollen selbstverständlich Relativpronomen verwenden.

Urlaub, den man nie vergißt.

REDEMITTEL

Hier seht ihr . . . , die . . .
Die Leute auf diesem Bild . . .
Links / rechts im Bild sind die . . . , die wir . . .
Das war in einem [Hotel], in dem / wo . . .

B **Gut und nicht so gut.** Was für Dinge (Menschen, Gegenstände, Ideen, usw.) finden Sie gut oder nicht so gut? Diskutieren Sie mit anderen Studenten darüber. Verwenden Sie Relativpronomen.

REDEMITTEL

Gut finde ich die [Kurse], die / in denen . . .
Nicht so gut finde ich das, was . . .
Ich halte viel / nichts von [Menschen], die . . .
Ich mag [Städte] (nicht), wo / in denen . . .

C **Zukunftswünsche.** Diskutieren Sie mit anderen Studenten über ihre Wünsche für die Zukunft.

REDEMITTEL

Ich suche vor allem einen Beruf, . . .
Natürlich möchte ich Kollegen haben, . . .
Vielleicht kann ich in einer Stadt / in einer Gegend wohnen, wo . . .
Hoffentlich lerne ich einen Mann / eine Frau kennen, . . .
Ich möchte selbstverständlich auch noch eine Familie haben, . . .
Ich möchte übrigens auch nichts / etwas erleben, was . . .

D **Eindrücke und Meinungen.** Fragen Sie andere Personen, was sie von gewissen bekannten oder berühmten Persönlichkeiten halten. Diskutieren Sie darüber.

REDEMITTEL

Was denken / halten Sie von . . . ?
Wie ist Ihr Eindruck von . . . ?
Ich halte ihn / sie für eine Person, die / der / deren . . .
Nun, (ich finde,) das ist ein Mensch, der / den / dem / dessen . . .
Er / sie kommt mir wie jemand vor, der . . .
Meiner Meinung nach hat er / sie etwas getan, was . . .
Nun, wer so etwas tut, der / den / dem . . .

* Schriftliche Themen

Tips zum Schreiben ***Using and Avoiding Relative Clauses***
Relative clauses work well in analytical writing; they enrich your prose by providing additional information about the persons and things you wish to discuss. Since relative clauses tend to interrupt the flow of a sentence, you should use them sparingly, however, particularly in fast-paced narratives or in compositions where the emphasis is on action(s) rather than explanation. Often a descriptive prepositional phrase can convey the same information (see **Tips zum Schreiben,** Chapter 10). For example, **die Familie, die in der nächsten Straße wohnt,** is expressed more succinctly by **die Familie in der nächsten Straße.** A relative clause with **haben** (for example, **die Studentin, die das Buch hatte**) can invariably be replaced by a prepositional phrase **(die Studentin mit dem Buch).** Relative clauses with the verb **sein (die Preise, die sehr hoch waren)** are even less desirable, since an adjective construction **(die sehr hohen Preise)** usually supplies the same information. (See also **Tips zum Schreiben** in Chapter 21).

A **Charakterbeschreibung.** Beschreiben Sie eine Person, die Sie kennen, oder einen unvergeßlichen Charakter aus einem Buch oder einem Film.

Beispiel: Oskar ist ein Mensch, der die Welt anders sieht als andere Menschen. Er redet auch dauernd von Dingen, die andere Menschen nicht interessieren. Wenn er z.B. . . .

B **Es war(en) einmal . . .** Schreiben Sie eine kleine Geschichte, die so anfängt. Verwenden Sie mindestens fünf verschiedene Relativpronomen.

C **Der Mensch.** Schreiben Sie einen Aufsatz mit diesem Titel. Vielleicht gibt Ihnen der folgende Textauszug *(excerpt)* ein paar Ideen.

Beispiel: Man könnte den Menschen geradezu *(frankly)* als ein Wesen *(being)* definieren, das nie zuhört . . . Jeder Mensch hat eine Leber, eine Milz *(spleen)*, eine Lunge und eine Fahne *(flag)* . . . Es soll Menschen ohne Leber, ohne Milz und mit halber Lunge geben; Menschen ohne Fahne gibt es nicht . . . Menschen miteinander gibt es nicht. Es gibt nur Menschen, die herrschen *(rule)*, und solche, die beherrscht werden . . . Im übrigen *(in other respects)* ist der Mensch ein Lebewesen, das klopft, schlechte Musik macht und seinen Hund bellen läßt . . . Neben den Menschen gibt es noch Sachsen *(Saxons)* und Amerikaner, aber die haben wir noch nicht gehabt und bekommen Zoologie erst in der nächsten Klasse. (Kurt Tucholsky, 1890–1935)

Wortschatz 26

der Apparat | das Gebäude
die Einrichtung | der Gegenstand
das Fahrzeug | das Gerät

\+ *other general categories of things*

The following words designate general categories of nouns. They are useful when classifying or defining items.

der Apparat, -e / **das Gerät, -e**	apparatus, tool, device, piece of equipment	**das Mittel, -**	means, medium
		das Möbel, -	*(piece of)* furniture
die Einrichtung, -en	layout, setup, contrivance; furnishings	**das Spiel, -e**	game
		das Brettspiel, -e	board game
		das Kartenspiel, -e	card game
das Fahrzeug, -e	vehicle	**das Spielzeug, -e**	toy
das Gebäude, -	building	**der Stoff, -e**	material, cloth, fabric
der Gegenstand, ¨e	object, thing, item	**das Transportmittel, -**	means of transportation
das Instrument, -e	instrument	**das Werkzeug, -e**	tool, implement
die Krankheit, -en	illness		
die Maschine, -n	machine		
das Medikament, -e	medicine, drug		

ÜBUNGEN

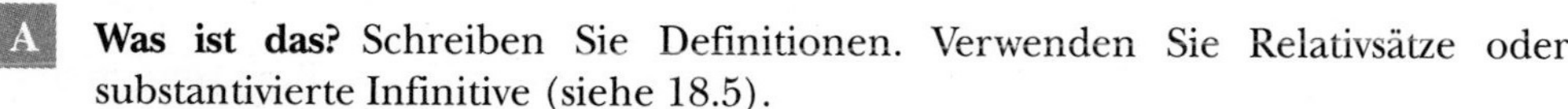

A **Was ist das?** Schreiben Sie Definitionen. Verwenden Sie Relativsätze oder substantivierte Infinitive (siehe 18.5).

Beispiele: das Klavier
Ein Klavier ist ein (Musik)instrument, das 88 Tasten (keys) *hat.*

die Schere *(scissors)*
Eine Schere ist ein Werkzeug zum Schneiden.

1. die Kirche
2. das Penizillin
3. (das) Poker
4. die Uhr
5. der Hammer
6. (die) Baumwolle *(cotton)*
7. die Schlaftablette
8. der Krebs *(cancer)*

Schreiben Sie fünf weitere Definitionen für Gegenstände aus fünf verschiedenen Kategorien.

B **Zurück in die Zukunft.** Was für technische Erfindungen *(inventions)* des 20. Jahrhunderts würde jemand aus einem früheren Jahrhundert gar nicht verstehen? Wie könnte man solche Erfindungen erklären?

VORSCHLÄGE

das Auto, -s
der Computer, -
der Fernseher, -
das Flugzeug, -e
das Penizillin
die Rolltreppe, -n
der Fernkopierer, - *(fax machine)*
der Satellit, -en *(weak noun, see 12.3)*
das Telefon, -e
der Videorecorder, -

Zusammenfassung 26

Rules to Remember

1. The relative pronouns **der, die, das,** and **die** (plural) agree with the word(s) they refer to in gender and number, but the case of the relative pronoun depends upon how it functions within its own clause.
2. A relative clause is a subordinate clause; the conjugated verb occupies final position.
3. Relative pronouns are often omitted in English, but they must not be omitted in German *(the woman [that] I helped;* **die Frau, der ich half).**
4. The neuter relative pronoun **was** is used instead of the relative pronoun **das** to refer to concepts (as opposed to specific objects) and entire clauses **(das Beste, was . . .; Sie läuft Ski, was mir gefällt.).**
5. A **wo-**compound may be used instead of a preposition + relative pronoun to refer to inanimate things **(der Bleistift, womit** [*or* **mit dem] ich schreibe).**

Learning Tip

Relative pronouns occur more in writing than in speaking. When speaking, they can often be avoided by using adjectives and/or by making two short sentences instead of one longer, complex sentence. Instead of saying **Ich suche ein Kleid, das schick aussieht und nicht zuviel kostet,** you might say **Ich suche ein schickes Kleid. Es darf aber nicht zuviel kosten.** However, it is important to be able to use relative pronouns with confidence when writing.

Activities

1 **Recognizing relative pronouns.** Pick two texts of two or more pages, one literary and one non-literary. Read through each quickly and underline all the relative pronouns. Determine the antecedent for each relative pronoun. Determine the case of each relative pronoun and the reason for this case.

2 **What kind of person are you?** Describe yourself in a series of eight to ten sentences containing relative pronouns.

Beispiele: *Ich bin ein Mensch, der . . .*
Ich mag Leute, die . . .

3 **Daffynitions.** Write humorous or cynical definitions about five or more objects or aspects of modern society. Share your "daffynitions" with the class.

Beispiele: *Ein Fernseher ist ein Apparat, der immer mehr kostet als er wert ist.*
Ein Hörsaal ist ein Zimmer, in dem man nachmittags leicht einschlafen kann.
Politiker sind Menschen, die . . .

4 **What you need or don't need.** Tell about five things that you feel you absolutely **(unbedingt)** need. What are five things you feel you do not need? Tell why you need or do not need these things by using relative pronouns.

Beispiele: *Ich brauche Geld, womit ich ein neues Auto kaufen kann.*
Ich brauche keine Kurse, in denen einer (der Lehrer) spricht und alle anderen schweigen oder schlafen.

5 **Cultural literacy.** Divide the class into two teams. Using relative pronouns, each team prepares ten written questions that test your American or German cultural IQ. Your team will receive one point for each question it poses correctly using a relative pronoun in the nominative case, two points for questions posed using relative pronouns in other cases. Each team receives two points for each question answered correctly, but loses two points for each incorrect answer or for no answer at all.

Beispiele: *Wie heißt der Autor / die Autorin, der / die [X] schrieb?*
Wie heißt der Fluß, der durch [X] fließt?
Wie heißt die Stadt, in der [X] stattfindet?

6 **Working with a text.** Using relative pronouns, discuss characters in a story you are reading.

27 Indirect Discourse Subjunctive

27.1 Indirect Discourse

1. Direct discourse **(direkte Rede)** involves repeating a person's words exactly as stated, in a direct quotation. Note the use of a colon and quotation marks to set off the speaker's words.

Die Lehrerin sagte: „Ich habe wenig Zeit zum Lesen."	*The teacher said, "I have little time for reading."*

2. Indirect discourse **(indirekte Rede)** involves restating another person's words as an indirect quotation: *Er / Sie sagte, (daß)* . . . Indirect discourse, also called indirect speech, requires certain changes in personal pronouns and tenses and can be introduced either with or without the word **daß.**

Direct Quotation	*Someone Else Reports*
Die Lehrerin sagte: „Ich habe wenig Zeit zum Lesen."	Die Lehrerin sagte, daß **sie** (*not:* **ich**) wenig Zeit zum Lesen hat. OR: Die Lehrerin sagte, **sie** hat wenig Zeit zum Lesen.

3. The *indicative* tends to be used in indirect discourse if persons relaying the information have no reason to distance themselves from this information or to question its validity.

Direct Quotation	*Someone Else Reports*
Herr Kunz sagte: „Ich habe jetzt gute Beziehungen in Ulm."	Herr Kunz sagte, daß er jetzt gute Beziehungen in Ulm **hat.** *(indicative)*

4. The *subjunctive* of indirect discourse is used if persons relaying the information wish to indicate that they are only reporting what someone else said but do not take any responsibility for the validity of the other person's statement.

   Someone Else Reports

   Herr Kunz behauptete, daß er jetzt gute Beziehungen in Ulm **hätte.** *(Subjunctive II)*

   Herr Kunz behauptete, daß er jetzt gute Beziehungen in Ulm **habe.** *(Subjunctive I)*

27.2 Forms of Present-Time Indirect Discourse Subjunctive

A. *Subjunctive II Forms*

One set of indirect discourse subjunctive forms consists of the present-time conditional subjunctive, known as Subjunctive II (see 20.1). Subjunctive II is formed by adding the endings **-e, -est, -e; -en, -et, -en** to the second principal part of a verb. Strong verbs require an umlaut if the past-tense stem vowel is an **a, o,** or **u.**

Subjunctive II Forms

	sein	haben	werden	müssen	lernen	nehmen
ich	wär**e**	hätt**e**	würd**e**	müßt**e**	lernt**e**	nähm**e**
du	wär**est**	hätt**est**	würd**est**	müßt**est**	lernt**est**	nähm**est**
er / sie / es	wär**e**	hätt**e**	würd**e**	müßt**e**	lernt**e**	nähm**e**
wir	wär**en**	hätt**en**	würd**en**	müßt**en**	lernt**en**	nähm**en**
ihr	wär**et**	hätt**et**	würd**et**	müßt**et**	lernt**et**	nähm**et**
sie / Sie	wär**en**	hätt**en**	würd**en**	müßt**en**	lernt**en**	nähm**en**

B. *Subjunctive I Forms*

1. In some situations, another form of the subjunctive, Subjunctive I, is used to report indirect discourse. It is formed by adding the same endings used with Subjunctive II to the infinitive stem of verbs, hence the name Subjunctive I.

Subjunctive I Forms

	haben	werden	müssen	lernen	nehmen
ich	hab **e**	werd **e**	müss **e**	lern **e**	nehm **e**
du	hab **est**	werd **est**	müss **est**	lern **est**	nehm **est**
er / sie / es	hab **e**	werd **e**	müss **e**	lern **e**	nehm **e**
wir	hab **en**	werd **en**	müss **en**	lern **en**	nehm **en**
ihr	hab **et**	werd **et**	müss **et**	lern **et**	nehm **et**
sie / Sie	hab **en**	werd **en**	müss **en**	lern **en**	nehm **en**

2. The Subjunctive I of **sein** is mildly irregular.

sein			
ich	sei	wir	sei**en**
du	sei**(e)st**	ihr	sei**et**
er / sie / es	sei	sie / Sie	sei**en**

3. Subjunctive I forms that are identical to the indicative are never used. Thus, aside from modal verbs and the verbs **wissen** and **sein,** only third-person-singular forms of Subjunctive I occur with any regularity.[1]

	Indicative	*Subjunctive I*	
ich	lerne	lerne	*(identical with the indicative)*
du	**lernst**	**lernest**	*(uncommon)*
er / sie / es	**lernt**	**lerne**	*(Subjunctive I used)*
wir	lernen	lernen	*(identical with the indicative)*
ihr	**lernt**	**lernet**	*(uncommon)*
sie / Sie	lernen	lernen	*(identical with the indicative)*

C. *The Choice Between Subjunctive I and II for Indirect Discourse*

1. Subjunctive II forms are identical in meaning with Subjunctive I forms when used in indirect discourse. Which subjunctive to use depends upon numerous factors, and actual usage deviates considerably from the prescriptions of grammarians.
2. Subjunctive II tends to be used in spoken indirect discourse, although it also occurs in writing.
3. Subjunctive I usually predominates in formal, written indirect discourse, especially in media reporting, where style and the impression of objectivity are important considerations and where the third person singular is mainly used.
4. If *either* Subjunctive I *or* Subjunctive II is identical with the indicative, the non-identical form is generally chosen.

Sie behauptete, sie **lerne** zu wenig. *(Subjunctive I, because Subjunctive II,* ***lernte,*** *would be identical with the past indicative)*	*She claimed she was learning too little.*

---

1. The second-person singular and plural Subjunctive I forms, while often distinct from the indicative, sound stilted and are simply not used. Germans use Subjunctive II instead.

Sie dachte, *du* **hättest** (*not:* **habest**) keine Zeit zum Schreiben.	*She thought you didn't have any time for writing.*

Sie meinte, daß die Kinder zu spät **kämen.** *(Subjunctive II, because Subjunctive I,* ***kommen,*** *would be identical with the present indicative)*	*She offered the opinion that the children were coming too late.*

5. If *both* subjunctives are identical with the indicative, then Subjunctive II tends to be used.

Sie meinte, daß die Kinder auch zu langsam **lernten.**	*She said that the children were also learning too slowly.*

6. In indirect discourse, a hypothetical statement (see 20.3) is always in Subjunctive II.

Direct Quotation
„Wir würden kommen, wenn wir Zeit hätten."

Indirect Quotation
Sie sagten, daß sie kommen **würden,** wenn sie Zeit **hätten.**
They said they would come if they had time.

7. For the reasons cited above, indirect discourse is inevitably a mix of both subjunctives.

Der Generalsekretär des Goethe-Instituts teilte mit, die Nachfrage nach Deutschkursen **sei** jetzt weltweit so stark, daß sie von den insgesamt 150 Auslandsinstituten nicht mehr befriedigt werden **könne.** Insbesondere in Polen, Ungarn und der [ehemaligen] Sowjetunion **wollten** die Menschen jetzt Deutsch lernen; in Polen allein **fehlten** etwa 1.000 Deutschlehrer. *(Deutschland Nachrichten)*

The General Secretary of the Goethe Institute reported that the demand for German courses is now so strong worldwide that it can no longer be satisfied by the present total of 150 institutes abroad. In particular in Poland, Hungary, and the [former] Soviet Union, people now want to learn German; in Poland alone there is a shortage of approximately 1,000 German teachers.

27.3 Present-Time, Past-Time, and Future-Time Indirect Discourse

A. Present-Time Indirect Discourse

If the original quotation is in the present tense, then the indirect quotation requires the present-time subjunctive—either Subjunctive I or II.

Direct Quotation
„Ich habe heute keine Zeit."

Indirect Quotation
Sie sagt, daß sie heute keine Zeit **habe / hätte.**
She says she has no time today.

Note that tense of the introductory verb **sagt** has no influence on the choice of forms in the indirect quotation.

Sie sagte,
Sie hat gesagt,
Sie hatte gesagt,
Sie wird sagen,
} sie **habe** heute keine Zeit.
sie **hätte** heute keine Zeit.

B. Past-Time Indirect Discourse

If the original quotation is in past *time* (simple past, present perfect, or past perfect tense), then the indirect quotation requires the past-time subjunctive. The past-time subjunctive is formed by using either Subjunctive I or II of the auxiliary **haben** or **sein** (see 3.2 for **haben** versus **sein**) + the past participle of the main verb.

Direct Quotation
„Ich schrieb ihm nicht."
„Ich habe / hatte ihm nicht geschrieben."

Indirect Quotation
Sie sagte, sie **habe / hätte** ihm nicht **geschrieben.**
She said (that) she has / had not written him.

Direct Quotation
„Ich ging am vorigen Abend ins Theater."
„Ich bin / war am vorigen Abend ins Theater gegangen."

Indirect Quotation
Sie erklärte, sie **sei / wäre** am vorigen Abend ins Theater **gegangen.**
She explained (that) she went / had gone to the theater the previous evening.

C. Future-Time Indirect Discourse

If the direct quotation refers to future *time* (future tense or present tense with future meaning), then the indirect statement requires future-time subjunctive. Future-time subjunctive is formed by using either Subjunctive I or II of **werden** + the main verb infinitive.

Direct Quotation
„Ich werde später mehr Zeit haben."

Indirect Quotation
Sie meinte, sie **werde / würde** später mehr Zeit **haben.**
She said (that) she will / would have more time later.

27.4 Uses of Indirect Discourse Subjunctive

A. Extended Indirect Discourse

In both English and German, indirect quotations are normally introduced by verbs of speaking, thinking, or opining such as **sagen** or **meinen** (see **Wortschatz 27**). In English, such introductory verbs must be repeated each time: *He said . . ., She remarked . . ., They replied . . .* German is more economical; continued use of the subjunctive signals continuing use of indirect discourse, and no introductory verbs are needed after the initial one.

Das Telefon klingelte, und schon redete ein erregter Leser auf mich ein. Er **sei** erschüttert, versicherte er mir. Man **dürfe** doch nicht von „Ladendiebstahl" *(store theft)* sprechen. Ob[2] ich **meinte,** daß man einen Laden stehlen **könne.** Richtig **müsse** es „Warendiebstahl" heißen, denn schließlich **würden** Waren und nicht der Laden gestohlen. (Eike Christian Hirsch, *Den Leuten aufs Maul*)

The telephone rang and immediately an excited reader began to lecture me. He was terribly upset, he assured me. [He said] one could not really talk about "shoplifting." [He wondered] whether I thought that a shop could be lifted. [He said] the correct thing to say was "ware lifting," because when you got right down to it wares were stolen, not the shop.

B. Indirect Questions

Questions are often reported in indirect discourse subjunctive. As with statements, Subjunctive II is more common in colloquial German, Subjunctive I in more formal usage. In most instances, the indicative is also possible. The conjunction **ob** *(whether)* introduces yes-no questions.

Direct Quotation
„Geht es meinem Patienten jetzt besser?"

Indirect Question
Die Ärztin fragte, ob es ihrem Patienten jetzt besser **gehe** / **ginge** (*or indicative:* **ging**).
The doctor inquired whether her patient was now better.

Direct Quotation
„Wer hat ein Radio mitgebracht?"

Indirect Question
Er wollte wissen, wer ein Radio mitgebracht **habe** / **hätte** (*or indicative:* **hatte**).
He wanted to know who had brought along a radio.

---

2. The word **ob** implies "he wanted to know whether" and is quite common in this usage.

C. Indirect Commands

The imperative is reported in indirect discourse subjunctive with either Subjunctive I or II of **sollen** (sometimes **müssen**). The indicative is also possible.

Direct Quotation
„Besuche uns bald!"

Indirect Statement
Sie sagten, daß er sie bald besuchen **solle** / **sollte**.
They said that he should visit them soon.

D. After **als ob / als wenn**

Indirect discourse Subjunctive I is sometimes used instead of Subjunctive II in **als ob** clauses (see 20.3E), although Subjunctive II is generally preferred.

Sie tat, als ob sie beleidigt **sei** / **wäre.**	*She acted as if she were insulted.*

E. Additional Uses of Subjunctive I

Since there are no imperative forms for the third person, German uses Subjunctive I in these instances. This construction is sometimes referred to as the exhortatory subjunctive.

Es **lebe** der König! Der König **lebe!**	*Long live the king!*
Man **nehme** zwei Eier. *(recipe)*	*Take two eggs.*
Edel **sei** der Mensch, hilfreich und gut! (Goethe)	*Noble be man(kind), helpful and good!*

* Übungen

A **Indirekte Rede analysieren.** Unterstreichen Sie die Konjunktivformen in dem folgenden Text. Erklären Sie, warum entweder Konjunktiv I oder Konjunktiv II verwendet wird.

Nach dem Erreichen der staatlichen Einheit im Oktober 1990 wachse Deutschland nun auch wirtschaftlich *(economically)* und gesellschaftlich *(socially)* zusammen, erklärte Bundeskanzler Helmut Kohl in seiner Neujahrsansprache. An die Westdeutschen richtete *(directed)* der Kanzler die Mahnung *(admonition)*, Wiedervereinigung heiße auch, daß die Sorgen der Menschen in den neuen Bundesländern das gemeinsame *(joint)* Anliegen *(concern)* aller Deutschen sein müßten: es dürfe kein „Hüben" *(over here)* und „Drüben" *(over there)* mehr geben. Innerhalb weniger Jahre werde im Osten Deutschlands einer der besten

Industriestandorte *(industrial sites)* Europas entstanden *(arisen)* sein, kündigte *(declared)* Kohl an. Bei allen Übergangsschwierigkeiten dürfe man nicht vergessen, daß es die Länder Osteuropas „viel, viel schwerer" hätten als die Deutschen. *(Deutschland Nachrichten)*

B **Von direkter Aussage zur indirekten Rede.** Geben Sie die Aussagen im Konjunktiv der indirekten Rede wieder.

Beispiel: Man lebt heutzutage ungesund.
Sie meinte, . . .
Sie meinte, man lebe heutzutage ungesund.

1. Im vergangenen Jahr hatten die Gastbetriebe *(eating establishments)* höhere Besucherzahlen.
   Das Fremdenverkehrsamt *(office of tourism)* gab bekannt, daß . . .
2. Vermutlich *(presumably)* sind auch in diesem Sommer mehr Touristen zu erwarten.
   Man meint jetzt, daß . . .
3. Es wird nicht mehr lange dauern, bis das Wohnproblem in der ehemaligen DDR gelöst ist.
   Politiker gaben der Hoffnung Ausdruck, es . . .
4. Wenn man jetzt nichts dagegen tut, wird das Straßenverkehrssystem in der deutschen Bundesrepublik in wenigen Jahren zusammenbrechen.
   Experten behaupten, . . .
5. Bleib fit, bleib gesund!
   Überall heißt es jetzt, man . . .
6. Früher brachten die Zeitungen meist schlechte Nachrichten.
   Viele sind der Meinung, . . .
7. Die besten Jahre sind jetzt.
   Manche denken, . . .
8. Die besten Jahre waren schon.
   Andere fragen, ob . . .
9. Wählervertrauen *(voter trust)* ist ein rohes Ei, man kann es nur einmal in die Pfanne hauen *(toss into the skillet)*.
   Der Redner bemerkte, . . .
10. Weil in der alten DDR die nötige Finanzierung fehlte, konnte der Staat viele Wohnhäuser nicht renovieren.
    Man erklärte die Sache so: . . .
11. „Man soll den Tag nicht vor dem Abend loben *(praise)*." (Sprichwort)
    Nach dem Sprichwort heißt es, man . . .
12. „Arbeite nur, die Freude kommt von selbst."
    Der Dichter Goethe empfahl, man . . .

C **Aus der Presse.** Berichten Sie, was die Presse berichtet. Verwenden Sie die indirekte Rede.

Auf den deutschen Straßen droht *(threatens)* der Verkehrskollaps. Die Autodichte *(automobile density)* in Westdeutschland ist mit 450 Fahrzeugen je 1.000

Einwohner inzwischen die höchste in Europa. Seit dem letzten Krieg hat man in Deutschland 150.000 Kilometer Straßen gebaut, aber für weitere Straßen ist in der eng besiedelten *(thickly settled)* Bundesrepublik kaum noch Platz, sofern man nicht *(unless one)* das ganze Land dem Straßenverkehr weihen *(dedicate)* will. Das führt dazu, daß auch auf den Autobahnen der Verkehr immer häufiger zum Stillstand kommt. Staus *(traffic jams)* von 100 Kilometer Länge sind, besonders zur Ferienzeit, keine Seltenheit mehr. *(Deutschland Nachrichten)*

Aus Deutschland wird berichtet, . . .

D **Aus Büchern.** Suchen Sie sieben deutsche Sätze aus Büchern oder Zeitungen. Setzen Sie diese Sätze in die indirekte Rede um. Geben Sie die Autoren oder Sprecher dieser Sätze an.

Beispiel: Bluthochdruck *(high blood pressure)* ist in den letzten Jahrzehnten zu einer richtigen Volkskrankheit geworden.

Mutter Theresa Berghammer schreibt, daß Bluthochdruck in den letzten Jahrzehnten zu einer richtigen Volkskrankheit geworden sei. (Gesundheit durch wiederentdeckte Hausmittel)

Anwendung

A **Worte der Woche.** Geben Sie einige wichtige Zitate der letzten Woche zu politischen Ereignissen in der indirekten Rede wieder.

REDEMITTEL

Es steht / stand in der Zeitung, (daß) . . .
Nach Angaben *(figures)* [des Pressesprechers] . . .
Die [Regierung] gab bekannt, (daß) . . .
Es heißt / hieß *(is / was said)* auch, (daß) . . .

B **Interview.** Interviewen Sie außerhalb des Kurses jemanden, der Deutsch spricht, und zwar über seine / ihre Meinungen zu einem aktuellen politischen Ereignis *(event)* oder Thema. Stellen Sie etwa sieben Fragen. Berichten Sie die Ergebnisse *(results)* Ihres Interviews im Kurs. Erklären Sie, welche Fragen Sie stellten, und geben Sie die Meinungen dieser Person in der indirekten Rede wieder.

REDEMITTEL

Fragen

Was halten Sie von . . . ?
Wie sehen Sie die Sache . . . ?
Darf ich Sie fragen, wie Sie zu den neuesten Ereignissen stehen?
Und wie beurteilen *(judge)* Sie . . . ?

Finden Sie es richtig / gut, daß . . . ?
Was für einen Eindruck hat . . . auf Sie gemacht?

Berichten

Er / Sie ist der Ansicht / Meinung, (daß) . . .
Er / Sie sagte auch, (daß) . . .
Bemerkt hat er / sie auch, (daß) . . .
Allerdings gab er / sie zu, (daß) . . .
Er / Sie gab der Hoffnung Ausdruck, (daß) . . .

* Schriftliche Themen

Tips zum Schreiben ***Paraphrasing***
Quoting a person directly can lend impact to a text. In compositions, however, you should use direct quotations sparingly. Instead, put the speaker's comments into your own words—a process known as paraphrasing. To make your reader aware that you are only paraphrasing what others say or said, in German you can use indirect discourse subjunctive. Remember that in writing, Subjunctive I forms are generally preferred, unless they are identical with the indicative. Also keep in mind that you do not have to preface every indirect statement with an introductory clause; the subjunctive alone can maintain the indirect discourse for two or three sentences at a time (see example, 27.3A). This approach will also allow you to avoid constant repetition of the word **daß.** When you do wish to introduce indirect statements, use a variety of verbs and expressions (see **Wortschatz 27**)—not just the verbs **sagen, meinen,** and **antworten.**

A **So steht es geschrieben.** Fassen Sie einen Artikel aus einer deutsch- oder englischsprachigen Zeitung kurz zusammen.

Beispiel: In diesem Artikel steht, daß im Freistaat Bayern 80,2 Prozent der Bevölkerung regelmäßige Biertrinker seien. Sie lägen damit an der Spitze aller Bundesländer. Die wenigsten Anhänger finde das Bier im Bundesland Bremen, wo nur 51,9 Prozent regelmäßig Bier trinken. Nach Ansicht des Autors, seien solche Statistiken irreführend *(misleading),* weil . . . Auch scheint er der Meinung zu sein, daß . . . usw.

B **Lebensansichten** *(views on life).* Gibt es jemanden, dessen Lebensphilosophie und Meinungen Sie für richtig oder besonders interessant halten? Erzählen Sie davon.

Beispiel: Der Philosoph Friedrich Nietzsche (1844–1900) meinte, es gebe starke und schwache Menschen auf der Welt. Aufgabe der Starken sei es, über die Schwachen zu herrschen. Nur so könne der Mensch . . . usw.

Wortschatz 27

andeuten
ankündigen
antworten auf
sich äußern
behaupten

+ *other verbs of speaking*

Most of the following verbs of speaking can introduce indirect discourse subjunctive. Many of them take a dative (indirect) object with persons and an accusative (direct) object or a prepositional phrase with things.

andeuten	to indicate
ankündigen	to declare, announce
antworten (auf)[3]	to answer
sich äußern (über[3] **/ zu)**	to express (one's opinion) (about)
behaupten	to assert, maintain
bekanntgeben	to announce
bemerken	to remark, say
sich beschweren (über)	to complain (about)
beteuern	to assure, swear
betonen	to emphasize
bitten um	to ask for
etwas einwenden (gegen)	to raise an objection (to)
entgegnen (auf)	to reply (to)
erklären	to explain
sich erkundigen (nach)	to inquire (about)
erläutern	to elucidate, elaborate
erwähnen	to mention
erwidern (auf)	to reply (to)
erzählen (von)	to tell (about)
fragen (nach)	to inquire, ask (about)
informieren	to inform
leugnen	to deny
meinen	to say, offer the opinion
mitteilen	to inform
plaudern	to chat
raten	to advise
reden (über / von)	to talk (about)
sagen (von)	to say, tell (about)
schwatzen / schwätzen	to chatter, prattle
sprechen (über / von)	to speak (about)
sich unterhalten (über)	to converse
verdeutlichen	to clarify
verkünden	to announce, proclaim
versichern	to assure
versprechen	to promise
wissen wollen	to want to know
zugeben	to admit, confess
zusammenfassen	to summarize

3. With verbs of speaking, the prepositions **auf** and **über** normally govern the accusative case.

Die Nachbarn haben **sich** über den Lärm von der Straße **beschwert.**	*The neighbors complained about the noise from the street.*
Sie **behauptete,** sie habe die Vase nicht zerbrochen.	*She maintained she had not broken the vase.*
Wer kann diesen Text kurz **zusammenfassen**?	*Who can briefly summarize this text?*

ÜBUNGEN

A **„Sagen" kann man das besser.** Drücken Sie den Inhalt der Sätze durch andere Verben anders (und präziser) aus.

Beispiel: Als er den Vorschlag *(suggestion)* machte, sagte niemand etwas.
Auf seinen Vorschlag erwiderte man nichts.

1. Sie sagte genau, wie der Text zu verstehen war.
2. Gegen diesen Plan kann ich nichts sagen.
3. Sie sagte, daß sie Unterstützung *(support)* brauche.
4. Der Chef sagte den Angestellten, daß man 100 Arbeitskräfte würde entlassen müssen.
5. Von ihren Problemen sagte sie nichts.
6. Sie sagte ihm, daß er nach Europa reisen sollte.
7. Der Bürgermeister sagte seine Meinung über die städtischen Baupläne.
8. Sie saßen am Teetisch und sagten allerlei *(all sorts of things)*.
9. Nachdem sie soviel über die Talente des Kindes gesagt hatte, glaubte man endlich daran.
10. Der Polizist sagte, daß er mehr über den Unfall erfahren *(find out)* wollte.

B **Synonyme.** Suchen Sie für jedes Verb andere Verben, die zu derselben Kategorie des Sprechens gehören. Natürlich werden diese Verben in ihren Bedeutungen nicht immer identisch sein. Bilden Sie Sätze mit einigen dieser Verben.

Beispiel: fragen
fragen: *Er fragte nach meiner Gesundheit.*
sich erkundigen: *Sie erkundigte sich nach seiner Adresse.*
wissen wollen: *Wir wollen wissen, wann das Konzert beginnt.*

1. reden
2. berichten
3. erklären
4. plaudern
5. antworten
6. versichern
7. verkünden

Zusammenfassung 27

Rules to Remember

1. Present-time indirect discourse is formed with either Subjunctive I or Subjunctive II of the verb **(er sei / wäre; habe / hätte; gehe / ginge; komme / käme,** etc.).
2. Past-time indirect discourse is formed with either Subjunctive I or Subjunctive II of the auxiliary verb **haben** or **sein** + the past participle of the main verb **(er habe / hätte getan; sie sei / wäre gegangen).**
3. Future-time indirect discourse is formed with either Subjunctive I or Subjunctive II of the future auxiliary **werden** + the infinitive of the main verb **(er werde / würde gehen).**
4. Subjunctive I occurs mainly in formal written indirect discourse, Subjunctive II mainly in spoken indirect discourse.

Activities

1 **Famous quotes.** Find famous quotations from five famous persons you admire. Write out the direct quotations, then tell other students about your quotations by using indirect discourse subjunctive.

Beispiel: *John F. Kennedy sagte, daß er ein Berliner wäre / sei.*[4]

2 **Unsolicited advice.** List some of the best and worst examples of advice parents, teachers, or other persons ever gave you. Use indirect discourse. Share your list with the class.

Beispiel: *[X] sagte einmal, ich solle / sollte . . .*

3 **Indirect discourse in texts.** Search through a German newspaper or an issue of *Deutschland Nachrichten* for examples of indirect discourse. Determine whether Subjunctive I or Subjunctive II was used in each example and why.

4 **Political statements.** Statements by politicians should be greeted with a degree of skepticism and reported in indirect discourse. What are some of the best whoppers you recall?

Beispiel: *Der New Yorker Senator [X] sagte, er habe / hätte . . .*

---

4. Kennedy should have said **daß** er Berliner wäre / sei (without the article **ein** [see 5.2C]), but then, of course, he never had the opportunity to use this **Handbuch.**

5 **Who said what?** Ten minutes before the end of class, see if you can recall some of the things your instructor and other students said during this class. Report these statements in indirect discourse subjunctive.

Beispiel: *Der Professor sagte, daß die indirekte Rede leicht wäre / sei.*
Die Studenten sagten, daß sie die indirekte Rede nicht gut verstünden.

6 **Working with a text.** Without looking at the text, can you recall statements made or questions asked by some of the characters in a story? Put these statements in indirect discourse and share them with the class.

28 Passive Voice

28.1 Passive Voice

A. *Formation*

1. German expresses the passive as a process, as something "becoming" done **(das Vorgangspassiv).** Thus the passive voice is formed with conjugated forms of the auxiliary **werden** in its various active voice tenses + a past participle of the main verb at the end of the sentence or clause. The past participle remains constant; only the forms of **werden** change.

	Present Tense	
ich **werde . . .**	geschickt	*I am sent / being sent*
du **wirst . . .**	geschickt	*you are sent / being sent*
er / sie / es **wird . . .**	geschickt	*he / she / it is sent / being sent*
wir **werden . . .**	geschickt	*we are sent / being sent*
ihr **werdet . . .**	geschickt	*you are sent / being sent*
sie / Sie **werden . . .**	geschickt	*they / you are sent / being sent*
	Past Tense	
ich **wurde . . .**	geschickt	*I was sent / was being sent*
du **wurdest . . .**	geschickt	*you were sent / were being sent*
etc.		
	Present Perfect Tense	
ich **bin . . .**	geschickt **worden**[1]	*I was sent / have been sent*
du **bist . . .**	geschickt **worden**	*you were sent / have been sent*
etc.		

1. Shortened from the past participle **geworden.**

Past Perfect Tense

ich **war** . . .	geschickt **worden**	*I had been sent*
du **warst** . . .	geschickt **worden**	*you had been sent*
etc.		

Future Tense

ich **werde** . . .	geschickt **werden**	*I will be sent*
du **wirst** . . .	geschickt **werden**	*you will be sent*
etc.		

2. The passive voice past participle stands at the end of main clauses, but is followed by the conjugated auxiliary in subordinate clauses.

Er **wurde** im Unfall nur leicht **verletzt.**	*He was only slightly injured in the accident.*
Ich weiß, daß er im Unfall nur leicht **verletzt wurde.**	*I know that he was only slightly injured in the accident.*

B. Use (Active Voice Versus Passive Voice)

1. In the active voice, the subject of a sentence performs the action, hence the term *active* voice. In the following sentence, the focus is on who does the action **(die Kinder).**

Die Kinder **singen** viele Lieder.	*The children are singing many songs.*

2. In the passive voice, the subject of the verb does *not* perform the action indicated by the verb, but rather receives the action, hence the term *passive* voice. The persons performing the action play a secondary role.

Viele Lieder **werden** von den Kindern **gesungen.**	*Many songs are being sung by the children.*

3. The passive voice is used chiefly to emphasize the occurrence of an *action* rather than who or what *did* the action. Indeed, who or what caused the action might not even be mentioned.

Auf dem Fest **wurden** viele Lieder **gesungen.**	*At the festival many songs were sung.*

C. Agents with the Passive

1. When the performer or *agent* of an action *is* expressed in a passive sentence, then this agent is named in a prepositional phrase.

COMPARE:

Active	*Passive*
Mein *Mann* **kocht** die Suppe.	Die Suppe **wird** *von meinem Mann* **gekocht.**
My husband cooks the soup.	*The soup is being cooked by my husband.*

In the first example, **Mann** is the subject; in the second sentence, **Suppe** is the subject and **Mann** is the agent. In other words, the direct object of the active sentence becomes the subject of the passive sentence, and the subject of the active sentence becomes the prepositional agent of the passive sentence.

2. **Von** *(by)* + dative is used to indicate the *agent* or *performer* of an action.

Das Papier wurde **von dem Chinesen Ts'ai Lun** erfunden.	*Paper was invented by the Chinese Ts'ai Lun.*
Sein Fahrrad ist **von einem Auto** überfahren worden.	*His bicycle was run over by a car.*

3. **Durch** *(by, through)* + accusative is used to indicate the *process* or *means* through which an action occurs.

Die Stadt Chicago wurde einmal **durch einen Brand** zerstört.	*The city of Chicago was once destroyed by a fire.*
Schwierigkeiten werden manchmal **durch Fleiß** überwunden.	*Difficulties are sometimes overcome through diligence.*

4. **Mit** *(with)* + dative is used to indicate the *instrument* or *tool* with which an action is performed.

Der Baum muß **mit einer Axt** gefällt werden.	*The tree has to be felled with an axe.*

D. *Passive with Introductory* es

1. In German, passive statements describing human activity often begin with an introductory **es,** a "dummy subject," followed by the conjugated auxiliary **werden** verb and the real sentence subject with which this auxiliary agrees.

Es wurden viele Brücken gebaut.	*Many bridges were (being) built.*

2. The introductory **es** is particularly common when there is no stated subject or object, that is, when only the occurrence of an activity is expressed. The conjugated auxiliary is then in the third person singular.

Es wird heute gearbeitet.	*There is work going on today.* (literally, *"it" is being worked today*)

Es wurde gestern viel getanzt. — *There was lots of dancing yesterday.* (literally, *"it" was danced a lot yesterday*)

3. The **es** is omitted if the sentence begins with another element.

Letztes Jahr wurden viele Brücken gebaut.
Gestern wurde viel getanzt.

E. Passive Voice with Modals

1. Modals themselves are never in the passive voice, but they can be combined with the passive. In such instances, the passive auxiliary **werden** is the infinitive that follows or complements the modal.

COMPARE:

Ich muß nach Hause **fahren.** *(active modal construction)* — *I must drive home.*
Ich muß nach Hause **gefahren werden.** *(passive modal construction)* — *I must be driven home.*

sie **muß** . . . gefahren **werden**	*she must be driven*
sie **mußte** . . . gefahren **werden**	*she had to be driven*
sie **hat** . . . gefahren **werden müssen**	*she has had to be driven*
sie **hatte** . . . gefahren **werden müssen**	*she had had to be driven*
sie **wird** . . . gefahren **werden müssen**	*she will have to be driven*

2. The present perfect, past perfect, and future tenses of modals seldom occur in the passive. The present and simple past tenses, as well as the subjunctive modals **müßte(n)** *(should, ought to),* **könnte(n)** *(could),* and **sollte(n)** *(should)* are quite common; they are often introduced by **es.**

Es **kann** mehr getan werden. *(present)* — *More can be done.*
Es **konnte** mehr getan werden. *(past)* — *More could / was able to be done.*
Es **könnte** mehr getan werden. *(subjunctive)* — *More could / might possibly be done.*

F. Passive with Dative Objects

1. An *accusative* object in an active sentence becomes a *nominative* subject in a passive sentence. A *dative* object, however, remains in the dative in both an active and a passive sentence.

Active

DAT. *ACC.*
Jemand schrieb **der Frau** *einen Brief.* — *Someone wrote the woman a letter.*

Passive

DAT. *NOM.*
Der Frau wurde *ein Brief* geschrieben.
NOM. *DAT.*
Ein Brief wurde **der Frau** geschrieben.
} *The woman was written a letter.*

2. Some verbs take a dative object only (see 4.5). When such a verb is used in the passive, the sentence is formed without any subject at all, though sometimes an introductory **es** is included. The conjugated verb is always in the third person singular.

Active
Man dankte ihm. — *They thanked him.*

Passive
Ihm wurde gedankt.
Es wurde **ihm** gedankt.
} *He was thanked.*

Active
Jemand hat **den Leuten** geholfen. — *Someone has helped the people.*

Passive
Den Leuten ist geholfen worden.
Es ist **den Leuten** geholfen worden.
} *The people have been helped.*

28.2 True Passive Versus Statal Passive

The verb **werden** in the passive voice always expresses the *process* of something happening; a sentence without **werden** is not a true passive.

COMPARE:

Der Computer **wird** repariert.	*The computer is being repaired. (It cannot be used now.)*
Der Computer **ist** repariert.	*The computer is repaired. (It can be used now.)*

The first example above contains the verb **werden** and is a true passive. The second sentence does not contain the verb **werden** and is known as a statal passive **(das Zustandspassiv).** The statal passive is not really a passive at all; the only verb is **ist,** and the past participle **repariert** is a predicate adjective (see 21.2) describing the state or condition of the computer. **Der Computer ist repariert** is structurally the same as **Der Computer ist neu.**

28.3 Substitutes for the Passive Voice

Since repeated use of the passive voice is considered poor style, one of several active-voice equivalents is often substituted.

A. Man

Man is a common alternative to the passive when no specific subject performs the action.

Hier raucht **man** nicht. (Hier wird nicht geraucht.)	*There is no smoking here.*
Wie macht **man** das? (Wie wird das gemacht?)	*How is that done?*

B. Reflexive Verbs

Reflexive constructions are used occasionally in place of the passive.

Das **lernt sich** leicht. (Das wird leicht gelernt.)	*That is easily learned.*
Wie **schreibt sich** das? (Wie wird das geschrieben?)	*How is that spelled?*

C. Sich lassen

The use of reflexive **sich lassen** with an infinitive expresses the idea that something can be done or that someone lets something *be done* (see **lassen,** 18.4).

Dieser Satz **läßt sich** nicht leicht **übersetzen.** (Dieser Satz kann nicht leicht übersetzt werden.)	*This sentence cannot be easily translated.* (that is, *it does not let itself be easily translated*).
Wir **lassen uns** nicht wieder **überlisten.**	*We are not letting ourselves be outwitted again.*

D. Sein . . . zu + *Infinitive*

Sein . . . zu + an infinitive can replace the passive to express that something *can* or *must be done.*

Das Spiel **ist** vielleicht noch **zu gewinnen.**
(Das Spiel **kann** vielleicht noch gewonnen werden.)
The game can perhaps still be won. (that is, *it is perhaps still to be won*)

Diese Videofilme **sind** bis morgen **zurückzubringen.**
(Diese Videofilme **müssen** bis morgen zurückgebracht werden.)
These videotapes must be returned by tomorrow. (that is, *they are to be returned by tomorrow*)

* Übungen

A **Das Passiv in verschiedenen Zeitformen.** Bilden Sie mit den folgenden Wörtern einen Satz zuerst im Passiv Präsens, dann in den weiter angegebenen Zeitformen.

Nach dem Krieg / werden / viele Häuser / bauen

1. Nach dem Krieg . . . (Passiv Präsens)
2. Nach dem Krieg . . . (Passiv Präteritum)
3. Nach dem Krieg . . . (Passiv Perfekt)
4. Nach dem Krieg . . . (Passiv Pluperfekt)
5. Nach dem Krieg . . . (Passiv Futur)

B **Kleinanzeigen.** Erklären Sie die kleinen Anzeigen *(advertisements)* im Passiv Präsens.

Beispiel: Autoreparatur – billig!
Autos werden billig repariert.

1. Suche Partnerin fürs Leben!
2. Alter VW Käfer *(Beetle)* zu verkaufen!
3. Ankauf *(purchase)* von Antiquitäten!
4. Fahrradverleih! (verleihen = *to rent*)
5. Mensa stellt Koch ein! (einstellen = *to hire*)
6. Studienprobleme? Wir beraten dich! (beraten = *to advise*)
7. Zimmervermittlung! (vermitteln = *to locate, find*)

„Wenn der Mensch alles leisten soll, was man von ihm fordert, so muß er sich für mehr halten, als er ist." (Goethe)

C **Große Leistungen** *(accomplishments).* Was wurde von wem getan? Antworten Sie im Passiv. Verwenden Sie die angegebenen Verben.

Beispiel: das Dynamit
Das Dynamit wurde im Jahre 1867 von Alfred Nobel erfunden.

besiegen	besteigen	entdecken	erfinden
erreichen	gründen	komponieren	verfassen

Was	*Von wem*
1. das *Kommunistische Manifest* (1848)	Henri Dunant
2. das *Weihnachts-Oratorium* (1734)	Johannes Gutenberg
3. die Buchdruckerkunst (1445)	Roald Amundsen
4. der Südpol (1911)	Karl Marx
5. das Rote Kreuz (1864)	J. S. Bach
6. Mount Everest (1953)	Edmund Hillary und Tenzing Norgay
7. der Tuberkel-Bazillus (1882)	Robert Koch
8. die Römer im Teutoburgerwald (9 nach Chr.)	Hermann der Cherusker (Arminius)

D **Historisches.** Wählen Sie aus fünf verschiedenen Jahrhunderten jeweils ein Jahr, in dem etwas besonders Wichtiges geschah. Erzählen Sie im Präteritum davon.

Beispiele: 1066: *England wurde im Jahre 1066 von den Normannen erobert* (conquered).
1914: *Der Erzherzog* (Archduke) *Franz Ferdinand von Österreich wurde 1914 in Sarajevo erschossen.*

E **Veränderungen in der Stadt.** Erzählen Sie im Perfekt von drei oder vier Veränderungen der letzten paar Jahre, welche die Lebensqualität Ihrer Heimatstadt verbessert oder verschlechtert haben.

Beispiele: *Viele neue Häuser sind gebaut worden.*
Eine Kirche ist renoviert worden.

F **Stadtplanung.** Welche Veränderungen sind in Ihrer Stadt für die Zukunft geplant? Machen Sie bitte Aussagen im Futur oder mit Modalverben.

Beispiele: *Ich glaube, daß bald ein neues Einkaufszentrum gebaut werden wird.*
Es soll auch eine neue Schule eröffnet werden.
Ich weiß nicht, was sonst gemacht werden wird.

G **Was alles getan werden mußte.** Einige Studenten fanden eine ziemlich heruntergekommene *(run down)* Wohnung. Was mußte getan werden, bevor sie einzogen? Verwenden Sie das Passiv mit oder ohne **es.**

Beispiele: Fenster ersetzen
Zwei kaputte Fenster mußten ersetzt werden.

Vorhänge *(curtains)* aufhängen
Es mußten auch Vorhänge aufgehängt werden.

1. die Küche sauber machen
2. die Gardinen *(drapes)* reinigen
3. das Badezimmer putzen
4. eine Tür reparieren
5. den Keller aufräumen

H **Das sollte getan werden.** Wie sieht es in Ihrer Wohnung oder in Ihrem Haus aus? Was könnte, sollte oder müßte in der Zukunft noch getan werden?

Beispiel: *Die Wände sollten gestrichen werden.*

I **Kartenverkauf: Passiv oder Zustandspassiv?** Drücken Sie die folgenden Sätze auf deutsch aus.

1. The concert was planned for April 7.
2. Tickets were sold two weeks before the concert.
3. After two days the best seats were sold.
4. Most of the tickets were sold to students.
5. By the **(bis zum)** day of the concert not all the tickets were sold.
6. By evening, however, the concert was sold out **(ausverkauft).**

J **Was wird dort gemacht?** Beantworten Sie die Fragen im Passiv und mit oder ohne **es.**

Beispiele: in einer Bibliothek
Es werden dort Bücher ausgeliehen.
Dort wird gelesen.

1. an einem Kiosk *(newsstand)*
2. in einem Bett
3. in einer Autowerkstatt
4. in einem Kino
5. in einer Disco
6. in einem Restaurant

Es wird weiter spekuliert

K **Passiv mit dem Dativ.** Drücken Sie die Sätze mit dem Passiv anders aus. Übersetzen Sie Ihre neuen Sätze.

Beispiel: Man hat der alten Frau geholfen.
Der alten Frau ist geholfen worden.
OR: *Es ist der alten Frau geholfen worden.*
(The old woman was / has been helped.)

1. Man erzählte den Kindern nichts davon.
2. Man hat den Gastgebern *(hosts)* gedankt.
3. Uns empfiehlt man, dieses Buch zu lesen.
4. Mir haben viele Leute zum Geburtstag gratuliert.
5. Man wird ihr wahrscheinlich raten, nichts zu sagen.

L **Anders ausdrücken.** Drücken Sie die Sätze durch andere Konstruktionen aus.

Beispiele: Das kann man nicht mit Sicherheit sagen.
Das läßt sich nicht mit Sicherheit sagen.
OR: *Das kann nicht mit Sicherheit gesagt werden.*
OR: *Man kann das nicht mit Sicherheit sagen.*

1. Wie buchstabiert man dieses Wort?
2. Autofahren ist leicht zu lernen.
3. Es konnte festgestellt *(ascertained)* werden, daß . . .
4. Solche Behauptungen *(assertions)* lassen sich nicht so einfach beweisen *(prove)*.

5. Änderungen an der chemischen Verbindung *(compound)* waren nicht zu erkennen *(recognize)*.
6. Das Wasser muß mindestens zwanzig Minuten gekocht werden.

* Anwendung

Klischeevorstellungen. Über fast jedes Volk und jedes Land auf der Welt gibt es Klischees. In Japan z.B. soll angeblich *(supposedly)* immer gearbeitet werden, in Amerika wird Energie verschwendet *(wasted)*, in Deutschland wird viel Bier getrunken, usw. An welche Klischees denken Sie? Welche Klischees halten Sie für richtig, welche für falsch? Diskutieren Sie mit anderen Personen darüber. Konzentrieren Sie sich dabei auf das Passiv und auch auf das Pronomen **man** als Passiversatz.

REDEMITTEL

Es wird behauptet, daß in Amerika / Deutschland . . . [getan] wird.
Manche meinen, es wird in Amerika / Deutschland . . . [getan].
Es wurde ja oft gesagt, daß . . .
In Amerika / Deutschland soll angeblich *(supposedly)* viel . . . [getan] werden.
Man kann nicht behaupten, daß . . .

REAKTIONEN

Damit stimme ich (nicht) überein.
Das halte ich für nicht ganz richtig / falsch.
Das finde ich (nicht) richtig.
Das ist ja Unsinn!
Das läßt sich nicht einfach so behaupten.
Das kann man auch anders sehen.

* Schriftliche Themen

Tips zum Schreiben ***Avoiding Overuse of the Passive***

The passive is often used in technical writing, where the agent of an action is not important, or in instances where the writer either does not know or does not wish to tell who performed the action. Most readers, however, find sentences in the active voice easier to read than sentences in the passive, where the doer, if there is one, is hidden in a prepositional phrase and thus takes longer to find. In addition, since the passive is wordy, it can deprive your prose of action and color. Use the passive sparingly, and only when the agent is unknown or when you wish to emphasize the occurrence of an action rather than its cause. Remember that you can avoid frequent repetition of the passive by using alternative constructions (see 28.3).

A **Eine interessante Veranstaltung** *(organized event)*. Erzählen Sie von einer Veranstaltung, bei der Sie einmal mitgemacht haben. Sie sollen nicht so sehr davon erzählen, *wer* was getan hat, sondern, *was* geschah oder gemacht wurde.

Beispiel: Einmal nahm ich an einer Protestaktion teil. Am Anfang organisierte man . . . Es wurden Transparente *(banners)* verteilt *(distributed)* . . . Es wurde viel geredet . . . Gegen Ende der Aktion marschierte man . . . Zum Schluß mußten alle Demonstranten . . . zurückgebracht werden.

B **Bessere Lebensqualität.** Was könnte oder müßte getan werden, um die Atmosphäre und die Lebensqualität an Ihrer Universität oder in Ihrer Stadt attraktiver zu machen?

Beispiel: Meiner Meinung nach könnte die Lebensqualität an dieser Universität durch renovierte Unterrichtsräume erheblich *(substantially)* verbessert werden. Man müßte auch mehr Räume einrichten *(set up)*, in denen man sich auch außerhalb der Unterrichtszeit treffen könnte. Vielleicht sollten auch mehr Parkplätze geschaffen werden, damit . . . Es ließe sich sicher noch viel mehr machen, um das Leben an dieser Universität angenehmer zu gestalten *(shape)*.

Wortschatz 28

schaffen, schaffte, geschafft
schaffen, schuf, geschaffen

1. As a weak verb, **schaffen (schaffte, hat geschafft)** means *to manage to do* or *accomplish* a task, often with considerable effort.

Sie wollten die Arbeit bis sechs Uhr beenden, und sie haben es **geschafft.**	*They wanted to finish work by six o'clock, and they managed to do so.*
Wir haben es **geschafft!**	*We did it!*

Schaffen can also mean *to work (hard)*.

Er hat sein ganzes Leben lang (schwer) **geschafft.**	*He worked (hard) his whole life.*

Schaffen sometimes means *to bring* or *get* an object to a particular place.

Der Gepäckträger hat die vielen Koffer in den Zug **geschafft.**	*The porter got the many suitcases into the train.*

2. When used as a strong verb, **schaffen (schuf, hat geschaffen)** means *to create, make,* or *bring about.*

Gott soll die Welt in sechs Tagen **geschaffen** haben.	*God is said to have created the world in six days.*
Er mußte etwas Ordnung in seinem Leben **schaffen.**	*He had to bring about some order into his life.*

3. The strong participle **geschaffen** occurs often as an adjective meaning *made* or *cut out for* something.

Sie ist für diese Rolle **geschaffen.**	*She is made for this role.* (that is, *it is the ideal role for her*)

ÜBUNGEN

A ***Geschaffen* oder *geschafft?*** Ergänzen Sie die Sätze durch das richtige Partizip.

1. Man sollte in zwei Stunden mit dem Examen fertig sein. Hast du es ge-____ ?
2. Haben die Kinder den Schnee vor der Haustür weg-____ ?
3. Diese Diskussion hat eine gute Atmosphäre ge-____ .
4. Dieser Posten ist für ihn wie ge-____ .
5. Ludwig van Beethoven hat viele unsterbliche Werke ge-____ .

B **Das habe ich getan.** Was haben Sie *geschafft* und *geschaffen?* Machen Sie zwei Aussagen mit jedem Partizip.

Beispiele: *Ich habe mehr Ruhe in meinem Leben* ***geschaffen.***
Ich habe es ***geschafft,*** *bisher alle meine Kurse zu bestehen* (pass).

Zusammenfassung 28

Rules to Remember

1. The passive is used mainly to express occurrences and actions where there is no "doer" or where the "doer" is of secondary importance.
2. The passive expresses a process **(Das Haus <u>wird</u> verkauft.),** the so-called statal passive describes a condition **(Das Haus <u>ist</u> verkauft.).**
3. The passive voice is formed with active voice conjugated forms of **werden** + past participle.
4. Agents of a passive action are expressed with the preposition **von** + the agent **(von der Polizei).** The means or processes through which an action is accomplished are expressed with **durch** + noun **(durch einen Sturm).** The instrument used to accomplish an action is shown with **mit** + noun **(mit einem Messer).**

Activities

1. **Recognizing the passive.** Find examples of passive voice in an issue of *Deutschland Nachrichten* or any other suitable text you have read recently in German. Can you find examples with modals or in indirect discourse? Present two or three of your examples to the class.

2. **Events and activities.** Describe the activities and events that usually take place at camp, on vacation, at your family reunion, or on the first day of the semester.

3. **From the newspaper.** Search through today's newspaper for five things that happened yesterday that you can express in the passive voice. Report these events in class.

4. **Important events.** Write in the passive what you consider to be the ten most important things that have happened in the world during your lifetime. Share your events with the class.

5. **Historical sketch.** Write a thumbnail historical sketch of a city, place, event, or technological development that interests you. Consult reference works if necessary. Use the passive voice in your sketch.

6. **Working with a text.** Make ten statements in the passive voice about events and occurrences in a story you have read in German.

Verb Prefixes

29.1 Separable Prefixes

A. *Separable Prefixes and Their Meanings*

1. German creates many verbs by adding prefixes to root verbs. A great number of such prefixes are "separable," meaning that they separate from the verb and appear at the end of the clause. Separable prefixes have a voiced stress and are usually prepositions or adverbs with specific meanings in their own right that either modify or completely change the meanings of the root verbs. Here are examples of the most common separable prefixes. Note that those marked with an asterisk can also be used inseparably (see 29.3).

Prefix	*Meaning*	*Example*	
ab-	*off, away, down*	abnehmen	*to take off weight*
an-	*on, at, to(ward)*	ansehen	*to look at*
auf-	*up, open, on*	aufmachen	*to open up*
aus-	*out*	aussterben	*to die out*
bei-	*by, with*	beistehen	*to stand by someone, aid*
ein-	*into*	einsteigen	*to get into, climb into*
***durch-**	*through*	durchsetzen	*to carry or put through*
fort-	*away*	fortgehen	*to go away*
her-	*(to) here*	herkommen	*to come (to) here*
hin-	*(to) there*	hingehen	*to go (to) there*
***hinter-**	*back, rear*	hintergehen	*to go to the back*
los-	*loose*	loslassen	*to turn loose*
mit-	*with, along*	mitsingen	*to sing along*
nach-	*after*	nachblicken	*to look or gaze after*
***über-**	*over; across*	überfließen	*to flow over*

Prefix	*Meaning*	*Example*	
***um-**	*around, about, over*	umdrehen	*to turn over*
***unter-**	*under*	untergehen	*to go down, set*
vor-	*before, ahead*	vorarbeiten	*to work ahead*
vorbei-	*by, past*	vorbeilaufen	*to run by*
weg-	*away*	weggehen	*to go away*
weiter-	*further, on*	weiterlaufen	*to run further*
***wider-**	*against*	widerhallen	*to echo*
***wieder-**	*again*	wiedersehen	*to see again*
zu-	*to, towards; to a shut position*	zumachen	*to shut*
zurück-	*back*	zurückrufen	*to call back*
zusammen-	*together*	zusammenstehen	*to stand together*

2. Some separable prefixes should be learned as pairs, since they form antonyms when combined with the same verb.

andrehen	*to turn on*	*vs*	**ab**drehen	*to turn off*
anziehen	*to put on (clothes)*		**aus**ziehen	*to take off*
aufmachen	*to open*		**zu**machen	*to close*
aufsteigen	*to climb up*		**ab**steigen	*to climb down*
einatmen	*to inhale*		**aus**atmen	*to exhale*
vorgehen	*to go ahead, precede*		**nach**gehen	*to go after, follow*
zunehmen	*to increase, gain*		**ab**nehmen	*to decrease, lose*

3. Occasionally another verb is a separable prefix.

kennenlernen	*to meet, make one's acquaintance*
spazierengehen	*to take a walk*
stehenbleiben	*to stop*

B. Use

1. A separable prefix is a verbal complement and stands in final position within a sentence (see 1.1F). Thus it separates from the conjugated form of its verb in a main clause but links up with this verb in a subordinate clause.

Das Konzert **fängt** / **fing** um acht Uhr **an.**	*The concert begins / began at eight o'clock.*
Ich weiß, daß das Konzert um acht Uhr **anfängt** / **anfing.**	*I know that the concert begins / began at eight o'clock.*

2. A separable prefix also separates from imperative forms of its verb.

Bleib bitte sofort **stehen!**	*Please stop immediately!*
Hören Sie mit diesem Unsinn **auf!**	*Stop this nonsense!*

3. In past participles, the **ge-** is inserted between the separable prefix and the rest of the participle.

Das Konzert hat um acht Uhr **angefangen.**	*The concert began at eight o'clock.*
Nachher sind wir **spazierengegangen.**	*Afterwards we went for a walk.*

4. If a separable prefix is added to a verb already having an inseparable prefix (see 29.2), no **ge-** is included in the past participle; the inseparable prefix takes its place.

Sie hat die Geschichte **weitererzählt.**	*She continued telling the story.*

5. In infinitive phrases (see 18.1), a **zu,** if present, is inserted between a separable prefix and its verb.

Die Kinder versuchen, die Wörter alphabetisch **einzuordnen.**	*The children are trying to arrange the words alphabetically.*
Wir hoffen, interessante Leute hier **kennenzulernen.**	*We hope to meet interesting people here.*

C. Hin- *and* her-

1. The separable prefixes **hin-** and **her-** are used mainly in combination with other separable prefixes to indicate specific direction *away from* (**hin-**) or *toward* (**her-**) the observer.

Common **hin-** and **her-** Combinations

hin(gehen)	*(to go) to*
her(kommen)	*(to come) from*
dorthin(gehen)	*(to go) to there*
hierher(kommen)	*(to come) to here*
hinein / hinaus(gehen)	*(to go) in / out*
herein / heraus(kommen)	*(to come) in / out*
hinauf / hinab(gehen)	*(to go) up / down*
herauf / herab(kommen)	*(to come) up / down*
hinüber(gehen)	*(to go) over to*
herüber(kommen)	*(to come) over to*
hinunter(gehen)	*(to go) down to*
herunter(kommen)	*(to come) down to*

2. Since they indicate direction, **hin-** and **her-** in combination with other prefixes usually make an action more specific than it would otherwise be.

Er geht **aus.** *(general action)*	*He is going out.*
Sie geht **hinaus.** *(away from the observer)*	*She goes out (of a room, house, etc.).*
Sie stieg aus dem Zug **(aus).** *(general action)*	*She got off the train.*
Sie stieg aus dem Zug **heraus.** *(toward the observer)*	*She got out of the train.*

3. Verbs of motion used with **hin-** and **her-** prefix combinations occasionally have an accusative noun that appears to be a direct object, but is really part of the adverbial expression.

Das Kind läuft **die Treppe hinunter.**	*The child runs down the stairs.*

29.2 Inseparable Prefixes

The prefixes **be-, emp-, ent-, er-, ge-, miß-, ver-,** and **zer-** are inseparable. Verbs with these prefixes do not have a **ge-** in the past participle: **hat besucht; haben verkauft.** These prefixes have no meanings by themselves, but most of them transform the meanings of root verbs in very specific ways.

A. Be-

1. A **be-** prefix verb is transitive, regardless of whether the root verb is transitive or intransitive.

antworten (auf)	*to answer*	**be**antworten	*to answer*
kämpfen (gegen)	*to fight against*	**be**kämpfen	*to fight against*
sprechen (über)	*to talk about*	**be**sprechen	*to discuss*

Wir **sprechen über** diese Probleme.	*We talk about these problems.*
Wir **besprechen** diese Probleme.	*We discuss these problems.*

2. The meaning of the verb may change considerably when a **be-** prefix is added.

kommen	*to come*	**be**kommen	*to receive*
sitzen	*to sit*	**be**sitzen	*to possess*
suchen	*to search*	**be**suchen	*to visit*

3. The prefix **be-** also creates transitive verbs from some nouns and adjectives.

der Freund	*friend*	**be**freunden	*to befriend*
die Frucht	*fruit*	**be**fruchten	*to fertilize, impregnate*
richtig	*correct*	**be**richtigen	*to correct*
ruhig	*calm*	**be**ruhigen	*to calm*

B. Ent-

When added to nouns, adjectives, or verbs, the prefix **ent-** expresses the idea of separation or removal. It is often equivalent to the English *de- (detach), dis- (disconnect),* or *un- (undo).*

das Fett	*fat, grease*	**ent**fetten	*to remove the fat*
die Kraft	*strength*	**ent**kräften	*to weaken*
fern	*far*	**ent**fernen	*to remove*
heilig	*sacred*	**ent**heiligen	*to desecrate*
decken	*to cover*	**ent**decken	*to discover*
falten	*to fold*	**ent**falten	*to unfold*
kommen	*to come*	**ent**kommen	*to escape, get away*

C. Er-

1. The prefix **er-** converts certain adjectives into verbs reflecting the quality expressed by the adjective.

hell	*bright*	**er**hellen	*to brighten*
hoch	*high*	**er**höhen	*to heighten*
möglich	*possible*	**er**möglichen	*to make possible*

2. The prefix **er-** also changes the meaning of certain root verbs to imply successful completion of an activity.

arbeiten	*to work*	**er**arbeiten	*to obtain through work*
finden	*to find*	**er**finden	*to invent*
raten	*to (take a) guess*	**er**raten	*to guess correctly*

With certain verbs, the "completion" of the action is death:

ermorden	*to murder*	erstechen	*to stab to death*
erschießen	*to shoot fatally*	ertrinken	*to die by drowning*
erschlagen	*to slay*		

D. Miß-

1. The prefix **miß-** indicates that something is done falsely or incorrectly. It often corresponds to the English *mis-* or *dis-* and is only used with about fifteen verbs in German.

behandeln	*to handle*	**miß**handeln	*to mistreat*
deuten	*to interpret*	**miß**deuten	*to misinterpret*
gefallen	*to be pleasing*	**miß**fallen	*to displease*
trauen	*to trust*	**miß**trauen	*to distrust*

Umweltveränderung

Leben im sauren Regen

Total verarmt nach 150 Jahren

2. When used with verbs that are already inseparable, the prefix **miß-** becomes stressed.

Er **mißversteht** die Frage. *He misunderstands the question.*

E. Ver-

1. The prefix **ver-** sometimes implies that the action of a root verb is done incorrectly.

fahren	*to drive*	sich **ver**fahren	*to take the wrong road*
führen	*to lead*	**ver**führen	*to seduce, lead astray*
legen	*to lay*	**ver**legen	*to mislay*
rechnen	*to calculate*	sich **ver**rechnen	*to miscalculate*
sprechen	*to speak*	sich **ver**sprechen	*to misspeak*

2. **Ver-** can also indicate that an action continues until something is used up or destroyed.

brauchen	*to use*	**ver**brauchen	*to use up*
brennen	*to burn*	**ver**brennen	*to burn up*
fallen	*to fall*	**ver**fallen	*to fall into ruin*
gehen	*to go*	**ver**gehen	*to pass* or *fade away*
schwinden	*to dwindle*	**ver**schwinden	*to disappear*
spielen	*to play*	**ver**spielen	*to gamble away*

3. In some instances, **ver-** indicates going, giving, or chasing away.

jagen	*to chase*	**ver**reisen	*to go away on a trip*
reisen	*to travel*	**ver**schenken	*to give away*
schenken	*to give as a gift*	**ver**jagen	*to chase away*
treiben	*to drive*	**ver**treiben	*to drive (s.o.) away*

4. Sometimes the prefix **ver-** simply intensifies, refines, or alters the action expressed by the root verb.

bergen	*to hide, cover*	**ver**bergen	*to hide, conceal*
gleichen	*to resemble*	**ver**gleichen	*to compare*
urteilen	*to judge*	**ver**urteilen	*to condemn*
zweifeln	*to doubt*	**ver**zweifeln	*to despair*

5. Finally, **ver-** converts many adjectives (often in the comparative form), a few adverbs, and an occasional noun into verbs.

anders	*different*	**ver**ändern	*to change*
besser	*better*	**ver**bessern	*to improve*
größer	*larger*	**ver**größern	*to enlarge*
länger	*longer*	**ver**längern	*to lengthen*
mehr	*more*	**ver**mehren	*to increase*
nicht	*not*	**ver**nichten	*to annihilate*
die Ursache	*cause*	**ver**ursachen	*to cause*

F. Zer-

The prefix **zer-** indicates destruction or dissolution through the action denoted by the verb.

brechen	*to break*	**zer**brechen	*to break into pieces, shatter*
fallen	*to fall*	**zer**fallen	*to fall into pieces*
gehen	*to go*	**zer**gehen	*to dissolve (in a liquid)*
legen	*to lay*	**zer**legen	*to take apart, disassemble*
reißen	*to tear*	**zer**reißen	*to tear to pieces*
stören	*to disturb*	**zer**stören	*to destroy*

29.3 Two-Way Prefixes

A. *Separable Versus Inseparable*

1. The separable prefixes **durch-** *(through),* **hinter-** *(back, rear),* **über-** *(over, across),* **um-** *(around, over),* **unter-** *(under),* **wider-** *(against),* and **wieder-** *(again)* are used separably with some verbs and inseparably with others. In some instances, these prefixes may also be used either separably or inseparably with the same verb, depending upon the meaning implied. Used separably, prefix verbs tend to have a fairly literal meaning corresponding to the basic meaning of the verb + prefix. Used inseparably, the prefix often gives the verb a more abstract or figurative meaning.

Der Fährmann hat die Reisenden **übergesetzt.** *(separable)*	*The ferryman ferried the travelers across.*
Sie hat den Artikel **übersetzt.** *(inseparable)*	*She translated the article.*

2. In general, all prefixes are stressed when used separably and unstressed when used inseparably.

Die Schule wurde während des Sommers **umgebaut.**	*The school was remodeled during the summer.*
Er hat seine Freundin **umarmt.**	*He hugged his girlfriend.*

3. When prefix verbs are used inseparably, they invariably make an intransitive verb transitive. In such instances, the auxiliary in the perfect tenses is **haben,** even when the verb without a prefix or with the separable prefix would take **sein.**

COMPARE:

Er **ist** durch den Park **gelaufen.** — *He ran through the park.*

Er **hat** den Park **durchlaufen.** — *He ran through the park from one end to the other.*

Wir **sind** auf die andere Seite **(hin)übergesprungen.** — *We jumped over onto the other side.*

Wir **haben** ein paar Kapitel im Buch **übersprungen.** — *We skipped a few chapters in the book.*

B. Use of the Two-Way Prefixes

1. Most (but not all) verbs with **durch-** are separable.

   Sie **macht** eine schlimme Zeit **durch.** — *She is going through a bad time.*

   Er **schaute** durch das Fenster **durch.** — *He saw through the window.*

   BUT:

   Er **durchschaute** den Plan seines Feindes. — *He saw through (recognized) the plan of his enemy.*

2. Five or six verbs normally used with **hinter-** are inseparable. Only two occur as separable verbs.

   Mutter hat eine Nachricht für euch **hinterlassen.** — *Mother left a message for you.*

   Er hat seine Freunde **hintergangen.** — *He deceived his friends.*

   BUT:

   Sie ist **hintergegangen.** — *She went to the rear.*

   Er **gießt** das Glas Bier **hinter.** — *He tosses down the glass of beer.*

3. Most (but not all) verbs with **über-** are inseparable.

   Er hat einen Hund **überfahren.** — *He ran over a dog.*

   Wir **überlassen** Ihnen die Entscheidung. — *We leave the decision (up) to you.*

   BUT:

   Der Topf ist **übergelaufen.** — *The pot boiled over.*

4. Some verbs with **um-** are separable, others are inseparable. Some verbs with **um-** can be either separable or inseparable, depending upon the meaning.

   Sie versucht, den Satz **umzuschreiben.** — *She tries to rewrite / revise the sentence.*

   Er versucht, den Satz zu **umschreiben.** — *He tries to paraphrase the sentence.*

5. Some verbs with **unter-** are separable, others are inseparable. Some verbs with **unter-** can be either separable or inseparable, depending upon the meaning.

Der Junge wurde in einem Kinderheim **untergebracht.**	*The boy was lodged in a children's home.*
Die schwere Arbeit hat seine Gesundheit **untergraben.**	*The difficult work undermined his health.*

6. All verbs with **wider-** are inseparable except for two.

Seine Aussage **widerspricht** den Tatsachen.	*His statement contradicts the facts.*
Niemand konnte sein Argument **widerlegen.**	*No one was able to refute his argument.*
BUT:	
Das Wasser **spiegelt** die Lichter **wider.**	*The water reflects the lights.*
Der Glockenton **hallte wider.**	*The sound of the bells echoed.*

7. All verbs with **wieder-** are separable except one.

Wann habt ihr eure Eltern **wiedergesehen?**	*When did you see your parents again?*
Der Student **holte** die Fragen **wieder.**	*The student fetched the questions again.*
BUT:	
Der Student **wiederholte** die Fragen.	*The student repeated the questions.*

* Übungen

A **Welches Verb paßt?** Ergänzen Sie die Sätze durch passende Präfixverben.

Beispiel: Ich möchte mir diese Schallplatte ____ . (hören)
Ich möchte mir diese Schallplatte ***anhören.***

1. Kinder, ich möchte jetzt schlafen. ____ das Licht bitte ____ . (machen)
2. Was er sagt, ist sehr wichtig. Ihr sollt gut ____ . (hören)
3. Du darfst mein Fahrrad benutzen, aber du mußt es heute abend ____ . (bringen)
4. Es regnet hier draußen. Kannst du mich bitte ____ ? (lassen)
5. Wer hat das Fenster ____ ? (schlagen)
6. Endstation! Alle bitte ____ ! (steigen)
7. Man ____ das alte Haus in wenigen Tagen ____ . (reißen: *tear*)

Statt Ausbau im Westen lieber Aufbau im Osten

B **Das Gegenteil.** Drücken Sie das Gegenteil dieser Sätze aus.

Beispiel: Können Sie das Fenster bitte *zumachen?*
Können Sie das Fenster bitte ***aufmachen?***

1. Ich muß den Koffer *packen.*
2. Kannst du bitte das Licht *anschalten?*
3. Habt ihr das Geld schon *ausgezahlt?*
4. Vergiß nicht, das Gas *abzudrehen.*
5. Du sollst dir die Schuhe noch *anziehen.*
6. Meine Uhr *geht vor.*
7. Der Lärm *nimmt* jetzt *ab.*

C **Dauernd** *(continually)* ***hin-*** **oder** ***her-***. Ergänzen Sie durch **hin-, her-** oder deren weitere Formen.

Beispiel: Die Nachbarn haben eine Party; gehen wir zu ihnen ____ .
Die Nachbarn haben eine Party; gehen wir zu ihnen ***hinüber.***

1. Klaus, ich brauche Hilfe. Komm bitte ____ !
2. Seine Eltern wohnen auf dem Land. Fahren wir morgen zu ihnen ____ ?
3. Vorsicht bitte, damit niemand in dieses Loch ____ -fällt.
4. Sie sahen weder nach links noch nach rechts, sondern nur vor sich ____ .
5. Wir fuhren ein paar Stunden in der Stadt ____ .
6. Ihr dürft euch selbstverständlich zu uns ____ -setzen.
7. Vati, kannst du meinen Drachen *(kite)* vom Baum ____ -holen?
8. Aus dem einsamen Tal *(valley)* tönte plötzlich Glockengeläute *(the chiming of bells)* zu den Bergwanderern ____ .

D **Anders ausdrücken.** Drücken Sie die Sätze durch Verben mit dem Präfix **be-** anders aus. Beachten Sie bitte, daß Verben mit dem Präfix **be-** immer transitiv sind.

Beispiel: Für seine Entscheidung hat er keinen *Grund gegeben.*
Er hat seine Entscheidung nicht ***begründet.***

1. Ich muß mein Schreiben jetzt *zu Ende bringen.*
2. Wer *gibt* ihm einen *Lohn* für seine Arbeit?
3. Die Nachricht von seinen Plänen hat uns sehr *unruhig gemacht.*
4. Niemand *dachte an* die Folgen einer solchen Politik.
5. Wir wollen mit jemand anders *über* dieses Problem *sprechen.*
6. Truppen *schossen auf* die feindlichen Stellen *(positions).*

E **Das richtige Verb.** Ergänzen Sie die Sätze durch passende Verben mit dem Präfix **ent-**.

1. Wenn ihnen die Blätter schmecken, können Raupen *(caterpillars)* einen Baum in wenigen Tagen ____ .
2. Geld hat einen bestimmten Wert, aber durch eine Inflation wird es ____ .

3. Wenn eine Firma zu viele Arbeiter hat, werden oft einige ____ .
4. Bevor man Meerwasser trinkt, muß man es zuerst ____ .
5. Dem Tod kann man nicht auf immer *(forever)* ____ .

F **Persönliche Fragen.** Beantworten Sie die Fragen. Verwenden Sie Verben mit dem Präfix **er-**.

1. Wer macht Ihnen das Studium möglich?
2. Was macht Sie besonders frisch?
3. Werden Sie rot, wenn Leute gut oder schlecht von Ihnen reden?
4. Was macht Sie besonders müde?

G **Mit oder ohne *er-*?** Ergänzen Sie die Sätze durch passende Verben aus den Verbpaaren.

frieren / erfrieren
leben / erleben
raten / erraten
reichen / erreichen
schießen / erschießen

1. Es ist kalt draußen. Es ____ . Sogar das Wasser im See ist zu Eis ____ .
2. Der Greis *(old man)* hatte lange ____ und viel ____ .
3. Dreimal darfst du ____ . —Ich habe es schon ____ .
4. Wir haben den Tunnel ____ . ____ mir bitte deine Taschenlampe.
5. Sie ____ mehrmals mit einer Pistole, aber glücklicherweise ____ sie niemand.

H **Verstehen Sie das?** Erklären Sie auf deutsch, was die folgenden Ausdrücke bedeuten.

1. ein Spiel verlängern
2. Flugblätter *(pamphlets)* verteilen
3. eine Frage verneinen
4. Pläne verwirklichen
5. sich zum Essen verspäten
6. eine Industrie verstaatlichen
7. etwas an einem Beispiel verdeutlichen

I **Alles mit *ver-*.** Ergänzen Sie die Sätze durch passende Verben mit dem Präfix **ver-**.

brauchen
gehen
jagen
legen
sinken
spielen
urteilen

1. In Las Vegas kann man leicht sein ganzes Geld ____ .
2. Ich kann meine Brille nicht finden. Vielleicht habe ich sie irgendwo ____ .
3. Dieser Wagen ____ zuviel Benzin.
4. Die Jahre sind schnell ____ .
5. Das Schiff ____ und wurde nie mehr gesehen.

6. Der Richter hat den Verbrecher zu einer Gefängnisstrafe *(imprisonment)* von sieben Jahren ____ .
7. Unser Hund ____ alle Katzen.

J **Alles in Stücke.** Beantworten Sie die Fragen. Verwenden Sie die folgenden Verben mit dem Präfix **zer-**.

Beispiel: Was tut ein Elefant im Porzellanladen?
Er zerbricht das ganze Porzellan.

brechen gehen legen reißen trampeln

1. Was kann ein sehr starker Mann mit einem Telefonbuch tun?
2. Was geschah, als Humpty Dumpty das Gleichgewicht *(balance)* verlor?
3. Was geschieht mit einer Pille, wenn sie im Wasser ist?
4. Was geschieht, wenn Kühe durch ein Blumenbeet *(flower bed)* gehen?
5. Was passiert mit Fröschen *(frogs)* im Biologielabor?

K **Trennbar oder untrennbar?** Bilden Sie kurze Sätze im Präsens mit den angegebenen Worten.

Beispiele: alle Zimmer im Haus durchsuchen *(to search)*
Die Polizei durchsucht alle Zimmer im Haus.

die Leine durchbeißen *(to bite through)*
Der Hund beißt die Leine durch.

1. durch das Fenster durchschauen *(to look through)*
2. den Betrug *(deceit)* durchschauen *(to see through)*
3. über die Straße (hin)übergehen *(to go across)*
4. mehrere Seiten im Buch übergehen *(to skip, pass over)*
5. bei der Prüfung durchfallen *(to fail)*
6. Dokumente unterschreiben *(to sign)*
7. dem Druck *(pressure)* widerstehen *(to resist)*
8. das Blatt umdrehen *(to turn over)*
9. die bissigen Bemerkungen ihres Freundes überhören *(to ignore)*

L **Vom Präsens ins Perfekt.** Setzen Sie Ihre Sätze von Übung K ins Perfekt.

Beispiel: Die Polizei durchsucht alle Zimmer im Haus
Die Polizei hat alle Zimmer im Haus durchsucht.

Der Hund beißt die Leine durch.
Der Hund hat die Leine durchgebissen.

M **Trennbar oder untrennbar?** Lesen Sie die Ausdrücke mit der richtigen Betonung vor. Erklären Sie, was die Ausdrücke bedeuten, indem Sie sie auf deutsch anders ausdrücken.

Beispiel: sich etwas überlegen (untrennbar)
bedeutet: über etwas nachdenken

1. ein paar Kapitel im Buch überspringen
2. seinen Willen durchsetzen
3. in eine andere politische Partei überwechseln
4. ein Gebot / Verbot übertreten
5. ein Buch / eine Zeitschrift durchblättern
6. ein Haus umbauen
7. einen Freund umarmen
8. den Fall *(case)* untersuchen
9. jemandem widersprechen

* Anwendung

Verben im Kontext. Unterstreichen Sie in einem kurzen Zeitungs- oder Zeitschriftenartikel alle Wörter mit untrennbaren Präfixen. Was bedeuten die Stammwörter *(root words)*? Auf welche Weise ändern die Präfixe die Bedeutungen dieser Stammwörter?

* Schriftliches Thema

Tips zum Schreiben ***Writing with Inseparable Prefix Verbs***

Inseparable prefix verbs are particularly useful for avoiding wordiness and for elevating your level of expression. For example, the sentence **Sie hat ihm das Studium möglich gemacht** is not incorrect, but it lacks the stylistic sophistication of **Sie hat ihm das Studium ermöglicht.** There is also nothing wrong with the statement **Wir sind in die falsche Richtung gefahren;** however, **Wir haben uns verfahren** says the same thing more concisely.

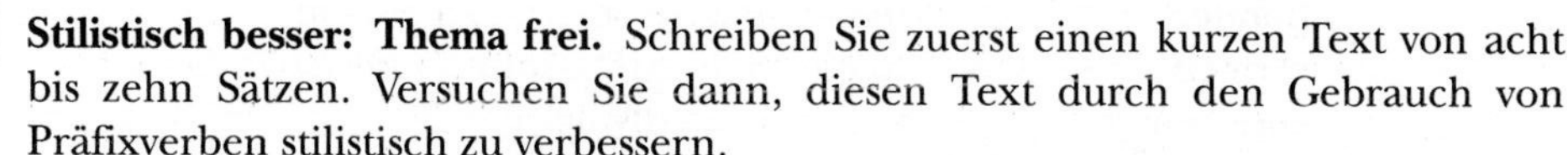

Stilistisch besser: Thema frei. Schreiben Sie zuerst einen kurzen Text von acht bis zehn Sätzen. Versuchen Sie dann, diesen Text durch den Gebrauch von Präfixverben stilistisch zu verbessern.

Wortschatz 29

arbeiten	erarbeiten
bearbeiten	verarbeiten

\+ *other verbs with* **be-, er-,** *and* **ver-** *prefixes*

Adding the prefixes **be-, er-,** and **ver-** to the verbs below changes their meaning as follows.[1]

1. **arbeiten**	to work
bearbeiten	to cultivate, work on; to treat
erarbeiten	to acquire through work
verarbeiten	to manufacture, process a *(raw)* material
2. **fahren**	to go, travel
befahren	to travel, to drive on or through something
erfahren	to find out, hear, discover, learn; to experience
sich verfahren	to take the wrong route, get lost
3. **greifen**	to seize, grasp, grab
begreifen	to comprehend, understand
ergreifen	to seize, take hold of; to touch deeply
4. **halten**	to hold (*see also* Wortschatz 15)
behalten	to keep, retain
erhalten	to receive (*see* Wortschatz 10)
sich verhalten	to (re)act, behave (*see* Wortschatz 20)
5. **kennen**	to know, be familiar with
bekennen	to confess, acknowledge, avow
erkennen	to recognize, make out, identify
verkennen	to mistake, fail to recognize correctly
6. **kommen**	to come
bekommen	to receive, get (*see* Wortschatz 10)
verkommen	to decay, go to ruin
7. **raten**	to advise, counsel; to take a guess
beraten	to advise, give advice to a person
erraten	to correctly guess, solve *(a riddle)*
verraten	to betray; to divulge
8. **schreiben**	to write
beschreiben	to describe
verschreiben	to prescribe *(medicine);* to miswrite *(a word)*
9. **setzen**	to set
besetzen	to occupy
ersetzen	to replace
versetzen	to transfer *(someone),* transplant *(plants)*

1. These definitions are not comprehensive; they cover only the most basic meanings of these verbs.

10.	**sprechen**	to speak
	besprechen	to discuss
	versprechen	to promise
	sich versprechen	to misspeak, use the wrong word
11.	**stehen**	to stand
	bestehen	to pass *(an examination),* survive an encounter
	erstehen	to buy, acquire *(at an auction)*
	verstehen	to understand
12.	**treten**	to step
	betreten	to set foot in / on, enter
	vertreten	to represent, act on behalf of; to advocate an intellectual position

ÜBUNGEN

A **Anders ausdrücken.** Setzen Sie das passende Verb ein.

1. Sie hat das Examen mit großem Erfolg ____ .
   Ich habe diese alte Lampe auf einer Auktion ____ .
2. Ich ____ den Standpunkt, daß es keine Todesstrafe *(capital punishment)* geben sollte.
   Den Rasen bitte nicht ____ !
3. Ich ____ nicht, wie man so etwas tun kann.
   Als das Feuer ausbrach, wurden viele Leute von Panik ____ .
4. Benedict Arnold hat sein Land ____ .
   Dreimal darfst du ____ , was ich dir zum Geburtstag schenke.
5. Wir haben seine gute Absicht *(intention)* leider ____ .
   Nach dem Unfall war Juliane so verändert, daß man sie kaum noch ____ konnte.
6. Meine Schwester wurde in eine andere Abteilung *(department)* in der Firma ____ .
   Heutzutage kann man eine kranke Niere *(kidney)* durch eine gesunde Niere ____ .
7. Durch Fleiß hat mein Bruder sich eine bessere Stelle ____ .
   In dieser Fabrik wird Leder zu Handtaschen ____ .
   Wenn man einen neuen Garten anlegt *(put in),* soll man vorher den Boden gut ____ .

B **Aussagen.** Schreiben Sie Beispielsätze mit den folgenden Wortpaaren.

Beispiel: besprechen / versprechen
Wir müssen das Problem noch besprechen.
Er hat ihr Liebe und Treue versprochen.

1. befahren / erfahren
2. betreten / vertreten
3. bekennen / erkennen
4. besetzen / ersetzen

Zusammenfassung 29

Rules to Remember

1. Separable prefixes separate from their verbs when these verbs are in first or second position in main clauses (**Sie geht am Abend aus**).
2. Separable prefixes do not separate from verb forms in final position (**Sie ist am Abend ausgegangen**). This includes all verb forms in subordinate clauses (. . . **daß sie am Abend ausgeht**).
3. Inseparable prefixes do not separate from their verbs.
4. Verbs with inseparable prefixes have no **ge-** in the past participle (**hat bearbeitet; hat verstanden**).
5. The three most common inseparable prefixes are **be-**, **er-**, and **ver-**. Other inseparable prefixes include **emp-**, **ent-**, **ge-**, **miß-**, and **zer-**.
6. The prefixes **durch-**, **hinter-**, **über-**, **um-**, **unter-**, **wider-**, and **wieder-** can be used either separably or inseparably, depending upon the verb and the intended meaning.

Activities

1 **One verb, many prefixes.** Prefixes are terrific vocabulary builders. Take a common strong verb. How many different separable and inseparable verbs do you think you can generate to combine with this verb? Write out a list, then look these verbs up in a German-English dictionary to see if they exist and what their meanings are. Present your verb and its many prefixes to the class. Some particularly good verbs for this activity are **brechen, fahren, fallen, gehen, halten, kommen, lassen, nehmen, schlagen, schreiben, sehen, sprechen, tragen, treten,** and **ziehen.**[2]

2 **Another verb, many prefixes.** Do Activity 1 using a very common weak verb such as **bauen, drücken, kaufen, machen, sagen, setzen, spielen,** or **stellen.**

3 **One prefix, many verbs.** Pick a separable prefix indicating direction (**ab, an, auf, aus, ein,** etc.). Generate a list of fifteen verbs (weak or strong) that can be combined with this prefix. What do you think each verb might mean? Check these verbs afterwards in a dictionary.

---

2. An excellent book of strong verbs and prefixes for advanced learners is Kläre Meil's *ABC der starken Verben,* Max Hueber Verlag, Munich. The first of many editions of this volume appeared in 1962. See also Kläre Meil and Margit Arndt's *ABC der schwachen Verben,* Hueber Verlag, latest edition.

4 **Prefix verbs in texts.** Pick two pages of a German text you have been reading and underline all *inseparable* verbs you find. Using the guidelines in this chapter, analyse each verb as to how the prefix helps determine its meaning.

5 **Prefixes in disguise.** Prefix combinations are not limited to verbs. Pick two pages of a German text you have been reading and underline all the words other than verbs (nouns, adjectives, or adverbs) that have separable or inseparable prefixes. Analyse how the prefixes help create the meanings of these words. Explain three of your words to the rest of the class.

6 **Working with a text.** Go through an issue of a German weekly newspaper such as the overseas edition of *Die Zeit*. Note five headlines containing separable or inseparable prefixes. Present your headlines to the class and see if they can guess the meanings of the headlines without looking up any words.

30 Prepositions as Verbal Complements

30.1 Prepositional Complements to Verbs

A. *Prepositional Phrases*

1. German verbs often complete their meaning with an additional sentence element. The most common verbal complements are other verbs, direct objects, and prepositional phrases. In the case of prepositional phrases, the preposition is not always what one might suspect on the basis of English usage. By way of illustration, the usual English equivalent for **an** is *on, at,* or *to* (see 10.3). Yet in the examples below, its English equivalents are quite different; the choice of **an** is determined by what this preposition conveys in combination with these particular verbs.

Sie denkt **an** ihre Mutter.	*She is thinking **of** her mother.*
Ich leide **an** Schlaflosigkeit.	*I am suffering **from** sleeplessness.*

2. In some instances, verbs may have a direct or indirect object *and* a prepositional complement.

Ich erkenne **ihn an seiner Stimme.**	*I recognize him by his voice.*
Sie hindert **mich am Arbeiten.**	*She is hindering me from working.*

B. *Prepositional* da-*Compounds*

When the prepositional object is expressed as a subordinate clause or an infinitive clause, a prepositional **da**-compound is used to link the verb with this object clause (see 19.2C).

Ich leide **daran,** daß ich nicht schlafen kann.	*I suffer from not being able to sleep.*

Sie denkt **daran,** ihrer Mutter zu schreiben. — *She thinks about writing to her mother.*

Almost all of the verbs in the next section can occur with **da**-compounds. Some occur more often with **da**-compounds than with nouns and pronouns.

30.2 Prepositions with Particular Verbs

A. An

Depending upon the verb with which it is used, **an** can govern either the accusative or dative case. Common examples include:

Accusative

denken an	*to think of*
jmdn. erinnern an	*to remind someone of*
sich erinnern an	*to remember*
sich gewöhnen an	*to get accustomed to*
glauben an	*to believe in*
grenzen an	*to border on*
sich richten an	*to direct (a comment or question) at*
sich wenden an	*to turn to, appeal to*

Dative

arbeiten an	*to work on / at*
jmdn. erkennen an	*to recognize s.o. by*
sich freuen an	*to delight in*
jmdn. hindern an	*to hinder / prevent s.o. from (doing)*
leiden an	*to suffer from*
sterben an	*to die of / from*
zweifeln an	*to doubt*

B. Auf

Auf occurs with a considerable number of verbs expressing the idea of physically or mentally looking or aiming at or towards something. In such usage, it almost always governs the accusative. Common examples include:

Accusative

achten auf	*to pay heed to*
antworten auf	*to answer, respond to*
aufpassen auf	*to keep an eye on, watch out for*
sich beschränken auf	*to limit oneself to*
sich beziehen auf	*to refer to*
blicken auf	*to glance at*
hoffen auf	*to hope for*
hören auf	*to listen to, heed*
sich konzentrieren auf	*to concentrate on*
reagieren auf	*to react to*
schießen auf	*to shoot at*
trinken auf	*to drink to*
vertrauen auf	*to trust in*
sich verlassen auf	*to rely upon*

sich freuen auf	*to look forward to* (see also **über,** 30.2H)	verzichten auf	*to forgo, renounce*
		warten auf	*to wait for*
(jmdn.) hinweisen auf	*to refer (s.o.) to*	zeigen auf	*to point to / at*

Dative

beruhen auf	*to be based upon*	bestehen auf	*to insist upon*

C. Aus

Aus is not nearly as common as **an** and **auf** in prepositional complements. It usually means *of* or *from,* and always governs the dative case. Common examples include:

Dative

bestehen aus	*to consist of*	werden aus	*to become of*
folgern aus	*to deduce from*		

D. Für

Für occurs with a number of common verbs and always governs the accusative case. Some common examples include:

Accusative

(jmdm.) danken für	*to thank (s.o.) for*	sich interessieren für	*to be interested in*
jmdn. / etwas halten für	*to regard s.o. / s.th. as* (see **Wortschatz 11**)	sorgen für	*to provide for, look after*
		stimmen für	*to vote for*
sich entscheiden für	*to decide on* (see **Wortschatz 17**)		

E. In

In occurs in the accusative with a few verbs expressing coming or getting into a situation or state. It also occurs occasionally in the dative with certain verbs. Common examples include:

Accusative

einwilligen in	*to agree to*	sich verlieben in	*to fall in love with*
geraten in	*to get or fall into (danger, difficulty, etc.)*	sich vertiefen in	*to delve into, become engrossed with*

Dative

sich irren in	*to err, be mistaken in / about*	sich täuschen in	*to be mistaken about*

F. Mit

Used with verbs, **mit** usually means *with.* It governs the dative. Common examples include:

Dative

aufhören mit	*to stop doing, cease*	sich verabreden mit	*to make an appointment with*
sich befassen mit	*to deal with*	verkehren mit	*to associate with, mix with*
sich beschäftigen mit	*to occupy o.s. with*	sich vertragen mit	*to get along (well) with*
handeln mit	*to trade or deal in*		
rechnen mit	*to count on*		
telephonieren mit	*to speak on the phone with*		

G. Nach

1. **Nach** tends to be used after verbs of longing, inquiry, or reaching for. It governs the dative. Some common examples include:

Dative

beurteilen nach	*to judge by / according to how*	greifen nach	*to reach for*
sich erkundigen nach	*to inquire about / after*	schicken nach	*to send for*
(jmdn.) fragen nach	*to ask (s.o.) about*	schreien nach	*to scream for*
forschen nach	*to search for, investigate*	sich sehnen nach	*to long for*
		streben nach	*to strive for*
		suchen nach	*to search for*
		sich umsehen nach	*to look around for*

2. **Nach** is also used after some verbs of looking, sounding, smelling, and tasting. In these cases it means that something looks, smells, sounds, or tastes *like* it might be.

aussehen nach	*to look like (something will happen)*	riechen nach	*to smell like*
klingen nach	*to sound like*	schmecken nach	*to taste like*
		stinken nach	*to stink of*

H. Über

Über occurs with a large number of verbs of speaking (see **Wortschatz 27**) and usually expresses the idea of *about.* **Über** always governs the accusative in these instances. Common examples include:

Accusative

sich ärgern über	*to be annoyed about / at*	reden über (*or* von)	*to speak about*
sich beklagen über	*to complain about*	sich schämen über	*to be ashamed about*
berichten über	*to report about / on*	spotten über	*to joke about, ridicule*
sich beschweren über	*to complain about*	sprechen über (*or* von)	*to speak about*
diskutieren über	*to discuss, talk about*	staunen über	*to be amazed at*
sich einigen über	*to agree upon*		
sich freuen über (*compare* sich freuen auf, an)	*to be happy about* (see also **auf,** 30.2B)	(sich) streiten über	*to quarrel (with one another) about*
sich lustig machen über	*to make fun of*	sich unterhalten über	*to converse about*
nachdenken über	*to think about, ponder*		

I. Um

Um is used with a number of verbs, particularly with those describing activities where something is at stake or being requested. **Um** governs the accusative. Examples include:

Accusative

sich bemühen um	*to take pains with*	sich kümmern um	*to look after, bother about*
jmdn. beneiden um	*to envy s.o. for*	sich sorgen um	*to be anxious / worried about*
sich bewerben um	*to apply for*		
jmdn. bitten um	*to ask s.o. for, request*	spielen um	*to play for (stakes)*
jmdn. bringen um	*to deprive or cause s.o. to lose*[1]	wetten um	*to bet for (stakes)*
		es geht um	*it is a matter of* (see **Wortschatz 19**)
kämpfen um	*to fight for*		
kommen um	*to lose, be deprived of*	es handelt sich um	*it is a matter of* (see **Wortschatz 19**)

1. This verb is not to be confused with the verb **umbringen,** *to take a person's life.*

J. Von

Von occurs with a wide range of verbs. It governs the dative. Examples include:

Dative

jmdn. abhalten von	*to keep, prevent s.o. from (doing)*	handeln von	*to be about* (see **Wortschatz 19**)
abhängen von	*to depend upon*	leben von	*to live on*
jmdm. abraten von	*to advise (s.o.) against*	reden von (or über)	*to speak about*
berichten von (*or* über)	*to report on*	sprechen von	*to talk about*
sich erholen von	*to recover from*	sich unterscheiden von	*to differ from*
erzählen von (*or* über)	*to tell about*	etwas verlangen von	*to demand s.th. from / of*
etwas fordern von	*to demand s.th. of / from*	etwas verstehen von	*to understand s.th. about*
halten (viel) von	*to think highly of* (see **Wortschatz 11**)	etwas wissen von	*to know s.th. about*

K. Vor

Vor occurs primarily with verbs of fearing, respecting, and protecting. In such instances, **vor** always governs the dative. Common examples include:

Dative

Achtung / Respekt haben vor	*to have respect for*	jmdn. schützen vor	*to protect (s.o.) from*
Angst haben vor	*to have fear of*	(sich) verstecken vor	*to hide (o.s.) from*
erschrecken vor	*to shrink at, be frightened of*	(jmdn.) warnen vor	*to warn (s.o.) of / against*
fliehen vor	*to flee from*	zittern vor	*to tremble with / from (fear, cold, etc.)*
sich fürchten vor	*to fear, be afraid of*		
sich hüten vor	*to watch out for, be on guard against*		
schreien vor	*to scream with / out of*		

L. Zu

Zu is used with a wide variety of verbs. It usually means *to, to the point of doing,* or *for the purpose of.* **Zu** governs the dative. Common examples include:

Dative

jmdn. beglückwünschen zu	*to congratulate s.o. on*	etwas meinen zu	*to have an opinion about s.th.*
(etwas) beitragen zu	*to contribute (s.th.) to*	neigen zu	*to tend to/toward*
jmdn. bringen zu	*to bring s.o. to the point of*	passen zu	*to match, be suited to*
dienen zu	*to serve a purpose as*	(jmdm.) raten zu	*to advise (s.o.) to*
sich entschließen zu	*to decide to* (see **Wortschatz 17**)	jmdn. überreden zu	*to persuade s.o.*
führen zu	*to lead to*	werden zu	*to become, turn into*
jmdm. gratulieren zu	*to congratulate s.o. on*	zwingen zu	*to force, compel to*

* Übungen

A **Ähnliche Verben.** Welches Verb paßt wegen der Präposition nicht in die Reihe?

1. beneiden sich bemühen berichten bitten
2. sich verabreden sich verstecken sich vertragen sich beschäftigen
3. suchen schicken spielen streben
4. zeigen blicken reagieren zwingen
5. sich freuen sich ärgern sich beklagen sich erholen
6. staunen warnen fliehen sich fürchten
7. sich erinnern abhängen glauben denken
8. leben leiden sprechen etwas verstehen
9. sich entschließen sich entscheiden beitragen passen

B ***An, nach, von, vor* oder *zu*?** Bilden Sie Sätze.

Beispiel: sich verstecken / Dieb / Polizei
Der Dieb versteckte sich vor der Polizei.

1. streben / Schüler / bessere Noten
2. passen / Hemd / Anzug
3. neigen / Studenten / Faulheit / manchmal
4. schmecken / Wurst / Knoblauch *(garlic)*
5. sich erholen / der Spieler / Verletzungen

6. leiden / viele Menschen / Krebs *(cancer)*
7. sich hüten / Menschen / Infektionen / sollen
8. überreden / der Autohändler / Kunden / Kauf eines Autos
9. fragen / Sohn / das Befinden seiner Eltern
10. abhalten / Kinder / ihre Mutter / die Arbeit

C **Und Sie?** Machen Sie Aussagen über sich selbst. Verwenden Sie die Präpositionen **an, nach, von, vor** oder **zu.**

Beispiel: denken
Ich denke gern an meine Kindheit.

1. streben
2. sich fürchten
3. glauben
4. sich erinnern
5. verstehen
6. halten
7. suchen
8. neigen

D ***Auf, für, mit, über* oder *um*?** Bilden Sie Sätze.

Beispiel: kämpfen / Soldaten / die Stadt
Die Soldaten kämpfen um die Stadt.

1. sich einigen / die Politiker / das neue Staatsbudget
2. sorgen / Mütter / Kinder / sollen
3. nachdenken / wir / dein Vorschlag / werden
4. sich sorgen / Mutter / ihr krankes Kind
5. sich bewerben / der Kandidat / mehrere Stellen
6. sich freuen / alle Arbeiter / das Wochenende
7. trinken / Männer / die Gesundheit ihres Freundes
8. halten / ich / dieser Politiker / Vollidiot
9. schicken / der verletzte Autofahrer / Arzt
10. sich unterhalten / ich / andere Studenten / unser Kurs

E **Und Sie?** Machen Sie Aussagen über sich selbst oder andere Menschen. Verwenden Sie die Präpositionen **auf, für, mit, über** oder **um.**

Beispiel: sich konzentrieren
Ich muß mich besser auf mein Studium konzentrieren.

1. sich ärgern
2. sich verlassen
3. sich interessieren
4. sich beschäftigen
5. bitten
6. aufhören

7. halten
8. diskutieren

F **Was fehlt?** Ergänzen Sie die Sätze durch eine Konstruktion mit **da** + Präposition.

Beispiel: Er strebte stets ____ , bessere Noten zu bekommen.
Er strebte stets danach, bessere Noten zu bekommen.

1. Sie neigt ____ , bei schweren Problemen zu schnell aufzugeben.
2. Ich zweifle ____ , ob ich die Prüfung bestehen kann.
3. Wer hat ihn ____ gebracht, uns zu helfen?
4. Manche Studenten haben Angst ____ , Prüfungen zu schreiben.
5. Darf ich Sie ____ bitten, diesen Platz frei zu halten?
6. Der Professor hat mich ____ abgeraten, seinen Kurs zu belegen.
7. Aber andere haben mir ____ geraten, den Kurs dieses Professors doch zu belegen.
8. Man sollte einen Menschen ____ beurteilen, wie er sich benimmt.
9. Ich möchte dich ____ erinnern, daß wir morgen keine Deutschstunde haben.

G **Wie geht es weiter?** Ergänzen Sie fünf Sätze durch eine Präposition mit einem Substantiv und fünf Sätze durch **da-** mit Präposition und einem Nebensatz.

Beispiel: Ich beglückwünsche . . .
Ich beglückwünsche Sie zum Geburtstag.
Ich beglückwünsche Sie dazu, daß Sie Ihr Studium jetzt beendet haben.

1. Der Wetterdienst warnt jetzt . . .
2. Hüten muß man sich im Winter . . .
3. Gute Studenten bemühen sich . . .
4. Ich weise Sie . . . hin, daß . . .
5. Ob wir morgen wandern gehen, hängt . . . ab
6. Manche Leute neigen . . .
7. Hm, es riecht hier . . .
8. Überreden möchte ich meine Freunde . . .
9. Niemand hindert dich . . .
10. Niemand zwingt dich . . .

* Anwendung

Verben im Kontext. Unterstreichen Sie in einem Text von etwa drei Seiten alle Präpositionen, die Ihrer Meinung nach mit bestimmten Verben idiomatisch verwendet werden. Sie werden vielleicht auch Verben finden, die nicht in diesem Kapitel vorkommen. Machen Sie eine Liste solcher Verben. Stellen Sie Ihre neuen Verben im Kurs vor.

* Schriftliches Thema

Tips zum Schreiben ***Categories of Writing***
Various types of writing require varying styles. What to say and how to say it normally dictate stylistic elements such as vocabulary, sentence structure, the use of metaphor, and other rhetorical devices. In general, you should attempt to write in a style (formal, informal, objective, rhetorical, argumentative, casual, exciting, etc.) befitting the topic or writing task, be it an objective analysis, a narrative, or an informal letter home. In all types of writing, the judicious use of verbs with prepositions often suggests an advanced level of linguistic and stylistic sophistication on the part of the author. Plan on using some verbs of this type in the writing task below.

Kategorien des Schreibens. Schreiben Sie über ein selbstgewähltes Thema, das in eine der folgenden Kategorien hineinpaßt. Schreiben Sie mindestens zwanzig Sätze.

KATEGORIEN	
analysieren	(ein Problem, einen Text, usw.)
argumentieren	(für oder gegen einen Plan, ein Gesetz, eine Situation, usw.)
berichten	(über ein Geschehen, einen Menschen, usw.)
beschreiben	(einen Ort, einen Gegenstand, einen Menschen, usw.)
erklären	(wie etwas gemacht wird, warum etwas geschehen ist, usw.)
erzählen	(eine Geschichte, eine Anekdote, einen Traum, ein Ereignis aus dem Leben, usw.)
überreden	(zu einer Handlung, einem Plan)
zusammenfassen	(ein literarisches Werk, einen Vortrag, einen Artikel in einer Zeitung oder einem Buch, eine Lebensphilosophie, usw.)

Wortschatz 30

es stellt sich heraus	es zeigt sich
sich herausstellen als	sich erweisen als

1. The expression **es stellt sich heraus** means that something *turns out to be, proves to be,* or *is seen to be.* The **es** anticipates the "something," which is expressed in a subsequent **daß-** or **ob-**clause. When the **es** comes after the conjugated verb, it is sometimes dropped.

Während der Untersuchung **stellte (es) sich heraus, daß** ein Zeuge falsch ausgesagt hatte.	*During the investigation it turned out that one witness had given false testimony.*

2. The verb **sich herausstellen (als)** may also be used with a subject other than **es.**

Unsere Versuche **stellten sich als** vergebens **heraus.**	*Our attempts proved to be in vain.*

3. The expression **es zeigt sich** is close in meaning to **es stellt sich heraus,** but sounds less formal.

Es wird **sich** noch **herausstellen** (*or* **zeigen**), ob sie sich richtig entschieden hat.	*It is still to be seen whether she made the right decision.*
Es zeigte sich (stellte sich heraus), daß er alles richtig gemacht hatte.	*It became evident that he had done everything correctly.*

4. The verb **sich erweisen als** conveys the same meaning as the expressions **sich herausstellen** and **sich zeigen,** but it usually does so with a specific subject rather than with an anticipatory **es** and a subsequent **daß**-clause.

COMPARE:

Das Gerücht **erweist sich als** falsch.	*The rumor turns out to be false.*
Es stellte sich heraus (*or* **zeigte sich**), daß das Gerücht falsch war.	*It turned out that the rumor was false.*
Lucy **erwies sich als** eine gute Freundin Beethovens.	*Lucy proved to be a good friend to Beethoven.*

ÜBUNG

Welche Ausdrücke passen am besten? Drücken Sie die Sätze durch Verben oder Ausdrücke aus **Wortschatz 30** anders aus.

Beispiel: Wir haben Karten gekauft, und jetzt erfahren wir, daß man das Konzert abgesagt hat.
Wir haben Karten gekauft, aber es stellt sich jetzt heraus, daß man das Konzert abgesagt hat.

1. Wir werden noch sehen, ob er recht hat oder nicht.
2. Zuerst hielt man die Rede der Politikerin für Unsinn, aber nachher wurde klar, daß sie sehr klug gesprochen hatte.
3. Liesl hat einen Computer gekauft, aber jetzt, wo sie ihn hat, braucht sie ihn nicht.
4. Wir haben für die Reise gespart, und jetzt erfahren wir, daß sie nicht mehr stattfinden wird.
5. Herr Voigt benahm sich wie ein Hauptmann *(captain),* aber später fand man heraus, daß er ein Betrüger *(imposter)* war.

Zusammenfassung 30

Rules to Remember

1. Many verbs must be followed by a specific preposition in idiomatic prepositional complements.
2. The rule determining case after two-way prepositions plays no role in idiomatic prepositional complements.
3. The prepositions **an** and **in** are followed by an accusative object after some verbs, a dative object after others.
4. The preposition **auf** almost always takes an accusative object in idiomatic prepositional complements.
5. The preposition **über** always takes an accusative object in idiomatic prepositional complements.
6. The preposition **vor** always takes a dative object in idiomatic prepositional complements.

Activities

1 **Brainstorming.** Working in small groups, consider the following prepositions: **an, auf, nach, über, um, vor,** and **zu.** For each preposition, make a list of five verbs that can precede it. Form short model sentences using each verb.

2 **Using da-compounds.** Using the verbs and prepositions in Activity 1, form model sentences containing **da**-compounds.

3 **Verbs and their prepositions.** Write on a card or slip of paper ten to fifteen verbs that can be followed by various prepositions. Do not include the preposition. Exchange papers with a partner, who then writes sentences using your verbs and suitable prepositional complements.

APPENDIX 1

Capitalization and Punctuation

I. Capitalization[1]

German capitalization varies from English usage in the following instances.

A. *Nouns and Adjectives*

1. Nouns and words used as nouns are capitalized in German.[2]

der Tisch *the table (noun)*
das Ich *the ego (pronoun used as a noun)*
ein Reicher *a rich man (adjective used as a noun)*
Schlechtes *bad things (adjective used as a noun)*
eine Vier *a four (number used as a noun)*
das Schreiben *writing (verb used as a noun)*
das Für und Wider *the pros and cons (prepositions used as nouns)*
das große Aber *the big but (conjunction used as a noun)*

---

1. In late 1996, a reformed system of orthography and capitalization was ratified by officials of Germany, Austria, and Switzerland. Most of the reforms concern hyphenation, the capitalization of nouns in adverbial phrases, the spelling of borrowed words, and the use of the comma. As adopted, rules for using the comma are now liberalized considerably; for example, most infinitive phrases are no longer set off by commas. One significant spelling change concerns the **ß** and **ss.** Under the old system, **ß** was written after long vowels and **ss** after short vowels. However if **ss** occurred at the end of a word it was written as **ß**. Under the new system, **ss** is to be written after all short vowels, regardless of location and **ß** after all long vowels. Thus Germans will no longer write **daß** and **muß,** but rather **dass** and **muss.** Since there is no assurance German speakers will actually abide by these reforms, we have not included them in this appendix.
2. In a few, very common adverbial phrases, the noun is not capitalized.

Sagen Sie das bitte auf **deutsch.**	*Please say that in German.*
BUT:	
Sprechen Sie **Deutsch?**	*Do you speak German?*

2. Proper adjectives are not capitalized unless they occur in titles (see 13.2E).

deutsche Autos	*German cars*
die Österreichischen Bundesbahnen	*the Austrian Federal Railway System*

B. Pronouns

1. The formal pronoun **Sie (Ihnen)** is capitalized, but its reflexive **(sich)** is not. The pronoun **ich** is capitalized only when it begins a sentence (see 16.1).
2. All forms of the pronouns **du** and **ihr,** including the reflexives, are capitalized in letters (see *Letter-Writing, Appendix 2*).

II. Punctuation

The most important punctuation rules in German concern the use or omission of the comma.

A. Comma (das Komma, -s)

1. Dependent (subordinate) clauses are always set off by commas.

Sie weiß, daß ich nicht kommen kann. *(subordinate clause; see 11.3)*	*She knows that I cannot come.*
Wir denken, der Plan ist zu gefährlich. *(subordinate clause without a conjunction)*	*We think the plan is too dangerous.*
Die Frau, die uns helfen könnte, ist nicht hier. *(relative clause, see 26.2)*	*The woman who could help us is not here.*
Er fragt, ob wir mitgehen wollen. *(indirect question; see 15.3)*	*He asks whether we want to go along.*

2. Clauses, phrases, or words linked by the coordinating conjunctions **denn, aber,** and **sondern** are set off by commas (see 11.1).

Das Wetter ist schön, aber kalt.	*The weather is nice, but cold.*
Unser Haus ist nicht weiß, sondern grün.	*Our house is not white, but (rather) green.*

3. Clauses linked by **und** or **oder** are separated by a comma, unless they share a common element such as a subject or a verb (see 11.1).

COMPARE:

Heinrich ist Maler, und er lebt in Köln. *(no shared element)*	*Henry is a painter, and he lives in Cologne.*
Franz sitzt zu Hause und liest ein Buch. *(shared subject)*	*Franz is sitting at home and reading a book.*
Michelle liest ein Buch und Nicole eine Zeitung. *(shared verb)*	*Michelle is reading a book and Nicole, a newspaper.*

4. In German, a comma is not used before **oder** or **und** in a series, whereas in English it is optional.

An diesem Institut kannst du Deutsch, Französisch, Russisch oder Italienisch lernen.	*At this institute you can learn German, French, Russian, or Italian.*
Sie wachte auf, stellte den Wecker ab und ging ins Badezimmer.	*She woke up, turned off the alarm, and went into the bathroom.*

5. Infinitive clauses consisting of more than just **zu** + infinitive (see 18.1) are normally set off by commas (but see footnote 2 on p. 403).

COMPARE:

Wir versprechen zu helfen.	*We promise to help.*
Wir versprechen, euch zu helfen.	*We promise to help you.*

6. Infinitive clauses introduced by **um . . . zu, ohne . . . zu,** and **(an) statt . . . zu** are always set off by commas regardless of length (see 18.2).

Wir gehen in die Stadt, um zu essen.	*We are going downtown (in order) to eat.*

7. Words in apposition are set off by commas.

Herr Castorp, der Kollege meines Vaters, besuchte uns oft.	*Mr. Castorp, my father's colleague, often visited us.*
Er war der Sohn Friedrichs des Ersten, König von Preußen.	*He was the son of Frederick the First, King of Prussia.*

8. Adverbs and adverbial phrases at the beginning of a sentence are not set off by a comma, as they may be in English (see 24.4).

Leider habe ich meinen Führerschein nicht mit.	*Unfortunately, I don't have my driver's license with me.*

9. The comma is used as a decimal point (see 22.1B).

6,5 (sechs Komma fünf)	*6.5 (six point five)*

10. Commas are not used to separate sets of digits in large numbers; German uses either periods or spaces (see 22.1B).

20 000 or 20.000 = 20,000

B. Other Punctuation Marks

1. A period **(der Punkt, -e)** is used with numerals to indicate an ordinal number + ending (see 22.2B).

   den 5. Juli (den fünften Juli) — *the fifth of July*

2. An exclamation point **(das Ausrufezeichen, -)** is occasionally used after a salutation in a letter. It is also used after emphatic imperatives (see 6.2B).

   Liebe Mutter! — *Dear Mother,*

   Seien Sie bitte ruhig! — *Please be calm!*

3. A question mark **(das Fragezeichen, -)** is used after questions, as in English.

4. Direct quotations (see 27.1) are preceded by a colon **(der Doppelpunkt, -e)** and enclosed by quotation marks (**die Anführungszeichen** [*pl.*]). In print and in handwriting, the initial quotation mark appears at the bottom of the line, while the final quotation mark is at the top of the line. Since computers and typewriters do not have the lower quotation marks, they put both marks above the line. The final quotation mark precedes a comma, but it follows a period.

   Sisyphus sagte: „Es ist hoffnungslos." — *Sisyphus said, "It is hopeless."*

   „Ich komme nicht", sagte sie. — *"I am not coming," she said.*

5. A hyphen **(der Bindestrich, -e)** is used to divide words at the end of a line. It is also used to indicate an omitted element common to two compound nouns in a pair.

   eine Nacht- und Nebelaktion (eine Nachtaktion und eine Nebelaktion) — *an operation under the cover of night and fog*

   Stadt- und Landbewohner (Stadtbewohner und Landbewohner) — *city and country dwellers*

6. A semicolon **(das Semikolon)** is seldom used in German.

APPENDIX 2

Letter-Writing

I. Formal Letters

In more formal correspondence, the heading, salutation, and closing are rather prescribed.

Hans-Jörg Möller

Ainmillerstraße 5
D-80801 München
13. November 19. .

(An)
Herrn / Frau S. Markstädter
Süddeutsche Zeitung
Sendlinger Straße 80
D-80331 München

Possible salutations:

Sehr geehrte Herren,
Sehr geehrter Herr (Dr.) Markstädter,
Sehr verehrte Frau (Dr.) Markstädter,

in der Wochenendausgabe Ihrer Zeitung vom 3. November 19. . stand ein Artikel über . . .

Mit freundlichen Grüßen

II. Informal Letters

In informal letters, the place and date are given in more abbreviated form, and there are also various choices for the salutation and the concluding sign-off.

Fulda, (den) 15. Oktober 19. .
OR: Fulda, 15.10.19. .

Common salutations:

Liebe Frau Schwarzenberger,
Lieber Horst,
Lieber Siegfried, liebe Ingrid,
Liebe Freunde,

vielen Dank für Deinen / Euren Brief. Es freut mich, daß Du / Ihr bald Deinen / Euren . . .

Sample closings (from more formal to less formal):

Mit freundlichen Grüßen

Herzliche Grüße
Dein / Euer

Herzlichst
Deine / Euere

III. *Points to Note* (See sample letters.)

1. In German dates, the day is always given before the month.
2. In addresses, the house number follows the street name.
3. The title **Herrn** is an accusative object of the preposition **an.** The accusative form is retained in addresses even if **an** is omitted.
4. The *D* before the zip code stands for Germany. Austria is *A,* and Switzerland is *CH.*
5. Salutations are normally followed by a comma; the first sentence of the letter begins with a lower-case letter. Salutations can also be followed by an exclamation point instead of a comma; in such instances, the first sentence of the letter begins with a capital letter.

   Liebe Freunde!
   Es hat mich sehr gefreut . . .

6. All forms of the pronouns **du** and **ihr,** including the reflexives, are capitalized.
7. There is no comma after the closing.
8. There are no indentations until the closing.

APPENDIX 3

Cognates

Both English and German belong to the Germanic branch of the Indo-European language family. Many words in both languages derive from a common root word and are called *cognates.* Sometimes such words have maintained a similar spelling and meaning in both languages and are quite obvious: **das Wort** *(word),* **finden** *(to find).* Frequently, however, the related meanings have diverged or become obscured over the centuries: **das Geld** *(money;* related cognate: *yield),* **schmerzen** *(to hurt, to pain;* related cognate: *to smart).*

One important linguistic development separating German from English is a shift in consonants known as the "second sound shift" **(die zweite Lautverschiebung).** Knowing the relationships between consonants in the two languages can help in identifying cognates and can make their meanings easier to remember.

Consonant Relationships

German	***English***	***Example***
t, tt	d	**Tür** door; **anstatt** instead
d	th	**drei** three; **Erde** earth
s, ss, ß	t	**das** that; **was** what
		essen eat; **lassen** let
		Fuß foot; **weiß** white
z, tz	t[1]	**zwanzig** twenty; **Herz** heart
		Katze cat; **sitzen** sit
b	v	**sieben** seven; **geben** give
ch	gh	**Licht** light; **lachen** laugh
ch	k	**brechen** break; **Woche** week
f, ff, pf	p(p)	**helfen** help; **hoffen** hope
		Apfel apple; **Pfeife** pipe
g	y	**sagen** say; **Weg** way
mm	mb	**Kammer** chamber; **Lamm** lamb

1. In *st* combinations, the consonant *t* remains the same in both languages: ***Sturm*** *(storm).*

German	English	Example
sch	sh	**Fleisch** flesh; **scharf** sharp
schl	sl	**schlafen** sleep
schm	sm	**Schmied** smith
schn	sn	**Schnee** snow
schw	sw	**schwimmen** swim

If you are trying to guess the meaning of a possible cognate, first try making one of the above consonant changes, retaining the German root vowels. Then pronounce the new word in German. Does it sound at all like an English word? Try substituting various similar vowels, and use your imagination.

Zeitung (newspaper) → Teidung → *tiding(s)*[2]
sterben (to die) → sterven → *to starve*[3]

Can you deduce the English meanings of the following words? The answers are at the bottom of page 412.

Beispiel: Herd *hearth (stove)*

leicht ***(easy)***

1. Seite
2. Pfund
3. Teufel
4. Heim(at)stadt
5. dachte
6. Zunge
7. grüßen
8. leicht
9. durch
10. Dieb
11. Auge
12. Feder
13. Witz
14. recht
15. Sicht
16. Harfe
17. anders
18. Kamm
19. gleiten
20. schmelzen

nicht mehr so leicht

1. Wert *(value)*
2. Zug
3. treten *(step)*
4. Bude *(stall)*
5. Knabe *(youth)*
6. Knecht *(farmhand, servant)*
7. Zweig *(branch)*
8. Frachter *(type of boat)*
9. Flasche
10. kurz
11. heben *(lift, elevate)*
12. teuer *(expensive)*
13. eben
14. bieten
15. Zoll *(customs)*
16. Becher *(goblet)*
17. Griff *(handle)*
18. suchte
19. Tier
20. Macht *(power, strength)*

---

2. The word **Zeitung** originally meant **news** in German. With the introduction of newspapers in the seventeenth century, the word took on its present-day meaning. The word *tiding* is preserved in English phrases such as "Christmas tidings" and "tidings of great joy."
3. In former times, starvation was one of the most common causes of death; to starve was to die.

recht schwierig

1. eitel *(vain)*
2. fahren
3. kühn *(bold)*
4. Zimmer
5. Schmutz *(dirt)*
6. Tal *(valley)*
7. Ziel *(goal)*
8. Herbst
9. riechen *(smell)*
10. laufen
11. teilen *(divide, distribute)*
12. wachsen
13. traurig
14. Mut *(courage)*
15. gleich
16. zwischen
17. Zaun *(fence)*
18. Dach *(roof)*
19. Baum
20. werfen *(throw)*

Answers **leicht:** 1. side 2. pound 3. devil 4. homestead 5. thought 6. tongue 7. greet 8. light 9. through 10. thief 11. blood 12. feather 13. wit 14. right 15. sight 16. harp 17. other 18. comb 19. glide 20. smelt

Answers **nicht mehr so leicht:** 1. worth 2. tug 3. tread 4. booth 5. knave 6. knight 7. twig 8. freighter 9. flask 10. curt 11. heave 12. dear 13. even 14. bid 15. toll 16. beaker 17. grip 18. sought 19. deer 20. might

Answers **recht schwierig:** 1. idle 2. fare (ye well) 3. keen 4. timber 5. smut 6. dale 7. (un)til 8. harvest 9. reek 10. lope 11. deal 12. waxing (moon) 13. dreary 14. mood 15. like 16. twixt 17. town (village with a wall around it) 18. thatch 19. boom (To "lower the boom" originally meant to let down the wooden barrier on a toll road, thus preventing travelers from proceeding without paying.) 20. warp

APPENDIX 4

Strong and Irregular Verbs

The boldfaced verbs are fairly common and should be learned for active use at the intermediate level. The other verbs are less frequent, but not uncommon. Irregular third person singular forms are indicated in parentheses after the infinitive. Verbs requiring the auxiliary **sein** rather than **haben** are indicated by the word **ist** before the past participle. Past participles preceded by **ist / hat** are normally intransitive, but they can be used transitively with the auxiliary **haben.**

Infinitive (3rd. Pers. Sing.)	*Simple Past*		*Past Participle*	*Subjunctive II*	*Meaning*
backen (bäckt)	buk / backte		gebacken	büke	*to bake*
befehlen (befiehlt)	befahl		befohlen	beföhle / befähle	*to command*
beginnen	**begann**		**begonnen**	begänne / begönne	*to begin*
beißen	**biß**		**gebissen**	bisse	*to bite*
betrügen	betrog		betrogen	betröge	*to deceive, cheat*
beweisen	bewies		bewiesen	bewiese	*to prove*
biegen	**bog**		**gebogen**	böge	*to bend*
bieten	**bot**		**geboten**	böte	*to offer*
binden	**band**		**gebunden**	bände	*to bind, tie*
bitten	**bat**		**gebeten**	bäte	*to ask (for), request*
blasen (bläst)	blies		geblasen	bliese	*to blow*
bleiben	**blieb**	ist	**geblieben**	bliebe	*to stay, remain*
braten (brät)	briet		gebraten	briete	*to roast, fry*
brechen (bricht)	**brach**		**gebrochen**	bräche	*to break*
brennen	**brannte**		**gebrannt**	brennte	*to burn*
bringen	**brachte**		**gebracht**	brächte	*to bring*
denken	**dachte**		**gedacht**	dächte	*to think*
dringen	drang	ist	gedrungen	dränge	*to penetrate, surge into*

Infinitive (3rd. Pers. Sing.)	*Simple Past*	*Past Participle*	*Subjunctive II*	*Meaning*
empfangen (empfängt)	empfing	empfangen	empfinge	*to receive*
empfehlen (empfiehlt)	**empfahl**	**empfohlen**	empföhle / empfähle	*to recommend*
empfinden	empfand	empfunden	empfände	*to feel*
erlöschen (erlischt)	erlosch	ist erloschen	erlösche	*to go out, become extinguished*
erschrecken (erschrickt)	erschrak	ist erschrocken	erschräke	*to be startled*
essen (ißt)	**aß**	**gegessen**	äße	*to eat*
fahren (fährt)	**fuhr**	**ist / hat gefahren**	führe	*to travel; to drive*
fallen (fällt)	**fiel**	**ist gefallen**	fiele	*to fall*
fangen (fängt)	**fing**	**gefangen**	finge	*to catch*
finden	**fand**	**gefunden**	fände	*to find*
fliegen	**flog**	**ist / hat geflogen**	flöge	*to fly*
fliehen	**floh**	**ist geflohen**	flöhe	*to flee*
fließen	**floß**	**ist geflossen**	flösse	*to flow*
fressen (frißt)	**fraß**	**gefressen**	fräße	*to eat (of animals)*
frieren	**fror**	**gefroren**	fröre	*to freeze, be cold*
gebären (gebiert)	gebar	geboren	gebäre	*to give birth*
geben (gibt)	**gab**	**gegeben**	gäbe	*to give*
gehen	**ging**	**ist gegangen**	ginge	*to go*
gelingen	**gelang**	**ist gelungen**	gelänge	*to succeed*
gelten (gilt)	galt	gegolten	gölte / gälte	*to be valid*
genießen	**genoß**	**genossen**	genösse	*to enjoy*
geraten (gerät)	geriet	geraten	geriete	*to fall into, get into*
geschehen (geschieht)	**geschah**	**ist geschehen**	geschähe	*to happen*
gewinnen	**gewann**	**gewonnen**	gewönne / gewänne	*to win*
gießen	**goß**	**gegossen**	gösse	*to pour*
gleichen	glich	geglichen	gliche	*to resemble; to equal*
gleiten	glitt	ist geglitten	glitte	*to glide, slide*
graben (gräbt)	**grub**	**gegraben**	grübe	*to dig*
greifen	**griff**	**gegriffen**	griffe	*to grip, grab, seize*
haben (hat)	**hatte**	**gehabt**	hätte	*to have*
halten (hält)	**hielt**	**gehalten**	hielte	*to hold; to stop*

Infinitive (3rd. Pers. Sing.)	*Simple Past*		*Past Participle*	*Subjunctive II*	*Meaning*
hängen	**hing**		**gehangen**	hinge	*to hang* (intransitive)
hauen	hieb / haute		gehauen	hiebe	*to hew, cut; to spank*
heben	hob		gehoben	höbe	*to lift*
heißen	**hieß**		**geheißen**	hieße	*to be called; to bid (do)*
helfen (hilft)	**half**		**geholfen**	hülfe	*to help*
kennen	**kannte**		**gekannt**	kennte	*to know, be acquainted with*
klingen	**klang**		**geklungen**	klänge	*to sound*
kneifen	kniff		gekniffen	kniffe	*to pinch*
kommen	**kam**	**ist**	**gekommen**	käme	*to come*
kriechen	kroch	ist	gekrochen	kröche	*to crawl*
laden (lädt)	**lud**		**geladen**	lüde	*to load*
lassen (läßt)	**ließ**		**gelassen**	ließe	*to let, leave*
laufen (läuft)	**lief**	**ist**	**gelaufen**	liefe	*to run, walk*
leiden	**litt**		**gelitten**	litte	*to suffer*
leihen	**lieh**		**geliehen**	liehe	*to lend*
lesen (liest)	**las**		**gelesen**	läse	*to read*
liegen	**lag**		**gelegen**	läge	*to lie, be situated*
lügen	**log**		**gelogen**	löge	*to (tell a) lie*
meiden	mied		gemieden	miede	*to avoid*
messen (mißt)	maß		gemessen	mäße	*to measure*
nehmen (nimmt)	**nahm**		**genommen**	nähme	*to take*
nennen	**nannte**		**genannt**	nennte	*to name, call*
pfeifen	**pfiff**		**gepfiffen**	pfiffe	*to whistle*
raten (rät)	riet		geraten	riete	*to advise; to (take a) guess*
reiben	rieb		gerieben	riebe	*to rub*
reißen	**riß**	**ist**	**gerissen**	risse	*to tear*
reiten	**ritt**	**ist / hat**	**geritten**	ritte	*to ride (on an animal)*
rennen	**rannte**	**ist**	**gerannt**	rennte	*to run*
riechen	**roch**		**gerochen**	röche	*to smell*
rinnen	rann	ist	geronnen	rönne / ränne	*to run, flow, trickle*
rufen	**rief**		**gerufen**	riefe	*to call*
saufen (säuft)	soff		gesoffen	söffe	*to drink (of animals)*

Infinitive (3rd. Pers. Sing.)	*Simple Past*	*Past Participle*	*Subjunctive II*	*Meaning*
saugen	sog / saugte	gesogen / gesaugt	söge	*to suck*
schaffen	schuf	geschaffen	schüfe	*to create*
	schaffte	geschafft	schaffte	*to do, accomplish*
scheiden	schied	geschieden	schiede	*to separate*
scheinen	schien	geschienen	schiene	*to shine; to seem*
schelten (schilt)	schalt	gescholten	schölte	*to scold*
schieben	**schob**	**geschoben**	schöbe	*to shove, push*
schießen	**schoß**	**geschossen**	schösse	*to shoot*
schlafen (schläft)	**schlief**	**geschlafen**	schliefe	*to sleep*
schlagen (schlägt)	**schlug**	**geschlagen**	schlüge	*to strike, hit, beat*
schleichen	schlich	ist geschlichen	schliche	*to creep, sneak*
schließen	**schloß**	**geschlossen**	schlösse	*to close*
schmeißen	schmiß	geschmissen	schmisse	*to fling, hurl*
schmelzen (schmilzt)	schmolz	ist / hat geschmolzen	schmölze	*to melt*
schneiden	**schnitt**	**geschnitten**	schnitte	*to cut*
schreiben	**schrieb**	**geschrieben**	schriebe	*to write*
schreien	**schrie**	**geschrie(e)n**	schriee	*to shout, scream*
schreiten	schritt	ist geschritten	schritte	*to stride*
schweigen	**schwieg**	**geschwiegen**	schwiege	*to be silent*
schwellen	schwoll	ist geschwollen	schwölle	*to swell*
schwimmen	**schwamm**	**hat / ist**[1] **geschwommen**	schwömme / schwämme	*to swim*
schwingen	schwang	geschwungen	schwänge	*to swing*
schwören	schwur / schwor	geschworen	schwüre	*to swear, vow*
sehen (sieht)	**sah**	**gesehen**	sähe	*to see*
sein (ist)	**war**	**ist gewesen**	wäre	*to be*
senden	**sandte**	**gesandt**	sendete	*to send*
	sendete	**gesendet**		*to transmit*
singen	**sang**	**gesungen**	sänge	*to sing*
sinken	**sank**	**ist gesunken**	sänke	*to sink*
sinnen	sann	gesonnen	sänne / sönne	*to think, reflect; to plot*
sitzen	**saß**	**gesessen**	säße	*to sit*

1. The use of **sein** as the auxiliary for **schwimmen** is characteristically Southern German, Austrian, or Swiss.

Infinitive (3rd. Pers. Sing.)	*Simple Past*		*Past Participle*	*Subjunctive II*	*Meaning*
spinnen	spann		gesponnen	spönne / spänne	*to spin; to be crazy*
sprechen (spricht)	**sprach**		**gesprochen**	spräche	*to speak, talk*
springen	**sprang**		**gesprungen**	spränge	*to jump*
stechen (sticht)	stach		gestochen	stäche	*to prick, sting*
stehen	**stand**	**hat /ist**[2]	**gestanden**	stünde / stände	*to stand*
stehlen (stiehlt)	**stahl**		**gestohlen**	stähle / stöhle	*to steal*
steigen	**stieg**	**ist**	**gestiegen**	stiege	*to climb, rise*
sterben (stirbt)	**starb**	**ist**	**gestorben**	stürbe	*to die*
stinken	stank		gestunken	stänke	*to stink*
stoßen (stößt)	stieß		gestoßen	stieße	*to push*
streichen	strich		gestrichen	striche	*to stroke; to paint*
streiten	stritt		gestritten	stritte	*to quarrel*
tragen (trägt)	**trug**		**getragen**	trüge	*to carry; to wear*
treffen (trifft)	**traf**		**getroffen**	träfe	*to meet; to hit (the target)*
treiben	**trieb**		**getrieben**	triebe	*to drive (cattle); to pursue (an activity)*
treten (tritt)	**trat**	**ist / hat**	**getreten**	träte	*to step, tread; to kick*
trinken	**trank**		**getrunken**	tränke	*to drink*
tun	**tat**		**getan**	täte	*to do*
verbergen	verbarg		verborgen	verbürge / verbärge	*to hide, conceal*
verderben (verdirbt)	verdarb		verdorben	verdürbe	*to spoil*
vergessen (vergißt)	**vergaß**		**vergessen**	vergäße	*to forget*
verlieren	**verlor**		**verloren**	verlöre	*to lose*
verschlingen	verschlang		verschlungen	verschlänge	*to devour, gobble up*
verschwinden	**verschwand**	**ist**	**verschwunden**	verschwände	*to disappear*
verzeihen	verzieh		verziehen	verziehe	*to forgive, pardon*
wachsen (wächst)	**wuchs**	**ist**	**gewachsen**	wüchse	*to grow*
waschen (wäscht)	**wusch**		**gewaschen**	wüsche	*to wash*

2. The use of **sein** with **stehen** is common in Southern Germany, Austria, and Switzerland.

Infinitive (3rd. Pers. Sing.)	*Simple Past*	*Past Participle*	*Subjunctive II*	*Meaning*
weisen	wies	gewiesen	wiese	*to point*
wenden	**wandte**	**gewandt**	wendete	*to turn*
	wendete	**gewendet**		*to turn (inside out)*
werben (wirbt)	warb	geworben	würbe	*to recruit, solicit*
werden (wird)	**wurde**	**ist geworden**	würde	*to become*
werfen (wirft)	**warf**	**geworfen**	würfe	*to throw*
wiegen	wog	gewogen	wöge	*to weigh*
winden	wand	gewunden	wände	*to wind, twist*
wissen (weiß)	**wußte**	**gewußt**	wüßte	*to know*
ziehen	**zog**	**gezogen**	zöge	*to pull, draw*
		ist gezogen		*to go, move*
zwingen	**zwang**	**gezwungen**	zwänge	*to force*

German-English Vocabulary

This vocabulary contains all words from the exercises and activities in this text except for pronouns, possessive adjectives, and numbers. Also not included are obvious cognates and words for which the English translation is provided in the text.

Nouns are listed with their plural endings: **die Auskunft, ¨e; das Messer, -.**

The genitive of weak nouns is given in parentheses before the plural: **der Experte, (-n), -n.**

Adjectival nouns are indicated as follows: **der Verwandte (ein Verwandter).**

Strong and irregular verbs are listed with their principal parts: **tragen (trägt), trug, getragen.** Strong verbs requiring the auxiliary **sein** are indicated by an **ist** before the participle: **kommen, kam, ist gekommen.** Weak verbs requiring the auxiliary **sein** are shown by **(ist)** after the infinitive: **passieren (ist).**

Separable prefixes are indicated by a raised dot: **ab·drehen.**

The following abbreviations are used:

acc.	accusative	*part.*	particle
adv.	adverb	*pl.*	plural
coll.	colloquial	*prep.*	preposition
coord. conj.	coordinating conjunction	*sing.*	singular
dat.	dative	*s.o.*	someone
fem.	feminine	*s.th.*	something
gen.	genitive	*sub. conj.*	subordinating conjunction
o.s.	oneself		

A

ab und zu now and then
ab·brechen (bricht ab), brach ab, abgebrochen to break off
ab·brennen, brannte ab, ist / hat abgebrannt to burn down
ab·bringen, brachte ab, abgebracht (von + *dat.***)** to divert from, dissuade from
ab·drehen to turn off
der Abend, -e evening; **abends** in the evening(s)
das Abendessen, - evening meal
das Abenteuer, - adventure
aber *(coord. conj.)* but; *(adv.)* however
ab·geben (gibt ab), gab ab, abgegeben to hand in
das Abitur graduation diploma from a German *Gymnasium*
ab·nehmen (nimmt ab), nahm ab, abgenommen to take off, lose weight
ab·reißen, riß ab, abgerissen to tear down
ab·sagen to cancel, call off; to decline *(an invitation)*
der Abschied, -e departure; **Abschied nehmen** to take one's leave
ab·schließen, schloß ab, abgeschlossen to lock up, shut; to conclude, complete
die Absicht, -en intention

ab•springen, sprang ab, ist abgesprungen to jump off
die Abtönungspartikel, -n modal ("flavoring") particle
sich ab•trocknen to dry oneself off
ab•warten to wait (*for something to happen*)
das Affenhirn, -e monkey's brain
ähneln *(dat.)* to resemble
aktuell of current interest, relevant
all- all
allerdings to be sure, by all means
alliiert allied
allmählich gradual(ly)
der Alltag everyday life
alltäglich everyday
die Alpen *(pl.)* Alps
als when, as; than
als ob as if
also thus, so, therefore
alt old
das Alter age
ältlich elderly
die Altstadt, ¨e old section of a city
amtieren to hold an office
sich amüsieren to have a good time, amuse o.s.
an *(prep. with acc. or dat.)* on (*vertical surface*), at, to
ander- other; **unter anderem** among other things
and(e)rerseits on the other hand
ändern to change (*s.th.*), modify; **sich ändern** to change
die Änderung, -en change
der Anfang, ¨e beginning; **am Anfang** in the beginning
an•fangen (fängt an), fing an, angefangen to begin, start
anfangs in / at the beginning
an•fassen to touch, take hold of
die Angabe, -n data, figure, statement
an•geben (gibt an), gab an, angegeben to indicate, give (*facts*); to brag
das Angebot, -e offer, bid
angeln to fish
angenehm pleasant, agreeable
der Angestellte (ein Angestellter) employee; *(fem.)* **die Angestellte**
an•greifen, griff an, angegriffen to attack
der Angriff, -e attack
die Angst, ¨e fear
an•halten (hält an), hielt an, angehalten to stop, bring to a stop
an•hören to hear, listen to; **sich** (*dat.*) **etwas an•hören** to listen to s.th.
an•kommen, kam an, ist angekommen to arrive; **an•kommen (auf** + *acc.*) to depend upon; **es kommt darauf an** it (all) depends
an•machen to turn on
die Annonce, -n ad, announcement
der Anorak, -s parka
an•probieren to try on
an•reden to address, speak to
an•regen to encourage, prompt
an•rufen, rief an, angerufen to call up, telephone
an•schalten to switch *or* turn on
an•sehen (sieht an), sah an, angesehen to see, look at; **sich** (*dat.*) **etwas an•sehen** to take a look at s.th.
die Ansicht, -en view, opinion
anstatt . . . zu instead of (doing); **anstatt daß** instead of (doing)
die Antwort, -en answer
antworten (auf + *acc.*) to answer
die Anweisung, -en instruction, direction
die Anwendung, -en application, use
an•ziehen, zog an, angezogen to dress; **sich an•ziehen** to get dressed
der Apfel, ¨ apple
die Arbeit, -en work, job; **arbeiten** to work
der Arbeiter, - worker
arbeitsam diligent, hard-working
das Arbeitsamt, ¨er employment office
die Arbeitskraft, ¨e worker; manpower
der Arbeitslohn, ¨e wage
die Arbeitsstelle, -n working place, job
der Arbeitstisch, -e desk
die Arbeitsweise, -n method of working
die Arche, -n ark
ärgern to annoy; **sich ärgern (über** + *acc.*) to be angry or annoyed with / about
arm poor
die Armut poverty
die Art, -en type, kind
der Arzt, ¨e doctor, physician; *(fem.)* **die Ärztin, -nen**
das Atomkraftwerk, -e nuclear plant
die Atomwaffe, -n atomic weapon
auch too, also; even
auch wenn even if
auf *(prep. with acc. or dat.)* on (*horizontal surface*), upon, at
auf einmal suddenly
auf•fressen (frißt auf), freß auf, aufgefressen to eat up (of beasts), devour
auf immer forever, for good
die Aufgabe, -n assignment, task
auf•halten (hält auf), hielt auf, aufgehalten to stop, halt; to detain, delay; **sich auf•halten** to stay, spend time
auf•hören to stop, cease
das Aufkommen rise
auf•legen to put *or* lay on
auf•machen to open
die Aufmerksamkeit, -en attention
auf•passen to watch out, pay attention
auf•räumen to clean *or* tidy up
auf•rufen, rief auf, aufgerufen to exhort, call upon, call up
der Aufsatz, ¨e composition

auf•schneiden, schnitt auf, aufgeschnitten to cut open
auf•schreiben, schrieb auf, aufgeschrieben to write *or* jot down
auf•stehen, stand auf, ist aufgestanden to get up, stand up
auf•stellen to put *or* set up
auf•wachen to wake up, awaken
auf•wachsen (wächst auf), wuchs auf, ist aufgewachsen to grow up
der Augenblick, -e moment
aus (*prep. with dat.*) out, out of, from
die Ausarbeitung completion, development
aus•brechen (bricht aus), brach aus, ist ausgebrochen to break out
der Ausdruck, ¨e expression; **zum Ausdruck bringen** to express
aus•drücken to express
der Ausflug, ¨e excursion; **einen Ausflug machen** to take an excursion
aus•führen to carry out
ausführlich in detail, detailed
aus•geben (gibt aus), gab aus, ausgegeben to spend (*money*)
aus•gehen, ging aus, ist ausgegangen to go out
die Auskunft, ¨e information
das Ausland abroad
der Ausländer, - foreigner; (*fem.*) **die Ausländerin, -nen**
aus•leihen, lieh aus, ausgeliehen to borrow; to lend out
aus•machen to turn off
aus•rechnen to calculate, figure out
die Ausrede, -n excuse
aus•reisen (ist) to leave (*a country*)
sich aus•ruhen to rest, take a rest
die Ausrüstung, -en outfit, equipment
die Aussage, -n statement
aus•schalten to switch *or* turn off
aus•sehen (sieht aus), sah aus, ausgesehen to look (like), appear
der Ausweis, -e identification (ID)
außer (*prep. with dat.*) except for, besides
außerdem moreover, in addition
außerhalb (*prep. with gen.*) outside of
äußern to express; **sich äußern** to express oneself *or* one's opinion
äußerst extremely
aus•sprechen (spricht aus), sprach aus, ausgesprochen to express, enunciate
aus•tauschen to exchange
aus•steigen, stieg aus, ist ausgestiegen to climb out, get out
aus•üben to practice (*a trade, profession, or activity*)
der Auswanderer, - emigrant
auswendig by heart, by memory
aus•zeichnen to honor, award a prize to s.o.
die Auszeichnung, -en award, distinction
aus•ziehen, zog aus, ausgezogen to undress (*s.o.*); **sich aus•ziehen** to get undressed
die Autobahn, -en expressway, superhighway
der Autoreifen, - automobile tire
die Autowerkstatt, ¨en automobile service shop

B

der Bach, ¨e brook, small stream
backen (bäckt), buk, gebacken to bake
der Backofen, ¨ oven
baden to bathe; **baden gehen** to go swimming
das Baggerschiff, -e dredging boat
die Bahn, -en track; railroad; **per Bahn** by rail
der Bahnhof, ¨e train station
bald soon
der Band, ¨e volume; **das Band, ¨er** tape, ribbon
die Bank, -en bank; **die Bank, ¨e** bench
das Bankkonto, -ten bank account
basteln to do handicrafts; to putter
der Bau, -ten building
bauen to build, construct
der Bauer, (-n), -n peasant, farmer; (*fem.*) **die Bäuerin, -nen** farmer's wife
der Bauernhof, ¨e farm
der Baum, ¨e tree
der Bauplan, ¨e construction plan
die Baustelle, -n construction site
bayerisch Bavarian
(das) Bayern Bavaria
die Bazille, -n germ
sich bedanken (bei + *dat.*) to express one's thanks to
die Bedeutung, -en meaning, significance, importance
bedürfen, bedarf, bedurft (*gen.*) to need
sich beeilen to hurry
beenden to end, complete, conclude
befahren (befährt), befuhr, befahren to travel *or* drive on *or* along
der Befehl, -e command
sich befinden, befand, befunden to be, to be located
befürchten to fear, suspect
begabt talented
begegnen (*dat.*) **(ist)** to meet, come across, encounter
die Begegnung, -en encounter
begeistert (von + *dat.*) enthusiastic about
begründen to provide a reason, substantiate
behaupten to claim, maintain

die Behauptung, -en assertion, claim
die Behörde, -n authority
bei *(prep. with dat.)* by, near, at; while
bei•bringen, brachte bei, beigebracht *(dat.)* to teach, impart knowledge
beid- both
das Bein, -e leg
das Beispiel, -e example; **zum Beispiel** (*abbrev.* **z.B.**) for example
beißen, biß, gebissen to bite
bei•tragen (trägt bei), trug bei, beigetragen (zu + *dat.*) to contribute to
bekannt familiar, known, well-known
der Bekannte (ein Bekannter) acquaintance; (*fem*) **die Bekannte**
bekannt•geben (gibt bekannt), gab bekannt, bekanntgegeben to announce, make public
bekennen, bekannte, bekannt to confess
bekommen, bekam, bekommen to get, receive
belegen (einen Kurs) to enroll *or* register (*for a course*)
beleuchtet illuminated
beliebt popular
bellen to bark
bemerken to observe, note
sich benehmen (benimmt), benahm, benommen to act, behave
benutzen to use
das Benzin gasoline
der *or* **das Bereich, -e** district, region; (*topic*) area
bereit (zu + *dat.*) ready for, prepared
bereuen to regret
der Berg, -e mountain
die Bergbahn, -en mountain cable car
das Bergmassiv, -e huge mountain
der Bergschuh, -e climbing boot
der Bericht, -e report
berichten to report
der Beruf, -e profession
beruflich occupational
sich beruhigen to calm down
berühmt famous, renowned
sich beschäftigen (mit + *dat.*) to occupy oneself with
beschäftigt occupied, busy
beschreiben, beschrieb, beschrieben to describe
die Beschreibung, -en description
sich beschweren (über + *acc.*) to complain about
beseitigen to remove, put an end to, clear away
besetzen to occupy
besichtigen to view, inspect
die Besichtigung, -en inspection; sightseeing
besiegen to conquer, overcome
besitzen, besaß, besessen to possess, own
der Besitzer, - owner
besonders especially
besser better
bestehen, bestand, bestanden to pass (*a course, test*); **bestehen (aus** + *dat.*) to consist of
besteigen, bestieg, bestiegen to ascend, climb (up)
bestellen to order
bestimmt definite; **bestimmter Artikel** definite article
der Besuch, -e visit
besuchen to visit
der Besucher, - visitor
betonen to emphasize, stress
der Betrag, ⸚e amount
betreiben, betrieb, betrieben to do, engage in
betreten (betritt), betrat, betreten to walk *or* step on *or* into
der Betrunkene (ein Betrunkener) drunk person; (*fem.*) **die Betrunkene**
sich betten to make a bed for o.s.
die Bevölkerung, -en population
bewegen to move (*s.o. or s.th.*); **sich bewegen** to move, stir
sich bewerben (bewirbt), bewarb, beworben (um + *acc.*) to apply for
die Bewertung, -en evaluation
der Bewohner, - dweller, inhabitant
bewundern to admire
bezahlen to pay for
bezweifeln to doubt
die Bibel, -n Bible
die Bibliothek, -en library
biegen, bog, gebogen to bend
die Biene, -n bee
der Bierdeckel, - beer coaster
bieten, bot, geboten to offer, bid
das Bild, -er picture
bilden to form, shape, construct; to constitute
die Bildgeschichte, -n picture story
billig cheap
bis *(prep. with acc.)* until; (*sub. conj.*) until
bisherig prior, previous
bissig biting
bißchen: ein bißchen a bit, a little bit
der Bittbrief, -e letter of request
bitte please; you're welcome (*in response to thanks*)
die Bitte, -n request
blaß pale
das Blatt, ⸚er leaf; sheet (*of paper*)
blau blue; **blaues Auge** black eye
bleiben, blieb, ist geblieben to remain, stay
der Bleistift, -e pencil
die Blume, -n flower
die Bluse, -n blouse
bluten bleed
der Bluthochdruck high blood pressure

der Boden, ⸚ ground, earth, soil; floor
der Bodensee Lake Constance (*in Southern Germany*)
der Bogen, - *or* ⸚ bow, arch
das Boot, -e boat
borgen to borrow; to lend
böse angry; evil; **böse (auf +** *acc.*) angry at
die Bowle, -n (punch) bowl; punch
der Brand, ⸚e fire
das Brandloch, ⸚er hole caused by something burning
brauchen to need; to use; **nicht zu tun brauchen** to not have to do
die Brauerei, -en brewery
braun brown
bremsen to brake
brennen, brannte, gebrannt to burn
das Brettspiel, -e board game
der Brief, -e letter
der Brieffreund, -e pen pal; (*fem.*) **die Brieffreundin, -nen**
die Briefmarke, -n stamp
die Brieftasche, -n pocketbook, wallet
der Briefträger, - letter carrier; (*fem.*) **die Briefträgerin, -nen**
die Brille, -n (eye)glasses, (pair of) glasses
die Brücke, -n bridge
der Brunnen, - fountain, well
das Buch, ⸚er book
die Buchdruckerkunst art of book printing
buchen to book
das Bücherregal, -e bookcase
die Buchhandlung, -en bookstore
buchstabieren to spell
die Buchung, -en booking
der Bundeskanzler Federal Chancellor of Germany
Bundesland, ⸚er federal state
Bundesstaat, -en federal state
der Bürger, - citizen
der Bürgerkrieg, -e civil war
der Bürgermeister, - mayor; (*fem.*) **die Bürgermeisterin, -nen**
das Büro, -s office

C

der Chef, -s head, director, manager; (*fem.*) **die Chefin, -nen**
der Chorgesang choir *or* chorus singing
das Christentum Christianity

D

da *(adv.)* here, there; then; (*sub. conj.*) since
dabei while doing (it); at the same time
das Dach, ⸚er roof
dafür for it / that; in return
dagegen on the other hand; against it / that
daher therefore, for that reason
damalig of that time
damals then, in those days
damit *(adv.)* with that; (*sub. conj.*) so that
danach after it / that; afterward(s)
der Dank thanks
danken *(dat.)* to thank
daran on it / that
darauf thereafter, thereupon
darüber about it / that
das Dasein existence, being
daß *(sub. conj.)* that
das Datum, -ten date (*of time*); (*pl.*) data, facts
dauern to last, endure
dauernd continual(ly)
davon from *or* about it / that
dazu to it / that, for it / that; in addition
die Decke, -n blanket, ceiling, cover
decken to cover; **den Tisch decken** to set the table
denkbar thinkable
denken, dachte, gedacht to think
die Denkweite expansive thought / thinking
denn for, because
dennoch nevertheless
dergleichen the like
derselb- the same
deshalb therefore, for that reason
deswegen therefore, for that reason
deuten to interpret, explain
deutlich clear, distinct
deutsch German
die Deutschstunde, -n German class
dick fat
der Dieb, -e thief
der Dienst, -e service
dies- (*sing.*) this; (*pl.*) these
die Diktatur, -en dictatorship
das Ding, -e thing
doch (*part.*) after all, really; oh, yes
das Dorf, ⸚er village
dort there
der Drache, (-n), -n dragon; **der Drachen, -** kite
dringend urgent, pressing
die Dummheit, -en stupidity, stupid thing
die Dunkelheit darkness
durch *(prep. with acc.)* through, by
durchblättern *(sep. or insep.)* to page through
durchaus nicht not at all, by no means
durch•führen to carry out
die Durchsage, -n broadcast announcement
durch•setzen (seinen Willen) to get one's way
dürfen (darf), durfte, gedurft to be permitted to, may
(sich) duschen to take a shower

E

eben (*adv. and part.*) just, precisely
ebenso . . . wie just as . . . as
echt real, genuine
die Ecke, -n corner

ehe *(sub. conj.)* before
die Ehe, -n marriage
ehemalig former, previous
der Ehemann, ¨er husband
ehrlich honest
das Ei, -er egg
eigen own
eigenartig peculiar, strange, queer
eigentlich actual(ly)
sich eignen to be suited
die Eile haste
ein paar a few
einander one another, each other
einäugig one-eyed
sich *(dat.)* **ein•bilden** to imagine, fancy o.s.
der Eindruck, ¨e impression
einfach simple
ein•führen to introduce, initiate
die Einheit, -en unity; unit
einig in agreement
einig- *(pl.)* some, a few; **einiges** some things
sich einigen (**über** + *acc.*) to agree on
der Einkauf, ¨e purchase
ein•kaufen to buy, purchase, shop for
die Einkaufstour, -en shopping trip
das Einkaufszentrum, -ren shopping center
ein•laden (lädt ein), lud ein, eingeladen to invite
die Einladung, -en invitation
die Einleitung, -en introduction
einmal once; **noch einmal** once more
einmalig unique, one-time
sich *(dat.)* **ein•reiben (das Gesicht), rieb ein, eingerieben** to rub s.th. into one's face
die Einrichtung, -en layout, setup; furnishings
ein•schlafen (schläft ein), schlief ein, ist eingeschlafen to fall asleep
einst once, one day (*past or future time*)
ein•treten (tritt ein), trat ein, ist eingetreten to step *or* walk in, enter
die Eintrittskarte, -n (admission) ticket
einverstanden in agreement
ein•wandern to immigrate
der Einwohner, - inhabitant
ein•zeichnen to mark *or* draw in
ein•ziehen, zog ein, ist eingezogen to move in
einzig only, sole, single
das Eis ice; ice cream
der Eisverkäufer, - ice cream man; (*fem.*) **die Eisverkäuferin, -nen**
die Eltern *(pl.)* parents
empfehlen (empfiehlt), empfahl, empfohlen to recommend
das Ende, -n end; **zu Ende** at *or* to an end, over
endlich finally
die Endung, -en ending (*grammar*)
die Energiesparpolitik energy-saving policy
der Engländer, - Englishman; (*fem.*) **die Engländerin, -nen**
das Enkelkind, -er grandchild
die Enkeltochter, ¨ granddaughter
entblättern to defoliate
entdecken to discover
die Entdeckung, -en discovery
enthalten (enthält), enthielt, enthalten to contain
entkommen, entkam, ist entkommen to escape; to avoid
entlang *(prep. with acc. or dat.)* along
entlassen (entläßt), entließ, entlassen to dismiss, release
entsagen *(dat.)* to renounce, give up
entsalzen to desalinate
(sich) entscheiden, entschied, entschieden to decide (*between options*), settle, make up one's mind
die Entscheidung, -en decision; **eine Entscheidung treffen** to come to *or* make a decision
sich entschließen, entschloß, entschlossen (zu + *dat.*) to decide (*to do*)
entschlossen resolved, determined
der Entschluß, ¨(ss)e decision, resolve; **einen Entschluß fassen** to make a decision
entschuldigen to excuse, pardon; **sich entschuldigen** to excuse oneself
die Entschuldigung, -en apology, excuse
das Entsetzen fright, horror
sich entsinnen, entsann, entsonnen *(gen.)* to remember, recall
entstammen (ist) *(dat.)* to be descended from
entweder . . . oder either . . . or
entwerten to devalue
entwickeln to develop s.th.; **sich entwickeln** to develop
die Entwicklung, -en development
erben to inherit
erblicken to see, catch sight of
die Erbschaft, -en inheritance
das Erdbeben, - earthquake
die Erde earth
sich ereignen to happen, occur, come to pass
das Ereignis, -se event, occurrence
erfahren (erfährt), erfuhr, erfahren to find out, hear, learn; to experience
die Erfahrung, -en (practical) experience
erfinden, erfand, erfunden to invent
die Erfindung, -en invention
der Erfolg, -e success
erfrieren, erfror, ist erfroren to freeze solid; to freeze to death

sich erfreuen *(gen.)* to enjoy, be the beneficiary of
erfunden imaginary, made up
ergänzen to complete
erhalten (erhält), erhielt, erhalten to receive, get
erhören to hear, answer *or* grant (*a request*)
sich erinnern (an + *acc.*) to remember, recall
sich erkälten to catch a cold
die Erkältung, -en cold (*illness*)
erkennen, erkannte, erkannt to recognize, discern
erklären to explain
die Erklärung, -en explanation; declaration
die Erkrankung, -en illness, affliction, disease
sich erkundigen (nach + *dat.*) to inquire about
erlauben to allow, permit
die Erlaubnis, -se permission
erleben to experience
das Erlebnis, -se (*personal*) experience, event, occurrence
-erlei kinds of
erlernen to learn, acquire
erlogen false, untrue
ermöglichen to make possible
erobern to conquer
eröffnen to open up
erraten (errät), erriet, erraten to guess correctly
erreichen to reach, attain
erscheinen, erschien, ist erschienen to appear
erschießen, erschoß, erschossen to shoot (*dead*)
erschlagen (erschlägt), erschlug, erschlagen to slay
erschweren to make more difficult
ersetzen to replace
erst only (*up to now*); not until
erstaunlich amazing
der Erwachsene (ein Erwachsener) adult; (*fem.*) **die Erwachsene**
erwähnen to mention
erwarten to expect
erweitert expanded
erzählen to tell, narrate
die Erzählskizze, -n narrative outline
die Erzählung, -en narrative, story
die Erziehung, -en upbringing, education
essen (ißt), aß, gegessen to eat
etwa approximately, about
etwas something; **etwas anderes** something else
eventuell possibly, perhaps
ewig eternal

F

fabelhaft fabulous, great
die Fabrik, -en factory
das Fach, ¨er field, subject, specialty
-fach -fold
fahren (fährt), fuhr, ist / hat gefahren to travel, ride; drive
der Fahrer, - driver; (*fem.*) **die Fahrerin, -nen**
das Fahrrad, ¨er bicycle
die Fahrt, -en ride, drive, trip
das Fahrzeug, -e vehicle
das Faktum, -ten fact
der Fall, ¨e case; **auf keinen Fall** by no means, in no case
fallen (fällt), fiel, ist gefallen to fall
fällen to fell (*a tree*)
falls in case, in the event
der Fallschirm, -e parachute
das Familienmitglied, -er family member
das Familienverhältnis, -se family relationship
der Fänger, - catcher
farbig in color, colorful
faul lazy, indolent; rotten
die Feder, -n feather; spring
fehlen to be missing, lacking
fehlend missing, lacking
der Fehler, - mistake, error
fehlerfrei error-free
feiern to celebrate
der Feiertag, -e holiday
die Ferien (*pl.*) vacation
das Feriendorf, ¨er vacation village
der Ferienort, -e vacation spot *or* village
die Ferienreise, -n vacation trip
die Ferienzeit vacation
das Ferienziel, -e vacation destination
fern•sehen (sieht fern), sah fern, ferngesehen to watch TV
das Fernsehen television
der Fernseher, - television set
die Fernsehsendung, -en television program
fertig finished; ready
das Fest, -e celebration, festive occasion, party
fest firm; **ein fester Freund** steady *or* close friend
die Festbeleuchtung festival lighting
fest•halten (hält fest), hielt fest, festgehalten to keep a firm grip on
der Fettdruck boldface; **fettgedruckt** printed in boldface
das Fieber fever
die Filmrezension, -en film review
der Filmschauspieler, - movie actor; (*fem.*) **die Filmschauspielerin, -nen**
finden, fand, gefunden to find
die Firma, -men firm, company
die Fläche, -n surface (*area*)
das Flachland flat country
die Flasche, -n bottle
der Fleck, -en spot, stain
der Fleiß diligence, hard work
fleißig industrious, diligent
die Fliege, -n fly
fliegen, flog, ist geflogen to fly
fliehen, floh, ist geflohen to flee
der Flug, ¨e (*air*) flight
der Flughafen, ¨ airport

das Flugzeug, -e airplane
die Flur, -en meadow, pasture; **der Flur, -e** hallway, corridor
der Fluß, ¨(ss)e river
die Flüssigkeit, -en fluid, liquid
die Folge, -n result
folgend following; **Folgendes** the following
fort•fahren, fuhr fort, ist fortgefahsen (zu tun) to continue (*to do*)
fort•setzen to continue (*s.th.*)
die Frage, -n question; **eine Frage stellen** to ask a question
fragen to ask
das Fragewort, ¨er question word
die Frau, -en woman
frei free; **im Freien** outdoors
frei•geben (gibt frei), gab frei, freigegeben to release, set free
die Freizeitbeschäftigung, -en leisure-time activity
fremd foreign, strange
der Fremde (ein Fremder) stranger, foreigner; (*fem.*) **die Fremde**
die Fremdsprache, -n foreign language
fressen (frißt), fraß, gefressen to eat (*of animals*)
die Freude, -n joy, delight
freuen to make happy; **sich freuen (auf** + *acc.*) to look forward to; **sich freuen (über** + *acc.*) to rejoice, be happy about
der Freund, -e friend; (*fem.*) **die Freundin, -nen**
der Freundeskreis, -e circle of friends
die Freundschaft friendship; **Freundschaft schließen** to make friends
der Friede(n), (-ns) peace
friedlich peaceful
frieren, fror, ist / hat gefroren to freeze
der Friseur, -e barber
froh happy, glad
früher earlier, previous
der Frühling, -e spring
das Frühstück, -e breakfast
frühstücken to eat breakfast
fühlen to feel; **sich (wohl) fühlen** to feel (fine)
führen to lead
für *(prep. with acc.)* for
sich fürchten (vor + *dat.*) to be afraid of
der Fuß, ¨e foot; **zu Fuß** on foot

G

ganz complete, whole, entire; quite
gar kein- not any at all; **gar nicht** not at all; **gar nichts** nothing at all
die Gärtnerlehre, -n gardening apprenticeship
die Gasse, -n street (*Southern German*)
der Gast, ¨e guest
der Gastgeber, - host
das Gasthaus, ¨er inn
die Gattung, -en genre
das Gebäck pastry
gebären (gebiert), gebar, geboren to give birth, bear
das Gebäude, - building
geben (gibt), gab, gegeben to give; **es gibt** there is / are
das Gebiet, -e area, territory, region
der Gebrauch, ¨e use, usage; custom
gebrauchen to use, make use of; **gebraucht** used
der Geburtstag, -e birthday
die Geburtstagsfeier, -n birthday celebration
das Geburtsjahr, -e birth year
gedenken *(gen.)*, **gedachte, gedacht** to remember, commemorate
das Gedicht, -e poem
die Gefahr, -en danger
gefährlich dangerous
gefallen (gefällt), gefiel, gefallen *(dat.)* to be pleasing
das Gefühl, -e feeling
gegen *(prep. with acc.)* toward; against
die Gegend, -en area, region
der Gegenspieler, - opponent
der Gegenstand, ¨e object, thing; subject matter, topic
gegenüber *(dat.)* across from, opposite
die Gegenwart present (*time*)
der Gehalt contents, ingredients
das Gehalt, ¨er salary
gehen, ging, ist gegangen to go; **es geht um** (*acc.*) it is about, it deals with, it is a matter of
gehorchen *(dat.)* to obey
gehören *(dat.)* to belong to
die Geige, -n fiddle
das Geld, -er money
der Geldverdiener, - wage earner
die Gelegenheit, -en opportunity
gelingen, gelang, ist gelungen to succeed; **es gelingt mir** I succeed
gelten (gilt), galt, gegolten to be valid *or* worth; to be directed at; **gelten für** to be considered (to be)
das Gemüse, - vegetable(s)
gemütlich cozy, snug; congenial, jolly
genau exact(ly), precise(ly)
genauso just as
genießen, genoß, genossen to enjoy
genug enough
genügen *(dat.)* to be enough, suffice
das Genus, -nera gender
gerade *(adj.)* straight; upright, even (*numbers*); (*adv.*) just, exactly
geradeaus straight ahead
geradezu downright
das Gerät, -e apparatus, device, piece of equipment
die Germanistik German studies
gern gladly; **gern tun** to like to do; **gern haben** to like (*s.o.* or *s.th.*)

das Geschäft, -e business; store
geschehen (geschieht), geschah, ist geschehen to happen
das Geschenk, -e gift
die Geschichte, -n history, story
die Geschwister *(pl.)* brother(s) and sister(s), siblings
die Gesellschaft, -en society
das Gesicht, -er face
gestalten to shape, form, structure
gestern yesterday
gestrig yesterday's
die Gesundheit health
das Gesundheitswesen health services
das Getränk, -e drink
die Getränkekarte, -n list of drinks
das Getreide grain
das Gewicht, -e weight
gewinnen, gewann, gewonnen to win
gewiß *(gen.)* sure of
gewöhnlich usual(ly)
gewöhnt (an + *acc.*) accustomed to
gibt: es gibt there is / are
gießen, goß, gegossen to pour
der Gipfel, - peak, summit
glauben (an + *acc.*) to believe (in)
gleich same, like
das Gleis, -e track
gleiten, glitt, ist geglitten to glide, slip
das Glockenspiel, -e carillon, chime(s)
das Glück happiness, good fortune
glücklich happy; fortunate, lucky
glücklicherweise fortunately
glühen to glow, be red hot
der Gott, ¨er god
der Graben, ¨ ditch
gratulieren *(dat.)* to congratulate
die Grenze, -n border
grenzen (an + *acc.*) to border on
groß big, large, great
die Großeltern *(pl.)* grandparents
die Großmutter, ¨ grandmother
die Großstadt, ¨e major city (*more than 100,000 inhabitants*)
der Grund, ¨e reason; **aus diesem Grunde** for this reason
gründen to found
die Grundzahl, -en cardinal number
die Gruppe, -n group
der Gruß, ¨e greeting
grüßen to greet
günstig favorable
gut *(adj.)* good; (*adv.*) well

H

das Haar, -e hair
haben (hat), hatte, gehabt to have
der Hafen, ¨ harbor
das Hafenviertel, - harbor district
der Häftling, -e prisoner
das Hallenbad, ¨er indoor pool
halt *(part.)* just
halten (hält), hielt, gehalten to hold; stop; **halten (für** + *acc.*) to consider, regard as; **halten (von** + *dat.*) to have an opinion of / about
handeln to act, take action; **handeln (von** + *dat.*) to be about; **es handelt sich um** (*acc.*) it is about
die Handelsmetropole, -n trading metropolis
hängen•bleiben, blieb hängen, ist hängengeblieben to get stuck
die Handtasche, -n purse
die Harfe, -n harp
hassen to hate
häufig frequent
der Hauptbahnhof, ¨e main train station
das Hauptfach, ¨er major field of study
die Hauptrolle, -n leading role
der Hauptsatz, ¨e main clause
die Hauptstadt, ¨e capital (*city*)
das Haus, ¨er house; **zu Hause** at home; **nach Hause** (*to go*) home
die Hausaufgabe, -n homework (*assignment*)
der Hausbesitzer, - homeowner
der Haushalt, -e household
der Hausherr, (-n), -en landlord; head of the house(hold)
das Haustier, -e house pet
die Haustür, -en front door
heben, hob, gehoben to lift, elevate, raise
das Heft, -e notebook
heim home, homewards
die Heimat, -en home; native land
der Heimatort, -e hometown
heiraten to marry, get married
heiß hot
heißen, hieß, geheißen to be called *or* named; to mean, signify; bid, tell (*s.o.*) to; **sie heißt** her name is; **das heißt** that is (to say); **es heißt** it is said (that)
der Held, (-en), -en hero, (*fem.*) **die Heldin, -nen**
die Heldentat, -en heroic deed
helfen (hilft), half, geholfen *(dat.)* to help
das Hemd, -en shirt
herauf•holen to bring up, haul up
heraus•finden, fand heraus, herausgefunden to find out, discover
heraus•fischen to fish out
sich heraus•stellen to turn out to be
der Herbst, -e fall, autumn
der Herd, -e stove
herein in(to)
herein•kommen, kam herein, ist hereingekommen to come in
herein•lassen (läßt herein), ließ herein, hereingelassen to let in
herein•treten (tritt herein), trat herein, ist hereingetreten to step in, enter

der Herr, (-n), -en Mr., gentleman; (*fem.*) **die Herrin, -nen** lady, mistress
die Herrenboutique (-butike), -n men's clothing store
herrlich magnificent, splendid
herrschen to prevail; to rule
herum around
herum•kommen, kam herum, ist herumgekommen to get around
herum•sitzen, saß herum, herumgesessen to sit around
das Herz (-ens), -en heart
herzlich cordial(ly)
heute today
heutig today's
heutzutage nowadays
die Hexe, -n witch
hier here
die Hilfe, -n help, assistance
die Himbeere, -n raspberry
der Himmel, - sky, heaven
das Himmelreich, -e heaven, heavenly kingdom
hinauf•fahren (fährt hinauf), fuhr hinauf, ist / hat hinaufgefahren to drive up
hinauf•kommen, kam hinauf, ist hinaufgekommen to come up
hinauf•steigen, stieg hinauf, ist hinaufgestiegen to climb up
hindurch through(out)
sich hin•setzen to sit down
hinter (*prep. with acc. or dat.*) behind
hinterlassen (hinterläßt), hinterließ, hinterlassen to leave behind
hinunter•schauen to look down
hin•weisen, wies hin, hingewiesen (auf + *acc.*) to indicate, point to
hinzu in addition, to this
hoch high; to the power of
das Hochhaus, ¨-er skyscraper
die Hochschule, -n university-level institution
höchst highly, very, extremely; **höchstens** at (the) most
höchstwahrscheinlich most likely
die Hochzeit, -en wedding
hoffen (auf + *acc.*) to hope for
hoffentlich hopefully
die Hoffnung, -en hope
höflich polite(ly)
die Höhe, -n height
die Höhenlage, -n elevation
die Höhensonne ultraviolet sunrays
holen to (go) fetch
das Holz wood
hören to hear
das Hörensagen hearsay
das Hörverständnis listening comprehension
die Hose, -n trousers
die Hosentasche, -n trouser pocket
hübsch pretty, lovely
der Hügel, - hill
der Hund, -e dog
der Hut, ¨-e hat

I

immer always; **immer noch** still
imponieren (*dat.*) to impress
in (*prep. with acc. or dat.*) in, into, inside
indem by [—]ing
die Informatik computer science
der Ingenieur, -e engineer; (*fem.*) **die Ingenieurin, -nen**
der Inhalt, -e content(s)
innerhalb (*prep. with gen.*) inside of, within
der Intelligenzquotient IQ
das Interesse, -n interest
sich interessieren (für + *acc.*) to be interested in
interessiert (an + *dat.*) interested in
inzwischen meanwhile
irgend- some . . . or other; any . . . at all
irgendjemand someone or other
irgendwo(hin) (to) somewhere
der Irrtum, ¨-er error, mistake

J

ja yes; (*part.*) you know, of course
die Jacke, -n jacket
jagen to chase, hunt
das Jahr, -e year
der Jahresverlauf course of the year
die Jahreszeit, -en season of the year
das Jahrhundert, -e century
das Jahrzehnt, -e decade
je ever
je . . . desto / umso the more . . . the more
jed- each, every
jedenfalls in any event
jedermann everyone, everybody
jederzeit (at) any time
jedesmal each time, every time
jemand someone; **jemand anders** someone else
jen- that
jenseits (*prep. with gen.*) on the other side of
jetzig present
jetzt now
jeweils in each case, respectively
der Jude, (-n), -n Jew; (*fem.*) **die Jüdin, -nen**
das Judentum Judaism
die Jugend youth
der Jugendliche (ein Jugendlicher) juvenile; (*fem.*) **die Jugendliche**
jung young
der Junge, (-n), -n boy, youth

K

der Kaffee coffee
der Käfig, -e cage
kalt cold
die Kälte cold(ness)
kämmen to comb
kämpfen to battle, struggle
das Kapitel, - chapter
kaputt broken, ruined, done for

die Karriere, -n career
die Karte, -n ticket; map
das Kartenspiel, -e card game; deck of cards
der Käse cheese
der Kassierer, - cashier; (*fem.*) **die Kassiererin, -nen**
die Katze, -n cat
der Kauf, ¨e purchase
kaufen to buy, purchase
das Kaufhaus, ¨er department store
kaum scarcely
keinesfalls by no means, not at all
der Keller, - cellar
der Kellner, - waiter; **die Kellnerin, -nen** waitress
kennen, kannte, gekannt to know, be acquainted with
kennen•lernen, lernte kennen, kennengelernt to get to know, become acquainted with
das Kind, -er children
der Kinderwagen, - baby carriage
die Kindheit, -en childhood
das Kino, -s cinema, movie theater, the movies
die Kirche, -n church
kitschig mawkish, trashy
die Klammer, -n parenthesis
klar clear
das Klavier, -e piano
der Klavierbauer, - piano maker
die Kleiderabteilung, -en clothing department
die Kleidung clothes, clothing
das Kleidungsstück, -e piece of clothing
klein small, little; short (*in height*)
klettern (ist) to climb, scramble
klingen, klang, geklungen to sound
klug intelligent, clever, astute
die Klugheit intelligence, cleverness
das Knie, - knee
der Knochen, - bone
kochen to cook
der Koffer, - suitcase, trunk, bag
der Kognat, -e cognate
die Kokospalme, -n coconut palm (tree)
der Kollege, (-n), -n colleague
komisch queer, strange, peculiar, comic(al)
kommen, kam, ist gekommen to come
der Kommissar, -e police inspector
komponieren to compose
der Komponist (-en), -en composer; (*fem.*) **die Komponistin, -nen**
der König, -e king; (*fem.*) **die Königin, -nen** queen
die Konjunktion, -en conjunction
können (kann), konnte, gekonnt to be able to, can
das Konzert, -e concert
der Kopf, ¨e head
der Korb, ¨e basket
der Körper, - body
krank sick, ill
das Krankenhaus, ¨er hospital
krankhaft pathological, abnormal
der Krebs cancer
kreisen to circle
(das) Kreta Crete
die Kreuzung, -en crossing, intersection
der Krieg, -e war; **Krieg führen** to wage war
die Kritik, -en criticism
der Kuchen, - cake
die Küche, -n kitchen
das Küchengerät, -e kitchen utensil *or* small appliance
die Kuh, ¨e cow
der Kühlschrank, ¨e refrigerator
das Küken, - baby chicken
sich kümmern (um + *acc.***)** to take care of, attend to
die Kunde news, notice, information
die Kunst, ¨e art; skill
künstlich artificial
der Kurs, -e course
kursiv (in) italics; **kursivgedruckt** printed in italics
kurz short, brief
die Kürze brevity
die Kusine, -n female cousin
der Kuß, ¨(ss)e kiss

L

lachen to laugh
die Lage, -n situation, position
die Lampe, -n lamp
das Land, ¨er land, country
die Landschaft, -en landscape
lang long; **lange** (*adv.*) for a long time
die Länge, -n length
langsam slow(ly)
sich langweilen to be bored
der Lärm noise
lassen (läßt), ließ, gelassen to let, leave
der Lauf, ¨e course, progress
laufen (läuft), lief, ist gelaufen to run, walk
der Läufer, - runner
läuten to ring
lauter *(adv.)* nothing but, purely
das Leben life; **ums Leben kommen** to die, perish
leben to live
der Lebenslauf, ¨e curriculum vitae
der Lebensstil, -e style of living
die Lebensweise, -n way of living
die Leber, -n liver
das Lebewesen, - creature
lecker tasty
der Ledermantel, ¨ leather coat
legen to lay, put; **sich legen** to lie down
das Lehrbuch, ¨er textbook
die Lehre, -n instruction, lesson, moral
lehren to teach
der Lehrer, - teacher; (*fem.*) **die Lehrerin, -nen**
lehrreich instructive
leicht easy, light

leid tun: es tut mir leid I am sorry
das Leiden, - sorrow, suffering
leider unfortunately
leihen, lieh, geliehen to loan, borrow
die Leine, -n leash
die Leistung, -en accomplishment
die Lektion, -en lesson
die Leseaufgabe, -n reading assignment
lesen (liest), las, gelesen to read
der Leserbrief, -e letter to the editor
letzt- last
die Leute *(pl.)* people
lieb dear
die Liebe love
lieber preferably; **lieber tun** to prefer to do
der Liebling, -e darling, dear
die Lieblingsspeise, -n favorite dish
liebst: am liebsten most / best of all; **am liebsten tun** to like to do most / best of all
das Lied, -er song
liegen, lag, gelegen to be situated, lie
liegen•lassen (läßt liegen), ließ liegen, liegen(ge)lassen to leave (lying about)
lila lilac (*color*)
links on the left; **nach links** to the left
das Lob praise
das Loch, ¨er hole
los: was ist los? what is the matter? what is going on?
lösen to loosen; to solve
der Lohn, ¨e wage
los•werden (wird los), wurde los, ist losgeworden to get rid of
der Lottogewinn, -e lottery winnings
die Luft, ¨e air
die Lüge, -n lie
die Lunge, -n lung
der Lungenkrebs lung cancer
die Lust desire, inclination; **(keine) Lust haben . . . zu tun** to have (no) desire to do
lustig merry, jolly, funny; **sich lustig machen** (**über** + *acc.*) to make fun of

M

machen to make; to do
die Macht, ¨e power, might
das Mädchen, - girl
das Mal, -e time; **zum ersten Mal** for the first time
mal *(adv.)* times (*math*); (*part.*) just
der Maler, - painter; (*fem.*) **die Malerin, -nen**
manch- *(sing.)* many a; (*pl.*) some
manchmal sometimes
der Mann, -ër man
die Mannschaft, -en team
der Mantel, ¨ coat
das Märchen, - fairy tale
die Maßeinheit, -en unit of measurement
die Mauer, -n (*masonry*) wall
das Maul, ¨er mouth (of animals)
das Medikament, -e medicine, drug
die Medizin (*science of*) medicine
das Meer, -e sea; ocean
der Meer(es)blick, -e view of the sea
mehr more
mehrere several
mehrmalig repeated
mehrmals several times
meinen to mean, think; to intend
die Meinung, -en opinion
die Meinungsäußerung, -en expression of opinion
meist- most; **meist** *or* **meistens** mostly
der Meister, - master; champion; (*fem.*) **die Meisterin, -nen**
melden to report
die Meldung, -en announcement
der Mensch, (-en), -en human, man (*species*)
die Menschheit mankind, humankind
menschlich human
merken to notice; **sich** (*dat.*) **merken** to take note
die Metropole, -n metropolis
die Miete, -n rent
mieten to rent
die Milch milk
die Milliarde, -n billion
mindestens at least (*with amounts*)
das Mißfallen displeasure
mit *(prep. with dat.)* with
mit•bringen, brachte mit, mitgebracht to bring along
mit•kommen, kam mit, ist mitgekommen to come along
mit•machen to participate
mit•nehmen (nimmt mit), nahm mit, mitgenommen to take along
der Mitspieler, - fellow player, teammate
der Mittag, -e noon; **zu Mittag** at noon
mit•teilen to communicate, impart, tell
die Mitteilung, -en notification, communication, announcement
das Mittel, - means, medium
das Mittelalter Middle Ages
möchte(n) would like (to)
die Modalpartikel, -n modal particle
das Modegeschäft, -e fashion shop
das Modell, -e model
mögen (mag), mochte, gemocht to like; may
möglich possible
die Möglichkeit, -en possibility
möglichst as . . . as possible
der Monat, -e month
der Mond, -e moon
der Morgen morning

morgen tomorrow; **heute morgen** this morning; **morgen früh** tomorrow morning
die Moschee, -n mosque
der Motor, -en motor
müde (*gen.*) tired of
der Mund, ¨er mouth
mündlich oral(ly)
die Münze, -n coin
das Museum, -seen museum
die Musik music
müssen (muß), mußte, gemußt to have to, must
die Mutter, ¨ mother; **Mutti, -s** mommy

N

nach (*prep. with dat.*) after; to(ward); according to
der Nachbar, (-s *or* **-n), -n** neighbor; (*fem.*) **die Nachbarin, -nen**
nachdem (*sub. conj.*) after
nacherzählen to retell
nachher afterward(s)
der Nachmittag, -e afternoon
die Nachricht, -en news, note, message, notice
nach•schlagen (schlägt nach), schlug nach, nachgeschlagen to look up (*in a book*)
nächst- next
die Nacht, ¨e night
die Nähe proximity; **in der Nähe** near, nearby
der Name, (-ns), -n name
nämlich namely, that is
die Nase, -n nose
natürlich of course, natural(ly)
neben (*prep. with acc. or dat.*) beside, next to
nebenan next door, in the next room, alongside
das Nebenfach, ¨er minor field of study
der Nebensatz, ¨e dependent clause
negieren to negate
nehmen (nimmt), nahm, genommen to take
der Neinsager, - person who says no
nennen, nannte, genannt to name
nett nice
neu new
neugierig curious
die Neujahrsansprache New Year's address
neulich recently
neuzeitlich modern, up-to-date
nicht not
nicht einmal not even
nicht wahr isn't it?, don't they?, etc.
nichts nothing
nie never
niedrig low
niemand no one, nobody; **niemand anders** no one else
noch still; **noch einmal** once more; **noch kein-** not any yet; **noch nicht** not yet; **noch nie** not ever (before)
normalerweise normally
die Note, -n grade
nötig necessary
die Notiz, -en note; **Notizen machen** to take notes
nur (*adv.*) only; (*part.*) just
nutzen *or* **nützen** to be of use
nützlich (*dat.*) useful
nutzlos useless

O

oberhalb (*prep. with gen.*) above
der Oberschullehrer, - high school teacher; (*fem.*) **die Oberschullehrerin, -nen**
obgleich (*sub. conj.*) although
obig above
obwohl (*sub. conj.*) although
oder or
öffnen to open (*s.th.*); **sich öffnen** to open
oft often
öfter often; more often
ohne (*prep. with acc.*) without
ohne . . . zu without [—]ing
ohne daß without [—]ing
die Oma, -s granny
der Onkel, - uncle
die Oper, -n opera
die Ordnung order, arrangement
die Ordnungszahl, -en ordinal number
der Ort, -e place
der Osten east
(das) Ostern Easter; **zu Ostern** at / for Easter
die Ostküste east coast
östlich eastern
die Ostsee Baltic Sea

P

paar: ein paar a few, several; **ein paarmal** a few times
das Paar, -e pair, couple
packen to pack; to grasp, pounce on
das Paket, -e package
der Panoramablick, -e panoramic view
der Papagei, (-s *or* **-en), -en** parrot
das Papier, -e paper
der Papst, ¨e Pope
die Partei, -en faction, party
das Partizip, -ien participle
die Party, -ies party
passen (*dat.*) to fit, suit
passend suitable, proper, fitting
passieren (ist) to happen, occur
die Pause, -n pause, break
das Pech bad luck (*literally:* pitch)
die Pension, -en bed and breakfast, inexpensive lodging
das Perfekt present perfect tense
das Pferd, -e horse
die Pflanze, -n plant
der Pflichtkurs, -e required course
der Pförtner, - doorman
das Pfund, -e pound

pilgern (ist) to go on a pilgrimage
der Plan, ⸚e plan
das Pläsierchen little pleasure
der Platz, ⸚e place, spot, site; room, space
plaudern to chat
plötzlich sudden(ly)
das Plusquamperfekt past perfect tense
die Politik politics; policy
der Politiker, - politician; (*fem.*) **die Politikerin, -nen**
die Polizei police
der Polizist, (-en), -en policeman; (*fem.*) **die Polizistin, -nen**
die Post mail; post office
das Postamt, ⸚er post office
der Posten, - post, position
das Präfix, -e prefix
das Präsens present tense
das Präteritum simple past tense
der Preis, -e price; prize, award
preiswert good value for the money
prima great
der Prominente (ein Prominenter) prominent person; (*fem.*) **die Prominente**
das Pronomen, - pronoun
der Prosaband, ⸚e volume of prose
die Protestaktion, -en protest march
der Protestierende (ein Protestierender) protester; (*fem.*) **die Protestierende**
der Proviant provisions, rations
der Prozeß, -(ss)e lawsuit
die Prüfung, -en examination
der Psychiater, - psychiatrist; (*fem.*) **die Psychiaterin, -nen**
das Publikum audience
der Punkt, -e point; period
putzen to clean, polish; **die Zähne putzen** to brush one's teeth

R

der Rabe, (-n), -n raven
das Rad, ⸚er wheel; bike
rad•fahren (fährt rad), fuhr rad, ist radgefahren ro ride a bicycle
der Rand, ⸚er edge, side
rasch swift, speedy, rapid
der Rasen lawn, grass; **den Rasen betreten** to walk on the grass
rasieren to shave (*s.o.*); **sich rasieren** to shave (o.s.)
der Rat advice
raten (rät), riet, geraten (*dat.*) to advise; to take a guess
das Rathaus, ⸚er city hall
der Ratschlag, ⸚e (*piece of*) advice, suggestion
das Rätsel, - riddle, puzzle
der Rattenfänger, - rat catcher
rauchen to smoke
räumlich spatial(ly)
rechnen (mit + *dat.*) to calculate, figure on
das Recht, -e right, privilege; justice
recht right; quite
rechts on the right; **nach rechts** to the right
der Rechtsanwalt, ⸚e lawyer
rechtzeitig on time
die Redaktion editorial staff
die Rede, -n speech
das Redemittel, - verbal strategy; useful verbal expression or structure
reden to talk
der Redner, - speaker
die Regel, -n rule; **in der Regel** as a rule
regelmäßig regular
der Regen rain
regieren to rule, govern
die Regierung, -en government
regnen to rain
reich rich
das Reich, -e empire
reichen to reach (for), hand
die Reihe, -n row; series
die Reise, -n trip, journey
das Reisebüro, -s travel agency
reisen to travel
der Reisende (ein Reisender) traveler; (*fem.*) **die Reisende**
der Reiseverkehr tourist travel
reißen, riß, gerissen to tear, rip
reiten, ritt, ist / hat geritten to ride (*an animal*)
die Reklame, -n advertisement; advertising
rennen, rannte, ist gerannt to run
das Restaurant, -s restaurant
richten (an + *acc.*) to direct at
richtig correct, right
riechen, roch, gerochen to smell
das Rollenspiel, -e role-play
die Rolltreppe, -n escalator
der Roman, -e novel
rosten to rust
(das) Rotkäppchen Little Red Riding Hood
der Rücken, - back
der Rucksack, ⸚e rucksack, knapsack
ruderlos without oars
der Ruf reputation
die Ruhe, -n peace, calm, rest
ruhig calm, quiet
das Ruhrgebiet Ruhr area (*industrial section of Germany*)
rund approximately, about, roughly; **rund um** around
der Rundbrief, -e a letter to be circulated
der Rundfunk radio

S

die Sache, -n thing, matter, subject
der Saft, ⸚e juice
die Sage, -n legend, fable
sagen to say
sammeln to collect
die Sammlung, -en collection
der Satz, ⸚e sentence
sauber clean, neat, tidy
das Schach chess

der Schäferhund, -e shepherd dog
schaffen, schuf, geschaffen to create
schaffen, schaffte, geschafft to do, accomplish, manage to do
die Schallplatte, -n record
der Schalter, - (ticket) window
sich schämen (über + *acc.*) to be ashamed of
die Schande disgrace
schauen to look
der Scheibenwischer, - windshield wiper
sich scheiden lassen, ließ, gelassen to get a divorce
der Schein, -e bill, banknote
scheinen, schien, geschienen to shine; to seem, appear
schenken to give (*as a present*)
schicken to send
schildern to depict, portray
schießen, schoß, geschossen to shoot
das Schiff, -e ship
der Schirm, -e screen
das Schläfchen, - nap
schlafen (schläft), schlief, geschlafen to sleep
das Schlafzimmer, - bedroom
schlagen (schlägt), schlug, geschlagen to strike, beat
die Schlange, -n snake
schlecht bad(ly)
schleichen, schlich, ist geschlichen to creep, slink, sneak
schleppen to drag; **sich schleppen** to drag o.s.
schließen, schloß, geschlossen to close
schließlich in the final analysis, in the end
schlimm bad, evil; severe, grave
der Schluß, ¨(ss)e end; **zum Schluß** finally, in the end; **Schluß machen** to stop doing, put an end to
schmecken (nach + *dat.*) to taste like
schmeicheln (*dat.*) to flatter
schmelzen (schmilzt), schmolz, ist / hat geschmolzen to melt
schmieren to smear
sich schminken to put on make-up
schmutzig dirty, filthy
der Schnee snow
schnell fast
schon (*adv.*) already
schrecklich terrible, frightful
schreiben, schrieb, geschrieben to write
der Schreiber, - clerk, copyist; (*fem.*) **die Schreiberin, -nen**
die Schreibmaschine, -n typewriter
schreien, schrie, geschrie(e)n to shout, scream
schriftlich written, in writing
schuften to labor, work hard
der Schuh, -e shoe
die Schule, -n school
der Schüler, - pupil
schützen to protect
schwach weak
die Schwäche, -n weakness
schwächlich weakly, feeble
schwarz black
schweigsam silent, taciturn
die Schweiz Switzerland
schwer heavy; difficult, hard
die Schwester, -n sister
schwierig difficult
die Schwierigkeit, -en difficulty; **in Schwierigkeiten geraten** to get into difficulty
schwimmen, schwamm, ist / hat geschwommen to swim
sechsstellig six-digit
der See, -n lake; **die See, -n** sea
segeln to sail
sehen (sieht), sah, gesehen to see
sehenswert worth seeing
die Sehenswürdigkeit, -en attraction
sein (ist), war, ist gewesen to be
seit (*prep. with dat.*) since *or* for (*temporal sense only*)
seit(dem) (*sub. conj.*) since
seitdem (*adv.*) (ever) since then
die Seite -n page; side
seither (ever) since then
selber (*emphatic*) myself, yourself, themselves, etc.
selbst (one)self; even
die Selbstaussage, -n statement about oneself
selbstverständlich obvious(ly), self-evident; it goes without saying
selten seldom
die Seltenheit, -en rarity
senden, sandte *or* **sendete, gesandt** *or* **gesendet** to send; to transmit
senken to lower, sink
setzen to set, put; **sich setzen** to sit down
sicher for sure; safe
die Sicherheit certainty, security
die Sicht sight, view, visibility
der Sieg, -e victory
siegen to conquer, be victorious
die Sinfonie, -n symphony
singen, sang, gesungen to sing
das Singspiel, -e operetta, musical comedy
der Sinn, -e sense; **nicht bei Sinnen sein** to be out of one's mind
sinnvoll meaningful; sensible
die Sitte, -n custom; **Sitten und Gebräuche** manners and customs
sitzen, saß, gesessen to sit
der Skat skat (*card game*)
sobald as soon as
sofort immediately
sogar even
solange as long as
solch- such; **ein solch-** such a
sollen (soll), sollte, gesollt to be supposed to, ought to; to be said to
sondern but (rather)
der Sonderpreis, -e special price
die Sonne, -n sun
der Sonnenbrand sunburn

sooft as often as
die Sorge, -n worry, care
sorgen (für + *acc.*) to care *or* provide for
sorgenlos without worries
sowieso anyway
sowohl . . . als auch both . . . and; as well as
spannend exciting
das Sparkonto, -ten savings account
der Spargel asparagus
sparsam thrifty, frugal
der Spaß fun; **Spaß machen** to be fun
spät late
spazieren•gehen, ging spazieren, ist spazierengegangen to take a walk
der Spaziergang, ¨e walk; **einen Spaziergang machen** to take a walk
spendieren to treat someone to, pay for s.th. for s.o.
der Spiegel, - mirror
das Spiel, -e game
spielen to play
der Spielfilm, -e feature movie
der Spielplatz, ¨e playground, playing field
die Spielsache, -n toy
die Spitze, -n point, tip, top, front
Sport treiben to do sports
das Sportangebot, -e sports offerings
das Sportgeschäft, -e sports store
der Sportler, - athlete
der Sportverein, -e sports club
die Sprachkürze terseness
die Spraydose, -n spray can
sprechen (spricht), sprach, gesprochen to speak
das Sprichwort, ¨er saying, proverb
springen, sprang, ist gesprungen to jump, leap
der Spruch, ¨e saying, proverb
spüren to feel, sense, perceive
der Staat, -en state
staatlich state, national
stabil rugged, sturdy
die Stadt, ¨e town, city
der Stadtplaner, - city planner; (*fem.*) **die Stadtplanerin, -nen**
der Stadtschreiber, - town clerk; (*fem.*) **die Stadtschreiberin, -nen**
der Stadtteil, -e section of a city
das Stadtzentrum, -ren city center
der Standpunkt, -e view, position; **einen Standpunkt vertreten** to take a position / view
stark strong
stattdessen instead (of that)
statt•finden, fand statt, stattgefunden to take place
stechen (sticht), stach, gestochen to prick; to sting, bite (*insect*)
stecken to stick, put
stehen, stand, gestanden to stand
stehlen (stiehlt), stahl, gestohlen to steal
die Steiermark Styria (*Austrian province*)
steigen, stieg, ist gestiegen to climb
der Stein, -e stone
die Stelle, -n position, spot, place; job
stellen to place; **eine Frage stellen** to ask a question
sterben (stirbt), starb, ist gestorben to die
stimmen to be correct; to be true
die Stimmung, -en atmosphere
der Stock, ¨e stick, pole; story *or* floor of a building
stolz proud
stören to disturb
stracks straight (away); without delay
der Strand, ¨e beach
die Straße, -n street
der Straßenarbeiter, - road repair worker
der Straßenrand, ¨er side of the road
der Straßenverkehr (road) traffic
der Strom, ¨e river, stream; electricity
das Studentenheim, -e student dorm
das Studentenlokal, -e student tavern
das Studium, -ien studies, course of studies
das Stück, -e piece
die Stunde, -n hour, class (hour); **stundenlang** for hours
der Stundenplan, ¨e schedule
der Sturm, ¨e storm
stürzen (ist) to fall, plunge; **(hat)** overthrow
die Styropackung, -en styrofoam packaging
das Substantiv, -e noun
suchen to seek, search
der Süden south
die Südseeinsel, -n South Sea island

T

der Tag, -e day; **eines Tages** one day
das Tagebuch, ¨er diary
die Tagesnachrichten (*pl.*) news of the day
die Tagesschau daily news program on German television
die Tageszeit, -en time of the day
täglich daily
tagsüber during the day
der Taler, - obsolete monetary unit
die Tankstelle, -n gas station
die Tante, -n aunt
der Tanz, ¨e dance
tanzen to dance
die Tasche, -n pocket
das Taschengeld spending money
die Taschenlampe, -n flashlight
der Taschenrechner, - pocket calculator
die Taschenuhr, -en pocket watch
die Tasse, -n cup

die Tätigkeit, -en activity
der Tatort, -e scene of the crime
die Tatsache, -n fact
taub deaf
tausend thousand
die Technik technology
der Teil, -e part, section
teilen to divide
teil•nehmen (nimmt teil), nahm teil, teilgenommen (an + *dat.*) to take part in, participate
der Tennisschläger, - tennis racket
der Teppich, -e rug, carpet
der Termin, -e fixed date; appointment
teuer expensive
der Teufel, - devil
das Thema, -men topic, subject, theme
die These, -n thesis
tief deep(ly)
die Tiefe, -n depth
die Tiefenpsychologie psychology of the subconscious
das Tier, -e animal
der Tiergarten, ⸚ zoo
der Tisch, -e table
der Titel, - title
die Tochter, ⸚ daughter
der Tod, -e death; **zu Tode** to death
toll crazy, insane; terrific, great
der Topf, ⸚e pot
das Tor, -e gate, portal; goal (*soccer*)
tot dead
der Tote (ein Toter) dead person; (*fem.*) **die Tote**
töten to kill
der Tourist, (-en), -en tourist
der Touristenführer, - tourist guide *or* guidebook
tragen (trägt), trug, getragen to carry; to wear
trauen (*dat.*) to trust
träumen to dream
traumhaft dreamlike, wonderful
traurig sad
treffen (trifft), traf, getroffen to meet; to hit; to affect
treffend apt, appropriate
treiben, trieb, getrieben to drive; to pursue an activity; **treiben (ist)** to drift, float
trinken, trank, getrunken to drink
trotz *(prep. with gen.)* in spite of
trotzdem *(adv.)* in spite of it / this, nevertheless; (*sub. conj.*) in spite of the fact that
tun (tut), tat, getan to do, act
die Tür, -en door
der Typ, -en type

U

über *(prep. with acc. or dat.)* over, across, above; about (*acc.*)
überall(hin) to everywhere
überein•stimmen to be in agreement
die Übergangsschwierigkeit, -en transitional difficulty
überhaupt in general, on the whole; **überhaupt nicht** not at all; **überhaupt nichts** nothing at all
überleben to survive
überlegen to ponder, consider; **sich etwas** (*dat.*) **überlegen** to think s.th. over
überraschen to surprise
die Überraschung, -en surprise
überreden to persuade
übersehen (übersieht), übersah, übersehen to overlook, ignore
übersetzen to translate
der Übersetzer, - translator; (*fem.*) **die Übersetzerin, -nen**
überspringen, übersprang, übersprungen to skip (over)
übertreiben, übertrieb, übertrieben to exaggerate
über•wechseln to change, go over
überzeugen to convince; **überzeugt** convinced
übrigens incidentally; **im übrigen** in other respects
die Übung, -en exercise
um (*prep. with acc.*) around; by (*with quantities*); **um sechs Uhr** at six o'clock
um . . . zu in order to
um . . . willen for . . . 's sake
umarmen to embrace, hug
um•bauen to remodel
um•fallen (fällt um), fiel um, ist umgefallen to fall over
umgekehrt vice versa
um•kippen to tip over
um•schreiben, schrieb um, umgeschrieben to rewrite, revise
sich um•sehen (sieht um), sah um, umgesehen to look around
der Umstand, ⸚e circumstance
die Umwelt environment
die Umweltverschmutzung environmental pollution
sich um•ziehen, zog um, umgezogen to change (clothes); **um•ziehen (ist)** to move, change one's residence
der Unabhängigkeitskrieg, -e war of independence
unbedingt absolutely
unbegrenzt without limitation
unbestimmter Artikel indefinite article
unerwartet unexpected
der Unfall, ⸚e accident
ungefähr approximately
ungesund unhealthy
unglaublich unbelievable
die Universität, -en university (*coll.:* **die Uni, -s**)
der Unsinn nonsense
unsterblich immortal
unten *(adv.)* below
unter *(prep. with acc. or dat.)* under, below, beneath; among; **unter anderem** among other things
unterbrechen (unterbricht), unterbrach, unterbrochen to interrupt
unterdessen meanwhile

unterdrücken to suppress, repress
unter•gehen, ging unter, ist untergegangen to set, go down; to perish
unterhalb *(prep. with gen.)* beneath
sich unterhalten (unterhält), unterhielt, unterhalten (über + *acc.*) to converse; to amuse o.s.
die Unterhaltung, -en amusement
die Unterkunft, ¨-e lodging
unternehmen (unternimmt), unternahm, unternommen to undertake
der Unterricht instruction
unterrichten to instruct, teach
der Unterrichtsraum, ¨-e instructional room
unterstreichen, unterstrich, unterstrichen to underline
unterstützen to support
die Unterstützung support
untersuchen to investigate, examine
unterwegs underway
unvergeßlich unforgettable
unverständlich incomprehensible
unvorsichtig careless, not cautious
das Unwesen, - awful creature
unwiderstehlich irresistible
der Urlaub, -e vacation
der Urlaubsort, -e vacation spot
urteilen to judge
usw. (und so weiter) etc.

V

der Vater, ¨ father; **Vati, -s** papa
sich verabschieden to take one's leave, say good-bye
verändern to change s.th.; **sich verändern** to become changed
die Veränderung, -en change
verantwortlich responsible
das Verb, -en verb
verbessern to improve
verbieten, verbot, verboten to forbid
verbinden, verband, verbunden to connect, combine; to bandage
das Verbot, -e ban, prohibition
der Verbrecher, - criminal
verbrennen, verbrannte, verbrannt to burn (up), scorch
verbringen, verbrachte, verbracht to spend *or* pass (*time*)
der Verdacht suspicion
verdeutlichen to make clear, illustrate
verdienen to earn, merit
vereinigt united
die Vereinigung unification
verfassen to write, compose
verfließen, verfloß, ist verflossen elapse, pass (*of time*)
vergangen past
die Vergangenheit past
vergessen (vergißt), vergaß, vergessen to forget
der Vergleich, -e comparison
vergleichend comparative
verhaften arrest, apprehend
sich verhalten to act, behave, react
das Verhältnis, -se relationship
verheiratet married
verhindern to stop, prevent
verkaufen to sell
der Verkäufer, - salesperson; (*fem.*) **die Verkäuferin, -nen**
der Verkehr traffic
die Verkehrsampel, -n traffic light
das Verkehrsmittel, - means of transportation
verkünden to proclaim, announce
der Verlag, -e publishing house
verlängern to extend, lengthen
verlassen (verläßt), verließ, verlassen *(with dir. obj.)* to leave, go away; **sich verlassen (auf +** *obj.*) to rely upon
der Verlauf, ¨-e course
verlaufen (verläuft), verlief, ist verlaufen to take its course, turn out; **sich verlaufen** to get lost, lose one's way
verletzen to injure, hurt; to insult, offend
die Verletzung, -en injury
sich verlieben (in + *acc.*) to fall in love with
verlieren, verlor, verloren to lose
der Verlobte (ein Verlobter) fiancé; (*fem.*) **die Verlobte**
der Verlust, -e loss
das Vermögen fortune
verneinen to answer in the negative
verpassen to miss (*a train; opportunity*)
verpflanzen to transplant
verrückt crazy; **verrückt (auf +** *acc.*) crazy about
versäumen to miss, neglect to do
verschieden various, different
verschlechtern to make worse
verschwenden to waste, squander
verschwinden, verschwand, ist verschwunden to disappear, vanish
versichern to assure; to insure
die Versicherung, -en insurance, assurance
sich verspäten to be *or* arrive late
die Verspätung, -en delay
versprechen (verspricht), versprach, versprochen to promise
verstaatlichen to nationalize
das Verständnis understanding, comprehension
verstärken to strengthen
verstehen, verstand, verstanden to understand
versuchen to try, attempt
verteilen to distribute
das Vertrauen trust, confidence

vertreiben, vertrieb, vertrieben to drive away, scatter; **die Zeit vertreiben** to pass the time
vertreten (vertritt), vertrat, vertreten to represent, act on behalf of
der Verwandte (ein Verwandter) relative; (*fem.*) **die Verwandte**
verwandtschaftlich pertaining to relatives
verwenden to use, make use of
verwirklichen to make come true, realize (*a goal*)
die Videospieldiskette, -n video game cassette
der Videospielfilm, -e video movie
viel (*sing.*) much; **viel-** (*pl.*) many
vielleicht perhaps
vielmals often, many times
der Vogel, ¨ bird
die Vokabel, -n (vocabulary) word
das Volk, ¨er people, nation, race
die Volkskrankheit, -en widespread illness
völlig total(ly), complete(ly)
die Vollpension lodging with all meals
von (*prep. with dat.*) from, of, by; about
vor (*prep. with dat. or acc.*) in front of, before; ago (*dat.*)
vor allem above all; **vor kurzem** recently
vorbei past; **an** (*dat.*) . . . **vorbei** (go) past
vor•bringen, brachte vor, vorgebracht to bring forward, bring up (*an argument*)
der Vorfahr, (-en), -en ancestor, forefather
vor•führen to demonstrate, display
vor•gehen, ging vor, ist vorgegangen to be fast (*of clocks*)
die Vorgeschichte, -n prior history
vor•haben to have in mind, intend
der Vorhang, ¨e curtain
vorher (*adv.*) before, previously
vorig previous
vor•lesen (liest vor), las vor, vorgelesen to read aloud
die Vorlesung, -en lecture (*course*)
der Vorschlag, ¨e suggestion
vor•schlagen (schlägt vor), schlug vor, vorgeschlagen to suggest
die Vorsicht caution, care
vorsichtig careful, cautious
vor•stellen to introduce; **sich** (*dat.*) **vor•stellen** to imagine
die Vorstellung, -en performance, show; conception
der Vortrag, ¨e lecture, talk
vorüber past, over
vorwärts forward
vorzüglich excellent, exquisite

W

wach awake
wachsen (wächst), wuchs, ist gewachsen to grow
der Wagen, - car; wagon
wählen to choose, select, vote
der Wähler, - voter
der Wahnsinn insanity
wahr true, real, genuine
während (*prep. with gen.*) during; (*sub. conj.*) while
die Wahrheit, -en truth
wahrscheinlich probably
der Wald, ¨er wood(s), forest
die Wanderausrüstung, -en hiking outfit
die Wanderkarte, -n trail map, hiking map
wandern to hike, wander, roam
die Wanderung, -en hike
wann (*interrog.*) when
die Ware, -n ware, product
warten (auf + *acc.*) to wait for
warum why
was für what kind of
das Waschbecken, - wash basin
waschen (wäscht), wusch, gewaschen to wash
das Waschpulver detergent
wasserdicht watertight, waterproof
der Wasserspiegel water surface
weder . . . noch neither . . . nor
weg away
wegen (*prep. with gen.*) on account of
weg•gehen, ging weg, ist weggegangen to leave, go away
weg•stellen to put away, put down
weh! woe!
(das) Weihnachten (*or pl.*) Christmas; **zu Weihnachten** at / for Christmas
weil (*sub. conj.*) because
die Weile while, (*amount of*) time
der Wein, -e wine
weise wise
weiter additional, further
weiter•fahren (fährt weiter), fuhr weiter, ist weitergefahren to drive on (farther)
weiter•gehen, ging weiter, ist weitergegangen to go on; to keep going
weiter•kommen, kam weiter, ist weitergekommen to get / come further; to keep coming
weiter•machen to keep doing
welch- which
die Welt, -en world
der Weltkrieg, -e world war
der Weltraum outer space
die Weltstadt, ¨e metropolis, major world city
wenden, wandte *or* **wendete, gewandt** *or* **gewendet** to turn
wenig (*sing.*) little; **wenig-** (*pl.*) few

wenn *(sub. conj.)* when(ever), if; **wenn . . . auch** even if, even though
wenn . . . kein / wenn . . . nicht unless
die Werbeschrift, -en advertising brochure
die Werbung, -en advertisement, advertising
werden (wird), wurde, ist geworden to become, get
werfen (wirft), warf, geworfen to throw, toss
das Werk, -e book, work; works, factory
das Werkzeug, -e tool, implement
wert *(dat.)* worth, of value to; *(gen.)* worth, worthy of
das Wesen, - being, creature
der Westen west
das Wetter weather
der Wetterdienst weather service
wichtig important
wider *(prep. with acc.)* against
widersprechen (widerspricht), widersprach, widersprochen *(dat.)* to contradict
wie lange how long
wie how; as
wieder again
wiederholen to repeat
die Wiedervereinigung, -en reunification
wieso how is it that
wieviel how much; **wie viele** how many
der Wille, (-ns), -n will
wirken to have an effect, work
wirklich real(ly)
die Wirtschaft economy
der Wirtschaftsplaner, - economic planner; *(fem.)* **die Wirtschaftsplanerin, -nen**
die Wirtschaftspolitik economic policy
wissen (weiß), wußte, gewußt to know
die Wissenschaft, -en science
der Wissenschaftler, - scientist; *(fem.)* **die Wissenschaftlerin, -nen**
wissenschaftlich scientific
der Witz, -e joke; wit
woanders elsewhere
das Wochenende, -n weekend
der Wochentag, -e weekday
wohin to where
wohl probably
wohnen to live, dwell
der Wohnort, -e place of residence
der Wohnsitz, -e official residence
die Wohnung, -en apartment, dwelling
wollen (will), wollte, gewollt to want to, intend
das Wort, ¨er individual word; **das Wort, -e** connected words
der Wortschatz, ¨e vocabulary
die Wunde, -n wound
das Wunderkind, -er child prodigy
der Wunsch, ¨e wish; **nach Wunsch** as desired
wünschen to wish
die Würze, -n spice
die Wüste, -n desert
wütend (auf) enraged at

Z

die Zahl, -en number
zahlen to pay
der Zahn, ¨e tooth
der Zahnarzt, ¨e dentist; *(fem.)* **die Zahnärztin, -nen**
der Zar, (-en), -en czar
die Zauberflöte magic flute
zauberhaft magical, enchanted
der Zaun, ¨e fence
zeigen to show
die Zeile, -n line
die Zeit, -en time
der Zeitausdruck, ¨e time expression
die Zeitform, -en verb tense
die Zeitschrift, -en magazine
die Zeitung, -en newspaper
das Zentrum, -ren center
zerbrechen (zerbricht), zerbrach, zerbrochen to break (into pieces), shatter
zerstören to destroy
die Zerstörung destruction
der Zettel, - scrap of paper; note
ziehen, zog, gezogen to pull; **ziehen (ist)** to move, go
ziemlich rather, fairly
das Zimmer, - room
der Zimmerschlüssel, - room key
der Zirkus, -se circus
das Zitat, -e quotation
zornig angry
zu *(prep. with dat.)* to, at; too
der Zucker sugar
zuerst (at) first
zufällig per chance, by accident
zufrieden satisfied
der Zug, ¨e train
das Zugabteil, -e train compartment
die Zugverbindung, -en train connection
zu•hören *(dat.)* to listen to
der Zuhörer, - listener
die Zukunft future
der Zukunftsplan, ¨e future plan
zuletzt at last, finally, in the end
zu•machen to close, shut
die Zunge, -n tongue
zurück•bringen, brachte zurück, zurückgebracht to bring back
zurück•führen (auf + *acc.***)** to trace back to, explain by
zurück•kehren (ist) to return
zurück•kommen, kam zurück, ist zurückgekommen to come back, return
zu•rufen, rief zu, zugerufen *(dat.)* to call to
zusammen together
zusammen•fassen to summarize

zusammen•halten (hält zusammen), hielt zusammen, zusammengehalten to hold *or* keep together
zusammen•stellen to put together
zusammen•wachsen (wächst zusammen), wuchs zusammen, ist zusammengewachsen to grow together
der Zuschauer, - spectator, onlooker
das Zustandspassiv, -e statal passive
zuviel too much
zuwenig too little
zu•winken *(dat.)* to wave at/to
zwar to be sure
zweifeln (**an** + *dat.*) to doubt, have doubts about
der Zwilling, -e twin
zwingen, zwang, gezwungen (**zu** + *dat.*) to force, compel
zwischen *(prep. with acc. or dat.)* between

Index

aber
  coordinating conjunction, 138–139
  modal particle, 319
Absolute comparatives and superlatives, 191–192
Accusative case, 40–41
  after **es gibt,** 40, 250
  after prepositions, 116, 124
  direct object, 41
  in greetings, 41
  in measurements, 41
  in time expressions, 300
  used reflexively, 224–226
  verbs with two accusatives, 40
  with distances, 40
Active voice, versus passive voice, 361
Addresses, in letters, 407–409
Adjectives
  after **all-,** 174
  after **andere, einige, mehrere, viele, wenige,** 173–174
  after **der-** and **ein-**words, 170–172
  after **viel, wenig, etwas,** 174
  comparative, 188–190
  governing cases, 175–176
  in extended modifiers, 277–278
  of reaction and emotion, 185–186
  participles used as, 277
  predicate adjective, 170
  suffixes, 177–178
  superlative, 188–190
  unpreceded, 172
  used as nouns, 277–279
  with dative and genitive, 175–176
  with prepositional complements, 176–177
Adjective nouns, 275–277
  from participles, 275–276
Adjective suffixes, *see* Suffixes
Adverbial conjunctions, 313
Adverbs
  comparative, 188–190
  of description, 310–311
  of manner, 310
  of place, 312
  of time, 308, 311–312
  suffix **-(er)weise,** 310–311
  superlative, 188–190, 191
  word order with Time-Manner-Place, 3, 313
Agents, with passive voice, 361–362
all-, 56–57
  adjective ending after, 174, 276
  ganz instead of, 57, 174
allerdings, 325
als
  = als ob, 263
  after comparative, 192
  subordinating conjunction, 141
  versus **wenn** and **wann,** 141
als ob / als wenn, 142
  conditional subjunctive after, 263, 265
also, modal particle, 320
an, preposition, 125
  after certain adjectives, 176
  after certain verbs, 391
  versus **auf,** 125
andere, 173
anders
  after **etwas, nichts, viel, wenig,** 276
  after **jemand** and **niemand,** 213
Animals, 164–166
anhalten, 208
(an)statt, preposition, 128
anstatt . . . zu, 237
Anticipatory **da**-compounds, 248–249
Anticipatory **es,** 251
Articles
  as pronouns, 59–60
  declension of **der-,** 53
  declension of **ein-,** 55
  inclusion or omission of definite article, 53–55
  inclusion or omission of indefinite article, 55–56
auch, modal particle, 320
auch wenn, *see* **wenn . . . auch**
auf, preposition, 125
  after certain adjectives, 176
  after certain verbs, 391–392
  versus **an,** 125
sich aufführen, 272
aufhalten, 208
aufhören, 208
aus, preposition, 119
  after certain verbs, 392
außer, 119
außerhalb, 128
äußerst, 193
Auxiliary verbs, *see* entries under various tenses

-bar, suffix, 178
be-, inseparable prefix, 376, 386–387
bei, preposition, 119–120
  dative after verbs beginning with, 43–44
bekommen, 136
sich benehmen, 272
beschließen, 233
bevor, subordinating conjunction, 142
bis
  preposition, 117
  subordinating conjunction, 142
bitte, with imperatives, 72
brauchen, with **nicht (zu),** 104

Capitalization (Appendix 1), 403–404
Cardinal numbers, 286–288
Cases, *see* entries under various cases
Categories of things, 343
-chen, diminutive suffix, 157
Cognate words (Appendix 3), 410–412
Colon (Appendix 1), 406
Comma, uses of (Appendix 1), 405–406
Commands, *see* Imperative
Comparative, forms of adjectives and adverbs, 188–190
Comparisons
  with **als,** 192
  with **immer,** 192
  with **je . . . desto / um so,** 192
  with **so . . . wie,** 192
Conditional subjunctive, *see* Subjunctive II (Conditional)
Conjunctions
  coordinating, 138–139
  correlative, 139–140
  subordinating, 140–146
Contractions, prepositions with definite article, 116, 119, 124
Contrary-to-fact conditions, *see* Subjunctive II (Conditional)
Countries, articles with, 54

da
  adverb of place, 312
  adverb of time, 312
  subordinating conjunction, 143
da-compounds, 247–248
  anticipatory, 248–249, 390–391
  in common expressions, 248
daher / dahin, as **da-**compounds, 249
damals, 311
damit
  subordinating conjunction, 143
  versus **so daß,** 143
darum, adverbial conjunction, 313
daß, subordinate conjunction, 143
  omission of, 5, 143
  after anticipatory **da-**compounds, 249
Dates, 302
Dative case
  after prepositions, 118, 124
  as indirect object, 41–42
  indicating possession, 44
  used reflexively, 226–227
  with adjectives, 175
  with certain verbs, 42–44
  with **gefallen,** 113
  with passive voice, 363–364
Dative of possession, 44
Days of the week, 299
Decimals, 287
Declensions
  definite articles, 53
  demonstrative pronouns, 214–216
  der- words, 56–57
  der- words as pronouns, 59–60
  ein- words, 58–59
  ein- words as pronouns, 60
  indefinite articles, 55
  jedermann / jemand / niemand, 213
  man, 213
  possessive adjectives, 58–59
  personal pronouns, 211
  reflexive pronouns, 223
  regular nouns, 38–39
  relative pronouns, 332
  weak nouns, 160–161
Definite article
  as pronoun, 59–60
  declension of, 53
  omission of, 55
  with geographical names and places, 54
Demonstrative pronouns, 214–216
denken an / von, 151–152
denn
  coordinating conjunction, 138
  modal particle, 320
dennoch, adverbial conjunction, 313
der-words, 56–58
  as pronouns, 59–60
derselbe / dieselbe / dasselbe, 215–216
  versus **der gleiche,** 216
deshalb, 313
dessen / deren
  as demonstratives, 215
  as relative pronouns, 332, 334
desto, 192
deswegen, 313
dies- / jen-, 56–57, 60
diesseits, preposition, 128
Diminutive noun suffixes, 157
Direct object, 40
  word order when used with indirect objects, 3, 42
doch
  modal particle, 320–321
  response to a question, 200
Double infinitives
  with future tense, 240
  with **hören, sehen, spüren, lassen,** 239–240
  with imperatives, 73
  with modal verbs, 106–108
du / ihr versus **Sie,** 211–212
durch
  preposition, 117
  two-way prefix, 380
  with agents in passive voice, 362
dürfen, modal verb, 101–103
  nicht dürfen, 102–103

eben, modal particle, 321
ehe, subordinating conjunction, 142
eigentlich, modal particle, 321–322
ein, as a numeral, 287
ein ander- / noch ein-, 220
einander, reciprocal pronoun, 228
einige, 173
ein-words, 58–59
  as pronouns, 60
endlich, versus **schließlich,** 316
ent-, inseparable prefix, 377
  dative after verbs beginning with, 43
entdecken, 283
entlang, preposition, 127
entscheiden / sich entscheiden, 232–233
Entscheidung: eine E. treffen, 233
sich entschließen, 233
Entschluß: einen E. fassen, 233
entweder . . . oder, 139–140
er-, inseparable prefix, 377, 386–387
erhalten, 136
-erlei, suffix, 288
-e(r)n, suffix, 178
erlöschen, 35
erschrecken, strong versus weak, 35
erst versus **nur,** 220
ertrinken versus **ertränken,** 35
es
  anticipatory, 251
  impersonal, 249–250
  introductory, 250–251
  with passive voice, 362–363
es gibt, 250
es handelt sich um, 255
etwa, 288
etwas
  adjective after, 174
  adjective noun after, 276
Exclamation point, 72, 406
Extended modifiers, 277–278

-fach, suffix, 288
fahren versus **führen,** 34
fallen versus **fällen,** 34
falls, 143
feststellen, 283
Flavoring particles, *see* Modal particles
fortfahren versus **fortsetzen,** 98
Fractions, 289–290
freilich, 325
fühlen with a following infinitive, 237
führen versus **fahren,** 34
für, preposition, 117
  after certain verbs, 117
Future perfect tense, 94–95
Future tense, 93–94
  modal verbs, 107–108

ganz instead of **all-,** 57, 174
gefallen, 113
gegen, preposition, 118, 303
gegenüber, 120
gehen, synonyms, 89–90
  es geht um etwas, 255
  with a following infinitive, 238
Gender, *see* Nouns
Genitive case, 44–45
  after certain verbs, 45
  after prepositions, 127–128
  von + dative as substitute, 45
  with adjectives, 175–176
gern: gern haben / tun, 112–113
  comparative and superlative, 190
gestern, in combinations, 299
gibt: es gibt, 250
glauben, 152
gleich: der gleiche, 216

haben
  as auxiliary verb, 28
  past participle, 25
  past-tense conjugation, 81
  present-tense conjugation, 14
  subjunctive II, 260
  versus **sein** as auxiliary, 28–29
-haft, suffix, 178
halb / die Hälfte, 290
halt, modal particle, 321
halten / anhalten, 207–208
halten von / halten für, 152
handeln, 272
  es handelt sich um, 255
handeln von, 255
hängen, strong versus weak, 34
heißen, 237
helfen, with a following infinitive, 237
herausfinden, 283
herausstellen, sich als, 399–400
herum, 118
heute, in combinations, 299
hin- / her-, 375–376
hinter
  preposition, 125
  two-way prefix, 380
höchst, 193
holen, 136
hören
  in double infinitives, 239
  used with following infinitive, 237
Hyphen (Appendix 1), 406

-ieren verbs
  past participle, 25
  present-tense conjugation, 11
-ig, suffix, 177, 302
ihr, instead of **Sie,** 212
immer + comparative, 192
Imperative
  forms, 70–72
  infinitives used as, 72
  with modal particles, 72–73
Impersonal verbs
  with **es,** 249–250
in, preposition, 125–126
  after certain verbs, 392
Indefinite articles
  declension, 55
  omission of, 56
Indefinite pronouns, 212–214
indem, subordinating conjunction, 144
Indicative versus Subjunctive, *see* Subjunctive I (Indirect Discourse)
Indirect discourse subjunctive, *see* Subjunctive I (Indirect Discourse)

Indirect object, 41–42
Indirect questions, 203–204
  with subjunctive, 351
Infinitives
  after **hören, sehen, lassen, helfen, lehren, lernen,** 237–238
  after modals, 102
  as imperatives, 72
  as nouns, 238–239
  double infinitives, 239–240
  with future tense, 93–94
  with **zu,** 236
  without **zu** after certain verbs, 237–238
Infinitive phrases
  after anticipatory **da-** compounds, 249
  punctuation, 236, (Appendix 1), 405
  with **um, ohne, (an)statt,** 237
innerhalb, 128
Inseparable prefixes, 376–379
  in present and past tenses, 14
  with past participles, 27
Instructions for exercises, 8–9
Interrogatives, 200–204
  adverbs (**wo, warum, wieviel,** etc.), 203
  pronouns, 201–203
  was für (ein-), 203
  welch-, 202
  wo-compounds, 202
Intransitive verbs
  examples of intransitive versus transitive, 34–35
  used with the auxiliary **sein,** 28–29
irgend, 214
Irregular weak verbs, *see* specific tenses
-isch, suffix, 177

ja, modal particle, 322
jed-, 57
jedermann (jeder), 213
je . . . desto / um so, 192
jemand, 213
jen- / dies-, 57, 60
jenseits, preposition, 128

kein- versus **nicht,** 69
kennen versus **wissen,** 20
können, modal verb, 101, 103
  use in subjunctive, 266
kriegen, 136

lassen, 238
  machen lassen, 238
  sich (machen) lassen, 365
  versus **verlassen,** 243–244
legen versus **liegen,** 34
lehren with a following infinitive, 237
-lein, diminutive suffix, 157
lernen
  versus **studieren,** 21
  with a following infinitive, 237
Letter-writing (Appendix 2), 407–409
-lich, suffix, 177, 301
liegen versus **legen,** 34
-los, suffix, 178
löschen, 35
(keine) Lust haben, 113

machen, with noun complements, 50
Mal, 308
mal, flavoring particle, 73, 323
-mal, suffix, 288, 307
-malig, suffix, 288
man, (einer, einen, einem), 213
  substitute for passive voice, 365
manch- / manch ein-, 57
Measurements, 290–292
mehr, no ending with, 190
mehrere, 173
meinen, 152
meinetwegen, 128
mindestens / wenigstens, 193
miß-, inseparable prefix, 377–378
mit, preposition, 120
  after certain verbs, 393
  with agents in passive voice, 362
möchten, 113
möchten, daß, 106
Modal (flavoring) particles, 319–325
  expressions with, 328
  with imperatives, 73
Modal verbs, 101–108
  future tense, 107–108
  meanings, 102–106
  passive voice, 363
  past tense, 101
  perfect tenses, 106–107
  present tense, 101
  subjunctive, 260, 265–266
mögen, modal verb, 101, 105–106, 112–113
Months of the year, 298
morgen, in combinations, 300
müssen, modal verb, 101, 103–104
  nicht müssen versus **nicht dürfen,** 104
  used in subjunctive, 266

nach, preposition, 120–121
  after certain adjectives, 176
  after certain verbs, 393
  dative after verbs beginning with, 43
nachdem, subordinating conjunction, 144
nachher, 144, 310
neben, preposition, 126
Negation
  kein-, 69
  nicht, 69–70
  nie(mals), 69–70
  positions of **nicht,** 70
  words and expressions, 77
Neuter adjective nouns, 276–277
nicht, 69–70
nicht nur . . . sondern auch, 139
nicht wahr, 200
nichts
  adjective noun after, 276
niemand, 213
noch ein- / ein ander-, 220
Nominative case, 39–40
Nouns
  collective with prefix **Ge-,** 157, 160
  compound nouns, 157

Nouns *cont.*
dual genders, 275–277, 297
from adjectives, 197, 275–277
from participles, 275–276
guidelines for genders, 155–158
plurals, 158–160
regular declensions, 38–39
weak nouns, 160–161
Noun suffixes, 155–157
Numerals
cardinal, 286–288
currencies, denominations and decades, 290–291
decimals, 287
fractions, 289–290
mathematical vocabulary and expressions, 296
ordinal, 289
percents, 287
nun, modal particle, 322–323
nur
modal particle, 73, 323
versus **erst,** 200

ob, subordinating conjunction, 144
in indirect discourse, 351
omission of with **als,** 263
oberhalb, 128
obgleich, obschon, obwohl, 144
oder, coordinating conjunction, 138–139
Official time, 303–304
ohne, preposition, 118
ohne . . . zu, 237
Ordinal numbers, 289
Ort, 66

Participial modifiers, 277–278
zu + present participle, 278
Participles
as adjectives, 277
as nouns, 275–277
Particles, *see* Modal particles
Passive voice
agents with **von, durch,** and **mit,** 361–362
dative objects, 363–364
es with the passive, 362–363
forms and tenses, 360–361
statal passive, 364
substitutes for, 365–366
versus active voice, 361
with modals, 363
Past participle
-ieren verbs, 25
irregular weak verbs, 25
modal verbs, 106
prefix verbs, 27
strong verbs, 26
used as adjective or noun, 277
weak verbs, 24
Past perfect tense, 83
of modal verbs, 106–107
Past tense, *see* Simple past tense
Percents, 287
Period, 287, 406
Personal pronouns,
declension, 211–212
possessive forms, 58–59
Platz, 66
Plurals, *see* Nouns
Possessive adjectives (pronouns), 58–59
Predicate adjective, 170
Predicate nominative, 39–40
Prefix Verbs
inseparable prefixes, 376–379
separable prefixes, 373–376
two-way prefixes, 379–381
Prepositions
after adjectives, 176
after reflexive verbs, 225–226
after verbs, 391–396
contractions with definite articles, 116, 119, 124
with accusative, 116–118
with accusative or dative (two-way), 124–127
with dative, 118–124
with genitive, 127–129
Prepositional complements, 390–396
Present participles
as adjectives or nouns, 277
in extended modifiers, 277–278
zu + present participle, 278
Present perfect tense, 24–29
haben versus **sein** as auxiliary, 28–29
irregular weak verbs, 25
modal verbs, 106
prefix verbs, 27
strong verbs, 26–27
weak verbs, 24–25
Present tense, 11–15
auxiliaries and **wissen,** 14
modal verbs, 101
prefix verbs, 14
used instead of present perfect, 15
verbs with stem-vowel changes, 12–13
with future meaning, 15
Principal parts of strong and irregular verbs, 25–27
(Appendix 4), 413–418
Pronouns
demonstrative, 214–216
der- and **ein-**words used as, 59–60
derselbe / dieselbe / dasselbe, 215–216
indefinite, 212–214
interrogative, 201–202
personal, 211–212
reciprocal, 228
reflexive, 224
relative, 331–336
Punctuation (Appendix 1), 404–406

Questions, 200–204, *see* Interrogatives
Quotation marks (Appendix 1), 406

Raum, 65
Reciprocal pronouns, 228
Reflexive pronouns
after prepositions, 226
declension, 223
position of, 224
used reciprocally, 228
Reflexive verbs
accusative reflexives, 224–226

Reflexive verbs *cont.*
dative reflexives, 226–227
substitute for passive voice, 365
-reich, suffix, 178
Relative clauses, 331
Relative pronouns
definite **(der / die / das),** 331–334
indefinite **(wer / was),** 335–336
was, 334
welch-, 332
wer / was *(whoever / whatever),* 336
wo-compounds, 334–335
word order, 332
Rivers, gender of, 156
rund, 288

Salutations, in letters, 407–408
sagen, synonyms for, 356–357
-sam, suffix, 178
schaffen: geschafft versus **geschaffen,** 370
schließlich versus **endlich,** 316
schon, modal particle, 323–324
with present tense, 15
Seasons of the year, 298
sehen
in double infinitives, 239
with a following infinitive, 237
sein, verb
imperative, 72
past participle, 26
past-tense conjugation, 81
present-tense conjugation, 14
versus **haben** as auxiliary, 28–29
+ **zu** + infinitive, 365
seit
preposition, 121–122
subordinating conjunction, 144–145
with present tense, 15
seit(dem)
adverb, 312
subordinating conjunction, 144–145
seither, 312
selbst / selber, 227–228
Semicolon (Appendix 1), 406
senden: gesendet versus **gesandt,** 25
senken versus **sinken,** 35
Separable prefix verbs, 373–376
past participles, 27, 375
past tense, 81
present tense, 14
Sexist language, avoiding, 219
sich, reflexive pronoun, 224
Sie, versus **du,** 211–212
Simple past tense, 80–83
irregular weak verbs, 80–81
modals, 101
separable prefix verbs, 81–82, 374
strong verbs, 81
versus present perfect tense, 82
weak verbs, 80
sinken versus **senken,** 35
sitzen versus **setzen,** 35
sobald, conjunction, 145
so daß, 143
so ein, 57
solch- / solch ein-, 57
sollen, modal verb, 101, 104
used in subjunctive, 266
sondern, coordinating conjunction, 138–139
so . . . wie, 192
sowohl . . . als auch, 139
springen versus **sprengen,** 35
spüren with a following infinitive, 237
Statal passive, 364
(an)statt, preposition, 128
anstatt . . . zu, 237
stattdessen, adverbial conjunction, 313
stehenbleiben, 208
Stelle, 66
stoppen, 208
Strong and irregular verbs, principal parts (Appendix 4), 413–418
studieren, 21
Subjunctive I (Indirect discourse)
choice between subjunctive I and II, 348–349
extended indirect discourse, 351
forms, 347–348
indirect commands, 352
indirect questions, 351
present, past, and future time, 349–350
uses of, 351–352
versus direct discourse, 346–347
versus indicative, 346–347
Subjunctive II (Conditional)
after **als (ob) / als (wenn),** 263, 265
conditional / hypothetical statements, 261–262, 264
forms, 258–260
past time, 264–265
present time, 257
requests, 263
versus indicative with modals, 266
wishes, 262–263, 265
würde(n) + infinitive, 260–261
Subordinate clauses, 5, 140–141
Subordinating conjunctions, 140–146
Suffixes
-bar, 178
-erlei, 288
-e(r)n, 178
-(er)weise, 310–311
-fach, 288
-haft, 178
-ig, 177, 302
-isch, 177
-lich, 177, 301
-mal, 288, 307
-malig, 288
-reich / voll, 178
-sam, 178
-tags, 299
-zeit, 308
with numerals, 288
with nouns, 155–157
with time expressions, 301–302
Superlative, adjectives and adverbs, 188–190
Superlative adverbs, 192

-tags, 299
Telling time, 303

Temperatures, 292
Tenses, *see* entries for each tense
Time expressions
  adverbs, 311–312
  clock time, 303–304
  dates, 302
  days and parts of the day, 299
  duration of time (accusative), 300
  heute, gestern, and **morgen,** 299–300
  indefinite time (genitive), 300–301
  months and seasons, 298
  specific time (accusative), 300
  suffixes with, 288
  -tags, 299
  units of time, 301
  years, 302
trotz, preposition, 128
trotzdem, adverbial conjunction, 313
tun, als ob, 272
Two-way prefixes, 379–381
Two-way prepositions, 124–127

über
  after certain verbs, 394
  preposition, 126
  two-way prefix, 380
überhaupt, modal particle, 324
um
  after certain verbs, 394–395
  in time expressions, 303
  preposition, 118
  two-way prefix, 380
um . . . zu, 237
und, coordinating conjunction, 138–139
ungefähr, 288
unter
  preposition, 126–127
  two-way prefix, 381
unterhalb, 128

ver-, inseparable prefix, 378, 386–387
Verbal complements, 3–4, 390–391
Verbs
  auxiliaries and **wissen,** 14
  impersonal, 250
  irregular weak, 25, 80–81
  modal, 101–108
  principal parts of strong and irregular, (Appendix 3), 413–418
  reflexive, 224–227
  strong, 26–27, 81
  used as nouns, 238–239
  weak, 24–25, 80
  with accusative and dative objects, 42
  with prepositional complements, 390–396
  with prefixes, 373–381
  with stem-vowel change in present tense, 12–13
Verbs of going, 89–90
Verbs of speaking, 356–357
sich verhalten, 272
verlassen, 244
verschwinden versus **verschwenden,** 35
viel
  adjective after, 174
  adjective noun after, 276
viele, 173–174
-voll, suffix, 178
von, preposition, 122
  after certain adjectives, 176
  after certain verbs, 395
  substitute for the genitive, 45
  with agents in passive voice, 362
von . . . an, 122
vor, preposition, 127
  after certain adjectives, 176
  after certain verbs, 395
  meaning *ago,* 127, 301

während
  preposition, 128
  subordinating conjunction, 145–146
wann, 203
  versus **als** and **wenn,** 141
warum, 203
was
  definite relative pronoun, 334
  indefinite relative pronoun, 335–336
  interrogative, 201–202
was für (ein-), 58, 203
weder . . . noch, 139
wegen, preposition, 128
weggehen, versus **verlassen,** 244
Weights, 291
weil, subordinating conjunction, 143
weiter(tun), 98
welch-
  der-word, 58
  interrogative, 202
  relative pronoun, 332
welch ein-, 58
wenden
  gewendet versus **gewandt,** 25
  versus **winden,** 35
wenig
  adjective after, 174
  adjective noun after, 276
  no ending in comparative, 190
wenige, 173
wenigstens versus **mindestens,** 193
wenn, versus **wann** and **als,** 141
wenn . . . auch / auch wenn, 146
wenn . . . nicht / wenn . . . kein, 146
wer (wessen, wem, wen)
  indefinite relative pronoun, 335–336
  interrogative, 201–202
werden
  future tense, 93
  imperative, 71
  passive voice, 360–361
  past-tense conjugation, 81
  present-tense conjugation, 14
  würde(n) + infinitive, 260–261
weshalb, 203
wider-, two-way prefix, 381
wie
  in comparisons, 192
  used instead of **als,** 141
wieder-, two-way prefix, 381

wissen
past-tense conjugation, 81
present-tense conjugation, 14
versus **kennen,** 20
wo, relative pronoun, 335
wo, wohin, woher, 203
wo-compounds
interrogatives, 202
relative pronouns, 335
wohl, 324
with future perfect tense, 94–95
wollen, modal verb, 101, 105
wollen, daß, 105
Word order
adverbs and prepositional phrases, 3, 313
after **als (=als ob),** 142, 263
after coordinating conjunctions, 2, 138
conjugated verbs, 2, 4–5
dependent clauses, 5, 140–141
double infinitives, 239–240
indirect questions, 203–204
main clauses, 1–2
nicht, 70
object nouns and pronouns, 2–3
past participles, 27
questions, 200–201
reflexive pronouns, 224
relative clauses, 5, 332
separable prefixes, 4, 14, 81, 374
subordinate clauses, 5, 140–141
Time-Manner-Place expressions, 3, 313
verbal complements, 4
Writing letters (Appendix 2), 407–409
würde(n) + infinitive, 260–261

Years, 302

zeigen: es zeigt sich, 400
Zeit, expressions with, 308
zer-, inseparable prefix, 379
zu, preposition, 123
after certain adjectives, 176
after certain verbs, 396
dative after verbs beginning with, 43–44
sein + **zu** + infinitive, 365
zu + present participle, 278
zuletzt, 316
zum ersten Mal, 308
zwar, 324–325
zwischen, preposition, 127